W9-BUK-038

GROLIER
ENCYCLOPEDIA
OF KNOWLEDGE

Grolier Incorporated
Danbury, Connecticut

Copyright © MCMXCI by Grolier Incorporated

All rights reserved. No part of this book may be reproduced
or transmitted in any form by any means electronic, mechanical,
or otherwise, whether now or hereafter devised, including
photocopying, recording, or by any information storage and
retrieval system without express written prior permission from
the publisher.

ISBN 0-7172-5300-7 (complete set)
ISBN 0-7172-5302-3 (volume 2)

Printed and manufactured in the United States of America.

This publication is an abridged version of the *Academic American Encyclopedia*.

10 9 8 7 6 5 4 3

anodizing [an'-oh-dyz-ing] Anodizing is a process in which the surface of a metal is converted by electrolytic oxidation into a coating. The metal usually used is aluminum, in which case the coating is aluminum oxide. Anodizing can be thought of as the opposite of ELECTROPLATING, in which a metallic coating is deposited on the surface of the metal. Because the coating is actually the converted surface of the aluminum, it has excellent adherence. The aluminum serves as the anode, and another metal, or carbon, serves as the cathode. The aluminum is placed into an acid, usually sulfuric or chromic, and an electric current is then applied. Anodized aluminum is used for structural and decorative material in buildings, for transportation and automotive parts, for consumer products, and for lighting fixtures and electrical applications.

anointing of the sick Anointing of the sick is a rite of Christian healing recognized as a SACRAMENT by the Roman Catholic and Orthodox churches. Its biblical basis is found in Mark 6:13 and James 5:14–15. The sacrament is intended for the seriously ill but is not restricted to those at the point of death; for that reason it is no longer known as "extreme unction." It consists of a laying on of hands by a priest, a prayer of faith, and an anointing with holy oil. It is believed that the sacrament grants forgiveness of sins, effects strength of soul, and even restores health should that be God's will. Anointing of the sick is included in the Episcopal Book of Common Prayer as a rite for the healing of spirit, mind, and body. It is also used by other Christians as part of a healing ministry.

Anoplura see LOUSE

anorexia nervosa [an-uh-rek'-see-uh nur-voh'-suh] Anorexia nervosa is a disorder typified by self-starvation. It occurs most commonly among adolescent females but is also observed in older women and in men. The disorder may appear when a young woman leaves home, or it may develop in connection with mental depression, peer pressure to lose weight, sexual temptation, the use of psychedelic drugs, or the discontinuance of oral contraceptives.

The patient stops menstruating and simply refuses to eat. She may lose weight to the point of life-threatening exhaustion. The patient remains physically active and believes she is much fatter than she actually is. In an associated condition called BULIMIA, the patient repeatedly gorges herself but expels the food through self-induced vomiting.

Anorexia nervosa may sometimes be associated with a disorder of the hypothalamus, a region of the brain that regulates menstruation, eating, body temperature, and sleep. About half of all anorexic patients recover permanently. About 10 percent die of self-starvation, and the rest have repeated relapses. (See PSYCHOSOMATIC MEDICINE.)

Anouilh, Jean [ah-noo-ee'] One of the most popular French dramatists since World War II, Jean Anouilh, b. June 23, 1910, d. Oct. 3, 1987, was sometimes called a mere entertainer. Choreography and music are often integrated into his plots, yet a seriousness and a pessimistic view of life lie beneath his farce and caricature. His protagonists usually reject compromise—and thus life. The result is either death or a retreat into untenable illusion.

Anouilh's collected works are color titled after the dominant mood of each. His two collections of *pièces noires*, or black plays, include *Eurydice* (1941), a modernization of the ORPHEUS legend, and *Antigone* (1944), an immensely popular rendition of Sophocles' play set in World War II France. The best of the pink, or lighter, plays are *Thieves' Carnival* (1938; Eng. trans., 1952) and *Time Remembered* (1939; Eng. trans., 1955). The witty *pièces brillantes*, or glittering plays, include *Ring Round the Moon* (1947; Eng. trans., 1950), *Colombe* (1951; Eng. trans., 1952) and *The Rehearsal* (1950; Eng. trans., 1961). The *pièces grinçantes*, or grating plays, return to the caustic earlier mood and include four devastating comedies: *Ardèle* (1949; Eng. trans., 1959), *The Waltz of the Toreadors* (1952; Eng. trans., 1956), *Ornifle* (1955; Eng. trans., 1970), and *Poor Bitos, or The Masked Dinner* (1956; Eng. trans., 1963). Of Anouilh's *pièces costumées*, or history plays, the most important are *The Lark* (1953; Eng. trans., 1955), about Joan of Arc, and *Becket, or The Honor of God* (1959; Eng. trans., 1962).

Anselm, Saint Saint Anselm, b. *c.*1033, d. Apr. 21, 1109, was an Italian-born archbishop of Canterbury and philosopher, considered the father of SCHOLASTICISM. He became a monk at the Benedictine school directed by LANFRANC in Normandy. After the Norman conquest of England (1066), Anselm followed Lanfranc to Canterbury. He was consecrated archbishop of Canterbury on Dec. 4, 1093. There followed a 13-year struggle between Anselm and the kings of England concerning the rights of the church over English sees, revenues, lay investiture

Saint Anselm, archbishop of Canterbury, is depicted in this medieval manuscript (c. 1150). As a philosopher and theologian, he was among the early proponents of scholasticism, a dominant school of philosophy during the Middle Ages.

(see INVESTITURE CONTROVERSY), property, and the primacy of the pope in the English church. During these years of church-state struggle, Anselm wrote his greatest theological work, *Cur Deus Homo* (Why God Became Man, 1098).

Perhaps no other medieval writing has received as much philosophical attention as Anselm's *Proslogion*, in which he presented the ontological proof for the existence of GOD. The argument holds that even one who denies the existence of God knows what is meant by the term, namely, "a being greater than which none can be conceived." However, since it is greater to exist both in the mind and in reality than in the mind alone, there must necessarily be in reality a being greater than which none can be conceived.

Although Anselm was never formally canonized, a calendar of Christ Church, Canterbury, dating before the martyrdom of Saint Thomas BECKET (Dec. 29, 1170), twice refers to Anselm as saint. He has been honored as a doctor of the church. Both as theologian and philosopher, Anselm is credited as having the most penetrating intellect between Saint AUGUSTINE, whom he closely followed, and Saint Thomas AQUINAS. Feast day: Apr. 21.

Ansermet, Ernest

[ahn-sair-may'] Ernest Ansermet, b. Nov. 11, 1883, d. Feb. 20, 1969, a Swiss conductor, founded (1918) the notable Orchestre de la Suisse Romande in Geneva, which he conducted until his retirement in 1967. On his many tours of Europe and the Americas, he was a brilliant interpretative advocate of such composers as Claude Debussy, Sergei Prokofiev, Maurice Ravel, and Igor Stravinsky.

A trained mathematician, Ansermet also studied music in Switzerland and Paris. An early meeting with Stravinsky led to his important collaboration with the Ballets Russes de Serge Diaghilev.

Anshan

(An-Shan) Anshan (1988 est. pop., 1,330,000) is a city in northeastern China in Liaoning province, part of the region of Manchuria. The site of China's largest iron and steel complex, Anshan's manufactures include farm machinery, building materials, chemicals, textiles, porcelain, and electrical appliances.

The city was first settled in 1387. After extensive destruction during the Boxer Rebellion, it was rebuilt in 1909 as an industrial city. In 1917–18 the Japanese established steelworks there. Invading Soviet forces dismantled the factories in 1945, but they were rebuilt in 1949. The blast furnaces were damaged again in 1967 during the Cultural Revolution but have since been rebuilt.

Ansky, Shloime

[an'-skee, shloy'-may] A Yiddish folklorist, dramatist, and author of many Hasidic tales and Jewish legends, Shloime Ansky, b. 1863, d. Nov. 8, 1920, attained fame among the Jews of his native Russia with his hymn "Di Shvue" (The Oath). It was composed for the Bund, the Jewish socialist movement founded in 1897. He rose to international fame with his tragedy *The Dybbuk* (1919), which has enjoyed thousands of performances in many languages since its Yiddish premiere in Vilna, Lithuania, in 1920. It was first filmed in 1934, has often been shown on television, was set as an opera in 1963, and was choreographed as a ballet in 1974. The dybbuk is a demon who takes possession of a young woman until exorcised. The play, with its tender love story, gives insight into the world of HASIDISM with its joy, longing for saintliness, and faith in divine justice.

ant

Ants are no doubt the most successful of all the social insects of the HYMENOPTERA, an order that also includes the social wasps and bees. Ants are colony makers and have inhabited the warmer environments of the Earth for at least 100 million years. Their numbers are prodigious: it has been estimated that at any one time there are at least 1 quadrillion (1×10^{15}) living ants on the Earth—a number so large that it is almost meaningless. These individuals are members of some 5,000, or perhaps as many as 10,000, species. Ants are remarkably adaptive and are found almost everywhere. In their feeding habits they range from species that specialize in feeding exclusively on ARTHROPOD eggs to those which feed indiscriminately on any living or dead animal.

Form and Function

Ant colonies may contain from a few to upward of 20 million individuals. They consist of two or more castes and subcastes of females, and males that are winged and appear only periodically in the life of the colony. The males are produced, as in all other Hymenoptera, from unfertilized eggs and serve only to fertilize the queens. The females, on the other hand, develop from fertilized eggs and are the functional mainstay of the colony. Most are wingless, nonreproductive workers and perform the life-maintaining tasks of the colony. Some are queens, usually winged; once inseminated, they produce large numbers of eggs from which the LARVAE hatch. These immature ants are fed and cared for by the workers. In some species the workers vary in size, and subcastes are sometimes distinguishable. This is especially true for the largest workers, which are often referred to as soldiers. In such species a division of labor correlated with worker size may be evident. Small workers may, for instance, tend the larvae, while the larger workers forage for food.

The body of an ant is divided into three major parts: a head, with elbowed or geniculate ANTENNAE and variable mandibles; an alitrunk, or mesosoma, which is part thorax and part abdomen and to which the wings (when present) and legs are attached; and a viscera-containing gaster, which is attached to the alitrunk by a one- or two-segmented waist. In addition to the unique metapleural glands, the queens and workers possess a crop that, when dammed by the proventriculus, serves as a storage tank for liquids. This storage capability makes it possible for these ants to regurgitate food for larvae and for other adults.

When new males and queens emerge from a colony, they usually engage in a nuptial flight, during which fertilization occurs. The male dies soon after the flight, but

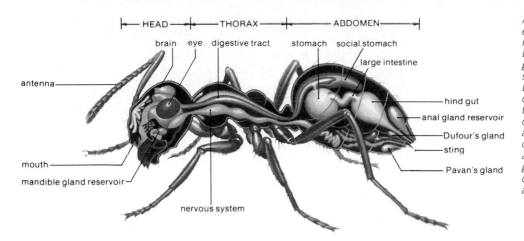

HEAD — THORAX — ABDOMEN

brain eye digestive tract stomach social stomach

large intestine

antenna

hind gut

anal gland reservoir

Dufour's gland

sting

Pavan's gland

mouth

mandible gland reservoir

nervous system

A diagram of a worker ant shows the inner structure of its body, including glands that secrete special chemicals. Dufour's gland produces a substance that other ants can detect and follow as a trail; Pavan's gland contains poison; and anal and mandibular glands secrete chemicals used as alarm signals.

the female drops to the ground, sheds her wings, and either is adopted by an existing colony or sequesters herself in a cavity, where she founds a new colony.

Ants pass through a developmental sequence that includes the egg, larva, pupa, and adult. Whether an egg will eventually develop into a worker or a queen depends mainly on the amount and kind of food fed to the larvae. As a colony matures, it eventually contains overlapping generations in which adults care for the young.

Ants have an elaborate system of communication, which includes visual, auditory, tactile, gustatory, and olfactory signals. Gustatory interaction is accomplished through the oral exchange of food, or trophallaxis, a behavior pattern of critical importance to social organization in ants. Olfactory communication is achieved through the release of chemicals called PHEROMONES, which permit ants to signal alarm, lay trails, and attract sister workers to new food sources.

Ants usually live in nests excavated in the soil or wood or housed in a variety of natural cavities. Some army ants, however, form temporary nests that consist entirely of the ants themselves, suspended from one another and a supporting object. The nest is a living ball or cylinder of ants. Other ants construct carton nests of macerated plant tissue. African weaver ants make nests of living leaves held in place by larval silk; when fashioning a nest, the workers carry the larvae about. Ants of the genus *Pseudomyrmex* live in the thorns of acacia trees and feed on the trees but also protect them from leaf-eating insects and competitive vegetation.

Specialized Colonies

Army Ants. Many ant species have specialized ways of obtaining food. Among the more dramatic is army ant behavior, which includes group predation and nomadism. The former involves both group raiding and group retrieval of prey. Because the workers forage en masse for food, they are able to overcome and capture other social insects and large arthropods. The colonies frequently migrate to new nesting sites where food is abundant.

Fungus-Growing Ants. Ants of the New World tribe Attini are highly specialized HERBIVORES that cultivate subterranean fungal gardens on fecal or plant-derived substrates. This fungus serves as the sole food of these ants. Attines of the genus *Atta* are called "leaf cutters" because they gather green leaves, which they masticate and on which they grow their fungus. *Atta* workers fertilize their gardens with fecal fluid, which contains amino acids and enzymes that help the fungus break down leaf proteins. Because the ants cannot digest the cellulose in these macerated leaves, and the fungus can, the ants gain access to the cellulose by eating the fungus.

Harvester Ants. Many ants feed on seeds. Some, called harvesters, live in arid environments and depend almost totally on seeds. Most harvesters construct elaborate subterranean nests that reach depths of 2 m (6 ft) or more. The nests contain some chambers devoted entirely to the storage of seeds and are sometimes topped by a mound of gravel and sand. Workers clear all vegetation from a circular space around the nest some 1 to 10 m (3 to 33 ft) wide. Harvesters generally husk the collected seeds before storing them.

Gatherers and Herders. Some ants gather plant liquids directly from wounds and nectaries. Still others collect honeydew—a substance excreted by insects such as APHIDS and TREEHOPPERS. These insects, of the order HOMOPTERA, feed on plant juices. Although the nutrient-rich juices first pass through the homopteran's digestive tract, the honeydew excreted through the anus still contains many nutrients. Some ants simply lick fallen honeydew, whereas others actively solicit it and directly imbibe the droplets as they form at the anal opening. The homopterans are protected from predators by the ants, which may even construct shelters over their "cows."

Parasitic and Slave-Making Ants. Some ants have entered into parasitic relations with other ants. Two or more species may form compound nests, in which the broods are maintained separately and the parasitic species obtains food from the host species. Although compound nests may be nonparasitic, another category, called mixed colonies, almost always results from social parasitism. In these the broods of the involved species are mixed and

In a colony of Australian bulldog ants, a queen (A) *lays her eggs, which hatch into larvae. Larvae* (B) *develop into pupae, spin cocoons* (C), *and emerge finally as adult ants. Female worker ants* (D) *tend the larvae and cocoons, and also forage aboveground for food and twigs to build up the nest. In a nuptial flight* (E), *a male fertilizes a queen ant with enough sperm to last for ten to fifteen years of producing eggs. The male dies soon after this flight, and the queen starts a new colony once she has dropped to the ground and shed her wings.*

cared for as one. Some parasitic ants are permanent residents of the host colony and are so specialized that they have lost the worker caste. Slave making also results in mixed colonies. Slave-making species raid other colonies and steal worker pupae, which they enslave to carry out the work of their colonies.

Ants and Humans

Ants can be both harmful and beneficial to humans. Pest species include ants that harbor and protect homopterans that in turn damage plants: *Atta* leaf cutters that defoliate entire trees and pose a threat to tropical agriculture; harvesters that can strip rangeland of vegetation and thus promote erosion; carpenter ants that can damage wooden structures; and the red fire ant, which inflicts a painful sting. On the other hand, Chinese citrus growers have for centuries used the predacious ant *Oecophylla smaragdina* in mandarin orange trees to destroy insect pests, and other ant species have been similarly used to protect crops elsewhere.

Classification and Origin

Ants form a single family, the Formicidae, in the order Hymenoptera. They differ from other Hymenoptera in possessing a pair of metapleural glands. Although the function of these thoracic glands remains unclear, it has been suggested that they produce an odor that distinguishes one colony from another.

Ants probably evolved from wasps resembling the present-day family Tiphiidae. In the fossil record, ants are known almost exclusively from Tertiary fossils, the oldest of which is of the Eocene Epoch (approximately 53 to 37 million years ago). These fossil ants are similar to contemporary ants.

See also: ANIMAL BEHAVIOR; ANIMAL COMMUNICATION; SOCIOBIOLOGY.

ant lion   Ant lion is the common name for any member of the insect genus *Myrmeleon* in the family Myrmeleontidae, order Neuroptera, and the name is also applied to some other genera of the family. The adults resemble damselflies but are softer bodied and have long, knobbed antennae. Their wingspan ranges from 2 to 16 cm (0.8 to 6.3 in). The larvae, called doodlebugs, have long, sickle-like jaws and move backward more easily than forward. They build a conical pit (as much as 50 mm/2 in deep) in sandy soils by tossing up the sand with their heads, then remain at the bottom with jaws above the surface and wait for ants (hence their name) or other insects to fall in. Ant lions are widely distributed in sandy areas, particularly those of the southern United States.

antacid Antacids are substances that reduce the degree of acidity in the stomach and upper digestive tract. They are among the most commonly used nonprescription drugs and are taken by persons feeling the distress of acid indigestion, sour stomach, and the esophageal pain known as heartburn. In strong doses, many of the same chemicals are used by physicians in the treatment of peptic ULCER.

All common antacids contain a weak base (see ACIDS AND BASES). Antacids containing easily absorbable cations, or positively charged ions, are called systemic. Sodium bicarbonate is the most familiar of these. Most antacids, however, are nonsystemic, in that only a small portion of the cation is absorbed. Calcium carbonate, which is fast-acting and continues to act for some time, is an example. Magnesium carbonate produces comparable effects, but less of the cation is absorbed. Like most other magnesium compounds, it has a cathartic effect. Antacids containing aluminum act slowly but also are of long duration. A more recently developed antacid, cimetidine, operates by blocking histamine receptors that stimulate gastric-acid secretion.

Antacids in themselves are not harmful to persons in good health. Their repeated use, however, can have harmful side effects. For example, excessive sodium (in bicarbonate) can contribute to hypertension, and excessive bicarbonate itself may lead to kidney stones and urinary-tract infections. Apparent gastric discomforts may also be symptoms of more severe problems that should be addressed instead of being masked by the use of antacids. Antacids should never be used for more than a short period of time.

Antananarivo [an-tuh-nan-uh-ree'-voh] Antananarivo (Tananarive) is the capital and largest city (1985 est. pop., 662,600) of Madagascar, the island state off the southeast coast of Africa. It is the country's commercial, industrial, and manufacturing center and is connected by rail to the Indian Ocean port of Toamasina (Tamatave).

Antarctica Antarctica is the fifth largest and southernmost continent. Its position at the South Pole, together with its elevation and ice-and-snow cover, generates the coldest climate on Earth. Its enormous ice sheet covers all but 2% to 3% of the continent and extends over the encircling ocean. If released by melting, this amount of water would cause the sea level to rise more than 60 m (200 ft) worldwide.

The summer population is several thousand, but only a few hundred scientists and support personnel stay during the winter. They live in semipermanent bases, the largest of which is the U.S. base at McMurdo, Ross Island.

The continent is more than half again as large as the United States and covers about 14,245,000 km² (5,500,000 mi²), including 1,640,000 km² (633,000 mi²) of floating ice shelves. At least a third of the coastline (about 30,000 km/18,600 mi) is hidden beneath perennial ice.

Most of the continent lies within the Antarctic Circle (lat. 66°30' S). It is completely isolated by the Antarctic Ocean. The South Shetland Islands adjoin the Antarctic Peninsula. Other islands in the Antarctic region, but removed from the continent itself, include South Georgia, South Sandwich, South Orkney, Bouvet, Heard, Balleny, Scott, and Peter. Islands such as the Kerguelen Islands that lie north of the Antarctic Convergence contain glaciers and are considered loosely within the Antarctic region. Because seasonal or perennial sea ice is found along all coasts, protected harbors are not available to ships much of the year.

The continent may be subdivided into two major parts on the basis of topography and geology: west Antarctica, which is south of South America, and east Antarctica, in the Eastern Hemisphere. The boundary between them roughly follows the 0°–180° meridian, from the east side of the Ronne-Filchner Ice Shelf in the WEDDELL SEA to the west side of the ROSS ICE SHELF in the Ross Sea. These enormous floating masses of PACK ICE are derived mostly from glaciers discharging from the continent; the Ronne Filchner Ice Shelf encompasses about 500,000 km² (193,050 mi²), and the Ross Ice Shelf about 538,720 km² (208,000 mi²). The Ross Ice Shelf alone is about equal to the area of Texas. Probably an additional 600,880 km² (232,000 mi²) of ice shelves fringe the coast of the continent.

In striking contrast to the ice cover are the "dry valley" areas of the continent, especially in Victoria Land, which receive little precipitation and do not have a continuous snow cover. The Transantarctic Mountains (2,000 to 4,572 m/6,562 to 15,000 ft) extend from Victoria Land southward along the west side of the Ross Sea to the Weddell Sea on the opposite side of the continent.

Coal, uranium, and a variety of metallic minerals have been found on land but are not considered economically exploitable. Offshore petroleum and natural gas have more economic potential. Fishing boats take whales, seals, and krill (small protein-rich crustaceans) from the surrounding ocean. Growing controversy surrounding the issues of environmental protection and resource development in Antarctica was fueled by oil spills there in 1989.

Topography

Antarctica has two topographies—one of perennial snow and ice (about 2 km/1.24 mi thick) and one of land. The snow-and-ice surface in east Antarctica is an irregularly shaped elliptical dome that rises to a maximum elevation of more than 4,267 m (14,000 ft). A deep bay in the margin of the continent at the Amery Ice Shelf and Lambert Glacier produces a topographic sag in the ice almost to the center of the dome. Broad topographic highs rise above both sides of it. In Queen Maud Land rugged mountains retain a high ice surface inland. The ice sur-

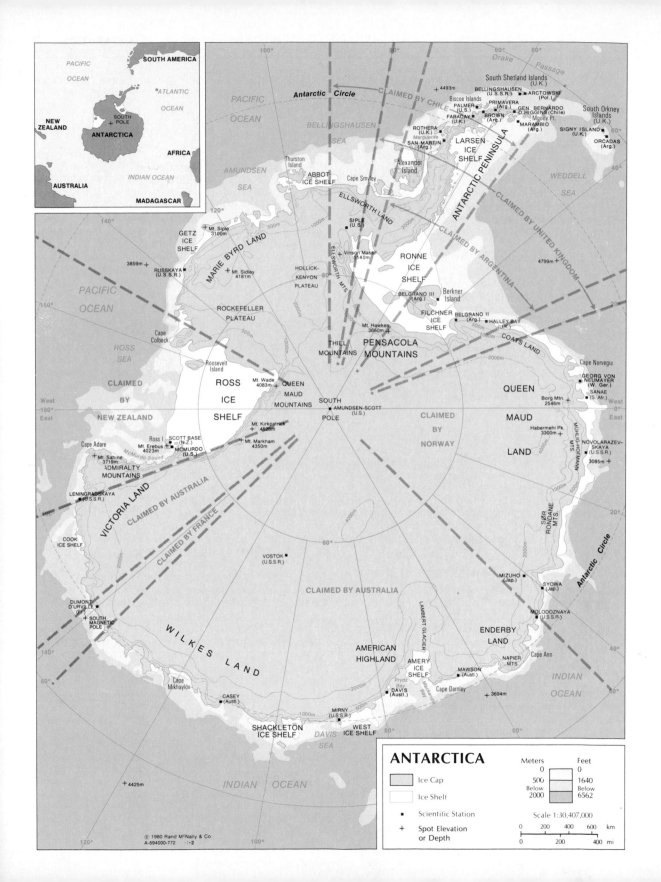

ANTARCTICA

Ice Cap

Ice Shelf

■ Scientific Station

+ Spot Elevation or Depth

Meters
0
500
Below
2000

Feet
0
1640
Below
6562

Scale 1:30,407,000

0   200   400   600 km

0   200   400 mi

© 1980 Rand McNally & Co.
A-594000-772

The U.S.S. Atka, an icebreaker, forges its way through the frozen waters of Mc-Murdo Sound. Antarctica is surrounded by a floating belt of pack ice that threatens ships as far as 1,500 km (900 mi) to the north.

face of the dome rises more gently from the coast south of New Zealand and Australia.

In west Antarctica a broad ice ridge extends from the center of the ice dome in east Antarctica past the South Pole and into the center of west Antarctica at the Ellsworth Mountains. Major ice flow is diverted to the Ronne-Filchner and Ross ice shelves on opposite sides of the ridge, and long shallow troughs follow that drainage. The only other large area of ice surface above 2,000 m (6,562 ft) is that in the Executive Committee Range near the coast between the Amundsen Sea and the Ross Sea. A broad saddle connects the Executive Committee Range and the ridge near the Ellsworth Mountains. A smaller area of ice slightly higher than 2,000 m (6,562 ft) lies at the base of the Antarctic Peninsula.

Most of Antarctica's bedrock topography is known only indirectly. The data collected thus far indicate an elongate basin, named the Wilkes Subglacial Basin, several hundred meters below sea level and parallel to and west of the Transantarctic Mountains of Victoria Land, in east Antarctica. The Polar Basin extends from the South Pole toward Queen Maud Land. In Wilkes Land deep embayments with small rises penetrate from the coast at longitude 145° and 115°. In those embayments preglacial shorelines would have extended many hundreds of kilometers into the present continent. A bedrock high above 3,000 m (9,842 ft) is centered at the Gamburtsev Mountains, near the Pole of Inaccessibility. In the rest of east Antarctica the bedrock topography ranges from about 1,000 m (3,280 ft) above to slightly below sea level.

Mount Erebus, one of Antarctica's five known active volcanoes, dominates the coastal landscape along McMurdo Sound. The volcano was first sighted during the 1840s by the James Clark Ross expedition.

brown skua

killer whale

blue-eyed cormorant

blue whale

Adelie penguin

king penguin

leopard seal

fur seal

Weddell seal

In contrast, much of the bedrock surface of west Antarctica is between sea level and −1,000 m (−3,280 ft), and depressions almost 3,000 m (9,842 ft) below sea level are known. In ranges where rock-surface elevations are between 1,000 and 3,000 m (3,281 and 9,842 ft), mountain peaks protrude above the ice surface. Most notable are the ranges in Marie Byrd Land and Eights Coast and the irregular ridge that extends from the Horlick Mountains through the Ellsworth Mountains to the Antarctic Peninsula. The highest point in Antarctica is Vinson Massif (5,140 m/16,863 ft) in the Sentinel Range.

The weight of ice has depressed the land by an average of 560 m (1,838 ft), roughly 0.28 times the average thickness of ice (2,000 m/6,562 ft). If the ice were removed, the land would rise until most of east Antarctica was above sea level, but west Antarctica would consist largely of a shallow sea.

By the time (1957–58) of the INTERNATIONAL GEOPHYSICAL YEAR (IGY), many land regions were still unknown. Now all major areas of rock outcrop have been seen or photographed from the air, if not actually studied on the ground.

Geology

A vast Precambrian continental shield makes up east Antarctica. High-grade metamorphic rocks dominate the coast. The Ross mobile belt includes the Transantarctic Mountains. An inner belt of sedimentary and volcanic rocks of the Gondwana System are Devonian to Jurassic in age; an outer belt is Precambrian to Cambrian in age. Cenozoic volcanic rocks are present on the west side of the Ross Sea.

In west Antarctica the Antarctic Peninsula and the coastal area to Marie Byrd Land make up the Andean mobile belt, of upper Paleozoic to Mesozoic rocks. The Ellsworth mobile belt (of mostly late Precambrian to late Paleozoic age) includes the Ellsworth and Whitmore mountains and a broad arc that swings out to the Filchner Ice Shelf.

Most plant and animal fossils are found in the sedimentary beds in the Transantarctic Mountains or in the low-grade metamorphic rocks of the Antarctic Peninsula. Fossils in rock structures of known age permit correlation of Antarctica with other continents believed to have been united in the ancestral continent of Gondwanaland. The discovery in 1982 of the fossil remains of the first land mammal found in Antarctica supports this theory. Other fossil evidence (including dinosaur remains, first found in 1986) indicates that Antarctica once had a climate milder than its present one.

The Kukri peneplain, an erosional surface on the Precambrian and lower Paleozoic basement rocks, has been identified throughout the Transantarctic Mountains. A Tertiary peneplain has been interpreted at several places in the Antarctic Peninsula and Pensacola, Shackleton, and Prince Charles mountains. Active volcanoes are confined to Victoria Land, Marie Byrd Land, and the South Shetland Islands. Block-faulted mountains are mostly in the Transantarctic Mountains, Queen Maud Land, and the Antarctic Peninsula.

Soils in Antarctica are limited to the ice-free areas, only 2% to 3% of the continent, and are patchy even there. They are thin, commonly alkaline, and have little humus, although they have many soil-forming bacteria. A "desert pavement" of rock fragments is common.

Climate

The Antarctic polar-climate boundary (10° C/50° F isotherm for the warmest month) encompasses about 12% of the surface of the globe, an area twice as large as that of the Arctic. It includes all of the Antarctic continent except the extreme northern tip of the Antarctic Peninsula. The vast area of snow and ice reflects about three-fourths of the incoming radiation. Vostok at 78°28' south latitude and 3,505 m (11,500 ft) elevation has an average temperature for the warmest month of only −33° C (−27° F), an absolute minimum of −88.3° C (−126.9° F), and an absolute maximum of −21° C (−5.8° F). The absolute minimum figure is the lowest temperature ever recorded on Earth. Coastal areas are much warmer, with annual mean temperatures of −15° to −10° C (5° to 14° F).

Most precipitation falls as snow. This amounts to only 50 mm (2 in) in the interior but is highly variable, from 500 to more than 1,000 mm (20 to 40 in), on the coast. The bulk of the precipitation comes from the cyclonic storms that diverge into the interior from the ocean.

In the mid-1980s, atmospheric studies showed that an ozone "hole"—a dramatic drop in ozone concentration in an area of the ozone layer above the continent—was appearing and then disappearing each Antarctic spring. Studies of past records revealed that this had been occurring for several years. Whether this "hole" is a product of human activities or a natural process is not yet known.

Scientists are also measuring the Antarctic ice in an attempt to determine whether the GREENHOUSE EFFECT, a global warming trend caused by rising levels of atmospheric carbon dioxide, is melting the Antarctic ice cap (which could raise global sea levels) or whether the warming air, because it can hold more moisture, is increasing snowfall over Antarctica, thus increasing the size of the continent.

Antarctic Life

Most of the life on and around the Antarctic continent is supported by the sea, because the continent itself is barren. The life consists primarily of a few species of lichens and mosses; some small floating plants called phytoplankton, which occur in certain freshwater lakes in ice-free desert areas; and a few arthropods, the most numerous of which are several groups of mites. The sea, on the other hand, is extremely rich because in many areas water movement is vertical and brings nutrients from the bottom to the surface for phytoplankton, which become food for small floating animals called zooplankton. Several species of zooplankton are important to the Antarctic marine ecosystem, particularly the krill, shrimplike organisms that feed directly on various small plants and are in turn an important food source for many fishes, birds, and mammals. Due to the exploitation of certain Antarctic species, several agreements to conserve Antarctica's living resources have been signed.

Robert F. Scott (standing, center) and his crew pose during their ill-fated 1912 expedition. The British explorers reached the South Pole only to find that Amundsen's Norwegian team had beaten them by more than a month. All members of the Scott expedition died during the return trip.(Below) Richard E. Byrd became the first person to fly over the South Pole, on Nov. 29, 1929.

A fairly large number of fish species are found in the Antarctic, but they are small in size or few in number. The birds of the Antarctic ecosystem include penguins, albatrosses, and petrels. Seven species of penguins are confined to the pack-ice region; they constitute more than 80% of the birds in the Antarctic region. The most common penguin is the Adélie, which nests in ice-free areas mostly on offshore islands around the Antarctic continent. Flying birds, such as albatrosses and petrels, nest on various offshore islands and on rock outcroppings.

Antarctic marine mammals include the whale and the seal. The whales can be classified into two groups, the baleen whales and the toothed whales. Four species of large baleen whales—blue, fin, sei, and humpback—inhabit Antarctic waters regularly. The two species of toothed whales considered most important are the large sperm whale, the only large-toothed whale to occupy the region, and the killer whale.

The following four species of seals are found in the pack-ice region: the crabeater, Weddell, leopard, and Ross's. The crabeater seal is by far the most abundant. The southern fur seal and the southern elephant seal are found farther north than the four species of true Antarctic seal.

Exploration and Territorial Claims

Although recent cartographic studies suggest that the broad outlines of the continent may have been known before the mid-16th century, it is generally thought that James Cook, on Jan. 16, 1773, was the first person to cross the Antarctic Circle, and Adm. Fabian von Bellingshausen and M. P. Lazarev, on Jan. 28, 1820, were probably the first to sight land in the Antarctic. John Davis, captain of the American sealer Huron, was the first to land, at Hughes Bay on the Antarctic Peninsula, on Feb. 7, 1821. On Jan. 23, 1895, Leonard Kristensen and Carsten Borchgrevink landed near Cape Adare, and they were thus the first to set foot on the main part of the continent.

In 1898, Borchgrevink led the first expedition to spend a winter on the continent, also at Cape Adare. Their stay ushered in the "heroic phase" of exploration by parties that wintered over for scientific purposes. Otto Nordenskjöld explored (1901–04) the east coast of the Antarctic Peninsula. Robert F. Scott and Ernest H. Shackleton led three scientific parties (1901–04, 1907–09, and 1910–13) from bases on Ross Island. In 1908, T. W. E. David of Scott's party ascended Mount Erebus (3,795 m/12,450 ft), and later reached the South Magnetic Pole (lat. 72°25' S, long. 155°16' E). The pole has since moved to the Adélie Coast. In 1909, Shackleton traversed the Ross Ice Shelf, ascended the Beardmore Glacier, and reached 88°23' south latitude on the polar ice sheet.

On Oct. 20, 1911, Roald Amundsen of Norway left from the Bay of Whales, on the east side of the Ross Ice Shelf, with four companions on skis and with dogsleds. They reached the South Pole (altitude 2,804 m/9,200 ft) on Dec. 14, 1911, via the Axel Heiberg Glacier. Scott started from Ross Island on Oct. 24, 1911, and followed Shackleton's route of 1909. Scott, Wilson, Bowers, Oates, and Evans man-hauled one sledge to the South Pole on Jan. 17, 1912; all perished on the return.

In 1911–14, Sir Douglas Mawson explored the Adélie Coast and Queen Mary Land. On Nov. 16, 1928, C. B. Eielson and Sir George Hubert Wilkins made the first airplane flight in Antarctica. Between 1926 and 1937, Lars Christensen made aerial surveys and mapped the coastal area from the Weddell Sea to the Shackleton Ice Shelf. Adm. Richard E. BYRD used aircraft extensively during four expeditions: 1928–30, 1933–35, 1939–41, and 1946–47. From a base at Little America, Byrd, Bernt Balchen, A. C. McKinley, and Harold June flew to the South Pole and back on Nov. 28–29, 1929. Between 1933 and 1939, Lincoln ELLSWORTH made four expeditions to Antarctica. In 1935 he flew from the tip of the Antarctic Peninsula to the Bay of Whales in the Ross Sea, landing four times during 12 days. In 1934–37 a British expedition used planes, boats, and dogs to study much of the Antarctic Peninsula, and in 1939 a German group photographed a large area in Queen Maud Land. In 1946–48, Comdr. Finn Ronne and a group, his wife among them, mapped a large area from the Antarctic Peninsula to the Filchner Ice Shelf. The Norwegian-British-Swedish expedition of 1949–52 conducted major scientific traverses into the interior and laid the foundation for the IGY.

During the IGY, 12 nations manned more than 50 wintering-over stations in Antarctica. The Pole of Inaccessibility (lat. 82°06′ S, long. 54°58′ E) was reached on Dec. 14, 1958, by a Soviet IGY tractor train. Between Nov. 24, 1957, and Mar. 2, 1958, Sir Vivian FUCHS's party crossed the continent from the Weddell Sea to the Ross Sea. In 1982, British explorers Sir Ranulph Fiennes and Charles Burton completed the first crossing of both poles in a single circumnavigation of the Earth.

The Special Committee on Antarctic Research (SCAR), set up in 1957, now coordinates all Antarctic research. Emphasis today is on long-term investigations of large-scale phenomena.

The United States and the USSR recognize no territorial claims in Antarctica and make none, although reserving the right to do so. The Antarctic Treaty was ratified on June 23, 1961, by the 12 IGY nations referred to above—Argentina, Australia, Chile, France, New Zealand, Norway, and the United Kingdom (all of which claim parts of the continent), plus Belgium, Japan, South Africa, the USSR, and the United States. Brazil, China, India, Poland, Uruguay, Italy, and Germany later became voting signatories; other nations not conducting major scientific activity in Antarctica have signed the document but do not have voting rights. Besides freezing all territorial claims until 1991, when it can be reviewed, the Antarctic Treaty states specifically that Antarctica shall be used for peaceful purposes only. In 1988 a convention to regulate the future exploitation of Antarctic mineral resources was negotiated. It was widely criticized by environmentalists, however, and by Third World nations demanding that the continent's resources be shared under United Nations supervision, and was later abandoned.

anteater   Anteaters are toothless mammals that feed mainly on ants. They belong to the family Myrmecophagidae, order Edentata ("without teeth"). The anteaters are the only edentates entirely lacking in teeth, the others (sloths and armadillos) having cheek teeth. Anteaters are found from Mexico to northern Argentina. Three genera

A giant anteater walks on its knuckles to protect its sharp claws. It uses its claws to tear apart ant and termite nests and then feeds on the insects with its long tongue.

exist, each with a single species. The giant anteater, or ant bear (*Myramacophaga tridactyla*), measures 183 cm (6 ft) from the long, cylindrical snout to the end of the bushy, cascading tail, and weighs up to 23 kg (50 lb). The powerful claws on the forefeet and the long (58-cm/23-in), extensible tongue are used to uncover and feed on ants, termites, and beetle larvae. The collared anteater, *Tamandua tetradactyla*, is about 56 cm (22 in) long, and its naked prehensile tail is as long again or longer. Chiefly nocturnal, it lives in trees and eats bees and ants. The two-toed pygmy anteater, *Cyclopes didactylus*, is 17 cm (6½ in) long and feeds in treetops at night.

antelope   Antelope are any of several hoofed, ruminant mammals, belonging to the family Bovidae, order Artiodactyla. This family also includes bison, buffalo, cattle, goats, and sheep. Although antelope resemble deer, they are much more closely related to cattle. Africa is the home of most antelope, although a few species survive in Asia and a close relative, the mountain goat, lives in North America. The numbers of antelope are sharply declining because of overhunting and habitat destruction. Habitats most common to antelope are grasslands, dry plains, and forests. Some antelope live in swamplands, on hot deserts, or at high mountain elevations.

Characteristics. Antelope are ruminants, or cud chewers. They lack incisors, or biting teeth, in the upper front jaw, and thus must tear off grass stems by exerting pressure with the lower teeth against the upper gum pad. This food is swallowed mainly unchewed and is later regurgitated from the stomach in small wads, or cuds, for thorough chewing with the molars.

Antelope have slender legs, with two-hoofed toes on each foot. Many of them have taller rumps than forequarters, with powerful rear-leg muscles to facilitate running and leaping. Some can attain speeds of about 60 km/h (35 mph). The rigid structure of the backbone enables them to run this fast and to jump high without injury to themselves. Their senses of smell and hearing are well developed, their vision less so.

These animals vary greatly in size. The largest, the giant ELAND of West Africa, may grow to a weight of more than 545 kg (1,200 lb) and a shoulder height of 1.8 m (6 ft). The smallest, the royal antelope of Africa's western

The hartebeest, native to African savannas, looks ungainly but runs with grace. The royal pygmy antelope, of West Africa, measures 20-25 cm (8-10 in) high. The greater kudu, of eastern Africa, is one of the most handsome of large antelopes. The white Arabian oryx, native to Sudan deserts, has horns that are almost as long as the oryx is tall. The gerenuk, of eastern Africa, is known as the giraffe antelope because of its long neck.

hartebeest

royal antelope

greater kudu

Arabian oryx

gerenuk

coastal regions, weighs about 6.8 kg (15 lb) and stands 25 cm (10 in) tall at the shoulder.

Horns of spectacular beauty adorn the heads of most antelope. Many horns are long and curved; some are ringed, and many are spiral, S-shaped, or lyre-shaped. The male four-horned antelope of Burma and India has two pairs of horns, one atop its head and the other on its forehead. Horns range in length from those of the royal antelope, which protrude less than 2.5 cm (1 in), to the corkscrew-shaped 1.5-m (5-ft) horns of the kudu of eastern and southern Africa. Antelope horns are nonbranching and have a bony core. They are not shed periodically, as are the antlers of deer.

Classification. It is generally agreed that the antelope group comprises about 50 genera and more than 100 species, including the GAZELLES. Among the largest and best-known antelopes are the ORYX, gnus (WILDEBEESTS), elands, kudus, hartebeests, sable antelope, and roan antelope of the African plains. The BONGO is a large antelope of African forests. Medium-sized antelope include the black buck of India and the African IMPALA and SPRINGBOK. The North American PRONGHORN, often called pronghorn antelope, is not a true antelope.

---

antenna (biology)   Antennae are the foremost pair of appendages on the heads of insects, myriapods, crustaceans, and onychophorans. Although their evolutionary origin from other body structures may vary, antennae are primarily organs of sensation.

A male emperor moth uses its antennae to locate the scent of a female who may be miles away. This moth's antennae are covered with thousands of minute olfactory hairs. Antennae help an animal feel, smell, and taste its surroundings.

Antennal structure and function are probably best understood among the insects. Insect antennae may be long and threadlike, featherlike, clubbed, or elbowed. They are typically composed of a basal scape that articulates with the head, a middle segment called the pedicel, and a comparatively long flagellum at the top. Antennae sometimes differ in males and females. They are typically covered with sensory hairs and pits (sensilla) involved especially with touch, smell, and taste; sensilla enabling insects to perceive temperature and moisture differences may also be present. A highly developed sense organ in the basal region of nearly all adult insect antennae senses movement of the flagellum, functioning in certain flies as a flight speed indicator, in male mosquitoes as a sound receiver helping them orient to female wingbeat sound, in aquatic whirligig beetles as a sensor of surface ripples, and in aquatic bugs as an aid in body orientation. Smell and taste sensilla help perceive stimuli involved with location of mates, hosts, food, egg-deposition sites, and the like. Antennae may play other than a sensory role; for example, larval water scavenger beetles capture and hold prey with their short, toothed antennae.

---

antenna (electronics)   An antenna, or aerial, is a device used in the transmission of ELECTROMAGNETIC RADIATION carrying some form of information. The principle by which it operates is based on James Clerk MAXWELL's theoretical discovery (1865) and its practical verification (1887) by Heinrich HERTZ that a moving electric charge generates electromagnetic radiation that propagates through space with the velocity of light.

Propagation of Signals. Various forms of communication use this propagation—for example, RADIO, broadcast television, radar, and COMMUNICATIONS SATELLITES. All such systems require antennas to transmit and receive the radiation through space. (Electrical signals can, however, be transmitted directly through electrical conductors without antennas, as in the telegraph, telephone, and cable television.) The radio is a good example of the functioning of antennas. The program from a radio station is first converted into electrical signals by a microphone or some other device. Then the transmitting antenna converts these signals into an electromagnetic wave, which spreads out from the transmitter in all directions. Each radio has a receiving antenna that can pick up the signal by intercepting the wave and reconverting it back into electrical signals, which are used to reconstruct the original program.

Antenna Types. Each type of antenna is designed to transmit or receive a specific type of radiation in a specific manner. The simplest type is a single wire called a monopole antenna. Another relatively simple form of antenna is the dipole, or doublet. It comprises two plates or rods connected by two straight wires.

Transmitting Antennas. An important characteristic of transmitting antennas is the amount of radiation that they can transmit. The distribution and direction of that radiation throughout space are also important. In antennas of relatively simple structure, the relative magnitude of the field strength at a point is proportional to the distance of

Indian villagers celebrate the arrival of their new dish antenna. Its parabolic shape is designed to capture satellite signals and reflect them into a receptor, or "feed antenna," at the center of the dish. The receptor is the actual antenna, a short piece of metal that transmits signals to the TV receivers linked to it by antenna cable.

the point from the center of the antenna. When antennas are near the Earth, however, the effect of ground reflections may considerably modify radiation patterns.

In many uses of radio it is desirable that the radiation transmitted or received be directional, or stronger in some directions than in others. Directional transmitting antennas are especially valuable with point-to-point communications.

The form of an antenna depends largely on the type of communication that is desired and the frequency used. For amplitude-modulated (AM) broadcasting, an omnidirectional antenna (one that transmits in all directions) is normally used. It comprises a vertical wire whose height is made about one-quarter of the wavelength being transmitted. Such an antenna radiates vertically polarized waves, or waves in which the direction of the electric field is vertical. Frequency-modulated (FM) antennas differ considerably from those used with amplitude MODULATION. Their frequency is about 100 times as great, and their waves are horizontally polarized. For very high frequencies (VHF) and ultra high frequencies (UHF), a parabolic reflector is used. Such a reflector has the shape of a paraboloid, with the property that if a radiator is placed at the focus of the paraboloid, then the radiation directed back into the dish will be reflected and will emerge in a narrow beam.

Receiving Antennas. Although in theory the two types are the same, receiving antennas and transmitting antennas differ considerably in their operating conditions. The power handled by receiving antennas is generally a minute fraction of the transmitted power; a fundamental goal of antenna design is to obtain maximum signal voltage at the receiving antenna.

Since the advent of portable radios with miniaturized circuitry, AM receiving antennas have been designed in the form of tuning coils wound over a ferrite rod inside the radio. The rod concentrates the magnetic component of the radiation field.

See also: SOUND RECORDING AND REPRODUCTION; TELEVISION TRANSMISSION.

anthelmintic drugs [ant-hel-min'-tik]   Anthelmintic drugs, also called vermifuges, are used to rid a host animal or person of parasitic worms, particularly those found in the intestines. These drugs either inhibit the parasite's ability to use nutrients it needs for survival or paralyze its neuromuscular system, making it unable to maintain its location. Anthelmintic drugs are more effective against tapeworms, pinworms, and roundworms in the gastrointestinal tract than they are against worms in other locations (for example, filaria or schistosomes in blood vessels and trichinae in muscles). Among the most effective of these drugs are thiabendazole, niclosamide, pyrvinium, pyrantel, ivermectin, and antimony compounds.

anthem   The anthem was developed in the Anglican church, as the English-language counterpart of the Roman Catholic Latin MOTET, a polyphonic choral work without accompaniment. During the English Reformation, composers adapted Latin pieces to syllabic English texts, keeping the original music. Thomas TALLIS was among the first to turn from adaptations to original compositions, writing full anthems unadorned by solos or instrumental accompaniment. Verse anthems, employing solo voices and instrumental accompaniment, appeared in the 16th century in the compositions of William BYRD, and became widely used in cathedral practice, where a choir of men and boys served. In the late 17th century, cantata-anthems added dance rhythms imported from France and the theatrical devices of recitative and aria. The form reached its peak with the works of Henry PURCELL. By the 18th century, the growth of parish-church choirs had resulted in a need for simpler pieces, and brevity again came to mark the form.

Early American tune books, whose contents were imported from England, contained some anthems. Native composers imitated their style, and the works of William BILLINGS were especially noteworthy. Imitation of European models developed greater variety and improved quality. A strong American market developed for anthems, so that several publishers concentrated solely on that medium.

Today the term *anthem* includes any brief choral piece used in a religious service. It is also applied to the principal patriotic song of a nation.

Anthemius of Tralles   see HAGIA SOPHIA

Anthony, Saint   Saint Anthony, *c.*251–355, was an Egyptian hermit who became the father of Christian monasticism. The son of well-to-do parents, he gave away his inheritance and joined a group of ascetics, but desiring greater solitude, he advanced by stages ever further into the desert. Disciples flocked to him and formed colonies of hermits, which he organized into the first communities of Christian monks. During the Middle Ages, Anthony was invoked against several types of inflammations of the skin known as "St. Anthony's Fire." Feast day: Jan. 17.

Anthony, Earl   The professional bowler Earl Roderick Anthony, b. Tacoma, Wash., Apr. 27, 1938, in the course of a relatively brief career (1970–83), won more tournaments (41) and more prize money (over $1,200,000) than any previous bowler. He was voted men's Bowler of the Year a record six times (1974–76, 1981–83) and achieved the highest seasonal per-game average a record five times (1973–75, 1980, 1983). He was elected to the Professional Bowlers Association Hall of Fame in 1981 and the American Bowling Congress Hall of Fame in 1986.

Anthony, Susan B.   Susan Brownell Anthony, b. Adams, Mass., Feb. 15, 1820, d. Mar. 13, 1906, was an American pioneer of women's rights. She was the daughter of a Quaker abolitionist. After completing her education in New York, she became a teacher. Dissatisfied teaching, she became assistant manager of the family farm in upstate New York. There she met and discussed with some of her father's guests the nature of American reform. Exposure to the views of William Lloyd Garrison, Wendell Phillips, and Frederick Douglass convinced her that she, too, could become an advocate of reform. However, as an agent for the Daughters of Temperance and for the American Anti-Slavery Society, she encountered discrimination against women.

Anthony's friendship with Elizabeth Cady STANTON proved crucial both for herself and for the feminist crusade. Influenced by Stanton's vigorous defense of women's rights, Anthony helped to found (1866) the American Equal Rights Association in order to work for women's

Susan B. Anthony led the 19th-century women's suffrage movement in the United States. For more than half a century, she directed a lobbying effort to secure women's rights in voting, education, and employment.

suffrage (see SUFFRAGE, WOMEN'S). She helped establish (1869) the National Woman Suffrage Association and in 1872 was arrested for attempting to vote, claiming that the provisions of the 14th and 15th Amendments applied to all citizens, male and female.

From 1892 to 1900, Anthony was president of the National American Woman Suffrage Association. She also helped to compile and edit the first four volumes of *The History of Woman Suffrage* (1881–1902). Anthony's ceaseless work and travel made women's suffrage a recognized cause in both America and Europe.

Anthony of Padua, Saint   Saint Anthony of Padua, b. Aug. 15, 1195, d. June 13, 1231, a Portuguese Franciscan theologian, had a reputation as a miracle worker. He is best known today as the patron saint invoked to find lost articles. After serving as a missionary in Morocco he returned to Europe, where he became distinguished as a biblical scholar and preacher. In art he is sometimes depicted with a book, symbolizing his great erudition. He was canonized in 1232 and declared a Doctor of the Church in 1946. His tomb is in Padua. Feast day: June 13.

anthracite   see COAL AND COAL MINING

anthrax   Anthrax is an infectious and often fatal disease caused by the bacterium *Bacillus anthracis*. It occurs in humans but is more common in such animals as cattle, goats, horses, sheep, and buffalo. Human infections usually result from the handling of animal hides, wool, and hair contaminated with anthrax spores. The bacterium typically enters through the skin and causes a swollen, pustular area, often with a black center, called a malignant pustule. General symptoms include fever and malaise. From the skin pustule the bacterium may invade the bloodstream and rapidly cause a fatal septicemia. Inhalation of spores may cause infection of the lungs, and the resultant pneumonia, called woolsorters' disease, is usually fatal. Anthrax spores may continue to be infectious for many years, even in articles made from infected animal products. Louis Pasteur developed an anthrax vaccine in 1881; new vaccines are now available for those at special risk. Treatment consists of administering large doses of antibiotics.

In 1979 more than 1,000 people were reported to have died from anthrax, after an explosion at a plant in the Russian city of Sverdlovsk. The plant is believed to have been manufacturing biological weapons (see CHEMICAL AND BIOLOGICAL WARFARE), among which anthrax has long been favored by both the USSR and the United States.

anthropological linguistics   Anthropological linguistics is the study of natural human languages—written or unwritten, contemporary or historical—as an intrinsic part of the general study of human culture. A traditional branch of ANTHROPOLOGY, it also includes three subareas: PSYCHOLINGUISTICS, ethnolinguistics, and SOCIOLINGUISTICS. Unlike the formal and deductive approaches to the study of language inaugurated by Noam CHOMSKY, anthropological study of languages describes the observable behaviors of speech communities from an inductive approach. Anthropological linguists also investigate primate systems of communication, sign languages of the deaf, language acquisition by children, pidgin and creole languages, the creation of national languages, bilingualism and dialects, oral literature of preliterate peoples, and ethnographic texts of all kinds.

Early Studies. Colonial expansion in the 19th century created an interest in mapping and understanding all that was found in the new lands, whether Russian-occupied Asia, Spanish colonial America, or American-occupied North America. This interest included an attempt to describe the peoples encountered there, particularly their cultures and languages. Thus until 100 years ago anthropological linguistics in the United States and Russia was a branch of ETHNOGRAPHY and anthropology.

Later Developments. Anthropologists had studied language competence and speech behavior generally; anthropological linguists focused on the way in which human language behavior dramatically reflects both human diversity and commonality in order to explore the range of potentialities and variations within the species. Attention continued to be concentrated upon the languages of peoples maximally different from the Europeans.

Distinguished Russian linguists such as Roman JAKOBSON and Nikolai Trubetskoy began by studying the ethnography and literature of non-Russians living within the tsarist Russian empire. In the United States, the Geological Survey, at first part of the government's attempt to map the newly acquired territories of the Louisiana Purchase and the West, collected word lists of the languages of the indigenous population.

After the Civil War in the United States, a significant contribution was made by John Wesley POWELL at the Bureau of American Ethnology. He developed a classification of the languages north of Mexico showing that, of the hundreds of languages and dialects, only 55 language families existed. This classification was essentially correct, although later studies have shown additional genetic relationships. Most scholars now believe that 10 large language families existed there, as well as a number of isolated languages.

The Twentieth Century. Like Powell, Americans such as Franz BOAS and his student Edward SAPIR studied customs, folklore, speech behavior, and language categories. They examined the grammatical structures and historical relationships of the native languages of the United States, including traditional oral literatures. One result of the studies of American Indian languages was the hypothesis developed by Benjamin Lee Whorf in association with Sapir, that language structures affect the speakers' perceptions.

General linguistic studies of recent decades have concentrated on the supposed genetically inherited human ability for language and on the mental rules shared by members of a speech community, called "competence." Studies in linguistic anthropology have, on the other hand, concentrated on the "performances," speech acts that manifest the innate competence. Structuralist-derived models (see STRUCTURALISM), however, are also now used in the interpretation of ethnographic materials and literary texts and in other SEMIOTIC investigations.

___

anthropology   Anthropology is the study of human differences, cultural and biological, against a background of the nature all humans share. Most anthropologists study human social life and CULTURE. Some, in the highly technical subfield of physical anthropology, study human evolutionary biology.

Nature and Scope of Anthropology

Anthropology began as a kind of natural history, a study of the peoples encountered along the frontiers of European expansion, and anthropologists have continued to use this approach. They record customs and collect artifacts in order to reconstruct the history of cultures. Since the 1930s, however, anthropology has been considered more directly related to the social sciences. Anthropologists analyze and compare societies and their ways of life in search of theoretical generalizations, regularities of process, and patterns of causal connection and covariation. Thus, anthropologists might look for connections between a people's political organization and the kinds of supernatural beings they posit; they might examine beliefs in sorcery and particular kinds of family structure to see if they are correlated; anthropologists might also try to determine whether the status of women in a society is related to the part they play in a subsistence economy. Such searches for regularities and connections in turn shed light on human differences and, through them, on human nature and universals that underlie diversity.

Anthropology differs from sociology, psychology, and the other social sciences in certain key respects. Until World War II anthropologists mainly studied tribal peoples—American Indians, Africans, Pacific Islanders, and Australian Aborigines—by living among them and by studying and participating in their ways of life. By contrast, the theories and methods of the other social sciences were primarily developed in Western societies. Since World War II, anthropologists, along with sociologists, political scientists, economists, and psychologists, have made studies in the Third World. Despite this convergence of interest, anthropological perspectives remain at least partly distinctive in their continuing concern with cultural differences and local ties of KINSHIP and community and in their style and method of research.

Cultural Anthropology

The comparative study of social and cultural systems is commonly (especially in the United States) referred to as cultural anthropology. This branch of anthropology is sometimes also called ethnology. In anthropology the term *culture* denotes a people's heritage of custom and belief. A culture is a system of ideas that has been trans-

The Tasaday, apparently unknown to the outside world until 1971, live in a remote rain forest of the Philippines. Some anthropologists believe them to be a hunting and gathering people who make their homes in caves and use primitive tools of stone and wood. Others believe them to be a hoax.

mitted down through the generations—assumptions about the world, rules and ways to act, goals and ways of achieving them. The cultural heritage of a people—their ideas about ways to live—shapes the ways they actually *do* live: for example, the ways they garden, herd, or hunt and the ways they organize their communities. The way in which cultural ideas are worked out in practice is also governed by the nature of the ecosystem in which people live, their diseases and diet, and the populations around them.

The organization of a people's communities—kinship and marriage networks, family structures, systems of property rights and political order—constitutes their SO-CIAL STRUCTURE. Many anthropologists, particularly those trained in the British tradition, are concerned primarily with the comparative study of social structure; they consider themselves social anthropologists (see SOCIAL AN-THROPOLOGY).

Subfields. Cultural anthropology is a broad category that sometimes includes *anthropological* LINGUISTICS, or the study of language in non-Western cultural settings, and prehistoric ARCHAEOLOGY, the study of the human past before written records. The narrow core of cultural anthropology, however, includes a number of subfields. These include *human ecology*, the comparative study of human adaptation to ecosystems; *political anthropology*, the comparative study of political institutions and processes; *economic anthropology*, the comparative study of systems of production and exchange; *structural-symbolist anthropology*, the study of the ways the mind imposes order on experience and organizes knowledge, particularly as expressed in ritual and myth; *psychological anthropology*, the study of psychological experience (especially in

childhood) and thought in non-Western societies; *legal anthropology*, the comparative study of social control, dispute settlement, and legal processes; URBAN ANTHRO-POLOGY, the study of human experience and social relations in urban settings; and *applied anthropology*, the applications of anthropology to practical problems (for example, the promotion of community reorganization and of bilingual and bicultural education).

As new interests crystallize, other subfields emerge in and outside anthropology. In recent years an anthropology of women, a comparative study of women's experience and status, has become prominent, as has medical anthropology—the comparative study of health, disease, and medicine.

Methodology. The core of the anthropological method is fieldwork: long residence in a community and close participation in its daily life. The observer usually records detailed information on kinship, marriage, social organization, and subsistence activities, even though the main focus may be on legal processes or religious ritual. Such analysis and documentation through fieldwork is called ETHNOGRAPHY.

Where possible and appropriate, anthropologists use the methods of the other social sciences—surveys, interviews, and computer analyses of data—to discover statistical patterns. Often, however, methods (such as questionnaires) that work in Western settings are unfeasible or inappropriate in the communities that anthropologists study.

Physical Anthropology

Physical anthropology is the specialized study of the evolutionary biology of our species, *Homo sapiens*. A central

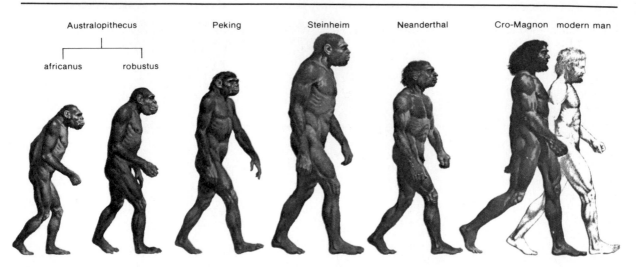

The early predecessors of modern humans, Australopithecus africanus *and* A. robustus, *belong to a species of prehuman creatures known as australo-pithecines, who lived in Africa 5.5 to 1.5 million years ago. They walked erect but had features similar to the chimpanzee. Peking man, a member of the species* Homo erectus, *lived in eastern Asia 500,000 to 250,000 years ago and probably used stone tools and fire. Steinheim man, usually classified as an early species of* Homo sapiens, *lived in Europe about 200,000 years ago. Neanderthal man,* Homo sapiens neanderthalensis, *who lived in Europe, Asia, and Africa between 100,000 and 40,000 years ago, is considered to have had high intelligence, compared with that of his ancestors. Cro-Magnon man,* Homo sapiens sapiens, *whose fossils have been discovered at numerous European sites, first appeared about 40,000 years ago. This anatomically modern human developed a culture that included stone and bone toolmaking, paintings and carvings, and elaborate rituals associated with hunting, birth, and death.*

task in physical anthropology has been to document the sequence whereby the human line (the hominids) evolved from early primate ancestors. The detective work that led to the discovery of the NEANDERTHALERS in Ice Age Europe, then to the HOMO ERECTUS fossils in Java and China, and finally to the much older AUSTRALOPITHECUS finds of Africa—pushing human origins successively back in time—is one of the exciting scientific adventure stories.

Reconstructing the evolution of the human lineage is an ongoing process of discovery; important new finds are made almost every year. Evidence from mineralized bones (fossils) is augmented by atomic-age technology to establish the age of ancient deposits and to compare the biochemistry of the PRIMATES, which include humans, apes, and monkeys. A more recent concern is the study of nonhuman primates—their behavior in the wild and in laboratories, their ability to learn and use communication systems taught by humans, and the organization of their social groups.

Physical anthropology is also concerned with the more recent evolutionary diversification of modern humans. The GENETICS of human populations and their adaptations to environmental pressures have been a main focus of modern studies. Traditional physical anthropology relied heavily on ANTHROPOMETRY, the measuring of skull shape, stature, and other physical characteristics. In the 1950s, emphasis shifted to genetic characteristics—blood groups, abnormal hemoglobin types, and other markers that have known genetic bases. By studying the genetics of human populations, anthropologists can gain information about their local histories of movement, intermarriage, and diversification.

Hopes that a comparison of genetic markers of the world's populations would demonstrate ancient origins and connections have not been borne out; the picture that has emerged is complicated, and it is obscured by the rapid change in gene frequencies in a population that sometimes takes place through NATURAL SELECTION. Some physical anthropologists have returned to the use of body measurement to study relationships between populations, but this time armed with computers and sophisticated statistical methods. In their studies of modern populations, they attempt to chart physical adaptations to environmental pressures—altitude, solar radiation, heat, cold, disease—through natural selection.

Populations of the same animal species that have diverged through adaptation to different local environments are called races. Physical anthropologists use the term RACE cautiously, if at all, in referring to humans. Sometimes populations that are very different genetically and have complex local evolutionary histories have been classed together as a race on the basis of external characteristics such as skin color or hair type. Modern evolutionary biologists are more concerned with process than with typology; some anthropologists believe that classing humans into races not only invites oversimplified typologies but encourages unfounded assertions about human inequality.

History of Anthropology

By the time of the Greeks and Romans, serious observations of "primitive" peoples at the margins of civilization had been recorded. The history of Western anthropology goes back more directly to the European thought of the

Enlightenment and to philosopher-scholars, notably Jean Jacques ROUSSEAU, who used fragmentary reports of exotic peoples to reflect on human nature, civilization, and society.

European expansion into the New World produced more substantial reports, which remain anthropological classics. The Spanish conquest of Mexico produced, amid destruction, superb ethnographic accounts of Aztec culture. Early Jesuits in North America recorded rich and often sympathetic accounts of Indian cultures. As European penetration of the hitherto unknown world accelerated, reports of alien peoples and customs—produced sometimes by explorers, but more often by missionary scholars—gradually accumulated.

Development of Anthropological Theory. In the second half of the 19th century, the growing body of information on so-called primitive peoples became increasingly incorporated into comparative theoretical schemes, partly because of sweeping theories in social philosophy and biology. The major theme was EVOLUTION: reconstructing the development of human cultures from the earliest "savage" state of primitive promiscuity, through the progressive evolution of "barbarism," and finally to "civilization."

Highly speculative schemes were advanced to explain reported customs of marriage and descent and to organize them into a single developmental sequence. Amid the speculation, profound scholarship emerged, notably in the brilliant interpretations of E. B. TYLOR, in the comparative studies of the English jurist Sir Henry Maine (1822–88), and in the penetrating analyses of ancient Greece and Rome by N. D. Fustel de Coulanges. In the United States, Lewis Henry MORGAN laid the foundations for a century of comparative study of kinship and the family.

By the turn of the century three developments—in England, in the United States, and on the Continent—had shaped the direction of things to come. In England W. H. R. Rivers' published research on the South Pacific pioneered field study of systems of kinship, descent, and marriage. His work was a kind of comparative sociology. In the United States, the work of Franz BOAS among the Eskimo had established a pattern of painstaking research on culture, language, and biology that dampened the quest for sweeping theories. In France, Émile DURKHEIM, Marcel MAUSS, and their colleagues had used the reports from the tribal frontier to interpret the interrelationships between the structure of society and the thought-worlds humans create in religion and ritual.

Social Anthropology in Britain. In Britain, A. R. RADCLIFFE-BROWN brought together the insights of Rivers on kinship and marriage and those of Durkheim on ritual. His important synthesis emphasized the systematic integration of society and the functions of ritual in reinforcing this cohesion. His vision of a scientific comparative sociology and his brilliance as a teacher stimulated a generation of theoretically oriented researchers.

A second force in British anthropology was the influence of Bronislaw MALINOWSKI, a Polish scholar whose field studies of the Trobriand Islands (in Papua New Guinea), magnetic manner, and forceful writing inspired a

Jane Goodall, known for her studies of chimpanzees, has contributed a wealth of information concerning primate behavior. As a result, many anthropologists have reevaluated theories about the intelligence of living primates and their ancestors.

tradition of superb field studies. The so-called functionalism of Malinowski, which stressed the needs of individuals, and that of Radcliffe-Brown, which stressed the integration of groups, were brought together by a generation of anthropologists (notably E. E. EVANS-PRITCHARD and Meyer Fortes) who documented African tribal societies with meticulous fieldwork and sociological insight.

American Traditions. In the United States, Boas founded the Department of Anthropology at Columbia University and trained or inspired the pioneers of American anthropology, including Ruth BENEDICT, A. L. KROEBER, Margaret MEAD, Edward SAPIR, Ralph Linton, and Robert Lowie. The cultural anthropology they developed in different ways stressed the overwhelming importance of culture in shaping human behavior and explored disciplinary borders with psychology and linguistics. It dominated the American scene through the 1950s. During the 1940s and '50s, American anthropology was influenced by psychoanalytic theory. Anthropologists began to look for relationships among culturally patterned childhood experience, adult personality, and cultural beliefs and customs. Another distinctly American contribution to anthropology has been the compiling of data on hundreds of peoples worldwide. This information has been used to test statistical associations between forms of social organization, modes of subsistence, religious beliefs and practices, and other customs. This so-called comparative

(Right) *Franz Boas's ethnographic studies of Eskimos and Indian groups inspired American anthropologists to develop controlled scientific methods in their research.*(Far Right) *Margaret Mead, shown in 1953 during a visit to Manus, became a popular symbol of anthropology as a result of her books on primitive cultures and her outspoken views on contemporary society.*

method had first been envisioned by the English anthropologist E. B. Tylor.

New Developments. The gap between the British tradition of social anthropology and the American tradition of cultural anthropology has been partly bridged since World War II. An international anthropological community has emerged, greatly expanded in number.

A concern with meaning and symbolism has been a unifying theme in modern anthropology, with the work of Edmund Leach, Victor Turner, and Mary Douglas in the British tradition and Clifford Geertz and David Schneider in the American being widely influential. The French anthropologist Claude LÉVI-STRAUSS, intellectual heir to Mauss, has advanced brilliant theories of how the structures of mind are spun out in the designs of culture. Anthropology has also become more genuinely international as the discipline has developed in the Third World. Indian, Nigerian, Mexican, Brazilian, and Indonesian anthropologists have made important contributions.

The strands of modern anthropological theory are too numerous and diverse to characterize easily. Some of them have been stimulated by the changes in the tribal world studied by earlier anthropologists—the decolonization of the Third World; the transformation of tribal peoples into peasants, wage laborers, and urbanites; and the processes of development. Evolutionary views of culture have reemerged in more sophisticated form in the studies of cultural adaptations to ecosystems, of the interplay of biology and culture, and of human social organization in the light of new findings on nonhuman primates. In the tradition of Boas, Americans have continued to explore the relationship between language and culture, particularly with the emergence in the 1960s of a cognitive anthropology that has sought to map the structure of cultures as systems of knowledge.

Anthropologists have become increasingly involved with other social science disciplines and with classic issues in social theory in recent decades. For instance, a serious application of Marxist ideas about "precapitalist modes of production" tied anthropology into the running controversies of social theory. Another development is a reexamination of the impact anthropologists have upon the groups that they study, and of the historic links between anthropology and colonialism. This development has been accompanied by a critical reassessment of the relationships between Western scholars and the societies of the Third World.

See also: PREHISTORIC HUMANS.

anthropometry [an-throh-pahm'-uh-tree] Anthropometry is the study of human body measurements, often for comparative purposes. Important to the field of ERGONOMICS, anthropometric measurements aid designers and manufacturers in the production of safe, efficient consumer goods that are comfortable to use. Anthropometric measurement of bones has proven especially useful to paleoanthropologists concerned with the study of PREHISTORIC HUMANS.

anthropomorphism Anthropomorphism is the assigning of human characteristics to animals, natural phenomena, inanimate objects, or abstract ideas. In the FIGURE OF SPEECH called personification, an object or abstraction is endowed with human qualities or feelings. The literary strategy of ALLEGORY often employs anthropomorphic personages: in *The Pilgrim's Progress*, for example, Death, Piety, and Fellowship are human companions of the hero, Christian. In the beast FABLE animals speak and evince human behavior and characteristics. The pathetic fallacy, a specialty of sentimental poetry, endows natural phenomena and objects with human emotions. In religion anthropomorphism occurs when a divinity is described as having a human body (the hand of God, out of God's mouth), or exhibits human behavior (Jove's wrath).

antiaircraft systems Antiaircraft systems are intended to destroy or neutralize attacking enemy aircraft and ballistic or guided missiles before they can reach and damage their intended targets. The history of these systems parallels the development of aviation. During World War I, belligerents used 75-mm and 105-mm artillery and machine guns against the low-flying, slow-moving

(Above) *Stinger, the portable antiaircraft missile, was supplied to Afghan insurgents by the United States and successfully used against Soviet planes during the Afghan conflict of the 1980s.*

(Left) *The U.S. Patriot system stores and fires radar-controlled missiles from its mobile launching station. Protective covers over the launching tubes lift away when the missiles are fired.*

aircraft of the day. Between the wars, aircraft improved faster than antiaircraft systems. A major innovation, introduced about 1940, was the director system of fire control; this system used a device to continuously compute the target's future position and to determine the gun and fuse settings necessary to fire. The system also had a height finder to determine target altitude, a telescope for the battery commander, and, for night defense, a sound locater, which controlled a searchlight beamed at the target. Another important and possibly decisive improvement was the electric detector (1943), which could use data from a RADAR system to aim heavy antiaircraft weapons such as the Allied 90-mm and 120-mm guns.

The great increase in aircraft speed since the end of World War II prompted a search for alternatives to gun systems. SURFACE-TO-AIR MISSILES have evolved from command-guided devices to sophisticated missiles capable of tracking an enemy plane with heat-seeking sensors, such as the shoulder-launched Stinger, or by radar (the Patriot and the Hawk). The FOG-M missile transmits a TV picture from a camera in its nose to the gunner, who controls it from the ground.

antiballistic missile The antiballistic missile (ABM) is a defensive weapon designed to intercept attacking BALLISTIC MISSILES. The SALT treaty of 1972 limited the United States and the USSR to no more than 100 ABMs apiece (see ARMS CONTROL). The Soviet system, about 64 ABM 1B Galosh missiles, is deployed around Moscow. The U.S. Safeguard system was deactivated in 1976. Both use nuclear-armed warheads and rely upon large radar arrays to warn of enemy missile launches (see BMEWS; MILITARY WARNING AND DETECTION SYSTEMS). In recent years the development of land-based ABMs has been

superseded by plans for missile defense systems based in space (see STRATEGIC DEFENSE INITIATIVE).

See also: NUCLEAR STRATEGY; ROCKETS AND MISSILES.

The United States Safeguard antiballistic missile system had two lines of defense. Area defense, provided by Spartan missiles (A), protected a region roughly 1,500 km by 1,000 km (930 mi by 620 mi), while high-speed Sprint missiles (B) provided a last-ditch, local defense. Perimeter Acquisition Radar (PAR) located the distant ICBM target and passed the information to the Missile Site Radar (MSR) for the Spartan to intercept the target outside the atmosphere. Had the target escaped destruction, a Sprint would have been launched to intercept it in its final seconds of descent. Although Safeguard was short-lived (5 months operational), it successfully demonstrated the means to destroy an oncoming intercontinental ballistic missile.

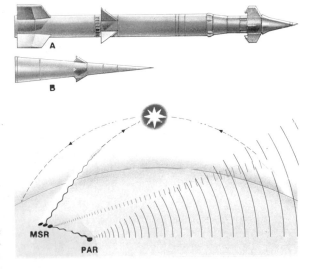

antibiotics   An antibiotic is a substance derived from living organisms, usually BACTERIA or molds, that kills microorganisms or inhibits their growth. Some antibiotics also interfere with life processes in higher organisms, but the term usually applies only to substances that act against microorganisms. Synthetic drugs also used to treat bacterial, fungal, or other parasitic infections may be called antibiotics, but strictly speaking the term is reserved for substances derived from living agents. The more general term might be *antibacterials* or *antimicrobials*.

History of Antibiotics

The use of moldy and fermented substances from dung and soybean curd to treat wounds and superficial swellings is described in the earliest medical records from China, Egypt, and Mesopotamia and dates back to at least 1500 BC. For more than 3,000 years, moderately effective methods for treating superficial infections were known, but ignorance of the causes of infectious disease precluded understanding of antibiosis.

In 1874, William Roberts (1830–99) of Manchester, England, noted that the growth of fungi was often antagonistic to that of bacteria, and vice versa. He specifically observed that a mold, *Penicillium glaucum*, was immune to bacterial infection. Shortly thereafter Louis PASTEUR and Jules François Joubert (1834–1910) noted that anthrax bacilli failed to grow if cultures became contaminated with airborne molds, and they suggested that this observation might have significant therapeutic implications. For about half a century, however, research on infectious diseases centered on immune serums, vaccines, and the use of chemical agents.

In 1928, Alexander FLEMING noticed that growth of the pus-producing bacterium, *Staphylococcus aureus*, had stopped around an area in which an airborne mold contaminant, *Penicillium notatum*, had begun to grow. Fleming determined that a chemical substance had diffused from the mold, and named it PENICILLIN. The small, impure amounts he initially extracted lacked potency, yielding disappointing results to early attempts to treat human infections with penicillin.

In the following years a number of researchers worked to purify penicillin and produce it in large quantities, efforts that gained urgency with the outbreak of World War II. Batches of partially purified penicillin became available for military use in 1943 but were so scarce that patients' urine was collected and the excreted penicillin recrystalized to be used again.

At the same time, efforts were under way to isolate other antibiotics. By 1944, Selman A. Waksman and his colleagues had isolated streptomycin and proved its effectiveness against the tubercle bacillus. By 1960 hundreds of antibiotics had been discovered, and many were eventually marketed.

In 1957 penicillin was synthesized in the laboratory. Complete synthesis of penicillins proved prohibitively expensive, but harvesting the basic molecules of penicillin from *Penicillium* molds and then tacking on diverse mol-

ecules proved feasible and led to a large number of tailor-made penicillin variants. During the 1960s there was a veritable explosion of so-called semisynthetic (part mold-made, part synthetic) penicillins, each designed to deal with the increasing problem of penicillin-resistant bacteria, to achieve better absorption and higher concentrations in the body, or to broaden the penicillins' effective antimicrobial spectrum.

The history of streptomycin and other major antibiotics is similar. During the period from 1960 to the present an enormous proliferation of laboratory-designed variations of the basic bacteria and molds isolated from nature has occurred, and a search through soil molds has yielded such antibiotics as the broad-spectrum carbapenems and the monobactams, which may prove particularly useful in dealing with hospital-derived infections (see also BIO-PHARMACEUTICALS).

Classification of Antibiotics

The most common classification is based on mechanism of action. Antibiotics that inhibit the growth of the bacterial cell wall include the commonly used penicillin and cephalothin groups, and such less-often-used antibiotics as vancomycin and bacitracin. Antibiotics that act like detergents on the cell membrane—and therefore disrupt the passage of nutrients into the bacterial cell—include the antibacterials polymyxin and colistin, and the antifungals mycostatin and amphotericin. Antibiotics that interfere with protein synthesis in the bacterial cell include the tetracyclines, the aminoglycosides (streptomycin, kanamycin, neomycin, gentamicin, and amikacin), and the macrolide group comprising erythromycin, lincomycin, and clindamycin. Antibacterials that disrupt bacterial-gene replication include the antifungal griseofulvin and the synthetic quinolone drugs.

Bactericidal and Bacteriostatic Effects. Another classification system is based on whether an antibiotic kills microorganisms (bactericidal effect) or merely inhibits growth (bacteriostatic effect). Penicillins, aminoglycosides, vancomycin, bacitracin, the polymyxins, and colistin are bactericidal. Tetracycline, on the other hand, is bacteriostatic. When susceptible bacteria are exposed to tetracycline, growth will cease temporarily and then resume. Chloramphenicol and the macrolides are also bacteriostatic. Lethal infectious diseases will respond only to bactericidal agents.

Spectrum of Activity. A further classification system rests on the effective target range (activity spectrum) of an antibiotic, as defined by two criteria: (1) the species of susceptible microorganisms (for example, *Staphylococcus, Streptococcus,* and *E. coli*), and (2) whether the species are gram-positive or gram-negative. Bacteria retaining a blue stain despite treatment with iodine and acid alcohol are called gram-positive, and those losing it are gram-negative. The penicillins are effective against most gram-positive bacteria, whereas aminoglycosides are chiefly effective against gram-negative bacteria. These two groups of antibiotics are therefore termed narrow-spectrum agents. Tetracyclines and chloramphenicol are effective against a broad range of gram-positive and gram-negative bacteria, rickettsia, and other microorganisms and are therefore called broad-spectrum antibiotics.

Bacterial Sensitivity

The susceptibility of a given bacterial species to an antibiotic is usually determined either from laboratory tests or from the result of treating an established infection.

In laboratory tests, bacteria isolated from an infected patient are inoculated into tubes containing a liquid culture medium enriched with graded concentrations of an antibiotic agent. The lowest concentration of antibiotic that inhibits microbial growth is termed the minimal inhibitory concentration (MIC). When this is compared with concentrations attainable in the body, one can judge whether the bacteria are sensitive, partly sensitive, or resistant to the antibiotic. Alternatively, the surface of a semisolid growth medium can be inoculated with bacteria, and antibiotic-impregnated filter-paper disks placed on that surface. The antibiotics leave clear zones around disks where growth of susceptible bacteria has been inhibited. The diameter of the inhibitory zones can be measured accurately and the results precisely interpreted.

Occasionally such tests do not correlate with clinical results, particularly when a person has a malignant disease, immune-system impairment, or severe injury, or is receiving drugs that reduce resistance to infection. Outcome may also be unpredictable because of failure to absorb the antibiotic, deterioration of the antibiotic during storage, or its inactivation by simultaneously administered drugs.

Resistance to Antibiotics

Innate properties and acquired mechanisms account for microbial resistance to antibiotics. Innate resistance depends on the mechanism of action of an antibiotic. Thus, penicillin may not be able to reach the cell wall of resistant gram-negative bacteria because the cells are protected by a slimy coating. Such resistance can be overcome if the penicillin molecule can be modified to penetrate the coating.

Resistance may be acquired by mutation or by the transfer of resistance genes from other bacteria. A mutation in the genetic apparatus of a bacterial cell may enable that cell to bypass the metabolic step blocked by an antibiotic or to eliminate a receptor within a microorganism required for the antibiotic to exert its effects. Mutants are usually disadvantaged for survival in nature, but if a mutation occurs while the bacterial population is under pressure from an antibiotic, then the resistant mutant survivors may propagate. Thus, for example, resistant bacteria readily accumulate in hospitals where antibiotics are used freely. When an antibiotic is later banned from use in the hospital, the natural, antibiotic-sensitive (wild) strains will gradually displace the resistant variants.

Sensitive bacteria can also acquire from resistant bacteria genes that code for the production of antibiotic-destroying enzymes. These genes, called resistance transfer

The antibiotic drug penicillin, a chemical that prevents the growth of infectious bacteria, was isolated from a green mold by Sir Alexander Fleming, a British bacteriologist. Antibiotics are among the most important chemotherapeutic agents.

factors, are frequently acquired in groups, and previously sensitive bacteria may suddenly become resistant to a broad variety of antibiotics. The extrachromosomal genes are contained in packages (plasmids) that replicate in synchrony with bacterial-cell replication but independently of the chromosomal genes. Plasmids are used in recombinant-DNA technology to alter the genetic makeup of bacterial cells (see GENETIC ENGINEERING).

Selection of an Antibiotic

An exact diagnosis of an infection can be established only by the demonstration of causative agents in a person's body fluids or tissues, or through the specific traces left by an infection in the antibody composition of the blood.

If the diagnosis of an infectious disease has been proved by laboratory tests or is strongly suspected, the physician must still decide whether available antibiotics can be used effectively to treat the infection and whether the potential benefits of treatment outweigh the risks and costs involved.

If a patient is so ill that the 24 to 48 hours required for diagnostic tests would probably result in further deterioration or even death, the physician immediately prescribes an antibiotic based on estimates of the most likely source of the infection. The physician first obtains specimens of blood, other body fluids, and any collections of infected material and sends them to the laboratory together with the available clinical information. The laboratory is thus guided to isolate and cultivate the most probable infectious agents and to perform antibiotic sensitivity tests. The physician can then make necessary adjustments in the antibiotic regimen.

If the risk entailed by delaying antibiotic therapy appears small, the physician can obtain all necessary specimens and suspend therapy until the infectious agent has been identified. The delay may protect the patient from unnecessary exposure to toxic or allergy-causing antibiotics, overgrowth by resistant microorganisms, and unnecessary expense.

Preventive Uses

Antibiotics have long been used in attempts to protect healthy persons against infection by specific bacteria to which they may be exposed, to reduce the risk of infection in people with chronic illnesses, and to limit or prevent infection in patients with traumatic or surgical wounds.

In the first case, prophylaxis, or prevention, usually succeeds when a single antibiotic will block infection by a specific microorganism or eradicate it shortly after it becomes established. Failure is common in other circumstances, since the objective is to prevent infection by any and all microorganisms, with neither targets nor weapons sharply defined. Misguided attempts at prophylaxis frequently result in an increased incidence of infections, with antibiotic-resistant microorganisms. Specialists estimate that at least 90 percent of antibiotic prescriptions are unnecessary or inappropriate.

Antibiotics are also added to commercial animal feed in minute quantities, both for prophylaxis and because growth in animals is markedly increased, but the practice raises the possibility of resistant strains being developed. This problem has been indicated in recent years by SALMONELLA outbreaks in human populations. Many countries restrict use of antibiotics in feed to those not prescribed to humans.

Commonly Used Antibiotics

Penicillin G, the first modern antibiotic to come into widespread use, is still the safest, most effective, and cheapest antibiotic. It is a bactericidal, narrow-spectrum antibiotic that is highly effective against gram-positive bacteria, especially staphylococci, which cause boils, osteomyelitis, wound infections, and infections of the heart and blood vessels; streptococci, which cause "strep" throat, predispose to rheumatic fever and acute glomerulonephritis, infect abrasions and wounds, and cause blood poisoning and childbed fever; pneumococci, which cause the most common form of bacterial pneumonia; and against the bacteria that cause syphilis, gonorrhea, and common forms of bacterial meningitis.

Nevertheless, penicillin G has several shortcomings. It is destroyed by stomach acid and by enzymes (penicillinases) produced by several microorganisms, its spectrum of activity is limited, and it frequently causes allergic reactions.

The phenoxy-penicillins, such as penicillin V, resist degradation by stomach acid and can therefore be taken by mouth. Antibacterial spectrum is roughly similar to that of penicillin G, and penicillin V is also destroyed by penicillinases.

Ampicillin is effective against a wider bacterial spectrum that includes some gram-negative bacteria, especially the typhoid bacillus and a *Hemophilus influenzae*, which causes the most common form of bacterial meningitis in infants between 6 months and 3 years of age, and many of the bacteria involved in urinary tract infections. Probably no more toxic than penicillin G, it does appear to be twice as likely to cause allergic skin rashes, and it often causes diarrhea. It is also destroyed by penicillinases. Amoxicillin is a very similar agent that is better

absorbed and less likely to cause diarrhea.

Methicillin (Staphcillin) resists penicillinase destruction and must be given by injection. It was the first penicillin effective against resistant "hospital staphylococcus," its only clinical indication. Oxacillin, cloxacillin, dicloxacillin, and nafcillin are similar in that they resist destruction by penicillinase and can be given by mouth.

Carbenicillin extends the antibacterial spectrum of the penicillins to cover *Pseudomonas* strains, its only clinical indication. These gram-negative bacteria cause serious infections in hospitalized and debilitated patients.

Mezlocillin, piperacillin, and ticarcillin are other extended-spectrum penicillins. Their main use is in treating *Pseudomonas* infection and as prophylaxis in immunocompromised patients, such as cancer patients, who are at serious risk of developing a gram-negative infection.

Cephalosporins. Cephalosporins are semisynthetic derivatives of cephalosporin C, which is produced by *Cephalosporium acremonium*, a fungus. They are very similar to penicillins in structure and activity and, in general, are active against many gram-positive, gram-negative, and some anaerobic bacteria.

First-generation cephalosporins were first available in the 1970s and, like penicillin G, are used against gram-positive organisms. Second-generation cephalosporins are generally active against organisms susceptible to first-generation agents, but their activity is expanded to include some gram-negative organisms. Third-generation agents have little activity against gram-positive organisms but are more active than second-generation agents against gram-negative organisms. Available only in the injectable form, they are used in hospitalized patients such as those with *Pseudomonas* infections.

Macrolides. Erythromycin is one of the safest antibiotics and rarely causes toxic reactions other than gastrointestinal irritation. The rare allergic reactions are usually limited to mild skin rashes, fever, and some changes in the cellular components of the blood. If the dosage is increased more than twofold beyond standard amounts, or if the chemical structure is altered to improve absorption, severe liver damage may occur. The principal use for erythromycin is in the treatment of mild to moderately severe gram-positive bacterial infections in patients allergic to penicillin, for the prevention of streptococcal infections in penicillin-allergic patients with a history of acute rheumatic fever, and for the treatment of pneumonia due to *Mycoplasma*.

Clindamycin, clinically similar to macrolides but chemically different, is effective against ANAEROBES that often cause wound infections following abdominal trauma or surgery. It has been known to cause massive diarrhea and colitis, in as many as 15 to 20 percent of treated patients, and is therefore reserved for treating severe, anaerobic infections.

Aminoglycosides. The aminoglycosides—streptomycin, neomycin, gentamicin, tobramycin, amikacin, netilmicin, and kanamycin—are second only to the penicillins in importance. Bactericidal, narrow-spectrum antibiotics, aminoglycosides are highly effective against most gram-negative bacteria. They are largely ineffective against gram-positive bacteria, with the exception of staphylococci, and they are ineffective against other forms of microbial life. All aminoglycosides are toxic to the auditory apparatus (the organs responsible for maintaining equilibrium) and the kidneys. All can cause allergic reactions, including fever, skin rashes, changes in the cellular composition of the blood, and—rarely—sudden death. The rapidity with which bacteria acquire resistance to these antibiotics has necessitated a continuing search for new aminoglycosides.

Tetracyclines. First discovered in the late 1940s, the tetracyclines are highly effective, broad-spectrum, bacteriostatic antibiotics. They are effective against a wide variety of gram-positive and gram-negative bacteria, rickettsia, and the large viruslike agents that cause trachoma and related diseases, and are partly effective against some biologically more complex protozoan parasites. The broad-spectrum activity of these agents results in eliminating much of the patient's normal microbial population, with consequent overgrowth of resistant remnants that are normally harmless. This has caused black, hairy tongue and fungal infections of the perineal area, the underarm area, and the gastrointestinal tract. A sore, red mouth may occur, probably due to vitamin deficiencies induced by elimination of the normal, vitamin-producing members of the host's microbial population. Tetracyclines are administered orally, usually for acne or urinary tract infections.

Chloramphenicol. Chloramphenicol is a highly effective, broad-spectrum bacteriostatic antibiotic with principal activity against gram-positive and gram-negative bacteria and rickettsia. One of the safest antibiotics, it has acquired a bad reputation because a few treated patients developed severe depression of bone marrow function (impaired red blood cell, white blood cell, and platelet production). Since substitutes exist for almost every indication where chloramphenicol might be considered, treatment with chloramphenicol can only be justified on the basis of demonstrated and documented need. Such can be found in the treatment of typhoid fever and bacterial meningitis.

▬

antibody   Antibodies are proteins in the blood that can combine with foreign substances (ANTIGENS) and assist in their removal from the body. The production of antibodies is part of the immune response against pathogens and is important in recovery from infectious diseases caused by bacteria or viruses.

The continued presence of antibody molecules in the blood after an infection is one reason for the long-lasting IMMUNITY to many such diseases. Individual antibody molecules have a high affinity for one particular antigen, but the body is able to produce many millions of different antibodies.

Another defensive function of antibodies is the protection of the newborn infant. The antibodies received across the placenta from the mother protect the newborn until it has developed its own antibodies. Antibodies are also present in the mother's milk and can be absorbed during breast feeding. In many mammals this is the newborn's only antibody source.

Antibody Production. Antibodies are secreted by specialized lymphoid cells (called plasma cells) in lymph nodes and in spleen and intestinal lymphoid tissue. They are divided according to their molecular structure into five major classes, called IgG, IgM, IgA, IgE, and IgD ("Ig" stands for immunoglobulin). The total antibody level of human serum is about 15 mg/ml, of which about 75 percent is IgG, 20 percent is IgA, and 5 percent is IgM. IgE and IgD are present in minute amounts only.

The basic structure of all antibody molecules is the same. As seen in the electron microscope, the structure is Y-shaped, with the antigen-combining sites located at the tips of the branches of the Y. The branches vary from one antibody to another. These branches are always attached to the same molecular handle, however; that is, to the leg of the Y.

Antibody Action. An antibody acts by first binding to the antigen with its specific combining sites, at least two of which are present on each antibody molecule. If the antigen is a harmful molecule (toxin) produced by a bacterium, as in diphtheria or tetanus infections, binding by antibody neutralizes the toxic effect. Viruses such as those causing influenza are directly neutralized by antibodies, which combine with them and prevent them from entering tissue cells.

In the case of infection with such bacteria as streptococci or staphylococci, however, antibodies act in cooperation with other defensive cells of the BLOOD called phagocytic white blood cells. The coating of these bacteria by antibodies enables the white cells to engulf and destroy them. Antibodies that perform this important role are called opsonins. They require another plasma-protein system called complement to assist them in this function.

Allergy and Autoimmunity. Antibodies are not always beneficial, however. Some are responsible for such allergic reactions as hay fever, asthma, and drug ALLERGY. Sometimes antibodies are produced against the body's own proteins or cells (autoantibodies) and cause AUTOIMMUNE DISEASES.

Antibodies can also be troublesome in blood transfusion. All individuals, except those of blood group AB, possess natural antibodies against the red blood cell (ABO) antigens other than their own type. Great care is therefore taken to match transfused blood with that of the patient. A serious disease involving antibodies to red blood cells is hemolytic disease of the newborn (Rhesus disease). Rhesus (RH FACTOR) is an antigen present in red cells. If an Rh-positive fetus is carried by an Rh-negative mother, she may produce antibodies against the Rh factor in fetal red cells. The antibodies cross the placenta and cause life-threatening anemia and jaundice.

Antibodies are detected by their ability to precipitate antigens from solution, agglutinate (clump together) bacteria or red cells, or activate the plasma complement system. They are used in typing blood and in such diagnostic tests as the Wassermann test for syphilis, the Widal test for typhoid fever, and the Paul-Bunnell test for infectious mononucleosis.

Monoclonal Antibodies. Production of a pure, single antibody in significant amounts for research and medicine has long been difficult. In 1975, however, British biologists Cesar Milstein and Georges Kohler announced the development of a method for CLONING antibodies by using myeloma cells, which keep secreting immunoglobulin of a single kind. By fusing a myeloma cell with an antibody-producing cell of a desired type, large quantities of specific monoclonal antibodies can be produced. Hybrid mouse-human antibodies increase the range of available types as well. New techniques are enabling drugs to be delivered to specific disease sites by monoclonal antibodies, which are also demonstrating their potential as catalytic agents that can speed up protein reactions in the body. Their uses in medicine and biology are expanding rapidly, from the diagnosis of infectious diseases to the detection, isolation, and analysis of biological materials. The genetic engineering of antibodies designed for very specific purposes, in fact, holds open the promise of their wide application as tailor-made enzymes in chemistry and other fields of technology. Catalytic antibodies, or "abzymes," are undergoing intensive research.

Antichrist   Antichrist is the designation for a cosmic power that opposes Jesus Christ. The Antichrist, an eschatological figure (see ESCHATOLOGY), is expected to come at the world's end to deceive and lead many followers of Christ astray. According to Christian literature, he will be defeated in the final conflict between good and evil at the SECOND COMING OF CHRIST.

The term *Antichrist* is used in only two New Testament books, 1 John (2:18, 22; 4:3) and 2 John (7). Although the term *Antichrist* is strictly Christian, similar concepts are expressed in ancient Persian and Babylonian mythology. The earliest Jewish antecedent is the reference to GOG AND MAGOG in Ezekiel 38–39.

anticoagulant   Anticoagulants inhibit the formation or action of one or more of the clotting factors involved in the sequence of reactions that causes BLOOD to coagulate. Most anticoagulants are essentially prophylactic, which means that they are used in the treatment of existing thrombosis (clot, or thrombus, formation) only to inhibit further clotting. Thrombolytic drugs relieve clots that have already formed. Heparin and the oral anticoagulants warfarin and dicumarol are equally effective in treating venous thromboembolisms, but only heparin is useful in treating arterial thrombosis. Thrombolytics developed in the 1980s include streptokinase, an enzyme that can be injected into the coronary artery to stop a heart attack; and tissue plasminogen activator (tPA), a blood protein now available in large quantities through recombinant-DNA techniques. The ongoing development of such drugs has been aided by the 1987 isolation of the body protein that initiates the blood-clotting process.

antidepressants   Antidepressants are used to treat the disorder called DEPRESSION, the symptoms of which include insomnia, listlessness, loss of appetite, and a dispirited or despondent emotional state. Some evidence indicates that chronic depression is caused by a deficiency in the neurotransmitter called norepinephrine, a natural stimulant of the central NERVOUS SYSTEM that is secreted at nerve endings. One group of antidepressant drugs, the monoamine oxidase (MAO) inhibitors, lessen the effect of one of the enzymes responsible for degrading natural stimulants, among them norepinephrine. An example of an MAO inhibitor is tranylcypromine (Parnate). The other group, called tricyclics, appear to act by diminishing the absorption of norepinephrine at nerve endings, thus maintaining proper blood levels of this stimulant. Examples of tricyclics are imipramine (Tofranil) and amitriptyline (Elavil). Drowsiness is an unexplained common side effect of these drugs. Since the resulting effect of using either group of drugs is a net increase in the amount of norepinephrine, it is medically dangerous to use both simultaneously. Irregular heartbeat and increased blood pressure may occur. Patients receiving MAO inhibitors must also avoid wine or aged cheese because these products contain tyramine, an autonomic-nervous-system stimulant that may cause similar adverse effects.

antidiuretic hormone   see HORMONE, ANIMAL

Antietam, Battle of   [an-tee'-tuhm]   The Battle of Antietam, in the U.S. Civil War, was fought on Sept. 17, 1862, between the U.S. Army of the Potomac under Gen. George B. McCLELLAN and the Confederate Army of Northern Virginia under Gen. Robert E. LEE. Lee's first invasion of the North culminated in the worst day of fighting to that time at Sharpsburg, Md., along Antietam Creek. McClellan concentrated near Sharpsburg after a rapid march from Washington. Lee, having dispersed his army for mopping-up operations from Harpers Ferry to Martinsburg, Va., also concentrated at Sharpsburg. Lee narrowly escaped defeat. Although Union casualties were heavier (12,000 men), Lee's loss of 10,000 men forced his retreat to Virginia.

Anti-Federalists   In U.S. history, the Anti-Federalists were those who opposed the ratification of the U.S. CONSTITUTION in 1787–88. Led by George Clinton, George MASON, Patrick HENRY, and Elbridge GERRY, they argued that the proposed Constitution gave excessive power to the federal government. The BILL OF RIGHTS was adopted partly to assuage their fears that individual liberties would be endangered. After the Constitution was ratified, the Anti-Federalists formed an opposition party in Congress, eventually fusing with the Jeffersonian Republicans in the Democratic-Republican party (see DEMOCRATIC PARTY).

antifreeze   Antifreeze is a substance that has the ability to lower the freezing point of any liquid to which it is added. It is added to the cooling system of many automobile engines to prevent the cooling liquid, usually water, from freezing in cold weather.

ETHYL ALCOHOL and METHYL ALCOHOL are common constituents of antifreeze because they lower the freezing point of water. A disadvantage of ethyl and methyl alcohol is that they evaporate in water solution and must be replaced each year. Permanent antifreeze, which usually contains ethylene GLYCOL, does not evaporate and so can retain its effectiveness through several seasons. Most antifreezes also contain various additives, such as rust inhibitors and lubricants. Antifreezes are also used in REFRIGERATION systems.

antigen [an'-ti-jen]   Antigens are substances capable of stimulating immune responses in living organisms. The essential property of an antigen is that it is a foreign material, usually a protein or a polysaccharide, in an organism that stimulates the production of ANTIBODIES, substances that combine with the specific invading material and inactivate it. Antigens are present in invading bacteria and viruses and are generally unique to the specific organism. Moreover, many organic molecules in the environment are antigenic. At least a million different substances may provoke immune responses.

Bacterial and viral antigens are useful in the identification and classification of these microorganisms and may be the very substances that cause disease (for example, the Vi antigen of SALMONELLA). In humans, antigens are present in red blood cells and tissue cells and cause problems in blood transfusion and transplantation. The major red-cell antigens are called the ABO antigens, and different individuals carry either the group A antigen, the group B antigen, both (group AB), or neither (group O). The existence of these strong antigenic differences means that, with certain exceptions, it is possible to transfuse blood only between individuals of the same blood group.

Individuals also differ in their tissue antigens (called histocompatibility, or HLA antigens). Because of these antigens, grafted organs such as kidneys usually fail to survive in the recipient unless donor and recipient are closely related, and thus have similar tissue types, or unless the immune response is suppressed by drugs.

See also: ANTIBODY; IMMUNITY (biology).

Antigone [an-tig'-uh-nee]   Antigone, the daughter of OEDIPUS, king of Thebes in Greek legend, was also the heroine of one of SOPHOCLES' greatest dramas. According to the legend, when Oedipus blinded himself after his marriage to his mother was revealed to him, Antigone shared her father's exile near Athens. After his death she returned to Thebes and attempted, with her sister Ismene, to reconcile her quarreling brothers Eteocles and Polynices. Both brothers were killed, but her uncle Creon, now king, forbade the burial of Polynices because he had betrayed Thebes. When Antigone secretly buried her brother against the edict of her uncle, she herself was buried alive.

Sophocles used the plot and characters of this legend in his tragedy *Antigone* (440 BC). The play has often been interpreted as a justification for civil disobedience. According to Euripides' version, fragments of which survive, Antigone escaped and married Haemon, the son of Creon.

Antigonus I Monophthalmus, Macedonian King [an-tig'-uh-nuhs, mahn-uhf-thal'-muhs]   The Macedonian Antigonus I, b. *c.*382 BC, was one of the successors (DIADOCHI) of ALEXANDER THE GREAT. He was governor of Phrygia under Alexander. After Alexander's death (323), he joined the alliance against PERDICCAS, killed EUMENES after a long war, and by 316 controlled the eastern provinces of the empire. Trying to conquer the western portion, he was opposed by the other Diadochi, although they were generally disunited. After a naval victory over PTOLEMY I by his son DEMETRIUS I POLIORCETES, he and Demetrius proclaimed themselves kings (307). Their opponents also assumed royal titles, thus ending the nominal unity of the empire. Successful in the field, Antigonus was unsuccessful in his diplomatic efforts to keep his enemies isolated. Their alliance defeated and killed him at Ipsus in Anatolia in 301.

BATTLE OF ANTIETAM
Sept. 17, 1862

Union position
Confed. position
Union attack
Confed. attack
Confed. retreat
Battle

HOOKER
McCLELLAN
Potomac R.
Antietam Creek

1) Dawn–10:30 AM: Hooker assaults Lee's left flank

EAST WOODS
WEST WOODS
CORN FIELD
LEE
JACKSON
SUMNER

2) 10 AM–1 PM: Confederates are forced from sunken road (Bloody Lane)

BLOODY LANE

Sharpsburg

LONGSTREET
BURNSIDE'S BRIDGE
BURNSIDE

3) 10 AM–1 PM: Burnside crosses Antietam Creek

A. P. HILL

0   ¼   ½   1 km
0   ¼   ½   mi

AT A GLANCE

ANTIGUA AND BARBUDA

Land: Area: 442 km^2 (171 mi^2). Capital and largest city: Saint John's (1982 est. pop., 30,000).

People: Population (1990 est.): 63,726. Density: 144 persons per km^2 (373 per mi^2). Distribution (1985): 31% urban, 69% rural. Official language: English. Major religion: Anglicanism.

Government: Type: parliamentary state. Legislature: Parliament. Political subdivisions: 6 parishes, 2 dependencies.

Economy: GDP (1989): $353 million; $5,550 per capita. Labor distribution (1980): commerce and services—82%; agriculture—11%; industry—7%; Foreign trade (1988): imports—$302 million; exports—$30 million. Currency: 1 East Caribbean dollar = 100 cents.

Education and Health: Literacy (1990): 90%. Universities (1989): none. Hospital beds (1984): 415. Physicians (1984) 33. Life expectancy (1990): women—74; men—70. Infant mortality (1990): 23 per 1,000 live births.

Antigua (city in Guatemala) [ahn-tee'-gwah]   Antigua (1982 pop., 27,014) is the capital city of Sacatepéquez department of south central Guatemala. Formerly the capital (1542–1776) of Guatemala, it is located in a fertile valley near several volcanoes. Coffee plantations are the mainstay of the economy. Antigua's Spanish colonial architecture, particularly churches, is a major tourist attraction.

Antigua and Barbuda [an-tee'-guh, bahr-bood'-uh]   Antigua and Barbuda, two of the Leeward Islands, together with the uninhabited islet of Redonda, became an independent state on Nov. 1, 1981. Southeast of Puerto Rico in the Caribbean Sea, it had been a self-governing associated state of the United Kingdom since 1967. SAINT JOHN'S, a deepwater port on Antigua, is the capital.

Largely deforested, Antigua is a partly volcanic and partly limestone coral island. Although generally low lying, it rises to a maximum elevation of 405 m (1,330 ft) at Boggy Peak. Barbuda is a low, flat coral island. The country has long been a popular tourist resort. The cultivation of fruits and vegetables, light industry, offshore banking, and fishing are also important to the economy.

Christopher Columbus discovered Antigua in 1493. The British colonized the land in the early 17th century. A successful sugarcane industry developed, but with the abolition of slavery in 1834 plantation agriculture became less profitable, and the economy fell into decline. Antigua has had a bicameral parliament since ending its status as a British colony in 1967. The British monarch, represented by a governor-general, is the ceremonial head of state. The Antigua Labor party, headed by Prime Minister Vere C. Bird, has dominated the government since independence.

anti-hero   An anti-hero is the central character in a drama, film, or prose work who lacks the traditional heroic qualities—strength, bravery, resourcefulness, good looks, and gallantry. He is often a seriocomic, graceless figure and an honorable failure. Antecedents are found in folk literature and in such picaresque novels as *Don Quixote* (1605, 1615). After World War II, the anti-hero became a commonplace in fiction and drama, embodying anguish, self-doubt, and distrust of society. Notable examples are Meursault in Albert Camus's absurdist novel The STRANGER (1942) and Yossarian in Joseph Heller's satiric novel CATCH-22 (1961).

antihistamine [an-ti-his'-tuh-meen]   Antihistamines are members of a varied group of drugs antagonistic to the effects of histamine, a chemical substance released at a tissue site or into the circulatory system as the result of tissue injury or in reaction to an ANTIGEN. Ragweed pollen is a common antigen; it causes the histamine reaction called hay fever. Histamine causes large blood vessels to constrict and smaller blood vessels, including capillaries, to dilate; it increases the permeability of capillaries, permitting the fluid part, or plasma, of the blood to escape and cause swelling; and it constricts small air passages, or bronchioles, in the lungs. Symptoms may include flushing, hives, headache, wheezing, facial puffiness, and lowered blood pressure.

Antihistamines act by blocking or displacing histamine at the H_1 receptor sites found in most tissues and organs, but particularly in the blood vessels, skin, uterus, and bronchioles. The efficacy of antihistamines is rarely complete because of the existence of other chemicals, such as serotonin, that have the same action as histamine. These chemicals have their own receptor sites, not blocked by antihistamines.

Another effect of histamine is the increased production of acid by specialized cells in the stomachs of mammals. The histamine action is on a different group of receptors, called H_2, and is not affected by standard antihistamines. Some newer drugs, called H_2 receptor antagonists, can modify histamine at these sites. Antihistamines are used in treating motion sickness and as a mild sedative.

Antilles, Greater and Lesser [an-til'-eez] The Antilles are a group of islands making up all of the West Indies except the Bahamas. They extend about 4,000 km (2,500 mi) from Florida to Venezuela, forming a natural breakwater between the Atlantic and the Caribbean. Cuba, Jamaica, Hispaniola, and Puerto Rico are known as the Greater Antilles. The remaining islands are the Lesser Antilles.

Anti-Masonic party The first third party in U.S. history, the Anti-Masonic party was formed in 1827 to counter the alleged subversion of public institutions by the Freemasons. Hostility toward the Masons erupted following the disappearance (1826) in upstate New York of William Morgan, the author of a purported exposé of the Masons. The party rapidly gained followers, and in 1831 it held a national nominating convention in Baltimore—the first time that practice was followed. Its presidential candidate, William Wirt, carried only one state (Vermont) in 1832, however, while Andrew Jackson, a Mason, won overwhelmingly. The party merged with the Whigs after 1838.

antimatter Antimatter is a form of matter in which each of the particles that compose ordinary matter—the proton, neutron, and electron—is replaced by its corresponding antiparticle, that is, the antiproton, antineutron, and POSITRON, respectively (see FUNDAMENTAL PARTICLES). Antiparticles have the same mass and spin as their respective particles, but they have opposite values of such electromagnetic properties as charge and MAGNETIC MOMENT.

The existence of antiparticles was first predicted by the British physicist Paul DIRAC in 1930. It was verified in 1932 by the U.S. physicist Carl David ANDERSON, who observed a particle with positive charge but the mass of an electron. Physicists later showed that any particle description consistent with special relativity and quantum theory necessarily implies the existence of antiparticles. For every type of subatomic particle that carries a property such as electric charge, there is a corresponding type of antiparticle.

Antiparticles can be produced in pairs with particles when enough energy is available. For example, when two protons with a total energy many times greater than the rest energy of a proton collide, a substantial probability exists that the collision products will contain a proton and antiproton in addition to the original protons. Antiprotons and antineutrons were produced in this way at high-energy accelerators starting in the 1950s. In the reverse process, when a particle and its corresponding antiparticle come near to one another, they annihilate rapidly and produce either lighter particles or radiation. As a result, matter and antimatter cannot coexist for any length of time under ordinary conditions. Small amounts of antimatter, however, have been stored for long periods in accelerator facilities by confining them through the use of magnetic forces.

Researchers are attempting to produce entire antiatoms. Astronomical observations indicate that little or no antimatter exists in the universe (see COSMOLOGY).

antimony [an'-ti-moh-nee] The chemical element antimony is a brittle silver-white metal in Group VA of the periodic table. Its chemical symbol is Sb, its atomic number is 51, and its atomic weight is 121.75. The chemical symbol Sb is derived from *stibium*, the Latin name for stibnite. The term *antimonium* first appeared in the 13th-century works of Geber. The abundance of antimony in the Earth's crust is 0.0001%. The principal minerals, stibnite (Sb_2S_3) and senarmontite (Sb_2O_3), are often associated with lead-, silver-, and copper-ore deposits. Antimony is obtained by roasting Sb_2S_3 in air to form Sb_2O_3. The metal is then recovered by reducing the oxide with carbon.

Metallic antimony melts at 630.5° C and boils at 1,380° C; its density is 6.69 g/ml. Its electrical conductivity is only 3.76% as great as silver. The three less stable ALLOTROPES are yellow, black, and the unusual so-called explosive antimony, a noncrystalline solid that transforms explosively to the metal upon mechanical shock.

Antimony forms stable compounds in the +3 and +5 oxidation states. The metal is unreactive to moist air, since it combines with water or oxygen only at high temperature.

Most of the antimony metal produced is used to form various alloys; antimony compounds are relatively unimportant. Addition of antimony to a soft metal such as lead produces an alloy of increased hardness and stiffness that is used mostly in the manufacture of grids for lead storage batteries. Another important alloy is type metal, which comprises variable amounts of antimony, tin, and lead, often with a trace of copper. Molten-type metal expands slightly on solidifying to give sharp reproduction in a mold or casting. High-purity antimony is used to make semiconducting materials.

The toxicity of different antimony compounds varies. The metal is inert, and substances such as antimony potassium tartrate (tartar emetic) have been used medicinally for centuries, but the volatile SbH_3 is extremely toxic.

Antioch [an'-tee-ahk]   Antioch (Antakya) is a city in Hatay province in southern Turkey. Situated on the banks of the Orontes River about 22 km (14 mi) from the Mediterranean, Antioch has a population of 109,233 (1985). Its economy depends on olives and tobacco.

Of major importance in the ancient world, the town of Antioch was established as the capital of the Greek province of Syria in 300 BC by SELEUCUS I NICATOR in memory of his father, Antiochus, and remained the center of the Seleucid kingdom until 64 BC, when it was taken over by the Romans. Eventually it became the third largest city in the Roman Empire. One of the earliest centers of Christianity, the city was the site of Saint Paul's first mission to the Gentiles; Saint Peter also preached at Antioch. The city was destroyed by earthquakes in AD 526 and 528. In 1517 it was taken by Selim I for the Ottoman Empire. Ancient ruins and buildings abound in Antioch.

Antioch College   Established in 1852, Antioch College is a private institution in Yellow Springs, Ohio. Its baccalaureate curriculum is a 4-year work-study program, and the government of the school is shared by students and faculty. The college is part of Antioch University (est. 1979), which also comprises the centers Antioch Seattle; Antioch New England Graduate School, Keene, N.H.; Antioch Southern California in Los Angeles and Santa Barbara; and the School for Adult and Experiential Learning and the Glen Helen Outdoor Education Center, both in Yellow Springs. Antioch's first president was Horace MANN.

Antiochus III, Seleucid King (Antiochus the Great) [an-ty'-uh-kuhs, suh-loo'-sid]   Antiochus III, c.242–187 BC, succeeded to the throne of the SELEUCIDS in 223, when the kingdom was controlled by a powerful minister and rebellion was spreading in Iran. He defeated the rebels, got rid of the minister, and conquered much of Phoenicia, Syria, and Palestine from the Ptolemies of Egypt. He withdrew, however, after losing the Battle of Raphia (217).

By 213, Antiochus had regained much of Anatolia. He then embarked on a major expedition (212–206) to reconquer the lost eastern provinces, ruled by independent dynasties. Marching with little fighting as far as India, he received the nominal homage of the eastern rulers without imposing firm control.

Antiochus next set himself to regain all the land held by Seleucus I. After the death (205) of Ptolemy IV, he retook what he had lost at Raphia, then advanced as a self-styled liberator through Anatolia and crossed to Thrace, where he rebuilt (196) the old capital of Lysimachus. The Roman general Titus Quinctius FLAMININUS, who had just defeated Philip V of Macedonia, then proclaimed the "freedom of all the Greeks" as a propaganda weapon against Antiochus. Defeated by Roman forces in Greece in 191 and in Anatolia in 190, Antiochus was forced to give up Anatolia (most of it to EUMENES II of Pergamum) and to accept humiliating terms that left him unable to deal with further rebellions.

Antiochus IV Epiphanes, Seleucid King [ee-pif'-uh-neez]   Antiochus IV, c.215–163 BC, was the SELEUCID king whose attempts to introduce pagan rites in Jerusalem led to the revolt (167) of the MACCABEES and the creation of a Jewish state. The son of Antiochus III, he had to defeat the usurper Heliodorus before taking power in 175. In 171 he invaded Egypt, but he was later driven out by the Romans. Antiochus also campaigned against the Parthians.

Antiope [an-ty'-oh-pee]   In Greek mythology, Antiope, a Theban princess, was seduced by the god Zeus, in the form of a satyr. Fleeing to Sicyon to escape the wrath of her father, she bore twin sons, Amphion and Zethus, both of whom were to become rulers of THEBES. Amphion was a master musician who built the wall around Thebes by charming the heavy stones into place with his lyre playing. Zethus was renowned as a warrior and married Thebe, for whom Thebes was named.

A second Antiope was a queen of the AMAZONS who was abducted by the hero THESEUS and became the mother of HIPPOLYTUS.

antioxidants   see FOOD ADDITIVES

Antipater [an-tip'-uh-tur]   The Macedonian Antipater, b. c.400, d. 319 BC, was prominent in war and diplomacy under PHILIP II of Macedonia, helped secure the succession of ALEXANDER THE GREAT, and served as the latter's viceroy in Europe, supporting friendly regimes and defeating a Spartan-led uprising. Though deposed by Alexander in 324, he retained his province after Alexander's death (323).

In 322, Antipater defeated a Greek rebellion and had DEMOSTHENES executed. Taking part in the attack on PERDICCAS, he was appointed regent after Perdiccas's death (321). He was the last regent to be recognized by all the DIADOCHI.

antiphon [an'-tuh-fahn]   Several types of Gregorian PLAINSONG are called antiphons. The principal type, among more than 1,200 examples in the repertory, is sung before and after psalms and canticles. Antiphonal singing, or the performance of music by two alternating choirs that may be stationed at a distance from each other in the church, is the common feature of all types of antiphon.

Antipodes Islands [an-tip'-uh-deez]   The Antipodes Islands are a group of uninhabited rocky islands in the

South Pacific Ocean, 564 km (350 mi) southeast of South Island, New Zealand. The islands, which belong to New Zealand, were discovered in 1800 by the British sea captain Henry Waterhouse during a voyage on the *Reliance*. They are named for their antipodal relationship (on diametrically opposite sides of the Earth) to GREENWICH, England.

This 18th century French clock, made of enameled porcelain, is from Strasbourg. Its curves and scrollwork are typical of the rococo period. (Victoria and Albert Museum, London.)

antique collecting Antique collecting has been a significant pastime since the early part of the 19th century, when old objects began to be venerated for their beauty as well as for their historical importance. Before 1966, U.S. customs law defined an antique as an object made before 1830. The Educational, Scientific, and Cultural Materials Act of 1966, however, permitted the importation, duty free, of "antiques made prior to 100 years before their date of entry," a definition that is also found in British customs law.

Canada requires that an antique must have been made before 1847 to be duty free. The term *antique* was originally used to describe the cultures of ancient Greece and Rome, and their time was and still is known as *antiquity*. As a noun, however, *antique* is loosely used to describe any object at least 100 years old.

Collectors and Collecting

Modern collectors are a large and varied group who seek an extensive, disparate array of ostensibly utilitarian objects that are not currently made and that have decorative value. Antique collectors usually favor such objects over more conventional art objects—paintings and sculpture—although some notable collectors are interested in all the arts. For collectors, an antique may be prehistoric or only a few years old. It may have been made as a purely utilitarian object, such as a century-old cobbler's bench that now serves as a coffee table or a decorative accessory. The fact that an object is old inspires many collectors, and they usually favor objects that bear signs of wear in texture and color. Although the quality of design is a prime consideration for some collectors, others specialize in objects that arouse nostalgia.

More obvious as antiques are masterpieces of the DECORATIVE ARTS—furniture, metalwork, ceramics, and glass—made in past centuries, objects whose design is a crucial consideration for serious collectors. They usually prefer objects made in the 17th, 18th, and 19th centuries. The exceptions are objects in such distinctive recent styles as turn-of-the-century ART NOUVEAU and ART DECO of the 1920s and '30s. These objects, however, as well as older artifacts of high quality, are too expensive for the casual collector because the styles are recognized, the objects are relatively rare, and they are coveted by a knowledgeable group of enthusiasts.

At the most popular level, antiques form a broad spectrum of out-of-date materials that can be used for decoration. Old bottles, tools, furniture, plumbing fixtures, and cracker boxes may be considered antiques, along with products of the more conventional decorative arts. Some are appealing because they are well designed; others are ugly but amusing reminders of life in the past. Such artifacts are offered for sale in small shops and fairs in most Western countries; they appeal to people who like antiques but who lack the resources and the consuming passion that characterize the avid collectors.

The latter dedicated group is concerned with specific styles or with such specific media as jewelry, glass, clocks, metalwork, ceramics, and furniture, all of which is meticulously classified by type within each category. In terms of the number of active collectors, glassware and clocks are the most popular objects. The most desirable objects are readily identifiable to these collectors and, if they are rare examples, familiar to specialists. American and English wares are the most well known in the United States, but French and Spanish goods are also significant to serious collectors. Specialists also concentrate on the products of Oriental, African, Middle Eastern, and primitive cultures. Of necessity, serious collectors must patronize the more prestigious antique shops and auction houses, since the objects they seek are becoming increasingly scarce, costly, and sought after.

Since originality or authenticity is essential, the an-

(Above) *This tin-glazed earthenware plate was made in Delft, Holland, an important pottery center since the 17th century. The plate is an example of the best-known type of delftware, characterized by Oriental motifs in Delft blue and white.*

flecting the taste of the period. In recent years the increasing interest in simple design has led many collectors to concentrate on FOLK ART. The unadorned, simple lines of Shaker chairs and chests, for example, attract many collectors. Ceramics, metalwork, glassware, and hand-woven textiles were the major media for folk artists of the past. Today's collectible pieces are more often the product of trained artists (see CRAFTS).

Although it is tempting to consider antique collecting a relatively modern phenomenon, documents prove that beautiful old objects have always been of interest. In ancient Rome new and old decorative wares were put on the auction block at the same sales. In the Renaissance, collections of curiosities included venerated objects, mainly valued because they were owned by important or famous people, but fine examples of the various decorative arts also found their way into princely collections. Art dealers of the 17th century offered paintings, sculpture, and precious silver objects that were both old and new, a tradition that continued for centuries. Shops advertising antiques are found listed in New York City directories as early as the 1840s. A dealer named Sypher sold old and new furniture at a time when the rococo and Renaissance revivals were just being introduced. The early interest in antique furniture was not restricted to American cities; it was based on the appreciation of the design of early pieces rather than on their associational value. The first books

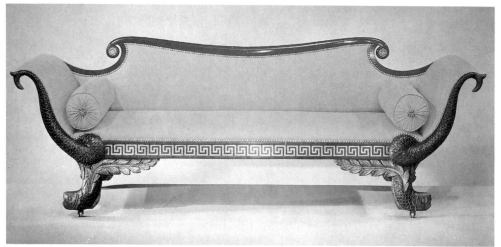

(Left) *The Empire-style dolphin sofa (c.1820) is an American version of the French Empire style. The frame is of carved mahogany with an inlaid design. (Metropolitan Museum of Art, New York City.)*

tique collector must be able to distinguish the real antique from later imitations, which can be either reproductions or fakes. Reproductions are later copies of objects made as exactly as possible without any intent to deceive. Fakes are copies made to look as old as the original in an attempt to fool the viewer. In some cases, revivals of early styles have inspired reproductions that have confused collectors because the reproductions acquired signs of age after a century.

Fashions in Collecting

Fashions in collecting shift focus from time to time, re-

on antique collecting began to appear in the 1870s; since then, collecting has been characterized by a continuing refinement of interests and knowledge and a broadening of public participation.

See also: CLOCKS AND WATCHES; FURNITURE; GLASSWARE, DECORATIVE; POTTERY AND PORCELAIN.

Antirent War   The Antirent War (1839–46) was a series of violent protests by tenant farmers in New York State against the semimanorial system of land tenure on the great Hudson Valley estates. The violence began when the heirs of Stephen Van Rensselaer, a landlord, tried to collect $400,000 in back rent. The tenants refused to pay and, disguised as Indians, resisted attempts to foreclose on their farms. The protests spread, and in 1845, after the death of a sheriff's deputy, Gov. Silas Wright of New York called out the militia. More than 50 men were arrested. Public opinion was on the side of the farmers, and in 1846 a new state constitution banned "feudal tenures."

anti-Semitism   Anti-Semitism, referring specifically to prejudice against JEWS, has manifested itself variously through history by hostile popular sentiment; discriminatory legislation; expulsion; and, in Nazi Germany, deliberate extermination.

From the beginning, their claim to be a chosen people, their refusal to worship other gods, and their insistence on special religious laws placed Jews in a vulnerable position. In the Roman Empire, very few Jews were admitted to Roman citizenship. Early Christians held the Jews responsible for the crucifixion of Christ, and this became the justification for anti-Semitism as Christianity spread throughout Europe.

During the Middle Ages periodic persecutions of Jews occurred. A large-scale persecution opened in Spain during the 13th century when Alfonso X of Castile (r. 1252-64), echoing the official church attitude, excluded Jews from public office. In 1278 a bill of Pope Nicholas III decreed that missionary efforts be directed to all European Jews. By the end of the 15th century the INQUISITION put to trial Jews and other nonconformists in Spain, culminating in the forced conversion or expulsion of Jews from that country. Similar oppressive measures were enforced in England, France, and Germany.

Jews were also forced to live in walled GHETTOS. Their segregation was motivated by fear of their influence on Christians and by the desire of merchants and artisans to restrict their economic activity. Outside the gates, they were obliged to wear identifying badges. Forced segregation was abolished only in the 19th century.

The settlement of Jews in eastern Europe began during the Crusades (from 1096 on); another wave of settlement occurred after the outbreak of the BLACK DEATH (1348) when it was rumored that Jews had poisoned wells. They enjoyed internal autonomy at first, but in 1648 persecutions began during a power struggle between the Polish Roman Catholics and the Ukrainian Orthodox. With the partitions of Poland (1772, 1793, 1795), masses of Jews were added to Russia, where the tsarist government established the "PALE of Settlement," a large territory in the western provinces. The POGROMS, or attacks on Jews, beginning in 1881 caused a mass emigration to the United States and the establishment of colonies in Palestine (see ZIONISM). In western Europe the Enlightenment in the 18th century and the French Revolution created sentiment for the separation of church and state that led to the emancipation of Jews, giving them equal legal status and religious freedom.

During the 19th century, anti-Semitism was again bolstered by pseudoscientific theories claiming the racial superiority of ARYANS. In Germany it became an organized movement during the late 19th century. In the 1930s, NAZISM turned anti-Semitism into an official government policy that within a decade led to the systematic extermination of nearly 6 million Jews (see HOLOCAUST).

In the United States and Western Europe, anti-Semitism waned after the defeat of Hitler and the creation of the national Jewish state of Israel. In 1961 the World Council of Churches condemned anti-Semitism as incompatible with the teachings of Christ, and in 1965 the Second Vatican Council formally repudiated the charge that all Jews are responsible for the death of Christ and condemned racism as un-Christian.

See also: CONCENTRATION CAMP; DREYFUS AFFAIR; PROTOCOLS OF THE ELDERS OF ZION.

antiseptic   Antiseptics are chemicals applied to body surfaces to reduce the infectious growth of bacteria, viruses, and fungi. The broader term *disinfectant* includes chemicals applied to nonliving objects for this purpose. In a sense, antisepsis was recognized in the ancient world, in that wine or vinegar was sometimes placed on wounds. This was done, however, without awareness of the existence of microorganisms. Such awareness came only in the 19th century with the work of Louis PASTEUR (see also MEDICINE, HISTORY OF).

Doctors routinely employ antiseptics in preparing a body area for surgery, blood withdrawal, or the injection of medicine. Common antiseptics include isopropyl alcohol, phenol (carbolic acid) and some derivatives, and certain compounds of chlorine and iodine. Silver nitrate is also still used to protect the eyes of newborn infants against gonorrheal infection. For home use, isopropyl alcohol is the most effective antiseptic, being applied around superficial wounds after they have been thoroughly cleaned. No antiseptic can kill all microorganisms, even if this were desirable, and many can cause increasingly severe reactions and tissue damage with increasing concentrations. For deeper wounds and for systemic protection against infection, ANTIBIOTICS are used. A number of local antibiotics are also available.

antitoxin   Antitoxins are ANTIBODIES found in the gamma globulin in blood protein. They are formed to inactivate poisons, or toxins, caused by infecting bacteria or other living organisms. In tetanus, for example, tetanus antitoxin can neutralize the toxin that causes muscle spasms and convulsions before it is bound to nerve cells. Antitoxins can be obtained from the blood of a human who has survived the disease; from the blood of animals (usually horses) that have been injected with either the bacterium or the toxin; and from the injection of toxoid, a bacterial culture that has been rendered noninfective but that retains enough characteristics to be antigenic, or capable of stimulating antibody production. In acute disease, antitoxin production is too slow after toxoid use, and an antitoxin is injected, as in tetanus or botulism. Injections of toxoids that prevent diphtheria and tetanus are usually given in the early years of life, with "boosters" at appropriate intervals, thus avoiding the need for antitoxin (see DISEASES, CHILDHOOD; VACCINATION).

antitrust laws   Antitrust laws are laws designed to prevent monopoly and unfair practices by businesses. U.S. laws include the ROBINSON-PATMAN ACT and the SHERMAN ANTI-TRUST ACT. (See also MONOPOLY AND COMPETITION.)

Antofagasta [ahn-toh-fah-gahs'-tah]   Antofagasta is the capital of Antofagasta province and the most important city and seaport of Chile's desert north. It is also landlocked Bolivia's main outlet to the sea. The city has a population of 203,100 (1986 est.). Minerals—chiefly copper, sulfur, and borax—and fish meal are the principal exports.

Antofagasta was founded in 1866 on Bolivian territory to supply the Chilean nitrate mines; it was given its official name in 1870 when it boomed after a silver discovery. Bolivia ceded Antofagasta province to Chile after the War of the Pacific (1879–82).

Antonello da Messina [ahn-toh-nel'-loh dah mes-see'-nah]   Antonello da Messina, one of the major artists of the Renaissance, was born in Messina, Sicily, c.1430. He was apprenticed in Naples, where Spanish and French rule guaranteed exposure to the works of Flemish artists. One of Antonello's earliest pictures, *St. Jerome in His Study* (c.1460; National Gallery, London), may have been inspired by a lost van Eyck panel of the same subject, known to have been in Naples in 1456. Of a similarly obvious Netherlandish cast is Antonello's earliest signed work, *Salvator Mundi* (1465; National Gallery, London).

His Venetian altarpiece *Madonna and Saints* (Kunsthistorisches Museum, Vienna), usually known as the *San*

Portrait of a Man (*or Presumed Self-Portrait*), *painted about 1475 by Antonello da Messina, is in the National Gallery, London. One of the earliest Italian masters to paint in oils, Antonello was famous for his insights into the personalities of his subjects.*

Cassiano Altarpiece, fundamentally influenced the subsequent development of painting in Venice. With its figures assembled symmetrically around the elevated throne of the Madonna, all placed within a large-scale architectural setting, Antonello's painting was emulated well into the 16th century by such artists as Giovanni Bellini (see BELLINI family), Lorenzo LOTTO, and GIORGIONE.

Antonello is particularly noted for his portraits, of which the *Portrait of a Man* (c.1475; National Gallery, London), perhaps a self-portrait, is an excellent example. He died in Messina sometime between Feb. 14 and 25, 1479.

Antonescu, Ion [ahn-toh-nes'-koo, yawn]   Ion Antonescu, b. June 15, 1882, was dictator of Romania during World War II. Chief of the army general staff, he was appointed (Sept. 5, 1940) premier by King CAROL II under German pressure. Supported by the fascist IRON GUARD, he immediately forced Carol's abdication in favor of Carol's son Michael and allied (November 1940) Romania with the Axis powers. On Aug. 23, 1944, with Soviet armies about to overrun the country, King Michael imprisoned Antonescu; he was executed on June 1, 1946, as a war criminal.

Antoninus Pius, Roman Emperor   Antoninus Pius, b. Sept. 19, 86, d. Mar. 7, 161, was Roman emperor from 138 to 161. After serving ably as proconsul in Asia, he was adopted (138) by HADRIAN, whom he succeeded as emperor. He consolidated and stabilized the government, deferring to a generally approving Senate, and brought economic prosperity to Rome and its provinces. In addition to governing well, he endowed Italy with a grand array of public buildings. Antoninus Pius adopted his wife's nephew, MARCUS AURELIUS, who peacefully succeeded him.

Antonioni, Michelangelo [ahn-toh-nee-oh'-nee, mee-kel-ahn'-jel-oh]   Michelangelo Antonioni, b. Sept. 29, 1912, an Italian director, began his career in the cinema as a film critic and scriptwriter. After working with Roberto Rossellini and Marcel Carné, he made his debut as a director in 1943 with the documentary *Gente del Po* (The People of the Po Valley). He is best known for the trilogy *L'Avventura* (The Adventure, 1959), *La Notte* (Night, 1960), and *L'Eclisse* (The Eclipse, 1962). In these films, and in the machine-dominated *Deserto Rosso* (Red Desert, 1964), his first color film, mystery and eroticism merge in landscapes of compelling beauty. Antonioni's subsequent English-language films, *Blow-Up* (1966), *Zabriskie Point* (1970), and *The Passenger* (1975), had less success with the critics despite their stylistic interest.

Antony, Mark   Mark Antony, or Marcus Antonius, was triumvir in Rome with Octavian (later Emperor AUGUSTUS) and Marcus Aemilius LEPIDUS after the murder of Julius

CAESAR. He is famous in literature for his liaison with the Egyptian queen CLEOPATRA, and figures in Shakespeare's *Antony and Cleopatra* and *Julius Caesar*.

A cousin of Julius Caesar through his mother, Antony was born in *c.*83 BC. As a young man he served in Palestine and Egypt and in Gaul, and in 48 commanded Caesar's left wing at Pharsalus. He was chosen Caesar's co-consul for 44 BC.

After Caesar's assassination, Antony avoided further bloodshed by restraining Lepidus and conciliating the conspirators. Nevertheless, efforts to strengthen his own position against both rival Caesarians and the republicans caused leaders in each group, such as Octavian and CICERO, to join forces against him. After Antony and Octavian were reconciled, they united with Lepidus to form the Second Triumvirate (November 43). Cicero and many others perished in the subsequent proscriptions. Antony then defeated CASSIUS LONGINUS and BRUTUS at Philippi (42 BC) and set out to reorganize the eastern provinces.

Antony's relationship with Octavian soon became strained, as each sought supremacy in Rome. Various reconciliations, including his marriage to Octavian's sister, Octavia (39), led to a 5-year extension of the Triumvirate. Antony, however, soon abandoned his wife for Cleopatra. The failure of his invasion (36) of Parthia made him more dependent upon Cleopatra's support, and his relationship with her led to an open breach with Octavian.

When Antony divorced (32) Octavia, Octavian obtained the annulment of Antony's powers as triumvir along with a declaration of war against Cleopatra. Battle was joined in September 31 BC at ACTIUM. Antony was defeated and fled with Cleopatra to Alexandria, where he committed suicide in August 30 BC.

Antwerp's Cathedral of Notre Dame, the largest cathedral in Belgium, houses several works by the Flemish master Peter Paul Rubens, who lived in the city.

Antwerp Antwerp is the second largest city and chief port of Belgium and one of Europe's busiest seaports. It lies on the SCHELDT RIVER 89 km (55 mi) from the North Sea. Its population is 476,044 (1987 est.). Located in the Flemish-speaking region of Belgium, it is known in Flemish as Antwerpen and in French as Anvers. Antwerp is linked by the Albert Canal with the Meuse River at Liège and also with the Rhine.

The Contemporary City. The old city contains a large market square (Groote Markt) surrounded by Renaissance guild houses and dominated by the 122-m (400-ft) spire of the Gothic cathedral of Notre Dame (begun in the 14th century).

The docks lie to the north of the old city. The first basins were constructed about 1800. In 1830, Belgium became an independent state, and the rapid expansion of manufacturing that followed led to the growth of Antwerp's docks. Antwerp now handles much of the transit traffic from France and Germany as well as much of the seaborne trade of Belgium. Manufacturing industries include oil refining, petrochemical production, the assembly of automobiles from imported parts, processing of imported foodstuffs, and shipbuilding.

History. Antwerp was a walled city by the 11th century. It later became a member of the HANSEATIC LEAGUE, specializing in the grain trade. The city rose to prominence in the 15th century as the chief port of FLANDERS, replacing Bruges, and soon became the chief banking and financial center in northern Europe. The city and its commerce suffered severely during the Dutch Revolt of the late 16th century, and in 1576 Antwerp was partially destroyed by mutinous Spanish soldiers. When the war ended, the independent Netherlands held the Scheldt estuary and denied seaborne ships the right to sail up the river to Antwerp. The port languished until the Scheldt was reopened by the French in 1792. The city and port subsequently grew steadily, despite considerable damage in both world wars.

Anu [ay'-noo] In Sumerian, Akkadian, and Babylonian mythology, Anu was the god of the heavens and the king of the gods. The Babylonians associated him with the trinity that also included Enlil (MARDUK), the earth god, and Enki (EA), the water god. The Babylonian king was considered his representative on Earth.

Anubis [uh-noo'-bis] In Egyptian mythology, Anubis was the jackal-headed god who took the souls of the dead to be weighed before the judge of the infernal regions.

Anuradhapura [uh-noo'-rahd-uh-poo'-ruh]   Anuradhapura, the capital of North Central province, Sri Lanka (formerly Ceylon), was the royal city of the Sinhalese kings of ancient Lanka for more than a millennium. Traditionally thought to have been founded in the 5th century BC and named for the constellation Anuradha, it became one of the major centers of Buddhism in Asia. It was destroyed AD 992 by the armies of the South Indian Chola dynasty.

Its ruins, discovered by the British in the 19th century, include gigantic STUPAS of the mother monasteries of the major Buddhist sects and the restored shrine of the Bodhi, or Bo tree, supposed originally to have been miraculously transported to Anuradhapura (c.245 BC) in the form of a branch of the sacred tree at Bodh Gaya, India.

Anuszkiewicz, Richard [ah-nuhs'-ke-vich]   The American painter Richard Anuszkiewicz, b. Erie, Pa., May 23, 1930, is a leading practitioner of OP ART. A student at Yale (1953–55) under Josef ALBERS, who stressed the importance of color interaction, Anuszkiewicz has since worked with combinations of often dazzling colors in hard-edged geometrical shapes. In his work he creates illusions of movement and afterimages through the use of alternating patterns and oscillating vibrations of color.

anxiety   Anxiety is an unpleasant emotion characterized by a feeling of vague, unspecified harm. Unlike FEAR, it is characterized by the absence of an apparent cause—the circumstance that precipitates anxiety is hidden and unknown to the person. When the cause for anxiety becomes known but the feeling of apprehension remains, it is called worry.

Anxiety has many symptoms, including rapid or pounding heartbeat, difficult breathing or breathlessness, tremulousness, sweating, dry mouth, tightness in the chest, sweaty palms, dizziness, weakness, nausea, diarrhea, cramps, insomnia, fatigue, headache, loss of appetite, and sexual disturbances. In addition to the uncomfortable bodily sensations associated with fear, anxiety results in a narrowing of one's time perspective so that only the present matters; it also results in an inability to attend to more than one task at a time or to organize thoughts and plans effectively. Although low levels of anxiety may temporarily increase a person's ability to do a simple task, due to the greater vigilance and narrowing of one's attention associated with anxiety, behavior becomes more disorganized and ineffective as anxiety increases.

Psychoanalytic Theory. Two types of anxiety are recognized in psychoanalysis. The first type, traumatic anxiety, results from overstimulation. Events happen faster than the mind can comprehend them; this produces a feeling of crisis. The second type, signal anxiety, is believed to arise from a person's need to guard against the disorganization of traumatic anxiety. The EGO appraises its own ability to cope with both external demands and the push of internal drives and wishes. When normal methods of coping with these pressures threaten to fail, the ego responds with anxiety, which then mobilizes the person to take new action.

Learning and Cognitive Theories. In LEARNING THEORY anxiety is seen both as a response to learned cues and as a drive, or motivator, of behavior. Most learning theorists maintain that anxiety is derived from reaction to PAIN. Anxiety can thus be reduced by removing or avoiding the source or sources of the situations that have produced pain. Avoidance may become firmly established and lead to constricted or bizarre behavior (see PHOBIA). Psychologists have recently focused on the role of cognition in the origin of anxiety (see COGNITIVE PSYCHOLOGY). Experiments have shown that the interpretation of a situation determines whether a person feels anxiety or some other emotion. Learning to substitute benign reappraisals for unrealistically negative "self-talk" reduces anxiety.

Physiological Theory. Evidence exists that some persons may be biochemically vulnerable to an extreme form of anxiety known as "panic attacks." Some medications relieve the panic, leading to the hope that anxiety can be understood physiologically, but the metabolic pathways are unknown and may be quite complex. A combination of medication and therapies, including relaxation training, provides the best treatment for panic attacks.

Anyang [ahn'-yahng]   Anyang (1982 pop., 250,000), a city in Henan province, north China, was the site of an important center of early Chinese civilization. From c.1400 BC, it was the last capital of the SHANG dynasty (c.1600–1027 BC).

One of the most extensively excavated sites in China, Anyang is still the richest repository of artifacts of the Bronze Age culture of Shang yet discovered. Enormous royal tombs, discovered in 1928, contained grave goods and the skeletons of wives, servants, and guards sacrificed for the service of the king in the next world. Archaeologists also found ORACLE BONES, on which appear the earliest form of Chinese writing, and stone sculptures far older than any previously known in China. Anyang was first excavated (1928–37) under the direction of the archaeologist Li Ji; since 1950, work has frequently been resumed at the site.

Anza, Juan Bautista de [ahn-zah', hwahn bow-tees'-tah day]   Juan Bautista de Anza, b. 1736, d. Dec. 19, 1788, was a Spanish explorer in the American West. Born in Mexico, he joined the army in 1752 and served on the northern frontier of Sonora. In 1774, Anza led an expedition from the presidio at Tubac (now in Arizona) to the mission at Monterey, Calif., proving that supplies could be transported overland to Upper California. The following year Anza set out from Tubac on a second California expedition during which he explored (March 1776) the San Francisco Bay region. There he chose the general location for the first European settlement, which was established later that year by José Joaquin Moraga. Anza returned to Mexico and later served (1777–87) as governor of New Mexico.

Anzio Anzio is a town on the Tyrrhenian Sea in Roma province of the Lazio (Latium) region in central Italy. It is a seaside resort about 48 km (30 mi) south of Rome, with a population of 27,094 (1981); its main industry is fishing. Older than Rome, by which it was conquered (*c.*340 BC), Anzio became a year-round resort for wealthy Romans. Emperors Nero and Caligula were born there. The city was abandoned in the early Middle Ages after being destroyed by the Saracens and was not revitalized until Pope Innocent XII ordered the construction of a new port in 1698. In World War II, American and British troops seriously damaged most of the old town when they landed at Anzio beach on Jan. 22, 1944, as part of their successful effort to break through to Rome.

Anzus Treaty Signed on Sept. 1, 1951, the Anzus Treaty is a mutual defense agreement between Australia, New Zealand, and the United States. The acronym Anzus is formed by the initial letters of the countries' names.

aorta [ay-ohrt'-uh] The aorta is the largest ARTERY in the human body. It is the primary vessel carrying blood from the HEART to the rest of the CIRCULATORY SYSTEM. The aorta arises from the base of the left ventricle of the heart. Blood is prevented from reentering the ventricle from the aorta by the aortic valve, which is located at the juncture of the aorta with the ventricle. The aorta then arches over and backward to the left front side of the vertebral column, or spine. It passes downward to the level of the fourth lumbar vertebra, then divides into the common iliac arteries, which supply blood to the extremities.

For descriptive purposes, the aorta is usually divided into the ascending aorta, the aortic arch, the thoracic descending aorta, and the abdominal aorta. Major branches serving the upper part of the body arise from the aortic arch. The renal arteries, mesenteric arteries, and many other branches arise from the abdominal aorta.

The walls of the aorta are quite thick and consist primarily of strong, elastic connective tissue. The distensibility of the aorta and its major branches is such that this central reservoir acts as a second heart pump.

The rise of aortic blood pressure is associated with the ejection of blood from the heart. The pressure remains constant when the ejection rate equals the rate of drainoff through the tissues. Following this, the heart relaxes to the point where pressure is greater in the aorta than in the ventricle, and the aortic valve closes. The following gradual decrease of pressure, the diastolic phase, is caused by the drainage of blood from the central reservoir through the tissues of the body.

The pressure PULSE is transmitted down the arterial tree as a pressure front. Since the tubes are distensible, the velocity of transmission of the pulse is relatively slow, about 5 m/sec (more than 16 ft/sec) in the aorta.

Apache [uh-pach'-ee] The Apache (from a Zuñi word meaning "enemy") are a North American Indian people of the Southwest. Their name for themselves is Inde, or Nde ("the people"). Together with the NAVAJO, they are classified as belonging to the Southern Athabascan linguistic family. The Apache were composed of six regional groups: the Western Apache (Coyotero), Chiricahua, Mescalero (Faraon), Jicarilla (Tinde), Lipan, and Kiowa Apache (Gataka), long associated with the KIOWA Plains Indians. Each group was made up of numerous localized bands.

Geronimo, the leader of a band of southern Chiricahua Apaches, appears in this photograph taken after his capture in 1886. One of the ablest Apache leaders, Geronimo led Apache warriors on raids against Mexicans, American settlers, and other Indian tribes of the Southwest.

On marriage, men customarily took up residence with their wives' kin. Maternal clans existed among the Western Apache, who depended more on cultivation than did other groups. All Apache relied primarily on hunting of wild game and gathering of cactus fruits and other wild plant foods. By 1688 they customarily supplemented their hunting and cultivating economies with raids on settlements of the Spanish and, later, on the westward-migrating American settlers. They attained their greatest fame as guerrilla fighters defending their homelands under the Chiricahua leaders COCHISE, GERONIMO, MANGAS COLORADAS, Victorio, and Juh. The surrender of Geronimo and Juh in 1886 marked the end of Apache resistance.

Today the Apache occupy reservations in New Mexico and Arizona, with some Chiricahua, Lipan, and Kiowa Apache in Oklahoma. In 1680 the Apache population was estimated at 5,000; in 1989 it was estimated at about 30,000, of whom most lived on reservations. The Apache on reservations have maintained many of their traditional social and ritual activities.

Apalachee [ap-uh-lach'-ee] The Apalachee were a tribe of North American Indians who inhabited the area around Apalachee Bay in northwest Florida; the tribe is now extinct. A Muskogean-speaking people, they raised maize, beans, and pumpkins. By 1655, when the tribe numbered about 7,000, eight Franciscan missions were established at their settlements near present-day Tallahassee, Fla.

Beginning about 1700 the Creek conducted raids against the Apalachee at the instigation of the English. In 1703 an English-Creek force destroyed their towns and missions, killing the Spanish garrison and more than 200 Apalachee warriors and taking 1,400 townspeople as slaves. About 400 Apalachee escaped to the French community at Mobile, Ala.; others fled to the Savannah River in Georgia. After Spain ceded Florida to England in 1763, most remaining Apalachee moved to Louisiana, where their numbers had drastically declined by the early 1800s.

apartheid [uh-pahr'-tayt] *Apartheid* (Afrikaans, "apartness") is the name given to the South African policy of "separate development," a rigid system of racial segregation designed to maintain white supremacy. The policy has been officially in effect since South Africa's National party came to power in 1948.

The South African population is legally classified into whites, constituting about 15%; Africans, 73%; Coloureds (of mixed descent), 9%; and Asians, 3%. In accordance with the theory of separate development, and to divide the black majority, the government has set aside certain economically poor areas as homelands for each of the officially recognized African ethnolinguistic groups. In the homelands the Africans have citizenship, exclusive rights to ownership of the land, and the expectation of political autonomy. By 1990, four of the ten homelands had been declared independent, although that independence is recognized only by the South African government. A majority of blacks work in white areas, living in segregated black townships, often separated from their families, and subject to many restrictions.

The implementation of apartheid over the years, involving massive resettlement of peoples and great hardship, has been widely condemned by the United Nations and the Commonwealth of Nations, among others. Since the late 1970s the government relaxed the apartheid laws slightly, lifting some occupational restrictions, desegregating certain public facilities, and in 1985 repealing the 1948 law prohibiting intermarriage. The Constitution of 1983 gave Coloureds and Asians limited representation in the formerly all-white parliament, and similar representation for blacks was proposed. The pass laws requiring blacks in white areas to carry permits were repealed in 1986, although the framework of white supremacy remained intact. In 1990, President F. W. DE KLERK committed his government to the abolition of apartheid, desegregating public facilities and negotiating with black leader Nelson MANDELA in an effort to satisfy black aspirations while protecting white interests.

apatite [ap'-uh-tyt] The very widely distributed calcium PHOSPHATE MINERAL apatite, $Ca_5(PO_4)_3(F, Cl, OH)$, is used as a mineral fertilizer and occasionally as a gemstone. Gem apatite occurs in sea-green to bluish or violet prismatic crystals (see HEXAGONAL SYSTEM) that have a vitreous luster. Hardness is 5 (soft for most gemstones); streak is white; and specific gravity is 3.1–3.2. Minute crystals of apatite are common as an accessory rock-forming mineral in IGNEOUS ROCKS; large crystals form in PEGMATITE. Collophane, a massive variety, is the principal component of fossil bone and PHOSPHORITE, much used for fertilizer.

Apatite is found with other minerals in nearly every kind of rock. The most abundant phosphate mineral, it includes several types that differ in their content of fluorine, chlorine, or hydroxyl ions. Fluoroapatite, the most common form, is used as a gem.

Apatosaurus [uh-pa-tuh-sawr'-uhs] *Apatosaurus* was one of a number of giant, plant-eating DINOSAURS that roamed western North America during the Jurassic Period, more than 140 million years ago (see GEOLOGIC TIME). The animal probably will remain better known for some time under the name *Brontosaurus*, because this name has been used in many books and films about dinosaurs. *Apatosaurus*, however, was the name with which the first fossil fragment of the animal was labeled, and by paleontologic convention the first name given is the one accepted. *Apatosaurus* and other giants such as BRACHIOSAURUS, DIPLODOCUS, and *Camarasaurus* constitute the suborder Sauropoda. These five-toed, long-necked dinosaurs, the dominant herbivores of their time, probably used their long necks to reach and browse on treetop foliage. Fossil remains, abundant in Utah, Colorado, and Wyoming, suggest that *Apatosaurus* had an enormous, barrellike body supported by thick, heavy legs. Its tail and neck were long and stout. More than 25 m (82 ft) in total length, it weighed 18–32 metric tons (20–35 U.S. tons). The skull was elongated, and the teeth short but pointed.

ape Apes are PRIMATES, and of all the primates they are the closest living relatives to humans. Two families exist: the Pongidae, or great apes, and the Hylobatidae, or lesser apes. Until fairly recently BABOONS and MONKEYS were also considered apes, and they are still often but unscientifically so called.

The great apes consist of the CHIMPANZEE, GORILLA, and ORANGUTAN, and the lesser apes of the GIBBON and SIA-

Apatosaurus, or Brontosaurus, *a plant-eating dinosaur of the late Jurassic time, was one of the largest land animals that ever lived. It weighed up to 32 metric tons. Here it is compared to the size of today's largest land animal, the African elephant.*

MANG. Two species of chimpanzee are known: *Pan troglodytes* and the rarer pygmy chimpanzee, *P. paniscus.* The single species of gorilla is divided into two subspecies: the western lowland gorilla, *Gorilla gorilla gorilla,* and the mountain gorilla, *G. gorilla beringei.* Only one species of orangutan exists, *Pongo pygmacus.* Four or five species of the gibbon genus, *Hylobates,* may be distinguished, according to different authorities, and two species of the siamang genus, *Symphalangus.*

Apes are the only primates considered hominoid, or humanlike, in various characteristics. In general they are larger than the other primates. They all have larger braincases, have opposable thumbs as humans do, and are tailless. Anatomically, gorillas and chimpanzees resemble each other more closely than they do humans, but genetic data suggest that chimpanzees are more closely related to humans than to gorillas. Such data also suggest that gibbons and siamangs branched from the family line leading to humans about 20 million years ago, orangutans about 15 million years ago, and gorillas and then chimpanzees within the last 10 million years.

Appearance. Chimpanzees stand about 1.0–1.7 m (3.0–5.5 ft) tall when erect. The spread of the arms is about half again as great as the animal's height. The body hair and face are black, and the hands, feet, nose, and ears are pinkish. The ears are large and flattened, and the brow ridge is prominent. Males weigh up to 80 kg (176 lb). The pygmy form is much smaller and is now recognized as a distinct species.

Gorillas stand up to 1.7 m (5.5 ft) tall with the knees slightly bent. The span of the arms may be as great as 2.7 m (9.0 ft), and the circumference of the chest is often as much as 1.75 m (5.75 ft). An adult male weighs 180–270 kg (400–600 lb). Gorillas have short muzzles, large nostrils, and coarse, black hair. The male has a sagittal crest—a ridge of bone above its eye sockets. Old males have silvery hair on their backs.

The orangutan is about 1.2–1.5 m (4.0–5.0 ft) tall. The arms have a span of 2.3 m (7.6 ft). Wild adult males weigh 75–90 kg (165–200 lb). The hair is reddish brown, and the forehead is sloping and high, with no brow ridge. Orangutans travel chiefly by swinging through trees by the arms (brachiation).

Gibbons and siamangs are much smaller than the great apes but have relatively longer arms, hands, and feet. The height of the gibbon is about 0.6 m (2.0 ft) and the weight up to 8 kg (18 lb). The siamang is larger than the gibbon.

Range. Apes live in equatorial Africa and Southeast Asia. Their numbers are in decline. The chimpanzee appears to be holding its own after having been pushed out of previous ranges. It inhabits tropical rain forests and woodlands in the Congo River Basin and elsewhere in tropical Africa. Gorillas also inhabit African equatorial forests. The lowland gorilla is found near the Congo, usually about 50 km (30 mi) from the coast. The mountain gorilla lives farther east at elevations of 2,300–3,500 m (about 7,500–11,500 ft). The orangutan lives only in Sumatra and Borneo. Overhunting and agricultural expansion have driven it into poor habitats. The gibbon and the siamang are found in the rain forests of Southeast Asia.

Behavior. All apes sleep at night. The siamang and gibbon sleep sitting erect on tree limbs, and the other apes make platforms in trees or nests on the ground. Apes are herbivores, although the chimpanzee has been known to kill animals for food. Gibbons and siamangs are the most agile of mammals in the trees, swinging and leaping briskly from branch to branch. Chimpanzees spend more of their time on the ground, and gorillas have almost completely abandoned trees. The great apes often walk on all fours with the knuckles on the ground. Siamangs and gibbons walk with their long arms held high or to the rear. Apes can rotate their arms widely in the sockets, an ability possessed by only a few of the higher mammals.

Apes bear a single offspring or, rarely, twins. In general they have a dangerously low rate of reproduction, given

Apes, which are humans' closest relatives, are much more intelligent than other monkeys. A lar gibbon (top left) displays its great agility, using its long arms to swing from tree to tree. The chimpanzee (top right) has been extensively studied in the wild and in captivity for its social behavior and intelligence. A few chimpanzees, trained in sign language of the deaf and other language systems, have been able to communicate with humans on a fairly complex level. The orangutan (bottom right) whose name means "man of the woods" in the Malay language, is probably as intelligent as a chimpanzee but is shy and more difficult to study. The gorilla (bottom left), the largest ape, is a shy animal, but the male will roar and beat its chest to threaten intruders.

their dwindling numbers in the face of human encroachments. Apes travel in family groups of 30 to 40. They live 30 years or more. Siamang and gibbon young cling to their mothers' waists. Orangutans, gorillas, and chimpanzees carry their infants in one arm, much as a human mother does, or place them on their upper backs. Chimpanzees are curious and extroverted, whereas gorillas are cautious. Despite folklore, which has characterized male apes as ferocious, these animals are in fact placid. When threatened, however, male gorillas stand erect, roar, beat their chests, and display other such threatening behav-iors. Apes are subject to many of the same diseases as humans. Albinism, Down's syndrome (with accompanying heart defects), and epilepsy have been observed, and both gorillas and orangutans may contract poliomyelitis. Apes may also have heart attacks and strokes. Apes and humans have similar blood types.

Learning and Intelligence. Ape intelligence is second only to that of humans. Chimpanzees and gorillas have demonstrated an ability to master a vocabulary of up to several hundred words in sign language (see ANIMAL COM-MUNICATION). Some researchers believe that the orangutan is equally intelligent but less inclined to follow directions or to display its abilities to humans. Apes and monkeys are unable to talk because their vocal apparatus is not capable of it. Chimpanzees have been observed using simple tools such as sticks to pry termites out of the ground, leaves to spoon up food and liquid, and boxes to stack and climb upon in order to reach food. Some researchers claim that apes are capable of performing simple mathematical calculations.

Apelles [uh-pel'-eez] Apelles, who was active from about 350 to 300 BC, was considered the greatest Greek painter by PLINY THE ELDER and others. He was court painter to and a friend of ALEXANDER THE GREAT and Alexander's father, the Macedonian king PHILIP II. Alexander refused to let any other painter portray him.

Apelles' style was noted for graceful figures and composition, spatial depth, fine line quality, and avoidance of excessive detail. He was much praised for his realism, although he used only four earth colors—white, black, yellow, and red. All of Apelles' works are lost, but in the Renaissance the Florentine painter Sandro BOTTICELLI tried to re-create two of them as described by Pliny and Lucian. Botticelli's versions are called *Birth of Venus* and *Calumny of Apelles*, both in the Uffizi in Florence.

Apennines [ap'-uh-nynz] The Apennine Range in central Italy is part of the greater Alpine mountain system. The range is a spur of the Ligurian Alps that extends 1,400 km (870 mi) along the Italian peninsula. Bordered by narrow coastal plains, it is between 40 and 201 km (25 and 125 mi) wide. The highest point, Monte Corno, is 2,914 m (9,560 ft) high.

The Apennines formed during the latter part of the Paleozoic Era and were shaped by erosion caused by numerous rivers. There are some minerals and deposits of natural gas. Scenic highways and numerous railroads traverse the mountains. Home of the Italic peoples since prehistoric times, the Apennines have recently lost population.

aperture see CAMERA; LENS

aperture synthesis see RADIO ASTRONOMY

aphasia [uh-fay'-zhuh] Aphasia is the loss or impairment of the ability to use spoken and written words. The disorder may follow damage to the dominant hemisphere of the BRAIN, which, in right-handed persons, is almost always the left hemisphere. The two broad classifications of aphasia are Broca's and Wernicke's. In Broca's aphasia—also known as expressive, motor, nonfluent, or telegrammatic aphasia—patients understand speech reasonably well but have difficulty in retrieving words and hence in naming objects or expressing themselves. In Wernicke's aphasia—also known as receptive, sensory, fluent, or jargon aphasia—patients produce fluent but nonsensical speech and comprehend poorly the speech of others.

The zebra plant, native to Brazil, is one of the most widely grown aphelandras. It has large, shiny, dark green leaves marked with whitish stripes, and the yellow flowers protrude from bracts with an orange hue.

aphelandra Aphelandra is both the common and the scientific name for about 200 species of flowering, evergreen shrubs. They constitute the genus *Aphelandra* in the family Acanthaceae (see ACANTHUS). The plants are native to tropical and subtropical regions of the Western Hemisphere and are widely cultivated for their showy flowers. The flowers grow on tall spikes and range in color from red to orange, yellow, and white. The floral bracts are also often brightly colored, and the leaves are large and sometimes lobed.

aphid Aphids are of several families of the order HOMOPTERA. The most common aphids are plant lice. They are small (usually less than 5 mm/0.2 in long), somewhat pear-shaped insects that feed on the sap of many kinds of plants. To procure their food, they pierce stems and leaves with their thin, tubelike mouthparts. Aphids secrete a sugary substance, called honeydew, which attracts ANTS and other insects. Some ants regularly tend aphids, obtaining honeydew by tickling an aphid's posterior to stimulate release of honeydew droplets.

Among some aphids, females during most of summer do not require males to reproduce (see PARTHENOGENESIS). Such aphids often have no egg stage but give birth to live young. In autumn these aphids usually produce winged forms of both sexes, which mate. The females' eggs overwinter on twigs and hatch in the spring.

Many aphids produce chemicals called alarm PHEROMONES when attacked by a predator. The injured aphid discharges a droplet of pheromone, which evaporates into the air. Nearby aphids react by fleeing. Because of their predilection for sap and their ability to reproduce rapidly in huge numbers, aphids become pests to a variety of crop and ornamental plants. They also transmit serious plant diseases. Aphids may be controlled biologically or with pesticides.

aphrodisiac [af-roh-dee'-zee-ak] Aphrodisiacs are agents reputed to stimulate or excite sexual desire. Although it is plausible that brain centers controlling sexual responses could be influenced by drugs, to date only inhibitory activity has been substantiated; most claims regarding aphrodisiacs have been dismissed as folklore.

Throughout the ages many foods have been considered sexual stimulants. Similar claims have been made for alcohol, amphetamines, cocaine, LSD, marijuana, morphine, opium, and mescaline. These substances break down inhibitions, the cause of much sexual malfunctioning; but if taken in large enough quantities, they diminish rather than enhance sexual capacity. Cantharides (Spanish fly) and yohimbine are also considered aphrodisiacs. The former, by irritating the genitourinary tract and concomitantly dilating the associated blood vessels, does produce a certain stimulation of the genitals, and yohimbine stimulates the spine nerve centers that control erection. Nevertheless, claims for their aphrodisiac effects are not substantiated. The same is true of amyl nitrite ("poppers"), a chemical used to dilate blood vessels.

Androgens, male hormones produced by both sexes, are the only substances known to increase sexual interest, drive, and performance in both sexes. Where deficiency exists, physicians may prescribe androgen therapy.

Aphrodite [af-roh-dy'-tee] In Greek mythology Aphrodite was the beautiful and voluptuous goddess of love. She was known to the Romans as VENUS. Aphrodite is variously described as being the daughter of ZEUS and Dione and as having been born from the foam of the sea. She had many lovers, among them ADONIS and the war-god ARES, but she was the wife of the smith-god HEPHAESTUS. She was the mother of EROS.

Aphrodite plays a major role in the so-called Judgment of PARIS, in which the young Trojan prince was asked to choose the fairest of the goddesses. He selected Aphrodite, who rewarded him by helping abduct HELEN OF TROY, provoking the TROJAN WAR. As the war neared its end, Aphrodite managed to rescue Paris from the grasp of MENELAUS. She also did what she could to assist the escape of her son AENEAS, whose father ANCHISES had been another of her lovers.

The myrtle was Aphrodite's sacred tree, and the dove her sacred bird. Among the most famous representations of Aphrodite are the statue known as the Aphrodite of Melos or Venus de Milo, and Botticelli's painting *The Birth of Venus*.

Apia Apia (1981 pop., 33,170) is the capital and only city of Western Samoa, an independent state in the South Pacific. Located near Mount Vaea on the northern coast of Upolu Island, the city is set on an open harbor, once an international naval port. Robert Louis STEVENSON is buried outside the city.

apiculture see BEEKEEPING

Apis In Egyptian mythology, Apis was the sacred bull of Memphis, believed to have been conceived by lightning on a moonbeam and to incarnate the soul of either OSIRIS or PTAH. Apis was worshiped as SERAPIS by the Greeks and Romans.

APL see COMPUTER LANGUAGES

apnea [ap'-nee-uh] Apnea, in medicine, is a temporary cessation of breathing. When periods of apnea alternate with periods of hyperpnea (increased rate and depth of inspiration), the syndrome is known as Cheyne-Stokes respiration.

The rate and depth of inspiration are controlled by the relative levels of oxygen and carbon dioxide in the blood. If the level of carbon dioxide becomes too high, the level of oxygen falls too low (anoxia), and apnea or Cheyne-Stokes breathing can result. Apneic spells may also arise from interferences with the respiratory centers of the brain. Such interferences include physical trauma, diabetic coma, intoxication (with alcohol, tranquilizers, or barbiturates), and the effects of metabolic toxins arising from liver or kidney damage or from congestive heart failure. Researchers think that respiratory-center lapses are also involved in obstructive sleep apnea, in which air passages in the throat are blocked by soft tissues during inspiration. The blockages lead to snoring and from 30 to several hundred apneic spells per night. Patients complain of insomnia and daytime sleepiness. Treatment consists of weight loss or of surgery to correct abnormalities in the soft tissues.

Apneic spells may also be part of the sudden infant death syndrome (see CRIB DEATH).

apocalyptic literature Apocalyptic literature consists of those parts of the Bible and other Jewish and Christian books which embody an apocalypse, or revelation, given through a symbolic vision of the future. They depict the final confrontation between God and the powers of evil. The conflict frequently culminates in a world catastrophe. Classic examples are the books of DANIEL and REVELATION. Passages such as Isaiah 24–27, Zechariah 9–14, and Mark 13 belong to this type of literature. Other examples are Enoch, Jubilees, and the Apocalypse of Baruch in the Jewish PSEUDEPIGRAPHA, as well as the Apocalypse of Peter in the Apocryphal New Testament.

Sometimes apocalypses, especially the Apocalypse of Adam and others in the literature of GNOSTICISM, contain elements drawn from Greek MYTHOLOGY.

Apocrypha The Apocrypha are books of the Old Testament included in Roman Catholic and Orthodox Bibles as deuterocanonical (added to the earlier canon), but excluded from the Hebrew Bible and from most Protestant Bibles. It is not certain why the term *apocrypha* (hidden things) was originally applied to them, but they were considered less authoritative than the other biblical books because of their relatively late origin (c.300 BC–AD 100). Except for 2 Esdras, which was in Latin, they were part of the SEPTUAGINT. The other books placed after the Old Testament in the Revised Standard Version are the following: 1 and 2 Esdras, TOBIT, JUDITH, Additions to the Book of ESTHER, WISDOM, SIRACH, BARUCH, Additions to DANIEL, the Prayer of Manasseh, and 1 and 2 MACCABEES. Roman Catholic Bibles also list 1 and 2 Esdras and the Prayer of Manasseh as apocryphal. The Greek Orthodox Bible omits 2 Esdras but adds 3 Maccabees and Psalm 151, with 4 Maccabees as an appendix. The Apocrypha are important sources for Jewish history and religious developments in the 1st and 2d centuries BC.

Apollinaire, Guillaume

Apollinaire, Guillaume [ah-pawl-ee-nayr'] Guillaume Apollinaire, b. Rome, Aug. 26, 1880, d. Nov. 9, 1918, was an art critic and poet who had a significant influence on the French avant-garde of the early 20th century. An important modernist figure, he is frequently linked with such diverse movements as CUBISM and FUTURISM and is said to have coined the terms Orphism and SURREALISM.

The son of a Polish aristocrat and an Italian army officer, Apollinaire was originally named Wilhelm Appollinaris de Kostrowitzki. His close association with scores of Parisian painters aided him in writing numerous influential essays, culminating in *The Cubist Painters: Aesthetic Meditations* (1913; Eng. trans., 1944; rev. ed., 1949). In 1913 he published a collection of poems, *Alcools* (Eng. trans., 1964), in which he radically blended traditional rhyme schemes with unpunctuated free verse. It was followed by *Calligrammes* (1918; Eng. trans., 1970), in which the visual shape of the poem corresponds to its subject matter: rain streams down a page, a fountain spurts up. He also wrote fiction, including *The Poet Assassinated* (1916; Eng. trans., 1923), and such surrealistic plays as *The Breasts of Tiresias* (1918; Eng. trans., 1966).

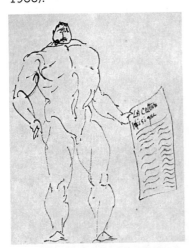

Guillaume Apollinaire, a French poet and art theorist, is caricatured as an athlete in a 1915 pen drawing by Pablo Picasso. Apollinaire was a major force in the avant-garde movements of early-20th-century art.

Apollo

Apollo In Greek mythology Apollo and his twin sister, ARTEMIS, were the children of ZEUS and LETO and were born on the island of DELOS. Hence, Apollo was often called the Delian god, and Delos long remained a center of his worship. He was also identified closely with DELPHI, in central Greece, where he killed the serpent PYTHON and founded the most renowned center for prophecy in the ancient world, the shrine of the Delphic Oracle. Areas of special concern to Apollo were prophecy, medicine, the fine arts, archery, beauty, flocks and herds, law, courage, and wisdom. Associated with him were the tripod, omphalos (a beehive-shaped stone at Delphi, designating that spot as the center or navel of the Earth), lyre, bow and arrows, laurel wreath, palm tree, wolf, hawk, crow, and fawn.

Apollo was the god who best embodied the Greek spirit. Later he became confused with the sun-god HELIOS and was considered the god of light. Of Apollo's many loves, one of the best known was DAPHNE, who fled his embraces and was turned into his tree, the laurel. From that time on, Apollo wore a laurel wreath. Laurel wreaths became the prize awarded in athletic and musical competitions.

In Roman mythology Apollo represented the literary and fine arts, culture, and the law. Augustus (r. 31 BC–AD 14) built a magnificent temple to him. Apollo was a favorite subject for artists of every medium. The walls of his temple at Delphi bore two Greek maxims, "Know Thyself" and "Nothing in Excess."

Apollo program

Apollo program The Apollo program was the successful conclusion of the U.S. effort to achieve, within the decade, the goal—set by President John F. Kennedy on May 25, 1961—of landing a man on the MOON and returning him safely to Earth. It followed the GEMINI manned-flight program conducted in 1966–67 to develop the necessary techniques of orbiting, docking, and extravehicular activity (EVA). The main elements of the Apollo project were the three-man Apollo spacecraft; the two-man LUNAR EXCURSION MODULE (LEM), or Lunar Module (LM); and the SATURN family of rockets, consisting of the Saturn 1, the Saturn 1B, and the Saturn 5. These units made up the first manned, interplanetary transportation system. Using this system, astronauts landed on the Moon, where they explored and collected samples at six sites on the near side between July 1969 and the end of December 1972. The total cost of developing and operating the Apollo-Saturn transportation system in the lunar program was $25 billion.

Between October 1968, when the Apollo-Saturn transportation system underwent its first full space test, and July 1975, when it was used for the last time, the National Aeronautics and Space Administration (NASA) launched 15 manned Apollo-Saturn flights. Eleven of these were missions in the lunar landing program, including two test flights in low Earth orbit, two test flights in lunar orbit, six landings, and one circumlunar flight, during which the planned landing was aborted. During the

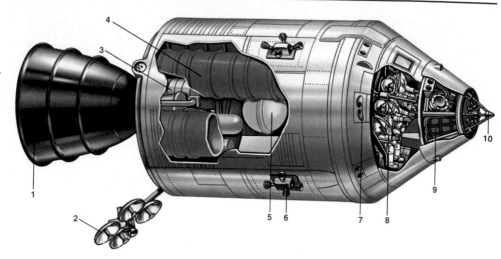

The Apollo Command and Service Module (CSM) remained in lunar orbit during Apollo missions. It transported the astronauts to the Moon and back. Prior to reentry, the service module was jettisoned; only the command module completed the journey. Shown are main engine nozzle (1); high-gain antenna (2); 9,670-kg-thrust (21,500-lb) main engine (3); fuel tanks (4); helium tanks (5); attitude (6) and pitch control engines (7); crew (8); parachutes (9); docking mechanism (10).

testing period three fatalities occurred on the launchpad at the Kennedy Space Center, Florida, but none in actual flight.

After completion of the lunar landing program, four flights were carried out: three were missions that ferried astronauts to and from the SKYLAB experimental space station in 1973–74, and one was a joint flight with Soviet cosmonauts in the APOLLO-SOYUZ TEST PROJECT in 1975.

The Apollo Spacecraft

Developed from Mercury and Gemini technology, the Apollo spacecraft itself consisted of the combined Command and Service Module (CSM). It was 10.4 m (34 ft) long and 3 m (10 ft) in diameter at the blunt end. A major advance over earlier spacecraft was the inertial guidance system developed by the Massachusetts Institute of Technology.

The CSM was actually two modules. The crew rode in the Command Module (CM), which contained three couches and was pressurized with oxygen at 0.35 kg/cm^2 (5 lb/in^2). For reentry, the CM separated from the Service Module; a heat shield protected it during reentry. During the first stage of the descent, the CM was stabilized by its own reaction control system. During the last stage it employed a drogue and three main parachutes.

Behind the CM was the Service Module (SM), which housed the main engine, of 9,670-kg (21,500-lb) thrust, the reaction-control system, fuel-cell batteries, oxygen and hydrogen tanks, and an environmental-control system. The main engine was used for course corrections and major changes in orbit, including the injection of the vehicle into lunar orbit and its escape from lunar orbit for return to Earth.

Manned Apollo Flights

The manned Apollo flights were preceded by testing, which began on May 28, 1964. Tragedy struck the program on Jan. 27, 1967, when fire erupted in the *Apollo 1* Command Module while a crew was performing a flight simulation. Dense fumes from burning plastics fatally

suffocated Col. Virgil I. "Gus" GRISSOM, Lt. Col. Edward H. White II, and Navy Lt. Comdr. Roger B. Chaffee.

On Oct. 11, 1968, *Apollo 7*, the first manned Apollo flight, was boosted by a Saturn 1B into low Earth orbit from the Kennedy Space Center. Navy Capt. Walter M. SCHIRRA, Jr., Air Force Maj. Donn F. Eisele, and Walter Cunningham demonstrated that the vehicle was spaceworthy for the duration of a lunar mission. The second manned Apollo-Saturn flight, *Apollo 8*, flew ten orbits of the Moon on Dec. 24, 1968. The eight-day mission (Dec. 21–28) served as a reconnaissance for landing sites. The *Apollo 9* mission (Mar. 3–13, 1969) tested the Lunar Module in Earth orbit and practiced docking with it. The Lunar Module was then tested in lunar orbit on the *Apollo 10* flight (May 18–26).

First Lunar Landing. Launched July 16, 1969, *Apollo 11* made the first manned lunar landing on July 20. As Lt. Col. Michael COLLINS orbited the Moon in the mother ship *Columbia*, Neil A. ARMSTRONG and Col. Edwin E. "Buzz" ALDRIN, Jr., touched down on the basaltic regolith of Mare Tranquillitatis (Sea of Tranquility) in the Lunar Module *Eagle* at 4:17:42 PM Eastern Daylight Time, with the historic report: "Houston, Tranquility Base here. The *Eagle* has landed." Armstrong was the first out: he stepped on the surface at 10:56:20 PM that day. Dropping the last meter from the ladder, he said: "That's one small step for [a] man, one giant leap for mankind."

On the Moon, Armstrong and Aldrin erected the American flag and set up scientific instruments, including a laser-beam reflector, a seismometer that later transmitted evidence of a moonquake, and a sheet of aluminum foil to trap SOLAR WIND particles. The astronauts took soil and rock photographs and collected 24.4 kg (53.61 lb) of rock and dirt samples. Armstrong, the first out and the last back into the Lunar Module, spent 2 hours and 13 minutes outside. The crew landed in the Pacific Ocean on July 24, 1969.

Scientific Exploration. Detailed scientific exploration began with the flight of *Apollo 12*, Nov. 14–24, 1969. Astronauts Charles Conrad, Jr., and Alan L. Bean made two sorties of extravehicular activity (EVA) on the surface, totaling 7 hours and 50 minutes. They unpacked the first Apollo Lunar Scientific Package (ALSEP), consisting of an array of scientific instruments, and brought back 33.9 kg (74.7 lb) of rocks and soil as well as pieces from the SURVEYOR 3 spacecraft.

Two days after *Apollo 13* was launched on Apr. 11, 1970, an oxygen tank exploded in the Service Module and crippled the vessel's power and life-support systems so badly that a planned landing in the Fra Mauro formation of the Moon was canceled. *Apollo 14* (Jan. 31–Feb. 9, 1971) reached the Fra Mauro uplands. After deploying ALSEP instruments, including a second laser reflector, Navy Capt. Alan B. Shepard, Jr., and Comdr. Edgar Dean Mitchell collected 42.9 kg (94.3 lb) of rocks and soil and spent 9 hours and 9 minutes outside on two EVAs. Quar-

(Left) *The planet Earth as seen from space. The photograph, taken at a distance of 185,000 km (115,000 mi) by the outgoing Apollo 11 astronauts, shows most of africa and parts of Europe and Asia*

(Left) *The ascent stage of the Apollo 11 Lunar Module* Eagle *nears rendezvous with the Command Service Module,* Columbia, *in lunar orbit.*

(Below left) *After the first lunar landing on July 20, 1969, astronaut Aldrin deploys experiments, with the* Eagle *in the background.*
(Right) *The Apollo 12 astronauts—(reclining, front to rear) Charles Conrad, Jr., commander; Richard F. Gordon, command-module pilot; Alan C. Bean, lunar-module pilot—undergo spacesuit check before their launch to the Moon on Nov. 14, 1969.*

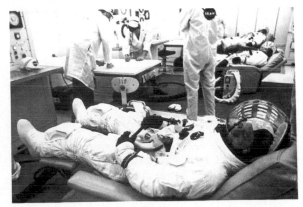

(Left) *The Lunar Rover became the first manned mobile vehicle on the Moon during the Apollo 15 mission, July 1971. It was powered electrically, and traveled at speeds up to 13 km/h (8 mph). Astronauts Irwin (pictured here with Mount Hadley in the background) and Scott used the Rover to explore the lunar surface. A Lunar Rover was also used in the Apollo 16 and 17 missions* (Right) *The Apollo Moon landing sites and dates were: Apollo 11, Sea of Tranquility, July 20, 1969; Apollo 12, Ocean of Storms, Nov. 19, 1969; Apollo 14, Fra Mauro region, Feb. 5, 1971; Apollo 15, Hadley Apennines, July 30, 1971; Apollo 16, Descartes highlands, April 20, 1972; and Apollo 17, Taurus Littrow, Dec. 11, 1972.*

antining returned lunar astronauts at Houston for 14 days after their departure from the Moon was terminated after this mission.

Apollo 15 (July 26–Aug. 7, 1971) brought the first manned surface vehicle—the Lunar Rover—to the Moon. It was carried with its wheels folded, in the descent stage of the LM *Falcon*. Two astronauts spent 18.5 hours roaming for more than 30 km (18.6 mi) on the surface in the Rover, setting up experiments, taking measurements, and collecting 77 kg (170 lb) of soil and rocks. A subsatellite containing instruments for measuring gamma- and X-radiation from the surface was deployed in lunar orbit for the first time by Maj. Alfred M. Worden.

The last two missions penetrated the lunar highlands. *Apollo 16* (Apr. 16–27, 1972) was targeted for the Descartes highlands in the Southern Hemisphere. Two astronauts covered 27 km (16.8 mi) in their Rover and collected 95.8 kg (210.8 lb) of samples in EVAs totaling 20 hours and 14 minutes. *Apollo 17* (Dec. 7–19, 1972) took the first geologist, Harrison H. Schmitt, to the Moon. He and Navy Capt. Eugene A. Cernan landed in the Taurus Mountains, near the Littrow crater, on December 11, in the LM *Challenger*. Comdr. Ronald E. Evans made observations from orbit in the CSM *America*. Cernan and Schmitt spent 22 hours outside in three EVAs and brought back 110 kg (242 lb) of rocks and soil cores, having traversed 35 km (22 mi) in their Rover. This was the final mission in the Apollo lunar-landing program.

See also: SPACE EXPLORATION.

Apollo-Soyuz Test Project [soi'-uhz]   The APOLLO PROGRAM, which started during a time of intense competition between the United States and the USSR, ended in a demonstration of détente in space: a joint orbital flight of the Apollo and SOYUZ spaceships, known as the Apollo-Soyuz Test Project (ASTP). Technically, the joint mission in low Earth orbit demonstrated intership crew transfer and space rescue. The project had been initiated by the United States in 1969 but did not gain Soviet approval until the Nixon-Kosygin summit conference in Moscow in 1972.

The total cost to NASA of the Apollo-Soyuz Test Project was $250 million. The Apollo crew consisted of Air Force Brig. Gen. Thomas P. Stafford; Vance D. Brand, a civilian; and D. K. SLAYTON, a civilian and one of the original seven Project Mercury astronauts. Aboard the smaller, two-man *Soyuz 19* were the pilot, Col. Aleksei LEONOV, and the engineer, Valery N. Kubasov.

Soyuz 19 was launched from Baikonur at 8:20 AM Eastern Daylight Time, on July 15, 1975, and Apollo was launched 7½ hours later from Florida. Because Apollo had the more powerful propulsion system, it carried the specially designed docking module to orbit. The vessels docked over a spot in the Atlantic Ocean about 1,030 km (640 mi) west of Portugal on July 17 at 12:09 PM Eastern Daylight Time. During the next two days, the crews made four transfers between the two ships and completed five planned experiments. The vessels separated July 19. Soyuz landed in Kazakh SSR on July 21, and Apollo in the Pacific Ocean on July 24. The nine-day mission was the last one of the Apollo program.

Apollodorus of Damascus [uh-pahl-uh-dor'-uhs] Apollodorus of Damascus was the chief architect for the Roman emperor TRAJAN (r. AD 98–117). He was skilled as a military architect and engineer and also as an urban planner. His masterpieces—Trajan's Forum and Column, the Basilica Ulpia, and Trajan's Markets—formed a vast ensemble in Rome. The many buildings integrated perfectly with the street pattern and the other forums, but they required the removal of a hill reputedly as high as Trajan's Column. Trajan's Markets survive virtually intact as a marvel of ingenious urban planning.

According to one account, when HADRIAN became emperor, he contrived Apollodorus's exile in AD 130 and later had him executed.

Apollonius of Perga [ap-uh-loh'-nee-uhs, pur'-guh] Apollonius of Perga, a Greek mathematician of the 3d and early 2d centuries BC, was known as the Great Geometer. In his *Conics*, an investigation of the mathematical properties of CONIC SECTIONS, Apollonius introduced the terms ELLIPSE, HYPERBOLA, and PARABOLA. He was also an important founder of Greek mathematical astronomy, which applied geometrical models to planetary theory.

Apollonius of Rhodes A Greek poet-scholar of the 3d century BC, Apollonius wrote the epic poem *Argonautica*, the story of Jason, Medea, and the quest for the Golden Fleece. The epics of HOMER were his models, but the poem shows an Alexandrian penchant for pedantry, allusiveness, and self-conscious contrivance. VERGIL's epic poem AENEID reflects the influence of Apollonius.

Apology see DIALOGUES OF PLATO

apostle [uh-pahs'-uhl] In the Bible apostle is a title conferred on one sent with a message. The term is applied primarily to the original Twelve called by Jesus to accompany him during his ministry (Matt. 10:2–4; Mark 3:16–19; Luke 6:13–16). In the Gospels other followers are called disciples. The title was gradually extended to others such as PAUL and BARNABAS (Acts 14:14; Rom. 9:1, 11:13); when this occurred, the Twelve were distinguished from all the apostles, as in 1 Corinthians 15:5–7. PETER, JAMES (the Greater), and JOHN formed an inner circle closest to Jesus; MATTHIAS was selected to replace JUDAS ISCARIOT (Acts 1:16). The others were MATTHEW, PHILIP, BARTHOLOMEW, THOMAS, JAMES (the Lesser), SIMON, and THADDEUS.

apostolic succession In its strict sense, apostolic succession refers to the doctrine by which the validity and authority of the Christian ministry is derived from the APOSTLES. Churches of the Catholic tradition hold that bishops form the necessary link in an unbroken chain of successors to the office of the apostles. The outward sign by which this connection is both symbolized and effected is the laying on of hands by the BISHOP at ordination.

In its broader sense, apostolic succession refers to the relationship between the Christian church today and the apostolic church of New Testament times. Understood in this way, the church's validity is derived from the apostolic message that it professes and from the apostolic witness that it lives.

apothecary [uh-pahth'-uh-kair-ee] The term *apothecary* refers to a person who sells spices and drugs. It is an old-fashioned term for pharmacist (see PHARMACY) that originated in Europe in the late 13th century.

In colonial America a pharmacy operated by an apothecary or a pharmacist was called an apothecary shop to distinguish it from a doctor's shop, a pharmacy operated by a medical practitioner. The term *apothecary* was recognized by the Continental Congress in 1775, when it established a medical department. Two years later the duties of the apothecary were restricted to pharmaceutical tasks for the first time in America.

In the United States today, the term *pharmacist* denotes one who is licensed to practice pharmacy. Some community pharmacists, however, have adopted the term *apothecary* to indicate that their pharmacies sell only pharmaceuticals and health service items, unlike other pharmacies that sell a wide variety of merchandise in addition to pharmaceuticals. This meaning dates from 1940, the year in which the American College of Apothecaries was organized.

See also: PHARMACOLOGY; PHARMACOPOEIA.

Appalachia [a-puh-lay'-chuh] Appalachia is a region in the eastern United States that takes its name from the Appalachian Mountains cutting through much of it. The region includes (often fairly isolated) parts of 12 states: Alabama, Georgia, Kentucky, Maryland, Ohio, New York, North Carolina, Pennsylvania, South Carolina, Tennessee, Virginia, and West Virginia. The term *Appalachia*, which came into common use in the 1960s, connotes certain economic and sociological characteristics of the region as well as the geography. It refers to economic deprivation and also to distinctive cultural aspects such as arts and crafts. Federal efforts to aid Appalachia culminated under President Lyndon Johnson in March 1965 with the Appalachian Regional Development Act, which provided $1.1 billion in federal funds for an economic-development plan, directed by the Appalachian Regional Commission (ARC).

Appalachian Mountains The Appalachian Mountains, formed about 250 million years ago, are an extensive and relatively narrow mountain system that parallels the eastern seacoast of North America for approximately 1,950 km (1,212 mi) from Newfoundland to Alabama. In Ohio, Pennsylvania, and West Virginia its width exceeds 320 km (199 mi), although in most places it rarely exceeds 160 km (99 mi). Rising out of coastal plains and separated from them by the FALL LINE, the Appalachian Mountains are made up of a broken chain of mountains, ridges, and dissected plateaus. The region is bordered on the west by the Interior Low Plateau, the Central Lowlands, and the St. Lawrence Lowlands, and a marked elevational difference usually indicates this separation. Large portions of the region are still covered with dense deciduous forests. The highest peak, Mount MITCHELL (2,037 m/6,684 ft), is in the BLACK MOUNTAINS in North Carolina.

This Appalachian valley lies at the foot of New Hampshire's Mt. Washington (1,917 m/6,288 ft), the highest point in the northeastern United States. The Appalachian Mountains parallel the Atlantic Coast from Newfoundland to Alabama.

Several prominent ranges are in the system. The GREAT SMOKY MOUNTAINS of Tennessee and North Carolina have peaks in excess of 1,830 m (6,004 ft). The BLUE RIDGE MOUNTAINS, the backbone of the whole system, extend from Georgia to Pennsylvania. Other ranges are the Lehigh, Allegheny, and Pocono mountains of Pennsylvania; the CATSKILL MOUNTAINS of New York; the BERKSHIRE HILLS, GREEN MOUNTAINS, WHITE MOUNTAINS, and Taconic Mountains of New England; the Notre Dame and Shickshock mountains of Quebec; and the Long Range Mountains of Newfoundland. The Appalachians can be viewed as five divisions: the PIEDMONT PLATEAU, the Blue Ridge, the Ridge and Valley, the Appalachian Plateaus, and the New England provinces. None of the boundaries is clearly definable, but each division has distinctive characteristics.

The Piedmont, which abuts the Coastal Plain at the fall line, is an upland region that slopes toward the higher Blue Ridge. It is composed mainly of igneous and metamorphic rocks of Precambrian and early Paleozoic age. The Blue Ridge includes many of the highest peaks and a bold east-facing frontal scarp. It is composed of folded metamorphic rocks with igneous intrusions and of early Paleozoic sedimentary rocks. The Ridge and Valley province is an extensive area of heavily dissected anticlinal and synclinal structures. The ridges are formed on the more resistant sedi-

mentary sandstone layers; the valleys usually overlie the more easily erodible limestone strata. The age of the rock varies from early to late Paleozoic. The Appalachian Plateaus comprise two main areas, the southern portion being the CUMBERLAND PLATEAU, and the northern, the Allegheny Plateau. Both are characterized as heavily dissected sedimentary layers of horizontal strata of the late Paleozoic Era. Bituminous coal is mined from these dissected plateaus. The New England upland is a continuation of these divisions, but its characteristics are not as clearly defined in the glacially subdued northern province.

Appalachian Trail   The Appalachian Trail is a mountain-hiking footpath along the crests of the Appalachian Mountains in the eastern United States. It extends about 3,300 km (2,050 mi) from Mount Katahdin in north central Maine to Springer Mountain in northern Georgia. The trail passes through 14 states and reaches its highest elevation (2,022 m/6,634 ft) on Clingmans Dome in the Great Smoky Mountains. The trail was completed, except for minor alterations, in 1937. In 1968 it was designated a national scenic trail. It is marked and maintained by hiking groups under the supervision of the Appalachian Trail Conference.

The Appaloosa horse was bred by the Nez Percé Indians along the Palouse River of the northwestern United States. It is distinguished by spots and striped hooves.

Appaloosa [ap-uh-loo'-suh] The Appaloosa is a breed of horse developed by the NEZ PERCÉ Indians. In October 1877, Chief Joseph and his Nez Percé band surrendered to the U.S. Army and were exiled to Oklahoma, taking with them 1,100 of their carefully bred Appaloosa horses. These beautiful spotted horses almost became extinct in the following years, surviving largely because their spectacular appearance made them popular for circuses and Wild West shows. The Appaloosa is 14–15 hands (142–152 cm/56–60 in) high and weighs 431–533 kg (950–1,175 lb).

appeal An appeal, in law, is the procedure in which a higher court is asked to review a decision of a lower court. In a civil suit, either party may appeal a court verdict; in a criminal case, only a convicted defendant has the right of appeal.

An appeal is usually based on grounds that the trial court erred in matters of law—for instance, by allowing or disallowing certain evidence or by giving prejudicial instructions to the jury. The discovery of new evidence is another basis for appeal. The interpretation of evidence—deciding whether the judge or jury drew the wrong conclusions from the evidence presented—is not ordinarily a basis for appeal.

The higher (appellate) court (see COURT OF APPEALS) may affirm or reverse the lower (trial) court decision, or it may remand—that is, send back—the case to the trial court for additional findings of fact and conclusions of law or, sometimes, for the taking of additional testimony. In remanding the case to a lower court, the higher court will state specifically whether it retains jurisdiction. In handing down rulings over the years, appellate courts build up a body of precedents, or judge-made law, that trial courts are obliged to follow.

After the highest appeals court in a state has ruled, an appeal may be carried to the U.S. federal courts only if it can be argued that federal law has been violated or constitutional rights denied. The court of last resort is the SUPREME COURT OF THE UNITED STATES, which grants review by permission only and deals primarily with legal, rather than factual, questions.

Appel, Karel Karel Appel, b. Amsterdam, Apr. 25, 1921, is one of Europe's leading abstract expressionist painters. He is one of the founders of the avant-garde artists' group CoBrA, whose members were born in Copenhagen, Brussels, and Amsterdam. Often mentioned with Willem DE KOONING as an exponent of Nordic ABSTRACT EXPRESSIONISM, Appel reaches back toward primitive mythic and biomorphic forms in his painting. His canvases, to which the paint is very thickly applied, have a rough, expressionistic appearance and look as if the paint had been sculpted. Appel's works are found in the collections of most major museums of contemporary art.

Scream for Freedom (1948) by Karel Appel demonstrates the influence of children's drawings on the international expressionist CoBrA group. (Stedelijk Museum, Amsterdam.)

appendix The appendix is a slender projection opening from the pouchlike portion of the large INTESTINE called the cecum. Located near the point where the ileum, or lower portion of the small intestine, empties into the large intestine, it is called the vermiform appendix, from the Latin *vermiform* meaning "wormlike," which describes its shape. It is 2–20 cm (1–8 in) long, about as thick as a pencil, and hollow; the free end is closed.

The appendix has no known function in human beings and is regarded as a vestigial organ, an evolutionary relic. The same structure appears in the anthropoid ape. Herbivorous animals have an extended cecum that resembles the appendix but is as long as the large intestine; it probably serves a digestive function. The human appendix consists mostly of lymphoid tissue, like the tonsils and adenoids, and is easily invaded by microorganisms. When the appendix is infected, the inflammatory response is called appendicitis, a medical emergency that is almost always treated by surgical removal of the appendix.

Appert, Nicolas   see CANNING

Appian Way   see ROMAN ROADS

apple   The most widely cultivated of all fruit trees, the apple (genus *Malus* of the family Rosaceae) is second only to the grape in its importance as a temperate-zone fruit. One of the oldest of cultivated fruits, varieties have been propagated for at least 2,000 years in Europe alone. Today about 7,500 varieties are grown worldwide, and about 2,500 can be found in the United States.

Apples grown for commercial use are generally classified as CIDER apples, grown chiefly for their juice; as cooking apples; or as eating (dessert) apples. Size, sweetness, aroma, and crispness vary greatly from one variety to another, and color ranges from shades of red to yellow or green. Smaller CRAB APPLE species of the genus *Malus* may also be eaten.

Trees are propagated by grafting or by budding. A 2-year-old tree, transplanted from nursery to orchard, may take up to 8 years to produce a commercial crop. Although traditional orchards have full-grown trees, a newer trend is to graft branches bearing full-sized fruit onto dwarf trees and train the branches against a trellis (see ESPALIER). This method allows more trees to be planted per hectare. Apple trees require careful pruning during the first 5 years of growth and seasonal protection from pests and parasites. Chemicals are used to thin out young fruit, to prevent ripe fruit from dropping before it is harvested, and to control the numerous insects and fungal diseases that attack apple trees. Because not every variety is self-fruitful, several varieties are usually planted together to ensure cross-pollination. The apple tree requires a period of dormancy and does not produce well in regions where winter temperatures average higher than 9° C (48° F).

Apples are usually harvested when fully ripe, because immature apples ripen poorly after picking. Fruit stored at temperatures below freezing and in high humidity, however, will remain fresh up to 10 months. Modern large-scale storage techniques enable some apple growers to maintain a year-round market for their produce. The USSR, the United States, and France harvest the largest

Red Delicious   Stayman

Rome Beauty   Jonathan

Golden Delicious   Rhode Island Greening

The common apple is grown in thousands of cultivated varieties. The Red Delicious, a sweet, juicy apple that is the most popular in the United States, is frequently used in salads. The Rome Beauty, although not as flavorful as other apples, is used to make baked apples, applesauce, or pies. The Golden Delicious, which is the second most popular apple, tastes sweet and slightly acid. An all-purpose apple, it is eaten raw, cooked, or baked. The Stayman, also used in cooking, is tart, crisp, and juicy. Two other popular apple varieties are the distinctively flavored Jonathan, used as a dessert and cooking apple, and the Rhode Island Greening, a tart apple used primarily for cooking and baking.

apple crops. Western Europe as a whole produces more apples than does any other region; Argentina, Chile, and Japan are also important producers.

Washington, Michigan, and New York produce most of the U.S. apples. About half the crop is eaten as fresh fruit; the remainder is canned as sauce or pie filling, or is made into cider, cider vinegar, juice, jelly, or apple butter.

Appleseed, Johnny   see CHAPMAN, JOHN

Appleton   Appleton (1990 pop., 65,695), a city on the Fox River in east central Wisconsin, is the seat of Outagamie County. It is a manufacturing center for paper and related products and was named for Samuel Appleton, father-in-law of Amos Lawrence, who founded Lawrence University there in 1847.

Appleton, Sir Edward Victor The British physicist Sir Edward Victor Appleton, b. Sept. 6, 1892, d. Apr. 21, 1965, won the 1947 Nobel Prize for physics for his discovery that the upper layer of the ionosphere, called the F-region or Appleton layer, reflects radio waves. The discovery established the possibility of radio communication over long distances. Appleton served (1924–36) as a professor of physics at King's College, University of London, taught (1936–39) at Cambridge University, and, while serving (1939–49) in the Department of Scientific and Industrial Research, aided in the development of radar and the atomic bomb. He was knighted in 1941.

Appleton, Nathan Nathan Appleton, b. New Ipswich, N.H., Oct. 6, 1779, d. July 14, 1861, played a prominent role in the development of the U.S. textile industry. A successful Boston merchant, he supported Francis C. Lowell in his effort to introduce the power loom and build a cotton mill in Waltham, Mass. The mill, completed in 1814, was the first in the country to perform all the operations necessary to turn raw cotton into cloth. Appleton served (1831–32 and 1841–42) in Congress, where he advocated protective duties that would enable the fledgling industry to develop without being threatened by cheaper imports.

Applications Technology Satellite The Applications Technology Satellite (ATS) was a series of six satellites (see SATELLITE, ARTIFICIAL) developed for the National Aeronautics and Space Administration (NASA) to test advanced techniques, control systems, and components for future communications, navigational, and meteorological satellites. They also gathered scientific data on the orbital environment and the ionosphere. The five first-generation satellites of the series, which was an outgrowth of project SYNCOM, were launched between 1966 and 1969; the more advanced ATS 6 was launched in May 1974. Only ATS 1, 3, and 6 were completely successful, and a proposed ATS 7 was canceled before it could be completed.

appliqué see NEEDLEWORK

Appomattox Court House [ap-uh-mat'-uhks] Appomattox Court House, a former village in Virginia 40 km (25 mi) east of Lynchburg, was the site of the surrender by Gen. Robert E. LEE of his Confederate Army of Northern Virginia on Apr. 9, 1865. Lee's forces, cut to barely 9,000 effective troops, were virtually surrounded by the Army of the Potomac under Gen. George MEADE. After a morning of heavy skirmishing, which revealed growing Union strength, Lee met Gen. Ulysses S. GRANT, commanding the Union armies, and surrendered his army. Pressed to surrender all Confederate armies, over which he held nominal command, Lee refused. However, surrender of the Army of Northern Virginia in itself was enough to spell the end of the Confederacy and of the U.S. CIVIL WAR. Appomattox Court House is now a national historical park.

apportionment Apportionment is the system by which representation in a legislature or other body is distributed. Political scientists distinguish five principal methods of apportionment: (1) on the basis of population, as in the U.S. House of Representatives, which operates on the principle of the larger the state, the greater its representation; (2) on the basis of governmental or geographical units, as in the U.S. Senate, where two senators represent each state, regardless of its size; (3) on the basis of occupational, ethnic, or social groups (at one time, a businessman with an office in the City of London was entitled to vote there even though he also voted at his place of residence elsewhere); (4) on the basis of wealth, as in the early years of the United States when states had property requirements for voting; and (5) on the basis of party voting strength (see PROPORTIONAL REPRESENTATION).

The U.S. Constitution requires that a census be taken every ten years to determine how many seats each state is entitled to in the House of Representatives but says nothing about the apportionment of state districts.

apprenticeship Apprenticeship is a method of training in which the learner works for a master craftsperson, receiving both training and a small income. Medieval craft GUILDS established apprenticeship programs, customarily lasting seven years, in which apprentices lived with the master in a quasi-familial relationship. At the completion of this period the apprentice became a journeyman: he was no longer tied to a master, but worked for a day's wage.

Trade unions have developed similar programs in which a young worker is employed at low pay while learning a craft. The National Apprenticeship Act of 1937 (the Fitzgerald Act) authorized federal coordination of programs in the United States. Apprenticeship programs must allow equality of opportunity. Training is done in phases, with examinations and pay increases marking the transitions from phase to phase. Facilities and supervision must be adequate.

apricot Apricots are the fruit of certain species of trees of the genus *Prunus*, which also includes almonds, cherries, nectarines, peaches, and plums. The common apricot, *P. armeniaca*, a native of China, grows to about 9 m (30 ft) high, has reddish bark, and bears oval-shaped leaves up to 8 cm (3 in) long and small white to pinkish flowers. The fruit is classified as a drupe—fleshy and one-seeded, with the seed enclosed in a stony endocarp called a pit (see FRUITS AND FRUIT CULTIVATION). The Japanese apricot, *P. mume*, bears a more sour fruit that is often used to produce a liqueur.

The common apricot is widely cultivated in the temperate zones; in the United States, California produces

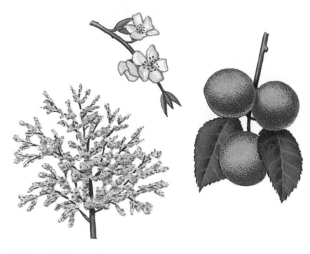

The apricot tree produces a sweet, thick-fleshed fruit that is often preserved in dried form. In the Middle East, sieved apricot pulp is sun dried into thin, chewy sheets that are eaten like candy.

about 95 percent of the crop. Because the trees bloom early in the season, commercial production is practical only in areas free from serious spring frost, and winter chilling is required to induce dormancy. The trees are propagated by GRAFTING onto apricot or peach seedling rootstock. The fruits develop rapidly and ripen early in the summer.

apse   see CATHEDRALS AND CHURCHES

apteryx   see KIWI (bird)

aptitude tests   see EDUCATIONAL MEASUREMENT

Apuleius [ap-oo-lay'-uhs]   Lucius Apuleius, AD 123–50, was a Latin philosopher who wrote the novel *Metamorphoses* (Transformations), known popularly as *The Golden Ass*. He was born at Madauros (North Africa), educated in Carthage and Athens, and traveled widely. When he married a wealthy widow in Tripoli, her relatives accused him of witchcraft. The speech he delivered in his own defense in court, *Apologia*, or *De magia*, tells much about occult science in the ancient world. Apuleius was acquitted and returned to Carthage, where he taught philosophy and rhetoric. In addition to *The Golden Ass*, the only extant complete novel in Latin, Apuleius's works include the Platonic essays *De Deo Socratis* (On Socrates' Personal God) and *Florida* (purple passages from his declamations).

Aqaba, Gulf of [ah'-kah-bah]   The Gulf of Aqaba is a narrow arm of the Red Sea extending northeast between Saudi Arabia and the Sinai Peninsula. It is approximately 160 km (100 mi) long and 19–27 km (12–17 mi) wide. At the head of the gulf are Aqaba and ELAT. Aqaba is Jor-

dan's only seaport, and Elat is Israel's only outlet to the Red Sea.

aquamarine   see BERYL

aquarium   An aquarium is a container for maintaining aquatic organisms for display or research. Aquarium facilities range from the relatively simple tanks kept by amateur enthusiasts to huge oceanariums, where undersea environments are reproduced.

Home Aquariums. Because of their attractiveness and easy maintenance, glass aquariums with capacities of up to 200 l (50 gal) are the most frequently used. The basic components of most modern home aquariums include, in addition to the tank, a heater to keep the water at the proper temperature (usually between 22° and 27° C/72° and 80° F, depending on the type of fish) and an air pump and filter combination that add oxygen and remove some of the impurities in the water. Some aquarists establish balanced tank communities in which little aeration and filtration are required. In these systems, the number of fish, the amount of food supplied, and the plant life are carefully balanced to achieve a simple ecological cycle. Wastes from the fish are converted to nutrients and harmless debris by bacteria. The plants take up the nutrients and produce enough oxygen for the needs of the fish.

The development of material that allows amateur aquarists to duplicate seawater synthetically has made it possible to raise saltwater organisms in a home tank. Colorful reef fishes are among the most popular, followed by a wide variety of invertebrates such as anemones, hermit crabs, and mollusks.

An aquarium requires careful control of water temperature, light, and oxygen. Standard equipment includes a glass tank with a metal frame, which can hold several gallons of water. A thermostatically regulated immersion heater maintains the proper temperature, which is checked by a thermometer. A filter of charcoal and glass wool cleans the water of debris, and an aerator replenishes the oxygen supply. With adequate amounts of light, aquatic plants photosynthetically convert the carbon dioxide expired by the fish into oxygen.

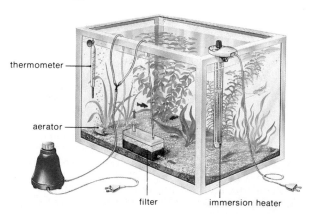

thermometer

aerator

filter

immersion heater

Public Aquariums. The first aquarium for publicly displaying fish was opened in 1853 at Regent's Park, England. Today there are about 500 public and commercial aquariums worldwide for displaying fish or for research. Modern aquariums may have both freshwater and marine tanks, with capacities of up to 4 million l (1 million gal). These huge tanks may hold a large number of different fish and invertebrate species as well as marine reptiles and birds. Some aquariums have tanks in which tides are simulated so that estuarine animals can also be maintained.

Oceanariums often maintain large tanks or holding areas directly on the ocean, stocked with such large marine forms as dolphins or sharks. Visitors view the ocean life through glassed areas on the tank walls and from overhead walkways.

Aquarius Aquarius the Water Bearer, or Water Carrier, is one of the CONSTELLATIONS of the ZODIAC, the band of sky through which the Sun, Moon, and planets appear to move. Most prominent during the autumn months in the Northern Hemisphere, Aquarius contains the globular cluster M 2, the planetary nebula NGC 7009, also known as the Saturn nebula, and NGC 7293, known as the Helix nebula. The Aquarid meteor showers appear to radiate from the constellation in May and July.

In ASTROLOGY, Aquarius governs the period between January 20 and February 18. Because of the precession of the equinoxes, the point where the Sun passes from the south to north of the celestial equator (the spring equinox) will move into Aquarius about AD 2200, giving rise to the phrase "the dawning of the age of Aquarius."

aquatint Aquatint is an intaglio ETCHING technique used by printmakers to create variations in tone similar to the wash effects of watercolors. It is achieved by applying a layer of resin to a copperplate, which is heated to fuse the grains to the plate's surface. When the plate is exposed to an acid solution, the unprotected metal between the fused grains is eaten away, and thousands of tiny cavities are formed. These hold the ink and print a variety of tones, depending on the depth of the acid "bite," which will vary according to the size of the grains and the length of time the plate is exposed to the acid.

In his *Los Caprichos* (1796–98), Goya demonstrated a mastery of aquatint. Later notable aquatint artists include Thomas Rowlandson, Georges Rouault, and Picasso.

aqueduct An aqueduct is a structure built to carry water from a source to a distant destination (see WATER SUPPLY). The modern aqueduct may involve a complex system of canals, tunnels, and pipelines, and it almost always uses pressure to force the water along some part of its route. The aqueducts of ancient times were less complicated structures and usually employed only the force of gravity to move the water.

In 691 BC, Sennacherib, king of Assyria, built a conduit to transport water from a river about 80 km (50 mi)

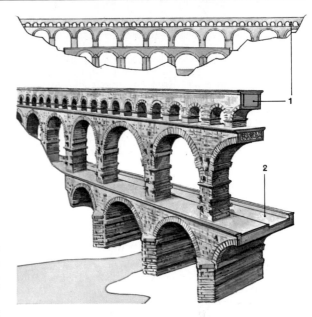

The Pont du Gard at Nîmes, France, is a splendid example of Roman aqueduct engineering. The structure is part of a 40-km (25-mi) aqueduct built about AD 14. Three tiers of arches support a water channel (1). A footbridge (2) runs above the first tier.

distant to his fields and gardens in Nineveh. A gently sloping masonry channel was constructed, and where it passed over a valley, an arched bridge 9 m (30 ft) high was built to support it. This was one of the earliest known aqueducts—although evidence indicates that aqueducts had been built in the Middle East as early as the 10th century BC—and it furnished a model for the Greek engineer Eupalinus when he built his aqueduct on the island of Samos in 530 BC.

Although elevated structures with arches formed a part of most ancient aqueducts, underground conduits were used in hilly or mountainous regions to tap GROUNDWATER supplies. Called *qanats* in the Near East, these tunnels sloped downward underground, pierced at regular intervals by vertical shafts to the surface and marked aboveground by piles of excavated material.

The most extensive ancient aqueduct system was that built by the city of Rome. It is described in detail by Sextus Julius FRONTINUS. Rome's 11 aqueducts totaled 479 km (298 mi) in length. The first, the Aqua Appia, was built in 312 BC.

Modern aqueducts use pipes that can carry water under high pressure, and pressure tunnels—built far underground, where the surrounding rock supplies pressure resistance—to handle even larger, faster water flows. The diameter of these tunnels can be quite large, 6 to 8 m (20 to 26 ft), whereas the average Roman conduit had a diameter of 1.5 m (5 ft). Pumping stations now lift great volumes of water up hundreds of meters, and the length of some newer aqueducts is measured in hundreds of kilometers.

aquifer [ak'-wi-fur]   An aquifer is any natural material that contains water recoverable in useful amounts by means of wells. Aquifers may be fractured zones in otherwise solid rock, layers of solid but porous rock, or loose sedimentary materials. Some of the most productive aquifers are thick beds of sandstone, geologically young limestones and basalts, and stream sands and gravels. Except in favored areas, most geologic materials are not aquifers. Clay and shale contain water, but, unless the beds are fractured, pore openings are too small to allow water movement. Many other rocks, such as granite, contain virtually no water.

See also: ARTESIAN WELL; GROUNDWATER; WATER RESOURCES.

Aquila [ak'-wil-uh]   Aquila the Eagle is a CONSTELLATION of stars prominent in the summer sky in the Northern Hemisphere. It contains the bright star Altair (α Aquilae), of visual magnitude 0.77 and spectral type A7. The so-called summer triangle is composed of Altair and the stars Vega in Lyra and Deneb in Cygnus. The Milky Way passes through Aquila and, because of dust clouds, appears to divide into two parts in this area.

Aquinas, Saint Thomas   Saint Thomas Aquinas, a Dominican theologian, met the challenge posed to Christian faith by the philosophical achievements of the Greeks and Arabs. He effected a philosophical synthesis of faith and reason that is one of the greatest achievements of medieval times.

Saint Thomas Aquinas, known as the Angelic Doctor, synthesized religious and philosophical thought during the Middle Ages. A fresco by Andrea da Firenze shows an enthroned Saint Thomas with the Spanish-Arabic philosopher Averroës sitting at his feet.

Life. Thomas d'Aquino, the son of a count, was born in his family's castle at Roccasecca, central Italy, in 1224. At about the age of five, Thomas was placed by his parents in the Benedictine monastery at Monte Cassino. When Monte Cassino became the scene of a battle between papal and imperial troops, Thomas withdrew and enrolled at the University of Naples. There he came into contact with members of the Dominican order and, against the violent opposition of his family, became a Dominican friar in 1244. He then went north to study (1245–52) at Paris and Cologne under ALBERTUS MAGNUS.

From 1252 to 1259, Thomas taught at the Dominican *studium generale* (house of studies) in Paris; he was named a master of theology in 1256. From 1259 to 1269 he was in Italy, attached to the papal court. A second Parisian period, 1269–72, was followed by his assignment to Naples to head the Dominican *studium generale* there. In 1274, going north again to attend the Council of Lyon, Thomas fell ill and died in the Cistercian abbey of Fossanova on March 7. His *Summa contra Gentiles* was written in 1258–60, and his greatest work, the SUMMA THEOLOGIAE, occupied him from 1267 to 1273.

Thought. Thomas's thought embodied the conviction that Christian revelation and human knowledge are facets of a single truth and cannot be in conflict with one another.

Humans know something when its truth is either immediately evident to them or can be made evident by appeal to immediately evident truths. They believe something when they accept its truth on authority. Religious faith is the acceptance of truths on the authority of God's REVELATION of them. Despite the fact that this seems to make knowledge and faith two utterly distinct realms, Thomas held that some of the things God has revealed are in fact knowable, including the existence of God and certain of his attributes, the immortality of the human soul, and some moral principles. The rest of what has been revealed he called "mysteries of faith," for example, the Trinity, the incarnation of God in Jesus Christ, the resurrection, and so on. He then argued that, if some of the things God has revealed can be known to be true, it is reasonable to accept the mysteries as true.

Thomas's conviction that truth is ultimately one because it has its source in God explains the confidence with which he approached the writings of non-Christian thinkers: ARISTOTLE, the Muslim Aristotelians AVERROËS and AVICENNA, and the Jewish philosopher MAIMONIDES.

Thomas argued that the existence of God can be proved by reasoning from sense data. He also held that there are first principles of moral reasoning (NATURAL LAW) that all humans grasp; many of them, however, have been revealed in the Ten Commandments.

Influence. In 1323, Thomas was canonized, and since that time his thought has become more or less the official doctrine of the Roman Catholic church. He was declared a Doctor of the Church in 1567. In the 19th century, under Pope Leo XIII, the modern revival of Thomism began.

Aquino, Corazon C. [ah-kee'-no]   Corazon Cojuangco Aquino, b. Jan. 25, 1933, the widow of Philippine opposition leader Benigno S. Aquino, Jr., became president of the Philippines in 1986. She served as her husband's link to the outside world during his eight years of imprisonment (1972–80) for opposition to President Ferdinand MARCOS and accompanied him into exile in the United States in 1980. After his assassination when he returned to the Philippines on Aug. 21, 1983, she became the rallying point for the fragmented opposition. In late 1985, when Marcos called for early presidential elections, she reluctantly agreed to head the opposition ticket. The National Assembly proclaimed Marcos the winner of the Feb. 7, 1986, elections. Aquino, charging that she had been deprived of victory by fraud and intimidation, mounted a campaign of nonviolent resistance to force Marcos from office. Marcos and Aquino held rival inaugurations on February 25. Later that day, with Marcos en route to exile in the United States, Aquino assumed de facto control of the government; on March 25 she assumed transitional legislative powers. Despite the ongoing problems of poverty, government corruption, and a Communist insurgency, the results of the Feb. 2, 1987, referendum on a new constitution confirmed her in office until June 30, 1992, and the May 11, 1987, elections gave her supporters control of Congress. She has survived several coup attempts.

Philippine president Corazon Aquino and her vice-president, Salvador Laurel, are shown in front of a portrait of Aquino's late husband, Benigno S. Aquino, Jr., whose 1983 assassination set off a wave of popular protests that brought the Marcos era to a dramatic end in February 1986.

Aquitaine [ak'-wi-tayn] Aquitaine (Latin: Aquitania), an area roughly corresponding to the southwestern third of France, was one of the three divisions of ancient GAUL. After 500 years of Roman rule, it fell to the Visigoths in the 5th century and then to the Franks when they defeated the Visigoths in 507. The Franks rarely maintained strong control over Aquitaine, and in about 725 it was raided by the Muslim conquerors of Spain. The Frankish leader CHARLES MARTEL crushed these invaders in 733, and Aquitaine became part of the Carolingian empire.

In the 9th century the leading counts and other nobility gradually freed themselves of royal control. Bernard

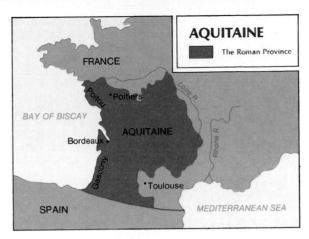

Aquitaine, a former Roman province comprising most of southwestern France, became a powerful duchy in the Middle Ages.

Plantevelue (r. 868–86) and his son, William I (r. 886–918), whose power was based in Auvergne, called themselves dukes of Aquitaine, but their state disintegrated. William V (r. 995–1030) founded a new duchy of Aquitaine based in Poitou. It reached its zenith under William VIII (r. 1058–86). When William X died (1137), his daughter ELEANOR OF AQUITAINE married Louis VII of France, whom she divorced in 1152 to marry Henry II of England. She maintained an elegant chivalric court at Poitiers. Her sons, Richard I and John, and their successors as kings of England were dukes of Aquitaine (later known as GUIENNE). The French conquered Poitou in 1224 and other parts of Aquitaine in the next century. English victories during the HUNDRED YEARS' WAR enabled Edward III to reconstruct the old duchy in the 1360s, but France finally conquered the remainder of it in 1453.

Arab-Israeli Wars Since the United Nations partition of Palestine in 1947 and the establishment of the modern state of Israel in 1948, there have been five major Arab-Israeli wars (1947–49, 1956, 1967, 1973, and 1982). Although Egypt and Israel signed a peace treaty in 1979, hostility between Israel and the rest of its Arab neighbors was complicated by the demands of Palestinian Arabs for an independent state in Israeli-occupied territory.

The First Palestine War (1947–49)

The first war began as a civil conflict between Palestinian Jews and Arabs following the United Nations recommendation of Nov. 29, 1947, to partition Palestine, then still under British mandate, into an Arab state and a Jewish state. Fighting quickly spread as Arab guerrillas attacked Jewish settlements to prevent implementation of the UN plan.

Jewish forces prevented seizure of most settlements, but Arab guerrillas, supported by the Transjordanian Arab Legion under the command of British officers, besieged Jerusalem. By April, Haganah, the principal Jewish military group, seized the offensive, scoring victories against the Arab Liberation Army in northern Palestine, Jaffa, and Jerusalem.

After the British had departed and the state of Israel had been established on May 15, 1948, under the premiership of David BEN-GURION, the Palestine Arab forces were joined by regular armies of Transjordan (now the kingdom of Jordan), Iraq, Lebanon, and Syria, with token support from Saudi Arabia. Efforts by the UN to halt the fighting resulted in a 4-week truce beginning June 11. When the Arab states refused to renew the truce, ten more days of fighting erupted, with Israel greatly extending the area under its control and breaking the siege of Jerusalem. Fighting on a smaller scale continued during a second UN truce, and Israel acquired more territory, especially in Galilee and the Negev. By January 1949, when the last battles ended, Israel had extended its frontiers by about 5,000 km^2 (1,930 mi^2) beyond the 15,500 km^2 (4,983 mi^2) allocated to the Jewish state in the UN partition resolution. It had also secured its independence. During 1949, armistice agreements were signed under UN auspices between Israel and Egypt, Jordan, Syria, and Lebanon. The armistice frontiers were unofficial boundaries until 1967.

Suez-Sinai War (1956)

Border conflicts between Israel and the Arabs continued despite provisions in the 1949 armistice agreements for peace negotiations. Hundreds of thousands of Palestinian Arabs who had left Israeli-held territory during the first war concentrated in refugee camps along Israel's frontiers and became a major source of friction when they attacked Israeli border settlements. A major tension point was the Egyptian-controlled GAZA STRIP, from which Arab guerrillas raided southern Israel. Egypt's blockade of Israeli shipping in the Suez Canal and Gulf of Aqaba intensified the hostilities.

These escalating tensions converged with the SUEZ CRISIS, caused by the nationalization of the Suez Canal by Egyptian president Gamal NASSER. Great Britain and France strenuously objected to Nasser's policies, and a joint military campaign was planned against Egypt with the understanding that Israel would take the initiative by seizing the Sinai Peninsula. The war began on Oct. 29, 1956, after an announcement that the armies of Egypt, Syria, and Jordan were to be integrated under the Egyptian commander in chief. Israel's Operation Kadesh, commanded by Moshe DAYAN, lasted less than a week; its forces reached the eastern bank of the Suez Canal in about 100 hours, seizing the Gaza Strip and nearly all the Sinai Peninsula. The Sinai operations were supplemented by an Anglo-French invasion of Egypt on November 5, giving the allies control of the northern sector of the Suez Canal.

The war was halted by a UN General Assembly resolution calling for an immediate cease-fire and withdrawal of all occupying forces from Egyptian territory. The General Assembly also established a United Nations Emergency Force (UNEF) to replace the allied troops on the Egyptian side of the borders in Suez, Sinai, and Gaza. By December 22 the last British and French troops had left Egypt.

Israel's forces were not withdrawn from Gaza until March 1957.

Six-Day War (1967)

In the following decade the Suez Canal remained closed to Israeli shipping, and periodic border clashes occurred between Israel, Syria, and Jordan. By 1967 the Arab confrontation states—Egypt, Syria, and Jordan—became impatient with the status quo, and border incidents increased. Tensions culminated in May when Egyptian forces massed in Sinai, and Cairo ordered the UNEF to leave Sinai and Gaza. President Nasser also announced that the Gulf of Aqaba would be closed again to Israeli shipping. At the end of May, Jordan placed its armed forces under Egyptian command. Efforts to deescalate the crisis were of no avail.

Believing that war was inevitable, the Israeli government approved preemptive strikes at Egyptian, Syrian, Jordanian, and Iraqi airfields on June 5, 1967. By the evening of June 6, Israel had destroyed the combat effectiveness of the major Arab air forces. Israel also swept into Sinai, reaching the Suez Canal and occupying most of the peninsula in less than four days.

King HUSSEIN of Jordon rejected an offer of neutrality and opened fire on Israeli forces in Jerusalem on June 5. But a lightning Israeli campaign placed all of Arab Jerusalem and the Jordanian West Bank in Israeli hands by June 8. As the war ended on the Jordanian and Egyptian fronts, Israel opened an attack on Syria in the north. In a little more than two days of fierce fighting, Syrian forces were driven from the Golan Heights, from which they had shelled Jewish settlements across the border. The Six-Day War ended on June 10 when the UN negotiated cease-fire agreements on all fronts. The Six-Day War increased severalfold the area under Israel's control, but the addition of more than 1,500,000 Palestinian Arabs to areas under Israeli control threatened internal security.

October War (1973)

Israel was the dominant military power in the region for the next six years. Led by Golda MEIR from 1969, it was generally satisfied with the status quo, but Arab leaders repeatedly warned that they would not accept continued Israeli occupation of the lands lost in 1967. After Anwar al-SADAT succeeded Nasser as president of Egypt in 1970, threats were more frequent, as was periodic massing of troops along the Suez Canal. Egyptian and Syrian forces underwent massive rearmament with sophisticated Soviet equipment. Sadat consolidated war preparations in secret agreements with President Hafez al-ASSAD of Syria for a joint attack and with King FAISAL of Saudi Arabia to finance the operations.

Egypt and Syria attacked on Oct. 6, 1973, pushing Israeli forces several kilometers behind the 1967 cease-fire lines. Israel was thrown off guard, partly because the attack came on Yom Kippur (the Day of Atonement), the most sacred Jewish religious day (coinciding with the Muslim fast of Ramadan). In counterattacks on the Egyptian front, Israel seized a major bridgehead behind the Egyptian lines on the west bank of the canal. In the north,

Israel drove a wedge into the Syrian lines. After 18 days of fighting in the longest Arab-Israeli war since 1948, hostilities were again halted by the UN.

The political phase of the 1973 war ended with disengagement agreements accepted by Israel, Egypt, and Syria after negotiations in 1974 and 1975 by U.S. secretary of state Henry A. KISSINGER. The agreements provided for Egyptian reoccupation of a strip of land in Sinai along the east bank of the Suez Canal and for Syrian control of a small area around the Golan Heights town of Kuneitra. UN forces were stationed on both fronts to oversee observance of the agreements.

Under an Egyptian-Israeli peace treaty signed on Mar. 26, 1979, Israel returned the Sinai peninsula to Egypt. Hopes for an expansion of the peace process to include other Arab nations waned, however, when Egypt and Israel were subsequently unable to agree on a formula for Palestinian self-rule in the West Bank and Gaza Strip. In the 1980s tensions were increased by conflicts between Israeli authorities and Palestinians in the occupied territories, by PALESTINE LIBERATION ORGANIZATION (PLO) guerrilla attacks on Israeli settlements in Galilee, and by Israeli retaliatory raids into Lebanon.

Operation "Peace for Galilee" (1982)

On June 6, 1982, Israel launched a full-scale invasion of Lebanon to destroy PLO bases there and to end the attacks across its borders. Meeting little resistance, Israeli commanders pushed northward, reaching the outskirts of Beirut within a week. Fighting with Syrian forces also erupted. By the end of June, Israel had captured most of southern Lebanon and besieged PLO and Syrian forces in West Beirut. The siege ended through U.S. mediation in August, when Israel agreed to leave Beirut provided Syrian and PLO forces also withdrew. A multinational force from the United States and Western Europe supervised the Syrian and PLO evacuation. On September 15, after the assassination of Lebanese president-elect Bashir Gemayel, Israel reoccupied Beirut and authorized Gemayel's Phalangist militia to "cleanse" Palestinian refugee camps of any remaining PLO fighters. The Phalange massacred hundreds of Palestinians, sparking Israeli protests against the war.

Israel signed an agreement with Lebanon ending the state of war in May 1983, but Lebanon renounced the pact under Syrian pressure in March 1984. Public pressures in Israel forced the government to begin a phased withdrawal. The government decided to complete withdrawal by June 1984, leaving 1,000 "security personnel" to assist its Lebanese allies. While Israel's borders remained secure, its internal stability was threatened by continued demands for Palestinian self-determination and by increasing unrest in the occupied territories, where activists launched a civil disobedience campaign in December 1987.

▬

Arab League The League of Arab States was formed in Cairo on Mar. 22, 1945, by Egypt, Saudi Arabia, Syria, Lebanon, Iraq, Transjordan (now Jordan), and Yemen.

The main aim of the league is to coordinate the political action and safeguard the sovereignty of the Arab states. In the council of the league, on which each member has one vote, only unanimous decisions are binding. In 1990 the league had 21 members, including Egypt, which was readmitted in 1989 after being suspended for 10 years due to the Egyptian-Israeli peace treaty of 1979. League headquarters, in Tunis from 1979, were to return to Cairo. In 1990 the Iraqi invasion of Kuwait split the League. Twelve of its members condemned Iraq and voted to send troops to Saudi Arabia.

▬

Arabia Arabia is a large peninsula separated from Africa by the Red Sea and the Gulf of Aden on the west and from Asia by the Persian Gulf and the Gulf of Oman on the east. The Indian Ocean forms the southern boundary, and the deserts of Jordan and Syria isolate the area from the north. For these reasons, the Arabs call the area Jazirat al-Arab ("the island of the Arabs"). More than 80% of the 2,590,000-km^2 (1,000,000-mi^2) peninsula is occupied by Saudi Arabia. The states of Yemen, Oman, the United Arab Emirates, Qatar, and Kuwait ring the peninsula on the south and east. The island state of Bahrain lies 21 km (13 mi) off the eastern coast of Saudi Arabia. The peninsula's population is 31,000,000 (1990 est.).

The Arabian Peninsula is a plateau composed of crystalline rock and overlain with sediments. It is bordered on all sides by a series of escarpments. Summer temperatures average more than 38° C (100° F). Annual rainfall averages less than 100 mm (4 in). Mountainous regions are found along the western and southern coasts. Most of the water used to support the production of millet, wheat, barley, and sheep comes from underground springs. More than one-fifth of the peninsula is covered by the Rub al-Khali ("Empty Quarter"), the largest continuous sand body in the world. Sand ridges hundreds of kilometers long and very high dunes are common features. Oil fields concentrated around the Persian Gulf account for about 20% of world petroleum production.

The Arabian peninsula was occupied by the wealthy Sabaean civilization (see SHEBA), then by the Babylonians and Egyptians. It was eventually united (7th century) under MUHAMMAD's caliphs and became the "cradle of Islam." The western Saudi Arabian province of Hejaz contains MECCA and MEDINA, the holiest cities of Islam.

▬

Arabian Desert The Arabian Desert (Eastern Desert) is located in Egypt between the Nile River and the Red Sea, with an extension south into Sudan. It has an area of about 222,500 km^2 (85,907 mi^2). The name Arabian Desert also is applied sometimes to the deserts of the Arabian Peninsula.

The Arabian Desert is known in Egypt as the Eastern Highlands and has many peaks that rise to more than 1,830 m (5,925 ft). Jabal Shayib, the highest mountain in Egypt, has an elevation of 2,183 m (7,161 ft). Travel is difficult, because the mountains are dissected deeply by wadis, riverbeds through which water flows only during the occasional winter rains. The area is so inaccessible that Saint ANTHONY, the first Christian monk, chose Deir al-Memun as the site for his monastery. A caravan route along Wadi al-Hammamat—connecting Thebes on the Nile with Qusayr on the Red Sea—was once an important link to the south. Most of the desert is barren and inhospitable (annual rainfall is less than 100 mm/4 in). The average January temperature is 18° C (65° F), and the summers are characterized by heat waves.

The Arabian Desert is inhabited by herders and traders—the Maaza, a nomadic tribe that arrived from Arabia in the 18th century; and the nomadic Ababda (who speak Arabic) and Bisharin, both of whom derive from the Hamitic-speaking Beja. No major cities or towns are located there. Since ancient times the desert has been a source of porphyry, a hard igneous rock. Petroleum, iron ore, manganese, and granite also occur in the region.

Arabian horse   The Arabian is an ancient breed of HORSE originating in the Middle East. For about 1,400 years Arabians have been crossed with other European strains, and the grace, hardiness, spirit, speed, and trimness of the Arabian have been passed on not only to the major breeds of lightweight horse—the American saddle horse, quarter horse, Standardbred, and Thoroughbred—but to some of the heavier breeds as well. The Arabian is rather small, about 14–15 hands (142–152 cm/56–60 in). The offspring of crosses with other breeds are nearly always larger. Other characteristics of the Arabian are a prominent chest and hindquarters; a short back; slender, small-boned legs; and a delicate, dished face with large, wide eyes. Arabians are characteristically bay in color, but gray or white ones are highly prized.

The Arabian is one of the finest of all racehorse breeds. It runs for long distances with great endurance. Bedouin tribes of the Arabian peninsula kept carefully controlled breeding practices for centuries in order to maintain pure lines.

The kemanje, which originated in Persia, is a spike fiddle with three strings. It is held downward like a small cello and is played with a bow. Pitches are produced by pressure against the strings.

Arabian music   Arabian music refers to that of the Islamic peoples of Arabia and aiso, in its broad sense, to that of Islamic peoples in North Africa, Persia, and Syria. Although the major writings on Arabian music appeared after the dawn of ISLAM (AD 622), music had already been cultivated for thousands of years.

Origins and Influences. The music of pre-Islamic Arabia was primarily vocal. It is alleged that singing originated with the caravan song (*huda*), from which developed a more sophisticated secular song (*nasb*). Instruments were used to accompany the singer. The short lute ('*ud*), long lute (*tunbur*), flute (*qussaba*), tambourine (*duff*), and drum (*tabl*) were popular.

With the coming of Islam and the Arab conquest of Syria, Egypt, and Persia, foreign musical influence began to be felt more strongly in Arabia. The tuning of the '*ud* was altered to afford it the range of the Persian lute. Works began to be written on musical theory, which borrowed from Syrian and Persian practices. Ibn Misjah (d. *c*.715) described eight melodic modes (*asabi*) and six rhythmic patterns (*iqaat*); these were modified and expanded in the following centuries. During the Umayyad dynasty (661–750) and the first hundred years of the Abbasid dynasty (750–847), Damascus and Baghdad, respectively, were the centers of culture. The caliphs, or rulers, were noted music patrons, and the classical art flourished at their courts. Al-Farabi (d. *c*.950) was one of the greatest music theorists of all time. His *Grand Book on Music* describes in detail the musical instruments of the age and explains the rhythmic modes then in use. The last of the caliphs had Safi al-Din (d. 1294) as principal court musician. In his treatises he included an early example of Arabic musical notation and formulated a new theoretical system that consisted of 12 primary melodic modes. By the 14th century the term *maqamat* (plural of *maqam*) referred to the 12 scales. During subsequent centuries additional melodic modes were admitted and different rhythmic patterns established, but the development of Arabian music had already reached its zenith, and the music of this period was built mainly on past achievements.

Musical Forms. The two major features of present-day Arabian music are much the same as those of a thousand years ago: a single, unharmonized melodic line, based upon one of the *maqamat*, and a repetitive rhythmic cycle (*iqa*). All performers make use of elaboration, embellishment, and improvisation. Programs of Arabian classical music often feature the *taqsim*, a nonmetrical, improvisatory solo instrumental form in a particular *maqam* but without rhythmic accompaniment. The *taqsim* may be self-contained, or it may preface a metrical solo song or suite (*nauba*). Another improvisatory form is the *layali*, performed vocally but otherwise similar to the *taqsim*. It is often followed by a composed piece or by a *mawwal*, which includes melodic improvisation on a poetic text.

The most important classical instrument is the *'ud*, a pear-shaped lute with four or more pairs of strings and a wooden soundboard. The most popular flute is the end-blown variety, the *nay* (a Persian term). The *qanun* is a zither with 72 strings in 3-string courses stretched over a trapezoidal box; it is played by plectra worn on each index finger. The two most representative percussion instruments are the tambourine (*duff*) and the vase drum (*darbuka*).

Arabian Nights   *The Arabian Nights*, also called *The Thousand and One Nights*, is a large collection of stories, mostly Arabian, Indian, or Persian, written in Arabic between the 14th and 16th centuries. They were introduced into Europe through Antoine Galland's French translation (1704–17). The best-known English version is by the explorer Sir Richard BURTON (1885–88).

The frame story, Persian in origin, turns on the woman-hating King Schahriah (Shahryar) who, after his queen's infidelity, marries a different woman each night and then slays her the next morning, ensuring her faithfulness. The bride SCHEHERAZADE (Shahrazad), however, beguiles the king with a series of stories for a thousand and one nights, withholding the ending of each story until the next night, and thus saving her life.

The elaborately plotted stories, filled with intrigue, are folkloric in origin. Three of the best known are "The History of Aladdin, or the Wonderful Lamp," "The History of Sinbad the Sailor," and "The History of Ali Baba and the Forty Thieves."

See also: ALADDIN; ALI BABA; ARABIC LITERATURE; PERSIAN LITERATURE.

Arabian Peninsula   see ARABIA

Arabian Sea   The Arabian Sea is the broad northern portion of the INDIAN OCEAN, between India and the Arabian Peninsula. It has an area of about 3,859,100 km^2 (1,490,300 mi^2) and a mean depth of 2,734 m (8,968 ft). The Arabian Sea remains unusually deep close to its shores, and its islands, such as SOCOTRA and the LACCADIVE ISLANDS, lie close to the coast. Trade winds blow northeast in winter and southwest in summer, a circumstance that has aided direct crossing of the sea since the time of early sailing ships. The water surface temperature is normally warm (24° C/75° F minimum), and fish life is abundant. The sea's main ports are Bombay and Karachi.

Arabic language   Arabic belongs to the Semitic branch of AFROASIATIC LANGUAGES and is the national language of about 175 million inhabitants of North Africa, the Arabian Peninsula, Syria, Lebanon, Jordan, and Iraq. Outside these areas, it is spoken by Arabs living in Israel, and in some parts of sub-Saharan Africa, North and South America, and Soviet Central Asia. Since it is the language of the KORAN, some limited knowledge of it exists throughout the Muslim world.

All Arabs have as their mother tongue some local variety of Arabic. These vernaculars differ so markedly that, for example, Moroccan Arabic is virtually unintelligible in Iraq. The local vernacular is used in everyday commerce but rarely written. In contrast with the vernaculars is standard Arabic, used for writing and formal speech. Because it must be learned at school, many Arabs do not command it sufficiently to use it themselves, although radio and other media are gradually spreading its comprehension. Standard Arabic has remained remarkably stable. In grammar and basic vocabulary the Arabic literature produced from the 8th century to the present is strikingly homogeneous; the works of the medieval writers differ from modern standard Arabic hardly more than Shakespeare's language differs from modern English.

Arabic literature   A written Arabic literature began to be known with the collection of the KORAN, the sacred book of Islam, in Arabia in the 7th century AD. With the spread of the Islamic faith into Asia, Africa, and Europe, the Arabic language soon became a major world language.

Even before the revelations of MUHAMMAD (*c.*570–632) were collected in the Koran, however, the Arabs possessed a highly developed poetry, composed for recitation and transmitted orally from generation to generation. The most famous examples are the elaborate odes, or *qasidahs*, of the *Mu'allaqat* ("the suspended ones"), beginning with those of Imru' al-Qais (fl. *c.*540). These poems reflected and praised the customs and values of the desert environment in which they arose.

Historical Periods. The history of Arabic literature is usually divided into periods marking the dynastic changes that took place within the Islamic world. During the Umayyad period (AD 661–750), Arabic prose literature was limited primarily to grammatical treatises, commentaries on the Koran, and the compiling of stories about Muhammad and his companions. The Umayyad poets, chief of whom were al-Akhtal (7th–8th century) and al-

Farazdaq (c.640–732), favored new poetic forms such as love lyrics (ghazals), wine songs, and hunting poems. These forms reflected the conditions of life and manners in the territories conquered by Islam.

In the early years of the Abbasid empire (750–1258), many forms were invented for Arabic literature, which then entered what is generally regarded its greatest period of development and achievement. It is certain that Persian influences contributed significantly to this development. For example, translations from the Persian, such as those of Ibn al-Muqaffa (d. 757), led to a new refinement in Arabic prose called adab, often sprinkled with poetry and using rhymed prose (saj'), the style of the Koran. The greatest masters of adab were al-JAHIZ (d. 868) and al-Hariri (d. 1122). An inventive type of folk literature, exemplified in The Thousand and One Nights (popularly known as the ARABIAN NIGHTS), drew upon the recitations of wandering storytellers called rawis.

ABU NUWAS (d. c.810) was acknowledged as foremost among the new poets who used the Arabic language with greater freedom and imagination. An experimental tradition now vied with a classical one, and some poets excelled in both; al-Maarri (973–1057) and al-MUTANABBI (915–965) are regarded as the greatest among them. In Spain an independent poetic tradition culminated in the lyrics of Ibn Zaydun and Ibn Quzman (d. 1160). The Romance of Antar, the closest work to an epic in Arabic, was also written at about this time.

Modern Period. During the centuries of Ottoman Turkish domination, Arabic literature declined. Not until the mid-19th century was it revived in the intellectual movement known as the nahdah ("reawakening"), which began in Syria and spread to Egypt. At first highly imitative of the themes and forms of European literature, modern Arabic literature has gradually freed itself from centuries of neglect and reassumed its place among the world's great literatures. Arabic writers of the past century have been extremely versatile. Most of their work shows a strong concern for social issues. Outstanding among recent Arabic novelists, dramatists, and essayists are Tawfiq al-HAKIM, Nobelist Naguib MAHFOUZ, and Taha Husayn. Among the poets, Iliya ABU MADI, Adonis, Ahmad Shawqi, Abu Shadi, and Abbas al-Aqqad excel.

Arabs   The term Arabs refers to the peoples who speak Arabic as their native language. A Semitic people like the Jews (see SEMITES), Arabs form the bulk of the population of Algeria, Bahrain, Egypt, Iraq, Jordan, Kuwait, Lebanon, Libya, Morocco, Oman, Qatar, Saudi Arabia, Sudan, Syria, Tunisia, the United Arab Emirates, and Yemen. In addition, there are about 1.7 million Palestinian Arabs living under Israeli rule in the WEST BANK and GAZA STRIP, territories occupied by Israel during the 1967 Arab-Israeli War (see ARAB-ISRAELI WARS), and more than 700,000 Arab citizens of Israel. Estimates of the total Arab population of the countries above range from 175 million to 200 million. The great majority of Arabs are Muslims, but there are significant numbers of Christian Arabs in Egypt (see COPTIC CHURCH), Lebanon, and Syria and among Pal-

This miniature painting, dated 1237, depicts a camel caravan of Arab pilgrims making their obligatory journey, or hajj, to the holy city of Mecca in Saudi Arabia. Every Muslim who can is expected to make this pilgrimage at least once.

estinians. In geographical terms the Arab world includes North Africa and most of the Middle East (excluding Turkey, Israel, and Iran), a region that has been a center of civilization and crossroads of trade since prehistoric times.

Arab History

References to Arabs as nomads and camel herders of northern ARABIA appear in Assyrian inscriptions of the 9th century BC. The name was subsequently applied to all inhabitants of the Arabian Peninsula. From time to time Arab kingdoms arose on the fringes of the desert, including the Nabataeans at PETRA in southern Jordan in the 2d century BC and PALMYRA in central Syria in the 3d century AD, but no great Arab empire emerged until ISLAM appeared in the 7th century AD.

Although a majority of Muslims today are not Arabs, the religion was born in the Arabian Peninsula and Arabic is its mother tongue. MECCA, in Saudi Arabia, was the birthplace of the Prophet of Islam, MUHAMMAD Ibn Abdullah (c.570–632 AD); the Muslim calendar begins with his flight to MEDINA in 622 because it marked the founding of a separate Muslim community. By the time of Muhammad's death, Mecca and nearly all the tribes of the peninsula had accepted Islam. A century later the lands of Islam, under Arab leadership, stretched from Spain in the west across North Africa and most of the modern Middle East into Central Asia and northern India.

There were two great Islamic dynasties of Arab origin, the UMAYYADS (661–750), centered in Damascus, and the ABBASIDS (750–1258), whose capital was Baghdad. Most Umayyad rulers insisted on Arab primacy over non-Arab converts to Islam, while the Abbasid caliphs (see CALIPHATE) accepted the principle of Arab and non-Arab equality

This mosque in Baghdad, the capital of modern Iraq, is a symbol of the city's rich history. Baghdad was the center of a great Arab Islamic empire during the reign of the Abbasids. The Abbasid caliphs, who ruled in the name of Islam, were directly descended from members of Muhammad's family.

as Muslims. At its height in the 8th and 9th centuries, the Abbasid caliphate was extraordinarily wealthy, dominating trade routes between Asia and Europe. Islamic civilization flourished during the Abbasid period (see ARABIC LITERATURE; ISLAMIC ART AND ARCHITECTURE) even though the political unity of the caliphate often shattered into rival dynasties. Greek philosophy was translated into Arabic and contributed to the expansion of Arab-Persian Islamic scholarship. Islamic treatises on medicine, philosophy, and science, including Arabic translations of Plato and Aristotle, greatly influenced Christian thinkers in Europe in the 12th century by way of Muslim Spain.

The power of the Arab Abbasid family declined from the 10th century onward due to internal political and religious rivalries and victories by Christian European crusaders (see CRUSADES; MIDDLE EAST, HISTORY OF THE) seeking to recapture territory lost to Islam. The Mongol invasion of the 13th century (see MONGOLS) led to the destruction of the Abbasid caliphate in 1258 and opened the way for the eventual rise of the great Turkish Muslim empire known as the OTTOMAN EMPIRE. The Ottomans took Constantinople (Istanbul) from the Byzantines in 1453 and had taken control of the Arab Middle East and most of North Africa by the end of the 16th century. Arabs remained subjects of the Ottoman Turks for over 300 years—into the 20th century.

The Arab world of today is the product of Ottoman decline, European colonialism, and Arab demands for freedom from European occupation. At the beginning of World War I all of North Africa was under the domination of France (Algeria, Tunisia, Morocco), Italy (Libya), or Great Britain (Egypt). After World War I the League of Nations divided the Arab lands that had remained Ottoman during the war between Britain and France, with the understanding that each power would encourage the de-

velopment of the peoples of the region toward self-rule. Iraq and PALESTINE (including part of what is now Jordan) went to Britain, and Syria and Lebanon to France. Britain had suggested to Arab leaders during the war that Palestine would be included in areas to be given Arab self-determination, but British officials then promised the region to the Zionist movement, which called for a Jewish state there. The Arab lands gained their independence in stages after World War II, sometimes, as in Algeria, after long and bitter struggles. Much of Palestine became the state of Israel in May 1948, setting the stage for the Arab-Israeli conflict, in which five wars have occurred (1948–49, 1956, 1967, 1973, and 1982), and contributing to the rise of the PALESTINE LIBERATION ORGANIZATION (PLO), which gained prominence after the humiliating Arab losses in the 1967 war.

People and Economy

Arabs have traditionally been considered nomads, epitomized by the BEDOUIN of Arabia. In fact, Bedouin are less than 10 percent of the total Arab population. Most Arab societies are heavily urbanized, particularly the oil-rich states of the Arabian Peninsula, largely because there is little agriculture in such societies. Major peasant populations are found in countries such as Egypt (see FELLAHIN), Syria, Algeria, and Iraq, where there is water for irrigation, but all these nations have heavy urban concentrations; Cairo, for example, has a population of 14 million and is still expanding.

The two basic elements uniting most Arabs are the Arabic language and Islam. Though spoken Arabic differs from country to country, the written language forms a cultural basis for all Arabs. Islam does the same for many, with Arabic being the language of the KORAN, the revealed word of God delivered through the Prophet Mu-

A Yemeni woman wears a veil in accordance with the traditional Islamic custom of purdah. This practice has enjoyed a resurgence in recent years.

(Left) *Pilgrims gather at Mecca, the birthplace of the Prophet Muhammad, fulfilling the requirement that every Muslim make the pilgrimage* (hajj) *at least once.* (Above) *The object of veneration in Mecca is the Kaaba, a shrine within the al-Haram, or Great Mosque, toward which all Muslims orient themselves when praying.*

hammad. Most Arabs are Sunni Muslims (see SUNNITES). A minority are SHIITES. The division of Islam into two main branches is the result of a dispute over succession to the caliphate that goes back to the 7th century and has led to certain doctrinal differences between the two branches. The major Shiite country is non-Arab Iran, but there are large numbers of Shiites in Iraq (where they form a majority) and in Lebanon (where Shiites are now the biggest single religious group). Shiite tensions are due partly to Iranian efforts to promote Shiite Islam in the aftermath of the 1979 revolution that brought Ayatollah Ruhollah KHOMEINI to power and partly to the fact that Shiites, who form the economic underclass in many Arab nations, feel that they have been discriminated against by the Sunnite majority.

Although traditional tribal life has nearly disappeared, tribal values and identity retain some importance, especially when linked to Islam. Descent from the clan of the Prophet Muhammad or from one of the first Arab tribes to accept Islam still carries great prestige, and blood ties contribute to the formation of political factions.

Nevertheless, the importance of kinship has been weakened by the rapid expansion of urban society, by modern educational systems, and by the creation of centralized governments whose bureaucracies are often the major source of employment for university graduates. Many educated young people choose spouses from among fellow classmates, a development that reflects especially the expansion of educational and professional opportunities for women.

The rapid pace of urbanization and social change has been encouraged by economic constraints found in many Arab societies. Except for oil, there are few natural resources to be exploited for industrial development. Agri-

cultural productivity is generally high in Arab countries, but productive land is scarce in some regions because of the lack of water, and droughts and rising demand have increased the possibility of conflicts over water resources shared by neighboring countries.

The rate of population growth in many Arab countries is near 3 percent annually, as compared to rates of increase in Western Europe of less than 1 percent. These growth rates reflect the impact of modern medicine and social services that have lessened infant mortality. The tendency to smaller families found in Western urban so-

Because lack of water limits agriculture in most oil-producing Arab countries, petroleum revenues have been invested abroad and in industrial projects. Many such projects, such as this oil refinery in Libya, are petroleum related.

cieties has not occurred because of the prevalence of traditional attitudes favoring large families, particularly among the poor and in areas where tribal values prevail. The United Arab Emirates has a growth rate approaching 9%, and even a rate of 2.7% for Egypt means that a million Egyptians are born every 9 months in a country where agricultural land constitutes only 12% of the total land area, forcing further urban congestion and the need to import more food to maintain subsistence levels. The inability to feed a nation's population from indigenous resources leads to increased indebtedness and a diversion of funds needed for development.

One final element in the socioeconomic equation is the large number of young people in these expanding populations. For example, 60% of all Tunisians are under 20 years of age, a not unrepresentative statistic suggesting that future problems of unemployment and food shortages will be greater than they are now. These population indices suggest great potential for social unrest, and the failure of many secular Arab regimes to fulfill their promises of economic prosperity and national strength have contributed to the increasing adherence to Islam by young people in some Arab societies. Among the young, in particular, Arab inability to regain the territories lost in the 1967 war with Israel led to questioning of the secular ideologies that had dominated regional politics during the post–World War II era, while a growing gap between rich and poor and the spread of education increased demands for greater participation in largely undemocratic political systems.

Modern Politics and Social Issues

The men who led the Arab independence movements after World War I were usually secularists. Although many of them, such as Egypt's Gamal Abdul NASSER, were Pan-Arab nationalists who advocated the creation of a single Arab nation, they believed it essential that their countries adopt many aspects of Western civilization, such as secular laws, parliamentary government, and the like. These views challenged the primacy of Islam in everyday life. Is-

Although a majority of Palestinian Arabs are not refugees, many of the more than 700,000 Arabs who left their homes during the first Arab-Israeli War live in refugee camps such as this one in Lebanon. These refugees— a majority of whom are too young to have seen what they consider their homeland— remain a symbol of injustice in the Arab world.

lamic law (see SHARIA) makes no distinction between religious and temporal power. Muslims believe that all law derives from the Koran, and that God's word must therefore apply to all aspects of life. The gradual relegation of Islam to the realm of personal status, a process that began during the period of Western dominance, continued as Arab nations gained independence under nationalist leaders who believed that Islam lacked answers to the problems confronting modern society and national development.

Many devout Arab Muslims disagreed. The Muslim Brotherhood, for example, was formed in Egypt as early as 1929 to meet the needs of Egyptians uprooted by modern economic and cultural inroads into traditional Egyptian life. A central tenet of all such Muslim groups is the belief that Western economic and social values cannot restore past Arab greatness, and that Muslim societies must be

In the nations of the Persian Gulf, such as Saudi Arabia, petroleum revenues have been used to build modern cities in what was once barren desert. The lavish spending of the oil-rich nations has tended to obscure the fact that most Arabs remain poor.

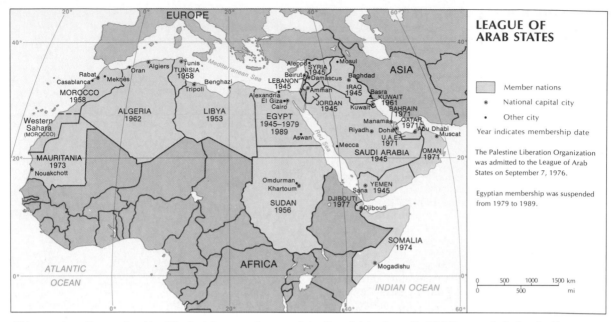

LEGEND:

LEAGUE OF ARAB STATES

- Member nations
⊕ National capital city
• Other city

Year indicates membership date

The Palestine Liberation Organization was admitted to the League of Arab States on September 7, 1976.

Egyptian membership was suspended from 1979 to 1989.

This map shows the membership of the Arab League, a loose confederation of states formed in 1945 to promote Arab unity. Egypt's membership was suspended in 1979 in protest against that country's conclusion of a peace treaty with Israel. It was restored in 1989.

based on principles derived from their own roots. Beyond this, such groups often differ on the type of society they envisage and how to achieve it. Some organizations advocate the violent overthrow of existing regimes, others the spread of their views by peaceful means. The call to Islam has special appeal to those who are the victims rather than the beneficiaries of modernization. Many others who have rejected membership in such groups have returned to the private religious duties of Islam, such as praying five times daily, fasting during the holy month of RA-MADAN, and making a pilgrimage to Mecca.

Muslim organizations see the West as the real threat to Islamic stability. Most see Israel as an agent of the West in the Middle East, depriving Palestinian Arabs of their rightful homeland. Even secular Arabs who admire the West and fear reintroduction of a Muslim theocracy nevertheless often feel angered at what they perceive as Western and especially American ignorance of Arab concerns. The Palestinian uprising (*intifada*) launched in December 1988 has created new awareness of the problem.

On the other hand, anti-Israeli pronouncements have often served to create a false impression of unity when real agreement was lacking. The ARAB LEAGUE, formed in 1945, has been more a forum for Arab infighting than a framework for cooperation. Arabs genuinely feel common bonds based on language and a shared historical and cultural legacy, but they also identify themselves as Egyptians, Iraqis, and so on. Their ideological differences reflect the wide range of governing systems in the Arab world, from socialist regimes to oil-rich monarchies.

Complicating factors for the GULF region have been the 1980–88 war between Iran and Iraq, increased ten-

sions between Iran and the Arab states of the Persian Gulf, and the war resulting from the 1990 Iraqi invasion of Kuwait.

As of 1987, more than 60% of the proved oil reserves of the globe could be found in the Middle East, particularly in Saudi Arabia, which contains nearly half of the world's reserves. Oil has been exported from the Arab world since the 1930s, but only with the creation of the ORGANIZATION OF PETROLEUM EXPORTING COUNTRIES (OPEC) in 1960 and the Libyan revolution of 1969 did these countries begin to determine oil prices themselves. Although only eight Arab nations are substantial oil producers and OPEC has several non-Arab members, the organization is usually associated with Arab oil; the oil shortages of 1973–74 resulted from Saudi anger at U.S. policy during the 1973 Arab-Israeli War. Overproduction drove down prices in the 1980s, weakening OPEC's clout and the ability of the oil-producing Arab states to provide aid and jobs for the poorer Arab nations. Oil experts believe, however, that the Arab world will long remain the center of world oil production, a fact that contributed to the international response to Iraq's effort to gain control of a larger share of the area's oil reserves.

Future Prospects

The Arab world holds potential for both growth and conflict. A solution to the Palestinian problem would defuse the likelihood of another Arab-Israeli war and permit allocation of resources to domestic sectors rather than to military outlays. Arab states, however, need to settle their own differences as well. Some efforts to promote more unified approaches to common problems have been made in recent years, including the formation of the Gulf Cooperation Council (Saudi Arabia, Bahrain, Kuwait, Oman, Qatar, and the United Arab Emirates) in 1981; the Arab Maghrib Union (Algeria, Libya, Mauritania, Morocco, and Tunisia) and the Arab Cooperation Council (Egypt, Iraq, Jordan, and Yemen) in 1989; and the union of the Yemens in 1990. Efforts to forge Arab unity have been strained by Iraq's efforts to seize leadership of the Arab world (opposed by Egypt, Syria, and the Gulf states) and regional involvement in strife-torn Lebanon. The impact of population growth on development and the success of Iraqi and Islamic revolutionary appeals to the disaffected are crucial to Arab prospects.

Arachne [uh-rak'-nee] In Greek mythology, Arachne was a woman of Lydia who was so skilled in weaving that she presumed to challenge the goddess ATHENA to a contest. After seeing the perfection of Arachne's work, Athena changed her into a spider.

arachnid [uh-rak'-nid] Arachnids are a major class of the ARTHROPOD phylum and include the SPIDER (order Ara-

neae); SCORPION (order Scorpiones); MITE and TICK (order Acarina); harvestman and daddy longlegs (order Opiliones, or Phelangida); whip scorpion and vinegaroon (order Uropygi); and sun spider, or wind scorpion (order Solifugae). The class comprises more than 60,000 species. Most dwell on land, a few in water. Most arachnids are nocturnal predators, feeding mostly on small arthropods; mites and ticks, however, are commonly either herbivorous or parasitic, and some harvestmen are scavengers.

Arachnids are usually small, less than 5 mm (2 in) long, with the exception of the sun spiders, the scorpions, the tailless whip scorpion, and some whip scorpions and spiders. Some mites are as small as 0.1 mm (0.004 in), but certain African scorpions attain a length of about 18 cm (7 in).

Arachnids have two major body parts: a posterior opisthosoma and an anterior prosoma with six pairs of appendages. These appendages include: a pair of chelicerae (often pincerlike, small, and associated with feeding), a pair of pedipalps (pincerlike limbs that scorpions use for holding prey, and male spiders use as a copulatory organ), and four pairs of walking legs. The prosoma houses the brain and usually bears up to six pairs of simple, never compound, eyes.

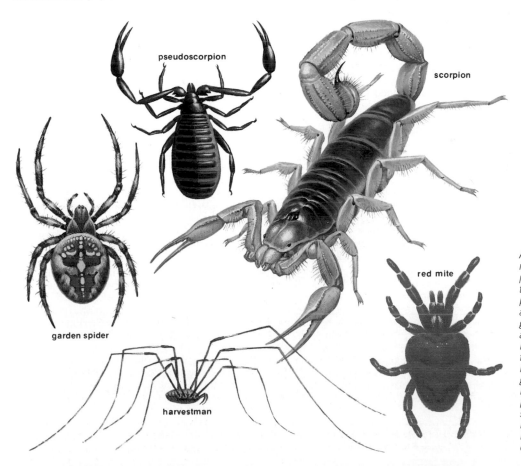

pseudoscorpion

scorpion

garden spider

red mite

harvestman

Arachnids commonly have four pairs of legs, no antennae, and two pairs of modified appendages for grasping, biting, and touching. Representatives of the Arachnid class include a European garden spider; a book scorpion, or pseudoscorpion; a scorpion; a harvestman, or daddy longlegs; and a red mite, or chigger.

Yasir Arafat, the head of the Palestine Liberation Organization (PLO), captured the attention of the United Nations General Assembly in 1974, when he delivered a plea for an independent Palestinian nation. His organization claimed to speak for all Palestinians of the Gaza Strip and West Bank of the Jordan River, as well as for others displaced by the Middle Eastern conflicts.

Arafat, Yasir [ahr'-ah-faht, yah-seer']   Yasir Arafat, b. 1929, is the leader of the PALESTINE LIBERATION ORGANIZATION (PLO). A native of Palestine, Arafat emigrated to Egypt after the establishment of the state of Israel and later became head of al-Fatah, an anti-Israeli guerrilla group. Named chairman of the PLO in 1969, he originally sought to replace Israel with a secular Palestinian state and was widely recognized as the chief spokesman for the Palestinian people. After Palestinians in the Israeli-occupied territories launched an uprising in December 1987, Arafat persuaded the PLO to declare (November 1988) an independent Palestinian state, renounced terrorism, and accepted UN Resolution 242 and Israel's right to exist. He was named president of the Palestinian government in exile in 1989, but his peace proposals were met with skepticism in Israel, and he faced opposition from dissidents within the PLO.

Aragon [air'-uh-gahn]   Aragon is a historic region and former kingdom in northeastern Spain. It covers an area of 47,650 km² (18,398 mi²). The population of 1,208,474 (1988 est.) is sparsely spread over most of the region, whose only large city is SARAGOSSA (Zaragoza). Aragon extends from the Pyrenees, which separate it from France, to the high plateaus that separate it from Castile. To the southeast is Catalonia. Aragon has three distinct regions: the southern flanks of the Pyrenees in the north, the wide plain of Aragon formed by the Ebro River and its tributaries, and the mountains and plateaus that border Castile.

The kingdom of Aragon was formed in the 11th century out of lands formerly controlled by the MOORS. It grew with the annexation of the county of Barcelona (Catalonia) in 1137 and Valencia in 1238. The marriage of FERDINAND II of Aragon and ISABELLA I of Castile led to the unification of Spain into a single kingdom in 1516.

Aragon, Louis [ahr-ah-gohn']   Louis Aragon, b. Oct. 3, 1897, d. Dec. 24, 1982, a French writer, began his career as an iconoclastic participant in DADA and then in SURREALISM. Leaving the surrealist movement after a visit to the USSR in 1930–31, he joined the Communist party and devoted himself mainly to realistic and political fiction.

The poems in Aragon's *La Grande Gaîté* (1929) illustrate surrealist poetic investigation through wordplay and contributed to the foundation of surrealist poetics. His novel *Le Paysan de Paris* (1926; *The Night Walker*, 1950) develops the surrealist concept of "the daily marvelous" (*le merveilleux quotidien*) through its evocation of the urban landscape of the French capital. In *Traité du style* (1928) he offered not a treatise on style but a virtuoso display of invective, inspired by the surrealist ethic. Aragon inaugurated his realistic fiction in 1934 with *Les Cloches de Bâle* (The Bells of Basel, 1936) and thereafter became increasingly Marxist.

Aral Sea [ar'-ul]   The Aral Sea is a large inland body of water located in the USSR on the border between the Kazakh republic to the north and the Uzbek republic to the south. The Ustyurt Plateau is to the west and the Kyzyl Kum desert to the southeast. The Aral Sea has no outlet. It is fed by two rivers, the SYR DARYA on the east and the AMU DARYA on the south. These rivers have been tapped extensively for irrigation, and their flow has been so drastically cut that the Aral Sea's area declined by about 40% between 1960 and 1990. Increasing salinity and pollution have destroyed the fishing industry; the former port of Muynak is now 48 km (30 mi) inland. Schemes proposed to halt the sea's shrinkage, which poses a severe environmental threat to the surrounding area, include reductions in water usage and the building of a canal to divert water from the IRTYSH RIVER into the Aral Sea.

The Aral Sea was known as the Khwarazan Sea to the Arabs as early as AD 903. Native Kazakhs were living in the area when the Russians first sighted the sea in the 17th century.

Arales [uh-ray'-leez]   The plant order Arales comprises the ARUM family, Araceae, or aroids, and the DUCKWEED family, Lemnaceae. Plants of this order are perennial herbs with small flowers on a fleshy spike, or spadix, wrapped in a reduced leaf called a spathe.

The aroids, which are found worldwide but mainly in the forests of tropical regions, number more than 100 genera and about 2,000 species. Some are important food plants—especially TARO, which is cultivated for its edible tuber. Familiar American species include the CALLA, JACK-IN-THE-PULPIT, and SKUNK CABBAGE. Many aroids make striking houseplants and are used as ornamentals. The leaves are extremely variable. In some genera, such as *Monstera*, they are large and may develop holes; in others they are compound. The flowers are often attractive but may have an unpleasant odor. Some species of *Anthurium* have masses of scarlet or vermilion spathes with protruding, creamy-white spadices. In the climbing aroids, aerial roots are common. They serve as supports and may also grow into the soil and function as roots.

The duckweeds, which number 4 genera and about 30 species, are common on ponds, lakes, and still streams in tropical and temperate regions, where they often form a thin green mat on the water's surface.

Aramaeans [air-uh-may'-uhnz] The Aramaeans were an ancient West Semitic people of the Syro-Palestinian area in the Near East. Originally seminomadic, they are known from about 1500 BC. Their population may have included tribal elements of other neighboring Semitic peoples, particularly the earliest Hebrews, whose ancestor Jacob is called "a wandering Aramaean" in Deuteronomy 26:5. Wandering Aramaeans continually harassed the inhabitants of northern Mesopotamia (ASSYRIA) and southern Mesopotamia (BABYLONIA), thereby seriously affecting the political stability of these areas. By about 1000 BC, however, large numbers of Aramaeans had settled permanently, creating small, city-state kingdoms in Syria and the Upper Euphrates region.

After 1000 BC, the Aramaic kingdoms around Damascus, as well as those in Palestinian border areas, interacted with the Israelites, sometimes as opponents and sometimes as expedient allies. Beginning in the late 8th century BC, Syrian Aramaic territories were incorporated into the Assyrian, Neo-Babylonian, and Persian empires.

Under the Persians (post-539 BC), and for centuries thereafter, Aramaic became the language of everyday affairs in the Near East. Thus Jesus spoke in Aramaic.

Aramaic language see AFROASIATIC LANGUAGES

Arany, János [aw'-rawn-yuh, yah'-nawsh] János Arany, b. Mar. 2, 1817, d. Oct. 22, 1882, was Hungary's greatest epic poet and, with Sándor Petőfi, the creator of a realistic poetry based on Hungarian folk traditions. He produced valuable literary treatises, landmark translations of Shakespeare and Aristophanes, and ballads unsurpassed in Hungarian literature. His Toldi trilogy—*Toldi* (1847), *Toldi szerelme* (Toldi's Love, 1848–79), and *Toldi estéje* (1854; Toldi's Evening, 1914)—an epic tracing the life of the 14th-century Hungarian hero, remains the best Hungarian narrative poem.

Arapaho [uh-rap'-uh-hoh] The Arapaho are a North American Indian people who, like their allies the Cheyenne, lived as nomadic buffalo hunters on the Great Plains in the 19th century. These Algonquian-speakers called themselves *Inuna-ina* ("our people").

At one time the Arapaho lived in agricultural villages in northern Minnesota. With the expansion of the fur trade and white settlements in this area, they migrated westward onto the Plains by the late 18th century. There they fought the Pawnee, Shoshoni, Ute, and other Indian tribes as well as white settlers crossing Indian territory. After 1830 they split into northern and southern divisions, living near the Platte River in Wyoming and the Arkansas River in Colorado.

As did many other tribes, the Arapaho made the SUN DANCE a major ceremonial event. A GHOST DANCE ritual was added later. The search for visions through communion with supernatural beings was also practiced. An estimated 4,000 southern Arapaho combined with Cheyenne live on a reservation in Oklahoma. About 3,800 northern Arapaho live on or near the reservation at Wind River, Wyo.

Arapesh [ar'-uh-pesh] The Arapesh, a people of the east Sepik district of Papua New Guinea, are dispersed over an area from the north bank of the river to the coast. Beach Arapesh live in large villages and practice some fishing but rely mainly on their gardens and sago (palm) patches for subsistence. Mountain Arapesh have small settlements, hunt occasionally, and make their gardens on steep hillsides as well as on the plains.

Hamlets traditionally are occupied by a land-owning clan made up of members of one family whose lineage is determined through male ancestry. Labor is divided between the sexes in taro and banana gardening; in the yam gardens men do almost all the work. Cooperation is the key to traditional Arapesh life, in which warfare has played a lesser role than among other Sepik peoples. Expressions of competitiveness and aggressiveness are deemphasized in the training of both boys and girls, although qualities of leadership, particularly trading ability, are encouraged. Traditional religion is based on the *tamberan* cult of ancestors and other spirits.

Ararat, Mount [ar'-uh-rat] Mount Ararat (Turkish: Ağbri Dağbi) consists of two volcanic peaks—Great Ararat, rising to 5,122 m (16,804 ft), and Little Ararat, at 3,896 m (12,782 ft)—on the Aras Plain in extreme eastern Turkey near Iran and the USSR. The highest point in Turkey, Great Ararat, according to tradition, is the place where Noah's ark landed. Earthquakes in 1840 destroyed a village, a convent, and a chapel on the mountain. Ararat is the Hebrew form for Urartu, the Assyrian name for a kingdom that existed in the region from the 9th to the 7th century BC.

Araucanians [ar-uh-kayn'-ee-uhnz] Araucanian is both a cultural and linguistic classification of the Picunche, Mapuche, and Huilliche Indians of South America. Most lived in Chile, but a large émigré population settled in the Argentine Andes after the Spanish conquest (1540). The Picunche are now extinct and the Huilliche have virtually disappeared. The Chilean Mapuche resisted control during the Spanish colonial and early republican periods. They were finally pacified and settled on more than 3,000 small reservations between 1884 and 1912, mainly in the provinces of Cautín and Malleco. Today they are the largest indigenous society in South America, with a population of about 675,000.

Mapuche determine descent and residence according to male ancestry; patterns of alliance, bride-price, and dowry are based on female descent and involve ritual obligations. These practices are buttressed by the Mapuche's traditional polytheistic religion.

An agricultural people whose main crops are wheat and potatoes, the Mapuche have been drawn into the regional Chilean cash-credit economy. Because of increasing population pressure on dwindling land reserves, many of the younger generation migrate to towns to become laborers.

Arawak [ah'-ruh-wahk]   The Arawak are a group of linguistically related but culturally diverse Indian peoples who inhabit the tropical forests of South America from the Andean foothills to the Antilles.

Before the Spanish conquest (1540), the Taino, an Arawakan group of the Greater Antilles, had established in this area a highly developed form of political organization, based on agriculture and the exploitation of rich maritime resources. Wealthy mainland Arawakan communities were large, consisting of several lineage-based households numbering as many as 2,000 people. Early in the colonial period the Antillean Arawak were absorbed into Spanish society.

The mainland Arawak who survived conquest continue to practice slash-and-burn horticulture and exploit river resources. They live in small communities of 100 to 200 persons. Settlements often consist of a single large multifamily dwelling. The Arawak believe in bush spirits and the power of local shamans. In the past, some Arawak societies had harvest ceremonies and messianic movements.

Arber, Werner   The Swiss scientist Werner Arber, b. June 3, 1929, is known for his investigations into the nature of the ENZYME group called restriction enzymes, or restriction endonucleases. Arber received the 1978 Nobel Prize for physiology or medicine, along with Hamilton Smith and Daniel Nathans, for their separate work on these enzymes. The enzymes are able to cleave, or cut, DNA molecules at specific sites and have therefore become important tools in genetic engineering. They are also used to study gene structure, the order of genes in chromosomes, and protein interactions with DNA bases. Arber's award-winning work was done while he was on the faculty of the University of Geneva (1962–70).

arbitrage [ahr'-bi-trahj]   Arbitrage is the buying and (often simultaneous) selling in another market of commodities, currencies, or securities in order to profit from price differences. In the stock market, risk arbitragers can make (and lose) large amounts by acting on takeover bids and imminent MERGERS. Arbitragers buy blocks of the target company's stock at a low price, hoping to sell at a higher price when the merger occurs.

arbitration (international law)   Arbitration, in international law, is the settlement of disputes among nations by referring them to a third party for decision. Arbitration has been practiced since ancient times, when it was used among the Greek city-states. In recent centuries territorial disputes have frequently been settled by arbitration. For example, JAY'S TREATY between Great Britain and the United States in 1794 set up an arbitral commission that settled the boundary dispute between Maine and New Brunswick. Two other commissions ruled on claims for property damages arising out of the American Revolution.

arbitration (labor-management and commercial)   Arbitration, the sending of a dispute to an impartial third party for a decision, is common in labor-management relations and in the commercial world. In a small number of cases, acceptance of the decision is voluntary; the usual practice, however, is to make acceptance compulsory.

Two types of labor-management arbitration are distinguished. The first, arbitration of rights, provides ways to settle disputes over the interpretation of the terms in a collective-bargaining agreement. It is used, for example, when a worker and a company disagree over a job classification. The second type, arbitration of interests, is used far less often, since it is considered a last step after a deadlock develops in negotiations on a new contract. Laws often compel arbitration in industries involving public utilities or municipal services, where public safety or convenience is involved, and many business contracts provide for arbitration.

The parties concerned agree to abide by the decision, although an arbitrator's award may generally be appealed to the courts if there is a question whether proper procedure was followed. The facts of the case, however, are usually not open to court review.

arborvitae [ahr-bur-vy'-tee]   Arborvitae (from Latin meaning "tree of life") is a common name for evergreen

The giant arborvitae, or western red cedar, flourishes in moist soil. It may reach heights of 60 m (200 ft) and live 1,000 years. Its wood is the primary source of shingles in the United States. The upright, seed-bearing cones (right) are 1.25 cm (0.5 in) long.

conifers that belong to the genus *Thuja* of the cypress family, Cupressaceae. Five species of these trees or shrubs, which have flexible branches and tiny, scalelike leaves, are found in eastern Asia and North America. The two native North American species, sometimes called cedars, should not be confused with the true CEDARS (genus *Cedrus*). American arborvitae, or white cedar, *T. occidentalis*, is found in northeastern North America, and giant arborvitae, or western red cedar, *T. plicata*, occurs in the Pacific Northwest. *T. occidentalis* is a popular landscape tree; more than 100 varieties have been cultivated. *T. plicata* is also used as an ornamental, and its wood, which is resistant to moisture and decay, is in great demand as a construction material.

Arbus, Diane   Photographer Diane Arbus, b. Diane Nemerov in New York City, Mar. 14, 1923, d. a suicide, July 26, 1971, became famous for her ability to spy out and capture in black and white the strangeness, craziness, and sadness of ordinary people. In the 1940s she and her husband photographed for U.S. fashion magazines. From the mid-1950s, however, she began to find new subjects on the city's streets, and by 1960 had embarked on a career as a free-lance photographer. Two Guggenheim fellowships (1963, 1966) supported her work. A 1967 exhibition at the Museum of Modern Art—and a posthumous show in 1972—proved her acceptance as a major talent.

arc   An arc is a continuous segment of a simple curve. More specifically, any segment of the circumference of a CIRCLE is called a circular arc. In a circle with center at O and two points A and B on the circumference, the ANGLE AOB is a central angle of the circle; the larger of the two arcs AB is a major arc of the circle; the smaller, a minor arc. If the two arcs AB are the same length, each arc is a semicircle. An arc is measured in angles or radians.

arc, electric   An electric arc, or arc discharge, is a continuous electrical conduction in gases between two separated conductors. It is characterized by high current density and relatively low potential difference, or voltage, in contrast to a spark, which is a relatively brief discharge with a high potential difference and low current density.
See also: DISCHARGE, ELECTRICAL; ELECTRIC FURNACE; LIGHTNING.

Arc de Triomphe de l'Étoile [ahrk duh tree-ohmf' duh lay-twahl']   The Arc de Triomphe de l'Étoile, the world's largest triumphal arch, surmounts the hill of Chaillot in Paris, at the center of a star-shaped configuration of 12 radiating avenues. It is the climax of a vista seen the length of the Champs Élysées from the smaller Arc de Triomphe du Carrousel.
In 1806, Napoleon I conceived of a triumphal arch patterned after those of ancient Rome and dedicated to

the glory of his imperial armies. The structure was designed by Jean François Thérèse Chalgrin (1739–1811) and completed in 1836 during the reign of Louis Philippe. Its deceptively simple design and immense size, 49.5 m (162 ft) in height, mark it unmistakably as a product of late 18th-century romantic NEOCLASSICISM. The most famous of its sculptural reliefs is *La Marseillaise* (1833–36) of François Rude. The arch has become an emblem of French patriotism; since 1920 it has sheltered the tomb of France's Unknown Soldier.

arcade   see ARCHITECTURE

Arcadia [ahr-kay'-dee-uh]   Arcadia is a mountainous area in the center of the Greek Peloponnesus that became celebrated in ancient literature for its rustic simplicity. The region was under Spartan domination from the 5th century BC until about 370 BC, when an anti-Spartan Arcadian League was formed on the advice of EPAMINONDAS. The capital of the league was MEGALOPOLIS.

Arcadius, Roman Emperor in the East [ahr-kay'-dee-uhs]   Flavius Arcadius, b. *c.*377, d. May 1, 408, was the first emperor of the Eastern, or Byzantine, empire after the permanent division of the Roman Empire on the death (395) of THEODOSIUS I. The oldest son of Theodosius, Arcadius inherited the east, and his brother HONORIUS received the west.
Arcadius was a weak ruler dominated by his ministers, notably Rufinus and Eutropius, and by his Frankish wife, Eudoxia. In 395, Greece was overrun by the Visigoths under ALARIC. A campaign against them by the general Flavius STILICHO was cut short when Arcadius ordered Stilicho out of the east. The emperor then made peace (397) with Alaric by making him supreme commander of Illyricum. In 399 the empire's Gothic mercenary troops revolted and held Constantinople for six months before they were defeated. Arcadius's court was repeatedly denounced for immorality by John CHRYSOSTOM, patriarch of Constantinople, whom the emperor banished in 404. Arcadius was succeeded by his son, Theodosius II.

Arcaro, Eddie [ahr-kair'-oh]   George Edward Arcaro, b. Cincinnati, Ohio, Feb. 19, 1916, a jockey, set a record by riding the Kentucky Derby winner five times (1938, 1941, 1945, 1948, and 1952). Arcaro also rode the Triple Crown winner (the Kentucky Derby, the Preakness, and the Belmont, all for 3-year-olds) two years, first with Whirlaway in 1941 and again with Citation in 1948. In a 31-year racing career that ended in 1962, he rode 4,779 winners, and his mounts earned $30,035,543 in stakes and purses.

arch and vault   The arch and vault were, until the 19th century, the only known construction methods for roofing buildings without the use of beams. They had be-

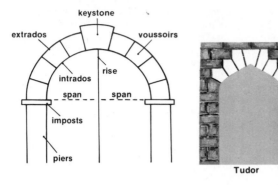

horseshoe   Gothic   segmental

The major parts of an arch are illustrated with four of the many different types of arches: a Tudor arch, an Islamic horseshoe arch, a pointed Gothic arch, and a segmental arch.

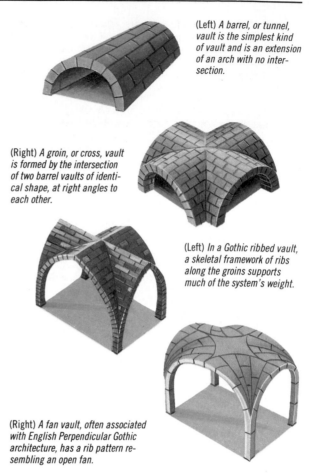

(Left) *A barrel, or tunnel, vault is the simplest kind of vault and is an extension of an arch with no intersection.*

(Right) *A groin, or cross, vault is formed by the intersection of two barrel vaults of identical shape, at right angles to each other.*

(Left) *In a Gothic ribbed vault, a skeletal framework of ribs along the groins supports much of the system's weight.*

(Right) *A fan vault, often associated with English Perpendicular Gothic architecture, has a rib pattern resembling an open fan.*

come a highly developed system with infinite variations over the centuries.

Arch. The arch is an architectural form used to span a window, a door, or other open space of any size. It can be semicircular (Roman and Romanesque), segmental (less than half a circle), or pointed (Gothic). The arch developed from the POST AND LINTEL. In this construction method, the spanning element, the lintel, is flat; the span is limited by the length of the lintel and the weight it can support.

Although the arch was known in ancient Egyptian and Greek architecture, the Romans were the first to give it monumental form. The semicircular arch of the Romans requires two supports (PIERS or COLUMNS) and a series of wedge-shaped, trimmed stones or bricks called voussoirs. Starting from each support, the voussoirs are laid one next to the other, building up each side equally until the space of a single voussoir remains in the center. A wooden scaffolding supports the voussoirs until the final stone, the keystone, is dropped in. The downward thrust of the keystone pushes the voussoirs outward and holds the arch in place. The advantages of the arch over the post-and-lintel system are the greater distances that may be spanned and the greater weight that, with adequate buttressing (see BUTTRESS) to counteract the outward thrust of the voussoirs, may be carried.

Vault. The vault is an elaboration of the arch. The simplest form, the barrel vault, is a series of semicircular arches placed adjacent to each other, to form a barrellike roof. This vault was known in Egypt and the eastern Mediterranean, but the Romans perfected it and used it extensively.

The barrel vault has limitations. It functions successfully in one architectural direction only and requires heavy buttressing to counteract the outward thrust of the voussoirs. The Romans solved this problem. They placed two barrel vaults together, intersecting at right angles, creating a new form, the groin vault. The groin vault dispersed the weight and thrust of the voussoirs onto four supports, along the outlines (groins) of the arches. This dispersion of the weight allowed a still greater space to be spanned, permitted two architectural directions to interpenetrate, and enabled more windows to be placed within the walls, since it reduced the need for buttressing.

During the Romanesque period (c.700–c.1150), ribs were added along the groins to reduce the need for scaffolding and to support some of the weight of the vault. The soaring interior spaces and numerous stained-glass windows in cathedrals of the Gothic period (c.1150–c.1600) were made possible by the ribbed vault.

Modern Developments of the Arch and Vault. In the 19th and 20th centuries the techniques and forms of the arch and vault changed radically as a result of the availability of new materials. Metal frames, prestressed concrete, and tensile structures reduced the power of the outward thrust. Spans could be much greater, and vast areas could be spanned.

See also: ARCHITECTURE; CATHEDRALS AND CHURCHES; DOME.

archaebacteria [ahr-kee-bak-tir'-ee-uh] Archaebacteria constitute a unique grouping of BACTERIA. In microscopes they resemble other bacterial forms, now collectively called eubacteria, and like them are procaryotes (organisms whose cells lack nuclei). In the 1970s, however, intensive studies were made of gene sequences in bacteria. They showed that at the molecular level the organisms now called archaebacteria bore as close a resemblance to all other organisms—the eucaryotes (organisms whose cells have nuclei)—as they did to eubacteria. The name was chosen because archaebacteria seem best suited to conditions found early in Earth's history. The three main types of archaebacteria are methane producers, sulfur metabolizers that thrive in hot and acid conditions, and forms that live in very salty environments (see ANAEROBE). Some biologists suggest that the archaebacteria, eubacteria, and eucaryotes all derived from a common ancestral group not yet known.

archaeoastronomy [ahr'-kee-oh-as-trahn'-uh-mee] Archaeoastronomy is an interdisciplinary science that concerns the recovery and study of evidence of the astro-

The dawning Sun, seen from the center of Stonehenge at the summer solstice on June 21, rises over the so-called Heel Stone. Many astronomers believe that people in prehistoric Britain used Stonehenge as a observatory.

nomical beliefs and practices of ancient or preliterate peoples. It is primarily a tool to gain insight into the intellectual achievements of remote cultures, for example, the builders of MEGALITHS (stone monuments) that have astronomical orientation or the makers of glyphs (symbolic figures) that have astronomical significance. Archaeoastronomical findings may also be of value to astronomers in documenting ancient celestial events.

Archaeoastronomical ideas were probably first applied to STONEHENGE in southern England, where in 1740 William Stukeley noted that the principal axis of the monument was oriented to the direction of sunrise at summer solstice (June 21). The field of archaeoastronomy is still actively studied in Western Europe, where scientists have demonstrated that a relatively high level of astronomical achievement existed among the Early Bronze Age inhabitants of the British Isles and Brittany (western France). More controversial are the suggestions that the Bronze Age builders used structures such as Stonehenge to predict the dates of lunar and solar eclipses and that a standard unit of length ("the megalithic yard") was used in laying out the megalithic stone circles.

Archaeoastronomy is especially important in the study of the ancient cultures of Latin America, where archaeologists and astronomers have worked together to interpret the astronomical significance of the remains of AZTEC, INCA, MAYA, and OLMEC civilizations. Considerable evidence suggests the fundamental importance of astronomy in the daily life of the Maya, for surviving books, called codices, include accurate tables of planetary positions. Maya calendar glyphs carved in stone also attest to the vital significance of astronomy in their measurement of time.

In North America, archaeoastronomy has been applied to the interpretation of stone artifacts called medicine wheels. Some of these stone structures, found on the high plains and mountains, show consistent astronomical alignments. Distinctive features of the Bighorn Medicine Wheel in Wyoming are aligned to the place of sunrise at summer solstice and to three bright stars of midsummer

Stonehenge, consisting of a ditch, 56 chalk-filled holes, and huge standing stones arranged in concentric circles, was built more than 4,000 years ago. Some of the stones are aligned with the rising Sun at the summer solstice; others line up with the rising or setting Sun and Moon on certain days of the year.

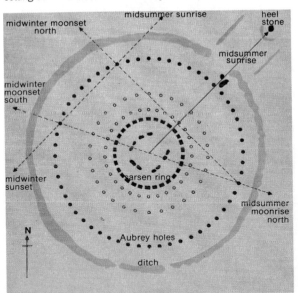

An aerial photograph of the Bighorn Medicine Wheel in Wyoming shows a circular pattern of stones assembled by the American Plains Indians more than 300 years ago. It appears to have been used to determine the positions of the Sun on the horizon at sunrise and at sunset when the summer solstice occurred.

dawn—Aldebaran, Rigel, and Sirius. Archaeological evidence suggests that this medicine wheel was built in stages, beginning perhaps 300 or 400 years ago.

Astronomical orientations have also been attributed to certain structures built in the central United States by MOUND BUILDERS 500 to 1,500 years ago and to stone structures such as Casa Rinconada at CHACO CANYON, in New Mexico, where the Anasazi Indians lived until about AD 1200. The symbol of the crescent moon with an adjacent starlike object, found painted or pecked onto rock surfaces throughout the southwestern United States and northern Mexico, has been interpreted as a depiction of the well-known exploding star, or SUPERNOVA, in the Crab Nebula, recorded by Chinese astronomers and depicted by other peoples in various forms. In North America, the supernova was first visible as a brilliant new star in the eastern sky, near the crescent Moon, on the morning of July 5, 1054.

archaeology [ahr-kee-ahl'-uh-jee]   Archaeology is the branch of the humanities and social sciences that studies the material remains of humankind. Benjamin Franklin coined the phrase, "man is a tool-making animal"; archaeology is concerned with tools and other artifacts of human CULTURE.

Scope of Archaeology

Archaeology is an immense and wide-ranging subject that covers a time span of at least 3 million years, from the first appearance of humankind to the present day. Writing, and therefore history in the strict sense, came into existence only 5,000 years ago in the valleys of the Tigris and Euphrates in Mesopotamia (modern Iraq) and of the Nile in Egypt. Two archaeologies are immediately obvious: the archaeology of everything preceding the earliest period of recorded history, or prehistoric archaeology; and the archaeology from the appearance of writing onward,

which is sometimes referred to as text-aided archaeology. For the first archaeology—that before writing—the French had already been using the term *préhistoire* in the early years of the 19th century, but the idea and the word were not commonly used in the English-speaking world until Sir Daniel Wilson (1816–92), a Scottish archaeologist, published *The Archaeology and Prehistoric Annals of Scotland* in 1851, and Sir John Lubbock published *Prehistoric Times As Illustrated by Ancient Remains and the Manners and Customs of Modern Savages* in 1865. Today, prehistoric archaeology, or PREHISTORY as it is sometimes called, is often viewed as part of the wider discipline of ANTHROPOLOGY.

The borders between prehistory and history are extremely vague and differ chronologically from place to place. In parts of the Near East, prehistory ends around 3000 BC; in parts of Europe it continues until the begin-

Archaeologists measure a terra-cotta figure from an excavation in China. The soldier, one of more than 6,000 sculptures of men and horses discovered at the site, is part of the funerary treasure near the tomb (210 BC) of Emperor Qin Shi Huang Di.

ning of the Christian Era and elsewhere even longer. Moreover, there is no immediate change from prehistory to history but rather a long transitional period, when both material and written sources form the raw data of archaeology. For this period the word *protohistory* is often used.

The only source for knowledge of humankind during the prehistoric period of roughly 3 million years is archaeology—the material remains. Both archaeology and written sources are combined to produce an account of human culture during the protohistoric period, and during the historic period written sources become more and more important. For example, the study of the Paleolithic caves in southern France and northern Spain is strictly prehistoric, as is the study of the OLMEC civilization of Mexico: archaeology is the only available source of knowledge about these topics. The development of city life out of peasant villages in Mesopotamia and Egypt from 3500 to 2500 BC and the subsequent establishment of two of the first civilizations are protohistoric subjects, the sources of which are twofold, namely, the archaeological remains and the inscriptions in Mesopotamian cuneiform writing and in Egyptian hieroglyphics. The Norman conquest of England is well attested by written records; archaeological evidence from domestic, military, and religious sites acts as a valuable supplement to the historical record.

Methods of Archaeology

The archaeologist attempts to reconstruct the past by analyzing, dating, and comparing systematically excavated sites and artifacts. Within the field of archaeology and parallel to the traditional subdivisions of history are separate areas of research and specialization, such as the following: EGYPTOLOGY, or the study of ancient Egypt; Meso-potamian archaeology; classical archaeology, or the study of ancient Greece and Rome; medieval archaeology; and American archaeology. As a methodology, however, archaeology has many more aspects in common with the natural sciences than with history. Excavation reports today would hardly be possible without the contributions of geologists, geophysicists, mineralogists, botanists, zoologists, physical anthropologists, chemists, physicists, and other specialists.

Current developments in archaeological methods are reflected in the academic training the archaeologist receives and in the daily practice of the profession. Alongside the contemporary professional archaeologist, the amateur archaeologist—who for a long time was the only archaeologist—continues to play an important role in locating sites, searching for and passing on archaeological finds, and often in assisting at the "dig," or excavation site.

Discovering the Site. Many archaeological sites are discovered by accident. Sometimes layers of soil are exposed by natural causes such as erosion. Most accidental finds, however, are unearthed in the course of human activities such as plowing fields, dredging waterways, or constructing foundations for buildings, roads, and reservoirs. In recent years a specialized field called SALVAGE ARCHAEOLOGY has developed in response to the need for the quick recovery and research of finds resulting from urban expansion and modernization projects throughout the world.

Sometimes indications on the surface of the earth suggest that an archaeological site is buried below. MIDDENS, burial mounds, and earthworks such as the famous Celtic field systems are examples. A study of old records, place names, and local folklore may also lead to the discovery of archaeological sites.

(Right) *Archaeologists plot the location of artifacts unearthed at Tule Springs, Nev. Excavations yielded crude stone implements and the skeletal remains of Indians who lived there more that 9,000 years ago. (Below) Louis S. B. Leakey, the famed British anthropologist and archaeologist, unearthed fossilized evidence that humanlike creatures inhabited the Olduvai Gorge in Tanzania more than 2 million years ago.*

Aerial photography, which often reveals features that are indistinguishable at ground level, has aided archaeologists in the search for ancient sites. The photograph, taken over southwestern England, shows a series of ditches that mark the boundaries of a Neolithic village.

Archaeological Prospecting. During the 20th century a separate branch of archaeology has developed that specializes in archaeological prospecting. The goal of this subfield is the systematic inventory of all sites in a given area. Aerial photography has revolutionized this search.

First employed on a limited scale during World War I, aerial photography was further developed by O. G. S. Crawford and others in England from 1920 to 1940. It received a strong impetus during World War II when many archaeologists, geologists, and geographers from Britain, the United States, Canada, and France were employed by military intelligence as air-photograph interpreters. During the past three decades the developments in aerial photography have made possible the discovery of thousands of previously unknown sites. Some of these are surface sites that could perhaps have been found by ordinary fieldwork, but most are visible only from the air, when shadows and crop and soil marks reveal partly destroyed earthworks and other types of archaeological evidence. With aerial photography, the landscape can be surveyed as a totality. The air photograph reveals certain details that cannot be seen from the ground, usually variations in soil color and differences in flora or crop densities that result from the influence of ancient construction on the drainage capacity of the soil.

Aerial photography has revolutionized archaeological prospecting. For example, until the mid-1920s prehistoric stone circles in Britain were regarded as a particular category of archaeological site. In 1927 a military pilot interested in archaeology saw and photographed not far from STONEHENGE on the Salisbury Plain of southern England what he described as "a ploughed-out round barrow [burial mound] with measles." Excavation revealed a series of circular postholes surrounding an Early Bronze Age burial; Sir Thomas Kendrick (1895–1979) later coined the name WOODHENGE for this monument. A few years later the same pilot found a similar monument in another location. As a result of these discoveries, archaeologists now define *henge monuments* as embanked and ditched circles of either stone or wooden pillars, and it is now widely understood that the famous stone circles of the British Isles are lithic, that is, stone translations of wooden circles. This piece of archaeology and prehistoric reconstruction could never have happened without the penetrating eye of the air camera.

The photoperiscope furnishes archaeology with another prospecting tool. First used in 1957 to probe Etruscan tombs at the cemetery of Monte Abbatone, Italy, the periscope was inserted into the burial chamber in order to photograph the walls and contents of the tomb. Other prospecting techniques applied to archaeology employ geophysical methods such as electromagnetic and resistivity surveying. Magnetic methods of prospecting make use of instruments such as the proton magnetometer, which measures variations in underground magnetism caused by the presence of stone foundations, brick walls, kilns, ovens, and other structures. The important Etruscan town of TARQUINIA, Italy, was discovered in 1967 by magnetic prospecting.

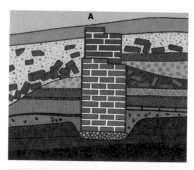

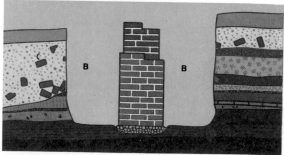

Stratigraphy, as shown by the diagram of a buried wall (A), is a means of establishing a relative chronology; in any undisturbed deposit, older objects lie in the lowest layers. Instead of indiscriminately removing soil, trenches (B) are dug to preserve the stratigraphic layers.

Archaeologists in scuba gear survey the remains of a Greek cargo ship off the coast of Cyprus. Despite difficulties of working underwater, standard methods of archaeological data-gathering are maintained. The gridlike structure of water-resistant tubing aids in mapping the site. Before the development of a practical aqualung by Jacques Cousteau, dredging, which is a particularly destructive technique, had been used to recover underwater artifacts.

Excavating the Site. The purpose of archaeological excavation is to discover as precisely as possible the basic sequence of occupation of a site and to examine various aspects of the artifacts and other remains found there. By combining horizontal and vertical cross-sections of the areas under examination, the archaeologist is able to study the structure, dimensions, and stratification of the terrain.

In most cases, once a topographical survey has been undertaken, experimental borings made, and trial ditches cut to determine the approximate expanse of the site, the excavation pits are dug. Most of the digging must be done carefully by hand with a shovel and a trowel. Digging machines are generally used only to remove the uppermost layer of soil.

All the data are registered as they are uncovered. Longitudinal and transverse cross-sections are drawn to scale and photographed, and the location and depth of various finds in relation to a fixed point are calculated. Often a contour line map of the elevation of the terrain is also drawn, and scale drawings of the site in the horizontal plane are made as the excavation proceeds downward. After the exact location of each find is registered as precisely as possible, the objects can be removed from the site, cleaned, analyzed, and stored for safekeeping. At excavation sites where the stratification is extremely complex, the digging is done layer by layer until the natural subsoil is reached. Often the completion of the excavation of visible monuments is followed by a process of restoration. When an important site is not menaced by general destruction, a part of the site is sometimes left untouched so that at some point in the future the conclusions that have been drawn can be reevaluated, possibly with the aid of improved methods.

Underwater Archaeology. Excavation is not confined to dry land. Underwater archaeology has been considerably developed in the 20th century. It involves many of the same techniques of observation and excavation required at land sites. In addition, of course, one must be trained as a diver.

Sponge divers made the first great archaeological discoveries in the Mediterranean. In 1942, Jacques Yves COUSTEAU developed the self-contained breathing apparatus known as the SCUBA, of which the most commonly used type is the aqualung. Cousteau's pioneering work near Marseilles and that of the American archaeologists George Bass (1932–) and Peter Throckmorton (1928–) off the coast of Turkey demonstrated the amazing possibilities of archaeology under the sea. Work on a Byzantine shipwreck near Yassi Ada, Turkey, from 1961 on led to the development of the photogrammetric mapping of shipwrecks and the launching in 1964 of the *Asherah*, a two-seated submarine specially designed for archaeological exploration.

Interpreting the Finds. Discovering and excavating the site, although primary and essential aspects of archaeology, are only part of the archaeologist's task. After the excavation work has been completed, the archaeologist must evaluate and interpret the results.

Archaeologists register an artifact from the excavations of Nippur in Iraq. The registration, classification, and publication of data is the accepted procedure by which archaeologists present their findings to colleagues.

In analyzing certain finds, the contemporary archaeologist often must rely on specialists in the natural sciences and other disciplines. The work of the British geologist H. H. Thomas (1876–1935) in the early 1920s showed that many of the "bluestones" used in the construction of Stonehenge in southern England came from the Preseli Mountains in southwestern Wales 320 km (200 mi) away. Petrological analysis of Neolithic stone axes in western Europe has enabled archaeologists to determine some of the sites where they were made.

Using spectroscopic techniques, it is now possible to "fingerprint" geological sources of obsidian by their trace-element composition. Obsidian is a volcanic glass highly prized for the manufacture of tools in prehistory. Elemental analyses of the artifacts themselves have shown that obsidian was widely traded in the Mediterranean and Near East, possibly as early as the 8th millennium BC.

Archaeologists view the sites they have excavated or the objects that arrive in their museums not as isolated finds but as material remains of the past that must be fitted into the appropriate environmental picture. The ecological approach to archaeology is one of the most im-

portant and interesting developments in the last quarter-century. The information in the specialized branch of botany called palynology (see POLLEN STRATIGRAPHY) is indispensable to the archaeologist in this regard. By taking pollen samples at the excavation site, it is possible to reconstruct the natural environment of the site at the time it was inhabited. Similarly, a zoologist can offer information about the types of animal that were hunted or domesticated by studying bones found on the site. Archaeology today is also closely linked to PALEOGEOGRAPHY, the physical geography of the geological past.

Archaeological Dating

A key problem in archaeology is dating. When studying Egyptian and Greek remains, or cathedrals and castles in medieval Europe, archaeologists have written dates to which they can refer. But in prehistoric Europe and Africa no written dates exist before the arrival of the Romans, and for North America and Australia, there are none before the explorations of Columbus and Captain Cook. Thus, a major problem for the archaeologist has been how to date the prehistoric remains of the world—how to put Stonehenge, Machu Picchu, Mohenjodaro, or the giant statues of Easter Island in meaningful temporal perspective.

Two different types of archaeological dating have been devised, one based on relative chronology and one based on absolute chronology. Relative chronology refers to the dating of archaeological matter in relation to other phenomena so that artifacts can be arranged in a chronological sequence. With this method, one can say that a certain object is older than another object, but one cannot say how much older in years. Absolute chronology, on the other hand, is the calculation of the actual age of archaeological objects in years.

In the late 19th century, Sir Flinders PETRIE invented the technique of cross-dating, relating undated materials to times that were dated in the Near East by written records. He found Egyptian artifacts in Mycenae and Mycenaean pottery in Egypt, and thus was able to suggest dates for the Mycenaean civilization of Greece based on the historical Egyptian chronology. This technique of cross-dating prehistoric southeastern Europe with historic Egypt was later extended by the Swedish archaeologist Oscar Montelius and the British archaeologist V. Gordon CHILDE to include central, western, and northern Europe.

The establishment of a relative chronology through cross-dating had great limitations. The dates given in the 1930s and 1940s for the beginning of agriculture and, for example, the construction of megalithic monuments, 3000 to 2000 BC, were to a certain extent the result of guesswork by archaeologists. The first absolute chronology based on nonhuman history was obtained by counting varved deposits—or geochronology, as it was called by its inventor, the Swedish geologist and archaeologist Baron Gerard de Geer. This method was based on counting the layers, or varves, deposited by the melting glaciers as the Ice Age came to an end. It gave a chronology of 18,000 years, which was more than three times as long as the chronology based on Egyptian and Mesopotamian king lists. The dating of trees by counting their annual growth

Heinrich Schliemann, a German merchant and linguist, located several archaeological sites through the study of classical literature. In 1870 his excavations of a Turkish hill resulted in the discovery of the fabled city of Troy. Schliemann followed this triumph with the discovery of a royal burial complex at Mycenae, Greece.

Therefore, it is not surprising that antiquarians of the 17th and 18th centuries attributed to the Druids the great megalithic monuments of France and Britain such as the CARNAC alignments, AVEBURY Circle, New Grange, and Stonehenge. The essential feature of archaeology is that the material remains are studied directly, by excavation and comparison, and answers concerning the name, nature, and date of these remains are sought from the remains themselves. Archaeology in this modern sense of the word began not more than 150 to 200 years ago, when carefully conducted excavations began to take place in England, France, and Denmark, and surveys of antiquities were being made, such as the exhaustive, brilliantly illustrated *Description de l'Egypte* (Description of Egypt) published by French scholars in 1809–13.

Origins in Classical Archaeology. The word *archaeology*, which comes from two Greek words meaning to talk about ancient things, seems to have been first used extensively in the 16th and 17th centuries. Although the material remains of past civilizations have always been sought after, the search was usually restricted to objects of intrinsic value, such as gold and silver utensils and ornaments and coins. During the Renaissance a growing interest in the

The Rosetta Stone, named for the site of its discovery in Egypt, held the key to deciphering hieroglyphics, a form of picture-writing used in Pharaonic Egypt. The stone was discovered by accident when French troops, repairing a wall of Fort St. Julien, noticed its inscriptions and preserved it for study. A French scholar, Jean-François Champollion, deciphered the ancient script in 1822.

rings, called DENDROCHRONOLOGY, was first applied to archaeology in 1929 by the American scientist A. E. Douglass. The technique depended on the use of trees in the construction of buildings in ancient times.

Willard F. LIBBY's discovery in 1948 of carbon-14 dating brought about a revolution in archaeological dating. By this method the radioactive carbon-14 (C-14) content of organic material is measured, and absolute dates as far back as 50,000 years ago can be obtained.

Other techniques of absolute dating have been developed, among them thermoluminescence (see LUMINESCENCE), used in dating earthenware products, and potassium-argon dating, by which it has been established that early humans existed in East Africa at least 3 million years ago.

History of Archaeology

The obvious material remains of the past, such as the Egyptian pyramids, Stonehenge, and Hadrian's Wall, had been noticed and discussed for centuries and were the object of antiquarian speculation. The medieval and later antiquaries, however, were not archaeologists. They tried to explain antiquities with reference to written sources, and this is why they attributed the existence of ancient monuments to biblical events such as the Flood or to the explanations that appeared in classical sources such as Caesar and Tacitus. The classical writers who described the pre-Roman inhabitants of France and Great Britain often referred to the DRUIDS—an ancient people who seemed to have been priests, judges, teachers, and sages.

Sir Arthur Evans, a British archaeologist, is remembered as the discoverer of the Royal Palace of Minos at Knossus, Crete. The excavations, which Evans supervised from 1899 to 1935, uncovered a palatial complex that had been the heart of the previously unknown Minoan civilization.

classical world of Greece and Rome was primarily concerned with art, both the written works of classical authors and the material works of classical sculpture and architecture. The search for and collection of these works of art gave rise to the oldest branch of archaeology, classical archaeology.

As early as the 15th century, Italian humanists collected antique statues. The LAOCOÖN group by Agesander (fl. 1st century BC), discovered in Rome in 1506, attracted much attention. The first systematic collection of classical antiquities was started in the Collegium Romanum in 1635. The art-historical phase of classical archaeology reached a peak in the exact precision of the work and commentary of J. J. WINCKELMANN, known as the father of classical archaeology.

In 1711 antique statuary was found at the site of ancient HERCULANEUM, which, along with POMPEII, had been destroyed during the eruption of Vesuvius in AD 79. In 1748, Charles IV, king of Naples (later CHARLES III of Spain), initiated excavation work at Pompeii, and for many years excavations were pursued there but without any systematic plan. A new era of serious scientific exploration in Pompeii and Herculaneum began in 1861 with the activities of Guiseppe Fiorelli. He was the first to note the location of the finds and make efforts to have them

carefully and conscientiously restored.

Other important large-scale excavations were undertaken in other areas of the Mediterranean during the mid-19th century. The ruins of the temple of Artemis, one of the SEVEN WONDERS OF THE WORLD, were excavated in 1869–74 at EPHESUS. In 1878, Karl Human (1839–96) began excavations at PERGAMUM, which yielded the famous Zeus altar and frieze, now in the Pergamon Museum, Berlin. In 1873 a team of French archaeologists began excavations on the island of DELOS, and the German archaeologist Alexander Conze (1831–1914) dug at SAMOTHRACE. The work begun by the German archaeologist Ernst Curtius in 1875 at OLYMPIA is considered one of the first truly scientific full-scale archaeological projects.

Archaeology's Heroic Age. A series of remarkable finds were made by the brilliant, wealthy German merchant-scientist Heinrich SCHLIEMANN, assisted by his friend and advisor, Wilhelm Dörpfeld. Schliemann helped shape certain basic principles of good excavation work. He preserved everything he found, realizing the importance of everyday objects in supplying an accurate archaeological picture of the past. He recorded carefully the levels at which all finds were made, had drawings or photographs made of every important find, and published his results quickly. His untiring efforts to prove that Homer's story of the battle of TROY was based on fact were rewarded in 1870 with the discovery of the Trojan fortress on the mound of present-day Hissarlik in Turkey. At MYCENAE he discovered the famous royal shaft graves in 1874, and in 1884 he excavated TIRYNS. These discoveries greatly enriched the knowledge of AEGEAN CIVILIZATION. He was unable to realize his plans for excavations at Crete, which he had to relinquish to the English archaeologist Arthur EVANS. Early in the 20th century, Evans discovered the labyrinthlike great palace at KNOSSOS and an ancient civilization he called Minoan. In 1952 an English architect and cryptographer, Michael Ventris, deciphered LINEAR B, one of the two types of hieroglyphic script that appeared on the clay tablets discovered by Evans at Knossos.

The foundation for the study of Egyptology was laid by experts and draftsmen who came to Egypt in the wake of Napoleon in 1798. During this expedition, a stone tablet was found at the town of Rosetta in the Nile delta; it bore the same inscription in three different kinds of writing: HIEROGLYPHICS, demotic characters, and Greek. The ROSETTA STONE enabled the French Egyptologist Jean François CHAMPOLLION to decipher Egyptian hieroglyphics in 1822. The first scientific excavations were undertaken in 1880 at Giza under the supervision of Petrie. In 1919 excavations were conducted in the VALLEY OF THE KINGS, led by Howard CARTER. This undertaking culminated in one of the most sensational finds of the 20th century: the discovery (1922) of the almost completely intact tomb of the pharaoh TUTANKHAMEN.

Archaeological expeditions to the Near East began in the early 17th century, when Pietro della Valle visited PERSEPOLIS. Later, Jean Chardin (1643–1713) and Engelbert Kempfer (1651–1716) studied the ruins of that ancient Persian capital. Georg Friedrich Grotefend provided the basis for the decipherment of clay tablets con-

Howard Carter, an English archaeologist, prepares to open the tomb of Tutankhamen. This royal tomb yielded a wealth of artifacts, including furniture, jewelry, and the mummified remains of Tutankhamen.

The funerary portrait mask of Tutankhamen, an Egyptian boy-king who reigned during the 14th century BC, suggests the vast wealth of the pharaohs. The mask is fashioned of beaten gold inlaid with glasslike paste and semiprecious jewels.

taining cuneiform writing at Persepolis—copied by Karsten Niebuhr—by comparing them with the decipherment of inscriptions in three languages found at BEHISTUN in Persia. The decipherment of cuneiform was completed in 1846 by H. C. Rawlinson. The first systematic excavations in the Near East took place in the 19th century. In 1843, Paul Émile Botta began archaeological research at KHORSABAD. In 1845, A. H. Layard did the same at Nimrud. From 1890 to 1900, an American expedition undertook excavations at NIPPUR; from 1899 to 1914, a German expedition led by Robert Koldewey worked at BABYLON. Important research was also conducted by Leonard WOOLLEY at ALALAKH (Tell Atchana; 1912–14) and at UR in Mesopotamia (1922–34). Among the most important discoveries of the 20th century were the Hebrew DEAD SEA SCROLLS (1947).

Development of Prehistoric Archaeology. The ideas underlying prehistoric archaeology originated in Europe at the beginning of the 19th century. According to long-standing antiquarian notions, human beings had existed for a very short time; calculations made from the dates given in the Bible suggested that the world and the human species were created in 4004 BC. The geologists of the 18th century firmly believed in this short chronology and explained the layering of rocks as a result of the Flood. This was the geologist William Bucklands's view

when he wrote *Reliquiae Diluvianae; or Observations on the Organic Remains Contained In Caves, Fissures, and Diluvial Gravel and on Other Geological Phenomena Attesting the Action of an Universal Deluge* (1823).

His pupil, Charles LYELL, reacted against this CATASTROPHISM interpretation of geology, although James HUTTON, in his book *Theory of the Earth* (1785), had already realized that the layering of rocks was due to ongoing processes in rivers, lakes, and oceans. "No processes are to be employed that are not natural to the globe," he wrote, "no action to be admitted except those of which we know the principle." This was the beginning of the theory of UNIFORMITARIANISM, which held that early geological processes do not substantially differ from those currently observable. A leading figure among the Fluvialists, as they were called, was Lyell, whose *Principles of Geology*, first published in 1830–33, was regarded by Charles DARWIN as a book that helped form his own thinking. Prehistoric archaeology could not have been born had not the short chronology of the antiquarians disappeared and the new fluviatile geology gained acceptance.

During the early years of the 19th century, in addition to a new geology, archaeology developed a new approach to artifacts that was provided by Scandinavian archaeologists. Excavators in the late 18th century had complained that although they found in their excavations objects of stone, bronze, and iron, they did not know in what sequence to place them. The ancient Greeks already had a vague notion that there had been a stone age in the past, but it was the Scandinavian archaeologists who created a complete revolution in antiquarian thought by postulating, on technological grounds, successive stages in the past. C. J. THOMSEN classified the material

(Right) *This Maya tomb with its glyph-covered walls was found in the jungles of northeastern Guatemala, at the Río Azul site. At Río Azul, in May 1984, an unlooted Maya tomb was discovered. Archaeologists have identified about 300 centers of Maya architecture overall, and they continue to study that mysterious civilization.* (Below) *A huge basalt head, carved by Olmec Indians, gazes over the countryside near Mexico's Gulf Coast. The Olmec culture, which flourished more than 3,000 years ago, was one of the major influences on the development of Mesoamerican civilizations.* (Below right) *Macchu Picchu, the "lost city of the Incas," was a landmark discovery, made in 1911 by Hiram Bingham, an American explorer. The easily defended citadel rests on an Andean precipice at an elevation of 2,742 m (8,997 ft). The complex, with its fountains and plaza, displays unusually advanced engineering techniques. The city is thought to have been a center of Inca culture during the 15th and 16th centuries.*

in the Copenhagen Museum, opened to the public in 1819, on the basis of three successive technological ages of stone, bronze, and iron. His pupil and successor, J. J. A. Worsaae, demonstrated the truth of this hypothesis by his excavations in the peat bogs and barrows of Denmark. The same was shown to be true in Switzerland, when low lake-levels revealed prehistoric LAKE DWELLINGS. Thomsen had demonstrated the succession of cultures and produced the three-age system. Worsaae demonstrated stratigraphy as applied to human remains. Geology was based on stratigraphy; now archaeology could also benefit from stratigraphical observation. More than a quarter of a century before the opening of the Copenhagen Museum, Thomas Jefferson had excavated a burial mound in Virginia and correctly observed its stratigraphy and the lessons to be drawn from it.

Prehistoric archaeology began with the three-age system. Lubbock, in his book *Prehistoric Times* (1865), invented the terms PALEOLITHIC and NEOLITHIC and turned the three-age system into a four-age system. Hodder Westropp (d. 1884) in 1866 proposed the term MESOLITHIC, and thus European prehistory became a fivefold system of Old Stone Age (Paleolithic Period), Middle Stone Age (Mesolithic Period), New Stone Age (Neolithic Period), Bronze Age, and Iron Age.

General Augustus Pitt-Rivers instituted the use of highly refined excavation methods in prehistoric archaeology. His numerous excavations of sites in Britain from 1880 to 1900 were notable for the emphasis he placed on precise stratigraphic observation and recording; detailed sectional drawings and plans of all his excavations were made, and scale models were constructed of major

An artist's illustration of life in a Paleolithic, or Old Stone Age, camp is based on evidence unearthed at Ostrava-Petrkovice in Moravia in Central Europe. The camp existed more than 25,000 years ago. Its inhabitants were nomadic hunters who traveled from campsite to campsite and whose lives depended on stalking native reindeer and mammoths. Cave paintings from other Paleolithic sites suggest that sewn animal skins were worn. Shelters at Ostrava-Petrkovice probably were little more than conical tents that could be dismantled and transported as the hunters continued their search for game. It is likely that these tents were fashioned from animal hides and buttressed against the elements with bones and tusks. The illustration depicts a tribesman (foreground) carving a talisman. This simple act has special significance, because a major achievement of Paleolithic culture was the introduction of plastic arts.

sites. His sumptuous 4-volume work, *Excavations in Cranborne Chase*, produced from 1887 to 1898, set a high standard for archaeological publications. Pitt-Rivers's approach was later adapted and perfected by the English archaeologist Mortimer Wheeler, as set forth in his book *Archaeology from the Earth* (1954).

Other Areas. In the Americas, the first reports concerning ancient civilizations date from the time of the Spanish conquistador Hernan CORTÉS. The expedition (1799–1804) to South and Central America headed by Alexander von HUMBOLDT led to renewed interest in the ancient American cultures. Count J. F. M. de Waldeck (1766–1875) and J. L. Stephens were among the first to study the Mayan cities. In 1912, Hiram Bingham discovered in the Urubamba valley of Peru the Inca town of MACHU PICCHU, spectacularly situated on a saddle in the Andes Mountains with a drop of 457 m (1500 ft) on either side.

In Africa, the state of Zimbabwe (formerly Rhodesia) is named after a great fortified site located on the plateau between the Limpopo and Zambesi rivers. It was formerly argued that the ZIMBABWE RUINS could not have been built by the local population but rather by an intrusive group of superior foreigners. Excavations, particularly those of Dr. Gertrude Caton-Thompson in 1929 and Peter Garlake in 1964–70, have shown, however, that this site was built and inhabited from AD 330 to 1450 by a prosperous farming and trading people indigenous to southern Africa.

For a long time archaeology was primarily concerned with the most ancient human past in the Old World. Gradually, however, archaeological interests and scholarly competence moved into diverse geographical regions and throughout the historical field. Now Anglo-Saxon and Merovingian archaeologists, medieval archaeologists, and postmedieval archaeologists are practicing members of the profession; a genuine interest has developed in the archaeology of the past 200 years, particularly in the development of industry, a discipline called industrial archaeology. Everything from the first stone tool to the garbage in yesterday's trash can is now a legitimate archaeological subject.

Archaeology in Perspective. How can the amount of energy, activity, and money now spent on archaeology in all parts of the world be justified? First, the cave paintings at Lascaux and Altamira, the temples of the Maya, the megalithic monuments of the Maltese, classical Greek architecture (even if the urban pollution in Athens is steadily destroying what remains of the masterpieces on the Acropolis), the art of the Celts and the Scythians, the cathedrals and the castles of the Middle Ages and of the Renaissance are all part of the universal heritage of humanity that must be guarded and understood. Second, humans' curiosity about their past and their remote origins justifies the search. Through the now well-dated record of the material past, the following facts about human history have been revealed: (1) humans themselves, the tool-making animals, have existed for at least 3 million years; (2) humans of the same physical type as modern humans, namely *Homo sapiens sapiens* (formerly called CRO-MAGNON MAN), have been in existence for at least 50,000 years, and cultural features associated with modern humans, such as careful burial of the dead, the production of art, and the decoration of objects of everyday use, date from this period; (3) humans moved slowly from being hunters, fishers, and food-gatherers to domesticators of animals and cultivators of foodstuffs in many different parts of the world, achieving what V. Gordon Childe called the Neolithic Revolution; (4) some agrarian communities brought into existence by the Neolithic Revolution went through a process whereby they became complex urban societies and developed into the first civilizations of Egypt, Mesopotamia, northwest India, and China in the Old World, and the Olmec, the Maya, and the Andean civilizations in the New World. This process, sometimes known as the Urban Revolution, took place 5,000 years ago in the ancient Near East. In America the oldest civilization, that of the Olmec, dates from about 1200 BC.

This is the pageant and perspective of human history now revealed by archaeology, and without doubt the last decade of the 20th century will make it more detailed and better documented. New discoveries are continually being made: only recently it has been learned that pottery in Japan dates from about 10,000 BC and that humans reached Australia by about 40,000 years ago.

In the 19th century, endless discussion centered on the nature of change revealed by archaeology. Was the advancement from a Stone Age to a Bronze Age, and from a Bronze Age to an Iron Age, something natural for all humankind? Did cultural evolution thus follow biological evolution, or were new ideas and techniques spread from one center? The battle between the proponents of independent evolution and of diffusion from a single cultural center was waged in archaeological books and meetings of learned societies for many years. Some scholars argued that nothing could be invented twice, and others, like Elliot Smith, proposed that all post-Stone Age discoveries and inventions came from ancient Egypt.

This Egyptocentric hyperdiffusionist dogma is no longer fashionable. It was replaced in the 1920s and '30s by a modified diffusionism advocated by V. Gordon Childe, in which most of the post-Paleolithic advances in human culture (such as the Neolithic Revolution and the Urban Revolution) were seen as coming from a number of centers in southwest Asia. Accurate dating and the study of prehistoric African, Chinese, and American archaeology have established that, although some ideas and processes were diffused—and undoubtedly extensive movement of peoples took place in prehistoric times—parallel cultures developed in many parts of the world.

What is referred to as the origin of agriculture was in fact the discrete development of crop raising in many parts of the world; and what is referred to as the origin of civilization is the independent growth of literate urban communities in many different parts of the world. Archaeology has made human history far more interesting and understandable.

See also: AFRICAN PREHISTORY; NORTH AMERICAN ARCHAEOLOGY; RADIOMETRIC AGE-DATING.

Archaeopteryx [ahr-kee-ahp'-tur-iks] *Archaeopteryx* (Greek: *archaios*, "ancient"; *pteryx*, "wing") is an extinct, primitive bird, possibly flightless, that lived about 150 million years ago. Among the oldest birds known, its fossilized remains, including the imprint of feathers, were found more than 100 years ago in limestone of the Jurassic Period in Solnhofen, Bavaria, Germany (see GEOLOGIC TIME). Fragmentary birdlike fossils of even greater age, dating from the Triassic Period, have since been found and given the name *Protoavis* (see BIRD). About the size of a crow, *Archaeopteryx* was birdlike in having a wishbone, a big toe rotated backward to oppose the others and allow the claw to grip, and some fused wristbones. Reptilian features, inherited from its DINOSAUR ancestors, included a long, whiplike tail, teeth, three complete clawed digits, and abdominal ribs. The limb bones were solid, lacking the air sacs that modern birds have, and the breastbone may or may not have had a birdlike keel. In the absence of other evidence, paleontologists cannot say for sure whether *Archaeopteryx* could fly or glide or was merely a

The Archaeopteryx, which flourished about 150 million years ago, was one of the first true (feathered) birds. It is an evolutionary link between birds and their reptilian ancestors.

fast runner, like its diminutive dinosaurian relative, *Compsognathus*.

Archangel   see ARKHANGELSK

archerfish   Archerfish, genus *Toxotes*, are perchlike fish in the order Perciformes, family Toxotidae. They live in coastal fresh, brackish, and marine waters from India to Australia, the Philippines, and Polynesia. They are up to about 25 cm (10 in) long. They use their large, expansive mouth to spit jets of water up to about 1.2 m (4 ft) above the surface, to dislodge small prey or other food into the water.

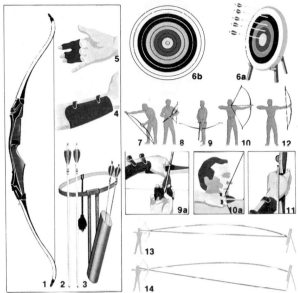

An archer's equipment typically includes a fiberglass-and-wood bow (1), aluminum arrows (2), a quiver (3) with a waistbelt, and an arm bracer (4) and a tab (5) to protect the drawing hand. Targets are divided into either five (6a) or ten (6b) scoring zones. To shoot, an archer strings the bow (7), nocks the arrow (8), prepares to draw (9; detail, 9a), draws (10; detail, 10a), aims (detail, 11), and shoots (12). Methods of aiming include line-of-sight (13) and point-of-aim (14).

An archerfish aims and shoots drops of water at an insect. It ejects jets of water from its gill chambers by rapidly compressing its gill covers.

archery   Archery, the skill of shooting arrows with a bow, was one of the earliest hunting techniques acquired by humans. The bow and arrow were used for this purpose more than 30,000 years ago. They were also principal weapons in warfare until superseded by gunpowder.

Hunting with the bow and arrow is still popular, and archery in the form of target shooting has developed into a national and international competitive sport. The Fédération Internationale de Tir à l'Arc (FITA) has continued to hold world championships since 1931. In 1933 it established separate competitions for men and women.

The average length of the modern bow is 1.8 m (6 ft) for men and 1.7 m (5.5 ft) for women. The force required to draw the bowstring to its extremity is called the bow weight. This is 14.5–19 kg (32–42 lb) for men and 11.8–15.4 kg (26–34 lb) for women. The string side of a bow is called the belly, and the other side is referred to as the back. The length of the modern arrow is 61–81 cm (24–32 in). An archer uses an arrow slightly longer than his or her arm. (See BOW AND ARROW.)

The standard target used in official competition is 122 cm (48 in) in diameter, and the bottom is 61 cm (24 in) from the ground. The target is divided into a center circle (the bull's-eye) and four concentric colored bands, further divided into two scoring rings in each band. From the center out the specified scoring for each

area is gold, 10–9; red, 8–7; blue, 6–5; black, 4–3; white, 2–1. In competition each archer is allowed a specified number of shots, which constitutes a round. In an FITA round, an archer must shoot 36 arrows each at 90, 70, 50, and 30 m for men (295, 230, 164, and 98 ft), and 70, 60 (197 ft), 50, and 30 m for women.

Other forms are flight shooting, strictly for distance; freestyle shooting (also for distance), in which the archer straps a 68-kg (150-lb) bow to the feet and lies down to draw the string with both hands; and field archery, employing the same skills as those used in bow hunting.

Archilochus [ahr-kil'-uh-kuhs]   Archilochus, a Greek poet who flourished between 680 and 640 BC, is best remembered for the sensual strength of his satiric verse and for his metrical innovations. He was born on the island of Paros, traveled extensively around the Aegean, and fought and died as a mercenary. Considered the first to have used iambic meter, he experimented with many metrical combinations as well as with the use of colloquial language. A sharp observer of nature, society, love, and war, Archilochus emerged as the first Western writer to express a strong sense of individuality in his poetry.

Archimedes [ahr-ki-mee'-deez]   Archimedes, b. *c.*298 BC, d. 212 BC, was the greatest mathematician of ancient times. A native of Syracuse, Sicily, he was killed during its capture by the Romans in the Second Punic War. Stories from Plutarch, Livy, and Polybius describe machines including the CATAPULT, the compound pulley, and a burning-mirror invented by Archimedes for the defense of Syracuse. He spent some time in Egypt, where he purportedly invented the device now known as ARCHIMEDES' SCREW.

Archimedes made many original contributions to geometry in his work on the areas of plane figures and the areas and volumes of curved surfaces. His methods anticipated INTEGRAL CALCULUS. Archimedes proved that the volume of a sphere is two-thirds the volume of a circumscribed cylinder. He was also known for his approximation of π.

In theoretical mechanics, Archimedes is responsible for fundamental theorems concerning the centers of gravity of plane figures and solids, and he is famous for his theorem on the weight of a body immersed in a liquid, called Archimedes' principle, which states that any object floating upon or submerged in a fluid is buoyed upward by a force equal to the weight of the displaced fluid.

Archimedes' screw

Archimedes' screw, also called a water snail, is a simple device that has been used since ancient times to lift water continuously for a distance of a few feet. Often used to direct water into an IRRIGATION channel, it was originally composed of a wooden beam, several feet long, around which a spiral SCREW thread was built of layers of flexible, pitch-covered wood strips. Over this thread were fastened tight-fitting narrow planks running the length of the beam and giving it the appearance of a tube. VITRUVIUS (1st century BC) described it as a "natural imitation of a spiral shell."

For the screw to operate, it must be angled into the water so that the underportions of the threads at the submerged end can cup and hold the water. When the screw is rotated on its axis in the proper direction, the cupped water is lifted up along the underside of the beam on the moving threads until it reaches and can flow out of the tube's raised end.

An Archimedes' screw is used in the screw pump. The pump comprises a treadmill-driven spiral that lifts water as it turns.

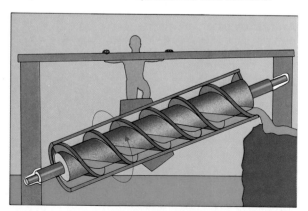

Archipenko, Aleksandr

[ahr-kuh-peng'-koh] The Russian-American Aleksandr Archipenko, b. Kiev, the Ukraine, May 30 (N.S.), 1887, d. Feb. 25, 1964, was a pioneer in abstract sculpture. From 1912 to 1917, while he was associated with Jacques VILLON's Section d'Or (Golden Section) group in Paris, Archipenko began to use cubist space and multiplanarity (use of many surfaces in one work). In accord with the futurists' idea of working with unorthodox materials, he also began to use polychrome glass, metal, and wood in a series of figural relief constructions that he called "sculpto-paintings." In 1913 he completed *Head: Construction of Crossing Planes* (Perls Gallery, New York), in which he transposed into three-dimensional form the type of cubist head painted by Pablo PICASSO and Georges BRAQUE. His work was included in the epic New York ARMORY SHOW of 1913. Archipenko's most original and accomplished works are those he produced between 1910 and 1920 in Paris, which may be seen in most major collections of 20th-century art.

architecture

Architecture is probably the oldest of the fine arts (see ART). Certainly it is the most useful and in some respects is a prerequisite for the other arts. Most early sacred texts associate buildings with deities; architecture was not only considered the highest art form, to which other arts were adornments, but some buildings were viewed as representing another, higher realm. In medieval illuminated manuscripts, God was frequently shown armed with compasses and a mason's square, as Architect of the Universe.

Architecture can be defined in at least four ways, all valid, all interrelated, and none truly satisfactory. It is the art and method of erecting structures; it is a planned entity, the result of a conscious act; it is a body or corpus of work; it is a way to build. A good definition was provided by the Roman architect VITRUVIUS in the 1st century AD and was translated from the Latin into English during the 17th century by Sir Henry Wotton (1568–1639). Vitruvius said that architecture was a building that incorporated *utilitas, firmitas*, and *venustas*, which Wotton translated as "commodotie, firmness, and delighte." This definition recognizes that architecture embraces functional, technological, and aesthetic requirements: it must have *commodotie* (utilitarian qualities), *firmness* (structural stability and sound construction), and *delighte* (attractive appearance).

Because the history of architecture concerns buildings substantial enough to survive (at least in part) or important enough to be recorded in some way (by drawings or written description), in practice it has been the history of significant buildings—CASTLES, CATHEDRALS AND CHURCHES, TEMPLES, and major institutional monuments.

This discussion will concentrate on the development of Western architecture. Nonwestern architecture, as well as more detailed consideration of each epoch in Western architecture, is treated elsewhere in the encyclopedia and may be found by culture, by country, by style, by type, by architect, and by building or monument.

Architects. Much more is known of ancient buildings than of the people who designed and built them. The names of a few Egyptian, Greek, and Roman architects have survived, but the identities of the great cathedral builders of the Middle Ages are mostly unknown. They are generally described as master masons, but they regarded themselves as architects and sometimes incorporated a LABYRINTH in their own memorial plaques to signify a link with DAEDALUS, the legendary first architect of the Greek world and the designer of the MINOTAUR's labyrinth.

The names of architects first began to be known in Italy during the RENAISSANCE in the 15th and 16th centuries. The idea of a professional architect with formal training and academic qualifications is a product of the 19th century. In 1819 architecture courses were instituted at the ÉCOLE DES BEAUX-ARTS (School of Fine Arts) in Paris; in 1847 a night school was established at the Architectural Association in London; courses in architecture were first offered at the Massachusetts Institute of Technology in 1868, at Cornell University in 1871, and at the University of Illinois in 1873. Until World War I, however, most architects were trained while working in the offices of practicing architects, and governments were slow to insist upon qualification tests. The state of Illinois passed the first licensing law for architects in 1897; Great Britain did not have such a law until 1931.

The Study of Architecture. Just as the architect as a professional is a recent phenomenon, so too is the evaluation of architecture itself. Not until the late 18th century did ancient Greek and Roman architecture cease to be regarded as an unassailable criterion of excellence throughout the Western world. Only when the hegemony of the classical styles began to be challenged did architects and scholars begin to consider the whole of the subject. The traditional approach was based on a closely observed study of architectural style, with considerable em-

The 4th-dynasty pyramid of Khafre at Gizeh is the 2nd largest of the three great Egyptian pyramids. It stands 141.3 m (c.465 ft) high and is the only one retaining some of its original limestone facing.

phasis on the differences of detail treatment from one country to another.

An alternate approach based on determinism has been developed over many years by a group of German-speaking scholars (including Jakob BURCKHARDT, Sir Nikolaus PEVSNER, Siegfried Giedion, and Heinrich WÖLFFLIN) who established an interpretation of architecture as an expression of the *Zeitgeist*, or spirit of the age. Burckhardt and Wölfflin introduced the *Zeitgeist* concept in their studies of the Italian Renaissance, but Giedion and Pevsner applied it to MODERN ARCHITECTURE, which they saw as expressing the spirit of a technological era. Another approach seeks to understand architecture in the same way as did the people who built it. During the 19th century this associative school of thought became central to architectural theory.

Contemporary architects and scholars emphasize the influences of technology on the development of buildings. The use of iron and steel beams and columns released the wall from its traditional load-bearing function and allowed architects to incorporate enormous windows and wide, open-plan floors, two of the most significant characteristics of modern architecture. No large modern building, however, would be practicable without the parallel development of ELEVATORS, central HEATING SYSTEMS and electric LIGHTING DEVICES.

Architectural History

Architecture is most readily grasped by studying its development in successive historical periods, noting the general characteristic of each, the development of building techniques from one era to the next as well as from one culture to the next, and noting the evolution of each successive architectural style. Following are brief summaries of the ten major cultural epochs in Western architecture from ancient Egypt and the Near East to the present time.

The great ziggurat at Ur, in Mesopotamia, built by Ur-Nammu and other 3d-dynasty Sumerian kings, is shown in this reconstruction. The Mesopotamian ziggurat is a stepped pyramid supporting a shrine and surrounded by a walled precinct.

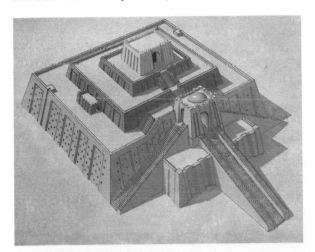

The Temple of Poseidon (c.460 BC) in Paestum, Italy, is among the best-preserved Greek Doric temples. The Doric temple form is derived from earlier wooden temple forms; it reveals the refinements of proportions used by the Greeks to achieve visual harmony.

Ancient Egyptian and Near Eastern Architecture. The construction of the most famous Egyptian structures, the PYRAMIDS, began in the 3d and 4th Dynasties of the Old Kingdom (c.2686–2498 BC). Temples in stone were built during the Middle Kingdom (c.2133–1786 BC), but most of the surviving examples date from the New Kingdom (1570–1085 BC) and the Ptolemaic Period (323–30 BC). Permanent building in stone was restricted to TOMBS, temples, and the associated statuary (OBELISKS and avenues of SPHINXES and lions), but the forms of these monumental stone structures seem to have been influenced by those of primitive Egyptian domestic architecture. Houses were formed of mud-brick walls with columns made from bundles of reeds lashed together. Thus, the walls of stone buildings were generally battered (thicker at the base and tapered), and the columns were short in proportion. The column heads or capitals were carved to represent lotus flowers or buds, palm leaves, and papyrus heads; the column shafts often had decorative bindings recalling the primitive lashed reeds.

Stone and timber were rare in the alluvial plains of the Tigris and Euphrates rivers; so MESOPOTAMIAN ARCHITECTURE was necessarily based on the use of clay BRICKS with an outer skin of often highly colored glazed bricks, exemplified by the ZIGGURAT at UR (c.2500 BC). Farther up the Mesopotamian rivers in ASSYRIA, stone was available, but it was used primarily as a wall covering to be decorated with BAS-RELIEF sculpture and inscriptions, from which much of the knowledge of Assyrian history is derived. The architecture of both the Babylonian (c.1900–c.1550 BC) and the Assyrian (c.1100–612 BC) empires was based on massive brick platforms raised above the floodplain and often further terraced to give the characteristic ziggurat form. The ancient Persian Empire (538–333 BC) adopted these features and supplemented them with the extensive use of columns, as in the palaces at PERSEPOLIS (518–c.460 BC)

Greek Architecture. Any consideration of Greek architecture must begin with mention of AEGEAN CIVILIZATION, typified by the great Minoan palaces on the island of CRETE, in particular the huge complex of KNOSSOS and the magnificently sited structures at PHAISTOS (both c.1700–c.1400 BC). Constructed of massive masonry, they were several stories high and incorporated large pillared halls, dozens of labyrinthine smaller rooms, sweeping terraces looking to the sea, and plumbing arrangements of astonishing modernity. The walls were decorated with brilliantly colored frescoes (see FRESCO PAINTING) and stucco bas-reliefs. The Minoans were conquered by the Mycenaeans of mainland Greece, whose architecture was subsequently strongly influenced by Cretan prototypes.

This early Greek architecture (3000–700 BC) is characterized by the use of massive stone blocks for walls and by the occasional use of corbeled masonry to make primitive forms of vaults and domes, as in the Lion Gate and so-called Treasury of Atreus at MYCENAE (1400–1200 BC).

(Left) The Doric order, the oldest of the classical Greek orders, established the refined proportions used in the later Ionic and Corinthian orders. One of these refinements is entasis, a slight convexity of the column shaft that subtly negates any optical illusion of concavity. (Right) These capitals represent the three classical Greek architectural orders: Doric, Ionic, and Corinthian. The Ionic capital is characterized by its typical volute, or spiral scroll, and the Corinthian is adorned with acanthus leaves.

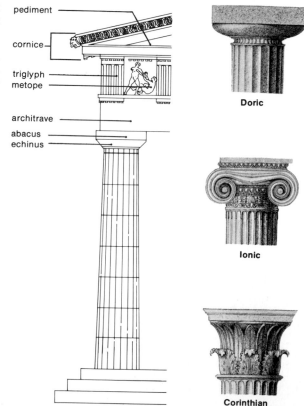

pediment
cornice
triglyph
metope
architrave
abacus
echinus

Doric

Ionic

Corinthian

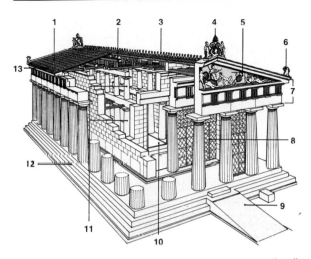

The Temple of Aphaia at Aegina (c.490 BC), shown in this reconstruction, displays the characteristics of a typical Greek Doric temple, which includes terra-cotta roof tiles (1); supporting roof timbers (2); ridge-beam antefix, an ornamental block covering the roof-tile ends (3); acroterion (4); pediment (5); water spout (6); entablature (7); pronaos, or entrance (8); entrance ramp (9); naos, or sanctuary (10); two-tiered interior columns (11); stylobate (12); eave antefix (13). All of the elements were painted in earth colors.

Columns sometimes were also used to frame doors and gateways and to provide internal colonnades for palaces, as in the courtyard at TIRYNS. It was, however, the column and the beam—POST AND LINTEL—that formed the basis of classical Greek architecture and that gave it the simple, straightforward character that, together with its details, has led many scholars to speculate on its origins in the construction of primitive wooden huts.

The Greeks developed a vocabulary of architectural detail in stone that was fundamental to European architecture for more than 2,000 years. The Greek "language of architecture" reached its zenith during the 5th century BC. Classical Greek architecture consisted of three orders—the Doric, Ionic, and Corinthian. Each represented the assembly of the basic components of a simple rectangular building with a pitched roof, that is, column, CAPITAL (or column head), entablature (the "beam" connecting the columns), and pediment (the triangular gable of the roof). Different proportions and decorative conventions imparted a distinctive character to each order, regardless of the bright colors applied to the original buildings or the subject matter of the sculptured decoration along the FRIEZE or in the triangular pediment (TYMPANUM). The proportions of each order were fixed within narrow limits, and, strictly speaking, the components of each order could be correctly assembled in only one way. The Greeks never mixed different orders on the same building. This, and other rules, were modified in Roman architecture. The Romans created two additional orders, the Tuscan and the Composite, and employed all five orders as decoration for buildings constructed on principles different from those the Greeks used.

The basic building material of the classical period was MARBLE, a strong stone that could be shaped to give great precision of line and detail. The basic temple form was also very simple: a rectangular chamber with a shallow-pitched gabled roof, surrounded by a row of columns (or fronted by a columned porch), standing on a podium of three steps. Given the simplicity of the construction system and the building form, the essential achievement of the Greeks was the refinement of the building and its components into an architectural system of proportion and decoration—exemplified by the buildings on the Athens ACROPOLIS, in particular the Parthenon (447–32 BC)—that remained the basis of the Western European architectural tradition until the mid-19th century.

Roman Architecture. During the 2d century BC the Romans, in conquering North Africa, Greece, Anatolia, and Spain, absorbed the architectural traditions of those areas (most significantly that of Greece), to which they added the constructional skills of the ETRUSCANS, their immediate neighbors in central Italy. The most significant achievements of the Romans were in their technology of building, their use of a much wider range of materials (including concrete, TERRA-COTTA, and fired bricks), and their refinements of the ARCH AND VAULT and the DOME—all of which had been pioneered by the Etruscans. Roman temples generally remained modeled on those of Greece, with the common addition of a high plinth (base or platform) and the frequent omission of the side and rear columns, typified by the Maison Carrée at Nîmes, France.

Roman civic monuments included a number of building types of unprecedented size and complexity, which could not have been built using the Greek beam-and-column construction system. AQUEDUCTS, thermae (such as the Baths of CARACALLA), BASILICAS (law courts), theaters, triumphal arches, amphitheaters (such as the COLOSSEUM), circuses, and palaces involved enclosing much larger spaces or bridging much greater distances than could be achieved by the use of timber or stone beams. The Ro-

The Maison Carrée in Nîmes, France, is a Roman temple begun in the late 1st century BC. Set on a high plinth the temple has an elaborately carved entablature carried by Corinthian columns.

Diocletian's Palace was built (c.300) in Spalato (modern Split), Yugoslavia. Intended for the emperor's retirement, the palace was actually a walled town.

man use of domed construction in mass concrete is best represented by the well-preserved PANTHEON in Rome (constructed AD 120–24), which subsequently became a Christian church. Later Roman or Early Christian churches (see EARLY CHRISTIAN ART AND ARCHITECTURE) generally took their form from the basilica, whose central nave, side aisles, triforium, and apse became characteristic features of the Romanesque and Gothic church. Emperor CON-

STANTINE I built huge basilican churches at all the major Christian sites in the Roman Empire in the 4th century, thus firmly establishing the basilica as the predominant form of Christian church architecture.

Byzantine Architecture. BYZANTINE ARCHITECTURE developed in the BYZANTINE EMPIRE founded by Constantine I when he moved the capital from Rome to Byzantium (subsequently Constantinople—present-day ISTANBUL) in

The Colosseum in Rome is the largest extant Roman amphitheater. Begun about AD 70 by Vespasian, it could accommodate more than 45,000 spectators. The central arena could be flooded for water games.

Hagia Sophia (Church of the Holy Wisdom) in Constantinople, built 532–37, is the masterpiece of Byzantine architecture. The square nave of the church is covered with a huge central dome supported on pendentives.

the 4th century. In southern and eastern Europe, in particular in those parts of Italy, Greece, and Anatolia that remained under the sway of the Byzantine Empire, the continuity of Roman plans and techniques was strong. Only slightly modified Roman basilican plans were used for such Italian churches as Sant' Apollinare in Classe, RAVENNA (534–39); in Constantinople itself huge domed churches, such as HAGIA SOPHIA (532–37), were built on a scale far larger than anything achieved by the Western Roman Empire.

Romanesque Architecture. In northern Europe, where Roman remains were less frequently encountered, greater freedom of experiment existed in MEROVINGIAN, CAROLINGIAN, and OTTONIAN ARCHITECTURE, as the early periods are known. From the mid-10th to the mid-12th century greater progress was made toward the development of a successor style—the Gothic. The primary characteristics of ROMANESQUE ARCHITECTURE (or NORMAN ARCHITECTURE, as northern Romanesque is often known) were Roman in origin, however: large internal spaces were spanned by barrel vaults on thick, squat columns and piers, windows and doors had round-headed arches, and most of the major churches were laid out on the basilican plan, modified by the addition of BUTTRESSES, transepts, and towers. The buildings are solid, heavy, and, because of the comparatively small windows, dimly lighted, exemplified by Durham Cathedral (begun 1023) in England. Portals, capitals, and altars are embellished with sculpture of superlative skill and powerful effect; STAINED GLASS first appeared in Europe, but on a limited scale, because of the restricted size of window openings.

Gothic Architecture. From the mid-12th century to the 16th century northern European architecture was characterized by the use of flying buttresses, pointed arches, ribbed vaults, and traceried windows. The thin walls, slender columns, and the very large areas of glass in Gothic buildings gave an impression of lightness that contrasted markedly with the Romanesque. GOTHIC ARCHITECTURE originated at the royal abbey church of SAINT DENIS, built by Abbot SUGER between 1137 and 1144. It was refined in the great churches of northern and central France, such as Amiens Cathedral (1220–70), notable for its great height and the slenderness of its columns, and the SAINTE-CHAPELLE in Paris (1247–48), in which exceptionally large wall areas were filled with glass and tracery. Indeed, Gothic architecture was most fully developed in France and England, where the style spread in the late 12th century. The spread of Gothic to Germany was delayed until the mid-13th century, and in this country only a few cathedrals, such as the one in Cologne (begun 1248), approached the size and quality of the northern French prototypes. The most thorough application of northern Gothic to Italy was in the Milan Cathedral, built at the end of the 14th century by French and German masons. In general, the Italians tended to use Gothic as a decorative feature rather than as a total building system.

Many Gothic secular buildings survive, some of the finest examples being the Bruges Town Hall (1376–1420) in Belgium, the Palazzo Pubblico (begun 1298) in Siena, Italy, and the Pont Valentré (early 14th century) in Cahors, France. The greatest concentration of Gothic sec-

The Norman (English Romanesque) Durham Cathedral (begun 1093) was the earliest church to have ribbed vaulting throughout. Much of this cathedral, including the Perpendicular Gothic towers, dates from the late Gothic period.

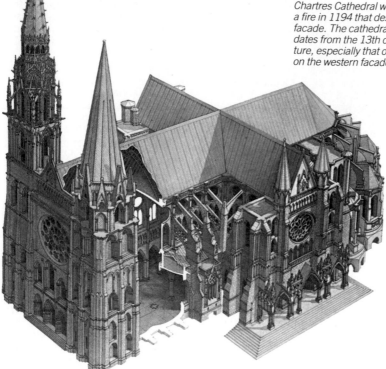

Chartres Cathedral was rebuilt in its present High Gothic form following a fire in 1194 that destroyed an earlier structure, except for the western facade. The cathedral is noted for its stained glass, most of which dates from the 13th century. It is also famous for its magnificent sculpture, especially that of the Early Gothic (mid-12th century) Royal Portal on the western facade.

(Above) The building of Amiens Cathedral in its present form was begun about 1220. Amiens, the largest Gothic cathedral in France, is notable for the height (42 m/138 ft) of its nave.

ular buildings is in Belgium, in what was then the most prosperous part of northwest Europe.

Renaissance Architecture. During the early 15th century, European culture became inspired by the rediscovery, known as the Renaissance, of classical literature, art, and architecture. Italy was the center of this rebirth, and in Florence, where the movement started, architecture was influenced by the use of the orders, the round arch, the barrel vault, and the dome—all Roman features. In north-

Filippo Brunelleschi's octagonal dome for Florence Cathedral (begun 1420) was the first great architectural achievement of the Renaissance.

ern Europe, where Gothic continued to flourish well into the 16th century, the Renaissance at first made only a superficial impact and was for a much longer time confined to decorative changes. In both France and England a truly classical style was not established until the first half of the 17th century: in France by François MANSART and in England by Inigo JONES.

The Florentine Renaissance did not initially mean the complete break with traditional practice that was implied in the Gothic north. For the church of Santo Spirito (begun c.1436), Filippo BRUNELLESCHI used a basilican plan, round arches, and a flat ceiling; but these traditional Italian Romanesque elements were combined with a new sense of proportion, the use of Corinthian columns, and a dome over the crossing of nave and transepts. Brunelleschi's later design for the vast, still unfinished cathedral of Santa Maria degli Angeli (also called the Duomo of Florence) took the form of a domed octagon with eight radiating chapels, a centralized plan that became the ideal among his contemporaries in Florence (Leon Battista ALBERTI and MICHELOZZO) and his followers in Rome. There, during the 16th century, a more monumental version of the style was developed by Donato BRAMANTE, RAPHAEL, and MICHELANGELO, as in their various plans for SAINT PETER'S BASILICA.

Baroque and Rococo Architecture. In the 15th century Florentine architecture relied for effect upon proportion, simple straight lines, and the correct use of classical details. During the 16th century, however, architects such

Giovanni Lorenzo Bernini's Piazza of St. Peter's (begun 1656), Rome, was designed to hold the vast crowds that come for the papal blessing. Commissioned by Pope Alexander VII, the keyhole-shaped piazza is surrounded by a free-standing colonnade.

as Michelangelo and GIULIO ROMANO abandoned this restraint for a more exciting, idiosyncratic version of the style, now called MANNERISM, in which the classical rules were deliberately flouted for effect. Giovanni Lorenzo BERNINI and Francesco BORROMINI further developed the style by introducing curvilinear forms and by incorporating sculpture and painting in their buildings to give a rich and dynamic version, known as BAROQUE, which spread during the 17th and 18th centuries from Rome to much of southern Europe and to South America.

In northern Europe, especially in Austria and Germany, baroque architecture achieved an exuberance and freedom unmatched elsewhere, climaxing in the ROCOCO, as in the Würzburg Residenz in West Germany. In France baroque and rococo were tempered by NEOCLASSICISM, with a resultant elegance and refinement in both architecture and decoration, exemplified by the 18th-century sections of the palace of VERSAILLES. The spread of neoclassical architecture during the 17th and 18th centuries was due in no small measure to the illustrated books that brought it to the attention of educated patrons. Although fine architecture has never been created by untalented architects, the rules of the classical orders enforced systematic convention in design that enabled many moderately competent architects to produce well-proportioned and finely detailed buildings. In part this explains the extraordinary success of the Palladian (see PALLADIO, Andrea) interpretation of Romanized Greek architecture. It was, for example, the source of almost all country-house building in England during the 18th century, as well as of numerous mansions, courthouses, state capitols, and universities along the eastern seaboard of North America.

The Age of Revivals. During the late 18th and 19th centuries, Europe and America witnessed a series of sty-

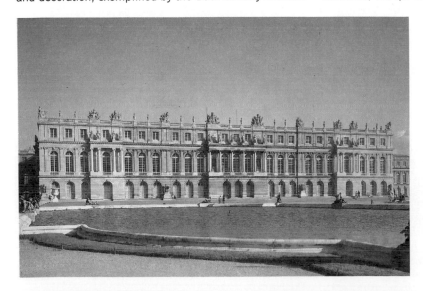

The garden facade of the Palace of Versailles (begun 1669) was designed by Louis Le Vau. The facade was altered in 1678 by Jules Hardouin-Mansart in order to add the famous Galerie des Glaces (Hall of Mirrors) on the main (2d) floor.

Johann Balthasar Neumann's Hofkirche (chapel) of the Würzburg Residenz (1732–41) is typical of the lavish German rococo style.

vived Gothic applied during the 19th century to private houses, office buildings, railroad stations, hospitals, and waterworks was by no means the same as the Gothic architecture of the northern medieval cathedrals. New engineering techniques and modern materials—in particular in CAST-IRON ARCHITECTURE—removed many of the age-old practical constraints on building design. Rapid urban growth during the 19th century produced a great many fine and essentially original buildings, the quality of which is only beginning to be appreciated.

Modern Architecture. Contemporary architecture takes a bewildering variety of forms and makes use of a far wider range of materials than ever before. The INTERNATIONAL STYLE, promulgated by Walter GROPIUS, LE CORBUSIER, and Ludwig MIES VAN DER ROHE in theory and practice, has dominated architecture in this century until very recently. Most of the earlier buildings by these architects were

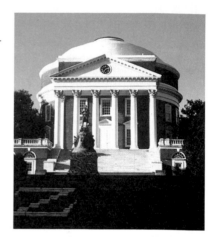

The neoclassical Rotunda is the focal point of Thomas Jefferson's design (1817–26) for the University of Virginia.

listic revivals. The period was dominated by the proponents of the classical (themselves split between "Greeks" and "Romans") and the northern Gothic. Buildings were also designed in self-conscious imitation of Byzantine, Oriental, Egyptian, Venetian Gothic, and Florentine Renaissance architecture, however. This was not, of course, the first time that ancient styles had been revived; the Italians of the 15th century and the architects of Charlemagne's court in the 9th century had incorporated classical motifs in their buildings. Both the revived classical and the GOTHIC REVIVAL, however, were essentially different from the architecture that inspired them.

The country mansion of England and colonial America bore a classical portico, but it was attached to a type of building never seen in ancient Rome or Greece. The re-

(Left) The Houses of Parliament, London, were built (1840–65) by Sir Charles Barry in the Gothic Revival style. Barry was assisted by A. W. N. Pugin, who was responsible for interior decoration and ornamental details. Big Ben is in the tower at the far right. (Right) Louis Sullivan's Carson, Pirie, Scott Store (1899–1904) in Chicago, is one of his most subtle buildings. The two lowest floors are ornamented with iron scrollwork; the upper floors are sheathed in light brick.

(Above) *The Kauf-mann House, "Fall-ingwater," at Bear Run, Pa., was designed (1936–37) by Frank Lloyd Wright. To integrate the house with its setting, the fer-roconcrete roots and terraces were cantilevered over the waterfall.* (Right) *Lever House (completed 1952) in New York City, designed by Gordon Bunshaft, uses glass curtain-wall construction and rises from a hori-zontal base that surrounds a roof-less garden court.*

small private houses, usually rectangular, with undeco-rated walls, flat roofs, and large areas of glass set in met-al frames. Conscious avoidance of any previous styles or recognizable antecedents was combined with highly sophisticated proportioning to achieve sleek, elegant structures, such as Mies's German Pavilion for the 1929 Barcelona Exhibition. To the dismay of its originators, the International Style was enthusiastically adopted by far lesser talents and profit-minded builders to produce nu-merous "modern" office buildings, apartment complexes, hospitals, and motels all over the world.

Not all contemporary architects subscribed to Mies's dictum of "less is more," and hence their work is difficult to classify as "modern."

Frank Lloyd WRIGHT, probably the outstanding Ameri-can architect of this century, Kenzo TANGE of Japan, Alvar AALTO of Finland, and the Finnish-Americans Eliel and Eero SAARINEN produced many buildings of great beauty and originality.

Although some of their work does reflect the Interna-tional Style, most of their buildings are instantly recog-nizable in their individuality, as were the great buildings of the past.

In short, these architects and others like them seem to be part of a continuing architectural tradition rejected by the practitioners of the International Style.

The social turmoil of the 1960s was emphatically re-flected in architecture. *Complexity and Contradiction in Modern Architecture* (1968) by the architect Robert VEN-TURI was a revolt against the ubiquitous glass boxes of the modernists, and it signaled the emergence of POSTMODERN ARCHITECTURE. Since that time, architects have found new strength in the traditions of the past, as well as in the ver-nacular architecture seen all about them.

See also: COLONIAL STYLES IN NORTH AMERICA; HISTORIC PRESERVATION; HOUSE IN WESTERN ARCHITECTURE; LANDSCAPE ARCHITECTURE; URBAN PLANNING.

architrave   see ARCHITECTURE

archon [ahr'-kahn]   In ancient Greek city-states, ar-chons were state magistrates of the highest order. Athens had at first three archons—one each to wield religious, military, and civil powers. In the 8th century BC their ten-ure was for ten years, but by 683 BC tenure was reduced to one year. Soon thereafter, six court magistrates (called *themosthetai*) were elected, in addition to the archons, to record judicial decisions. The nine positions were the fo-cus of fierce political rivalry in the 7th and 6th centuries BC. After 487 BC archons were chosen by lot from all three social classes, and their importance diminished. Ex-ar-chons became lifetime members of the AREOPAGUS.

Arcimboldo, Giuseppe [ahr-cheem-bohl'-doh] Giuseppe Arcimboldo, b. Milan, c.1527, d. July 11, 1593, an Italian MANNERIST painter, is best known for his paintings of bizarre heads formed by combinations of fruits, flowers, animals, or fish. In his youth he painted for the Milan Cathedral. In 1562 he entered the service of the Habsburgs in Vienna and Prague and became court painter to Maximilian II and Rudolf II. Works painted in the grotesque style for which he is famous include a Four Seasons series (1563; Kunsthistorisches Museum, Vien-na) and a portrait of John Calvin (1566; Gripsholm Cas-tle, Sweden).

Arctic   The Arctic is the northernmost region of the Earth. Centering on the North Pole, the region includes the ARCTIC OCEAN, the northernmost sections of North America and Eurasia, and the numerous islands and ar-chipelagoes that fringe the northern coasts of these two continents. The region thus encompasses all of GREEN-LAND (a Danish territory) and all the northern parts of Can-ada, Alaska (U.S.), the USSR, Finland, Sweden, and Norway. The major islands are those of the Canadian Ar-chipelago (including BAFFIN, ELLESMERE, VICTORIA, Banks,

An Eskimo hunter hunts seals from a kayak as his dog team waits on the shore. The Eskimo, whose name is derived from an Algonquian Indian term meaning "eaters of raw meat," prefer to be called Inuit.

Sverdrup, Parry, Prince of Wales, and Axel-Heiberg); the Norwegian island group of SVALBARD (including Spitsbergen); and FRANZ JOSEF LAND, NOVAYA ZEMLYA, and the New Siberian Islands, all of which are part of the USSR. Whether Iceland is placed within, or excluded from, the Arctic depends on the criteria used to define the southern limit of the region.

The southern limit of the Arctic region is most commonly placed at the Arctic Circle (lat. 60°30' N); this is also the southernmost limit of the midnight sun, or 24-hour summer day. Some experts, however, regard the tree line as the edge of the Arctic. Others place the edge of the region along the 10° C (50° F) isotherm (a line connecting points of equal temperature) for the warmest month of the year, or along the –4° C (25° F) annual isotherm.

The name *Arctic* is derived from the Greek word *arktos*, meaning "bear," and is a reference to the constellation Ursa Major, or Great Bear, which appears prominently in the northern sky.

Physical Geography

The Arctic, unlike Antarctica, is mostly free of snow and ice cover in the summer months. Glaciers are common throughout the archipelagoes, but the only permanent ice sheet, that of Greenland, is about one-eighth the size of the ANTARCTICA ice sheet. In the Arctic, snow is subject to melting and evaporation more than in Antarctica, and thus ice buildup is less. The region's long, cold winters do produce an all-year layer of drifting ice, 5–7 m (16–23 ft) thick, on the central (and some coastal) areas of the Arc-

tic Ocean. This ice covers a larger area in winter than in summer, but open water exists even in the winter months. PERMAFROST, or permanently frozen ground, occurs in all Arctic lands and commonly extends to a depth hundreds of meters below the surface. In warmer areas a shallow layer may thaw in summer, and the meltwater will form vast marshy areas and myriads of lakes.

Topography. At one time or another during the Pleistocene Epoch (2,000,000 to 10,000 years ago), most of the Arctic was covered by ice sheets, although some areas such as northern Alaska and parts of SIBERIA appear to have escaped glaciation. Glaciation dissected the existing mountain ranges, but the Arctic was a region of low average elevation before the Pleistocene Epoch began.

The continental fringes bordering the Arctic Ocean in both North America and Eurasia are generally low-lying. Four major rivers—the MACKENZIE in North America and the LENA, OB, and YENISEI in Eurasia—flow north to the Arctic Ocean.

By contrast, many of the Arctic islands are relatively rugged, and low mountains rise precipitously from the sea. Baffin, Devon, Ellesmere, and Axel-Heiberg, the four islands in the Canadian Archipelago where the principal glaciers are found, rise to about 2,000 m (6,600 ft.). Approximately 80% of the even higher island of Greenland is also covered by ice. More than half of the islands of Svalbard, the most westerly of the Arctic islands, are buried under glaciers, as are about 85% of Franz Josef Land and 25% of Novaya Zemlya, off the coast of the USSR. About half of Severnaya Zemlya, an archipelago north of central Siberia, is also covered by ice. Small glaciers are found in the northeastern New Siberian Islands, off the coast of eastern Siberia, although the highest point is only 374 m (1,227 ft) above sea level.

Mineral Resources. The Arctic is the site of many valuable mineral deposits. The USSR mines gold, tin, tungsten, diamonds, nickel, copper, and coal in the Arctic. Coal is mined in Svalbard, and iron ore is mined in northern Sweden. In 1968 vast oil and natural-gas deposits were found on the North Slope at PRUDHOE BAY, Alaska. Geologic exploration continues throughout the North American Arctic.

Climate. Climatically, the Arctic is a cold desert; that is, it receives (with local exceptions) less than 250 mm (10 in) of precipitation annually. Indeed, some areas of the Arctic, such as Peary Land in northern Greenland, are drier than the world's tropical deserts. Generally, precipitation ranges from 250 mm (10 in) in the southern regions to less than 125 mm (5 in) in the north. Most precipitation falls as snow (an annual average of about 300–600 mm/12–24 in) in the autumn and the early spring.

Arctic winters are long and cold, and summers are short and cool. The region receives minimal solar heat owing to the low angle at which the Sun's rays strike the

Earth even during the long summer days; in winter the Sun does not rise above the horizon.

The Arctic Ocean, which receives relatively warm north-flowing currents from the Atlantic and Pacific, acts as a moderating influence, especially on the surrounding shores and islands. A temperature INVERSION exists over the region during much of the year, the result of relatively warm air coming into contact with a lower layer cooled by the ground. In summer, especially, this is associated with cloud cover and fog. Smog, probably from Eurasian industrial areas, has accumulated over parts of the Arctic; some scientists think such pollution will affect the climate. Thinning of the OZONE LAYER above the Arctic has also been observed.

The Greenland ice sheet and the Arctic Ocean maintain cold temperatures throughout the year, but the tundra-covered coastal fringes warm up each summer for a brief period. Minimum temperatures of –70° C (–94° F) are approached or reached in Greenland and have been recorded at Verkhoyansk, in Siberia; maximum temperatures of about –5° C (23° F) to 2° C (36° F) are common on the ice sheet, and highs of 20°–40° C (70°–100° F) on land areas. The annual temperature range is greatest

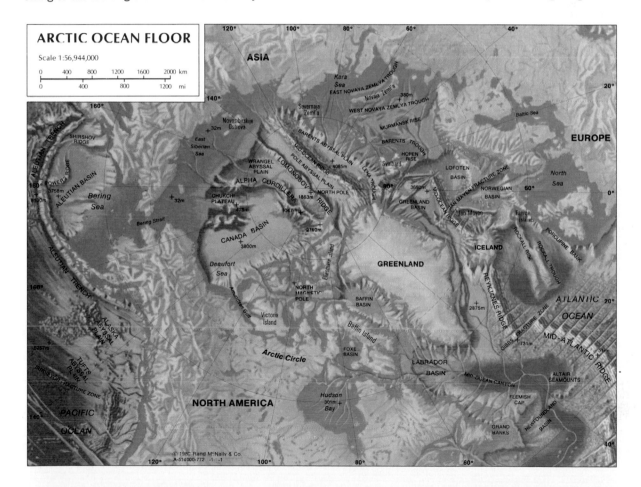

peregrine falcon

caribou

wolves

wolverine

musk-oxen

snowy owl

short-tail weasel

snowshoe hare

ORR

in parts of Siberia, approaching 100 C degrees (180 F degrees). Arctic winds are less prevalent and strong than those of Antarctica, but coasts are subject to cyclonic storms.

Flora and Fauna

Despite the Arctic's harsh environment, the zone contains a varied plant and animal life. Cycles of overpopulation and food scarcity characterize Arctic ecology. Humans living in the Arctic have long had a stable relationship with their environment, but modern technology threatens this relationship.

Plants. Arctic plants have evolved many specialized adaptations for life on the windswept tundra, with its low precipitation and long, severe winters. Trees and shrubs that grow there are much smaller than related forms to the south, and their tissues are far more resistant to freezing and thawing. (The recent discovery of a fossil forest in the Canadian Arctic indicates that trees were more substantial in the past.) Arctic plants have short roots because of permafrost. Mosses and lichens are the most common plant life, the lichens helping to break down surface rocks into soil. During the brief summer, grasses and attractive flowering plants appear, sometimes completing their entire life cycle within one month.

Animals. Arctic animal life is more familiarly represented by the polar bear, which roams the snow and ice, and the caribou, which migrates in vast herds across the

(Opposite page) Snow buntings migrate to the Arctic in April and are considered by Greenlanders to be signs of spring. Peregrine falcons, found in almost all habitats of the world, patrol the Arctic sky in pursuit of smaller birds or dive and attack lemmings and hares. Caribou are Canadian reindeer of subarctic tundras. They annually migrate toward the Barren Grounds, a subarctic prairie west of Hudson Bay. Wolves, headed by an experienced leader, chase the caribou and prey upon the lame, weak, and sick members of the herd. Musk-oxen can withstand the full blast of Arctic winters after other animals have hibernated or migrated south. Musk-oxen are protected by heavy wool coats and are well armed with huge, curved horns and heavy hooves. The wolverine of Old and New World subarctic tundras is considered by Eskimos, Lapps, and Mongols as the embodiment of evil because it is a fearless, vicious killer of almost all animals. A snowy owl clutches its prey, a snowshoe hare, as a short-tail weasel looks on. The owl, hare, and weasel all have white coats in winter and brown coats in summer. (Below) Along an Arctic shore a polar bear strikes its prey, the ringed seal, with its huge paw. This bear lives a nomadic life along arctic shores and on pack ice, following the migrations of the seal. Arctic foxes feed on seal carcasses left by the bear. The polar bear fears only killer whales and walruses as it swims along the shore. A walrus, which feeds on small marine mollusks, using its tusks to tear its foe, has no enemies but humans. Even killer whales, which hunt in packs for sea animals, avoid an adult walrus and attack only walrus infants. Storms have forced migrating walruses to travel as far as 33 km (20.5 miles) over the snow.

killer whale

walrus

arctic fox

polar bear

ringed seal

Fridtjof Nansen's Fram *("Forward") is held fast in the Arctic ice during his voyage of 1893–96. The Norwegian explorer failed in his attempt to drift to Greenland in the pack ice, but, on foot, led a team within 472 km (272 mi) of the North Pole.*

tundra in search of food. Besides caribou and polar bears, large Arctic land mammals include other bears and muskoxen. Among the several small Arctic land mammals are rodents such as voles and lemmings; weasels such as ermines, martins, and sables; foxes; squirrels; and hares.

Arctic sea mammals such as the narwhal, walrus, seal, and sea lion usually migrate, but fishes such as cod, salmon, and char are found in Arctic waters and below the ice cap throughout the year. Insects and other invertebrate species inhabit milder regions of the zone. Generally, the adult insect forms stay below the snow in winter, but their eggs and pupae can survive below the surface. The high GLYCEROL content of some adult insects enables them to withstand extreme cold without freezing. The absence of predatory reptiles, together with the long summer days and the abundance of insects, makes the tundra an ideal breeding place for ground-nesting birds. These include many kinds of waterfowl, sandpipers, plovers, and some hawks, ptarmigans, cranes, owls, larks, and finches.

As the Arctic winter approaches, all herbivorous mammals and many carnivores acquire fat reserves. Besides acting as an energy reserve, the fat serves as excellent insulation. In addition to fat, the larger land mammals have thick coats of fur. The hair seals and walruses, lacking a dense coat of fur, are equipped with a thick blubber layer, as are the Arctic whales. A dominant characteristic of most Arctic animals is their white color, the degree of which is related to the winter climate in a given region.

Some animals, such as the polar bear and snowy owl, are white the year round; others, such as the Arctic fox, alternate with a darker summer color. The color helps conceal both predator and prey in winter.

People

The harsh Arctic environment supports a sparse but varied population. In North America the principal Arctic inhabitants are the small numbers of miners, technicians, and government workers who come north for short periods of service and a far larger number of ESKIMO, or as they prefer to be called, Inuit. The principal inhabitants of the European Arctic are the LAPPS, a people of Finno-Ugrian origin, who now occupy the northern parts of Norway, Sweden, Finland, and the northwestern USSR collectively referred to as Lapland. The Arctic reaches of the central and northeastern USSR are occupied by numerous ethnic groups, including a small number of YAKUT, Eskimo, Chukchi, and Samoyed.

Exploration

The recorded history of the Arctic lands dates from the early 9th century when, according to Icelandic sagas, Irish monks were living in Iceland. In about AD 850, Norsemen settled in Iceland. The first reported sighting of Greenland was by Gunnbjörn Ulfsson, but the credit for actual exploration of the island goes to ERIC THE RED, who visited the western coast about 982 and, in about 986, set up a colony in the southwestern part of the island that survived for several centuries. Spitsbergen was discovered in 1194 and was used as a base by Norsemen who explored eastward as far as the island Novaya Zemlya.

In the 15th and 16th centuries, in their search for a northern sea route to China, explorers rediscovered many of the Arctic islands. Martin FROBISHER, who commanded the first (1576) of numerous British expeditions charged with finding a NORTHWEST PASSAGE, discovered in the course of his voyages Frobisher Bay in southern Baffin Island and accurately mapped for the first time parts of Greenland and the Canadian Archipelago.

Willem BARENTS, a Dutch navigator for whom the Barents Sea is named, searched for a NORTHEAST PASSAGE in 1596–97. His expedition rediscovered Spitsbergen and wintered on Novaya Zemlya, the first (in recorded history) to survive the hardships of an Arctic winter. Henry HUDSON led the first expedition to survive the winter (1610–11) in Hudson Bay.

Exploration of the Russian Arctic occurred during the conquest of Siberia beginning in the 17th century. Between 1728 and 1741, Vitus BERING, a Dane in Russian service, became the first to sail through the strait between Asia and North America that now bears his name.

In the 19th century there was a renewed interest in Arctic exploration. In 1818, Sir William Edward PARRY and Sir John Ross retraced the 1615–16 voyage of William BAFFIN and opened up an extensive area of Baffin Bay to whaling interests. In 1831, Sir James Clark ROSS, a nephew of John Ross, became the first man to reach the north magnetic pole.

In 1847, Sir John FRANKLIN became the first man to

The U.S. Navy commander Robert E. Peary (above), *his associate Matthew A. Henson* (below), *and four Eskimo became the first people to reach the North Pole, on Apr. 6, 1909, although Peary's imprecise records later raised questions about his claim. Henson, b. 1866, d. Mar. 9, 1955, accompanied Peary on each of his eight Arctic voyages and was noted for his technical skills and his ability to communicate with the Eskimo. The son of a tenant farmer, he went to sea at the age of 12. Henson's long association with Peary began in 1887, on a surveying mission to Nicaragua. His account of the famous final dash to the pole,* A Negro at the North Pole, *was published in 1912.*

and allowed the ship, frozen into the ice, to drift for three years across the ocean. Their scientific observations set new standards for oceanographic and Arctic research. Nansen left the icebound *Fram* in 1895 and, with Hjalmar Johansen, made an unsuccessful effort to reach the North Pole by dogsled and kayak, setting a new record for northward exploration by reaching 86°14' north latitude.

Vilhjalmur Stefansson explored many parts of the Arctic in the early part of the 20th century, and Knud RASMUSSEN's 1921–24 studies of the American Eskimo are recorded in his famous book, *Across Arctic America* (1927). The *Gjoa*, under the command of Roald AMUNDSEN, became the first ship to successfully navigate the Northwest Passage; Amundsen also navigated (1918–1920) the Northeast Passage.

Robert E. PEARY, after several unsuccessful attempts, finally reached the North Pole for the first time on Apr. 6, 1909. On May 9, 1926, Admiral Richard E. BYRD and Floyd BENNETT became the first men to fly to the pole by airplane; and, just three days later, Lincoln ELLSWORTH, Umberto Nobile, and Roald Amundsen crossed the pole for the first time in a dirigible. Sir Hubert WILKINS and Carl Eielson were the first to cross the Arctic Ocean by fixed-wing airplane in 1928. In 1958 two U.S. Navy submarines crossed the North Pole under the Arctic Ocean ice pack. Wally Herbert's British Trans-Arctic Expedition (1968–69) made the first successful surface crossing of the Arctic Ocean. On May 1, 1978, the Japanese explorer Naomi Uemura made the first one-person expedition to the North Pole. A Canadian team surveyed the Alpha Ridge, a huge underwater mountain range, in 1983.

Many nations have expressed interest in the Arctic's resources and concern for the Arctic environment. The Inuit (Eskimo People's) Circumpolar Conference, founded in 1980, has worked to formulate an Arctic policy on oil development, military maneuvers, and weapons testing that will preserve the traditional Inuit way of life.

find a sea passage through the North American Arctic, but it was blocked by ice and unnavigable. After Franklin's death the members of his party set out on foot, and all perished. Relief expeditions sent out to find or to learn the fate of the missing Franklin party brought much new knowledge of the region. On one such expedition, Sir Robert McClure made the first traverse (1853) of a route by foot and boat that, if not icebound, would have realized the British dream of a Northwest Passage. Richard Collinson discovered another sea route, but it, too, was icebound and unnavigable. Interest in the Eurasian Arctic was similarly renewed in the 19th century, and in 1878–79, Adolf Erik Nordenskjöld successfully navigated the Northeast Passage for the first time.

International polar conferences in 1879 and 1880 advanced the idea of international cooperation in conducting systematic meteorologic and magnetic observations in the Arctic. Starting in 1882 observation stations were set up by several countries.

In 1888, Fridtjof NANSEN, Otto Sverdrup, and others became the first people known to have crossed Greenland. In 1893, Nansen and Sverdrup sailed the *Fram* into the Arctic Ocean pack ice off the New Siberian Islands

Arctic Ocean

Arctic Ocean   The Arctic Ocean, located entirely in the North Pole region, is the smallest of the world's oceans. It occupies a roughly circular basin and covers an area of about 14,090,000 km² (5,440,000 mi²). Nearly landlocked, the ocean is surrounded by the landmasses of Europe, Asia, North America, and Greenland and a number of islands, as well as by the BARENTS, BEAUFORT, Chukchi, Kara, Laptev, East Siberian, Lincoln, Wandel, Greenland, and Norwegian seas. It is connected to the Pacific Ocean by the BERING STRAIT and to the Atlantic Ocean through the Greenland Sea.

An underwater ridge, the LOMONOSOV RIDGE, divides the Arctic Ocean into two basins: the Eurasian, or Nansen, Basin, which is between 4,000 and 4,500 m (13,000 and 15,000 ft) deep, and the North American, or Hyperborean, Basin, which is about 4,000 m deep. The topography of the ocean bottom is marked by ridges, plains of the abyssal zone, and basins.

The greatest inflow of water comes from the Atlantic via the Norwegian Current, which then flows along the Eurasian coast. Water also enters from the Pacific via the

The S.S. Manhattan, *a 150,000-ton icebreaking tanker, proceeds slowly through the frozen Arctic Ocean. In 1969 it became the first merchant ship to navigate the Northwest Passage, showing the possibility of using that route to transport petroleum.*

Bering Strait. The East Greenland Current carries the major outflow.

Temperature and salinity vary seasonally as the ice cover melts and freezes. Ice covers most of the ocean surface year-round, causing subfreezing temperatures much of the time. The Arctic is a major source of very cold air that inevitably moves toward the equator, meeting with warmer air in the middle latitudes and causing rain and snow. Little marine life exists where the ocean surface is covered with ice throughout the year. Marine life abounds in open areas, especially the more southerly waters. The ocean's major ports are the Soviet cities of MURMANSK and ARKHANGELSK (Archangel). The Arctic Ocean is strategically important as the shortest route between North America and the USSR.

Ardennes [ahr-den'] The Ardennes is a region of heavily wooded dissected plateaus and rounded peaks, located mostly in southwestern Belgium and extending into Luxembourg and northeastern France. Rising to the east of the Meuse River valley, the plateau reaches 694 m (2,277 ft) at Botrange, in Belgium. The Ardennes's proximity to major corridors of Western Europe has often made it a battleground, notably in 1914 and 1918 during World War I, and it was the site of the Battle of the Bulge (1944) during World War II. The infertile and frequently boggy soil is unsuitable for most agriculture, but tourism is important at such resorts as Spa, Belgium.

Arduino, Giovanni [ahr-dwee'-noh] Giovanni Arduino, b. Oct. 16, 1714, d. Mar. 21, 1795, an Italian geologist, pioneered the classification of rocks into chronological sequences (see STRATIGRAPHY). Although his par-

ents were poor, a noble's patronage permitted him to study at Verona and to become a mining expert. Commissioned (1769) by the Republic of Venice to develop its agriculture and industry and later to study its mines, he also worked for several mining companies in Italy and taught mineralogy and metallurgy in Venice. In 1759, Arduino published his observation that mountains comprise groups of rock formations uplifted at different times. About the same time, the German chemist Johann Gottlob Lehmann made a similar, independent announcement. From observations in the Alps, Arduino divided the rocks of the Earth's crust into primary, secondary, tertiary, and quaternary groups. He recognized that fossils change according to the age of the rocks in which they occur, and he explained upheaval and subsidence of the Earth's surface as having been produced by volcanoes.

area Area is a measure of the size of a closed region. It is expressed as the number of square units contained in the region. A unit of area is a square of a unit of length. Areas of many irregular figures or other figures whose areas could not be calculated directly were calculated in the past by a limiting process called the method of exhaustion. Such areas are now calculated by methods of INTEGRAL CALCULUS. Formulas for the areas of many plane geometric figures are given in separate articles on each figure.

Arecibo Observatory [ah-ray-see'-boh] Arecibo Observatory, located 15 km (9 mi) south of Arecibo, Puerto Rico, is part of the National Astronomy and Ionosphere Center. Conceived in 1958 by William E. Gordon,

The Arecibo Observatory in northern Puerto Rico operates a radio telescope capable not only of intercepting radio waves from the far reaches of the universe, but also of bouncing radar signals off planets, satellites, and particulate matter in the atmosphere.

a Cornell University professor of electrical engineering, the radio observatory has been operated, since its completion in 1963, by Cornell under contract with the National Science Foundation. Its chief instrument is a 1,000-ft-wide (305-m) immobile radio telescope, composed of 38,778 individual panels, each attached to a network of steel cables stretched across a natural valley. Three towers support a 600-ton triangular platform that hovers over the dish and collects or transmits radio signals. Another smaller telescope is used in conjunction with the main reflector for interferometric studies.

Major research programs at Arecibo include studies of the Earth's middle atmosphere and ionosphere to an elevation of 5,000 km (3,100 mi), investigations of planetary surfaces through the analysis of reflected radar signals, and observations of radio objects within and outside our own galaxy.

Arendt, Hannah [ar'-ent]

Hannah Arendt, b. Hanover, Germany, Oct. 14, 1906, d. Dec. 4, 1975, was a teacher, writer, and political philosopher. Arendt was educated at the universities of Marburg, Freiburg, and Heidelberg. In 1933 she left Germany for France; in 1941, fleeing the Nazis, she went to the United States. She worked for Jewish relief agencies until 1952, afterward devoting herself primarily to university teaching and writing. She held professorial positions at Princeton, the University of Chicago, and the New School for Social Research. Her books, which viewed the human condition pessimistically, generated extensive controversy when they appeared. They included *The Origins of Totalitarianism* (1951), *The Human Condition* (1958), *Eichmann in Jerusalem* (1963), *On Revolution* (1963), *On Violence* (1970), *Crises of the Republic* (1972), and *The Life of the Mind* (1977).

Arensky, Anton Stepanovich [uh-rayn'-skee]

Anton Stepanovich Arensky, b. July 12, 1861, d. Feb. 25, 1906, was a Russian composer whose lyrical style marked him as a follower of Peter Ilich Tchaikovsky. After studying musical composition with Nikolai Rimsky-Korsakov in St. Petersburg (Leningrad), he taught music theory in the Moscow Conservatory. Among Arensky's pupils was Sergei Rachmaninoff. Arensky composed three operas, two symphonies, considerable chamber music, including the popular *Piano Trio* dedicated to Tchaikovsky's memory, numerous vocal works, and many piano compositions. His *Variations on a Theme of Tchaikovsky* for string orchestra is frequently heard in concert.

Areopagitica   see MILTON, JOHN

Areopagus [ar-ee-ahp'-uh-guhs]

The Areopagus was the principal council of ancient ATHENS. It took its name from the Hill (Greek, *pagos*) of Ares, just northwest of the Acropolis, where it convened. It probably began as the king's advisory council, but its judicial and legislative power increased as the monarchy declined. It ruled in murder cases and had important religious functions as well as censorship powers over state officers. After 487 BC, with democratic changes in government, the choosing of the ARCHONS (chief magistrates) by lot, and the advance of naval power, the influence of the Areopagus began to decline. It retained its religious functions and its position as a homicide court, however, and survived into the 4th century AD.

Ares [air'-eez]

In Greek mythology, Ares, the son of ZEUS and brother of ERIS, was the god of war. Although he was not greatly admired among the Olympian gods, he was loved by APHRODITE, by whom he became the father of several children. In Homer's ILIAD, Ares is depicted as a warrior god who exults in bloodshed and violence. Called variously the avenger, the slayer, and the curse, Ares used a spear as his emblem. The vulture and the dog were sacred to him. In the TROJAN WAR, he favored the Trojans. In Roman mythology, he was identified with MARS.

Aretino, Pietro [ah-ray-tee'-noh]

Pietro Aretino, b. Apr. 20, 1492, d. Oct. 21, 1556, was an Italian satirist whose forthright, witty, and often wicked pen earned him the sobriquet "Scourge of Princes." Forced to leave Rome, in spite of papal protection, because of the enmity aroused by his journalistic exposures, he settled in Venice in 1527. Thereafter he devoted himself in equal measure to a lavish libertinism (supported by blackmail) and serious literary pursuits. *I ragionamenti* (The Harlot's Dialogues, 1534–36), illustrated by the painter GIULIO ROMANO, colorfully demonstrates Aretino's dual concerns. His spoof of Roman corruption in *The Courtesan* (1534; Eng. trans., 1926) and his *Lettere* (1537–57) demonstrate his intimate knowledge of the mores of High Renaissance Italy.

Argelander, Friedrich Wilhelm August

A German astronomer who pioneered in the field of variable stars, Friedrich Argelander, b. Mar. 22, 1799, d. Feb. 17, 1875, compiled the last extensive star catalog made without the aid of photography and cofounded the Astronomische Gesellschaft, the first significant international organization of astronomers. His *Uranometria Nova* (1843), a star catalog, superseded Johann Bayer's *Uranometria* (1603); his monumental *Bonner Durchmusterung* (1859–62), a catalog of more than 324,000 stars brighter than magnitude 9.5, is still used.

Argenteuil [ahr-zhahn-toy']

Argenteuil (1982 pop., 95,347) is a suburban industrial city in northern France located on the Seine River about 8 km (5 mi) northwest of Paris. Industries produce metal, chemicals, transportation equipment, and furniture. The town grew around a 7th-century convent, where, in the 12th century, Heloïse served as prioress during her romance with Peter ABELARD.

AT A GLANCE

ARGENTINE REPUBLIC

Land: Area: 2,766,889 km² (1,068,301 mi²). Capital and largest city: Buenos Aires (1982 est. pop., 2,879,000).

People: Population (1990 est.): 32,291,000. Density: 11.6 persons per km² (30.2 per mi²). Distribution (1989): 85% urban,15% rural. Official language: Spanish. Major religion: Roman Catholicism.

Government: Type: republic. Legislature: Congress. Political subdivisions: 22 provinces, 1 federal district, 1 national territory.

Economy: GNP (1989): $72 billion; $2,217 per capita. Labor distribution (1985 est.): services—57%; industry—31%; agriculture—12%. Foreign trade (1989): imports—$4.3 billion; exports—$9.6 billion. Currency: 1 austral = 100 centavos.

Education and Health: Literacy (1988): 94% of adult population. Universities (1988): 52. Hospital beds (1980):151,568. Physicians (1984): 81,260. Life expectancy (1990): women—74; men—67. Infant mortality (1990): 32 per 1,000 live births.

A seamless robe given by Charlemagne, thought to have been worn by Jesus, is enshrined in St.-Denis Basilica (1866). Argenteuil was a favorite subject of the impressionist painters.

Argentina   Argentina, the second largest (after Brazil) and the third most populous country (after Brazil and Mexico) in Latin America, occupies most of the southern portion of South America. It is bordered by Chile to the east (with whom it shares the island of TIERRA DEL FUEGO), Bolivia and Paraguay to the north, and Brazil and Uruguay to the northeast. On its east and south, Argentina has an extensive Atlantic coastline. Its north-south length is about 3,500 km (2,175 mi), and its greatest width is about 1,400 km (870 mi). BUENOS AIRES, the capital, is one of the world's great cities.

Argentina is among the more highly developed countries in the Western Hemisphere. Its economy has gradually shifted from an exclusive dependence on the large-scale production of livestock and agricultural goods to one in which the industrial and service sectors are now dominant. Since the 1950s, it has been one of the world's principal trading nations.

Land and Resources

Physical Regions. Argentina is primarily a country of lowlands, although the ANDES, which occupy its western periphery, rise to an elevation of 6,960 m (22,834 ft) in the peak of ACONCAGUA, the highest point in the Western Hemisphere. There are four main topographical regions: the PAMPAS, PATAGONIA, the Andes and their foothills, and the Northeast.

The flat, fertile Pampas of east and central Argentina comprise approximately one-fourth of the total area. The eastern, humid Pampas receive as much as 1,000 mm (40 in) of precipitation a year, while in the dry Pampas to the west the average rainfall is less than 500 mm (20 in). To the south of the Pampas, south of the Río Colorado, lies Patagonia, with arid, windy plateaus. The Andean and plateau region in the western part of the country includes most of the ranges, or cordilleras, of the Andes, the hills of the Sierra de Córdoba, and the desert and mountains of the old colonial region in the northwest. The northeast, one-fifth of the country's area, comprises the forested plains of the CHACO, the subtropical Misiones, and the floodplains and gently rolling land Mesopotamia, between the PARANÁ and URUGUAY rivers.

Soils. The soils of the Pampas, among the richest in the world, consist of an accumulation of loose, wind-blown materials (LOESS), resting upon granite and other ancient crystalline rock, entirely free of stones. Argentina's less productive soils range from LATERITE in the north to desert sands in the west.

Climate. Most of Argentina has a temperate climate. The extreme heat of the northern Chaco, which has an annual mean temperature of 23° C (74° F) with about 14 days a year of nearly 45° C (113° F), and the high hu-

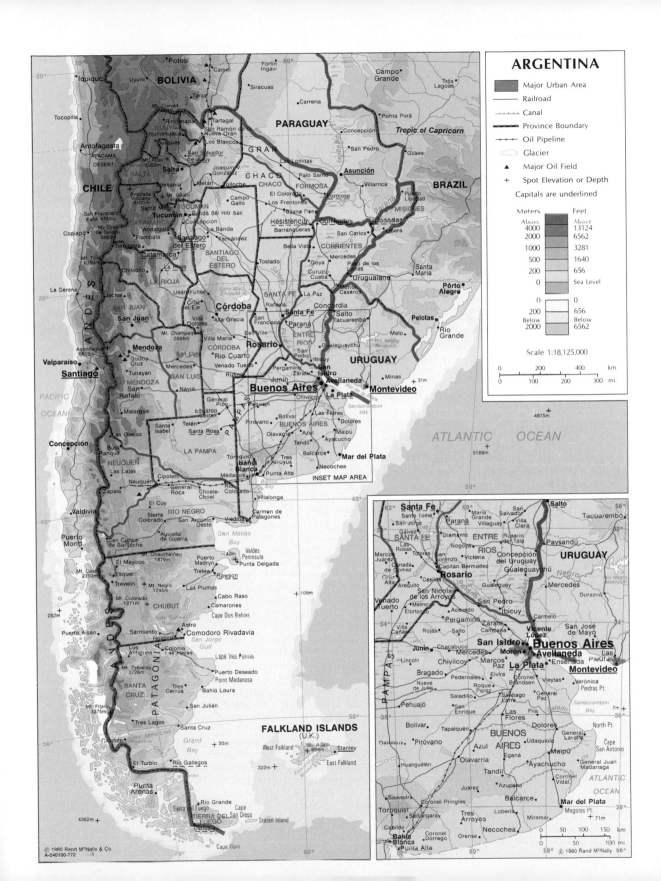

ARGENTINA

Major Urban Area
Railroad
Canal
Province Boundary
Oil Pipeline
Glacier
▲ Major Oil Field
+ Spot Elevation or Depth
Capitals are underlined

Meters	Feet
Above 4000	Above 13124
2000	6562
1000	3281
500	1640
200	656
0	Sea Level
0	0
200	656
Below 2000	Below 6562

Scale 1:18,125,000

0 200 400 km
0 100 200 300 mi

INSET MAP AREA

PACIFIC OCEAN

ATLANTIC OCEAN

FALKLAND ISLANDS (U.K.)
West Falkland   East Falkland
Stanley
Mt. Adam 698m

© 1980 Rand McNally & Co.
A-540100-772 -1

© 1980 Rand McNally

The Palace of the National Congress in Buenos Aires is the seat of the Argentine legislature. More than one-third of the nation's population lives within the city's metropolitan area, making Buenos Aires the largest city in the Southern Hemisphere.

midity of the northeast (85%–90% during the winter) are gradually ameliorated toward the central Pampas, which enjoy an annual mean temperature of 16° C (60° F) and humidity of 76%. Farther south, the cool, windy, and dry climate of Patagonia turns into glacial cold at higher altitudes in the Andes.

In the northern two-thirds of the country, winter (May to August) is the driest period of the year. Rainfall diminishes from east to west and toward the south, with about 2,000 mm (80 in) a year in Misiones, 940 mm (37 in) in Buenos Aires, and 750 mm (30 in) in the Chaco. Annual precipitation is less than 250 mm (10 in) in Patagonia, and only 50 mm (2 in) in the far west and the northwest of the country.

Drainage. Argentina's five great river systems drain eastward into the Atlantic Ocean. The largest is the Paraná, Paraguay, and Uruguay system in the north, which empties into the Río de la Plata estuary. All these rivers are more or less navigable. Large areas of the Pampas are poorly drained. At a zone of marshes southwest of Rosario and Buenos Aires the water table rises during the wet season (October to April) so that much of the surface becomes marshy with shallow lakes. The Colorado, Negro, and Chubut are the principal rivers of Patagonia.

Vegetation and Animal Life. Argentina has a wide variety of vegetation. With their cold, dry climate, Patagonia and Tierra del Fuego have few trees and are covered by low shrubs and grasses. The Pampas constitute South America's largest area of grassland. The Chaco region is characterized by both forests (including quebracho and carob trees) and savanna. In the temperate northeast are forests of carob and palm, and in the more humid Andes deciduous forests flourish. Animal life in Argentina is especially rich. Llama and vicuña inhabit the Andean tracts; jaguars, pumas, monkeys, deer, foxes, and wild boars are found at lower elevations. Birds, including the condor,

and fish are particularly numerous, and the country is one of the richest in dinosaur fossils.

Resources. Argentina's mineral deposits are mostly small and in remote regions. Petroleum is the only mineral produced in a substantial quantity, and about 21 million metric tons (over 23 million U.S. tons) are extracted each year, making Argentina nearly self-sufficient in liquid fuels.

People

Most Argentinians are descendants of either the Spaniards who settled in the 16th century or the millions of European immigrants who arrived in the late 19th and early 20th centuries. The MESTIZO (mixed Indian and European) and Indian populations, once a majority, now number only about 30,000. Blacks were originally brought in as slaves but as a separate racial group have virtually disappeared. The largest groups of immigrants entering Argentina between 1857 and 1940 were Italians (44%) and Spaniards (31%). Other western Europeans, such as the French, Germans, Austrians, British, Swiss, and Portuguese, accounted for fewer than 10% of the immigrants. Eastern Europeans, including Poles, Russians, Hungarians, Turks, and Yugoslavs, made up about 9% of the new population. Since the mid-20th century many Paraguayans, Bolivians, and Chileans have crossed the border into Argentina. The Argentine Jewish population is the largest in Latin America and among the largest in the world.

Language. Spanish is both the official and the popular language. It is a distinctly Argentine Spanish, with its own expressions and pronunciation. A dialect called Spanish Lunfardo, developed in Buenos Aires before 1900, has many borrowed words from Italian and Portuguese. Bilingualism among immigrants and their descendants is considerable; in the Buenos Aires area there are a dozen community newspapers printed in languages other than Spanish. Indian languages, including Guaraní, Quechua, and Tehuelche, are spoken by only about 1 person in 1,000.

Religion. More than 90% of the Argentine people identify themselves as Roman Catholics, 2% as Protestants, and fewer than 2% as Jewish. Freedom of worship is guaranteed, but the Roman Catholic church is recognized as the established church, and the president and vice-president must belong to it.

Demography. Argentina has one of the lowest growth rates in Latin America. There is, however, an imbalance of population distribution: fewer than one-fifth of the people are dispersed over the vast rural landscape; more than one-third live in metropolitan Buenos Aires; and nearly half live in the five largest metropolitan cities—Buenos Aires, Rosario, CÓRDOBA, LA PLATA, and Mendoza. The country lacks middle-sized cities, towns, and villages.

Argentina ranks above the United States as one of the most extensively urbanized countries in the Western Hemisphere. However, the overall population density is one of the lowest in Latin America and less than one-third the world average.

Education and Health. Free compulsory education ensures that most people go through elementary schools. Large numbers enter secondary schools, but only a minority graduate. The University of Buenos Aires, the largest university in Latin America, has 105,000 students. There are 25 other national universities and several private universities in the country. Medical facilities (especially those in urban areas) are generally excellent.

Cultural Activities. Argentina has long been noted for the high quality of its intellectual life and for its many artistic influences. One of the major literary figures was Jorge Luis BORGES. Others of international reputation included Julio CORTÁZAR and Manuel PUIG. (See also LATIN AMERICAN LITERATURE.)

Drama, music, painting, and sculpture have flourished, especially in Buenos Aires, although political and economic turmoil since the 1950s has acted as a deter-

rent to the development of the arts. Buenos Aires, however, is still the scene of some of the world's major international music events, many of which take place at the famous Teatro Colón.

Economic Activity

Foreign trade and commerce have been major components of the country's economy since the earliest times. Several, sometimes overlapping, economic periods can be distinguished in Argentine economic history. From 1600 to 1750, wild cattle and horses were hunted for hides; from 1700 to 1850, large herds of semidomesticated animals became the backbone of the *estancia* (large-scale ranch) system. From the colonial period to the end of the 19th century, fats and salted meats were processed in large vats and sold as food for slaves on plantations in the Americas and as food to be eaten on sailing ships. Between 1830 and 1900, extensive sheep ranches were established.

During 1850–1900 rapid expansion of crop farming coincided with the influx of European immigrants. By the late 1920s, Argentina had attained the highest level of economic development in Latin America and ranked alongside many European countries. Industrial development began in the 1930s and has continued as an important element of the national economy. Since the 1940s, however, economic growth has been hampered by inflation, by foreign-trade deficits, and by large-scale foreign borrowing. In an attempt to reverse a financial crisis related to hyperinflation and the foreign debt, the government introduced stringent economic reforms in 1985 and established a new currency, the austral.

Manufacturing, Mining, and Energy. Manufacturing employs about one-fourth of the labor force. Meat packing and food processing are among the major manufacturing industries, as are the production of textiles, cement, petroleum, chemicals, iron and steel, automobiles, and machinery. Mining employs a minute percentage of the labor

A gaucho, the Argentine equivalent of the American cowboy, herds cattle in the Pampas. Argentina is one of the world's great cattle-producing nations.

(Above) *Ushuaia, a port on the Beagle Channel, is the territorial capital of Tierra del Fuego.* (Right) *Mounted shepherds and trained dogs watch their flock on the wind- scoured plains of Patagonia.*

force, and minerals account for about 2% of the GNP.

Most of the energy generated is consumed in the city and province of Buenos Aires, which is far from the sources of power. Argentina's oil and gas fields are located in Patagonia and near the Bolivian border, and hydroelectric sites are located principally in the Andes and on the Brazilian frontier. By 1986 hydroelectric power provided about 40% of electricity requirements.

With substantial reserves of uranium, Argentina is the leading nuclear power in Latin America. In 1985, 11% of the country's energy needs were provided from this source.

Agriculture, Forestry, and Fishing. Argentina ranks among the world's top dozen producers of wheat, rye, maize (corn), and linseed. Livestock production is also among the world's highest.

Nearly 60% of Argentina's land area is used for agriculture. About half of all farms are privately owned; the rest are mostly in corporate, cooperative, state, or institutional ownership.

About 25% of the land is covered by forests, which are mainly in the northern subtropical Misiones and Chaco. The most valuable timber, however, is in Patagonia, where araucarian forests as well as cypress, pine, larch, and oak are found. The quebracho tree is valued for its tannin.

The fishing industry has expanded since the early 1960s. Argentinian dietary habits, which traditionally favored meat, have changed considerably, and fish catches—mostly of hake, mackerel, and anchovies—nearly doubled between 1972 and 1982. Most fishing is off the northern half of the Atlantic coast.

Transportation. Argentina has the most extensive transportation system in Latin America. Roads are used to carry a large percentage of the freight and passenger traffic, with Buenos Aires the focus of the transport network.

Trade. Historically, Argentina has enjoyed a favorable balance of trade, but during the 1970s there were frequent trade deficits. In an attempt to control the problem,

import volume was cut and currency controls were imposed in the early 1980s. Current imports are mainly raw materials, chemicals, and machinery.

Government

Argentina is a federal republic made up of 22 provinces, one territory, and the federal capital. The country is governed under the constitution of 1853, with amendments. During much of the period since 1930, however, Argentina has been ruled by a series of military governments that have suspended many constitutional provisions. Although a separation of powers is provided for, the president has considerable control over legislative and judicial matters. The president introduces bills in congress, appoints cabinet members and other officials without the consent of the legislature, and has the power to declare a state of siege and thereby legally suspend constitutional guarantees.

Congress consists of two chambers, a Senate and a House of Deputies. Members of the latter serve 4-year terms and members of the former, 9-year terms. The president, elected for 4 years, cannot serve two consecutive terms. Federal judicial power is vested in a supreme court of justice appointed by the president with the consent of the Senate. Provincial governments have some autonomy, but the federal government can intervene in order to ensure a republican form of government.

History

At the beginning of the 16th century, before the arrival of Europeans, the area that is now Argentina had a population of about 300,000 mostly nomadic Indians.

Colonization. In 1516, the Spaniard Juan Díaz de Solís, in search of a southwest passage to the Orient, became the first European to set foot on Argentine territory. He sailed up the Río de la Plata estuary and claimed the land on both sides for Spain. In 1526, Sebastian CABOT, in the employ of the Spanish, ascended the Paraná and Paraguay rivers. He was impressed by the silver ornaments of the Indians, and this may account for the names *Río de la Plata* ("Silver River") and *Argentina* ("silvery"). When the country did not yield the silver that had been anticipated, the Spanish crown lost interest.

Buenos Aires was founded in 1536 by Pedro de MENDOZA, but because of Indian attacks, was abandoned within a few years in favor of ASUNCIÓN, Paraguay. In the second half of the 16th century, Spanish colonists moved in over the Andes, founding Santiago del Estero (1553), Mendoza (1561), San Juan (1562), Tucumán (1565), CÓRDOBA (1573), Salta (1582), La Rioja (1591), and San Luis (1596). The pattern of settlement, from west to east, was opposite to that of the United States.

Permanently resettled in 1580, Buenos Aires began to reap the benefits of its location both as an east-coast port and as a buffer to the southward expansion of the Portuguese colony of Brazil. The creation, in 1776, of the Viceroyalty of La Plata (including present-day Argentina, Uruguay, Paraguay, and southern Bolivia), with its capital in Buenos Aires, further enhanced the city's prestige. Up to this time Argentina was part of the Viceroyalty of Peru.

Independence. In 1806, during the Napoleonic Wars, Buenos Aires was occupied by the British. Although the colonial militia led by Jacques de Liniers (1753–1810) restored Spanish rule, Spain's ties with its American colonies were weakened in the tumultuous period, especially after Napoleon's deposition of Ferdinand VII. On May 25, 1810, a revolt occurred in Buenos Aires, and a junta was appointed to rule in the name of the deposed king. A full independence movement led by Manuel BELGRANO soon gathered force, however; the royalists were defeated, and a proclamation of independence was signed at Tucumán on July 9, 1816. Independence was followed by almost continuous civil war. Conflict developed between the centralists (or unitarians), who favored a strongly centralized government at Buenos Aires, and the federalists, who, with the support of gaucho troops, supported provincial autonomy. The federalist Juan Manuel de ROSAS, governor of Buenos Aires, consolidated his power to rule as virtual dictator of the country from 1835 to 1852 and managed to preserve a national unity. Following his overthrow, the present constitution was adopted (1853), but it was not until 1862 that Buenos Aires became a fully integrated province in the federal structure provided for by the constitution.

Economic Expansion. Despite political turmoil in the 19th century, much economic progress was made. Under presidents Bartolomé MITRE (1862–68) and Domingo Faustino SARMIENTO (1868–74) immigration was encouraged, a public education system was established, railroads were built, and livestock breeding was improved. Gen. Julio A. ROCA (president 1880–86, 1898–1904) vanquished the Indians in 1879, opening the Pampas to settlement.

With the support of immigrant groups and the urban middle class, the Radical party was formed, and in 1912 it won the adoption of universal male suffrage and election by secret ballot. In 1916 the Radical candidate Hipólito Irigoyen (c.1850–1933) became the first Argentine president to be elected by popular vote. Irigoyen continued Argentina's policy of neutrality in World War I.

Recent History. Disillusion with the Radical party's ineffectualness grew, and in 1930, Irigoyen was deposed from his second term by a coup. Conservatives then ruled the country until 1943, when another coup replaced the president with a military dictatorship. Argentina remained neutral through most of World War II, but eventually declared war (March 1945) on Germany. In 1946, with the strong support of labor and the Roman Catholic church, Juan D. PERÓN was elected president. During his 9 years in power, Perón established an authoritarian regime. He and his second wife, Eva, cultivated an extraordinary popularity with the workers.

Even after the armed forces ousted him in 1955, Perón continued to be a force in Argentine politics. Of the succession of military and civilian presidents that followed, none completed a full term. Then, after 18 years of exile, Perón was again elected president in 1973. By that time, however, his followers were bitterly divided; urban guerrillas (both leftist and rightist) were active, and Perón was old and ailing. He died the following year, leaving his third wife, Isabel, who was his vice-president, to succeed him. Unable to unite the divided Peronistas, contain mounting violence, or control inflation, she was overthrown by the armed forces in March 1976. The military then conducted a ruthless purge against the leftist guerrillas in which thousands of persons disappeared. The economic situation worsened.

After an unsuccessful war (1982) with Great Britain over possession of the FALKLAND ISLANDS, civilian government returned with the election of a Radical, Raúl ALFONSÍN, as president in 1983. Alfonsín took office in December in the midst of an economic crisis, with annual inflation rate running at more than 500% and an enormous foreign debt. In June 1985, with inflation above 1,000% annually, he instituted the Austral austerity program. Overall inflation decreased dramatically but then crept upward, forcing the government to take further measures to control it—and to manage the foreign debt. Alfonsín's government also prosecuted officers responsible for the disappearance of more than 9,000 persons. Late in 1985 ex-presidents Jorge Rafael VIDELA and Roberto Viola and three others received prison sentences. In 1987 military pressure led to granting immunity to most officers. Separately, former president Leopoldo Galtieri was convicted in 1986 of negligence in conducting the Falklands War. The government crushed military rebellions in April 1987 and January 1988. Presidential elections were held in May 1989 at a time of economic disintegration. The Peronist candidate, Carlos Saúl MENEM, handily won. Menem was sworn in on July 8, with Alfonsín retiring five months early due to the economic crisis. Menem, who pardoned the three former military leaders in 1989 and restored ties with Britain in 1990, launched an economic austerity plan that failed to halt inflation. Although his free-market economic policies were opposed by many Peronists, he was named leader of the Peronist party in August 1990.

Argo Argo, also known as Argo Navis, is an ancient name for a Southern Hemisphere CONSTELLATION that contains Canopus (α Carinae), the brightest star in the sky after Sirius. It was named for the ship in Greek mythology in which Jason and the Argonauts sought the Golden Fleece. Because Argo covered such a large area of the sky, in modern times it has been divided into smaller constellations representing parts of the ship, including Puppis (the Stern), Carina (the Keel), Vela (the Sails), and Pyxis (the Compass). Some of the most brilliant parts of the Milky Way pass through Vela and Carina.

argon Argon is a chemical element—a monatomic gas—the third of the INERT GASES in Group 0 of the periodic table. Its symbol is Ar, its atomic number is 18, and its atomic weight is 39.948. Argon is the most abundant of the inert, or so-called noble, gases in the atmosphere, being present to the extent of 0.94% by volume. It was first separated by fractional distillation of liquid air by Lord Rayleigh and Sir William Ramsay in 1894.

Argon has a melting point of −189.2° C and a boiling point of −185.7° C. The element does not appear to form true compounds.

Argon is obtained commercially from the distillation of liquid air. It is used to fill electric light bulbs, fluorescent tubes, phototubes, and glow tubes. Argon is also used as an inert gas shield for electric arc welding and cutting, and as an inert atmosphere for growing silicon and germanium crystals.

argonaut see NAUTILUS

Argonauts see JASON

Argonne [ahr-guhn'] The Argonne is a plateau region in northeastern France between the Meuse River on the east and the Aisne River on the west. About 350 m (1,150 ft) in elevation, it is rocky and heavily forested. It was the site of battles in 1792 and in both world wars.

Argos Argos was an ancient Greek city in the northeastern Peloponnesus, near modern Nauplia. Inhabited since prehistoric times, it became the most powerful of the Greek city-states by the 7th century BC, when King Pheidon defeated Sparta. Argos fought intermittently with Sparta and was often allied with Athens. Cleomenes I of Sparta defeated Argos in 494 BC. The city joined the Achaean League (see ACHAEA) in 229 BC and was conquered by Rome in 146 BC. Important archaeological remains include a complex of sanctuaries of the mother goddess Hera, which contained sculptures by POLYCLITUS, and extensive Roman ruins.

Argus In Greek mythology Argus was a monster with 100 eyes, also called Panoptes ("all-seeing"). It guarded

Io, a mortal maiden loved by Zeus whom he changed into a heifer. Argus was also the name of the old dog of the epic hero Odysseus.

Argyll [ahr-gyl'] Argyll is a former county in the western highlands of Scotland. Its deeply indented, island-dotted coastline is bordered by the Atlantic Ocean and the North Channel. The county town was Inveraray, and the main islands include Mull, Islay, Iona, and Jura. Argyll is mountainous away from the coast, with its highest point, Ben Cruachan, reaching an altitude of 1,124 m (3,689 ft). Fishing is important along the coast, livestock is raised inland, and distilleries, woolen textile mills, and timber mills are located in the main towns of Campbeltown, Oban, Dunoon, and Inveraray. Tourism is also important. Early Celtic Christian ruins dating from the 6th century are located on Iona. In 1975, during the reorganization of Scottish local government, Argyll was divided between the administrative regions of Highland and Strathclyde.

Århus [awr'-hoos] Århus is a seaport in eastern Jutland, Denmark, about 121 km (75 mi) north of Odense, on Århus Bay. The seat of Århus County, it is the second largest city in Denmark, with a population of 258,028 (1988 est.). Industries include beer, machinery, textiles, chemicals, tobacco, and shipbuilding. Århus is a commercial center, and the city has several fine examples of modern Danish architecture. Notable buildings are the cathedral of Saint Clement (13th century), the town hall (1938–42), and the University of Århus (1928). Cultural institutions include an open-air museum, a theater, and a music academy.

Århus became a bishopric in 948. It was a trade center until the Reformation, when its political status declined. During the 19th century, efforts were made to improve the harbor, and eventually Århus grew to its present importance.

aria The aria is a long, complex, accompanied vocal solo, found usually in the OPERA but also in the ORATORIO and the CANTATA. The antithesis of the RECITATIVE, it has little part in moving the plot forward, for its emphasis is on music.

The da capo aria in BAROQUE MUSIC returns to its opening section (A) after a contrasting section (B), *da capo* meaning "repeat from the beginning." A favorite with singers, the da capo idea was condemned by other musicians and critics because it interrupted the dramatic flow. After the mid-18th century, arias were emotionally and dramatically integrated into operatic scenes. Such works as Richard Wagner's *Tristan und Isolde* obliterated the distinction between recitative and aria; melody and narrative unfolded continuously. The prominent position of more conventional 19th-century opera in the standard repertoire is due, in great part, to its high percentage of attractive arias.

Ariadne [air-ee-ad'-nee]   In Greek mythology Ariadne was the daughter of Minos, the king of Crete. She fell in love with THESEUS and helped him slay the Minotaur by providing Theseus with a thread to find his way out of the monster's labyrinth. Theseus took Ariadne with him when he sailed for Athens but soon abandoned her, leaving her asleep on the island of Naxos. There, Dionysus, the god of wine, wooed and later wed her.

Ariane [ahr-ee-ahn']   Ariane is a rocket designed by the EUROPEAN SPACE AGENCY (ESA) to give Europe greater independence in the launching of satellites. Its private marketing company, Arianespace, has headquarters in Every, France, and a launch facility at the French Space Center, Kourou, French Guiana. The French space agency is the company's principal shareholder, along with 36 European aerospace firms and 11 European banks.

The prototype *Ariane 1* was designed to place a payload of up to 1,700 kg (3,750 lb) into geosynchronous orbit. The rocket's first successful launch took place on June 16, 1983, when the fifth *Ariane 1* orbited two satellites. Following several other *Ariane 1* flights, the first *Ariane 3* lifted two satellites into space on Aug. 4, 1984. The new model of the rocket differed in several features, including the use of two solid strap-on boosters.

The more powerful *Ariane 4* model offers a multiple-payload launch capability. On its first launch, on June 15, 1988, it orbited three satellites. One version of *Ariane 5*, a heavy lift launcher set to operate by the mid-1990s, will be used to orbit ESA's planned Hermes spaceplane (see SPACE PROGRAMS, NATIONAL).

See also: ROCKETS AND MISSILES.

Arianism [air'-ee-uhn-izm]   Arianism was a 4th-century teaching on the nature of Christ named for Arius (*c*.250–*c*.336), a priest in Alexandria. Arius denied the full deity of a preexistent Son of God who became incarnate in Jesus Christ. He held that the Son, while divine and like God, was created by God as the agent through whom he created the universe. Arius said of the Son, "there was a time when he was not."

Arianism became so widespread in the Christian church and resulted in such disunity that the emperor Constantine convoked a church council at Nicaea in 325 (see NICAEA, COUNCILS OF). Led by ATHANASIUS, bishop of Alexandria, the council condemned Arianism and stated that the Son was consubstantial (of one and the same substance or being) and coeternal with the Father.

Nonetheless, the conflict continued, aided by the conflicting politics of the empire after the death of Constantine (337). Three types of Arianism emerged: radical Arianism, which asserted that the Son was "dissimilar" to the Father; homoeanism, which held that the Son was similar to the Father; and semi-Arianism, which shaded off into orthodoxy and held that the Son was similar yet distinct from the Father. After an initial victory of the homoean party in 357, the semi-Arians joined the ranks of orthodoxy, which finally triumphed except in Teutonic Christianity, where Arianism survived until after the conversion (496) of the Franks.

Arias Sánchez, Oscar [ah'-ree-ahs sahn'-chays]   Oscar Arias Sánchez, b. Sept. 13, 1941, a former minister of planning and a professor, was president of Costa Rica from 1986 to 1990. He was the main architect of the peace plan for CENTRAL AMERICA that he signed on Aug. 7, 1987, with the presidents of strife-torn El Salvador, Guatemala, Honduras, and Nicaragua. Although peace has proved elusive, Arias won the 1987 Nobel Peace Prize for his persistent efforts.

Arica [ah-ree'-kah]   Arica (1987 est. pop., 169,774) is a port city of Tarapacá province in northern Chile. Located just south of the Chilean-Peruvian border, it lies at the edge of the ATACAMA DESERT. In 1954, Arica was made a free port, and it handles a great deal of foreign trade for landlocked Bolivia and for Peru. Its fishing industry is also important. Chile's claim to Arica, which originally belonged to Peru, was not settled until 1929.

arid climate   Zones of arid climate are defined as areas where, from one year to the next, more water is lost by EVAPOTRANSPIRATION than is returned by precipitation. Arid climates occur in either tropical or mid-latitude zones: (1) between 20° and 30° latitude, on the east side of persistent, HIGH-PRESSURE REGIONS, where subsiding air is continually heated and dried by compression; or (2) between 30° and 40° latitude, in continental interiors far from oceanic influences or in the rain shadows behind mountain ranges.

All arid climates share extreme temperature ranges and unpredictable or variable rainfall (see DESERT; DROUGHT). The amount of SOLAR RADIATION received is high, as are average temperatures. Because terrestrial reradiation is also high, daily temperatures vary greatly. Similarly, rainfall may be so variable that annual values cannot be used to predict climatic conditions.

Aries [air'-eez]   Aries, the Ram, is one of the CONSTELLATIONS of the ZODIAC, the band of sky through which the Sun, Moon, and planets appear to move. Most prominent during the autumn in the Northern Hemisphere, it contains no stars brighter than 2d magnitude. In ASTROLOGY, Aries governs the period between March 21 and April 19. Celestial right ascension (analogous to terrestrial longitude) is measured from the so-called first point of Aries, or vernal equinox, where the Sun crosses the celestial equator from south to north during the spring equinox. Because of precession, this point now lies in Pisces.

Arikara [uh-rik'-uh-ruh]   The Arikara, a Cadoan-speaking North American Indian tribe, inhabited the area of the upper Missouri River as early as 1100; after about 1750 they moved to North Dakota. In language and way of life, they are closely related to the Skidi division of the PAWNEE Indians of Nebraska.

The semisedentary Arikara lived in earth-covered lodges, grew maize (corn) and other crops, and twice yearly left their villages to hunt buffalo. Like other upper–Missouri River peoples, the Arikara population was largely destroyed by wars, especially with the Dakota, and by smallpox epidemics in the late 18th and early 19th centuries. From an estimated population of 15,000 in the mid-1700s, they declined to about 2,600 in 1804. In 1990 about 3,000 Arikara, MANDAN, and HIDATSA, known as the Three Affiliated Tribes, lived on the Fort Berthold Reservation in North Dakota.

Ariosto, Ludovico

Ariosto, Ludovico [ah-ree-aws'-toh, loo-dohvee'-koh] The Italian poet Ludovico Ariosto, b. Sept. 8, 1474, d. July 6, 1533, wrote the important epic *Orlando Furioso* (1516; final form, 1532). He was the son of a captain in the service of the Este dukes of Ferrara. After his father's death in 1500, he entered the service of Cardinal Ippolito d'Este, who sent him on numerous diplomatic missions, among them, to Popes Julius II and Leo X. He became governor of the Garfagnana in 1522 and directed the theater at the court of Ferrara.

His *Orlando Furioso* continues Matteo Maria Boiardo's uncompleted epic *Orlando Innamorato* (1483). His *Satires* (1519–25), in triple rhyme with Horatian overtones, affords a glimpse into the poet's private life. As director of the newly erected court theater at Ferrara, Ariosto presented the first regular Italian comedies on the stage, among them his own *I suppositi* (1509), *Il negromante* (1520), and *La Lena* (1529), reminiscent of the comedies of Plautus and Terence.

Aristaeus

Aristaeus [ar-i-stee'-uhs] In Greek mythology Aristaeus, the son of APOLLO and Cyrene, was a guardian of herds and a beekeeper. He fell in love with Eurydice, wife of ORPHEUS, and tried to seduce her. As she fled from Aristaeus, his bees pursued her; she accidentally stepped on a snake and died of its bite. Thereafter, all his bees died. Aristaeus consulted PROTEUS, a seer, and on his advice offered sacrifices and funeral honors to Eurydice, and new swarms of bees were then generated. Aristaeus spent his last days teaching the skill of beekeeping.

Aristarchus of Samos

Aristarchus of Samos [ar-i-stahr'-kuhs, say'-mahs] The Greek mathematician and astronomer Aristarchus, c.310–230 BC, is celebrated as the exponent of a Sun-centered universe and for his pioneering attempt to determine the sizes and distances of the Sun and Moon. A student of Strato of Lampsacus, third head of Aristotle's Lyceum, Aristarchus was in the generation between Euclid and Archimedes. Little evidence exists concerning the origin of his belief in a HELIOCENTRIC WORLD SYSTEM.

The only surviving work of Aristarchus, *On the Sizes and Distances of the Sun and Moon*, provides the details of his remarkable geometric argument, based on observation, whereby he determined that the Sun was about 20 times as distant from the Earth as the Moon, and 20 times the Moon's size. Both these estimates were an order of magnitude too small.

See also: DISTANCE, ASTRONOMICAL.

Aristides

Aristides [ar-i-sty'-deez] Aristides, c.530–c.467 BC, was an Athenian general and political leader, surnamed "the Just." He served (490) in the Battle of Marathon but was later ostracized (482) after a quarrel with THEMISTOCLES. Recalled to Athens, he played a significant part in the Greek victory over the Persians at Salamis (480). Aristides was also central in the formation (478) of the DELIAN LEAGUE and was chosen to assess the contributions to be paid by the member states. Thereafter he remained an influential figure in Athenian politics.

aristocracy

aristocracy The word *aristocracy*, from the Greek *aristos* ("best") and *kratos* ("rule"), originally meant rule by the best people of the country. In later times it came to mean rule by any privileged group, usually a hereditary landowning nobility. In a broader sense, aristocracy may mean a group that is superior in wealth, power, or intellect and is able to pass these on to successive generations.

Modern political aristocracies have included the British landed gentry who governed England until the mid-19th century, the French nobility who lost power after 1789, and the Russian nobility who clung to power until 1917.

Aristophanes

Aristophanes [ar-i-stahf'-uh-neez] Aristophanes, b. c.445 BC, d. c.385 BC, the greatest comic dramatist of ancient times and the only extant representative of the Athenian style known as Old Attic Comedy, refined his genre to its highest point of sophistication and virtuosity. In his last two plays, examples of Middle Comedy, he also bridged the gap between the comic forms born of religious ritual and the domestically oriented New Comedy of the Hellenistic period, which, by way of its Roman imitators, determined the course comedy would take in Elizabethan and modern times.

Although Aristophanes was much influenced by earlier comic poets, especially Cratinus, his use of the traditional elements of Old Comedy, which had been an integral feature of the annual Athenian state festivals in honor of DIONYSUS since 487 BC, was inventive and subtle, and he voiced justifiable pride in his original treatment of themes. Like other comic poets, Aristophanes was critical of the pomposity, imposture, wrongheadedness, and corruption he observed in society. His targets were prominent people from all walks of life. Because he wrote for a wide and diverse audience, his plays commonly appeal to popu-

Imaginative costumes and surrealistic sets are used in this modern performance of Aristophanes' The Birds, *a fantasy about a city in the sky. Aristophanes wrote more than 40 plays, 11 of which have survived.*

lar sentiments hostile to major cultural innovations and to those responsible for them. His heroes (or sympathetic characters) often look to an idealized Athenian past, with its traditional pleasures, civic virtues, and social solidarity. The hero is commonly an "everyman," who may be positively ruthless in attaining his goals but whose successful struggles to debunk or best authority figures must have given Aristophanes' audiences great vicarious pleasure.

The plays produced during the first decade of Athens's 27-year war against Sparta, the PELOPONNESIAN WAR (431–404 BC), are particularly rich in topical references and use the chorus in a relatively uniform way. In general, the entry of the chorus (*parodos*), the set debate (*agon*), and the chorus's address to the audience (*parabasis*) constitute the first half of the play; in the second half a series of episodes is articulated by choral songs. In later plays there are progressive changes in these structures until, in the last plays, the role of the chorus has been drastically curtailed and the number of topical references greatly reduced.

Aristophanes is believed to have written more than 40 plays, although only 11 survive. In *The Clouds* (423; rev. 418), Socrates is aligned with the Sophists, contemporary teachers of rhetoric and masters of specious reasoning, and attacked as an evil influence on society. *The Wasps* (422) ridicules the mania for litigation and paid jury service exhibited by the senior citizens of Athens. In *The Birds* (414), a clever Athenian dropout persuades the birds to build a utopian city in the sky (Cloudcuckooland) and forces the gods to cede him their prerogatives. Aris-

tophanes' third comment on the Peloponnesian War, LYSISTRATA (411), has women from everywhere in Greece uniting to compel their men, by means of a sex strike, to conclude peace. EURIPIDES is twice his target, in *The Frogs* (405) and in *The Thesmophoriazusae* (411).

Aristophanes was adept in a variety of techniques, including burlesque, caricature, parody, satire, exaggeration, and fantasy. In ancient times he was most admired for the choiceness of his language, including his elaborate wordplay, and his mastery of lyric poetry. His style could be by turns grandiloquent or colloquial, solemn or bawdy; his humor, broad or subtle. In an age of giants he had no rival among comic playwrights, and there have been few, if any, who have equaled the inventiveness and rhythmical beauty of his work.

Aristotle

Aristotle [ar-is-taht'-uhl]   With the possible exception of Plato, Aristotle, 384–322 BC, is the most influential philosopher in the history of Western thought. Logic into the present century was basically Aristotelian logic. The study of the natural sciences was dominated by Aristotle until early modern times, and modern physics was developed in reaction to the Aristotelian tradition. Aristotle also was the founder of biology; Charles Darwin regarded him as the most important contributor to the subject. Aristotle's Poetics, the first formal work of literary criticism, had a strong influence on the theory and practice of modern classical drama. Aristotle's immense influence is due primarily to the fact that he seemed to offer an all-encompassing system, which, although lacking in certain respects, was as a whole formidably imposing and unrivaled in its comprehensiveness.

Life

Aristotle was born in 384 BC in Stagira in northern Greece. His father, Nicomachus, was a physician with close connections to the Macedonian court. In 367, Aristotle went to Athens to join Plato's Academy, first as a student, then as a teacher. Plato had gathered around him a group of outstanding men who shared no common doctrine but who were united by the systematic effort to organize human knowledge on a firm theoretical basis and expand it in all directions. This effort characterizes Aristotle's own work.

It was also part of the Academy's program to train young men for a political career and to provide advice to rulers. Thus, after Plato's death, Aristotle joined (347) the court of Hermias of Atarneus, and later went (343) to the court of Philip II of Macedonia, where he became tutor to the young Alexander the Great. In 335, Aristotle returned to Athens to found his own school, the Lyceum, or Peripatus. The Peripatus under Aristotle and his successor, THEOPHRASTUS, pursued a wider range of subjects than the Academy ever had. In particular, prominence was given to the detailed study of nature. After the death of Alexander the Great in 323, anti-Macedonian feeling in Athens rose, and Aristotle retired to Chalcis, where he died the following year.

Aristotle (384-322 BC), one of the greatest Greek thinkers, wrote philosophical treatises that have exerted a major influence on Western thought. He advocated moderation in behavior and the use of logic as the proper tool of investigation.

Writings

All Aristotle's writings for a larger audience, mainly dialogues, have been lost except for some fragments. What remains are treatises apparently meant for use within the school. These form the so-called *Corpus Aristotelicum*. In addition, there survives a mutilated version of his *Constitution of Athens*, some letters of doubtful authenticity, and some poems, including an elegy on Plato.

The texts of the treatises raise serious problems. Some of them so clearly contain later thought and language that they cannot possibly be by Aristotle; others are of doubtful authenticity.

Underlying the order of the treatises in the *Corpus* is the traditional division of philosophy into logic, physics, and ethics. The *Metaphysics*, and the *Rhetoric* and the *Poetics*, do not easily fit this scheme. These are appended to the physical and the ethical writings, respectively. Thus the following classification of Aristotle's writings is observed: (1) Logical writings—*Categories, On Interpretation, Prior and Posterior Analytics, Topics, Sophistical Refutations*; (2) Physical writings—*Physics, On Generation and Corruption, On the Heavens, Meteorologica, On the Soul, Parva Naturalia, History of Animals, Parts of Animals, Generation of Animals, Motion of Animals*; (3) *Metaphysics*; (4) Ethical writings—*Nicomachean Ethics, Eudemean Ethics, Magna Moralia, Politics*; (5) *Rhetoric, Poetics*.

Thought

Logic. Logic, the theory of formal truth and validity, originated in reflections on the practice of DIALECTIC, the kind of debate found in Plato's dialogues. Dialogue was regarded as the appropriate form for philosophical argu-

ments, and hence the acquisition of dialectical skill was regarded as crucial for students of philosophy. Aristotle's first great achievement was probably a handbook, now entitled *Topics* and *Sophistical Refutations*, in which he provided the first general analysis of dialectic and formulated rules for success in this kind of argument. In the *Prior and Posterior Analytics* Aristotle tried to work out which kind of premises are needed to gain scientific knowledge and which formal conditions an argument must satisfy to be incontestably valid (see LOGIC). According to the *Posterior Analytics*, the ultimate premises or principles of a science are necessary truths. Human knowledge of these truths is based on experience; it is not itself a matter of experience, however, but rather of reason. When a subject is sufficiently familiar, its governing principles become evident to reason. Deduction from these principles provides not only the knowledge that something is true, but also the reasons why it is true. For Aristotle, both are required for scientific knowledge.

Aristotle's ideal of a science as a deductive system based on evident axioms had a considerable influence on the history of science. In the *Prior Analytics* he examines the conditions an argument must satisfy in order to be incontestably valid. Because he is primarily concerned with the arguments whose propositions are scientific, and because he only regards general categorical propositions as scientific, his theory applies only to a small class of logically valid arguments, the so-called categorical SYLLOGISMS.

Natural Sciences. The natural sciences are concerned with natural objects that are characterized by the fact that they are subject to change. Change is therefore the basic phenomenon with which physics has to deal. Hence Aristotle's work in physics is devoted to an analysis of change and a discussion of its presuppositions. Matter and form are the material and the formal cause, respectively, of what comes to be. A cause is a factor, and a true statement about that factor helps to explain the being of what is caused. Aristotle distinguishes four kinds of causes. If a house comes into being, its efficient cause is the builder, its formal cause is the structure by virtue of which it is a house, its material cause is the matter that has received this structure, and its final cause is the end or purpose for which houses exist, namely the protection of people and property.

The form of an object helps to account for its behavior. Aristotle calls the forms of living things "souls," which are of three kinds: vegetative (plants), sensitive (animals), or rational (human beings). Because Aristotle believed that the soul is merely a set of defining features, he did not regard the body and the soul as two separate entities that mysteriously combine to form an organism. Hence it is not clear what he had in mind when he described an active intellect whose activity is presupposed by the activity of the human mind and that is supposed to be able to exist independently of the body.

Most of Aristotle's work in biology was devoted to zoology. In Aristotle's study of biology the doctrine of TELEOLOGY is particularly prominent. This doctrine, that the form of natural objects is determined by their final ends or purposes, has frequently been misunderstood as an assertion that there is a universal design in nature. Aristotle simply insists that the structure and the behavior of things also has to be understood as contributing to their individual being and function.

Metaphysics. Whereas sciences deal with particular kinds of beings, metaphysics is concerned with beings as such. According to Aristotle there is no such thing as mere being; to be is always to be a SUBSTANCE or object, a quantity, a quality, or a member of some other basic category. Substances are prior to nonsubstances because qualities or quantities are determined by substances. Such substances as God may, however, lack quantities and qualities. Hence an account of beings is, in the first place, an account of substances. To understand substance, it is necessary to consider immaterial substantial forms, ultimately God. Only then can humans understand what it is to be a substance, and what it is to exist. Ultimately, then, the study of metaphysics becomes in part theological.

Ethics. The end, or good, of humankind is not merely to live, but to lead a good, flourishing life that manifests the rational nature of humanity and thus satisfies human needs. The pursuit of happiness is a search for the good life, which is composed of virtuous actions. Aristotle offers no simple definition of goodness, but he advises that virtue is a mean, lying between extremes. Generosity, for example, consists in giving neither too little nor too much. Aristotle also describes intellectual virtue and moral virtue, which correspond to the rational and the irrational parts of the soul. The most important of the intellectual virtues are theoretical and practical wisdom. To the extent that the irrational part of a person's soul is subject to reason and has reasonable desires and feelings, that person is characterized by such moral virtues as justice, courage, and magnanimity.

Humans are by nature gregarious and are disposed to form political associations to fulfill their desires. The aim of the state is the good life of its citizens. In the *Politics*, Aristotle evaluates different forms of government in the light of these assumptions. His views are profoundly influenced by the belief that only certain people are endowed with the capacity to lead the good life and undertake the responsibilities of citizens, and that fewer still are capable of holding public office. Thus a Greek DEMOCRACY (which was nonrepresentational and in which offices rotated) imposed severe limitations on the rights to citizenship.

Rhetoric and Poetics. Aristotle in his *Rhetoric* makes use of traditional rhetorical methods, but he deals with the subject in a more systematic and theoretical fashion than specialists in RHETORIC AND ORATORY. Priority is given to the orator's ability to invent arguments, to see what is plausible in a given case. Only then does Aristotle turn to the strategy and verbal form of the plea.

In the *Poetics*, Aristotle defends poetry against Plato's criticisms. Whereas Plato had spoken of the imitative character of the arts, Aristotle regarded the poet's creations as imaginative, ideal truths closer to reality than the records of historiography. He also rejected the view that poetry should be judged by the morality of what it depicts. The interpretation of Aristotle's observation in the *Poetics*, that tragic drama, by engendering pity and fear, can purge the emotions, has always been disputed.

Aristotelian Tradition

During the Hellenistic period the Aristotelian tradition was continued by the Peripatetic school (see PERIPATETICS). Because of the eclecticism and neoclassicism that arose during the 1st century BC, Aristotle became an authority for all philosophers, especially in logic and in natural sciences. The leading philosophy from the 3d century AD onward, however, came to be Platonism, which better suited the religious temperament of the age. Nevertheless, the history of scholastic philosophy (see SCHOLASTICISM) is primarily the history of the assimilation of Aristotelianism despite the opposition of theologians. It was because of the close association of Aristotelianism and scholasticism that Aristotelianism fell into disrepute in early modern times. During the 19th century, however, Aristotelianism was revived.

arithmetic Arithmetic is a branch of mathematics. The term can be used to refer to everything from simple numerical computations to abstract NUMBER THEORY. The two fundamental operations of arithmetic are addition and multiplication. The result of adding two numbers is called the sum of the numbers. The result of multiplying two numbers is called the product. Subtraction is the inverse operation, or the undoing, of addition; the result is called the difference. The inverse, or undoing, of multiplication is division; the result is called the quotient. Arithmetic of REAL NUMBERS—that is, rational and irrational numbers—is based on a number of properties called field properties. They include the following:

1. Closure property of addition. For any real numbers a and b, $a + b$ is a real number.
2. Closure property of multiplication. For any real numbers a and b, $a \times b$ is a real number.
3. Associative law of addition. For any real numbers a, b, and c, $(a + b) + c = a + (b + c)$.
4. Associative law of multiplication. For any real numbers a, b, and c, $(a \times b) \times c = a \times (b \times c)$.
5. Commutative law of addition. For any real numbers a and b, $a + b = b + a$.
6. Commutative law of multiplication. For any real numbers a and b, $a \times b = b \times a$.
7. Additive identity property. For any real number a, $0 + a = a + 0 = a$.
8. Multiplicative identity property. For any real number a, $1 \times a = a \times 1 = a$.
9. Additive inverse property. For any real number a, there is a unique real number $-a$ such that $-a + a = 0$.
10. Multiplicative inverse property. For any nonzero real number a, there is a unique real number $1/a$ such that $(1/a) \times a = 1$.
11. Distributive law of multiplication over addition. For any real numbers a, b, and c, $a \times (b + c) = (a \times b) + (a \times c)$.

Scope of Subject. Different types of NUMBERS answer different types of questions. Whole numbers (0, 1, 2, 3,...) answer these questions: How much? How far? The answer to the question "How many?" can be no less than "none," which is represented by ZERO.

When questions ask for the direction of a number but still deal with complete units only, the system of integers is used. Integers are often called signed numbers or directed numbers. They include all whole numbers as well as the negative, or additive inverse, of every whole number. Thus the integers are . . . -3, -2, -1, 0, 1, 2, 3,... in which zero no longer represents nothing but is the middle number of the system.

RATIONAL NUMBERS include integers as well as fractional numbers (FRACTIONS), which lie between integers. A rational number can be represented by any integer (called the numerator) divided by a nonzero integer (called the denominator) or by a repeating or terminating decimal fraction. In order to measure all distances, the real-number system, which includes both rational numbers and IRRATIONAL NUMBERS, is needed. The system of real numbers includes all possible distances—positive, negative, and zero—and complete units and parts of units. This system is called a complete ordered field.

History. More than 4,000 years ago the Babylonians were proficient in arithmetic. They developed a numeration system that used 60 as a base and included place values. This base-60 system was effective in dealing with time.

The present Hindu-Arabic system of numeration was developed by the Hindus and brought to Europe by the Arabs before 1200, but Europe did not fully adopt this system and abandon Roman NUMERALS until the 17th century.

See also: ALGEBRA; DUODECIMAL SYSTEM; GROUP THEORY; MATHEMATICS, HISTORY OF.

—

Arizona

Arizona, the sixth largest state of the United States, in terms of area, is located in the Southwest. It is bordered by Utah on the north, by Colorado on the northeast, by New Mexico on the east, by Mexico on the south, and by California and Nevada on the west; its northeast corner is the only point in the United States shared by four state boundaries. Known as the Grand Canyon State, Arizona is one of the fastest developing states of the U.S. Sunbelt. Its population is increasing at a rapid rate, and its diversified economy is dominated by service and manufacturing industries. Arizona's name is derived from the Pima Indian village of Arizonac (formerly located in what is now Mexico, near modern Nogales, Ariz.), where silver was found by Spaniards about 1736. The word *Arizonac* probably means "place of the small spring."

Land and Resources

Arizona includes many areas of great natural beauty and geological interest. The highest point in the state is Humphreys Peak (3,851 m/12,633 ft), near FLAGSTAFF, and the lowest point is 21 m (70 ft) above sea level, in the southwest along the Colorado River. The approximate mean elevation of Arizona is 1,250 m (4,100 ft). About 43% of the state's land area is owned by the federal government and includes about 20 Indian reservations.

Physiographic Regions. Arizona may be divided into two major geographic regions, each of which is part of a larger physiographic area. In the north is a section of the COLORADO PLATEAU, and in the south and west is a part of the Basin and Range Region.

The Colorado Plateau area, about two-fifths of the state, comprises a series of generally level plateaus, mostly separated by steep-sided chasms. The elevation is mainly between 1,525 and 2,440 m (5,000 and 8,000 ft), although some areas, such as the extensive Kaibab Plateau (2,835 m/9,300 ft high) and the volcanic San Francisco Peaks (one of which is Humphreys Peak), are higher. Other notable features of the Colorado Plateau include the 1.6-km-deep (1-mi) GRAND CANYON of the Colorado River; the CANYON DE CHELLY, with sheer red cliffs; the PAINTED DESERT, an extensive area of colorful sand and rock formations; the PETRIFIED FOREST, with great "logs" of jasper and agate; and MONUMENT VALLEY (astride the border with Utah), containing monumental red-sandstone buttes.

The Mogollon Rim, an escarpment (about 609 m/2,000 ft high) that extends diagonally from central Arizona to southwest New Mexico, in part separates the Colorado Plateau from the Basin and Range Region. The latter comprises several northwest-southeast–trending mountain ranges. Ranges in the central region include the Black, Hualapai, Mazatzal, Superstition, and Gila Bend mountains; crest elevations are generally from 2,135 to 3,355 m (7,000 to 11,000 ft). The southern Arizona ranges include the Pinaleño, Chiricahua, Huachuca, Santa Rita, Santa Catalina, and Mohawk mountains; elevations are generally less than 11,340 m (4,400 ft), but isolated peaks rise more than 2,700 m (9,000 ft). In the southwest is the Sonoran Desert.

Soils. Soils suitable for agriculture cover only about 10% of Arizona's land area. The Colorado Plateau region of the north has very little arable land, but some of the broad basins of the south contain gray and red soils that, with the addition of fertilizer, can support productive irrigated farming.

Rivers and Lakes. The COLORADO RIVER (rising in Colorado) and its tributaries drain most of Arizona. The Colorado flows for about 1,127 km (700 mi) in the state, entering in the north, then winding westward (in part through the Grand Canyon) before turning south to form most of Arizona's western boundary. Important components of the Colorado system in Arizona include the GILA, Little Colorado, Bill Williams, Verde, Salt, and Santa Cruz rivers. Most of the state's rivers and streams are intermittent, flowing only after a rainfall; the Colorado flows at all times, however.

Arizona's few natural lakes are small and situated in mountain areas. But the state has several very large artificial lakes, created by damming rivers. These lakes include Lake MEAD and Lake Mohave (both partly in Nevada), Lake Powell (mostly in Utah), and Havasu Lake (partly in California), all on the Colorado River; Theodore

AT A GLANCE

ARIZONA

Land: Area: 295,260 km² (114,000 mi²); rank: 6th. Capital and largest city: Phoenix (1990 pop., 983,403). Counties: 15. Elevations: highest—3,851 m (12,633 ft), at Humphreys Peak; lowest—21 m (70 ft), at the Colorado River.

People: Population (1990): 3,677,985; rank: 24th; density: 12.5 persons per km² (32.3 per mi²). Distribution (1988 est.): 76.4% metropolitan, 23.6% nonmetropolitan. Average annual change (1980–90): +3.3%.

Government (1990): Governor: Rose Mofford, Democrat. U.S. Congress: Senate—1 Democrat, 1 Republican; House—1 Democrat, 4 Republicans. Electoral college votes: 8. State legislature: 30 senators, 60 representatives.

Economy: State personal income (1988): $52.2 billion; rank: 25th. Median family income (1979): $19,017; rank: 30th. Agriculture: income (1988)—$1.96 billion. Forestry: sawtimber volume (1987)—30.4 billion board feet. Mining: value (1987, nonfuels only)—$1.8 billion. Manufacturing: value added (1987)—$11.2 billion. Services: value (1987)—$13.9 billion.

Miscellany: Statehood: Feb. 14, 1912; the 48th state. Nickname: Grand Canyon State; bird: cactus wren; flower: Saguaro cactus blossom; tree: paloverde; motto: *Ditat Deus* ("God Enriches"); songs: "Arizona March Song" and "Arizona."

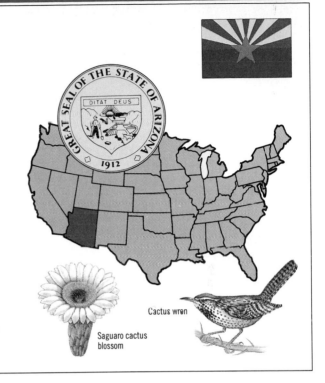

Cactus wren

Saguaro cactus blossom

Roosevelt Lake, on the Salt River; and San Carlos Lake, on the Gila River. The long-term Central Arizona Project, to carry scarce water eastward from the Colorado, connected with Phoenix in 1985 and is scheduled to reach Tucson in 1991.

Climate. Because of its wide range of elevation and relief, Arizona has a varied climate pattern. The Colorado Plateau region has cool to cold winters and warm summers. In Flagstaff the mean January temperature is -3° C (28° F), and the average July temperature is 19° C (66° F). The Basin and Range Region has mild winters and hot summers. In Phoenix, the centrally located state capital, the mean January temperature is 11° C (52° F), and the July average is 33° C (91° F). Each year the city receives about 86% of the possible sunshine.

Arizona as a whole gets about 330 mm (13 in) of precipitation yearly. High mountains and plateaus receive somewhat more moisture (510–1015 mm/20–40 in per year, with up to 1.5 m/5 ft of snow), while the southwest gets much less precipitation (50–130 mm/2–5 in annually).

Vegetation and Animal Life. Vegetation in Arizona forms distinct zones, largely according to elevation. Lowland deserts, dominated by creosote bushes and sagebrush, include many cacti, notably the giant saguaro (whose blossom is the state flower), and yucca, such as the tall Joshua tree. The useful mesquite tree is also found in desert regions. Grasslands, some pure and others shrub-dotted, are common at somewhat higher elevations. The grasslands merge into woodlands of oak and chaparral in the warmer areas and into woodlands of piñon, juniper, and other pine trees in the cooler locations. Above the woodlands, from about 2,135 to 2,745 m (7,000–9,000 ft), are dense stands of valuable ponderosa pine. At high altitudes are forests of Douglas fir and spruce mixed with such deciduous trees as aspen, oak, and maple.

Altogether, about 25% of Arizona is forested, but less than 20% of this area has commercial value. Virtually all the commercial timberland is controlled by the federal government, mostly in the state's seven national forests.

Arizona has large numbers of wildlife. Bigger animals include black bear, mountain lions, desert bighorn sheep, mule deer, white-tailed deer, antelopes, and elk. Among the smaller wild animals are jackrabbits, beavers, squirrels, and chipmunks. The state's numerous reptiles include the poisonous Gila monster and other kinds of lizards; rattlesnakes; and coral snakes. More than 400 species of birds, including both rarities, such as the elegant trogon, and common types, such as the roadrunner, are found there.

Mineral Resources. Arizona has great copper deposits, principally located at Morenci, San Manuel, Ajo, Bagdad, and the area south of Tucson. Deposits of asbestos, coal, gemstones, gold, gypsum, helium, lead, molybdenum,

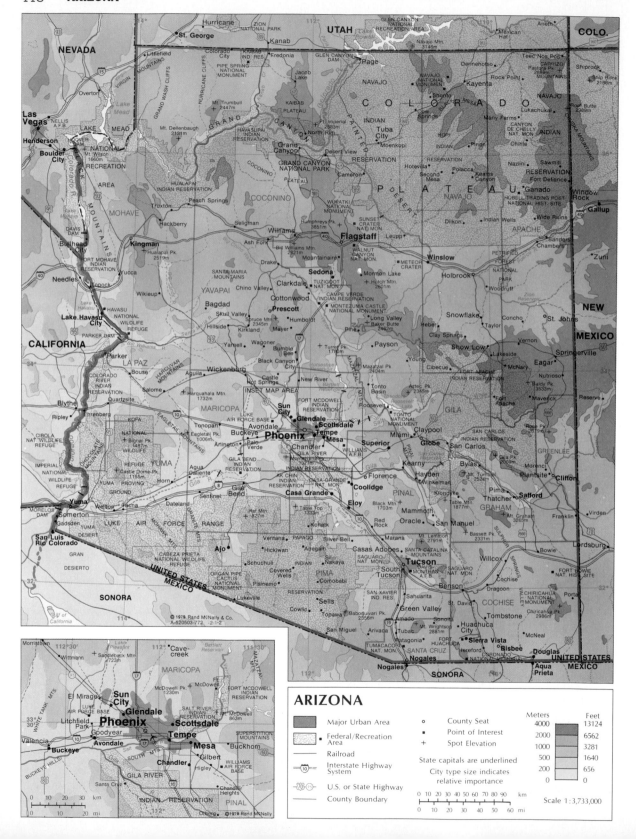

ARIZONA

	Major Urban Area
	Federal/Recreation Area
	Railroad
	Interstate Highway System
	U.S. or State Highway
	County Boundary

- ○ County Seat
- ■ Point of Interest
- + Spot Elevation

State capitals are underlined
City type size indicates relative importance

Meters	Feet
4000	13124
2000	6562
1000	3281
500	1640
200	656
0	0

0 10 20 30 40 50 60 70 80 90 km
0 10 20 30 40 50 60 mi

Scale 1:3,733,000

© 1979 Rand McNally & Co.
A-520503-772 -2-1-2
©1979 Rand McNally

pyrites, sand and gravel, silver, uranium, and zinc are also found.

People

The 1990 population of Arizona was 3,677,985, giving the state an average population density of 12.5 persons per km^2 (32.3 per mi^2). The number of inhabitants increased by 53.1% during 1970–80 and by 35.3% during 1980–90, far greater than the national rate for those periods. Arizona's growth was mainly the result of persons moving to the state for its employment opportunities and for its healthful warm, dry climate. Approximately 83% of Arizona's population are classified as urban; the principal cities are Chandler, Flagstaff, Glendale, MESA, PHOENIX, PRESCOTT, Scottsdale, Sierra Vista, Tempe, TUCSON, and YUMA.

The great majority of Arizonans are white. The state has about 441,000 citizens of Hispanic background; almost all of them are Mexican-Americans, concentrated in southern cities and mining centers. The Indian population of about 153,000 is exceeded in size only by those of Oklahoma and California. Larger Indian groups in Arizona are the NAVAJO, HOPI, YUMA, APACHE, Yavapai, PIMA, and PAPAGO. Blacks, about 3% of the population, live mainly in the Phoenix and Tucson areas.

In religion, most Arizonans are Protestant, but large numbers are Roman Catholics and Mormons.

Education and Cultural Activity

The first public schools in Arizona were established in the early 1870s, but the school system became sizable only well after statehood was granted in 1912. In the late 1980s, about 534,000 pupils annually attended the state's public elementary and secondary schools. Arizona has numerous public two-year colleges, including Navajo Community College (opened 1969), at Tsaile, the first U.S. college established on an Indian reservation. Other institutions of higher education in the state include Arizona State University (1885), at Tempe; Grand Canyon College (1949), at Phoenix; Northern Arizona University (1899), at Flagstaff; and the University of Arizona (1885), at Tucson. Lowell Observatory (founded 1894), at Flagstaff, is a noted center of astronomy. KITT PEAK NATIONAL OBSERVATORY, with several large reflecting telescopes and the world's biggest solar telescope, is situated near Tucson.

Cultural Institutions. Arizona has several museums with historical or anthropological emphasis: the Arizona State Museum, near Tucson; the Heard Museum, in Phoenix; the Museum of Northern Arizona, in Flagstaff; and the Amerind Foundation, near Dragoon. The principal libraries in Arizona are the state library (1,155,000 volumes), at Phoenix, and the University of Arizona Library (2,900,000 volumes), at Tucson.

Historic Sites. Arizona has several highly interesting remains of past Indian cultures. These include cliff dwellings in MONTEZUMA CASTLE NATIONAL MONUMENT, near Camp Verde; Navajo National Monument, near Tonalea; Tonto National Monument, at Roosevelt; and Walnut Canyon National Monument, near Flagstaff. Also of his-

torical interest are the 800-year-old Hopi Indian pueblo of ORAIBI and ruins of pueblos in Tuzigoot National Monument, near Clarkdale, and Wupatki National Monument, near Flagstaff. Among other historic sites are the Spanish Roman Catholic mission of San Xavier del Bac near Tucson and the city of TOMBSTONE, containing many reminders of the time when it was a lawless silver-mining boom town. The noted American architect Frank Lloyd WRIGHT lived for many years in Arizona, and buildings he designed in the state include TALIESIN WEST, in Scottsdale.

Communications. Arizona's communications media in the mid-1980s included 11 commercial television stations and 92 radio stations. In 1987 there were 19 daily English-language newspapers, with a combined daily circulation of 704,000 copies. Influential dailies included the *Phoenix Arizona Republic*, the *Phoenix Gazette*, the *Tucson Citizen*, and the *Tucson Arizona Daily Star*. Arizona's first newspaper was the *Weekly Arizonian*, founded in 1859 at Tubac.

Government and Politics

Arizona is governed under a constitution of 1911, as amended. The chief executive of the state is a governor, elected to a 4-year term; the number of terms a governor may serve is unlimited. Arizona has a bicameral legislature, comprising a 30-member Senate and a 60-member House of Representatives. All the legislators are elected to 2-year terms. Two populous counties, Maricopa (including Phoenix) and Pima (including Tucson), together elect about three-fourths of the members of each chamber. The highest tribunal in the state is the supreme court, comprising five justices elected to 6-year terms. The state also has a Court of Appeals, and each of Arizona's 15 counties has a Superior Court. The government of each county is overseen by an elected board of supervisors. Arizona elects two U.S. senators and six representatives; it has eight electoral votes in presidential elections.

The Democratic party dominated state and local politics in Arizona until the early 1950s. Since that time the Republican party has attracted a large proportion of the state's many immigrants, and Republicans have held

A monolith of wind-eroded sandstone rises more than 300 m (1,000 ft) above the desert floor of Monument Valley in northeastern Arizona. Monument Valley Navajo Tribal Park lies within the largest Indian reservation in the United States.

The Grand Canyon, in north central Arizona, is one of the natural wonders of the world. This spectacular chasm, cut in sandstone over millions of years by the eroding forces of the Colorado River and the wind, is 347 km (217 mi) long and more than 1.6 km (1 mi) deep.

their share of governorships since 1950. A similar pattern has occurred in presidential elections. In 1964 U.S. Sen. Barry M. GOLDWATER of Arizona was the Republican candidate for president.

Economy

In the first half of the 20th century Arizona's economy was dominated by copper, cattle, cotton, and climate (which lured tourists). Beginning in the 1940s, however, many factories were built; eventually, the electronics industry greatly boosted Arizona's manufacturing. By the late 1980s the service industries (including trade and financial services) contributed about 75% of the gross state product.

Agriculture and Forestry. Although now proportionately much less important, agriculture still contributes significantly to Arizona's economy. The most valuable agricultural commodities are cattle, cotton, hay, and lettuce; maize, potatoes, citrus fruit, hogs, sheep, milk, and eggs also are produced in sizable quantities. Agricultural holdings in Arizona generally are very large, and most of the farmland is used to raise livestock. Ranches are situated in the Colorado Plateau region, in the central mountains, and in the southeast. Most cattle are fattened in feedlots, concentrated in the Phoenix area. Crops are grown intensively on irrigated land. The Salt River Valley is the leading crop-producing region; it is irrigated in large part with waters from the Theodore Roosevelt Dam.

Arizona has a relatively small forest-products industry. The chief trees cut are softwoods like yellow pine, Douglas fir, and ponderosa pine.

Mining. Arizona has an important mining industry. Copper ore is by far the most valuable mineral. Arizona produces more than half of the total U.S. copper output, mostly from open-pit mines. Significant amounts of gold, silver, and molybdenum are recovered through the processing of copper ore. Other mineral products include coal, sand and gravel, stone, asbestos, perlite, pumice, pyrites, and gemstones.

Manufacturing. Arizona's manufacturing has grown tremendously since the 1940s, most recently in high-technology areas, and now produces about 15% of the gross state product. The leading goods produced in the state's factories, mostly located in the Phoenix and Tucson metropolitan areas, are electrical machinery and electronic devices, followed by nonelectrical machinery, transportation equipment, and primary metals (mainly refined copper ore).

Tourism. Tourism is one of Arizona's major economic activities. Winter visitors are attracted mainly by the warm and dry climate in the southern part of the state, and summer tourists are lured principally by the state's areas of great natural beauty. The state's parks and monuments are primary attractions. There are also luxurious private resort hotels (notably in Scottsdale) and some dude ranches.

Transportation. Arizona is well equipped to move persons and freight by road, railroad, and air transport. Most major roads and railroad lines run east-west. There are about 200 airports, the busiest being at Phoenix.

Energy. In the mid-1980s Arizona had an installed electric generating capacity of 13.7 million kW, and the annual production of electricity was about 51 billion kW h. About two-thirds was produced in thermal plants; much of the rest was generated by hydroelectric facilities (notably HOOVER, Glen Canyon, Davis, and Parker dams, on the Colorado).

History

Indians first inhabited the region that is now Arizona between about 25,000 and 10,000 years ago. By AD 700 the HOHOKAM CULTURE, centered in the lower Salt and middle Gila river basins, was among the most sophisticated Indian groups north of present-day Mexico. Another highly developed culture group, the ANASAZI (of which the Hopi are descendants), lived on the Colorado Plateau. These people constructed many cliff dwellings that still exist. During the 16th and 17th centuries the Athapascan-speaking Apache and Navajo moved into eastern Arizona; by this time the Hohokam had abandoned their lands.

Spanish Presence. The first white person to enter Arizona was probably the Spanish explorer Álvar Núñez CABEZA DE VACA, in 1536. Three years later the Franciscan friar Marcos de Niza and the black slave Estavan passed through the San Pedro valley in search of the fabled Seven Cities of CIBOLA, reputed to contain great amounts of gold. In 1540–42, members of a party led by Francisco Vásquez de CORONADO, also attempting to find the Seven Cities, visited the Grand Canyon of the Colorado River and some Hopi villages. During the following 100 years several Spanish explorers and missionaries traveled in Arizona. One such visitor was Juan de OÑATE, who went down the lower Colorado in 1605. In the early 17th century missions were established among the Hopi, Papago, and Pima Indians; the Hopi later ousted the missionaries during a great Indian revolt in 1680.

In the 1690s and early 1700s the Jesuit Eusebio KINO founded missions at Tumacacori, Guevavi, and Bac (which is now called San Xavier and is still active), in the Santa Cruz valley, and at Quiburi, in the San Pedro valley. In 1752, Spanish soldiers established Arizona's first white settlement, a presidio at Tubac, and in 1776 the presidio was transferred to Tucson. During the 18th century warfare occurred between the Spanish and Indians and between the Apache and other Indians. The whites and Apache were at peace from about 1790 to 1822, but in the later 1820s much fighting occurred in Arizona, since 1821 a part of independent Mexico.

Phoenix, in the "Valley of the Sun," is Arizona's capital and largest city. Nearly 50% of the state's population resides within the city's metropolitan area.

Glen Canyon Dam in northern Arizona, was completed in 1964 and measures 216 m (710 ft) in height. Lake Powell, created behind the dam, extends 297 km (186 mi) into southern Utah.

U.S. Annexations. As a result of the MEXICAN WAR (1846–48) the United States annexed Arizona north of the Gila River, and the area was made part of the New Mexico Territory in 1850. The United States also sought the region south of the Gila, partly as a transportation route to California, and it gained this territory from Mexico through the GADSDEN PURCHASE (1853). In the late 1850s silver was mined near Tubac, and copper was produced at Ajo. Southern Arizona was settled mainly by Americans from the South, and during the Civil War considerable sentiment for the Confederacy existed.

On Feb. 24, 1863, the separate Union territory of Arizona was created. In the 1860s several agricultural settlements, such as Gila Bend (1864), Phoenix (late 1860s), and Florence (1866), were founded, and in the 1870s and '80s many large cattle and sheep ranches were established. In 1877 much silver was discovered at what became (1879) Tombstone. Also in the 1870s, the Mormons founded a number of settlements on the Colorado Plateau and in the Salt and upper Gila river valleys. In 1878 the railroad reached Yuma from California, and during 1881–83 a rail line was built westward across northern Arizona. From the 1860s to 1880s fighting occurred between whites and the Apache, led by chiefs MANGAS COLORADAS, COCHISE, and GERONIMO (surrendered 1886).

In the 1880s and '90s several corporations opened large-scale copper mines. The completion, in 1911, of Theodore Roosevelt Dam on the Salt River resulted in a considerable growth of irrigated farming. With a growing economy and population, Arizona was admitted (Feb. 14, 1912) to the Union as the 48th state.

Statehood. The first governor of the state was George W. P. Hunt, a Democrat; he held the office for seven 2-year terms before his death in 1934. The copper-mining industry grew during this period. In the 1920s and '30s commercial agriculture expanded as new irrigation projects were constructed.

Arizona's economy received a great boost during World War II when many defense installations (notably air bases) and industries were established in the state. In the postwar period manufacturing became the leading segment of the economy, and agriculture, mining, and tourism also expanded rapidly. The population increased from 499,261 in 1940 to 3,677,985 in 1990. With the great economic and population growth came a need for more fresh water. In 1963 the U.S. Supreme Court ruled that Arizona was entitled to 3.45 billion m³ (2.8 million acre-ft) of water per year from the Colorado River, and in 1968 the U.S. Congress authorized the great Central Arizona Project. The project delivered water from the Colorado to Phoenix in 1985; it is scheduled to reach Tucson in 1991. In February 1988 the Arizona house voted to impeach Gov. Evan Mecham, a Republican; the state senate then convicted him on two charges of official misconduct and removed him from office. Only the seventh U.S. governor to have been impeached and removed from office, Mecham was succeeded by Arizona secretary of state Rose Mofford, a Democrat.

ark In the biblical story of NOAH, the ark was a large vessel that saved Noah's family and pairs of all living creatures at the time of the DELUGE. Genesis 6:14–16 gives a description of this floating houseboat. It was made of "gopher" wood, had three decks, and was approximately 137 by 23 by 14 m (450 by 75 by 45 ft) in size. The Sumerian-Babylonian Epic of GILGAMESH gives a similar but more detailed account of an ark and a deluge.

ark of the covenant The ark of the covenant was originally a portable wooden chest containing the two stone tablets of the TEN COMMANDMENTS. In ancient Israel's history and cult, it served as a symbol of God's presence and as a military rallying point. It was carried at the head of the column when the Jews fled from Egypt, and before the army in battle. Later, DAVID brought the ark, by then an ornate golden shrine, to Jerusalem, where it eventually resided in the temple's inner sanctuary. Today, a holy ark can be found in every synagogue. It is placed in the wall facing Jerusalem (the eastern wall in Europe and America) and contains the TORAH scrolls.

Arkansas [ahr'-kuhn-saw] Arkansas, one of the Southern states of the United States, is bordered by Missouri on the north and northeast, by Tennessee and Mississippi on the east, by Louisiana on the south, and by Texas and Oklahoma on the west. The region of Arkansas was first visited by Europeans in 1541–42, when Hernando DE SOTO, a Spanish explorer, led a party through the area. Acquired (1803) by the United States as part of the LOUISIANA PURCHASE, Arkansas became the 25th state in 1836. Long an agricultural region, the state industrialized rapidly after 1940, and by the late 1970s its economy was dominated by the manufacturing sector. The name *Arkansas* is derived from a Quapaw Indian word meaning "downstream people"; the name was formerly also spelled *Arkansa* and *Arkansaw*.

Land and Resources

Arkansas encompasses a picturesque region, with much forestland and several major rivers. The highest point is Magazine Mountain (839 m/2,753 ft high), in the western part of the state, and the lowest point, along the Ouachita River in the south, has an elevation of 17 m (55 ft); the approximate mean elevation is 198 m (650 ft). About 10% of the state's land area is owned by the federal government.

Physiographic Regions. Arkansas comprises two major regions—the Interior Highlands of much of the west and north and the Lowlands of the south and east.

The Interior Highlands comprise the Ozark Plateau (see OZARK MOUNTAINS) in the north and the Ouachita Mountains. The Ozarks, ranging in elevation in Arkansas from 150 to 786 m (492 to 2,579 ft), comprise mainly the Springfield and Salem plateaus, in the north, and the Boston Mountains, in the south. The plateaus are gently rolling, except where swift-flowing streams have cut deep valleys. Much of this area is forested and also has good farmland. The wooded Boston Mountains are interlaced by numerous river gorges.

The Ouachita Mountains comprise a series of parallel east-west valleys and ridges. Included in the Ouachitas is the Arkansas Valley, through which runs the Arkansas River. Although generally less elevated than the rest of the region, the valley contains several lofty points, including Magazine Mountain, which at 839 m (2,753 ft) is the highest point in the state, and Petit Jean Mountain. The Ouachita Mountains region contains many mineral springs, such as those at HOT SPRINGS.

The Lowlands region is composed of the West Gulf Coastal Plain, in the south, and the Mississippi Alluvial Plain, in the east; the terrain is mostly level and from 30 to 90 m (98 to 295 ft) in elevation. The coastal plain has extensive pine forests and important deposits of bauxite, petroleum, and natural gas; the soil is generally sandy. The alluvial plain, adjacent to the Mississippi River, has a deep fill of unconsolidated river-deposited sediments, sometimes with a shallow hardpan that permits irrigated rice farming. Crowleys Ridge, a narrow north-south band of hills covered with loess, is in the center of the alluvial plain.

Rivers and Lakes. Arkansas contains several major rivers. The MISSISSIPPI RIVER forms most of the state's eastern boundary, and the ARKANSAS RIVER flows diagonally across the state from the Oklahoma border to its confluence with the Mississippi, in the southeast. Other rivers include the White River, which traverses much of northern and eastern Arkansas before entering the Mississippi; the Ouachita River, which rises in western Arkansas and flows south into Louisiana; and the Red River, which forms part of the boundary with Texas.

Arkansas has few big natural lakes; the largest is Lake Chicot, in the southeast, an oxbow lake near the Mississippi River. The state has several major artificial lakes, created by dams on rivers: Lakes Ouachita, Hamilton, and Catherine, on the Ouachita River; Millwood Lake, on the Little River; Nimrod Lake, on the Fourche La Fave River; and

AT A GLANCE

ARKANSAS

Land: Area: 137,754 km² (53,187 mi²); rank: 27th. Capital and largest city: Little Rock (1990 pop., 175,795). Counties: 75. Elevations: highest—839 m (2,753 ft), at Magazine Mountain; lowest—17 m (55 ft), at the Ouachita River.

People: Population (1990): 2,362,239; rank: 33d; density: 17.1 persons per km² (44.4 per mi²). Distribution (1988 est.): 39.7% metropolitan, 60.3% nonmetropolitan. Average annual change (1980–90): +0.2%.

Government (1991): Governor: Bill Clinton, Democrat. U.S. Congress: Senate—2 Democrats; House—3 Democrats, 1 Republican. Electoral college votes: 6. State legislature: 35 senators, 100 representatives.

Economy: State personal income (1988): $29.3 billion; rank: 32d. Median family income (1979): $14,641; rank: 49th. Agriculture: income (1988)—$4 billion. Forestry: sawtimber volume (1987)—64.5 billion board feet. Mining: value (1987, nonfuels only)—$264 million. Manufacturing: value added (1987)—$10.6 billion. Services: value (1987)—$5.5 billion.

Miscellany: Statehood: June 15, 1836; the 25th state. Nickname: Land of Opportunity, State; bird: mocking bird; flower: apple blossom;tree: pine; motto: *Regnat Populus* ("The People Rule"); song: "Arkansas."

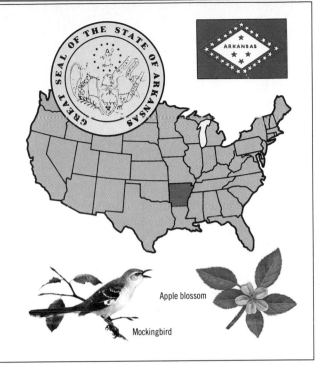

Apple blossom

Mockingbird

Ozark Reservoir and Dardanelle Lake on the Arkansas River.

Climate. The climate of Arkansas is mild, with warm to hot summers and cool winters. Annual precipitation averages from 1,016 to 1,524 mm (40 to 60 in) and comes mostly during winter and spring. December and January are usually the wettest months in the south, and March through May is the wet period in the north. The Interior Highlands are somewhat cooler than the Lowlands and receive small amounts of snow in the winter. Tornadoes occur in the warm seasons, especially in the extreme northwest and in the low-lying southeast. LITTLE ROCK, in the center of the state, has a mean January temperature of 4° C (40° F) and a mean July temperature of 27° C (81° F).

Vegetation and Animal Life. About 50% of the state is covered with forestland, most of which is privately owned. The state has three national forests. Approximately two-thirds of the forests comprise hardwoods, such as oak, white ash, cypress, elm, and hickory; these are located mainly in the Interior Highlands and in the Mississippi Alluvial Plain. The West Gulf Coastal Plain contains softwood forests, chiefly composed of loblolly pine and short-leaf pine. Tulip trees grow on Crowleys Ridge. The state has many kinds of wild flowers, including American bellflowers, yellow jasmines, orchids, water lilies, and hydrangea.

The plentiful animal life includes whitetail deer, red foxes, rabbits, squirrels, bobcats, weasels, and muskrat.

Among the numerous game birds are ducks, geese, pheasant, woodcocks, and quail. Rivers and lakes are well stocked with fish, such as bass, perch, catfish, bream, and sturgeon.

Mineral Resources. Arkansas has several valuable mineral deposits. Bauxite is found in great quantity near Little Rock, and deposits of petroleum, natural gas, and bromine are located in the West Gulf Coastal Plain. The Arkansas River Valley has coal and natural gas deposits. There are deposits of diamonds near Murfreesboro, but nearly all the diamonds were recovered during 1908–25 and the area is now a state park; individuals can search for diamonds and occasionally find them near the surface. The state's other mineral resources include stone, sand and gravel, lime, clay, barite, and gypsum.

People

During the census period 1980–90 the population of Arkansas increased by 3.3% (the national growth rate during 1980–90 was 10.2%). The proportion of urban population has steadily increased since the 1940s. The largest communities in Arkansas are Little Rock (the capital), FORT SMITH, North Little Rock, PINE BLUFF, Fayetteville, Hot Springs, Jonesboro, West Memphis, Jacksonville, El Dorado, and Blytheville. In 1980 about 83% of the state's inhabitants were white, and about 16% were black; approximately 9,400 of the inhabitants were Indians.

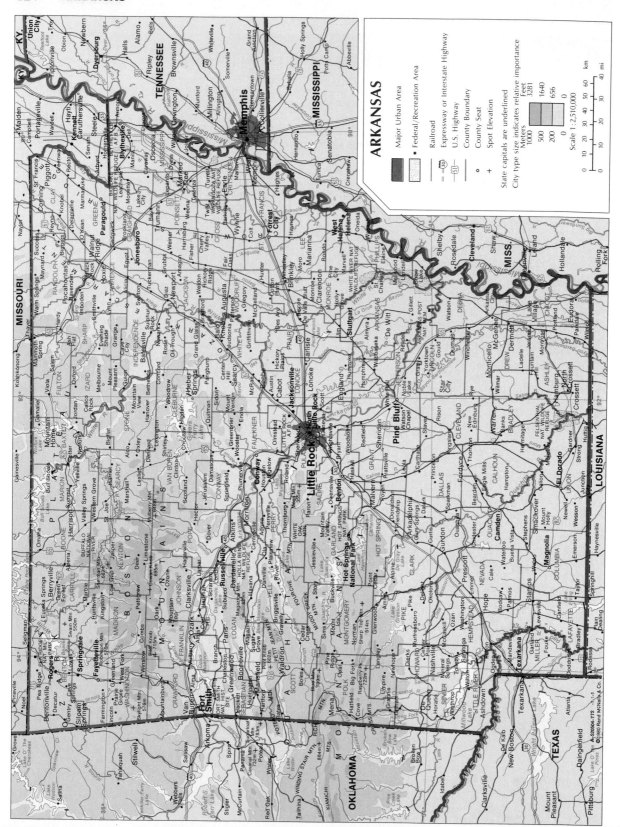

ARKANSAS

Major Urban Area

Federal/Recreation Area

Railroad

Expressway or Interstate Highway

U.S. Highway

County Boundary

County Seat

Spot Elevation

State capitals are underlined

City type size indicates relative importance

Meters	Feet
1000	3281
500	1640
200	656
0	0

Scale 1:2,510,000

© 1980 Rand MNally & Co.
A-500504-772   -7-1-1

A substantial majority of Arkansans are Protestant, mainly Baptist and Methodist. A sizable number of inhabitants are Roman Catholics, and a much smaller number Jewish.

Education. The first school established in Arkansas was the Dwight Mission (opened in 1822 near modern Russellville), whose initial students were Cherokee Indians. In 1843 the state legislature provided for a system of public schools, but private academies dominated education until the 1870s.

Among the institutions of higher education in the state are Arkansas Tech University (1909), at Russellville; Arkansas State University (1909), at State University; Harding University (1924), at Searcy; Henderson State University (1890) and Ouachita Baptist University (1886), both at Arkadelphia; Southern Arkansas University (1909), at Magnolia; the University of Arkansas (1871), at Fayetteville; the University of Arkansas at Little Rock (1927); the University of Arkansas at Monticello (1909); the University of Arkansas at Pine Bluff (1873); the University of Central Arkansas (1907), at Conway; and Westark Community College (1928), at Fort Smith.

Cultural Institutions. The leading libraries in Arkansas are at the University of Arkansas at Fayetteville and at the University of Arkansas at Little Rock. The Arkansas Library Commission maintains about 35 regional public libraries. Notable museums in the state include the Arkansas Arts Center, the Arkansas Museum of History, and the Museum of Science and Natural History, all in Little Rock; the University of Arkansas Museum, with displays on the state's history, in Fayetteville; a noted museum of firearms, in Berryville; and a museum of Indian artifacts, near Wilson. Little Rock supports several musical groups, including a symphony orchestra.

Historical Sites. Among the places of historical interest in Arkansas are Arkansas Post National Memorial, including the site of the first permanent white settlement (founded 1686) in Arkansas; Fort Smith National Historic Site, encompassing one of the first U.S. military posts in the Louisiana Territory; Pea Ridge National Military Park, taking in the battlefield where Union forces scored an important victory (Mar. 7–8, 1862) during the Civil War; and the capitol, in Little Rock, of the old Arkansaw Territory.

Communications. The residents of Arkansas are served by numerous radio stations (the first one began operation in Pine Bluff in 1920); commercial television broadcasting is augmented by cable systems. Among the more influential daily newspapers are the *Fort Smith Southwest Times Record*; the *Hot Springs National Park Sentinel-Record*; the *Jonesboro Sun*; the *Little Rock Arkansas Democrat* and *Arkansas Gazette*; and the *Pine Bluff Commercial*. The state's first newspaper was the *Arkansas Gazette*, initially published in 1819 at Arkansas Post and moved in 1821 to Little Rock.

Economy

The economy of Arkansas was overwhelmingly agricultural until the middle of the 20th century when industrial enterprises began to be established in large numbers.

Agriculture. The value of farm output in Arkansas totals several billion dollars annually. Leading as the most valuable crops are soybeans, rice, cotton, and hay; other important crops include wheat, oats, sorghum grain, spinach, tomatoes, potatoes, watermelons, apples, and peaches. Arkansas leads the nation in the production of broilers (young chickens) and is a leading producer of chickens, chicken eggs, and turkeys. The state also has a sizable dairy industry and produces large numbers of beef cattle and hogs. The principal cropland is located in eastern Arkansas; livestock farms are situated mainly in the north and northwest.

Forestry and Fishing. Arkansas has a substantial forest-products industry. The commercially valuable softwood is used for pulp and plywood; much hardwood is also cut.

Arkansas has a small but significant fishing industry—perhaps unexpected for an inland state. Millions of pounds of fish are caught by commercial concerns in the Mississippi and its tributaries. The chief species landed are catfish, buffalo fish, carp, gizzard shad, paddlefish, sheepshead, and garfish.

Mining. Arkansas has an important mining sector. The

Canoeing, fishing, and camping draw people to the Buffalo River in northern Arkansas. This Ozark waterway is known for the steep bluffs along its course. In 1972, Congress designated a 209-km (130-mi) section of the Buffalo as the first U.S. national river.

(Left) *Little Rock, a port city on the Arkansas River, is the state's capital and largest city. A focus of economic and commercial activity, Little Rock is a marketing center for the agricultural produce of central Arkansas.* (Below) *The state capitol of Arkansas, modeled after the national Capitol, lies in the commercial district of Little Rock. The golden-domed structure, made of marble and granite, was completed in 1915.*

most valuable mineral recovered is petroleum; the chief petroleum production sites in Arkansas are in Union and Columbia counties in the south. Other valuable minerals include bromine, natural gas, and stone. Arkansas is the leading U.S. state in the production of bromine as well as bauxite and vanadium. Other minerals produced in significant quantities include coal, clay, lime, and sand and gravel.

Manufacturing. The leading branch of the economy of Arkansas is manufacturing. The chief products are processed food, electrical equipment, and forest products. Other manufactures include refined petroleum, clothing, printed materials, and metals. Arkansas, with its abundant water, power, and mineral resources, has been developing chemical-processing industries. The chief industrial centers are Little Rock-North Little Rock, Pine Bluff, and Fort Smith.

Tourism. Arkansas has a large tourist industry. Notable attractions include Hot Springs National Park, with 47 hot springs used by people seeking relief from illness or injury; Buffalo National River, an unpolluted stream that flows past multicolored bluffs and many caves and springs; and a variety of state parks and recreation areas. Arkansas's many lakes, rivers, and streams and wilderness areas attract sizable numbers of out-of-state sport fishermen and hunters.

Transportation. Road, water, and air transport are the chief means of carrying persons and freight in Arkansas. Although railroad mileage has diminished since early in the 20th century, a number of cities have rail freight service. Among the major navigable waterways are the Arkansas, Ouachita and White rivers. Major airlines serve the state's largest cities; Arkansas's other centers are adequately connected by small feeder lines.

Energy. Most of Arkansas's electricity is produced in thermal plants using refined petroleum. The state has several hydroelectric facilities, notably on the White and Little Red rivers, and a nuclear-power plant at Rus-

sellville, in the north central part of the state near the Arkansas River.

Government and Politics

Arkansas is governed under a constitution of 1874, as amended; previous charters had been adopted in 1836, 1861, 1864, and 1868. The chief executive of the state is a governor, elected to a 4-year term (raised from 2 years by voter approval in 1984). The state's bicameral legislature, called the General Assembly, comprises a 35-member Senate and 100-member House of Representatives; senators are elected to 4-year terms, and representatives are elected to 2-year terms. The highest tribunal in Arkansas is the supreme court, composed of a chief justice and six associate justices, all elected to 8-year terms. Arkansas is divided into 75 counties, each of which is administered by an elected county judge. Each county judge presides over a quorum court, a legislative body whose chief function is to draw up and approve the county budget.

The Democratic party dominates state and local government in Arkansas; Republicans have served as governor only in 1868-74 (during the era of RECONSTRUCTION), 1967-71 (when Winthrop Rockefeller held the office), and 1981-83 (when Frank D. White served one term). In presidential elections, the Democratic nominee carried Arkansas in all elections except 1868, 1872, 1972, 1980, and 1984, when the Republican candidate won, and 1968, when the American Independent party nominee won.

History

Among the earliest inhabitants of present-day Arkansas were the Bluff Dweller Indians, who probably lived in the northwestern part of the state before 1000 BC. About 2,000 years later, Indians known as MOUND BUILDERS settled along the Mississippi River. When the first Europeans arrived, in the mid-16th century, the QUAPAW lived

The Reynolds Aluminum plant in Patterson smelts ore from strip mines near Little Rock. More than 90 percent of all bauxite mined in the United States comes from a small area in central Arkansas.

near the mouth of the Arkansas River, and the OSAGE lived to the north of the river; the CADDO Indians, an agricultural people who constructed distinctive beehive-shaped dwellings, lived in the southwest.

European Exploration and Early Settlement. The first Europeans to enter Arkansas were members of a party led by the Spanish explorer Hernando de Soto; they traversed the central and southern parts of the state in 1541–42. In 1673 a group under Jacques MARQUETTE and Louis JOLLIET traveled down the Mississippi as far as the Arkansas River. In 1682 a party headed by Robert Cavelier, sieur de LA SALLE, journeyed down the Mississippi to its mouth. La Salle claimed the Mississippi Valley, including modern Arkansas, for Louis XIV of France and called it Louisiana. One of La Salle's aides, Henri de TONTY, established (1686) Aux Ares, the first permanent white settlement in Arkansas, near the mouth of the Arkansas River; the community later became known as Arkansas Post. In 1719–20 a colony of Germans was established nearby

as part of the abortive French MISSISSIPPI SCHEME. In 1762 France ceded Arkansas and its other possessions west of the Mississippi to Spain. The Spanish encouraged white settlement in the region, but when they returned the area to France in 1800, fewer than 1,000 persons lived in Arkansas. In 1803 the United States acquired Arkansas as part of the Louisiana Purchase.

U.S. Territory and Statehood. Arkansas was part of the Louisiana District (1804–05), the Louisiana Territory (1805–12), and the Missouri Territory (1812–19) before being constituted, in 1819, as the Arkansaw Territory, which also included part of present-day Oklahoma. Settlement of Arkansas was slow until the later 1820s, when the CHEROKEE and CHOCTAW Indians who had become embroiled in disputes with whites were removed from the territory. By 1835 Arkansas had 50,000 white inhabitants, and on June 15, 1836, it entered the Union as the 25th state. Black slaves supplied most of the labor for the productive cotton plantations of eastern and southern Arkansas.

The city of Hot Springs, in the Ouachita Mountains, is a major resort area and tourist attraction. The locale is known for its 47 thermal mineral springs. Since 1921, Hot Springs Spa has been owned and operated by the federal government.

The Civil War and Reconstruction. On the eve of the CIVIL WAR, Arkansas was almost equally divided between secessionists and antisecessionists. In March 1861, a state convention voted against leaving the Union, but in May 1861, a month after the Civil War had begun, the convention voted for secession and Arkansas joined the CONFEDERATE STATES OF AMERICA. In March 1862, Union troops won a bloody battle at Pea Ridge (Elkhorn Tavern), and by early 1864 Confederate forces were confined to southern Arkansas, where they made the town of Washington the new state capital. A Union regime administered most of Arkansas from Little Rock.

The war ended in 1865, but during 1866–67 former secessionists controlled the state legislature and passed several measures restricting the rights of the recently emancipated blacks. As a result Arkansas was placed under federal military rule in 1867. The state was readmitted to the Union in mid-1868.

Economic Hardships and Recovery. During the late 19th century agriculture (especially cotton cultivation) and business expanded, fostered in part by large-scale railroad construction. Because of low prices and crop failures, farmers faced hard times in the 1880s, however, and, organized in such groups as the Agricultural Wheel, dissatisfied farmers almost gained the governorship in the 1888 election. In the 1890s several laws were adopted that severely restricted the civil rights of blacks in Arkansas. In 1901–07, under Gov. Jeff Davis, a charismatic, Populist-style politician, the state's educational and penal systems were reformed and its debt largely retired.

In 1921 petroleum was discovered near El Dorado, but Arkansas remained overwhelmingly agricultural until manufacturing enterprises began to be established in sizable numbers during the 1940s. Farmers suffered from low cotton prices in the 1920s, a situation compounded by destructive flooding by the Arkansas and Mississippi rivers in 1927 and by a severe drought that began in 1930. The Depression of the 1930s created widespread unemployment and hardship in the state, and many "Arkies" headed west in search of better living conditions. Recovery in the state began during World War II when new industries (such as bauxite processing) were started and several military bases were established. During the war, J. William FULBRIGHT first gained national prominence as a representative of Arkansas in the U.S. Congress.

Civil Rights and Recent Trends. In 1954 the U.S. Supreme Court ruled that segregating black and white pupils in separate public schools was unconstitutional. Arkansas resisted implementing the ruling, and in September 1957 the state received national attention when Gov. Orval E. Faubus (in office 1955–67) tried to prevent the integration of Little Rock Central High School. President Dwight D. Eisenhower quickly intervened, in part by sending federal troops to Little Rock, and several black students were enrolled at the high school. Resistance by whites to school integration continued into the 1960s and '70s, but by the late 1970s blacks had equal access to virtually all public educational institutions in the state. In 1981, Little Rock elected its first black mayor.

From 1940 to 1960 the population of Arkansas de-

clined by more than 8%, because many persons, particularly blacks, left the state for better employment opportunities elsewhere. In the 1960s the state's population began to increase at a substantial rate, and the trend has continued. By the late 1970s the manufacturing sector dominated the economy, but during the 1980s Arkansas did not make significant economic strides despite efforts centered on education, economic development, and fiscal modernization.

Arkansas (Indian tribe)   see QUAPAW

——

Arkansas River [ahr'-kuhn-saw or ahr-kan'-zuhs] The Arkansas River, a major western tributary of the Mississippi River system, rises in the Rocky Mountains of central Colorado. It flows east into Kansas, turns southeast through northern Oklahoma, and crosses Arkansas to enter the Mississippi. It is 2,333 km (1,450 mi) long, and its drainage area is about 415,700 km^2 (160,500 mi^2). From its source to its mouth, it falls 3,475 m (11,400 ft) and has a relatively rapid current.

The principal tributaries of the Arkansas are the Canadian, Cimarron, and Verdigris rivers. Dams on the Arkansas have created reservoirs, including the John Martin in Colorado, the Keystone in Oklahoma, and the Dardanelle in Arkansas. Widening the river has made it navigable 1,210 km (750 mi) from its mouth. Important cities on its course are Pueblo, Colo.; Wichita, Kans.; Tulsa, Okla.; and Fort Smith and Little Rock, Ark. Arkansas Post, near the river's mouth, was settled by the French in 1686 and was one of the first European communities in the lower Mississippi River valley.

——

Arkhangelsk [ahr-kan'-gelsk] Arkhangelsk (English: Archangel) is a city in the northwestern USSR, situated on both sides of the Northern Dvina River about 48 km (30 mi) from its mouth in the White Sea. It has a population of 408,000 (1985 est.). Its harbor is frozen for six months a year but can be kept open by icebreakers; the city is an important shipping point for lumber and wood products.

The city was founded in 1584 on the site of an earlier Norse settlement. Originally called Novo-Kholmogory, the city was renamed in 1613 for a monastery of the archangel Michael. Arkhangelsk served as Russia's only foreign trade port until the founding of Saint Petersburg in 1703, whereupon it declined. A railroad completed to the city from Moscow in 1898 revived port activity.

——

Arkwright, Sir Richard The English inventor Richard Arkwright, b. Dec. 23, 1732, d. Aug. 3, 1792, is best known for designing the SPINNING frame. In 1769 he invented a mechanical thread-spinner capable of drawing carded cotton into hard-twisted threads of any desired thickness. This machine supplanted the earlier spinning jenny, because the stronger threads it produced could be used as the warp—or fixed, lengthwise threads—in weaving cotton cloth. Water-driven cotton mills using the spinning frame were built throughout the British Isles. Arkwright built many himself and established one of Britain's first industrial empires.

Arlen, Harold Harold Arlen, b. Hyman Arluck in Buffalo, N.Y., Feb. 15, 1905, d. Apr. 23, 1986, was a blues and popular-song composer. His success began in 1933 with "Stormy Weather," introduced by Ethel Waters in Harlem's Cotton Club. In 1939 his "Over the Rainbow" from *The Wizard of Oz* won an Oscar and became Judy Garland's musical trademark. Among his other motion-picture songs were "Blues in the Night," "One for My Baby," "That Old Black Magic," and "It's Only a Paper Moon." Broadway shows for which he wrote the music include *Bloomer Girl* and *Jamaica*.

Arlington Arlington (1990 pop., 261,721) is a city in northern Texas, between Dallas and Fort Worth. It is a center of the aerospace and automotive industries; steel and electronics equipment are also manufactured there. Arlington is the site of Six Flags Over Texas, a historical amusement park.

Arlington National Cemetery The Arlington National Cemetery, located across the Potomac River from Washington, D.C., in Arlington, Va., is the burial place for many Americans who were killed in war or who died while in the service of their country. Established in 1864, the 200-ha (500-acre) site also contains the Tomb of the Unknowns, the Confederate Monument, and the Custis-Lee mansion. Presidents Taft and Kennedy and Generals Pershing, Marshall, and Bradley are buried there.

Armada, Spanish see SPANISH ARMADA

armadillo Armadillos are nocturnal, burrowing New World mammals with a distinctive armor-encased body. They belong to the family Dasypodidae, order Edentata. They comprise 9 genera and about 20 species. The name *armadillo* was first used by the early Spanish explorers and means "small armored one." A patterned, hornlike, brown to pink armor composed of bony plates covers the upper and side surfaces and parts of the legs and under-

A nine-banded armadillo can hold its breath for up to six minutes during periods of exertion because of its extensive air passages and highly efficient circulatory system.

sides. If overtaken by an enemy, armadillos draw in their feet and nose, and some species roll into a ball.

The nine-banded armadillo, *Dasypus novemcinctus*, is found from the United States to South America. Its head and body are about 41 cm (16 in) long, the tail is an additional 36 cm (14 in), and the weight is up to 8 kg (18 lb). This species feeds at night on frogs, snakes, insects, and carrion.

All other armadillos live in Central and South America. The largest, which is often 150 cm (5 ft) long and weighs up to 60 kg (130 lb), is the giant armadillo, *Priodontes giganteus*, of eastern South America.

Armageddon [ahr-muh-ged'-uhn] Armageddon is the place named in the Book of REVELATION (16:16) where the kings of the Earth, the forces of good and evil, were to assemble for battle on the day of divine judgment. The biblical writer notes that *Armageddon* is the Greek transliteration of a Hebrew word. The term may mean "the mountain of Megiddo," referring to Mount CARMEL overlooking the plain of Megiddo, where many Old Testament battles were fought.

Armagh [ahr-mah'] Armagh, a district of Northern Ireland established in 1974, is a part of a former county of the same name. Bordering the Republic of Ireland on the south, Armagh has an area of 674 km² (260 mi²) and a population of 49,200 (1988 est.). The district town, Armagh, has been the ecclesiastical center of Ireland since the 5th century when Saint PATRICK is said to have founded his first mission settlement there; it is the seat of both the Church of Ireland and Roman Catholic archbishops. Apples and strawberries are grown in the district's northern lowlands.

Inhabited since prehistoric times, Armagh was an important political, religious, and cultural center during the Middle Ages. The area prospered during the 18th century.

armature see GENERATOR; MOTOR

armed services see AIR FORCE; ARMY; DEFENSE, NATIONAL; MARINE CORPS, U.S.; NAVY

Armenia [ahr-mee'-nee-uh] The historic Armenian homeland lies in eastern Anatolia and southern Transcaucasia (Soviet Armenia and adjacent parts of eastern Turkey). About 3 million Armenians live in Soviet Armenia, and another 1.4 million live in other parts of the USSR; an estimated 2 million more are dispersed throughout the world, primarily in the United States, Iran, France, Lebanon, Syria, and Turkey.

The Armenians are an Indo-European people who migrated to Armenia from the west, probably in the 7th century BC, intermingling with the peoples of URARTU. Ruled by kings of the Orontid dynasty, Armenia was one of the satrapies of the Persian empire until the defeat (4th century BC) of Persia by ALEXANDER THE GREAT, when it came

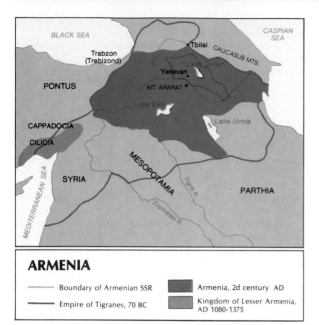

ARMENIA

| ——— Boundary of Armenian SSR | ▓ Armenia, 2d century AD |
| ——— Empire of Tigranes, 70 BC | ▓ Kingdom of Lesser Armenia, AD 1080-1375 |

under the nominal suzerainty of the Seleucids. During the Hellenistic and Roman periods it was an autonomous buffer state between the Parthian empire (2d century BC–3d century AD) and the Greco-Roman powers in the west. Under the Artaxiad king TIGRANES I (c.95–55 BC), the Armenian state reached its greatest expansion, extending from Georgia in the north into Mesopotamia and Syria in the south. Tigranes, however, was forced to become a tributary of Rome in 66 BC.

About AD 300, Tiridates III adopted Christianity as the religion of his kingdom, making Armenia the first Christian state. Christianization led to the development of a unique Armenian culture, a blend of Hellenistic and Iranian influences. In the early 5th century, Saint Mesrop, an Armenian churchman, devised an alphabet for the ARMENIAN LANGUAGE, initiating a period of literary and intellectual activity exemplified by the work of such historians as Athangelos and Koriun and the 5th-century philosopher and theologian Eznik of Kolb.

In the 5th and 6th centuries some parts of Armenia were nominally subject to the Eastern Roman (Byzantine) emperor, and others to the Sassanians of Persia, but the country was actually controlled by native clan leaders known as nakharars. Although at times the nobles were able to fight together to repel an external foe, as they did against the Sassanians at Avarair (451), much of medieval Armenian history was marked by disunity and division, intrigues and revolts by dynastic princes, and periodic invasions. In 640 the Muslim Arabs invaded Armenia and captured Dvin, its principal town. Under their patronage, the Bagratid family rose to prominence and established a line of kings in 886. Bagratid power reached its height in the 10th century, fostering a cultural renewal that included the work of such writers as Grig-

or Narekatsi and Hovhannes Draskhankertsi.

In the 11th century Armenia was conquered first by the Byzantines and then by the Seljuk Turks. Fleeing from the Turks, a group of Armenian nobles and their followers settled in Byzantine CILICIA, where they established a state known as Lesser, or Little, Armenia; it attained the status of a kingdom in 1198 and survived until 1375. The Armenians of Cilicia allied themselves with the European crusaders and developed a culture strongly influenced by the West.

The original Armenian homeland was conquered by the Ottoman Turks in the 16th century and—except for a portion seized by Persia in the early 17th century—remained under Ottoman rule for the next 400 years. The Armenians and other non-Orthodox eastern Christians were governed by the patriarch of the Armenian church, who lived at Istanbul and was responsible to the Ottoman sultan. Armenian society was dominated by wealthy bankers and businessmen—the sarafs and amiras; culture and literature were maintained by the church until the revival of national consciousness in the mid-19th century.

The annexation of Persian Armenia by Russia in 1828 and the growing influence of European thought among educated Armenians led to the development of a nationalist literature, outstanding examples of which were the novels of Khachatur Abovian (1805–48) and Hagop Melik-Agopian, known as "Raffi" (1835–88)—and to the formation of revolutionary political parties, the Hnchaks and the Dashnaks. Turkish atrocities against Christians led Armenians to undertake their self-defense and to call for autonomy or independence. European diplomats expressed concern about the "Armenian Question," but little was done when thousands of Armenians were massacred in 1894–96. During World War I the Turkish government, considering the Armenians sympathetic to its Russian foe, deported them en masse from Anatolia. Massacres and the hardships of the journey resulted in the deaths of between 600,000 and 1,000,000 Armenians in what has been called the "first genocide of modern times." Thousands migrated to Russian Armenia, where in 1918 an independent Republic of Armenia was established under Dashnak administration. For the duration of the republic the Dashnaks struggled to gain international recognition, solve chronic economic problems, and stave off attacks by Turkey. In December 1920 they turned the government over to the Communists rather than surrender to the Turks, and the Soviet Republic of Armenia came into being.

The frustration of Armenian nationalist aspirations has since provided motivation for terrorist activity directed against Turkey, and for the civil disturbances that convulsed Soviet Armenia in the late 1980s.

Armenia (Soviet republic)   Armenia is one of the 15 constituent republics of the USSR. It is located in Transcaucasia, on the borders of Turkey and Iran, and incorporates part of historic ARMENIA. The area is 29,800 km^2 (11,500 mi^2), and the population, 3,305,000 (1990 est.). The republic's capital is YEREVAN, with a population of 1,218,000 (1990 est.).

Soviet Armenia is a mountainous region, with 90% of its area at elevations of 1,000 m (3,300 ft) or more. The climate is dry and continental, with warm summers and cold winters. The only major lowland suitable for agriculture is the Ararat plain at the foot of Mount ARARAT, which is across the border in Turkey. The most prominent physical feature of Armenia is Lake Sevan, one of the world's largest mountain lakes, which covers 5% of its area. The outflowing Razdan River is used for power generation and irrigation.

The Armenians, who make up 90% of the population, speak a language that is a distinctive branch of the Indo-European family of languages. Russians constitute less than 5% of the population. More than 65% of the population are classified as urban, living mostly in small towns.

Armenia is one of the USSR's principal producers of copper, molybdenum, and gold. The chemical industry is concentrated in Yerevan and Kirovakan. A nuclear power station, opened in 1976, contributes much of the electricity. Agriculture, which is concentrated in the Ararat plain, specializes in vineyards, fruits, tobacco, and essential oils.

Beginning in 1988, Armenia was involved in a conflict with neighboring Azerbaijan over control of Nagorno-Karabakh, an Armenian enclave within Azerbaijan. In August 1990 the republic declared its independence of the USSR, changing its name from the Armenian Soviet Socialist Republic to the Republic of Armenia.

Armenian church   The Armenian church, also known as the Armenian Apostolic or Gregorian church, is an independent Christian church embracing the majority of the Armenian people. At the end of the 3d century, the king of Armenia, Tiridates III, was converted to Christianity by Saint Gregory the Illuminator. Since the 5th century the Armenian church has embraced MONOPHYSITISM, a doctrine that states that Christ has a single human and divine nature, separating it from other Christian groups. In other respects, most practices of the Armenian church resemble those of the ORTHODOX CHURCH. The head of the church is called the supreme catholicos. His permanent residence is at Echmiadzin in the USSR.

Armenian language   Modern Armenian, spoken by between 5 and 6 million people, comprises two main dialects: the Eastern, spoken in the USSR and Iran and the official language of the Armenian Soviet Republic, and the Western, spoken in Armenian communities in other parts of the Middle East, Europe, and the Western Hemisphere. Grabar, the classical Armenian dialect of the 5th century, survives as the language of the Armenian church. Armenian has its own alphabet, originally 36 letters (now 38), which was mainly derived from the Greek alphabet but with distinct innovations. The language is not closely akin to any surviving Indo-European dialect. Older theories relating it to the so-called Thraco-Phrygian group are no longer accepted, although it may have some relation to the Phrygian language itself. Current theory suggests a closer relation to Greek, however.

Arminianism   [ahr-min'-ee-uhn-izm]   Arminianism, which takes its name from Jacobus Arminius (Jakob Harmensen), is a moderate theological revision of CALVINISM that limits the significance of predestination. Arminius (1560–1609) was a Dutch Reformed theologian who studied at Leiden and Geneva. He became a professor at Leiden in 1603 and spent the rest of his life defending against strict Calvinists his position that God's sovereignty and man's free will are compatible.

A Remonstrance in 1610 gave the name REMONSTRANTS to the Arminian party. They were condemned by the Synod of Dort (1618–19) but later received toleration. English revisionist theology of the 17th century was called Arminian, although possibly without direct influence from Holland. John WESLEY accepted the term for his theological position and published the *Arminian Magazine*. The tension between the Arminian and Calvinist positions in theology became quiescent until Karl BARTH sparked its revival in the 20th century.

Arminius   [ahr-min'-ee-uhs]   Arminius, c.18 BC–AD 19, was a chief of the German Cherusci tribe who won a victory over the Roman army of Publius Quinctilius Varus in the Teutoburg Forest in AD 9. This battle, in which three Roman legions were destroyed, halted the Roman advance into Germany at the Rhine. Arminius, also called Hermann, was regarded as a German national hero.

Armistice Day   Armistice Day commemorates the signing of the armistice that ended World War I on Nov. 11, 1918. It was proclaimed an annual day of mourning in the United States by President Woodrow Wilson in 1919. The name was changed to Veterans Day in 1954, honoring the fallen in all U.S. wars.

Armitage, Kenneth   Kenneth Armitage, b. July 18, 1916, is a leading English sculptor. After study at the Leeds College of Art and the Slade School of Fine Art, London, he entered the British army in 1939. His military service completed in 1945, he became head of the sculpture department at the Bath Academy of Art the following year. By 1952, the year of his first one-man show in London, his striking mature style was evident. Although deeply affected by the modern drive toward abstraction, Armitage nearly always presents recognizably human forms, sometimes joining them with the forms of animals or furniture. The results are massive and highly stylized, with an archaic flavor that points to Armitage's interest in Egyptian and Cycladic art.

armor   Armor is covering worn to protect the body against assault by weapons. Although most often associated with the equipment worn by KNIGHTS in the Age of Chivalry, the first armor was probably a rudimentary wood and hide shield used in Neolithic times. The materials used for armor have ranged from tightly woven fibers to wood, metal, and—in our time—plastics. The wearing of armor became significant for the military about 1600 BC, when Greek foot-soldiers, or HOPLITES, began to wear protective equipment consisting of a round shield large enough to hide the body when kneeling, a bronze helmet, a cuirass (breastplate and backplate), and greaves (shin guards). This equipment plus a spear and short sword weighed more than 30 kg (about 70 lb). The magnificent Macedonian army of 331 BC was similarly armored, but individual overlapping metal plates known as scale armor were used. A significant Macedonian contribution was the use of scale armor to protect the heads and chests of warhorses, a practice known as barding. Armor was relatively unchanged during the next millennium, through the Roman period.

The importance of improvements in armor was demonstrated at the Battle of HASTINGS (1066), where Norman horsemen, protected by interlocking iron rings known as chain mail, and armored infantry soundly defeated the numerically superior English infantry, whose only protection was kite-shaped shields of Viking origin. This event marked the emergence of the armored horseman as the premier fighting force. In the next 400 years, however, the use of chain mail dwindled as technical advances allowed armorers to forge large single plates, or plate armor. Armor production increased and armor-related nomenclature became widely established.

Single-plate body armor reached its highest level of development during the 15th and 16th centuries, as German and Italian armorers vied to achieve the ultimate in technical, structural, and decorative craftsmanship. In the 17th century, the increasing efficiency of firearms in the West began to make armor obsolete; it had to be so heavy to withstand shot that troops refused to wear it for any length of time. In the Orient, mail and plate armor were significant during the first millennium BC, and continued in use even through the 19th century.

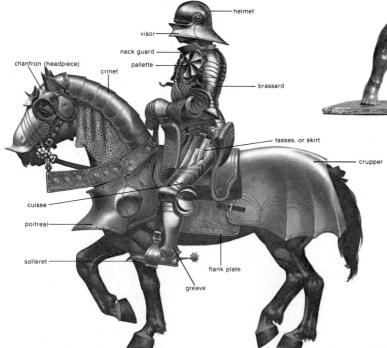

(Above) *Greek armor of the 6th century BC changed little in the following centuries. Made of bronze, it provided maximum protection to head and torso. The shield covered the body from neck to knees.* (Left) *At the height of its development in 16th-century Europe, plate steel armor was worn by the horse as well as the horseman. Protection was so complete that an armored knight was virtually indestructible when attacked with a sword. The only way to put him out of action was to knock him off his horse. Plate steel armor was little defense against gunpowder or cannonballs, however, and the kind of armor pictured here was used largely for purposes of prestige or ceremony by the end of the 16th century.*

helmet

visor

neck guard

chanfron (headpiece)   pallette

crinet

brassard

tasses, or skirt

crupper

cuisse

poitreal

flank plate

solleret

greave

(Left) *The "Corinthian" helmet was the type used most widely in classical Greece. Covering the head, face, and the nape of the neck, it left only the eyes and mouth unprotected. Its shape restricted hearing and side vision, however.*

The Polynesian warrior chief (center) wore armor of woven sisal cord and carried a sword edged with shark's teeth. His head was protected from the projectiles thrown by his own troops, who were arrayed in a mass behind him. Armor made of woven fibers was often used in societies that did not have metal weapons. The suit of the Japanese samurai (right) required the skills of many craftsmen. The armor itself was made of thin steel plates laced together by cords of silk. The shoes were made from a bear's pelt. The bronze face mask was attached to the helmet by a cord and served not only to protect the lower face but, with its ferocious features, to instill terror in the samurai's opponent.

Only two forms of armor, the helmet and the cuirass, survive to link the knights' armor with present-day protection. The shape of the earliest helmets and the helmets worn by today's soldiers are strikingly similar. The cuirass continued to be used by cavalry units and is still worn as ceremonial dress. During World War I it was briefly resurrected for infantry as protective body armor, especially for snipers and machine gunners.

World War II rekindled interest in body armor, and today many armies use a close relative of the cuirass in the form of a protective fabric vest containing plastic-encased metal plates. Commonly called a flak jacket, it originated during World War II, when experimental models were worn by American airmen to protect them from antiaircraft fire, known as flak.

In 1974 a stronger-than-steel fiber called Kevlar was developed for use as a puncture-resistant component of automobile tires. When combined in layers inside clothing, it was discovered that Kevlar acts as a kind of armor, bulletproofing the covered portions of the body (23 Kevlar layers can stop a submachine-gun bullet). The fiber was used at first in vests but is now made in almost every form of apparel. Body armor is bought by police officers, businesspersons, celebrities, and others who feel subject to attack, as well as by criminals. Many firms selling body armor require references or a gun permit from the buyer. Kevlar padding is also used to bulletproof automobiles.

armored vehicle Of basic importance in modern land warfare, armored vehicles include a variety of military equipment: tanks, infantry combat vehicles, armored personnel carriers, command vehicles, and self-propelled weapons, which are essentially mobile guns that carry their crews inside protective armor (see ARTILLERY). Most armored vehicles are propelled on caterpillar tracks capable of supporting and moving the heavy weights of these machines over rough terrain, and have an offensive capability in the form of guns or missiles.

Development of the Tank

Armored cars, the first modern armored fighting vehicles, were used in the opening years of World War I for reconnaissance and as self-propelled guns. The British began production of the Mark I tank in 1916, and tank designs—both French and British—were constantly refined and improved in speed and steerability as the war progressed. By the end of the war the British had built approximately 2,350 tanks of 13 different types, and the French about 4,000 smaller vehicles. Tanks fought effectively in all the final Allied offensives of World War I.

In the period between the wars, tank engines and components were greatly improved, and tank design began to take on its contemporary shape: an armored hull supported by tracks and topped by a turret mounting cannon and machine guns. Speeds took a quantum leap, to between 32 and 48 km/h (20–30 mph). Special-duty variants, such as light scouting tanks, began to appear.

The German attack on Poland in September 1939 combined devastating attacks by the German air force with *panzer* ("armored") units using *blitzkrieg* ("lightning war") techniques against the Polish lines. In 1940 Germany used blitzkrieg tactics to invade France and the Low Countries. Later in the war the heavy Russian T-34

Mark IV, World War I (Britain)

M-4A3E8 Sherman, World War II (U.S.)

Royal Tiger, World War II (Germany)

T-54, 1949 (U.S.S.R.)

M-60 A2, 1971 (U.S.)

XM-1, 1976 (U.S.)

The Mark IV was the most widely used British tank in service in World War I (about 1,000 were built). Its use en masse at the Battle of Cambrai (Nov. 20, 1917) first demonstrated the effectiveness of such a strategy. The Sherman tank, weighing more than 35 tons and traveling at a speed of 45 km/h (28 mph), was the main U.S. battle tank in World War II. This model, fielded in late 1944, had a 76-mm (3-in) turret gun and a 2½-in (6.35-cm) armor basis—the thickness of the hull front. The German Royal Tiger of late 1944 was a formidable weapon. It had a 6-in (15.24-cm) armor basis and an 88-mm (3.46-in) gun, but its 68-ton weight restricted its mobility. The T-54 (4-in/10.16-cm armor basis; 100-mm/3.94-in gun) was the backbone of the Soviet tank fleet in the 1950s, and tens of thousands are still held in their war reserves. The M-60A2 was an experimental tank using a turret with a missile launcher atop the proven M-60 hull. The U.S. XM-1 is an earlier version of the 1982 M-1 Abrams tank. It has new, laminate armor and a 105-mm (4.13-in) turret gun. Designed for easy maintenance, it travels at speeds of up to 70 km/h (43 mph).

proved effective against the lighter German tanks. Some 40,000 T-34s were produced by war's end, and the model continued as the main battle tank of the USSR until it was phased out in the mid-1950s and replaced by the T-54.

The mechanical reliability of the U.S. M-4 Sherman tank gave it an advantage over many other tanks, and it saw more service than any other Allied armored vehicle. More than 49,000 Shermans were produced during the war.

The U.S. drive to design improved tanks during World War II led to the production of superior tanks in the post-war period. The M-60 series, produced from 1960 to 1983, is still in use. The M-1 Abrams, the current U.S. main battle tank, is armored with laminated steel and

nonferrous materials. Its laser range finder, coupled with sophisticated fire control, gives it the ability to shell targets at ranges in excess of 4,000 m (4,374 yd). With the scheduled completion of 7,000 M-1s, the United States will have a total of 15,000 tanks. Current USSR field models, the T-64, -72, and -80, are—like all Soviet tanks—robust and easy to produce. Tank technology must also change rapidly in response to antitank weaponry developments.

Personnel Carriers

Armored personnel carriers (APCs) were originally simply shielded vehicles. In the 1960s, however, they were

M-109, 1970

M-3, World War II (U.S.)

LVTP-7 (1972)

The U.S. M-109, a self-propelled howitzer, is capable of firing a nuclear shell. More than 41,000 M-3 half-tracks were built during World War II. The amphibious LVTP-7 armored personnel carrier can transport 25 troops in water—where it is propelled by water jets—and on land.

armed with machine guns or small cannons and with gun ports along the sides that allowed firing from inside the vehicle. In 1967 the USSR introduced the BMP-1, considered the first true Infantry Fighting Vehicle (IFV). It carries a crew of three plus eight infantry. The current U.S. IFV, the XM2, carries six infantry and a crew of three, and is equipped with a 25-mm cannon, antitank missiles, and sophisticated targeting equipment. Like the BMP-1, it is amphibious and is propelled in the water by its tracks. APCs continue to be used for specialized purposes, such as the amphibious landing role carried out by the U.S. Marines' LVTP-7.

Armory Show The Armory Show is the popular name for the International Exposition of Modern Art that took place at the 69th Regiment Armory in New York City from Feb. 17 to Mar. 15, 1913. The exhibition, which afforded the American public its first look at European modernist art, was instigated by about 25 American artists, primarily from the ASHCAN and STIEGLITZ groups.

Among the chief organizers were Arthur B. DAVIES, Walt Kuhn, and Walter Pach. Their aim was to protest the academic art that then dominated exhibitions in the United States. About 1,500 paintings and sculptures were included; approximately 1,000 were by Americans. Some of the European works introduced CUBISM and FAUVISM in the United States.

Critics, the press, and the general public had strongly negative reactions to the show, particularly to the work of such Europeans as Marcel DUCHAMP, whose painting *Nude Descending a Staircase* was the object of much ridicule. The show had a significant impact, however, on a small group of American artists. More than any other single event, it stimulated American interest in ABSTRACT ART.

Armour, Philip Danforth Philip Danforth Armour, b. Stockbridge, N.Y., May 16, 1832, d. Jan. 6, 1901, was a meat packer who developed the Chicago stockyards. Beginning as a miner, farmer, and wholesale grocer, Armour went into meat packing in 1870. He pioneered in shipping hogs to Chicago for slaughter and in canning and exporting meat. He purchased his own refrigerator cars in order to ship fresh meat to the East Coast. Toward the end of his life he was charged, along with other packers, with selling chemically treated inferior meat to the armed forces. After his death his son, J. Ogden Armour, built Armour and Company into the world's largest meat-packing firm.

arms control Arms control refers to the voluntary limitation or reduction of weapons and their means of delivery, between and among countries, through negotiation. It is distinct from disarmament, which seeks to eliminate, also by international agreement, the means by which countries wage war. The goal of eliminating war goes far back in history, but in modern times disarmament came into focus with the HAGUE CONFERENCES in 1899 and 1907. These and subsequent efforts—the WASHINGTON CONFERENCE (1921–22) and the GENEVA CONFERENCE (1932)—met with only modest success.

The three objectives of arms control are to reduce the likelihood of war, to limit the extent of damage should war occur, and to reduce expenditures on military forces. It is only with respect to the first of the three objectives—reducing the likelihood of war—that proponents of arms control can claim any real measure of success.

Nuclear Arms Controversy. Nuclear arms control has aroused controversy from the outset. The Limited Test Ban Treaty, signed by representatives of the United States, the United Kingdom, and the Soviet Union in

The SALT II agreement was signed by President Jimmy Carter and Soviet leader Leonid Brezhnev in June 1979. Although never ratified by the U.S. Senate, many of the agreement's provisions were followed by both sides.

1963, provoked sharp debate when President John F. Kennedy later submitted this arms-control "first" for approval to the U.S. Senate. The treaty, which prohibits the testing of nuclear weapons above ground, under water, and in space, was seen by some critics as unenforceable, leading to speculation that the Soviet Union would violate the agreement. Despite opposition the treaty was ratified and fears of Soviet noncompliance proved unfounded. More favorably received in the United States was the 1968 United Nations-sponsored Nuclear Non-Proliferation Treaty (NPT), which seeks to restrict the size of the "nuclear club" by inducing non–nuclear-weapons states to renounce the acquisition of such weapons in exchange for a commitment on the part of the two superpowers to reduce their own arsenals (see NUCLEAR STRATEGY).

SALT Negotiations. The NPT was of critical importance in facilitating the start of bilateral U.S.-Soviet negotiations in 1969 to limit so-called central strategic forces. Known by the acronym SALT, for Strategic Arms Limitation Talks, these negotiations resulted in two arms-control agreements in May 1972. The first was the Anti-Ballistic Missile (ABM) Treaty, by which the two countries agreed to limit ABM sites and thus not deploy nationwide defensive systems to protect their homelands against nuclear attack. The second accord, the Interim Agreement on Offensive Weapons, was a five-year freeze on long-range land- and sea-based ballistic missile "launchers" (underground silos for the former and submarine tubes for the latter). Both agreements served to affirm the logic of nuclear deterrence, by which each superpower sought to deter the outbreak of nuclear war by having the capacity to deliver a devastating retaliatory blow following an enemy first strike.

The second phase of the negotiations, lasting from 1972 to 1979, led to the signing of the SALT II treaty, which attempted to extend and refine many of the provisions of the Interim Offensive agreement. Even though the Senate never ratified the treaty, the United States and the Soviet Union have abided by most of the agreement's provisions.

Later Negotiations. Negotiations on U.S. and Soviet central strategic systems, renamed the Strategic Arms Reduction Talks (START) by President Ronald Reagan's administration, resumed in 1982. The two sides reached consensus on many key points, including the desirability of 50 percent reductions in nuclear weapons. Among unresolved issues were exact procedures for ensuring effective verification of any new agreement and the preferred relationship between strategic offensive and defensive forces. The United States favored the rapid development and eventual deployment of nationwide defensive systems, as indicated by its support of the STRATEGIC DEFENSE INITIATIVE (SDI). The Soviet Union was sharply critical of SDI.

Major Breakthroughs. The rise to power of Soviet leader Mikhail Gorbachev in 1985 marked the beginning of a new era in arms-control efforts. Gorbachev's policy was to end the struggle between the USSR and the West. The first result of this policy was the Intermediate-Range Nuclear Forces (INF) Treaty, concluded in 1987, which eliminated all U.S. and Soviet land-based missiles with ranges of between 500 and 5,500 km (310 and 3,415 mi). This was followed in 1990 by a conventional arms treaty—signed by the 34-nation Conference on Security and Cooperation in Europe—that called for an unprecedented reduction in armaments and was billed as signaling the end of the cold war. The USSR renounced its overwhelming superiority in conventional arms on the European continent, agreeing to a parity between NATO and Warsaw Pact forces of 20,000 tanks, 20,000 artillery pieces, and 30,000 armored vehicles. At the same time, U.S. and Soviet negotiators reached agreement on a START treaty that effected a 50 percent reduction in strategic nuclear forces on each side, and included mutually satisfactory procedures for verification and inspection. Troop level reductions were also planned by both sides, and when Germany was reunited (1990) the Soviets pledged to withdraw all of their forces from that country by 1994.

While the future of arms control cannot be predicted, it is certain that efforts to limit and reduce both nuclear and conventional weapons will continue.

Armstrong, Edwin Edwin Howard Armstrong, b. New York City, Dec. 18, 1890, d. Feb. 1, 1954, was an American inventor and electrical engineer who made fundamental contributions to radio. His invention of the regenerative (FEEDBACK) circuit in 1912, while he was still in college, was challenged by Lee DE FOREST in a series of lengthy patent suits. Although Armstrong lost the case, the scientific community continued to support his claims. In 1918 he invented the superheterodyne circuit, which uses the HETERODYNE PRINCIPLE. His invention (1925–33) of the system of FREQUENCY MODULATION (FM) eliminated radio static. This invention, however, was also challenged in a patent suit. In poor health, with most of his money gone, he committed suicide. Armstrong has posthumously received increasing recognition for his many important inventions.

Armstrong, Henry Henry Armstrong, b. Columbus, Miss., Dec. 12, 1912, d. Oct. 22, 1988, is the only professional boxer to have held three world titles simultaneously. Originally named Henry Jackson, "Hammerin' Hank" adopted a ring name, Honey Mellody, and had a modest career up to 1937, when singer Al Jolson bought his contract. In October of that year, he won the featherweight title; he added the welterweight title in May 1938 and the lightweight crown in August 1938. He continued to win 46 straight matches into 1939. Armstrong fought until 1945, finishing his career with 152 victories and 100 knockouts in 181 bouts.

Armstrong, John John Armstrong, b. Carlisle, Pa., Nov. 25, 1758, d. Apr. 1, 1843, was U.S. secretary of war (1813–14) during the War of 1812. He was the son of another John Armstrong (1717–95), famous for his exploits in the French and Indian War. Both served in the American Revolution, and at its conclusion the younger wrote the anonymous "Newburgh Addresses" (1783), suggesting that the army use force if necessary to secure back pay. He was elected to the Continental Congress (1787), served in the U.S. Senate (1800–04), and was minister in Paris (1804–10).

When the War of 1812 began, Armstrong became a brigadier general and was charged with the defense of New York City. Appointed secretary of war, he was blamed for the disastrous 1813 expedition against Montreal. He was forced to resign when the British captured (1814) Washington. He later wrote *Notices of the War of 1812* (1836–40).

Armstrong, Louis Louis "Satchmo" Armstrong, b. New Orleans, July 4, 1900, d. July 6, 1971, was a brilliant American jazz cornet and trumpet soloist. He began to play at the age of 13, as a member of the band of the New Orleans Waifs' home. A cornetist in New Orleans and in Mississippi riverboat bands, he was first heard by a

Louis Armstrong, the great American jazz trumpet soloist, was also a band leader, composer, and vocalist who popularized the "scat" style in singing. He gained an international following during his many tours abroad. The name "Satchmo" caught on in 1932 after a music editor inadvertently garbled his earlier nickname, "Satchel mouth."

larger audience when he joined King OLIVER's group, in Chicago in 1922. His 1923 recordings with Oliver were among the first to feature black performers. In 1925, after playing as a solo artist with Fletcher HENDERSON's New York band, he returned to Chicago and formed his own group, Louis Armstrong's Hot Five (or occasionally, Hot Seven), which made a series of recordings still prized today as classic Chicago Dixieland.

In 1932, Armstrong made the first of many successful European tours. His popularity was heightened through appearances on radio, in films, and, later, on television. His unique "scat" singing style became as well known as his trumpet tone, and today he remains one of the most famous of all American jazz musicians.

Armstrong, Neil A. The American astronaut Neil Alden Armstrong, b. Wapakoneta, Ohio, Aug. 5, 1930, was the first person to walk on the Moon. Armstrong received his pilot's license on his 16th birthday. After two years at Purdue University, he joined the navy and flew combat missions over Korea. He returned to Purdue, obtained his aeronautical engineering degree in 1955, and became a test pilot. At Edwards Air Force base he flew the X-15 rocket plane a total of seven times. In 1962 he was selected as an astronaut. His first flight (1966) was as commander of GEMINI 8.

Neil A. Armstrong, commander of the U.S. Apollo 11 mission, became the first man to walk on the Moon, on July 20, 1969.

Armstrong was later assigned as commander of APOLLO 11, the first U.S. attempt to land on the Moon. On July 20, 1969, Armstrong and lunar-module pilot Col. Edwin E. "Buzz" ALDRIN landed the *Apollo 11* lunar module *Eagle* on the Moon at the Sea of Tranquility. At 10:56:20 PM Eastern Daylight Time (EDT), he planted his left foot on the lunar surface and proclaimed: "That's one small step for [a] man, one giant leap for mankind." After becoming NASA deputy associate administrator for aeronautics, Armstrong retired from NASA in 1971 to become a professor of engineering at the University of Cincinnati.

army An army is a large, organized land force trained to fight wars under military discipline. Usually an army is in the service of a national government or some other political group. In a more limited sense, an army is a tactical and administrative unit within the land forces of a country, capable of independent employment and generally made up of two or more corps—for example, the U.S. Army, Europe, which has its headquarters in Heidelberg, Germany.

Armies of the Past

Armies of some sort appear to have existed as long ago as 3500 BC. Pictures and other artifacts from prehistoric times show organized fighting groups, or at least groups that were armed, uniformly dressed, and moving in an ordered manner to confront an enemy.

Ancient Armies. Before 600 BC, highly disciplined and well-equipped armies existed in China, Egypt, Assyria, and Persia. Compact formations of foot soldiers, armed with swords and spears and protected by shields of hide, formed the basic unit, the infantry. Horsemen and chariots complemented the infantry. By the 4th century BC, siege machines were in existence. Together, these corresponded to the principal forces of modern armies: INFANTRY, CAVALRY, and ARTILLERY. The Greek army of ALEXANDER THE GREAT was able to conquer the known world in an 11-year campaign (334–23 BC). After Alexander's death, Carthaginian and then Roman armies replaced the Greek forces as the most formidable armed organizations in the Western world. A Carthaginian general, HANNIBAL, led his army of nearly 30,000 men together with horses and elephants through Spain and over the European Alps into Italy to attack Rome in the Second PUNIC WAR (218–201 BC). The Roman army captured Carthage at the end of the Third Punic War (149–146 BC), destroyed the city, and annexed its territory as the province of Africa. The strength of the Roman army was in its flexible and disciplined formations, called legions, (see LEGION, ROMAN), and in its ability to construct fortifications quickly and to defend them. Julius CAESAR's reputation as a brilliant general was largely derived from his army's feats of military engineering.

In the millennium after the decline of Rome, the armies of the Western world relied upon the horse, the bow, and ill-disciplined masses of foot soldiers. Commanders such as ATTILA THE HUN (5th century), BELISARIUS (6th century), CHARLEMAGNE (8th and 9th centuries), and the MONGOL khans (12th and 13th centuries), with large armies that at times consisted of 100,000 to 200,000 men, conquered extensive areas by defeating smaller and less-disciplined armed forces that opposed them.

Medieval and Early Modern Armies. In the period from the 12th to the 18th century, armies were slowly transformed through an increase in discipline, the introduction of gunpowder, and the emergence of the modern state. The horse, which had been the principal force of the armies of the great barbarian conquerors, was used in the 12th century by KNIGHTS, who served their feudal lords both by engaging in individual combat and by combining with other knights in feudal armies. The individual knights were generally well trained, but when formed into small armies they lacked cohesiveness and organization. This weakness was capitalized upon by the Swiss, who discovered in the 13th and 14th centuries that a highly compact, well-trained, disciplined formation of infantrymen could defeat the mounted warrior. The Swiss armed their foot soldiers with the pike (a long spear) and the halberd (an axhead with added points and barbs, mounted on a shaft).

Another dimension was added to warfare in the 14th and 15th centuries with the spread of GUNPOWDER. CANNONS, capable of destroying walled fortifications, were used with considerable success by King CHARLES VIII of France in his invasion of Italy in 1494. Handguns, called arquebuses, helped the Spanish under Gonzalo FERNÁNDEZ DE CÓRDOBA defeat the French in 1503. (See FIREARMS.)

The French and Spanish military successes in Italy led Nicolò MACHIAVELLI to advocate the creation of a MILITIA for Florence that would replace undisciplined and unreliable MERCENARIES with soldiers drawn from the populace. He had seen militias elsewhere and concluded that soldiers who had a cause other than material gain would provide Florence with a more reliable and effective army. Organization, discipline, the use of technological innovations, and the affiliation of soldiers with the state for which they were fighting were effectively combined by King GUSTAV II ADOLF of Sweden to create the most formidable army of the early 17th century. Later in the 17th century, standing armies were created to serve states and monarchs throughout Europe; none, however, could compare in discipline and training with the Prussian army that later won victories for FREDERICK II (Frederick the Great).

Conscripted Armies. The French Revolution (1789) brought dramatic changes, not only in the government and society of France but in the armies of Western civilization. The fundamental idea of the equality of all men and the compelling need to raise armies large enough to stop the combined forces of Europe that were arrayed against the new French republic led the revolutionary government to call for nationwide CONSCRIPTION. The result was a nation at arms and a return to the idea that every male citizen has the obligation to serve in the armed forces of his country. Since then, all the major powers have employed citizen armies to fight their great wars. The Industrial Revolution that began late in the 18th century made it possible to equip these mass conscript armies with weapons and other military necessities.

Mechanized Armies. Changes in technology have had profound effects on armies in the era since the French Revolution. Steam power increased the speed and ease with which armies could be transported—first by railroad and later in the 19th century by steamship. The development of rifling, breechloading, and smokeless powder made possible the creation of weapons of greater range, accuracy, and rapidity of fire than ever before (see MA-

(Above) *At the Battle of Waterloo (1815), the Scots Greys, a British cavalry regiment, charge the French infantry.*

(Below) *With their speed and mobility, airborne infantry are vital to tactical modern warfare.*

CHINE GUN; RIFLE). The telegraph, telephone, and radio made it possible for commanders to communicate almost instantly with their troops and governments.

The internal-combustion engine brought greater mobility to armies both on and off the battlefield, and the development of the airplane added another dimension to land warfare. Improved battle wagons, or tanks as they were named when the British introduced them during World War I, led to the creation of fully mechanized armored forces, capable of rapid advance and a new style of fighting called *blitzkrieg*, or "lightning war," by the Germans (see ARMORED VEHICLE). Jet engines, long-range rockets, and detection systems such as radar and sonar were introduced during World War II, extending the range, destructiveness, and surveillance of the modern army. The invention of the ATOMIC BOMB, with its capability of massive destruction, stimulated development of other devices in the decades since—and also changed essential aspects of defense planning (see DEFENSE, NATIONAL).

Space-satellite tracking stations, laser detection and guidance devices, intercontinental ballistic missiles, surface-to-air missiles, and complex electronic information systems are some of the tools that armies must now be able to use and manage in an organized and disciplined way (see BALLISTIC MISSILE; ROCKETS AND MISSILES).

The United States Army

The U.S. Army traces its origins to June 14, 1775, when the Second Continental Congress authorized the formation of an American Continental Army and appointed George Washington commander of the Troops of the United Provinces of North America. Since that day the army has been frequently and pervasively reorganized. The one exception has been in the position of commander in chief of the armed forces, the title given to the president of the United States by the Constitution. The National Security Act of July 16, 1947, as amended in 1949, established a Department of the Army along with a Department of the Navy and a Department of the Air Force, within the Office of the Secretary of Defense. The Department of the Army is headed by a civilian, the secretary of the army; his principal military advisor is the chief of staff of the army, a four-star general who is the army's senior military officer. The army chief of staff is also a member of the Joint Chiefs of Staff, along with his counterparts from the navy and air force; the Joint Chiefs of Staff is the principal military advisory body to the secretary of defense and the president.

The U.S. Army is organized into nine major commands plus others that belong to unified land, sea, and air commands. The first and largest of the commands is the Forces Command; it is responsible for all army forces, including reserve forces, within the territorial United States. The Forces Command is composed of five U.S. Army areas.

The Training and Doctrine Command, headquartered at Fort Monroe, Va., is the army's second major command; it develops and supervises the training of the active army, the Army Reserve, and the National Guard. The Materiel Development and Readiness Command, headquartered at Alexandria, Va., provides equipment and related services to the army and to some foreign agencies. The other six commands are the U.S. Army Information Systems Command; Intelligence and Security Command; Health Services Command; Criminal Investigation Command; Military Traffic Management Command, headquartered at Washington, D.C.; and the Military District of Washington. The Corps of Engineers is separate from the Army command structure, as are three additional overseas commands: the U.S. Army, Europe; the U.S. Army, Japan; and the Eighth U.S. Army, in South Korea. These belong to the three-service commands under the Department of Defense.

The U.S. Army maintains more than 300 installations in the United States, more than 175 in Germany, more than 150 in Japan and South Korea, and others in Belgium, the Canal Zone, the Netherlands, Puerto Rico, and the United Kingdom. Some of the better-known installations in the United States include the following: Fort Hood, Tex., the largest armored post in the Western world; Fort Bragg, N.C., the home of the airborne forces; Fort Benning, Ga., home of the Infantry School; Fort Knox, Ky., which has the Armor School; and Fort Sill, Okla., the location of the Field Artillery School. Advanced schooling in the army is conducted at the Command and General Staff College of Fort Leavenworth, Kans., and at the Army War College at Carlisle Barracks, Pa. Training for the volunteers who enlist in the army today takes place at such basic training posts as Fort Leonard Wood, Mo.

See also: MILITARY STRATEGY AND TACTICS; RESERVE OFFICERS TRAINING CORPS; UNITED STATES MILITARY ACADEMY.

The first authorized uniforms for infantrymen in the U.S. Army were worn by soldiers in the Continental Army during the American Revolution. Before 1782, however, uniforms differed from regiment to regiment. The flamboyant uniform adopted during the War of 1812 gave way to the practical fatigues introduced during the Mexican War and the functional uniforms of the Civil War. Uniforms were first standardized during the Spanish-American War. The uniform of World War I included a rigid helmet of British design. Since World War II, uniforms have changed only slightly. The major improvements have been the use of lighter, stronger fabrics and the introduction of a new helmet.

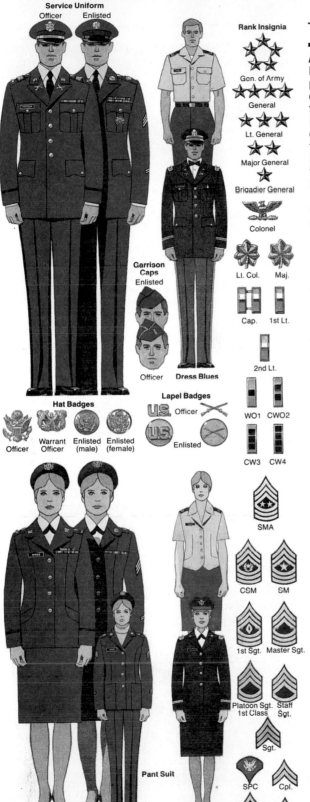

Service Uniform
Officer   Enlisted

Rank Insignia

Gen. of Army

General

Lt. General

Major General

Brigadier General

Colonel

Lt. Col.   Maj.

Garrison
Caps
Enlisted

Officer   Dress Blues

Cap.   1st Lt.

2nd Lt.

Lapel Badges

Hat Badges

U.S. Officer

US
Enlisted

WO1   CWO2

CW3   CW4

Officer   Warrant   Enlisted   Enlisted
Officer   (male)   (female)

SMA

CSM   SM

1st Sgt.   Master Sgt.

Platoon Sgt.   Staff
1st Class   Sgt.

Sgt.

Pant Suit

SPC   Cpl.

Officer   Enlisted   Dress Blues   Pfc.   Pv. 2

Arnauld, Antoine [ahr-noh'] Antoine Arnauld, b. Feb. 6, 1612, d. Aug. 8, 1694, was the single most important leader of French JANSENISM during the later 17th century and a contributor to rationalist philosophical thought (see RATIONALISM). His sister Angelique, known as Mere Angelique (b. Sept. 8, 1591, d. Aug. 6, 1661), became abbess of the Cistercian convent of Port-Royal at the age of 11. She reformed the convent along Jansenist lines and it became the primary retreat for members of the movement, including, among many other members of her family, the youngest son, Antoine.

Antoine became a priest (1641) and also obtained his doctorate in theology. He became the foremost proponent of Jansenism with the publication of the treatise *Frequent Communion* (1643). Persecuted by the Jesuits, he fled to Brussels (1679) where he died in exile. Best known for his hundreds of theological tracts, his critiques also helped clarify the thought of Descartes, Malebranche, and Leibniz. His own methodological position was summarized in the *Port-Royal Logic*, (1662) written with Pierre Nicole.

Arnaut Daniel   see DANIEL, ARNAUT

Arne, Thomas [ahrn] Thomas Augustine Arne, b. Mar. 12, 1710, d. Mar. 5, 1778, was a prominent English composer of songs and dramatic music, including "Rule, Britannia!" (1740). His music for the masques *Comus* (1738) and *The Judgment of Paris* (1740), the opera *Artaxerxes* (1762), and his settings for songs from Shakespeare's plays made him one of the most celebrated composers of the period. His other works include the oratorio *Judith* (1761), concertos, sonatas, overtures, and chamber music.

Arnhem [ahrn'-hem] Arnhem is the capital of Gelderland province in the Lower Rhine district of the Netherlands. It is located on the north bank of the Rhine River near its juncture with the IJssel, about 35 km (20 mi) from the German border. The 1988 population was estimated to be 128,107. Manufactures include scientific instruments, drugs, and textiles.

The site of the city may have been that of the Roman town of Arenacum. A trading center in the Middle Ages, Arnhem was the home of the dukes of Gelderland until the 16th century. It was occupied by France (1672 and 1795), Prussia (1813), and Germany (1940). In World War II it was the scene (1944) of a major battle between the British and the Germans. Several outstanding parks and museums in the Arnhem area include the Kröller-Müller Museum at Otterloo, which contains more than 300 works by van Gogh.

Arnhem Land [ahrn'-hem] A sparsely populated area of 80,808 km^2 (31,200 mi^2) in northeastern NORTHERN TERRITORY, Australia, Arnhem Land extends from the Van

Diemen Gulf southeast to the Gulf of Carpentaria and the Groote Eylandt. The area constitutes the largest of 17 Aboriginal reservations. Arnhem Land was discovered in 1623 by the Dutch explorer Jan Carstensz, who named it for his ship *Arnhem*. The name was first used to designate the entire region between the Roper and Victoria rivers. Arnhem Land is largely tropical plateau and rain forest. Elevation ranges from more than 1,000 m (3,300 ft) to sea level.

Arno, Peter

Peter Arno was the pen name of Curtis Arnoux Peters, b. New York City, Jan. 8, 1904, d. Feb. 22, 1968, an American cartoonist whose distinctive charcoal-and-wash satiric drawings regularly graced the pages of the *New Yorker* and *Esquire* for more than 40 years. Arno was best known for his depiction of New York society. His deceptively simple vignettes brought to comic life a world inhabited by bibulous executiyes, sabled dowagers, lecherous clubmen, and buxom young women. Collections of his cartoons include *Man in the Shower* (1944), *Sizzling Platter* (1949), and *Lady in the Shower* (1967).

Arno River

The principal river of TUSCANY, in central Italy, the Arno flows 242 km (150 mi) from the hills of Monte Falterona in the Tuscan Apennines to the Ligurian Sea 11 km (7 mi) west of Pisa. The river is navigable to FLORENCE but is used mainly for irrigation. It has a drainage basin of 8,247 km^2 (3,184 mi^2). The Arno has changed course several times over the centuries. Although flood-control measures have been taken, the river still causes considerable damage; for example, its destructive flooding of Florence in 1966. Noted for its beauty, the river has a rich history in myth and art.

Arnold, Benedict

Benedict Arnold, b. Norwich, Conn., Jan. 14, 1741, was an American Revolutionary general and America's most infamous traitor. At the age of 14, Arnold was a druggist's apprentice, but he ran away twice to serve in the colonial militia during the French and Indian War (1754–63). When the AMERICAN REVOLUTION broke out, Arnold marched his Connecticut militia company to Massachusetts, where he was made a colonel. His force, along with Ethan Allen's Green Mountain Boys, captured TICONDEROGA on May 10, 1775.

Arnold then led a force of 1,100 men through Maine in the dead of winter to invade Canada. There he led an unsuccessful attack on Quebec in December and was wounded. A promotion to brigadier general followed in January 1776.

Before his defection, Arnold had a brilliant career in the Continental Army. He particularly distinguished himself in the Saratoga campaign as second in command to Horatio GATES. During the second battle of Saratoga on Oct. 7, 1777, Arnold led a charge and was again wounded.

Arnold suffered many disappointments that embit-

Benedict Arnold, a brilliant but embittered general in the American Revolution, sought to betray American military secrets to the British. In this engraving he tells his accomplice, the British officer John André, to hide the documents in his boot.

tered him. When he was promoted to major general in February 1777, others he thought less deserving preceded him in rank. Gates received the credit for the victory at Saratoga. Named (June 1778) commander in Philadelphia, Arnold was accused of overstepping his authority. His second marriage (1779) to Margaret Shippen, the daughter of a Loyalist, also aroused suspicions.

His bitterness, along with a need for money to pay heavy debts, led Arnold to negotiate with the British. He offered to betray West Point, a post he commanded. When his treachery was revealed, Arnold escaped to the enemy lines, was commissioned a brigadier general in the British army, and was paid about $10,000. He led two British expeditions, one that burned Richmond, Va., and the other against New London, Conn.

Arnold went to England in 1781 and turned to trade. Worn by depression and suffering from a nervous disease, he died in London on June 14, 1801.

See also: SARATOGA, BATTLES OF.

Arnold, Henry Harley

As commanding general of the U.S. Army Air Forces during World War II, Henry Harley "Hap" Arnold, b. Gladwyne, Pa., June 15, 1886, d. Jan. 15, 1950, built up the world's largest air force. Arnold joined the infant aviation section of the army in 1911 and organized the air defense of the Panama Canal in World War I.

Chief of the Army Air Forces throughout World War II, Arnold was a member of the Joint Chiefs of Staff from 1942 and a 5-star general of the army from 1944. From 1944 to 1946 he was in direct command of the new 20th Air Force, whose B-29s carried out saturation bombing of Japanese cities. In 1949 he was made a 5-star general of the U.S. Air Force (created as a separate unit in 1947).

Arnold, Matthew

Matthew Arnold, b. Dec. 24, 1822, d. Apr. 15, 1888, was a major Victorian poet, principal English literary critic of his time, an important commentator on society and culture, and an effective government official. His father was Thomas Arnold, headmaster of Rugby School. After graduation from Oxford, Matthew Arnold went to London as private secretary to a member of the government. In 1851 he was appointed an inspector of schools, and for 35 years visited teacher-training schools to ensure they met government standards. He also visited schools on the continent, writing several reports that urged state support and supervision of education.

Arnold began his literary career in 1849 with a volume of poems, *The Strayed Reveller and Other Poems*. The title poem of his second volume (1852), "Empedocles on Etna," is about the suicide of a 5th-century BC Greek philosopher who in a changing time no longer believes that his work is making headway against ignorance and confusion. For a time Arnold withdrew this poem because, as he wrote in a preface to his collection, *Poems* (1853), it did not fulfill the inspirational function of poetry. Yet many of his most characteristic poems, including "Dover Beach" and "The Scholar Gipsy," concern the difficulty of knowing and acting in an age when conventional ideas and institutions have lost their authority.

Arnold began to publish literary criticism after his appointment in 1857 as professor of poetry at Oxford. In his lectures *On Translating Homer* (1861), the two series of *Essays in Criticism* (1865, 1888), and other essays he argued that literature could elevate a skeptical and materialistic age. Because it expressed its time, the literature of the present could not rise above that time to save it. But the literature of the past was grander, and the task of literary criticism was to make this literature effective in the present. When Arnold turned to social criticism, especially in CULTURE AND ANARCHY (1869), he similarly argued that a knowledge of "the best that has been thought and said" would provide standards to resist contemporary

errors and corruptions. In *St. Paul and Protestantism* (1870), he enlisted religion in his argument by trying to separate belief in a reality higher than our own from sectarian doctrines. In his poetry Arnold often expressed the sadness of living in an age in which what one loved most was in jeopardy. In his prose he tried to reestablish the authority of institutions—schools, the state, literature, religion—in which his contemporaries could learn how to know and live up to what was best in human experience.

Arnold, Thomas

Thomas Arnold, b. June 13, 1795, d. June 12, 1842, was a headmaster of RUGBY SCHOOL whose innovations made it the prototype of the Victorian school for gentlemen. A Fellow of Oriel College, Oxford, 1815–19, he accepted the headmastership of Rugby and was also ordained a priest in the Church of England in 1828.

The basis of education at Rugby was the classics. To these Arnold added mathematics, modern languages, and modern history. He felt, however, that the formation of character was more important than intellectual achievement. As headmaster, Arnold is portrayed in Thomas Hughes's *Tom Brown's Schooldays* (1857).

Arnold's achievements as a scholar earned him election to Regius Professor of History at Oxford shortly before his death. His son was the poet and critic Matthew ARNOLD.

Arnold of Brescia

[bray'-shah] Arnold of Brescia, c.1100–1155, was an Italian reformer. After studying at Paris, he became an Augustinian monk. Attacking the worldliness of the church he advocated radical church reforms, including a life of poverty for the clergy and the abandonment of wealth and temporal power by the church. He also rejected the idea of confession of sins to a priest. In 1139 the Second Lateran Council condemned these views, and Pope Innocent II ordered Arnold exiled and his books burned.

Arnold returned to Italy after a reconciliation with Pope Eugene III. He remained in Rome until 1155, when Pope Adrian IV banished him. Within the year he was captured and hanged. His body was burned, and the ashes thrown into the Tiber River.

Matthew Arnold, a 19th-century British poet and critic, appears in the painting by George F. Watts. Arnold, whose writings evoke a sense of spiritual desolation, expressed concern for what he felt to be a decline of society's values as a result of modern industrialism.

Arnolfo di Cambio

[ahr-nohl'-foh dee kahm'-bee-oh] The Florentine sculptor and architect Arnolfo di Cambio, 1255–1302, was one of the foremost artists of the Gothic period in Italy. Among his major sculptural projects was the original decoration of the facade of the Cathedral of Santa Maria del Fiore (or the Duomo) in Florence (after 1296; surviving fragments in the Cathedral Museum). Arnolfo was the original architect of the vast Cathedral of Florence (begun 1296), and may also have designed the Church of the Badia (begun 1284) and Santa Croce (begun 1295), two of the most important Gothic churches in Florence.

aromatic compounds   One of the major groups of organic compounds, aromatic compounds contain atoms of carbon linked to form a closed ring. (ALIPHATIC COMPOUNDS, in contrast, have open, chainlike structures.) The compounds were named aromatic because many of them have a strong odor. In modern chemistry, however, aromaticity means a distinctive type of chemical stability or low reactivity (see RESONANCE). BENZENE, C_6H_6, is the simplest aromatic compound.

Many aromatic compounds (such as benzene) have a hexagonal structure with six carbon atoms forming a ring. Each carbon atom is joined to one adjacent carbon atom by a single bond and to the other adjacent carbon atom by a double bond. Of the two pairs of electrons involved in carbon-carbon double bonds, one pair is designated as sigma electrons and the other as pi electrons. (For a more complete explanation, see CARBON.) In an aromatic compound the pi electrons are delocalized—that is, they are not associated only with the pair of carbon atoms that are doubly bonded but are shared by all the atoms of the aromatic group, forming a cloud of electrons. This configuration is responsible for the stability and low reactivity of the compounds.

Other atoms or functional groups can be attached to an aromatic compound without impairing its aromaticity. Aromatic rings can also be fused (attached side-to-side) so that the two rings have common carbon atoms. Fused rings lose some stability, and thus naphthalene is somewhat more reactive than benzene.

HETEROCYCLIC COMPOUNDS, or those containing rings with one or more atoms other than carbon, may also be aromatic. An example is pyridine, C_5H_5N, an unpleasant-smelling liquid used in laboratories as a solvent.

Aronson, Boris [air'-uhn-suhn]   The Russian-born American theatrical designer Boris Aronson, b. Oct. 15, 1900, d. Nov. 16, 1980, designed sets and costumes for more than 100 plays, ballets, and operas. From the 1960s he was a major designer of Broadway musicals.

Aronson went to the United States in 1923 and began designing for the Yiddish Art Theater. His semiabstract and often symbolic style reflected the fantastic and cubistic influences of Marc Chagall. Productions designed by Aronson included *South Pacific* (1943), *Cabaret* (1966), *Zorba* (1968), *Pacific Overtures* (1976), and *The Nutcracker* (1976–77). He won five Tony Awards.

Aroostook War [uh-roos'-tuk]   The Aroostook War, 1838–39, was a small border conflict between the inhabitants of Maine and New Brunswick, Canada, over the Aroostook Valley. The Treaty of Paris (1783) ending the American Revolution was unclear about the border, but no one paid much attention until exploration for proposed railroads and the frontier movement made the valley seem worth fighting for. When New Brunswick began granting land titles and claiming jurisdiction, the citizens

of Maine started the war. The fighting was halted by Gen. Winfield SCOTT in March 1839, and the border was settled by the WEBSTER-ASHBURTON TREATY of 1842.

Arp, Jean   The French painter, sculptor, and poet Jean Hans Arp, b. Sept. 16, 1887, d. June 7, 1966, is a leading figure in 20th-century avant-garde art. Having exhibited with the BLAUE REITER (Blue Rider) group in 1912, and in the *Erste Herbstsalon* (First Autumn Exhibition) in Berlin in 1913 with leading EXPRESSIONIST artists, Arp became associated with Guillaume APOLLINAIRE's circle of artists, including Pablo PICASSO. After exhibiting abstract, rectilinear works in 1915 in Zurich, Arp turned to arrangements of objects according to the laws of chance.

The marble Human Concretion *(1934) by French artist Jean Arp is one of his series of abstract sculptures called "Concretions," derived from basic organic shapes. (Musée National d'Art Moderne, Paris.)*

In 1916, in Zurich, he became a cofounder of DADA with Hugo Ball, Richard Huelsenbeck, Marcel Janco, and Tristan TZARA. Arp, who had written poetry since his youth, contributed both poetry and illustrations to all the Dada publications. In 1923 he contributed to Kurt SCHWITTERS's review *Merz*, and in 1925 he published, with El LISSITZKY, a work about all the contemporary art movements called *The Isms of Art*.

Becoming a member of the SURREALIST group, Arp began a long residency in Meudon near Paris in 1926. He joined (1930) the Cercle et Carre (Circle and Square) group, taking part in its international exhibition, and in 1931 he cofounded the Abstraction-Creation group in Paris. Arp invented (1930) a new kind of COLLAGE, using pieces of colored paper that were torn rather than cut and then arranged according to chance. The torn pieces were dropped on a sheet of paper, adjusted into configurations, and then attached. Arp called these works "organic concretions," avoiding the term *abstraction* because of its implications of discipline. Around 1930 he also began doing sculptures in full round, the compositions of organic shapes in wood for which he is perhaps best known. Arp is represented in most major collections of contemporary art.

Arrabal, Fernando [ah rah bahl'] The plays of the Spanish dramatist Fernando Arrabal, b. Aug. 11, 1932, belong to the THEATER OF THE ABSURD by way of the theater of cruelty. Arrabal exiled himself from Franco's Spain to France in 1955. His plays, notable for exhibiting extremes of cruelty, obscenity, and blasphemy, have outraged audiences. Yet there are many who see in his work a liberating quality, in the tradition of the theater movement that began with Antonin ARTAUD. Arrabal himself invented the "theater of panic," surreal, ceremonial, and exemplified by his best-known play, *The Architect and the Emperor of Assyria* (1967; Eng. trans., 1969). Some of his other successful works include *The Automobile Graveyard* (1958; Eng. trans., 1960) and *And They Put Handcuffs on the Flowers* (1967; Eng. trans., 1969), the latter a protest against political oppression in Spain. Arrabal has written a number of novels, of which the first, *Baal Babylon* (1959; Eng. trans., 1961), found a large readership.

arraignment see CRIMINAL JUSTICE

Arras Arras (1982 pop., 41,736) is a city in northern France and is the capital of Pas-de-Calais department. Vegetable-oil processing and other diversified light manufacturing take place here. Of Gallo-Roman origin, Arras became the capital of ARTOIS. During the Middle Ages it was an important cultural and commercial center famous for tapestry production. Arras was fought over many times until 1659, when it became a permanent part of France. Much of the city was destroyed during the French Revolution, and again during both world wars.

Arrau, Claudio [ahr-rah'-oo, klow'-dee-oh] Claudio Arrau, b. Chillán, Chile, Feb. 6, 1903, d. June 9, 1991, was one of the best-known of contemporary pianists. He first studied the piano in Santiago; his recital debut at the age of five led to a 10-year Chilean government scholarship to study in Berlin with Martin Krause, one of Franz Liszt's last pupils. Arrau performed throughout the world with leading conductors and orchestras, and he was still performing regularly almost until the time of his death. He was regarded as one of the foremost interpreters of Beethoven and the romantic composers.

arrest see CRIMINAL JUSTICE

Arrhenius, Svante August [ahr-ray'-nee-uhs, sfahn'-tu how'-gust] The Swedish physical chemist Svante Arrhenius, b. Feb. 19, 1859, d. Oct. 2, 1927, is best known for his theory of electrolytic dissociation, or ionization. The theory was initially developed (1884) in his doctoral dissertation at the University of Uppsala, in which he argued that many molecules, such as sodium chloride (NaCl), break apart spontaneously in solution to give ions. This was a major discovery. It helped establish the new field of physical chemistry, and Arrhenius received the Nobel Prize for chemistry for it in 1903.

arrowhead (artifact) An arrowhead, the penetrative tip of a projectile shot by a bow, is similar in shape and function to a spearpoint, although generally smaller. Small, preformed, chipped flint projectile points appear in MOUSTERIAN sites, suggesting that the BOW AND ARROW were in use more than 30,000 years ago. Direct evidence, in the form of arrow shafts, dates back only about 10,500 years. Magdalenian cultures of western Europe and Late Stone Age cultures in Africa may have used a series of small flint blades set at an angle in a wooden arrow. The rock paintings of Spain and the Sahara conclusively demonstrate the use of the bow and arrow by 8000 BC. In the New World, arrows did not replace javelin darts until about AD 500.

arrowroot Arrowroot is an edible starch, the product of the rhizomes, or rootstocks, of several tropical plants. West Indian arrowroot, *Maranta arundinacea*, family Marantaceae, is a perennial plant that produces genuine arrowroot starch in large (20–40 cm / 9–14 in) rhizomes. These are peeled and grated into water, and the starch is extracted. It is used as a thickener in cooking; its blandness and digestibility make it particularly useful for invalid diets. Tous-les-mois (tulema) arrowroot is made from *Canna edulis*; Brazilian arrowroot comes from the MANIOC plant, which is also the source of tapioca.

arrowworm Arrowworms are slender, active sea WORMS with transparent bodies 5 to 140 mm (0.2 to 1.6 in) long. Most dart about, capturing minute marine creatures as prey. They belong to the phylum Chaetognatha, the name of which means "bristle jaws." It refers to the stiff bristles on two muscular lobes beside the mouth, with which the arrowworm captures and devours its prey.

Arsacids [ahr-sas'-idz] The Arsacids were a Parthian dynasty that ruled in Iran from about 238 BC to AD 224. The first ruler was called Arsaces, and all his successors adopted that as their throne name. The principal rulers of the Arsacid dynasty were Mithradates I (r. *c.*171–138 BC), who expanded the boundaries of PARTHIA into Mesopotamia, and Mithradates II (r. *c.*128–87 BC), who established Parthian boundaries to the east in present-day Afghanistan. Under their successors the dynasty continually fought the Romans, defeating them at Carrhae in 53 BC. Although many times later defeated by the Romans, the Arsacids kept their independence until their final defeat by the SASSANIANS in AD 224.

arsenic [ahrs'-nik]   Arsenic is a metallic chemical element in Group VA of the periodic table. Its symbol is As, its atomic number is 33, and its atomic weight is 74.9216. The Earth's crust contains only about 5.5 parts arsenic per million.

Arsenic exists in three allotropic modifications: the yellow (α); the black (β); and the metallic, or gray (γ). Normally arsenic is found in its metallic form, which is the most stable and at normal pressure does not melt but sublimes at about 615° C. It forms alloys with other metals. The α and β modifications have no metallic properties. Arsenic is fairly reactive. Above 400° C it burns with a bluish flame, forming arsenic trioxide, As_2O_3. This compound is known as white arsenic and is used as a rat poison.

The toxic quality of arsenic has been known since ancient times. In the human body it accumulates in the nails and the hair, where it can be detected—even in the bodies of persons long dead—by the Marsh test. The acute symptoms are diarrhea and cramps. In cases of chronic poisoning, anemia and paralysis may appear. If there is prolonged contact with the skin, malignant skin tumors can develop. In medicine, 4-aminobenzene arsenic and 4-hydroxybenzene arsenic compounds are used to treat certain infections. The best known is Salvarsan, an antisyphilis drug. Commercially, arsenic is added to lead to harden it and is used in the production of herbicides and pesticides.

arson   Arson is the malicious burning of property for some illegal purpose such as destroying evidence, collecting insurance, or injuring someone. In English common law it originally meant the burning of a house, but in modern statute law the definition has been expanded to include the burning of any property.

Most laws recognize several degrees of arson. The first degree includes burning an inhabited dwelling at night. The second degree is burning a building other than a dwelling at night. The third degree includes burning personal as well as real property for illegal purposes.

art   All cultures throughout history have produced art. The impulse to create, to realize form and order out of mere matter—to recognize order in the world or to generate it oneself—is universal and perpetual.

Aspects of Art

Every work of art has two aspects: it is a present experience as well as a record of the past, and it is valued, preserved, and studied for both identities. As present experi-

This Paleolithic bison carving (c.12,000 BC) was used as a form of hunting magic. For the artist, the creation of an animal image was intended to bring a materialization of the animal itself. (Musée des Antiquités Nationales, St. Germaine-en Laye, France.)

ence, artworks afford people the pleasures, the tensions, the dramas, and ultimately the satisfaction to the senses of pure form—in the visual arts the relationships among colors, lines, and masses in space.

The meaning of the word *art*, derived from the Latin *ars*, meaning "skill," has changed through history. In medieval Europe, proficiency in the "liberal arts" was the goal of an educated person; only by the 19th century did the word come to denote painting, drawing, sculpture, graphic arts, and decorative arts. A distinction then arose between *artist* and *artisan*, the latter denoting a skilled manual worker, the former connoting capacity for imaginative invention. Although *the arts* may be taken today as encompassing the musical and verbal as well as the visual, *art* or *fine arts* is usually assumed to mean the visual arts—PAINTING, SCULPTURE, ARCHITECTURE, and, by extension, printmaking, DRAWING, DECORATIVE ARTS, and PHOTOGRAPHY.

The concept of a history of art is relatively recent. In the mid-16th century Giorgio VASARI compiled information about Renaissance artists' lives and works in *Lives of the Artists*. Modern art history may be thought of as beginning in the mid-18th century with Johann Joachim WINCKELMANN, who applied a conception of history as cyclical to what remained of the art of ancient Greece and Rome. Heinrich WÖLFLIN provided, in the early 20th century, a technique for understanding style by comparing two works of different periods and noting their differences; this is still the most widely used heuristic (interpretative) approach today.

Art history, a distinct discipline in the humanities since the late 19th century, is now largely nontheoretical. Historians examine works and documents about the works in order to place them appropriately in the present set of recognized groupings. Broadly, the four most general categories for Western art are ancient, medieval, Renaissance, and modern. In the past, the humanistic, classical art of Greece served as a positive standard by which works were judged. Today, art historians are neutral with regard to different styles—none is superior or inferior; all are worthy of study.

History of Western Art

STONEHENGE on the Salisbury Plain in England is the remaining monument of a prehistoric people now otherwise unknown. Built c.2000 BC, the post-and-lintel circles of massive rock were probably intended to be functional rather than artistic, like most PREHISTORIC ART. The cave paintings of LASCAUX in France and ALTAMIRA in Spain, or fertility figures such as the VENUS OF WILLENDORF from Austria, far older than Stonehenge, have in common with it a significance and even necessity in the rituals and beliefs of their makers. For more detailed consideration of prehistoric art—and the art and architecture of non-Western cultures and nations—see individual articles by country, by style, by type, by artist, and by building or monument.

The Ancient World. The advanced social, political, religious, and linguistic structures that constitute Western civilization appeared first in Mesopotamia and Egypt c.3000 BC. Egypt remained relatively stable as a state for the better part of 3,000 years and was able to generate and maintain a distinctive artistic style in all media. The monumental style of Egyptian art (see EGYPT, ANCIENT) is most powerful in 4th-dynasty sculpture, such as the seated pharaoh Khafre in the Egyptian Museum, Cairo. The figure seems contained, as if still confined within the block from which it was carved. The style and its formal properties make sense when seen in light of the beliefs to which the style is responsive. The sculpture was, in effect, a new and immortal dwelling for the spirit of the dead pharaoh, and as such was beyond the world.

Egyptian architecture includes not only the great PYRAMIDS at Giza but also a number of TEMPLES featuring long, low colonnades deployed on a central axis line, as at the temple complexes at KARNAK (c.1570–1085 BC) and LUXOR (c.1570–1200 BC). The temples were built so that the interior captures one's architectural interest as one proceeds from chamber to chamber, each more protected and secret than the one before. Incorporated in these massive architectural monuments were many wall paintings and BAS-RELIEF sculptures.

Much less stable than Egypt were the several civilizations of the Tigris and Euphrates valleys, and hence their art is more various. The extensive reliefs that adorned royal palaces like that of Ashurnasirpal II at Nimrud (9th century BC) have a firmness and authority of execution and cogent use of conventional stylizations—particularly in the musculature of the animals and men, the profile eyes, and the repeated contour lines of the horses—that are the hallmarks of a mature style. The imagery of the reliefs—the ruler's prowess as a warrior—reflects the concern with which these often warring states treated arms and power. At the opposite pole from these monuments of public propaganda were tiny mementos of individual distinction—cylinder seals, usually of semiprecious stone and about 2.5 cm (1 in) long, carved to leave an imprint of a god or mythological figure when rolled in soft clay.

Contemporary with the civilizations of the Fertile Crescent were the AEGEAN CIVILIZATIONS of the Minoans on the island of Crete and the Mycenaeans on the Greek mainland. Relatively little of their art is preserved, but in the fragments of wall paintings and the bright, lively style of Kamares-ware pottery one can sense the ebullient freedom of design and organic motifs that animate MINOAN ART. The ruins of their palaces, such as at KNOSSOS and MYCENAE, give evidence of their highly developed cultures.

For many artists and historians of the past, GREEK ART was artistic perfection. No other ancient style lingered on in the Western consciousness to reemerge so frequently or to condition aesthetic perception so pervasively. After an era of geometric abstraction in pottery and of archaic freestanding sculpture (korai, or female, and kouroi, or

In Michelangelo's Creation of Adam (1508–12), a detail of the ceiling of the Sistine Chapel in Rome, God's hand brings man to life. The creative power of the artist was often regarded as divine.

(Above) *In Frank Stella's* Sinjerli Variation IV *(1968) art ceases to imitate nature and becomes an entity in itself. (Collection of Mr. and Mrs. Burton Tremaine, Meriden, Conn.)*

(Above) *At Stonehenge, on the Salisbury Plain in southern England, massive post-and-lintel stones were placed in circles by an unknown prehistoric people. Built about 2000 BC, Stonehenge may have been used as a religious structure or for astronomical observations. (Left) The diorite statue of the pharaoh Khafre dates from the 4th dynasty of Egypt. Conceived as a still, solid mass rather than as a living being, the figure reflects the emphasis of Egyptian art on the promise of eternal life after death. (Egyptian Museum, Cairo.)*

male, figures) that partook of the same monumental abstraction as that of Egypt and Mesopotamia, the golden age of Greek art emerged in the 5th century BC. Of the painting, all that remains are painted vases, many of the highest quality.

As in the earlier cultures, architectural monuments and the sculpture that adorned them are the principal surviving achievements. The Parthenon (447–432 BC) on the ACROPOLIS in Athens incorporates in its design and sculptural embellishments the epitome of the classical style. All architectural components are brought into perfect balance to achieve the structure's stately firmness and tranquil grace. The sculptural works of PHIDIAS and his school, now called the ELGIN MARBLES and housed in London's BRITISH MUSEUM, use images of the gods to show the idealized human body in motion and at rest.

In freestanding sculpture, the stylized and monumental archaic style was replaced in the 5th century BC with one reflecting the natural rhythms of the body as it reacts to gravity. The *Hermes Holding the Infant Dionysus* of PRAXITELES (4th century BC; Olympia Museum, Greece) is posed in *contrapposto*, that is, the weight of the body is supported on one leg so that the hips and shoulders slant in opposite directions as a result. The proportions of such figures as this formed a canon that would remain in use hundreds of years later.

ROMAN ART had the same humanistic basis as Greek; in fact, most Greek sculptures are known to us through Roman copies. The realistic portrait sculpture produced by the Romans is important, since it superseded the Greek emphasis on the ideal. In architecture, new conceptions and new structural possibilities were developed, as shown in the huge domed PANTHEON (AD *c*.118–28) in Rome.

The Advent of Christianity. During the first centuries of Christianity, the classical world and its styles atrophied as the Western Roman Empire slipped into decline. EARLY CHRISTIAN ART, oriented toward intangible spirituality, de-

This late-8th-century BC Assyrian bas-relief from the palace of Sargon II at Khorsabad in modern Iraq represents a horse trainer bringing two steeds as tribute to the king. (Metropolitan Museum of Art, New York. Gift of John D. Rockefeller, Jr., 1933.)

veloped into the stylized abstraction characteristic of BYZANTINE ART, the product of the flourishing BYZANTINE EMPIRE, as the Eastern Roman Empire is known. In the West, Christian art proceeded through a series of styles splendidly chronicled in the applied arts—the IVORIES, TEXTILES, MOSAICS, ILLUMINATED MANUSCRIPTS, metalwork, and various liturgical implements of the MEROVINGIAN, CAROLINGIAN, and OTTONIAN periods. Christian architecture, and the sculpture that adorned it, gained prominence in the ROMANESQUE and GOTHIC eras. Large churches such as Saint Sernin (11th century) in Toulouse, France, synthesized elements from the earlier Carolingian and Ottonian periods. Romanesque churches employed barrel vaults to support the roof, with heavy masonry walls and BUTTRESSES. In plan these 11th- and 12th-century structures resembled a cross because the long nave was intersected by transepts. Pilgrims could move through the church down side aisles and through the ambulatory around the periphery of the apse, where the altar and shrine were housed. (See CATHEDRALS AND CHURCHES.)

The elaborate sculptural programs of the churches represented biblical figures and theological ideas. Although most of the worshipers were probably illiterate, they understood the sculptured scenes well enough. The artists/craftsmen of the Middle Ages charged their relief sculptures with great emotional power, executing them in a style that owes little or nothing to the classical tradition. In the TYMPANUM relief (early 12th century) over the west entrance to the Cathedral of Saint Lazare in Autun, France, the saved souls are shown approaching heaven on the left, while on the right devils capture souls as they are torn from their graves at the Last Judgment, a warning to the mortals who pass beneath it into the cathedral.

In the later 12th and through the 13th centuries, principally in France, the cathedrals were built that still make the Gothic style a feature of the urban landscape. The great height of the nave of CHARTRES CATHEDRAL

(1194–1220) draws the gaze in and up. The arcade, the triforium above it, the CLERESTORY windows, and finally the vaulting proceed from one to the next with grace and structural logic, just as the nave continues toward the altar with the regularly spaced intervals of the thick clustered piers. STAINED GLASS in the great windows diffuses a rich and gentle light throughout the nave.

While at all times compatible with the architecture, the sculpture at Chartres illustrates the variety of sculptural styles that developed in the Gothic era. The west facade displays an orderly array of elongated jamb figures, especially notable in the central Royal Portal. The statues seem to be squeezed into a tight fit with the adjacent columns, as if the figures were still columns. Yet they are conceived as sculptures in the round rather than in relief and thus reintroduce large-scale sculpture, virtually absent for a millennium. The feverish energy of the Autun tympanum is replaced in the corresponding relief at Chartres with serene calm, showing Christ giving blessing, surrounded by the symmetrically disposed symbols of the four Gospels. The portals of the south transept are later (c.1215) and show the relaxed naturalism of High Gothic sculpture. The jamb figures have a greater suggestion of space around them than their columnar predecessors on the Royal Portal. They are more mobile in space, with

Praxiteles' Hermes Holding the Infant Dionysus (4th century BC) is the only extant statue by one of the great Greek sculptors. The grace of the marble statue and the S-curve pose are characteristic of his work. (Olympia Museum, Greece.)

The typanum of the central Royal Portal at Chartres Cathedral depicts the figure of Christ with the symbols of the four Evangelists. The Gothic relief, dating from 1145, is the focal point of the west facade.

axes that hint at a slight S-curve of the body instead of maintaining the strict verticality of the earlier figures.

In Italy the Gothic style was never as pervasive as it was in the nations to the north. Manuscript illumination had been the chief outlet for painting in the north (culminating in the Gothic International Style at the beginning of the 15th century), but panel and fresco painting dominated in Italy. The development of painting most clearly traces changes in Italian art, just as developments in architecture and architectural sculpture do in France.

The Renaissance. After centuries under the dominance of the abstract Byzantine style, Italian (more specifically Sienese and Florentine) painters began to create altarpieces in which the figures became less and less stately and psychologically distant. The backgrounds were done in gold leaf, the rest in tempera, and the frames were elaborate gilded structures patterned on Gothic ornament. Key stylistic features shifted in the time from the late 13th to the early 14th centuries: the illusion of space was strengthened by the use of architectural backgrounds that imply and divide spatial areas. The receding diagonals of the setting unite and extend the space in the painting. Duccio's *Maestà*; (1308–11; Museo dell' Opera del Duomo, Siena), a polyptych (multipaneled altarpiece) commissioned by the Cathedral of Siena and installed in 1311, shows a point in the transition from the earlier frontal, hieratic style of Cimabue to the later spatial and volumetric style of Giotto—a change that implies a shift in the conception and portrayal of religious personages from embodiments of abstract spirits to sentient, recognizable human beings. Giotto initiated a great age of Fresco Painting with his cycles in the Arena Chapel in Padua and the Church of Saint Francis in Assisi, both from the first third of the 14th century. Since the Francis series is based in part on history (Francis had lived just a century before), the iconographic formulae of the past had to be abandoned in favor of new compositions.

A century later, the new tangibility of painted figures and settings was taken up by Masaccio and other Florentines as the Renaissance gathered momentum. Filippo Brunelleschi's Pazzi Chapel (c.1430–33), an elegant addition to the church of Santa Croce (Holy Cross) in Florence, is of simple and sober design, especially when weighed against the dramatic energy and awesome scale of the adjoining Gothic church. The chapel is laid out in multiples of a basic square module. The arches are round and the chapel domed, intentionally recalling Roman architecture.

The development of naturalism and individualism in the Renaissance is easily recognized in Florentine sculpture. As early as 1401, Lorenzo Ghiberti adapted antique Roman figural naturalism in his bronze reliefs for the Florence Baptistery doors. Large-scale bronze casting came back into practice with Donatello's equestrian Gattamelata (1445–50) in Padua. The horse and rider, although

The central panel from Duccio di Buoninsegna's Maestà altarpiece (1308–11) depicts the Virgin and Child surrounded by angels, the Apostles, and various saints. The huge altarpiece is the only authenticated work by Duccio. (Cathedral Museum, Siena.)

Perugino's Delivery of the Keys to St. Peter *(1482) is a wall fresco in the Vatican's Sistine Chapel in Rome. The sense of deep space is achieved through the use of perspective and the placement of figures, buildings, and trees on receding parallel planes.*

patterned on the 2d-century bronze statue of Marcus Aurelius in Rome, is strongly individual. The Renaissance esteem for strength of character and personal presence is quintessentially expressed in Andrea del VERROCCHIO's Colleoni Monument (1483–88) in Venice. The robust horse and rider exude the physical firmness that is at once seen as fortitude of will. The strong interests in anatomical correctness of structure and motion and in authority of execution reached their apogee in the work of MICHELANGELO in the next century—in sculpture, such as his DAVID (1501–04; Accademia, Florence), in painting, such as his ceiling of the SISTINE CHAPEL (1508–12; Vatican, Rome), and in architecture, such as the Farnese Palace (1546).

Italian painters shared the sculptors' concern for figural naturalism. As interest in the observable world increased, it was accompanied by the perfection of a regular system of spatial structure, or PERSPECTIVE, a primary concern of painters throughout the 15th century. Duccio's compressed and approximate space becomes, through Leon Battista ALBERTI's mathematical research and the experiments of such painters as Paolo UCCELLO and PIERO DELLA FRANCESCA, the orderly and precise space of PERUGINO's *Delivery of the Keys to St. Peter* (1482), a wall fresco in the Sistine Chapel.

Toward the end of the 15th century, the increasing availability of important papal commissions in Rome caused the Renaissance center of gravity to shift there from northern Italy. RAPHAEL and Michelangelo, along with LEONARDO DA VINCI, were the outstanding figures of the High Renaissance. More and more, the personality of the artist, his uniqueness, and his artistic sensibility became an important factor to those who sought works of art as well as those who made them. In the artist's workshop (*bottega*), staffed by assistants and apprentices, the dis-

tinction between the master's hand and that of his underlings became more noteworthy.

The linear quality of Renaissance painting, the clarity by which every detail is perfected to the same degree and discloses itself to the viewer to the same extent, was supplanted in the 16th century by a style featuring CHIAROSCURO—soft, mellow light, deep shadows, and greater awareness of the texture and handling of the paint itself. Color took on new prominence—subtle oil glazes enrich the color and hence the mood; earlier fresco and tempera works sometimes seem chalky, harsh, and arid by comparison. Lighting, once even and unobtrusive, became more selective and emphatic. The Venetian painter TITIAN combined intense hues with vivid action in his *Bacchus*

Andrea del Verrocchio's Colleoni Monument *(1483–88) in Venice is a bronze equestrian statue honoring the condottiere (soldier of fortune) Bartolomeo Colleoni. The revival of large-scale bronze casting was one of the great artistic accomplishments of the Italian Renaissance.*

Titian's Bacchus and Ariadne *(1522) illustrates the Venetian school's use of brilliant color. One of many works by Titian on mythological subjects, the painting reflects the intense Renaissance interest in the pagan classical world. (National Gallery, London.)*

and Ariadne (1522; National Gallery, London). Well illustrated in this canvas is the continuing Renaissance interest in anatomy, while the pagan theme testifies to the new options that competed with Christian subjects.

In the essentially Gothic north of Europe, the impact of the Renaissance is best seen in the work of Albrecht DÜRER, the preeminent figure outside of Italy. A tradition of superb craftsmanship and dazzling realism had been established a century before by the Flemish artist Jan van EYCK, particularly in the resplendent polyptych *Adoration of the Holy Lamb* (1432; St. Bavon, Ghent), and even before that with a succession of unsurpassed manuscript illuminators, such as the LIMBOURG BROTHERS of the Burgundian court, working up to the second decade of the 15th century. During that century the development and large-scale use of WOODCUTS AND ENGRAVINGS also occurred; these printing techniques increased the accessi-

bility of art with their ease in distribution, thanks to their modest cost, small scale, and innate reproducibility. Dürer's engraving *Knight, Death, and the Devil* (1513), an allegory with starting imagery, shows the high point of verisimilitude and tonal richness to which Dürer elevated the GRAPHIC ARTS. Even more than before, GENRE, LANDSCAPE, and STILL-LIFE PAINTING grew toward independence as categories and emerged, fully individual, in the 17th century.

The Baroque Age. In the 17th century, the BAROQUE age, the styles of the arts were at their most diverse. Large-scale mural and ceiling paintings with dizzying *trompe l'oeil* ("eye-fooling") ILLUSIONISM glorified Roman Catholicism in Italy; by contrast, diminutive still lifes recorded the austere tenor of Protestantism in The Netherlands. The Flemish master Peter Paul RUBENS, a diplomat as well as an artist, filled acres of canvas with his vigorous, splendidly colored scenes, typified by the 21 huge paintings (1622–25; Louvre, Paris) allegorizing the life of Marie de Médicis. Nicolas POUSSIN pursued his own stately classical style that kept Renaissance values alive in Paris and Rome, evidenced by his large *Triumph of Neptune and Amphitrite* (c.1636; Philadelphia Museum of Art).

Set against the grand and highly public baroque style are such subtle, intimate, and personally revealing works as REMBRANDT's tiny drawing of a child guided in his first steps (1660–62; British Museum, London). Sketches, once regarded as the unimportant preparatory debris of larger finished works, emerged in the 17th century as expressive and uninhibiting outlets for the artist.

The personal element is present, too, in such royal commissions as Diego VELÁZQUEZ's *Las Meninas* (*The Maids of Honor*; 1656, Prado Museum, Madrid), where the artist depicts himself at work in the Spanish king's household. The king and queen, seen reflected in the mirror on the back wall, force an awareness in the viewer of the world beyond the painting as well as the world within it.

Baroque architecture retained antique forms but modified their syntax or architectural language, developing new combinations that resulted in strikingly dramatic buildings, often on a large scale, impelled by Michelangelo's and Andrea PALLADIO's 16th-century redirection

Woman Bathing in a Stream *(1655) illustrates Rembrandt's masterful handling of chiaroscuro, the contrast of light and shadow. (National Gallery, London.)*

Knight, Death, and the Devil *(1513) exemplifies the brilliant technique and startling imagery characteristic of Albrecht Dürer's allegorical engravings. (Museum of Fine Arts, Boston.)*

and elaboration of Renaissance classicism. SAINT PETER'S BASILICA in Rome was so vast a project that several architects were responsible for its progress in the 16th and 17th centuries. Giovanni Lorenzo BERNINI finished the work in the mid-17th century by adding the gigantic colonnade embracing the vast piazza, bringing order to the urban environment by sculpturing the space in front of the church.

Sculpture, too, took a turn toward the dramatic, as the intense, even theatrical *The Ecstasy of St. Teresa* (1645–52; Cornaro Chapel, Santa Maria della Vittoria, Rome) well illustrates. In this complex work, Bernini combines the force of the sculpture with that of the architecture around it, even controlling the light, which comes from above as if to make into real light the gilded wood rays Bernini added. Combined with the illusionistic painting above, the whole ensemble exemplifies the baroque desire to maximize illusionistic effects and to integrate the arts.

The ROCOCO STYLE, the joyous child of the baroque, had different tones and emphases in different countries, especially in Germany and Austria, but was initially and most prominently French. In painting, the bombastic heaviness of court styles was softened and lightened in the painterly tradition of Rubens. Pastel pinks, blues, and greens were used to depict such images of pleasure as Antoine WATTEAU's *Embarkation for the Island of Cythera*

(1717; Louvre, Paris) and Jean Honoré FRAGONARD's series *The Progress of Love* (1771–73; Frick Collection, New York). In England, the 18th century was a rich one for a land where the verbal arts had long predominated over the visual. William HOGARTH invented a new genre with his moralizing paintings organized in series and commenting on contemporary values, such as in the eight paintings depicting *The Rake's Progress* (1735; Soane Museum, London). Sir Joshua REYNOLDS, the first president of the Royal Academy (founded in 1768), developed academic painting, drawing on its French incarnation and on Sir Anthony van DYCK's style, both from the previous century. Thomas GAINSBOROUGH produced elegant portraits, frequently with a rococo flavor to the handling. His *Robert Andrews and Wife* (1748–50; The National Gallery, London) combines portraiture with Dutch-inspired landscape painting, showing the gentleman farmer and his wife comfortably at home.

Rococo architecture radiates from Paris, where its curvilinear decoration was most fully developed by such artists as Jules HARDOUIN MANSART, Robert de COTTE, and Germain Boffrand. In southern Germany it was sumptuously expressed in the palaces and churches of François CUVILLIÉS and Balthasar NEUMANN. Rococo decoration—light in color, exuberant in mood, effortless in structure—was usually divorced from architectural function.

The Modern World. By the end of the 18th century, there were crosscurrents of different fundamental orientations to the possibilities provided by previous generations. Antonio CANOVA's sculpture of Pauline Borghese, *Venus Victrix* (1808; Borghese Gallery, Rome), epitomizes the tranquil repose of the neoclassical outlook. The marble seems to give up its own material nature as stone and assume that of the opulent flesh it represents. Outside Italy, NEOCLASSICISM gathered even greater strength, as in Jacques Louis DAVID's large neoclassical paintings such as his *Oath of the Horatii* (1784; Louvre, Paris), in

Giovanni Lorenzo Bernini's The Ecstasy of St. Teresa *(1645–52) combines sculpture, painting, and architecture to convey the saint's beatific vision in a typically complex baroque composition. (Cornaro Chapel, Santa Maria della Vittoria, Rome.)*

In Robert Andrews and Wife *(1748–50), Thomas Gainsborough combines an elegant and fashionable portrait, the type of painting for which he became famous, with his favorite type, landscape painting. (National Gallery, London.)*

Francisco de Goya's The Third of May, 1808 (c.1814) depicts French reprisals against the Spaniards during Napoleon's invasion of Spain. In this condemnation of human cruelty, Goya uses violent contrasts of light and dark to convey the violence and horror of the wanton killings. (Prado Museum, Madrid.)

the 1780s and '90s—archaeologically exact in detail (ancient POMPEII was rediscovered in 1748) but contemporary in its implicit political message in revolutionary France.

The romantic impulse emerged with those artists usually thought of as intense and often solitary personalities. It appeared at much the same time with William BLAKE and Henry FUSELI in England, Caspar David FRIEDRICH and Philipp Otto RUNGE in Germany, and Eugène DELACROIX and Théodore GÉRICAULT in France. Thus, the term RO-MANTICISM, as a name for a style, really describes a shared sensibility in the context of different national traditions, whereas the term baroque encompasses many divergent attitudes in one historical style.

The Spaniard Francisco de GOYA's Third of May, 1808 (c.1814; Prado Museum, Madrid) embodies key features of the romantic outlook: the paint application reveals the personal, energetic brushstroke of the artist; contrasting masses of light and dark give a spotlit effect to maximize the drama; the action of the scene is at its frantic peak; the subject—the systematic murder of civilians—stirs our sympathy at the same time that it excites our morbid curiosity.

The United States had produced artists, such as John Singleton COPLEY and Benjamin WEST, who gravitated toward the capitals of Europe, but early in the 19th century an indigenous group of landscapists, called the HUDSON RIVER SCHOOL, emerged under the leadership of Thomas COLE. Frederic Edwin CHURCH's Niagara Falls (1857; Corcoran Gallery, Washington, D.C.), typical of this school, shows the sublime magnitude and power of nature in an untamed, primeval land.

Niagara Falls (1857) by Frederick Church typifies the ability of the Hudson River school landscape artists to convey the grandeur of nature on canvas. (Corcoran Gallery of Art, Washington, D.C.)

The Crystal Palace, constructed of iron and glass, was designed by Sir Joseph Paxton for the London Exposition of 1851. It was reerected in a London suburb but destroyed by fire in 1936.

Constantin Brancusi's bronze Bird in Space (c.1924) is one of several versions of this theme. In his work, Brancusi seeks to represent, in abstract form, the concept of flight and soaring movement. (Philadelphia Museum of Art.)

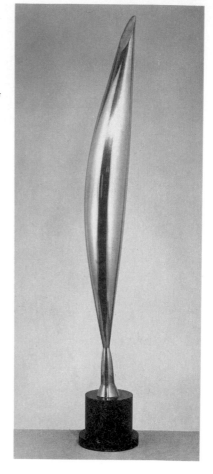

The profusion and diversity of styles in the 19th century is reflected in its architecture. The austerity of neoclassicism followed on the heels of rococo indulgence and spread rapidly from France to England and then to the United States, exemplified by buildings such as Thomas Jefferson's MONTICELLO in Charlottesville, Va. Revivalism caused a recapitulation of recent, older, and exotic styles, including the GOTHIC REVIVAL, as seen in Sir Charles BARRY's and Augustus PUGIN's Houses of Parliament in Lon-

Balzac (1892–97), Auguste Rodin's bronze tribute to the French novelist, created a furor when it was first shown, since it represented a radical break with 19th-century academic sculptural traditions. It is now seen as a presage of 20th-century sculptural expressionism. (Museum of Modern Art, New York.)

don (begun 1836), which found wide favor for the first time since it was eclipsed by the Renaissance.

The 19th century was characterized by stylistic upheavals for another reason—the Industrial Revolution and modern technology had begun to change the way structures could be built and hence changed how they looked. Sir Joseph PAXTON's CRYSTAL PALACE (1851; destroyed 1936) utilized the tensile strength of iron to free the walls from the function of support and thus allowed enormous areas of glass (see CAST-IRON ARCHITECTURE). In the modern world, regularity, uniformity, order, and a frequent respect for the structural properties of materials has created economical, functional buildings. This is true of Walter GROPIUS's BAUHAUS buildings at Dessau (1925–26) as well as of Ludwig MIES VAN DER ROHE's Lake Shore Drive apartments (1948–51) in Chicago, which achieve a reposeful monumentality and feature a predominantly glass curtain wall with understated vertical shafts.

Academic sculpture, reiterating classical works by rote, was shaken up in the late 19th century by the powerful presence of Auguste RODIN, who invested bronze sculpture in particular with new energy and new freedom in handling. *Balzac* (1892–97; Museum of Modern Art, New York) is a virtual column of upward force, a singular mass, with facial features deeply cut and intensely expressive. With the 20th century, direct carving of stone regained its popularity, and modeling in clay for bronze casting declined. The new aesthetic brought with it geometric abstraction and resulted in sculpture with the grace and refinement of Constantin BRANCUSI's yellow marble *Bird in Space* (1919; Philadelphia Museum of Art), in which the subject is pared down to its formal essence. The third way of making sculpture—assembling different materials and constructing it—was explored by Aleksandr ARCHIPENKO, Naum GABO, and many others, who brought new materials into the sculptor's vocabulary—glass, plastic, sheet metal, and the like. The metal constructions of David SMITH followed in that modernist tradition.

The late 19th century was also characterized by the rise of the avant-garde in the arts and by the birth of the "isms" that named the principal trends. Claude MONET's *Water Lilies* (1899; Louvre, Paris) shows his and the other impressionists' concern with light—the way it can change from hour to hour or day to day, the idea that material things are known to us only by light in its infinite permutations and hence may seem no more substantial than the atmosphere around them. The artists who matured after the first wave of IMPRESSIONISM altered its rationale. Georges SEURAT attempted to measure scientifically the effects of light, Paul GAUGUIN and Vincent VAN GOGH explored the mysteries of the self, and Paul CÉZANNE created a painted structure echoing the structure of the visible world. All four are now considered leaders of POST-IMPRESSIONISM.

In the first decade of this century, abstraction, oriented toward problems of composition or pictorial structure, was the preeminent artistic movement, originating, as had most of the important developments of the previous century, in Paris. CUBISM had by far the greatest impact. Pablo PICASSO's *Demoiselles d'Avignon* (1906–07; Museum of Modern Art, New York) creates a new logic of structure for the figures—one that does not depend on their relative appearance from any one point. The rebuilding of the figures also allows new boldness in composition, now that color and shape are freed from functioning purely for description. Also evident is Picasso's interest in AFRICAN ART, in particular carved masks and wood sculptures, reflected in the grotesque faces of the women.

Composition with Red, Blue, and Yellow (1930; Collection of Mr. and Mrs. Armand P. Batos, New York) by Piet MONDRIAN, one of the founders of the neoplastic DE STIJL group and also working in Paris, gives up representation entirely for an ABSTRACT ART dependent on pure relationships of forms and primary colors. In FAUVISM and EXPRESSIONISM artists sought to utilize the medium for subjective expression and evidence of personal involvement, while Mondrian and other artists created works that eschewed such features for those of reflective tranquility and formal precision. In a sense, the painting of this century may be understood as progressive self-examination and reduction, in quest of the deepest innate character of the medium. Alternatively, it may be seen as a response to the new, industrial, fast-paced, insecure world, or as the revelation of intuitions that are no longer suppressed by convention, as in SURREALISM, in which the inner world becomes the real world.

Water Lilies *(c.1910), by the French impressionist Claude Monet, is one of a large series of similar studies he painted in his gardens at Giverny. Monet approached abstraction in his rendering of the lilies in a shimmering stream of water. (Bührle Collection, Zurich.)*

In Three Dancers *(1925), Pablo Picasso uses cubist fragmentation and distortion of the human figure to represent the energy of the dance. (Tate Gallery, London.)*

An aerial view of Robert Smithson's Spiral Jetty *(1970) shows a huge spiral of rock and salt crystals projecting into Great Salt Lake, Utah. An example of earthworks art, the structure was made of natural materials that eventually eroded away.*

American artists began their own experiments in what came to be called MODERN ART a few years after such work appeared in Europe, sparked by New York's famous ARMORY SHOW of 1913. This culminated with the emergence of New York as the artistic world capital, supplanting Paris, with the development of ABSTRACT EXPRESSIONISM after World War II. Willem DE KOONING, Franz KLINE, Robert MOTHERWELL, Jackson POLLOCK, Mark ROTHKO, and Clyfford STILL were among the pioneers of this dynamic movement.

Today, the distinction between media is being blurred; *sculpture* seems an outmoded term for assembled pieces, and *painting* no longer applies if only a document is left, the artwork having become an act rather than an artifact. With such vanguard movements as conceptual art and, certainly, EARTHWORKS, the work transcends gallery walls. These and additional recent trends, including PERFORMANCE ART and VIDEO ART, not only further blur the distinction between media but also extend the traditional definitions of art.

See also: BRONZES; ENAMEL; FURNITURE; GLASSWARE, DECORATIVE; GOLD AND SILVER WORK; HOUSE (IN WESTERN ARCHITECTURE); INTERIOR DESIGN; JEWELRY; MUSEUMS, ART; SCULPTURE TECHNIQUES.

art collectors and patrons Humanists of the Italian Renaissance often advocated support of art and artists. Their most frequently cited precedent was Gaius MAECENAS, a Roman statesman of the 1st century BC, who was the patron of the poets Horace and Vergil. In the Middle Ages, artists were usually relegated to anonymity as artisans, so patronage in the modern sense appeared only when artists began to gain renown for their individual accomplishments. In 1334, the commune of Florence granted commissions to GIOTTO DI BONDONE on the basis of his personal reputation. During the Renaissance the principal patrons were the church and the aristocracy, and a few wealthy individuals such as Giovanni Rucellai (1403–81), a Florentine merchant.

The leading 15th-century Florentine patron was Cosimo de Medici (see MEDICI family). Cosimo's grandson, Lorenzo the Magnificent, carried on the Medici tradition until his death in 1492, whereupon the center of patronage shifted from Florence to Rome. In particular, Pope JULIUS II was adept at employing artists on projects that both advanced the cause of religion and helped the church compete with the growing power of secular government and the mercantile classes.

During the 16th century, FRANCIS I of France, MAXIMILIAN I, Holy Roman emperor from 1493 to 1519, and HENRY VIII of England supported the careers of many northern European painters. In 1560 Elector Augustus of Saxony (1526–86) began assembling his Dresden Kunstkammer, a collection that became the nucleus of the famed Dresden State Art Collection. In 1623, with the beginning of URBAN VIII's pontificate, Rome became once again the center of art patronage for all of Europe.

Some of the most active patrons and collectors from northern Europe were diplomats. Sir Dudley Carleton

(1573–1632), CHARLES I's ambassador to The Hague, was a major collector of Rubens's paintings. Joseph Smith (1682–1770), British consul at Venice, had become the leading art patron and collector of his day.

The founding of the Royal Academy in 1769 in London signaled the beginning of a period in which ACADEMIES OF ART became the conduits for the patronage of national governments and the steadily rising middle classes. As a result, most patrons, both governmental and private, supported only art officially approved by the academies; avant-garde artists often spent their early careers without benefit of any subsidy. Early collectors of the IMPRESSIONISTS and the POSTIMPRESSIONISTS were often sophisticated Parisian dealers such as Ambroise VOLLARD, Paul Durand-Ruel, and Georges Petit. One of the most important collections of this period was assembled by a wealthy colleague of the impressionists, the painter Gustave Caillebotte.

Important early collections of contemporary art were formed in the United States by Gertrude Vanderbilt WHITNEY, John Quinn (1870–1924), Walter Arensberg (1878–1954), and others. At the time of their founding, New York's MUSEUM OF MODERN ART (1929) and WHITNEY MUSEUM OF AMERICAN ART (1931) were attempts to provide the avant-garde with the kind of backing that was still being made available to conservative art by the METROPOLITAN MUSEUM OF ART and other long-established institutions. In 1937 the GUGGENHEIM MUSEUM joined the Modern and the Whitney. By the end of the 1950s, these museums, working in concert with such collectors as Peggy GUGGENHEIM, Philip JOHNSON, and Nelson ROCKEFELLER, had insured the place of the avant-garde in the postwar era.

In the 1970s three art patrons emerged as dominant in the United States. The oil magnate J. Paul GETTY left the bulk of his immense estate to the GETTY MUSEUM in Malibu, Calif., making it by far the wealthiest museum in the world. The philanthropist Paul MELLON added the $100-million East Wing to Washington's NATIONAL GALLERY OF ART. The industrialist Joseph H. Hirshhorn (1899–1981) donated all of his huge art collection to the nation. It is housed in the Hirshhorn Museum and Sculpture Garden in Washington, D.C. During the 1980s other extensive private art collections were opened to the public, including the outstanding 20th-century art collection of Dominique de Menil, housed in Houston, Tex.

Patronage of museums and private collectors has been supplemented in recent years by extensive programs of governmental grants. Precedent for this was set in the WORKS PROGRESS ADMINISTRATION of the 1930s in which the federal government employed artists, awarding them monthly stipends. A further source of patronage has recently appeared—corporations wishing to present a favorable image to the general public. Corporate patrons either provide grants of money to museums and other arts organizations or support artists directly through the formation of corporate collections.

art conservation and restoration Art conservation and restoration involve the examination, analysis, and treatment of artworks and artifacts by highly trained specialists called conservators. Art conservators are also concerned with the storage, shipment, and exhibition of artworks and with control of the environment in which the objects are kept. If an artwork is damaged—by physical deterioration, accident, or vandalism—the conservator must attempt to repair the object and, if possible, restore it to its original appearance, or at least to a state in which it can be exhibited.

Artworks are cared for and treated according to the nature of their materials. These fall into three broad categories: organic materials (animal skin, papyrus, paper, textiles, wood, bone, ivory, and most paints); metals (gold, silver, copper, lead, iron, steel, bronze, and brass); and siliceous and related materials (stone, ceramics, and glass). A great many artworks combine elements from these categories.

History. Use of the term *art conservation* appears to date from an international conference on the conservation of paintings held in Rome in 1930, but artists have been employed to restore works of art since ancient times. Such famous artists as Pausanias, Giorgio VASARI, and Peter Paul RUBENS have been associated with art conservation; generally, however, this kind of work appears to have been relegated to unrecorded artists. In 1543 an official cleaner was appointed to care for the ceiling and wall frescoes of the SISTINE CHAPEL in the Vatican. The first recorded transfer of paint from one canvas to another was performed in 1729 by the artist Domenico Michelini in Rome. Lining a canvas support with an additional canvas became standard procedure in the 18th and 19th centuries and is still practiced.

An art restorer in Venice works on an 18th-century painting by the Venetian artist Magiotto. The restoration process involves intensive laboratory analysis, cleaning or removal of old varnish, and retouching of damaged areas.

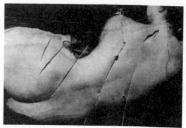

(Above) *A detail of Diego Velázquez's Rokeby Venus (c.1650; National Gallery, London) reveals the damage inflicted in 1914 when the painting was slashed.* (Left) *The painting was retouched and cleaned to restore its former splendor.*

The scientific method began to influence restoration procedures in the 18th and 19th centuries. In 1809, the French chemist Jean Antoine Chaptal analyzed colors found at POMPEII, and in 1815 the British physicist Sir Humphry DAVY analyzed other pigments used in ancient times. The first cleaning of pictures at the National Gallery in London began in 1846. A government commission was set up (1850) to investigate the condition of the paintings; one of its members, the eminent scientist Michael FARADAY, made deterioration studies, including a study of the deleterious effects of train smoke and illuminating gas on paintings. The first museum laboratory for treating and restoring art and antiquities was established in 1888 at the Staatliche Museen, Berlin. In 1896, only a year after Wilhelm Konrad ROENTGEN discovered the X RAY, radiography was used to detect alterations in an oil painting. The British Museum laboratory was set up in 1919, and the first scientific museum laboratory in America began operation in the Fogg Art Museum at Harvard University nine years later. The International Institute for Conservation of Historic and Artistic Works (IIC) was established in 1950; the American Group of the IIC held its first regular meeting in 1960, and in 1972 became the American Institute for Conservation of Historic and Artistic Works (AIC).

Apprenticeship was the only means of entering the profession until 1960, when the first American graduate training program in fine art conservation was established at the Institute of Fine Arts of New York University. A three-year graduate program in conservation was established in 1970 at the Cooperstown Graduate Program under the auspices of the State University of New York College at Oneonta and the New York State Historical Association; in 1974 a similar program was inaugurated at the University of Delaware under the joint sponsorship of the university and the Winterthur Museum.

Examination, Analysis, and Treatment. Before restoration or other treatment is initiated, an art object is carefully examined and, when necessary, component materials are analyzed. Photographic and written documentation before, during, and after treatment is es-

sential. Various techniques are available to the conservator, including ULTRAVIOLET LIGHT fluorescence, infrared photography (see INFRARED RADIATION), photomacrography (a technique for obtaining slightly enlarged pictures without a microscope), and beta-radiography (see BETATRON). All these processes have the advantage of being nondestructive. Microsamples can also be taken from the art object in order to study its structure and material. More advanced techniques of analysis used in conservation

A spectrographic analysis is used in a laboratory at the Louvre to determine the composition of a bronze sphinx. The statue is subjected to high-frequency rays that cause the work to emit radiations characteristic of its alloy.

may include X-ray fluorescence, X-ray diffraction, CHRO-MATOGRAPHY, spectrography (see SPECTROSCOPY), NEUTRON activation analysis, RADIOMETRIC AGE-DATING, and thermoluminescent dating (see LUMINESCENCE).

Restoration methods for artworks are as complex and varied as the materials from which works of art have been constructed. An important general principle is that the materials used should be reversible. An oil painting, for example, should never be retouched or "inpainted" in an oil medium that would become as insoluble as the surrounding original paint. A more easily soluble acrylic or watercolor vehicle would be recommended instead.

Typical treatment procedures include lining or relining oil paintings on canvas with an additional fabric, using a wax-resin or synthetic adhesive; deacidifying and relaxing distorted paper supports; using carefully analyzed adhesives to consolidate flaking gouache (gum-based watercolor) on paper, oil paint on canvas, painted gesso (a plasterlike substance) on wood, and paint on glass or metal; removing dirt and stains from textiles or paper; removing corrosion products from metals and stained glass; and mending torn paper, split canvas, fraying textiles, broken ceramics, damaged metal, split wood, and cracked marble or plaster.

Environment and Conservation. A work of art is a complex assemblage of different organic and inorganic materials, each of which reacts to the environment according to its natural properties. Sudden changes in temperature or humidity may immediately aggravate existing incompatibilities within the components of the object. These factors must be considered during all arrangements for storage, shipment, and exhibition of artworks. Generally a temperature of 21° C (70° F) and a relative humidity of about 50 percent constitute a stable environment for the maintenance of most art objects.

Paper, photographs, parchment, leather, and textiles are extremely sensitive to excessive moisture and are susceptible to fungus attack. Exposure to sunlight may cause immediate fading of watercolors, textiles, and wallpaper. One day of 90 percent relative humidity may cause corrosion in polished metals, which would be aggravated by the presence of any polish residue. Variations in humidity cause warping and checking of wood, especially in large objects and veneered furniture. Ivory, crizzled glass, salt-infused archaeological pottery, and painted, gilded, and gessoed wood all react unfavorably to moisture, which may be further catalyzed by heat, light, and atmospheric pollutants. The museum conservator must supervise the maintenance of stable environmental control as well as provide first aid or complete restoration of damaged or deteriorated artworks.

See also: FRESCO PAINTING; MURAL PAINTING; PAINTING TECHNIQUES; SCULPTURE TECHNIQUES.

Art Deco   Art Deco is an architectural and decorative-arts style, popular from 1910 to 1940, that is characterized by highly stylized natural and geometric forms and ornaments, usually strongly symmetrical. Outstanding

American examples of Art Deco are the CHRYSLER BUILDING and Radio City Music Hall in New York City. Artists such as Pablo PICASSO, Fernand LÉGER, and Wassily KANDINSKY produced work in the style, as did designers of furnishings, textiles, jewelry, and advertising.

Art Deco themes were often classical motifs reduced to geometric stylizations. Edgar Brandt decorated wrought-iron screens with symmetrical fountains; Emil Ruhlman inlaid ebony cabinets with ivory to depict floral arrangements of geometrical precision; René LALIQUE etched scenes, such as a gracefully striding female with a wolfhound or a gazelle, into crystal or frosted glass; and Jean Puiforcat and Daum depicted abstract geometric forms.

The term *Art Deco*, coined in the 1960s when interest in the style revived, was derived from *L'Exposition Internationale des Arts Decoratifs et Industriels Modernes*. This Paris exhibition of 1925 came midway in Art Deco's development and was a definitive display of the style. At this time Art Deco was also known as "Art Moderne" or "Modernistic"; later it was called "Jazz Pattern" or "Skyscraper Modern."

The INTERNATIONAL STYLE in architecture developed at the same time, and after 1925 it considerably influenced the final phase of Art Deco. Along with CUBIST painting and the German BAUHAUS school, the work of LE CORBUSIER and other International Style architects effected a change from the earlier, more decorative phase of Art Deco toward a simpler, bolder approach typical of the 1930s.

Art Deco emerged as a reaction to ART NOUVEAU. Its two forerunners were Charles Rennie MACKINTOSH of Scotland and Josef HOFFMANN of Vienna, whose works in 1900 were an indication of what was to appear in the next decades.

Hoffman's austere Palais Stoclet in Brussels (1905-11), with its mosaic murals by Gustave KLIMT, advanced for its time, marked the transition from Art Nouveau to Art Deco. In 1903, Hoffman founded the Wiener Werkstätte, a workshop that produced some of the earliest Art Deco designs.

These concepts were introduced in Paris in 1910 with an exhibition of decorative arts from Munich and Vienna at the Louvre. On display was a new style based on a simplification of the early 19th-century neoclassical BIEDERMEIER style and of peasant art, or FOLK ART, quite the antithesis of Art Nouveau. Another significant event in Paris in 1910 was the presentation by the BALLETS RUSSES DE SERGE DIAGHILEV of *Schéhérazade*. Léon BAKST had concocted oriental sets and costumes in dazzling, barbaric colors; this brought a demand in the fashion world for exoticism, soon answered by the couturier Paul Poiret. In 1912, Poiret created his own design school, the Atelier Martine, to further his Art Deco ideas. By the 1920s the effects of cubist painting were seen in advertising and product designs. Coco CHANEL used cubist colors and forms in creating women's fashions, which she adorned with Art Deco jewelry.

African sculpture and ancient Egyptian and Southwest American Indian arts all had their influence on Art Deco

Examples of furnishing accessories created in the Art Deco style early in the 20th century include: (1) a parchment and bronze lamp in the form of a parachutist; (2) a French ceramic inkwell made during the late 1920s; (3) a plastic and chrome candlestick; (4) a smoked glass Senlis vase (c.1925) designed by the French artist René Lalique; (5) a Fauré vase shaped like an African gourd and embellished with a triangle-and-stripe design in turquoise and cobalt-blue enamel; (6) a plastic imitation-amber scent bottle; (7) a crystal perfume flask (c.1925) from the French glassworks factory at Baccarat; (8) a marble clock by F. Priess with a silver and bronze face, mountings, and the figure of an Amazon; (9) a silver-gilt teapot (c.1937) with a rock-crystal handle and knob designed by Jean Puiforcat. Art Deco design was also used in the fashion accessories of the period, for example, (10) a silver, lacquer, and eggshell cigarette case by Raymond Templier; (11) a two-tone shoe with a stylized sunray motif; (12) a fan from the 1920s with designs inspired by cubist painting; (13) a plastic belt buckle (c.1935) from Paris; (14) two wood-and-ivory buttons (c.1935) probably made in England.

in this decade, as did Archaic Greek art. With the influence of the Bauhaus and the International Style after 1925, Art Deco arrived at a final development that reflected the industrial age, thus achieving a reconciliation of the arts and machine production that had troubled artists and designers since the Industrial Revolution began.

art forgery   SEE FORGERY IN ART

Art Nouveau [ahr noo-voh']   Art Nouveau, a French term meaning new art, refers to a style of ARCHITECTURE, of commercial and DECORATIVE ART, and, to some extent, a style of PAINTING and SCULPTURE that was popular about 1900. Although the style was then thought of as modern and was given the title "new art," it was adapted from older styles and art forms. Much was derived from the GOTHIC and ROCOCO and from the arts of Java and Japan. The movement was also inspired by Celtic manuscripts and the drawings of William BLAKE. Persian pottery and ancient Roman glass also served as models for some Art Nouveau craftsmen.

The style's patterns and motifs were taken primarily

Patterns and motifs inspired by nature appear in the metal and jewelry design of the Art Nouveau period. Examples include (1) a corsage ornament made of gold, enamel, opals, and other precious stones by René Lalique; (2) a pewter plaque with a typical nymph motif; (3) a corsage ornament of gold, enamel, opals, and chrysoprase by Lalique, once worn by Sarah Bernhardt; (4) a brass picture frame with a curvilinear flower motif; (5) a brooch of gold and enamel (1901) by C. Dessosiers; (6) a silver pillbox with a motif executed in multicolored enamel; (7) a silver and gilt spoon by Bogdar Karageorgevitch; and (8) a silver spoon in the form of a plant, by Karageorgevitch.

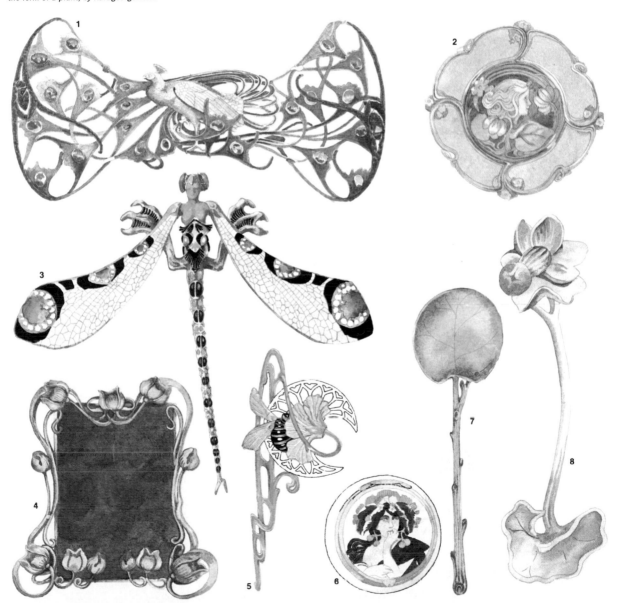

Alfons Mucha's Job *poster was designed about 1897 as an advertisement for a brand of cigarette paper. The elegant young woman with long flowing hair was a prominent motif of the Art Nouveau style.*

from nature and were often carried out with unrestrained exuberance of form, color, and especially line, a flowing curvilinear. A favorite Art Nouveau theme was a nymph with flowers in her abundant streaming hair. She appeared on the posters of Alfons Mucha and among the opals and moonstones of René Lalique's jewelry. Other favorites were peacocks, dragonflies, and moths. Morning glories glimmered through the stained glass of Louis Comfort Tiffany. Irises were inlaid in the marquetry cabinets of Louis Majorelle (1859–1926).

Art Nouveau was a rich, voluptuous style that appealed to an enlightened elite, to personalities such as Sarah Bernhardt and Loie Fuller, and to the *nouveaux riches*, who uninhibited by tradition, encouraged designers to stylistic excesses. The style's patrons grew bored with it, however, and it declined in fashion within a decade.

Yet not all Art Nouveau was frivolous and evanescent. Its serious adherents viewed it as the answer to a serious problem that had become apparent by the end of the 19th century: to find a style suitable for the industrial age rather than, as the academically trained architects of the Parisian École des Beaux-Arts were doing, applying past styles to contemporary works.

In 1861 the English designer William Morris started the Arts and Crafts movement in an effort to overcome the banality of industrially produced decorative arts by fostering a return to medieval craftsmanship. The Arts and Crafts movement was the parent of Art Nouveau, but it persisted into the new period and after 1900 merged into the mainstream of the newer style. This was also true of symbolism, a Continental movement in poetry and painting that appeared in the 1870s. Much of the enigmatic form and color of Art Nouveau is related to the spirit of symbolism, as are such motifs as Medusa heads, Pans, and woodland nymphs. The atmosphere of decadent cynicism found in the drawings and paintings of Aubrey Beardsley, Henri de Toulouse-Lautrec, and Edvard

Munch, as well as the otherworldly qualities found in the works of Paul Gauguin, Odilon Redon, and Gustav Klimt, were derived from the symbolist poets, yet the rendering in color and line related to Art Nouveau.

One other development that influenced Art Nouveau was the Aesthetic Movement, an English decorative-arts style created by followers of William Morris during the 1880s. The Aesthetic Movement took its sources from medieval art, as did its Arts and Crafts movement counterpart, but it adapted the newly discovered arts of Japan as well. It survived for only a decade, and much of the style was absorbed into Art Nouveau. Some of the Morris-inspired fabrics and wallpapers of Walter Crane, Charles Voysey, and Arthur Macmurdo (1851–1942), designed in 1882, could easily be taken for Art Nouveau circa 1895.

In fact, the British developments attracted interest on the Continent. The Belgian architects Victor Horta and Henri Van de Velde introduced the works of the English designers in a Brussels exhibition in 1892. They were considered very advanced and were called "Style Anglais." Also, in 1892, when Horta designed a home in Brussels for a Professor Tassel, he amalgamated these recent influences and thus created the first Art Nouveau architecture. The French architect Hector Guimard was aware of the work of Horta and Van de Velde, and in 1900 Guimard made brilliant use of Art Nouveau in his design for the entrances to the new Paris subway system, the Métro.

Architects in other parts of the world had been leaning in the direction of Art Nouveau even before 1890. One was the American architect Louis Sullivan, the teacher of Frank Lloyd Wright. Sullivan made use of ancient Celtic

Hector Guimard, a French Art Nouveau architect, created the Metro stations for the Paris subway system. Most of these metal and glass structures, designed about 1900, have been destroyed.

designs, incorporating them in the decoration of his otherwise functional buildings, such as the Auditorium Building (1889) and the Carson Pirie Scott Department Store, both in Chicago. In Barcelona the Spanish architect Antonio GAUDÍ was another precursor of Art Nouveau. Employing medieval Spanish traditions, Gaudí, like Sullivan, created a uniquely personal style. He combined typical Spanish materials such as wrought iron and colorful tile with cast concrete to create fantastic structures in an unusual Art Nouveau idiom.

Émile Gallé, the French designer of glass and furniture, was following William Morris's precepts before 1880. Inspired by Chinese cameo glass, he created glassware that was to influence Tiffany in the United States. During the 1890s Arthur Lasenby Liberty's shops in London and Paris were outlets for the modern style. Italians called Art Nouveau "Stile Liberty" and "Stile Floreale." The Germans referred to it as "Jugendstil," after the avant-garde art periodical *Jugend* (Youth). But the present-day label is derived from Maison de l'art nouveau, a shop opened by the dealer Siegfried Bing in 1896.

A rational architectural approach to the style was achieved by Charles Rennie MACKINTOSH, a Scotsman. His work so impressed Josef HOFFMANN and the Viennese SECESSION MOVEMENT that they adapted a similar modification of Art Nouveau, and in doing so created a new style that many decades later became known as ART DECO.

Art Nouveau was out of fashion before World War I had begun. From the 1920s to the 1950s it was considered by critics a moribund, even ugly, style. About 1960, however, a reappraisal began. In reaction to the unimaginative glass-and-steel rectangular architecture of the 1950s, critics began to turn back to the style of 1900 with favorable reconsideration. Art Nouveau was incorporated in the rebellious psychedelic style of the 1960s and finally achieved its place as a significant style in the history of modern art.

Artaud, Antonin [ahr-toh', ahn-ton-nan']

Antonin Artaud, b. Sept. 4, 1896, d. Mar. 4, 1948, was a visionary French actor, playwright, poet, and theorist. His idea of a theater of cruelty, set down in his work *Le théâtre et son double* (1938–45; *The Theatre and Its Double*, 1958), has significantly influenced modern notions of theatrical performance.

As a child, Artaud suffered from meningitis, and throughout his life he was afflicted with mental disorders. During the 1920s he wrote poems in the manner of the surrealists, acted in plays under such directors as Charles Dullin and in films such as Abel GANCE's *Napoléon* (1927), and began to write his own plays and essays. He left the surrealists to form his Théâtre Alfred Jarry (1926) with Roger Vitrac and Robert Aron, staging plays by such writers as Strindberg and Claudel. In essays and manifestos, Artaud advocated a metaphysical theater, linking spectator and spectacle. At certain points he likened theater to a plague that attacks the audience, breaks down its resistance, and cleanses it morally and spiritually. In the only play that he wrote and directed according to his

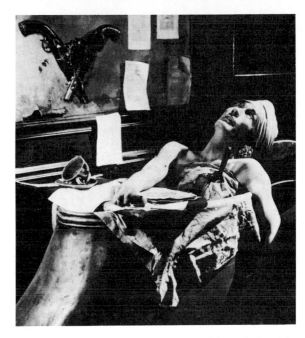

Antonin Artaud, a French actor, director, and dramatic theorist, appears as Jean Paul Marat in the 1927 film Napoléon. Artaud, whose chronic mental disorders resulted in a medical diagnosis of insanity in 1936, pioneered in the "theater of cruelty." This movement, which stresses the use of nonverbal aspects of the stage, seeks to outrage audiences.

precepts, *Les Cenci* (1935; Eng. trans., 1970), based on works by Percy Bysshe SHELLEY and STENDHAL, Artaud emphasized space, physicality, color, and sensual awareness over text and language. When his production was deemed a failure, Artaud went to Mexico in 1936 to study the ways of the Tarahumaras Indians. When he returned to France in 1937, he suffered a severe mental breakdown and was confined to the sanatorium at Rodez until 1946.

Artaud's theories influenced such theater artists as Jean Louis BARRAULT, Roger Blin, Peter BROOK, the LIVING THEATER, and the entire movement known as experimental theater (see IMPROVISATIONAL AND EXPERIMENTAL THEATER). Although Artaud was more a seer than a practical artist, his suggestive ideas are continually being defined and redefined.

Artaxerxes I, King of Persia [ahr-tuh-zurk'-seez]

Artaxerxes I was an Achaemenid king of Persia who ruled from 465 to 424 BC. He came to the throne after the assassination of his father, Xerxes I, and his elder brother Darius. Court intrigues at the beginning of his reign were followed by revolts in the provinces of Bactria and Egypt, which were put down after much fighting. A peace treaty was also signed (449) with Athens, and Ezra and Nehemiah codified the laws of Israel by order of Artaxerxes.

Artaxerxes II, King of Persia Artaxerxes II, the son of Darius II, was an Achaemenid king of Persia (404–359 BC). His younger brother CYRUS THE YOUNGER revolted against him at the outset of his reign but was killed (401) in battle. At the same time, Egypt became independent of Persian rule and remained so throughout his reign. After much fighting with the Greeks, Artaxerxes secured the King's Peace (also called the Peace of Antalcidas) in 387, whereby the Ionian cities of Anatolia were returned to Persian rule. Attempts to regain Egypt failed, and local revolts became frequent. Threats from the Greeks and Egyptians failed, however, because of dissension among them. In inscriptions at Susa and PERSEPOLIS, Artaxerxes invoked the aid of the gods Mithra and Anahite, as well as of Ahura Mazda, indicating a new development in the Persian religion of ZOROASTRIANISM.

Artemis [ahr'-tuh-mis] In Greek mythology Artemis was goddess of the hunt—the mistress of wild things—and the protectress of youth and women. In contrast to the voluptuous Aphrodite, Artemis was associated with chaste love; she is usually depicted as lean and athletic and is frequently accompanied by a deer. She was the twin sister of Apollo and the daughter of Zeus and Leto. Artemis was also identified with the Moon, and for that reason she was later identified with the moon goddess SELENE. Another of her names was Cynthia, bestowed because she was assumed to have been born on Mount Cynthus on the island of Delos. To the Romans she was DIANA.

arteriosclerosis [ahr-tir-ee-oh-skluh-roh'-sis] The term *arteriosclerosis* refers to several diseases that involve both arteries of different sizes and different layers of the walls of the arteries. From Greek words that mean "hardening of the arteries," the term originally signified the tendency of arteries to become hard and brittle through the depositing of calcium in their walls. This is not, however, an important characteristic of the most familiar form of arteriosclerosis, ATHEROSCLEROSIS, which involves the buildup of fatty deposits in the innermost lining of large and medium-sized arteries. Atherosclerosis can lead to coronary HEART DISEASE, STROKES, and other disorders brought about by the tendency of blood clots to form in the narrowed arteries; hardening of the arteries occurs only in advanced stages. A second form of the disease is medial, or Mönckeberg's, sclerosis, which involves calcium buildup in the medial layer of arteries in the extremities, leading to higher blood pressure. A third form of the disease is arteriolar sclerosis, involving the inner and medial layers of small arteries, which can decrease the blood flow to the limbs, eyes, and internal organs.

A sign of possible arteriosclerosis is high blood pressure, or hypertension; conversely, hypertension can aggravate arteriosclerosis. Although arteriosclerotic drugs are on the market, physicians most often aim at preventing the disease by treating the causative factors, which include not only hypertension but also diabetes mellitus, smoking, and obesity.

artery An artery is any blood vessel that carries blood from the HEART toward the capillaries, in contrast to a VEIN, which carries blood from the capillaries toward the heart. The largest artery is the AORTA, which receives blood from the left ventricle of the heart. Several main arteries branch from the aorta and successively branch into vessels of smaller diameter, culminating in tiny arteries called arterioles. These deliver blood to the capillaries, the network of microscopic blood vessels that brings blood close to all the cells of the body. The capillaries collect into venules, which are the beginning of the venous system for return of blood to the heart.

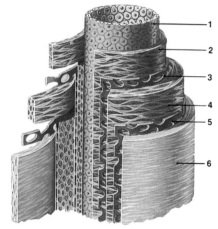

The artery wall is composed of three layers of tissue. The tunica intima, which is the innermost layer, comprises a sheet of endothelial cells (1) and a sheet (2) of connective tissue and some muscle cells. The tunica media comprises two layers of elastic tissue (3 and 5), with a layer (4) of smooth muscle and some connective tissue in between. The tunica adventitia is a thick outer layer (6) of connective tissue.

Arteries have three concentric layers of tissue. The innermost consists of a smooth endothelial lining, connective tissue, and a few muscle cells. The middle layer comprises primarily muscle cells and elastic fibers for expansion during a PULSE of blood set in motion by heart contraction. The outer layer is mainly fibrous connective tissue that prevents overexpansion during the pulse. Large arteries near the heart have a large amount of elastic tissue but little muscle, allowing them to resist the high pressures that occur during heart contraction; between contractions, the elastic recoil keeps the blood moving. Smaller arteries and arterioles have a thick muscular layer, which can contract or relax under control of the nervous system. This variation helps regulate BLOOD PRESSURE and blood distribution in various regions of the body.

See also: ANEURYSM; CIRCULATORY SYSTEM.

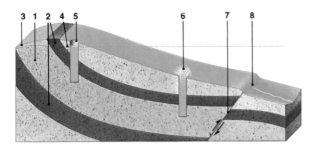

Artesian water exists where groundwater enters an inclined layer of porous rock (1), called an aquifer, confined between two impermeable rock layers (2). The confined water is under pressure that is determined by its depth below the source area (3). In any opening water can therefore rise to approximately the level (4) of the source area. A well (5) drilled from above this level will be nonflowing, whereas a well (6) drilled from below will fountain out under pressure. A fault line, or fracture (7), will permit water to seep upward to form an artesian spring (8). Artesian water is generally warm and pure.

artesian well   An artesian well taps water in an AQUIFER, or water-bearing layer of rock, that lies between rock layers impermeable to water. Such GROUNDWATER is under enough pressure to rise above the aquifer and often to the surface of the ground, producing a flowing well. As the artesian pressure decreases, however, the well may have to be pumped. The name *artesian* is derived from Artois, France, where such wells bored during the Middle Ages became well known, although similar wells have existed since ancient times.

The geological formations in which artesian wells can be sunk are usually only several square kilometers in extent, but a few are quite large. The Great Australian Artesian Basin is the most extensive, covering about 1,750,000 km² (676,250 mi²). In the United States a similar basin exists in North and South Dakota and neighboring areas.

arthritis   *Arthritis* is a general term for approximately 100 diseases that produce either INFLAMMATION of connective tissues, particularly in joints, or noninflammatory degeneration of these tissues. The word means "joint inflammation," but because other structures are also affected, the diseases are often called connective-tissue diseases. The terms *rheumatism* and *rheumatic diseases* are also used. Besides conditions so named, the diseases include gout, lupus erythematosus, ankylosing spondylitis, degenerative joint disease, LYME DISEASE and many others. Causes of these disorders include immune-system reactions and the wear and tear of aging; research indicates that the nervous system may often be equally involved. About one out of seven Americans exhibits some form of arthritis.

Inflammatory Connective Tissue Diseases

This varied group of diseases produces inflammation in the connective tissues, particularly in the joints. The signs of inflammation—warmth, redness, swelling, and pain—may be apparent. Microscopic examination of the lesions reveals prominent blood vessels, abnormal accumulations of white blood cells, and varying degrees of wound healing with scarring. In some diseases, the inflammation is clearly an immune reaction, the body's defense against invading microorganisms. In others, the cause is different or unknown.

Infectious Arthritis. This disease is most common in young adults. Infection in a joint is usually caused by bacteria or other microorganisms that invade the joint from its blood vessels. Within hours or a few days the joint, usually the knee or the elbow, becomes inflamed. There is an abnormal accumulation of synovial, or joint, fluid, which may be cloudy and contain large numbers of white blood cells.

Gonococcal arthritis, a complication of gonorrhea, is the most common form of infectious arthritis. Treatment with antibiotics and aspiration of synovial fluid is usually promptly effective, and only minor residual damage is done to the joint. Occasionally the infection is prolonged and produces joint destruction and requires surgery.

Rheumatic Fever. This form of infectious arthritis, caused by a streptococcal bacterium, is most common in children aged 5 to 15 years. The inflammatory process may involve the heart and produce rheumatic heart disease.

The symptoms of RHEUMATIC FEVER usually occur 2 to 3 weeks after the onset of a severe streptococcal sore throat. Acute pain and swelling "migrate" from joint to joint over a period of several days. The inflammation, which persists for less than 3 months, can usually be controlled by aspirin and rest, and it produces no residual deformity. Less than 1 percent of children with streptococcal sore throats develop rheumatic fever, and a small number of these will develop rheumatic heart disease. Rheumatic fever only rarely occurs if the streptococcal sore throat is treated early with an antibiotic.

Gout and Pseudogout. The inflammatory process in these diseases is unrelated to infection. Rather, inflammation is incited by the deposition in the joint of uric acid present in the bloodstream. An attack of acute gouty arthritis is caused by the formation of needlelike crystals of the deposited uric acid. When these crystals are ingested by white blood cells, the cells release enzymes that evoke inflammations.

Uric acid is a normal breakdown product of purine metabolism. Abnormally elevated blood levels of uric acid, which are associated with gouty arthritis, arise through either excessive production of uric acid or decreased excretion of uric acid by the kidneys. Some cases of hyperuricemia and gout are caused by known specific enzymatic defects. Many are associated with metabolic alterations that occur in obesity. When extreme, the gouty process results in large deposits of uric acid, or tophi, around joints. Acute attacks subside when the patient receives anti-inflammatory drugs. Further attacks may be prevented by the drug colchicine. Serum uric acid levels decline and tophi resolve when the excess uric acid production is controlled by weight reduction and by drugs. The disease usually affects men over age 40.

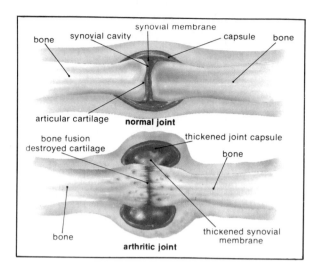

Arthritis, a painful degenerative disorder of bones, occurs when joints become stiffened and inflamed. Normally, two bones are cushioned by articular cartilage and encased by an articular capsule and synovial membrane, which are lubricated by synovial fluid. In an arthritic joint, the cartilage is worn away and the bones fuse. The capsule and synovial membrane swell and become irritated from lack of lubrication.

The symptoms of pseudogout may mimic GOUT but are initiated by crystals of calcium pyrophosphate. These can be distinguished from uric acid crystals by polarization microscopy. The disease is treated with anti-inflammatory drugs.

Rheumatoid Arthritis. The symptoms of rheumatoid arthritis arise from inflammation of connective tissues, and at least in some instances the onset of arthritic episodes of this sort may be related to previous infections.

In rheumatoid arthritis, the synovial membranes, or inner linings of the joint capsules, are chronically inflamed. The synovial mass proliferates and thereby destroys cartilage, bone, and adjacent structures. The widespread inflammatory process also involves other tissues such as blood vessels, skin, nerves, muscles, heart, and lungs. The result is painful joints, loss of mobility, and generalized soreness and depression.

Rheumatoid arthritis is predominantly a disease of women between the ages of 20 and 60. Probably many individuals have such a mild form of the disease that they never seek medical care. The typical newly diagnosed patient is a 35-year-old woman who has been complaining for months of generalized aches and stiffness, particularly in her hands and fingers, for an hour after arising; swelling and pain in fingers, hands, wrists, and elbows; distressing fatigue in the early afternoon; and difficulty in sleeping. The affected joints are tender. The fingers have a sausagelike appearance because of swelling at the proximal interphalangeal joints. The wrists, too, are swollen by overgrowth of the synovial mass.

Although rheumatoid arthritis may prove to be infectious, it is not a conventional contagious disease. Studies indicate that the presence of certain genes may predis-

pose some individuals to develop chronic rheumatoid arthritis. Inappropriate autoimmune responses are clearly important. Rheumatoid factors (anti-antibodies) form immune complexes that incite inflammation, and lymphocyte accumulations cause swelling of tissues, including synovia.

Systemic LUPUS ERYTHEMATOSUS has an even stronger predilection for women, especially those of child-bearing age. It is characterized by inflammation of blood vessels and potential involvement of several tissues and organs, particularly the skin, joints, kidneys, lungs, heart, nervous system, and blood cells. Some patients are acutely affected with a febrile disease that is life threatening because of renal disease, nervous system disease, or accompanying infections. Most have a more indolent disease that produces moderate disability from nondeforming arthritis, skin eruptions, and fatigue.

As in rheumatoid arthritis, the body seems to react against itself rather than against an invading microorganism. Antiself antibodies react with intact blood cells, nuclear components, and blood-vessel walls. The complexes that form in the patient's blood precipitate in basement membranes of skin, kidneys, and nervous system and thus cause inflammation.

Juvenile rheumatoid arthritis usually begins by age 5 or in the early teens. In most cases tests for rheumatoid factors are negative and the disease becomes inactive by age 15. Ankylosing SPONDYLITIS occurs more commonly in men than in women; it affects the spine and sacroiliac joints in particular, with resultant fusion of vertebrae and immobility.

Noninflammatory Connective-Tissue Diseases

The joints and other connective tissues can be involved by trauma, endocrine disorders, metabolic abnormalities, congenital deformities, and other disease processes. The most important of these is degenerative joint disease (OSTEOARTHRITIS).

Degenerative joint disease is the most common form of arthritis and affects virtually all older adults to one degree or another. Most have few, if any, associated symptoms, and the disease is diagnosed only because X rays of the vertebrae show characteristic spurs or because the fingers are knobbed by bony proliferations (Heberden's nodes) at the distal interphalangeal joints. In some the spurs encroach on nerves as they emerge from the spinal canal and produce nerve-root syndromes. In others the malpositioned joints are a source of ligamentous strain and abnormal muscular tension. The result is pain that becomes worse as the day goes on.

Occasionally a severe form of the disease affects the hips. The destructive process results in restricted mobility of the hip joints and disabling pain, and major surgery may be required in which destroyed tissue is replaced with a new joint made of plastic. Degenerative processes also affect the ligaments and intervertebral disks of the spine. If a disk slips out, the syndrome of herniated disk may ensue. This is common in middle-aged men and usually affects the lumbar vertebrae, producing nerve-root irritation and ligamentous strain with resultant low-back pain and neurological deficits. Unless the symptoms remit with rest and analgesics, the disk may need to be surgically removed.

These degenerative processes are in part caused by wear and tear. They affect primarily weight-bearing joints and joints subject to trauma or to malpositioned anatomy. Joints damaged by other forms of arthritis are prone to later degenerative joint disease. Heberden's nodes are more prominent in the right hand of right-handed individuals and in the fingers of typists. Traumas produce microfractures in the cartilage that lines the articulating surfaces, exposing raw underlying bone. The bone cells then release enzymes that destroy the protein and polysaccharide components of bone. Frayed pieces of cartilage may be taken up by white blood cells and thus add an element of inflammation.

Treatment of Arthritis

Infectious arthritis usually responds dramatically to appropriate antibiotics. The noninfectious inflammatory diseases are treated with drugs that suppress inflammation. Many of these drugs—for example, aspirin, indomethacin, and ibuprofen—appear to work by inhibiting synthesis of prostaglandins that mediate inflammation. Although certain adrenal cortical steroids are powerful inhibitors of inflammation, toxic side effects limit their usefulness. Similarly, drugs that inhibit undesirable inflammation may also inhibit desired inflammatory responses. A result is a high frequency of secondary infections. More specific therapy, as for gout, depends on knowledge of the precise biochemical mechanisms of disease pathogens.

Despite the wear-and-tear origin of degenerative joint disease, it, too, may respond well to so-called anti-inflammatory drugs. Perhaps these are acting primarily as analgesics (painkillers), or they may act by decreasing the secondary inflammation that follows joint trauma.

arthropod [ahr'-throh-pahd] An arthropod is any member of the phylum Arthropoda, which includes the CENTIPEDES, CRUSTACEANS, INSECTS, MILLIPEDES, MITES, SCORPIONS, SPIDERS, and other related forms. Arthropods constitute about 75 percent of known animal species. More than 930,000 have been described, and the total has been estimated at more than 6,000,000. Arthropods are characterized by a resistant integument, or cuticle, forming an exoskeleton, a segmented body, and jointed appendages; the name *Arthropoda* means "jointed legs." Other characteristics include bilateral symmetry, growth by MOLTING, the presence of specialized cuticular sense organs, blood-filled spaces in the body (the hemocoel), and a greatly reduced body cavity (coelom). Respiratory tracheae, or book lungs, occur in most terrestrial forms. Eyes are simple or compound; both types may occur in the same animal.

Millions of years before animal life succeeded in colonizing the land, the primeval oceans were teeming with arthropods. These had probably evolved from segmented, wormlike forms similar to the polychaete ANNELIDS of today, but fossil evidence is lacking. It is now generally accepted, however, that the phylum is polyphyletic; that is, some of its distinctive features—an exoskeleton, tracheal respiration, Malpighian excretory tubules, compound eyes, and others—must have originated from at least three separate ancestral lines.

Paths of Evolution. From the wormlike ancestor, one evolutionary path led to the extinct TRILOBITES and the chelicerates. Trilobites were marine organisms that were particularly numerous in the Cambrian Period, 570 million to 500 million years ago. They had flattened bodies molded longitudinally into three lobes whose segments bore paired limbs with fringed hairs. The chelicerates include ARACHNIDS—false scorpions, harvestmen, mites, scorpions, solifugids (sun spiders), and spiders—as well as king crabs (Xiphosura), SEA SPIDERS (Pycnogonida), and the Eurypterida—gigantic, scorpionlike marine animals, now extinct. The body of a chelicerate is divided into an anterior cephalothorax and a posterior abdomen. It has no distinct head and lacks ANTENNAE. It bears pincerlike chelicerae (jaws) and sometimes pedipalps. These may take the form of claws in scorpions and false scorpions; tactile and feeding organs in solifugids, harvestmen, and mites; or reproductive organs in male spiders.

The second evolutionary path led to the crustacea—BARNACLES, brine shrimps, COPEPODS, CRABS, LOBSTERS, ostracods, SHRIMPS, WATERFLEAS, and their allies. With the exception of wood lice, slaters, and land crabs, crustaceans are mostly aquatic, respiring by means of gills. They are equipped with two pairs of antennae; the eyes, when present, may be stalked or unstalked, and the limbs are often specialized.

The third path has evolved through animals such as the PERIPATUS, which retains many wormlike characteristics, to millipedes, symphylans, centipedes, and SPRINGTAILS and other insects. These groups possess one pair of antennae and simple and compound eyes. Like crustaceans, they feed with the aid of mandibles; but the crustacea use the basal part of a modified limb for masticating their food, whereas in the groups under discussion an entire limb has become a jaw, and its tip is used for biting. The crustaceans also resemble the arachnids in that the excretory coxal glands are divided from coelomoducts, whereas the Malphigian tubules of insects and their allies are outgrowths from the alimentary canal.

Body Systems. Many small and primitive arthropods, such as those that enjoy a hidden mode of life, respire through the body wall. The sites of gaseous exchange in crustaceans are varied. Many arachnids make use of book lungs, which contain numerous leatlike respiratory filaments. Tracheae and tracheoles, tiny breathing tubes that lead directly to the tissues, are the routes by which oxygen enters the body of most terrestrial arthropods. These tubes are present in their most primitive condition in the peripatus and are the principal respiratory organs of insects, myriapods, and some arachnids.

Feeding modes are even more diverse. Some arthropods are vegetarians, some are carnivores, and many of the crustaceans are filter feeders; others feed on fluids

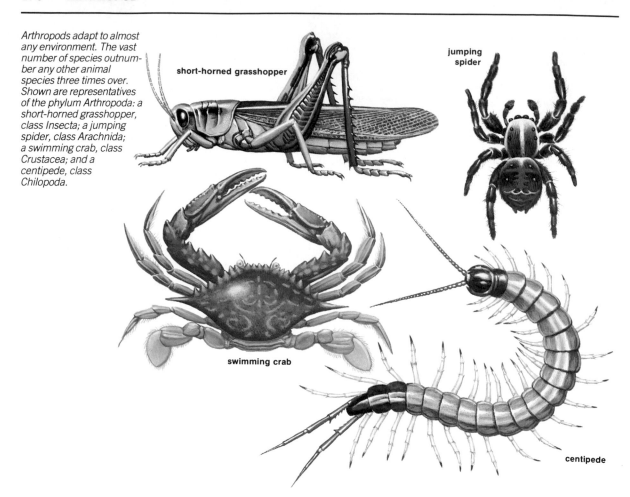

Arthropods adapt to almost any environment. The vast number of species outnumber any other animal species three times over. Shown are representatives of the phylum Arthropoda: a short-horned grasshopper, class Insecta; a jumping spider, class Arachnida; a swimming crab, class Crustacea; and a centipede, class Chilopoda.

short-horned grasshopper

jumping spider

swimming crab

centipede

obtained from the sap of plants or the blood of other animals. In these, different parts of the alimentary canal may be modified as sucking pumps—the foregut in arachnids, the pharynx in insects.

The basic pattern of the nervous system is as follows. From an anterior dorsal brain a pair of nerve cords passes ventrally, one on each side of the gut; each cord continues posteriorly to the extremity of the body. Paired ganglia in successive segments fuse together to produce more complex nerve masses from which segmental nerves lead off to the limbs and other appendages. Apart from the eyes, the sense organs of arthropods occur mainly in the form of hairs, the function of which may be tactile, auditory, chemoreceptive, or proprioceptive (responding to internal stimuli). Color change, retinal pigment migration, GROWTH, molting, METAMORPHOSIS, and sexual development are controlled by HORMONES.

In arthropods whose limbs are moved by their own muscles, the coelom is greatly reduced, and the functional body cavity is a blood-filled space known as the hemocoel. At the time of molting, arthropods swallow air or

water. The pressure induced is distributed by the blood so that when the new cuticle hardens, the entire body will have expanded.

Sex and Life Cycle. With few exceptions, the sexes are separate. Sex ducts open near the rear of the body in peripatus, centipedes, and insects. Among crustaceans, they nearly always open at the hind end of the thorax. In millipedes, pauropods, and symphylans the opening is not far behind the head. In arachnids the sex ducts open near the middle of the body. The abdomen of the sea spiders is so reduced that it contains little more than part of the alimentary canal, and the gonads are displaced into segments of the legs.

Spermatozoa are usually transferred to the female arthropod in sealed packets known as spermatophores. In this way the sperms are not diluted by the surrounding medium in the case of aquatic forms, nor do they suffer from desiccation on land. Transfer of spermatozoa is often accompanied by ritual courtship and mating ceremonies. In some groups there has been a specialization toward indirect sperm transfer, resulting in dissociation of the male and female. In some springtails, for instance, the male deposits spermatophores at random; these are later picked up casually by passing females.

Most arthropods lay eggs in masses, but in some species the eggs hatch inside the body of the mother and the young are born alive. Newly hatched arthropods are often very different from the adults in appearance and habits. In this way competition is avoided, and alternative food sources can be exploited. Many crustaceans have larval development stages that are planktonic; these play an important role in dispersal. Among endopterygote insects, the larvae are entirely different from the adults and pass through a pupal, or chrysalis, stage, during which metamorphosis occurs. In the case of exopterygote insects, the nymphal stages, although wingless, are essentially similar to the adults, as they are in most arachnids.

Limits to Size. Chief among the characteristics to which the arthropods owe their success is the presence of a rigid and almost impervious exoskeleton; this assists in the osmotic regulation of aquatic forms and enables many terrestrial species to become almost independent of water.

Animals encased in armored skeletons can grow only by molting, or ecdysis. The need for this also limits absolute size, because in larger animals, a considerable increase in weight results in a relatively small gain in linear dimensions. Molting is a hazardous process at all times. If everything does not go exactly right, the animal may die, for it is extremely vulnerable to enemies until its new cuticle has hardened. The benefits conferred by an exoskeleton are increasingly offset by its disadvantages as the size of the animal increases.

Among arthropods, only aquatic forms whose bodies are supported by seawater are able to attain any great size or weight. Crustacean integuments are heavy because they are strongly calcified, and weight is advantageous to bottom-dwelling aquatic animals. The cuticles of terrestrial arthropods, such as centipedes, insects, and arachnids, are strengthened by sclerotization, a chemical process analogous to the tanning of leather. In this way they become tough and rigid but at the same time remain light in weight.

Tracheal respiration is another deterrent to large size, because it depends on the slow process of gaseous diffusion. It is significant that the biggest insects either have long, slender bodies, as in dragonflies and mantids, or else tend to be sluggish, like the Goliath beetle and Hercules beetle.

The largest of the arachnids, which respire by means of book lungs, are not restricted in this way because their blood contains a respiratory pigment, hemocyanin, that stores oxygen, enabling them to indulge in sudden bursts of activity.

Adaptations to Land Life. Terrestrial arthropods face a number of problems not experienced by aquatic forms. Larger species require structural support; respiratory organs must be modified for breathing air; there is no surrounding water into which toxic excretory products can freely diffuse; and mechanisms for the conservation of water and maintenance of a constant internal medium must be developed.

Arthropods have successfully exploited the terrestrial environment by many adaptive changes. Each aspect of their adaptation to life on land has been affected by other aspects. Prevention of water loss by the evolution of an impervious integument has raised problems of respiration, which in turn have been solved by the development of book lungs and tracheae. Limitations to growth, engendered by the rigid integument, have been overcome by molting, but this, of course, has also set a limit to size. Many primitive land arthropods have not evolved a discrete layer of waterproof wax on their cuticles, as insects and arachnids have. Consequently, they soon dry up unless they remain hidden in damp, dark habitats; they can emerge only at night, when the temperature drops and the relative humidity of the atmosphere increases.

Aquatic animals can safely excrete toxic nitrogenous waste compounds, such as ammonia, but the necessity for water economy in terrestrial species generally requires the excretion of some dry, nontoxic compound. In terrestrial arthropods this problem has been solved by the evolution of insoluble, nontoxic excretory products—uric acid in the case of myriapods and insects and guanine in arachnids.

Arthur, Chester Alan   Chester Alan Arthur became the 21st president of the United States (1881–85) on the death of James A. GARFIELD on Sept. 19, 1881. An influential member of Roscoe CONKLING's political organization in New York State before he won the vice-presidency in 1880, Arthur made a competent president.

Early Political Career. Arthur was born in North Fairfield, Vt., on Oct. 5, 1829, the son of a Baptist clergyman and schoolteacher. He graduated from Union College in Schenectady, N.Y., in 1848 and was admitted to the bar in 1854. Practicing in New York City, he defended fugitive slaves and joined the Republican party. In 1859 he married Ellen Lewis Herndon, and they had three children.

For the first two years of the Civil War, Arthur served as assistant quartermaster general, supplying food and equipment for the New York militia, then inspector general, and finally quartermaster general for New York. He won praise for his organizing ability and his overall contribution to the war effort.

In 1863, Arthur returned to his law practice, working in Roscoe Conkling's New York political organization for the next decade. Within the Republican party he was a skilled manager and mediator. In 1871, President Ulysses S. Grant appointed Arthur collector of the port of New York, a post that involved the handling of two-thirds of U.S. tariff revenues. It was the most profitable and powerful patronage job in the nation, and Arthur was as honest, efficient, and partisan as the position allowed. When Conkling and President Rutherford B. HAYES quarreled over civil service reform and party supremacy in 1878, Arthur was removed.

After the Republicans nominated James A. Garfield of Ohio for president in 1880, they offered Arthur the vice-presidency, hoping he would help carry New York in the election. In the campaign he raised funds by assessing

AT A GLANCE

CHESTER ALAN ARTHUR
21st President of the United States (1881-1885)

Nickname: "The Gentleman Boss"

Born: Oct. 5, 1829, North Fairfield, Vt.

Education: Union College (graduated 1848)

Profession: Lawyer

Religious Affiliation: Episcopalian

Marriage: Oct. 25, 1859, to Ellen Lewis Herndon (1837-1880)

Children: William Lewis Herndon Arthur (1860-1863); Chester Alan Arthur (1864-1937); Ellen Herndon Arthur (1871-1915)

Political Affiliation: Republican

Died: Nov. 18, 1886, New York City

Buried: Albany, N.Y.

Vice President: None

officeholders and personally oversaw the successful Republican canvass of New York State. His services, a colleague recalled, "were of the highest importance" to the party.

Presidency. Garfield was shot on July 2, 1881, and died two and a half months later. In a brief inaugural address, Arthur said, "Men may die, but the fabric of our free institutions remains unshaken." The administration that followed was competent but uninspired. Mrs. Arthur had died in 1880, and a sister served as First Lady. The tall, urbane president, who wore sideburns and expensive clothes, shone in society.

A stalemated party system and a divided Congress limited the achievements of Arthur's term. He prosecuted grafters in the Post Office and vetoed (1882) rivers and harbors legislation, but Congress overrode his veto. Arthur also vetoed (1882) a bill that restricted Chinese immigration, compelling the lawmakers to pass an improved and less harsh measure. After the Republicans lost the midterm congressional elections of 1882, Congress enacted, with Arthur's support, the Pendleton Law that created a Civil Service Commission and a classified merit system. His support of a lower tariff failed when Congress enacted the high protective tariff of 1883.

Arthur's tepid record and lack of stong support within his own party cost him the presidential nomination in 1884. Moreover, he was ill with Bright's disease and knew that he could not live out a second term. His race for the nomination was only symbolic, and the party chose James G. BLAINE. Arthur died 21 months after leaving office. At a time when the presidency was held in

low esteem, he had been both respectable and admirable in office. Conscientious though not inspiring, he had demonstrated that men of modest background and attainments could grow in the White House.

Arthur and Arthurian legend   Arthur, the focus of an extensive medieval cycle of legends and romances, was probably a Celtic British king or chieftain of the 6th century AD who fought against the Saxon invaders of England. Arthur is first mentioned in the Welsh poem *Gododdin* (c.600), is referred to by the Welsh chronicler Nennius (c.800), and appears in the compilation *Annales Cambriae* (10th century). His popularity was equally great in Cornwall and Brittany, and it was through the Bretons that the legends spread orally to the rest of Europe.

By the 12th century, Arthur had become an English national hero. Given full-bodied shape by GEOFFREY OF MONMOUTH, he appears in the *Historia regum Britanniae* (1137) as the master of a European empire. The French poet Wace fleshed out the details of Arthur's fame in *Le Roman de Brut* (1155), to which the English poet LAYAMON added in his epic narrative *Brut* at the end of the century. The French poet CHRÉTIEN DE TROYES (fl. late 12th century) used the court of King Arthur as the setting for his intense, tragic romances of individual knights such as LANCELOT and Percival. These in turn influenced the German renderings of the PARSIFAL legend produced by WOLFRAM VON ESCHENBACH and the Tristan legend (see TRISTAN AND ISOLDE) produced by GOTTFRIED VON STRASS-

BURG (both 13th century); Chrétien de Troyes's romances also contributed to the mystique of COURTLY LOVE and the ideals of CHIVALRY then in vogue among the French aristocracy.

In the 13th century, the Arthurian legends, especially those concerning the Holy GRAIL, increasingly took on Christian overtones; pagan and religious elements survived in interpretive re-creations through the 19th century, most notably in Alfred, Lord TENNYSON's *Idylls of the King* (1859–85) and Richard WAGNER's opera *Parsifal* (1882). SIR GAWAIN AND THE GREEN KNIGHT was an important 14th-century English addition to Arthurian literature.

Arthur and his knights assumed nearly definitive form in the heroic prose epic Morte Darthur of Sir Thomas MALORY—a form that has served as a source of inspiration for the poets Edmund Spenser and Algernon Charles Swinburne as well as for such takeoffs as Mark Twain's *Connecticut Yankee in King Arthur's Court* (1899), T. H. WHITE's *Once and Future King* (1958), and the Alan Jay Lerner–Frederick Loewe musical *Camelot* (1960; see LERNER, ALAN JAY, AND LOEWE, FREDERICK). Elements include Arthur's birth to Igraine and King Uther Pendragon; his tutelage by the magician MERLIN; his assumption of the English throne after extracting the sword Excalibur from a rock; the institution of the round table at Caerleon, or CAMELOT; the adulterous love affair between his queen, Guinevere, and the noble Lancelot; the treachery of his nephew Mordred (or Modred); his mortal combat with Mordred at the battle of Camlan; his mysterious translation to the island of Avalon; the quest of Sir GALAHAD for the Holy Grail; and the adventures of GAWAIN, Gareth, Kay, Bedivere, Tristram, and others.

A 15th-century French manuscript depicts a youthful Arthur as he draws a magic sword from the stone in which it had been set. According to medieval legends, this feat won him acknowledgment as the rightful king of England.

artichoke [ahr'-ti-chohk]   The globe artichoke, *Cynara scolymus*, is grown for its bud, which is eaten as a vegetable. A member of the thistle tribe of the Compositae family, it is native to the Mediterranean area, where it is still economically important. The U.S. crop is produced in the midcoastal area of California, where the moderate climate affords ideal conditions for growth.

Artichokes grow to about 1.5 m (5 ft); blue green leaves and flower stalks bearing a central bud and two or

The bud of the globe, or French, artichoke has been a celebrated gourmet item for centuries. Illustrated are leaves, stalks, bud starting to flower (left), and detail of the bud (right).

three secondary buds arise from the base of the plant. The immature buds, surrounded by leaflike bracts, are the harvested portions.

Articles of Confederation   The Articles of Confederation, drafted by the Continental Congress in 1777 and ratified in 1781, became the first constitution of the United States. The original draft, prepared by John DICKINSON in 1776, contained provisions for a strong and possibly viable national government, but state jealousies and widespread distrust of central authority led to the emasculation of that document (see STATE RIGHTS).

As adopted, the articles provided only for a "firm league of friendship" in which each of the 13 states expressly retained "its sovereignty, freedom, and independence." Citizens of each state were given equal privileges and immunities, freedom of movement was guaranteed, and procedures for the extradition of accused criminals were outlined. The articles established a national legislature called the Congress, consisting of two to seven delegates from each state; each state had one vote, irrespective of its size or population. No executive or judicial branches were provided for. Congress was charged with responsibility for conducting foreign relations, declaring war or peace, maintaining an army and navy, settling boundary disputes, establishing and maintaining a postal service, and various lesser functions. Some of these responsibilities were shared with the states, and in one way or another Congress was dependent upon the cooperation of the states for carrying out any of them.

Four broad weaknesses of the articles, apart from those of organization, made it impossible for Congress to execute its constitutional duties. These were brilliantly analyzed in numbers 15–22 of The FEDERALIST, the political essays in which Alexander Hamilton, James Madison, and John Jay argued the case for the U.S. Constitution of 1787. The first and fundamental weakness was that Congress could legislate only for states, not for individuals;

thus it could not enforce legislation. Second, Congress had no power to tax. Instead, it was to estimate its expenses and apportion those among the states on the basis of the value of land. States were then to tax their own citizens to raise the money for these requisitions and turn the proceeds over to Congress. They could not be forced to do so, and in practice they rarely met their obligations. Third, Congress lacked the power to regulate commerce—without which its power to conduct foreign relations was meaningless, since most treaties except those of peace were concerned mainly with trade. The fourth weakness ensured the demise of the Confederation by making it too difficult to remedy the first three. Amendments could have rectified any of the weaknesses, but amendments required ratification by all 13 state legislatures. None of the several amendments that were proposed met that requirement.

In 1786 the ANNAPOLIS CONVENTION met to discuss the problem of interstate commerce. Out of it came the proposal for the CONSTITUTIONAL CONVENTION that met in Philadelphia in 1787 and drafted the new Constitution. To ensure its adoption, the amendment procedure of the articles was simply ignored.

■

artificial insemination Artificial insemination is the injection of SEMEN into the vagina by instrumental means. The first artificial inseminations of viviparous (live-bearing) animals were performed by the 18th-century Italian physiologist Lazzaro Spallanzani, who proved that the male contribution to reproduction resided in the semen. Pioneering work in the artificial insemination of dairy and beef animals was done in Russia about the time of the Revolutions of 1917. By the 1930s the technique was being practiced throughout Europe and the United States. Its principal advantage over natural breeding is that a single male of superior genetic quality can be used to impregnate thousands of females, thereby improving herds and increasing dairy and meat production. In addition, dairy farmers need not risk the deterioration of their herds from excessive inbreeding, nor incur the expense of maintaining their own bulls.

In humans artificial insemination is used to achieve pregnancy when an anatomical impediment prevents direct fertilization. When the male is sterile, semen is collected from an anonymous donor who is known by the physician to have a family history free of genetic disease and to bear some resemblance to one parent. The same precautions are taken when, as in recent years, artificial insemination has been used as a means of providing a child to a couple where the woman cannot conceive. In such cases the husband's sperm is used to fertilize a surrogate mother, who has volunteered to bear the child, usually for a fee, and to give it up immediately after its birth. At question are the legal aspects of SURROGATE MOTHERHOOD as well as unresolved moral and religious issues.

In cases where a woman is unable to conceive as a result of defective oviducts, an egg can be removed surgically from her ovary and fertilized "in vitro": in a petri dish under laboratory conditions that simulate the environment inside the oviduct where fertilization normally takes place. The embryo is then transferred to the woman's uterus to develop normally. The first human "test-tube baby" was born in 1978, under the supervision of Drs. Patrick C. Steptoe and Robert G. Edwards in England. Numerous babies have are now been conceived in this manner, and in vitro fertilization (IVF) clinics are proliferating. In the 1980s the possibilities for artificial insemination were further increased by various advances in technique, such as development of the ability to implant, nonsurgically, the fertilized ovum of one woman in another woman's uterus or fallopian tubes. Researchers also learned how to accomplish IVF births following the freezing of an embryo for months, a feat of significance for future storage systems in IVF clinics.

In the United States the operation of some IVF clinics outside of the medical regulatory structure has raised ethical questions and, in some states, potential legal and insurance problems. The Roman Catholic church has condemned IVF because the practice has required masturbation; in 1987 the Vatican issued a doctrinal statement against IVF, surrogate motherhood, and other practices involving embryos.

See also: EUGENICS; FERTILITY, HUMAN.

■

artificial intelligence Artificial intelligence (AI) is the ability of an artificial mechanism to exhibit intelligent behavior and also the name of the field in which artificial mechanisms that exhibit intelligence are developed and studied.

AI programs are primitive when compared to the kinds of intuitive reasoning and induction of which the human brain is capable. AI has shown great promise in the area of EXPERT SYSTEMS, or knowledge-based expert programs.

Examples of artificially intelligent systems include computer programs that perform medical diagnoses, mineral prospecting, legal reasoning, speech understanding, vision interpretation, natural-language processing, problem solving, and learning. Most of these systems are far from being perfected but have proven valuable.

Characteristics of AI

No generally accepted theories have yet emerged within the field of AI, due in part to the fact that AI is a very young science. However, it is assumed that on the highest level, an AI system must receive input from its environment, determine an action or response, and deliver an output to its environment. A mechanism for interpreting the input is needed. This leads to research in speech understanding, vision, and natural language (see PATTERN RECOGNITION). The interpretation must be represented in some form that can be manipulated by the machine. For this problem, techniques of knowledge representation are invoked. The interpretation, together with knowledge obtained previously, is internally manipulated by a mechanism or algorithm to arrive at an internal representation of the response or action. Finally, the system must construct an effective response. This requires techniques of natural-language generation.

History of AI

The term *artificial intelligence* was coined in 1956, when a group of interested scientists met for an initial summer workshop. Early work in AI consisted of attempts to simulate the NEURAL NETWORKS of the brain with numerically modeled nerve cells called perceptrons. In the late 1950s and early 1960s, scientists introduced symbolic processing (see COGNITIVE PSYCHOLOGY).

Scores of AI systems have been built as a means for uncovering and facing the problems of producing intelligent behavior. Explosive growth occurred in the 1970s. Progress was made in the interpretation of visual input. A method was developed for representing actions in a less ambiguous way, advancing the capabilities of natural-language–understanding programs. A rudimentary speech recognition system, capable of identifying spoken words, was also developed. The first knowledge-based expert program was written in the mid-1960s. Called Dendral, it could predict the structures of unknown chemical compounds based on routine analyses.

Recent Trends in AI

A large number of problems in the AI field have been associated with robotics (see AUTOMATA, THEORY OF; ROBOT). In addition to the mechanical problems of getting a machine to make very precise or delicate movements, there is the problem of determining the sequence of movements.

One of the most useful ideas that has emerged from AI research is that facts and rules (declarative knowledge) can be represented separately from decision-making algorithms (procedural knowledge). This realization has had a profound effect both on the way that scientists approach problems and on the engineering techniques used to produce AI systems. By adopting a particular procedural element, called an inference engine, development of an AI system is reduced to obtaining and codifying sufficient rules and facts from the problem domain. This codification process is called knowledge engineering.

An impediment to building even more useful systems is the problem of input, in particular, the feeding of raw data into an AI system. A second problem is in obtaining knowledge from an expert. To this end, efforts are currently being devoted to learning and knowledge acquisition. Following the idea of representing knowledge declaratively, logic programming, such as the COMPUTER LANGUAGE PROLOG, was developed.

Hopes for breakthroughs in AI hinge on a number of factors, such as the growing number of scientists involved in AI, the continuing identification of useful techniques, and advances in computer science, including PARALLEL PROCESSING.

See also: AUTOMATION; BIONICS; CYBERNETICS; IMAGE PROCESSING.

---

artificial limbs Artificial legs, arms, and hands have been used for more than 2,000 years, the earliest (*c.*300 BC) known being an artificial leg made of metal plates surrounding a wooden core. Artificial limbs have been im-

A technician assembles artificial hands at various stages of completion. A finished product (left) looks like a real hand and is capable of several motor-driven functions.

proved over the centuries, largely by surgeons and PROSTHETICS experts working to remake bodies damaged in war. Surgeons now can amputate limbs so that the remaining stump not only bears weight but has sufficient musculature to manipulate the artificial replacement.

Hand and arm replacements are usually operated by voluntary muscle control. An artificial hand, for example, may be held closed with a built-in spring; the fingers and thumb are pulled apart by a pull from straps connected to the opposite shoulder. The utility hook, however, has been found to be a more useful prosthesis than the artificial hand. In the early 1960s, Soviet scientists created an artificial hand controlled through the same nerve routes that had linked the brain to the severed hand. Later, American researchers succeeded in making an entire arm that works by similar myoelectric control (*myo*- means muscle). Current research in prosthetics is exploring the more sophisticated control and feedback systems made possible by microelectronics.

---

artificial organs Artificial organs are materials or devices designed either for implantation in the body to permanently replace faulty organs or for external use to temporarily take over the functions of organs. The artificial kidney, for example, is a machine that is connected externally to filter wastes from the blood of patients who have impaired kidney function or to remove poisons from the body in cases of attempted suicide or accidental poisoning. Another temporary artificial organ, the HEART-LUNG MACHINE, is used during heart surgery. A temporary "artificial lung" that can halve the burden on ailing lungs by removing carbon dioxide and adding oxygen to the blood when it is inserted into the body's largest vein, the inferior vena cava, is undergoing tests on human beings. The artificial LARYNX, or "voice box," is an electrically powered device used externally. The cochlear implant is an electrode or electrodes implanted in the cochlea of the inner ear of some profoundly deaf adults with undamaged auditory nerves (see HEARING AID).

Segments of diseased arteries can be replaced by tubes of various synthetic materials. Permanent artificial hearts have been implanted in patients, but thus far with limited success; they can also be used temporarily until a human heart becomes available for transplant. Artificial SKIN made of animal protein fiber and silicon has been developed for burn victims, and BLOOD substitutes have had limited use in patients who cannot accept natural blood.

Other body parts have been replaced with various plastics, metals, and synthetic fibers. Artificial joints have been successfully implanted in persons whose natural joints were damaged by arthritic disease or accidents. Artificial heart valves and cardiac pacemakers have been implanted in many thousands who were afflicted by crippling heart disease.

See also: BIONICS; HEART, ARTIFICIAL; IRON LUNG; KIDNEY, ARTIFICIAL; PACEMAKER, ARTIFICIAL; PROSTHETICS.

artificial respiration SEE CARDIOPULMONARY RESUSCITATION; FIRST AID

Artigas, José Gervasio [ahr-tee'-gahs, hoh-say' hair-vah'-seeoh] José Gervasio Artigas, b. June 19, 1764, d. Sept. 23, 1850, was a military and political leader of the people of the Banda Oriental (the area of modern URUGUAY) in the Latin American wars of independence. He is revered as Uruguay's national hero.

When the Argentine wars of independence broke out in 1811, Artigas raised a force of Uruguayans to support the revolutionaries in Buenos Aires, and by 1812 he controlled all of Uruguay except Montevideo. When his demand for representation in the proposed confederation of Río de la Plata provinces was rebuffed (1813) by the junta in Buenos Aires, Artigas allied himself with some Argentine inland provinces in opposition to the authority of Buenos Aires. In 1816 the Portuguese reoccupied the Banda Oriental, and Artigas fought them for four years but was defeated in 1820 and fled to Paraguay. Although Uruguay achieved its independence eight years later, Artigas never returned to his homeland.

artillery Artillery is one of the three main branches of an ARMY, along with the INFANTRY and the CAVALRY. Artillery refers both to the personnel who transport and serve its weapons and to the weapons themselves. Traditionally, artillery weapons include larger firearms, such as guns, HOWITZERS, MORTARS, and rocket launchers. In the United States, artillery weapons are those which use ammunition larger than 25.4 mm (1 in), except for portable rocket launchers, such as the BAZOOKA, the RECOILLESS RIFLE, and small mortars.

Development of Artillery. The term *artillery* once applied to all weapons that used projectiles: the bow and arrow, the slingshot, and the many variations of the catapult. Soon after GUNPOWDER was introduced in Europe in

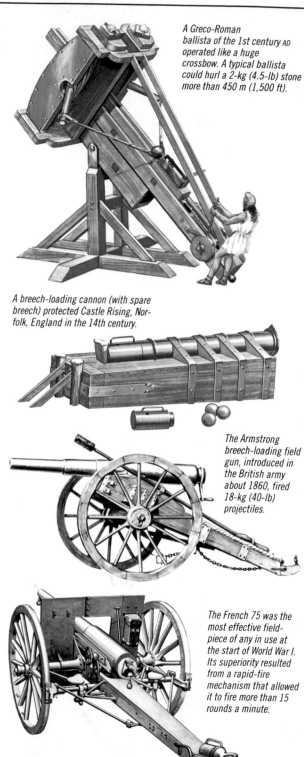

A Greco-Roman ballista of the 1st century AD operated like a huge crossbow. A typical ballista could hurl a 2-kg (4.5-lb) stone more than 450 m (1,500 ft).

A breech-loading cannon (with spare breech) protected Castle Rising, Norfolk, England in the 14th century.

The Armstrong breech-loading field gun, introduced in the British army about 1860, fired 18-kg (40-lb) projectiles.

The French 75 was the most effective field-piece of any in use at the start of World War I. Its superiority resulted from a rapid-fire mechanism that allowed it to fire more than 15 rounds a minute.

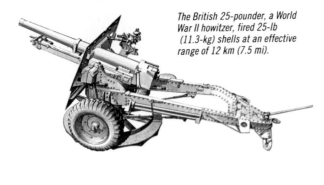

The British 25-pounder, a World War II howitzer, fired 25-lb (11.3-kg) shells at an effective range of 12 km (7.5 mi).

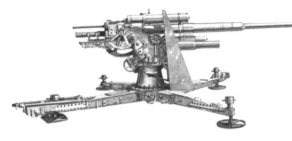

The German 88-mm antiaircraft gun, Germany's main air-defense weapon during World War II, fired approximately twenty 9-kg (20-lb) shells a minute.

The British army Abbot 105-mm gun fires twelve 15-kg (33-lb) shells a minute at a range of about 17 km (10.5 mi).

The U.S. M-107, a self-propelled 175-mm gun developed in the early 1960s, fired a 67-kg (147-lb) shell a maximum distance of 32.7 km (20 mi).

the 13th century, machinery for utilizing it in warfare began to be devised. During the 16th century the use and development of artillery increased. In 1509 the younger duke of Ferrara used his artillery to destroy the Venetian fleet that had sailed up the Po River. Henry VIII patronized the art of gun founding in England and encouraged the development of hollow shells filled with powder.

As the standing-army principle that began about 1500 came into general use, artillery became an organized arm of the military. Louis XIV of France raised a regiment of artillerymen in 1671 and established schools of artillery instruction. In 1715, Britain organized the Royal Regiment of Artillery, consisting of two permanent companies. During the Seven Years' War (1756–63), Frederick the Great of Prussia developed a horse artillery to accompany his cavalry.

Cannon began to change rapidly during the 19th century. Improvements included the rifled barrel, breech-loading mechanisms, smokeless powder, recoil-absorbing systems, and better metallurgy. By the latter half of the 19th century, modernizing armies were buying the cast steel, breech-loaded cannons produced by the German firm of Alfred Krupp (see KRUPP family).

Twentieth-Century Artillery. The science of mechanics contributed to the development of a gun mount that could absorb recoil—the backward movement of the gun caused by firing the projectile. Compression cylinders were used to absorb the recoil, and heavy springs returned the barrel to its original position. Because the recoil force could also be harnessed to open the breech and eject the shell, the French developed a 75-mm cannon that was capable of firing 15 rounds a minute; its rapid fire compensated for its lighter projectiles. The Germans developed heavier guns and howitzers, with longer ranges and larger bores. The largest used in World War I, "Big Bertha," was a 420-mm howitzer that fired an 800-kg (1,764-lb) shell about 10 km (6 mi).

The heavy artillery used in World War I was well suited to trench warfare, where mobility was a secondary need. During World War II, however, both sides devised improved methods for mounting guns on mobile carriers. The Germans developed a self-propelled howitzer of two large calibers, 540 mm and 600 mm. The U.S. Army's versatile 105-mm howitzer was eventually made in self-propelled wheeled and tracked versions as well as in its original truck-towed design.

Postwar developments have begun to erase the distinction between artillery and other forms of armament. Shoulder-carried recoilless rifles and ground-launched rockets and missiles are included within the definition of artillery, which is usually classified into three main groups: field artillery includes howitzers, mortars, and large recoilless weapons; antiaircraft artillery comprises cannon, medium-caliber automatic weapons, rockets, and SURFACE-TO-AIR MISSILES; antitank artillery includes ROCKETS AND MISSILES and cannon. Most U.S. artillery weapons are protected by an armored, wheel- or track-mounted chassis, and are self-propelled.

See also: AMMUNITION; ARMORED VEHICLE; NAVAL VESSELS; WEAPONS.

artiodactyl [ahr-tee-uh-dak'-tul]   Artiodactyls are even-toed ungulate, or hoofed, mammals of the order Artiodactyla, which includes about 150 species. The animals have either two- or four-toed hooves on each foot. They are native to all parts of the world except Australia, New Zealand, Antarctica, and some islands. They have been introduced almost everywhere because of their great importance to humans.

Members of the largest of the nine living artiodactyl families, Bovidae, are all RUMINANTS; that is, they have a complex multichambered stomach and chew their food again after it has been partly broken down. The family includes cattle, bison, buffalo, goats, antelope, and sheep. The family Suidae includes pigs and babirusas. Suids are nonruminating and omnivorous. The family Tayassuidae includes only the piglike, nonruminant peccary of the Americas. The family Camelidae includes the camels of the Old World and the llama, vicuña, alpaca, and guanaco of South America, which are all ruminants. The two hippopotamus species (Hippopotamidae), nonruminants, are native to Africa. The deer of Asia, Europe, and the Americas (Cervidae), the African and Asian chevrotains (Tragulidae), the African giraffes and okapis (Giraffidae), and the North American pronghorn (Antilocapridae) are all ruminants.

Artois [ahr-twah']   A former province in northern France, Artois is roughly equivalent to the present department of Pas-de-Calais (6,638 km²/2,363 mi²). ARRAS, the major town, was its capital. Artois is bounded by Flanders on the northeast, by Picardy on the south and southwest, and by the English Channel on the northwest. Coal mining and agriculture are the principal economic activities. Originally part of Flanders, Artois came under French control for the first time in 1180, through the marriage of King Philip II to Isabel of Hainaut. Artois passed to Burgundy in 1329. It became a possession of the Habsburgs in 1477 and a province of Spain in 1493. It was reconquered by the French in 1640; French possession was confirmed by the treaties of the Pyrenees (1659), Nijmegen (1678), and Utrecht (1713). Because of its strategic importance, Artois was the scene of heavy fighting during World War I.

Arts and Crafts movement   The Arts and Crafts movement originated in England in the second half of the 19th century as a revolt against the mass-produced furniture, household objects, and architecture that flooded the country following the Great Exhibition of 1851 at the Crystal Palace in London. The theorists of the movement were the writer John RUSKIN and the artist-poet William MORRIS, who, with the PRE-RAPHAELITE artists Ford Madox BROWN, Edward BURNE-JONES, and Dante Gabriel ROSSETTI and the architect Philip Webb, preached a return to the traditions of anonymous medieval artisans and recently discovered Japanese artists and craftsmen. Their aim was "honest" art: superior design and execution applied to utilitarian objects as well as to decorative objects. The

The English artist, poet, and designer William Morris created the wallpaper pattern "Blackthorn" in 1892. Morris and the other members of the Arts and Crafts movement rejected industrial mass production of the decorative arts in favor of a return to the high standards of medieval artisans.

beauty and high quality of the work they produced was undeniable, but critics of the time felt that the quality made the works costly and impractical.

Just as the movement seemed to fail, the Arts and Crafts Exhibition Society emerged in London. Beginning in 1888, it launched a series of exhibitions that finally aroused broad public interest, and the movement spread rapidly to Europe and the United States. In England and Scotland its principles were evident in the work of such architect-designers as Charles Rennie MACKINTOSH, C. F. A. VOYSEY, and Arthur H. Mackmurdo. In the United States the movement's influence can be seen in the work of Louis SULLIVAN and Frank Lloyd WRIGHT, and somewhat later, in the architecture of Greene and Greene. By the turn of the century the Arts and Crafts movement had become a major influence throughout the Western world and had led to the widespread popularity of ART NOUVEAU.

See also: ART DECO; GLASSWARE, DECORATIVE; INDUSTRIAL DESIGN; INTERIOR DESIGN; SECESSION MOVEMENT.

Aruba [ah-roo'-bah]   Aruba is an island in the Caribbean Sea, formerly part of the NETHERLANDS ANTILLES, lying about 32 km (20 mi) off the coast of Venezuela. On Jan. 1, 1986, Aruba separated from the Netherlands Antilles and became an autonomous member of the Kingdom of the Netherlands, with full independence scheduled for 1996.

Aruba, with an area of 186 km² (72 mi²) and a population of 62,000 (1987 est.), has a tropical, semiarid climate. It rises to 188 m (617 ft) at Jamanota, the highest point. Oranjestad, the largest city, is the administrative center. The population is mostly of mixed Dutch and Indian heritage, and Dutch is the official language. Papiamento, derived from Spanish, Portuguese, and Dutch, is also widely spoken.

Aruba's economy depended for decades on tourism and the refining of oil imported from Venezuela. Since 1960, when employment in oil refining and shipping began to decline, diversified tourism has been stressed. The closing in 1985 of the main refinery dimmed not only Aruba's economic future but also its hopes for eventual autonomy or independence.

Aruba was claimed by the Spanish in 1499, but the Dutch seized the island in 1634 and, except for brief periods during the Napoleonic Wars, have held it ever since.

---

arum [ar'-uhm]   Arum is the common name for Araceae, a large family of herbaceous or woody plants. Most arums are native to the tropics, although a few genera are found in temperate regions. Arum flowers are crowded on a spike (spadix), which is enfolded by a vaselike leaf (spathe). Many species of arum contain acrid and sometimes milky juices; the tubers of the familiar JACK-IN-THE-PULPIT contain needlelike crystals that are irritating if eaten raw. The aromatic rhizome of *Acorus calamus* is used in toilet powders, and an oil from it is used in perfumes. Three arums are grown extensively for a starchy food made from their corms or tubers: TARO (*Colocasia esculenta*) and dasheen (*C. esculenta*), both widely cultivated in Southeast Asia and Polynesia, and yautia (*Xanthosoma sagittifolium*), native to tropical America and the West Indies. Common houseplants in the arum family are species of DIEFFENBACHIA, PHILODENDRON, and *Spathiphyllum*.

The Italian arum is a herbaceous plant from southeastern Europe. It is used medicinally as well as being an ornamental. The calla lily (right) is grown as a houseplant wherever the climate is too cold to set it in gardens.

Aryan [air'-ee-uhn]   Aryan is a term formerly used to denote both a linguistic and an assumed racial category related to the language family now known as INDO-EUROPEAN. Early scholars, struck by similarities among ancient Indian languages such as Sanskrit and ancient European languages such as Latin and Greek, hypothesized the existence not only of a proto–Indo-European language but also of a proto–Indo-European racial group, the Aryans. This group, it was thought, had spread into South Asia and Europe from a Central Asian homeland in a series of migrations during the 2d millennium BC. Thus it was argued that, in contrast to the darker-skinned Dravidians of southern India, the northern Indians were, racially speaking, Aryans, sharing a common descent with the peoples of Western Europe.

Today, such arguments about racial origins are usually seen as little more than speculation. The term *Aryan* is now used to designate a family of languages that includes such modern South Asian examples as Bengali, Hindi, Punjabi, and Sinhalese. It was among the Aryan-speaking peoples of northern India during the 2d and 1st millennia BC that the religion of Hinduism and the institutions of CASTE first developed.

---

asbestos   Asbestos is the name given to certain inorganic minerals when they occur in fibrous form. Such fibers can be processed into a variety of materials that are uniquely resistant to fire, heat, and corrosion. Chrysotile, the fibrous form of SERPENTINE, is the most important source; it is mined principally in Quebec, Canada, and in the USSR. Fibrous forms of certain AMPHIBOLE minerals constitute a less important source. Usually excavated from open-pit mines, asbestos rock is crushed to free the fibers. These can be spun and woven into textiles, matted into insulating materials, or used with other substances to make numerous products, including brake linings, clutch pads, and roofing and flooring materials. For many of these products, asbestos is almost irreplaceable because no other substance provides its positive characteristics.

Nevertheless, manufacturers are developing replacement materials, because inhalation of asbestos's extremely fine fibers over a period of years has been linked to cancers of the lung or lung-cavity lining and to asbestosis, a severe lung impairment. The Environmental Protection Agency (EPA) has estimated that 3,000 to 12,000 cases of cancer, usually fatal, are caused annually in the United States by asbestos exposure. A 1964 U.S. study of World War II shipyard workers had proved this connection between airborne asbestos and the development of disease 20 or more years after exposure. In 1971 asbestos became the first material to be regulated by the U.S. Occupational Safety and Health Administration (OSHA); in 1986 OSHA drastically reduced permissible work-exposure levels. In 1989, the EPA ordered that the manufacture, use, and export of asbestos be reduced by 94 percent over a 7-year period, ending asbestos use for building materials and brake linings. Controversy continues to surround the EPA's assessment of asbestos insulation as a strong health hazard. Critics also maintain that chrysotile asbestos, unlike the amphibole form, is not a health hazard in the workplace.

Thousands of asbestos-related claims have been filed against asbestos manufacturers. The U.S. government is also the target of suits, because exposure standards it set in World War II shipyards were known at the time to be ineffective.

Asbury, Francis   Francis Asbury, b. Aug. 20, 1745, d. Mar. 31, 1816, an English-born American Methodist bishop, was the leader of the Methodist Episcopal Church, which through mergers with other denominations became the United Methodist Church in 1968. After experiencing trials in school and employment, Asbury underwent a spiritual conversion and joined a Methodist society at the age of 16. When he was 26, John Wesley appointed him missionary to the American colonies. Asbury's ship landed at Philadelphia on Oct. 27, 1771.

For the rest of his life, Asbury traveled on horseback, gathering congregations in schoolhouses, cabins, and taverns. He provided a model for CIRCUIT RIDERS, or itinerant preachers. His journal records in detail his travels in the eastern United States and across the Appalachian Mountains, more than 8,000 km (about 5,000 mi) a year. He was a leading figure in the formation of the Methodist Episcopal Church in 1784, when he was ordained and elected superintendent, or bishop, as he came to be known.

ascariasis [as-kuh-ry'-uh-sis]   Ascariasis is a debilitating human disease caused by the roundworm *Ascaris lumbricoides*; other species of *Ascaris* are parasitic in domestic animals (see NEMATODE). Perhaps as many as one-fourth of the world's people are infected, but ascariasis is particularly prevalent in tropical regions and in areas of poor hygiene. Infection occurs through ingestion of food contaminated with fecal matter containing *Ascaris* eggs. The larvae burrow through the intestine, reach the lungs, migrate up the respiratory tract, are reswallowed, and mature in the intestine, growing up to 30 cm (12 in) in length and anchoring themselves to the intestinal wall. Infections may be accompanied by inflammation, fever, and diarrhea. Serious problems may develop if the worms migrate to other parts of the body. They are easily killed by ANTHELMINTIC DRUGS.

Ascension of Christ   Described in the Bible as the lifting up of JESUS CHRIST into heaven 40 days after the RESURRECTION (Mark 16:19; Luke 24:51; Acts 1:9), the ascension signifies the exaltation of Christ as Lord of the universe and is thus closely associated with the resurrection. Ascension Thursday, kept 40 days after EASTER, is one of the major feasts of the Christian church.

Ascension Island   Ascension Island is a volcanic island about 10° below the equator in the South Atlantic between Africa and South America. With SAINT HELENA, 1,125 km (700 mi) to the south, it forms a British colony. Ascension's area is 88 km² (34 mi²), and its population is 1,535 (1984 est.). The Portuguese navigator João da Nova Castella discovered the island on Ascension Day

in 1501. About 650 mm (26 in) of rain falls in the mountains, where a little vegetation grows in the poor soil. Most of the rest of the island is dry and barren. Britain established a naval base on the island in 1815 that grew into the main settlement, Georgetown. A cable station, satellite tracking station, and missile base are now located on the island.

asceticism [uh-set'-uh-sizm]   Asceticism, derived from the Greek word for "exercise," denotes a system of practices that aims at the development of virtue and strength of character through self-denial and mortification. It has been an aspect of most religious traditions and of many philosophies, such as Stoicism. Methods of asceticism generally include such exercises as celibacy, fasting, upright posture, periods of silence, performance of unpleasant tasks, and withdrawal from human companionship. It is thought that these practices gradually free a person's spiritual element from the body's demands. Once control has been achieved a harmony of the whole person is experienced. Forms of self-mutilation, flagellation, and castration have been used in extreme practices of asceticism. Adherents of Jainism in India sometimes even starve themselves to death in striving for sainthood. Among Christians ascetic practices receive greater emphasis in the Roman Catholic, Orthodox, and Anglo-Catholic traditions than in the Protestant churches.

Asch, Sholem   Sholem (or Shalom) Asch, b. Kutno, Poland, Nov. 1, 1880, d. July 10, 1957, was the first Yiddish novelist and dramatist to attain world fame. Under the influence of Isaac Peretz, he wrote the novella *The Little Town* (1904; Eng. trans., 1907) and the tragedy *God of Vengeance* (1907; Eng. trans., 1918). Twenty plays followed. In 1907, Asch visited Palestine; he described its biblical sites and Zionist pioneers in short stories and in the novel *Song of the Valley* (1938; Eng. trans., 1939).

Asch spent many years in France, England, and the United States, where he was naturalized, but lived in Israel after 1954. His early work includes the novels *Mottke the Vagabond* (1917; Eng. trans., 1935), later dramatized, and *Uncle Moses* (1918; Eng. trans., 1920), about New York City. His trilogy *Three Cities* (1929–32; Eng. trans., 1932) is about Russian Jewry before and during the revolution. Asch's Christological novels—*The Nazarene* (1939), *The Apostle* (1943), and *Mary* (1949)—offended some Jewish readers. His biblical novels *Moses* (1951) and *The Prophet* (1955) returned to traditional subjects.

Ascham, Roger [as'-kuhm]   The English scholar and educator Roger Ascham, b. 1515, d. Dec. 30, 1568, taught at Cambridge University and subsequently served (1548–50) as tutor to the future Queen Elizabeth I and as secretary to King Edward VI. In *Toxophilus* (1545), a treatise on training archers, he stressed the benefits of physical training, championed the principles of HUMANISM, and recommended a vernacular style. His best-known work, *The Scholemaster* (1570), discusses methods of teaching Latin composition and denounces overelaborate English, but it is generally concerned with the shaping of character through enlightened principles of education that renounce corporal punishment.

Asclepius [as-klee'-pee-uhs]   In Greek mythology Asclepius, son of Apollo, the god of healing, was a famous physician. His mother, Coronis, a princess of Thessaly, died when he was an infant. Apollo entrusted the child's education to CHIRON, a centaur, who taught Asclepius the healing arts. Asclepius, when grown, became so skilled in surgery and the use of medicinal plants that he could even restore the dead to life. Hades, ruler of the dead, became alarmed at this and complained to Zeus, who killed Asclepius with a thunderbolt. The most famous shrine of Asclepius was at EPIDAURUS, where pilgrims came to be cured of their illnesses.

ascorbic acid   SEE VITAMINS AND MINERALS

ASEAN   The Association of Southeast Asian Nations (ASEAN) was established in 1967 by the governments of Indonesia, Malaysia, the Philippines, Singapore, and Thailand to promote economic growth, social and cultural development, and a balance of power in the Southeast Asian region. ASEAN was formed during the Vietnam War and supported the unsuccessful U.S. effort to prevent the establishment of a Communist government in Vietnam. Since then it has worked to improve economic ties among its members. Brunei joined ASEAN in 1984.

Asgard   In Norse mythology Asgard was the home of the gods, located in the heavens and accessible only over the rainbow bridge, Bifrost. Asgard had many gold and silver halls or palaces, the most splendid of which was VALHALLA, the residence of Odin.

ash   An ash is a deciduous hardwood tree belonging to the Oleaceae, or olive, family and to the genus *Fraxinus*. Of the 65 species, most occur in the northern temperate zone. Ashes have opposite pinnate leaves, which have 3 to 11 oval to elliptical leaflets that are usually sawtoothed. The bark is furrowed or scaly. Male and female flowers, both usually minute and greenish, are borne on separate trees. The fruit is a single oar-shaped wing with a seed capsule at the base.

The species *F. excelsior* is an important timber tree in Europe; it is also planted in the United States as a landscaping tree. Another native European and Asiatic tree, *F. ornus*, is commonly planted in the Pacific Northwest. A medicinal substance, manna, is extracted from this species. White ash, *F. americana*, is the most common and the largest ash in North America. Ashes are subject to at-

The white ash (top) *is about 25 m (82 ft) tall and has staminate and pistillate flowers* (shown below the tree). *The compound leaves* (top right) *usually have seven leaflets. The winged fruit, called samaras, are 2.5-5 cm (1-2 in) long. The flowering, or manna, ash* (center right) *is about 10 m (33 ft) in height and spread and has conspicuous bisexual flowers* (center). *The fruit are 2.5 cm (1 in) long. The European ash* (bottom) *grows to 40 m (130 ft) and is one of the Continent's largest deciduous trees.*

tack by some organism—perhaps a mycoplasma—that usually kills the trees within 10 years. The disease, for which no preventive or cure yet exists, is slowly but steadily spreading across North America.

The principal uses of ash wood are furniture, handles, motor-vehicle parts, barrels and crates, sporting and athletic goods, railroad ties, veneer, and fuel.

Ash Wednesday   In the Western church, Ash Wednesday is the first day of LENT and the seventh Wednesday before Easter. Its name comes from the practice of placing ashes on the foreheads of worshipers to symbolize death and sorrow for sin. In the Orthodox church, Lent begins on a Monday rather than on Ash Wednesday.

Ashanti [ah-shahn'-tee]   The Ashanti are an AKAN-speaking people of central Ghana and neighboring regions of Togo and Ivory Coast, in West Africa, numbering more than 1,000,000. They subsist primarily by farming, with cacao a major cash crop. Produce and handicraft articles are exchanged in local markets.

Formerly an independent kingdom subdivided into provinces, districts, and villages, the Ashanti state was headed by the chieftain of the Oyoko clan by the late 17th century. With its capital at Kumasi, the Ashanti kingdom was active in the slave trade in the 18th century. Conflicts arose with the British in the 19th century, resulting in Britain's annexation of Ashanti territory in 1901.

Ashanti traditionally worship a supreme deity, many minor spirits, and their ancestors. Ancestry is traced through the mother's line, but Ashanti believe that a child's spirit comes from the father, who is responsible for much of the child's training. Ashanti artistic creations include a wealth of myths and tales and distinguished plastic art forms of wood, bronze, and gold. The Golden Stool, the royal throne, symbolized the sovereign's power and was thought to contain the souls of the Ashanti people. The queen mother played an important role in politics.

Ashbery, John   John Lawrence Ashbery, b. Rochester, N.Y., July 28, 1927, an American poet, is noted for his experimental verse and vivid imagery. After studying at Harvard and Columbia, he published his first book of poems, *Turandot*, in 1953. Later volumes include *The Tennis Court Oath* (1962), *Self-Portrait in a Convex Mirror* (1975; Pulitzer Prize), *Houseboat Days* (1977), *The Wave* (1984), and *April Galleons* (1987). Ashbery has also written a novel (with James Schuyler), *A Nest of Ninnies* (1969), and three plays, *The Heroes* (1952), *The Compromise* (1956), and *The Philosopher* (unproduced; publ. 1964). Most critics consider Ashbery's work highly original and inventive, but many have complained about its obscurity and abnormal syntax. Ashbery himself likens his poetry to music, in which the structure carries the argument, "though the terms of this argument remain unknown quantities."

Ashcan school   The Ashcan school is the term subsequently applied to the American rebel group of painters originally known as The Eight, who exhibited together in New York City in 1908 and who are identified chiefly with the introduction of REALISM and urban subjects in American painting. They had considerable influence on other American artists, notably George BELLOWS. Their leader, Robert HENRI, and members of the group, including John SLOAN, George LUKS, William GLACKENS, Everett SHINN, Maurice PRENDERGAST, Arthur B. DAVIES, and Ernest Lawson, had little in common stylistically but shared an aversion to the pervasive academic paintings then fashionable. The movement reflected the new American interest in naturalism, which ranged from Theodore Roosevelt's political style to the novels of Stephen Crane and Theodore Dreiser.

John Sloan, a member of the Ashcan school, painted Backyards, Greenwich Village *in 1914. The work captures the flavor of what was then the center of New York's bohemian life. (Whitney Museum of American Art, New York City.)*

Except for Davies, who specialized in romantic pastorals laced with allegory, and Lawson, who favored misty river landscapes, all could be called realists. Sloan, who was also an illustrator, is known for his vivid New York street scenes, especially the views of slum backyards, alleys, and rooftops, which gave rise to the "ashcan" label, first used by the critics Holger Cahill and Alfred BARR in 1934.

Ashcroft, Dame Peggy   Peggy Ashcroft was the stage name of Edith Hutchinson, b. Dec. 22, 1907, d. June 14, 1991, an English actress noted for her performances in both classical and contemporary drama.

Among her most famous roles were Desdemona to Paul Robeson's Othello (1930), Cecily Cardew in *The Importance of Being Earnest* (1939), the lead in *Hedda Gabler* (1954), and also the lead in *The Duchess of Malfi* (1961). She also played numerous parts for the Royal Shakespeare Company. Her film credits include *The Thirty-Nine Steps* (1935), *The Nun's Story* (1959), and *A Passage to India* (1984; Academy Award, supporting actress), and she appeared in the television dramatization *The Jewel in the Crown* (1984).

Ashe, Arthur [ash]   Arthur Robert Ashe, b. Richmond, Va., July 10, 1943, became the first black player to win a major men's tennis title by triumphing in the U.S. National Amateur singles competition in 1968. That year he also won the U.S. Open and became the first black to play on the U.S. Davis Cup team. Ashe turned professional in 1969, won the Australian Open in 1970, and in 1975 won the Wimbledon title and the world championship of professional tennis. He was inducted into the International Tennis Hall of Fame in 1985. His book *Hard Road to Glory* (3 vols., 1988) is a history of African-American athletes.

Arthur Ashe, the first black tennis player to win a major men's singles tournament, holds the trophy he won by defeating Jimmy Connors in the 1975 Wimbledon final. He announced his retirement from competitive tennis in April 1980, but was named non-playing captain of the U.S. Davis Cup team in September 1980. The team won the Cup in 1981–82.

Asheville   Asheville is a city in west central North Carolina and the seat of Buncombe County. The population of the city proper is 61,607 (1990), and that of the metropolitan area is 174,821 (1990). The eastern gateway to the Great Smoky Mountains, Asheville is a tobacco and livestock center and a producer of textiles, furniture, and paper products. Settled and laid out in 1794, it was subsequently named Asheville for Gov. Samuel Ashe. Landmarks include Biltmore, the great Vanderbilt mansion, and Thomas Wolfe's birthplace, now a museum.

Ashi [ah-shee']   Ashi, AD 352–427, a Babylonian rabbi, was the primary editor of the Babylonian Talmud, or compilations of and commentaries on the oral teachings of the Jews. He revived the Sura rabbinical academy and headed it for more than 50 years while gathering material for his work. Ashi's edition of the Talmud was completed several decades after his death by Rabina II, head of the school of Sura from 474 to 499.

Ashkenazi, Vladimir   Russian pianist Vladimir Davidovich Ashkenazi, b. July 6, 1937, is known for the sensitivity and imagination of his playing, and especially for his interpretations of Mozart. Born into a family of musicians, he studied at the Central Music School of Moscow and the Moscow State Conservatory. His first U.S. tour was in 1958. He became an Icelandic citizen in 1972. He published his autobiography in 1985.

Ashkenazim [ash-kuh-naz'-im]   The Ashkenazim are one of the two major divisions of the Jews, the other being the SEPHARDIM. The division is based on geographic, linguistic, and cultural distinctions. The term *Ashkenazim* was derived from Ashkenaz, great-grandson of Noah (Gen. 10:3). Medieval rabbis, to explain Jewish settlements in the Rhineland predating the Roman Empire, claimed that Ashkenaz went to Germany after the DELUGE.

The language identified with Ashkenazic culture is Yiddish, a mélange of Middle German, Laaz, Slavic, and Hebrew, written in Hebrew characters. Before the 12th century, RASHI, Gershom ben Judah, and other scholars made Speyer, Worms, and Mainz centers of Jewish learning. Later, during the persecutions in the 17th century, large numbers of Eastern Jews settled in Western Europe.

Today the term *Ashkenazim* applies to Jews whose ancestors originally lived in German lands; *Sephardim* applies to Jews whose ancestors resided in the Iberian Peninsula. Ashkenazi Jews constitute more than 80 percent of the world Jewish population.

Ashley, William Henry   William Henry Ashley, b. Powhatan County, Va., c.1778, d. Mar. 26, 1838, was a financier and a participant in the development of the American West. Having emigrated from Virginia to Missouri by 1808, he served as lieutenant governor there before joining Andrew Henry in 1822 in a famous expedition from St. Louis to establish fur-trading posts on the upper Missouri River. When Indians resisting intrusion forced abandonment of the posts, Ashley and Henry in 1825 devised a rendezvous system in which company agents met independent trappers each summer to exchange trade goods for beaver pelts. By the time he retired in 1826, Ashley had made a fortune and had revolutionized the fur trade. He was congressman for Missouri from 1831 to 1837.

Ashton, Sir Frederick

Ashton, Sir Frederick   Sir Frederick William Mallandaine Ashton, b. Guayaquil, Ecuador, Sept. 17, 1904, d. Aug. 18, 1988, was a choreographer and director of Britain's Royal Ballet. After Marie Rambert encouraged him to choreograph his first ballet, *A Tragedy of Fashion*, in 1926, he made ballets for Rambert's small company and for the Vic-Wells Ballet, founded in 1931 by Ninette de Valois. De Valois engaged Ashton as resident choreographer and principal dancer in 1935. Most of his works were made for that company, which became the Royal Ballet in 1956. In 1963, Ashton succeeded de Valois as director of the company, an office he held until his retirement in 1970.

More than any other choreographer, Ashton developed and defined the British national style in classic ballet with such works as *Les Patineurs* (1937), *Symphonic Variations* (1946), *Scènes de ballet* (1948), *Cinderella* (1948), *Daphnis and Chloe* (1951), *Ondine* (1958), *La Fille mal gardée* (1960), and *The Dream* (1964). As a dancer, Ashton was never a virtuoso, but he will be remembered for such portrayals as Kástchei in Igor Stravinsky's *Firebird* and the timid stepsister in his own version of Sergei Prokofiev's *Cinderella*.

Ashurbanipal, King of Assyria

Ashurbanipal, King of Assyria [ah-shoor-bah'-nuh-pahl]   Ashurbanipal was the last great king of Assyria. During his reign (668–626 BC), the Assyrian empire reached its fullest extent (*c.*663) and then rapidly declined. Ashurbanipal was the son of ESARHADDON, by whom he was chosen to be king. His brother, Shamash-shum-ukin, was made king of Babylonia.

In the early years of Ashurbanipal's reign, a successful Egyptian campaign took the Assyrians all the way to Thebes in the south and established PSAMTIK I of Saîs as virtual viceroy of Egypt. When Gyges of Lydia sought an alliance with Ashurbanipal about the same time, Assyrian influence extended across Anatolia to the Aegean Sea. Later, when Shamash-shum-ukin allied himself with the Elamites against his brother (652 BC), Ashurbanipal was engaged in four years of civil war to win back Babylonia. In the meantime Egypt had become independent, the alliance with Lydia ended, and ELAM and MEDIA ceased to be tributary to Assyria. Ashurbanipal was a great, if unsuccessful, warrior king, but he was also a scholar. The enormous library of cuneiform literature—Babylonian, Assyrian, Sumerian—that he collected at NINEVEH (rediscovered by A. H. Layard in 1850) is a fitting monument to his memory.

Asia

Asia   Asia is the largest of all the continents and includes within its limits an area of 44,444,100 km^2 (17,159,995 mi^2), or about 33% of the world's total land surface and the greater part of the Eurasian landmass. The border between Europe is traditionally drawn as an imaginary zigzag line passing down the spine of the URAL MOUNTAINS and through the CASPIAN SEA, CAUCASUS MOUN-

TAINS, and BLACK SEA. The boundary dividing Asia and Africa is generally placed along the SUEZ CANAL, and the boundary between Asia and Australasia is usually placed between the island of New Guinea and Australia.

Asia is by far the most populous of all the continents, with nearly 60% of the world's total population. The population is diverse and divided by language, race, religion, politics, economics, and cultural origins into a complex cultural mosaic.

The nations of Asia are usually grouped into six main geographical and political-cultural subdivisions:

1. Southwest Asia, which includes Afghanistan, Bahrain, Cyprus, Iran, Iraq, Israel, Jordan, Kuwait, Lebanon, Oman, Qatar, Saudi Arabia, Syria, United Arab Emirates, and Yemen, plus Asian Turkey and Egypt east of the Suez Canal (Sinai Peninsula);
2. South Asia, which includes Bangladesh, Bhutan, India, Maldives, Nepal, Pakistan, and Sri Lanka (formerly Ceylon);
3. East Asia, which includes most of the People's Republic of China, Japan, North Korea (Democratic People's Republic of Korea), South Korea (Republic of Korea), and Taiwan (Republic of China);
4. Southeast Asia, which includes Brunei, Burma (Myanmar), Cambodia, Indonesia, Laos, Malaysia, the Philippines, Singapore, Thailand, and Vietnam;
5. Soviet Asia, which includes all of Siberia and the republics of the USSR located in Asia (Armenia, Azerbaijan, Georgia, Kazakhstan, Kirghizia, Tadzhikistan, Turkmenia, and Uzbekistan), and several smaller autonomous areas;
6. Central Asia, which includes Mongolia and three of the five autonomous regions of China (Inner Mongolia, Tibet, and Xinjiang-Uygur).

Land and Resources

Topography. The topography of Asia comprises a series of high mountain belts, which are the dominant landforms, and a related complex of plateaus, basins, island arcs, and alluvial lowlands. The highest point is Mount EVEREST, which towers to 8,848 m (29,028 ft) in Nepal; the lowest point is 395 m (1,296 ft) below sea level along the shores of the DEAD SEA in Israel and Jordan. The Ural Mountains on the western edge of Asia trend in a north-south direction, but most other belts extend across the continent in a general west-east direction and converge in a knot of high mountains in the PAMIRS, located where the borders of the USSR, China, and Afghanistan come together. West of the Pamirs, two main mountain belts are discernible. The southern one crosses the island of Cyprus, enters the mainland to form the TAURUS MOUNTAINS along the southern edge of Turkey, swings along the southern edge of the Iranian Plateau to form the ZAGROS MOUNTAINS, and continues on into Pakistan before turning north to become the HINDU KUSH and join the Pamirs. The northern mountain belt in Asia west of the Pamirs enters the continent at the Crimean Peninsula, swings eastward

AT A GLANCE

ASIA

Area: 44,444,100 km² (17,159,995 mi²); 33% of the world's land area.

Population: 3,116,000,000 (1990 est.); 60% of the total world population. *Density*—70 persons per km² (181 per mi²).

Elevation: *Highest*—Mount Everest (Zchomolungma), 8,848 m (29,028 ft); *lowest*—Dead Sea (shore of), 395 m (1,296 ft) below sea level.

Northernmost Point: Cape Chelyuskin, USSR, 77°45′N.

Southernmost Mainland Point: Cape Piai, Malaysia, 1°15′N.

Easternmost Point: Cape Dezhneva, USSR, 169°40′W.

Westernmost Point: Cape Baba, Turkey, 26°04′E.

Principal Rivers: Chang Jiang (Yangtze), Tigris-Euphrates, Indus, Ganges, Brahmaputra, Huang He (Hwang Ho), Irrawaddy, Salween, Mekong, Xi (Hsi), Amur, Lena, Yenisei, Ob, Syr Darya.

Principal Lakes: Caspian Sea, Aral Sea, Baikal, Balkhash.

Principal Mountain Ranges: Himalayas, Taurus, Caucasus, Urals, Hindu Kush, Zagros, Pamirs, Karakoram, Sulaiman, Arakan Yoma, Kunlun, Tian Shan (T'ien Shan), Altai, Da Hinggan (Greater Khingan).

Principal Deserts: Deserts of Arabia, Gobi, Syrian Desert, Taklimakan (Takla Makan), Thar, Kara Kum, Kyzyl Kum.

Political Divisions: 40 entire countries; part of the USSR; part of Turkey; part of Egypt.

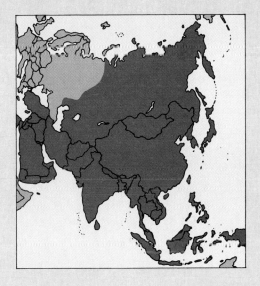

to form the Caucasus Mountains between the Black and Caspian seas, continues south of the Caspian Sea as the ELBURZ MOUNTAINS of Iran and the Kopet Mountains on the Iran-USSR border, and crosses into Afghanistan to merge with the Hindu Kush and the Pamirs.

East of the Pamirs, three mountain belts are discernible. One trends northeastward toward the Pacific Ocean and forms the Alai Range in the USSR, the TIAN SHAN and Da Hinggan (Greater Khinghan) Range in China, and the ALTAI, Sayan, YABLONOVY, and STANOVOI mountains in the USSR. A second mountain belt, located farther south, extends eastward from the Pamirs to form the KUNLUN MOUNTAINS, Astin Tagh, and Nan Shan in China and continues across the middle of China, separating North China from South China, as the Qin Ling (Tsinling).

The third and most southerly of the mountain belts radiating eastward from the Pamirs turns southeastward to form the KARAKORAM RANGE and the broad arc of the HIMALAYAS and then abruptly southward at the eastern end of the Tibetan Plateau, where it splits into a number of lesser ranges that continue southward as the Arakan Yoma in Burma, the mountainous rib of the Malay Peninsula, and the Annam Mountains in Vietnam.

Numerous plateaus and structural basins are located within or along the margins of these mountain ranges. The highest is the Tibetan Plateau, which has an average elevation of more than 4,000 m (13,000 ft) and is bordered by some of the world's highest mountains, including the Himalayas on the south, the Karakoram on the west, and the Kunlun Mountains on the north. This entire complex of high mountains and plateaus is often referred to as the "roof of the world." To the north of Tibet are three important Chinese basins: the Qaidam Pendi (Tsaidam Basin), the Tarim (TAKLI MAKAN) Basin, and the Junggar Pendi (Dzungarian Basin).

Also important to China are the Sichuan (Red) Basin, located in the western Chinese province of Sichuan; the Gobi Plateau, a vast, semidesert upland located in Mongolia and China's Inner Mongolian Autonomous Region (see GOBI); and the Loess Plateau, located south of the Gobi, which is covered with an immense thickness of windblown loess deposits derived from the Gobi. Other plateaus in Asia are the Anatolian Plateau, in Turkey; the Arabian Plateau, mainly in Saudi Arabia; the DECCAN PLATEAU, in peninsular India; and the Vitim and Aldan plateaus, in the USSR.

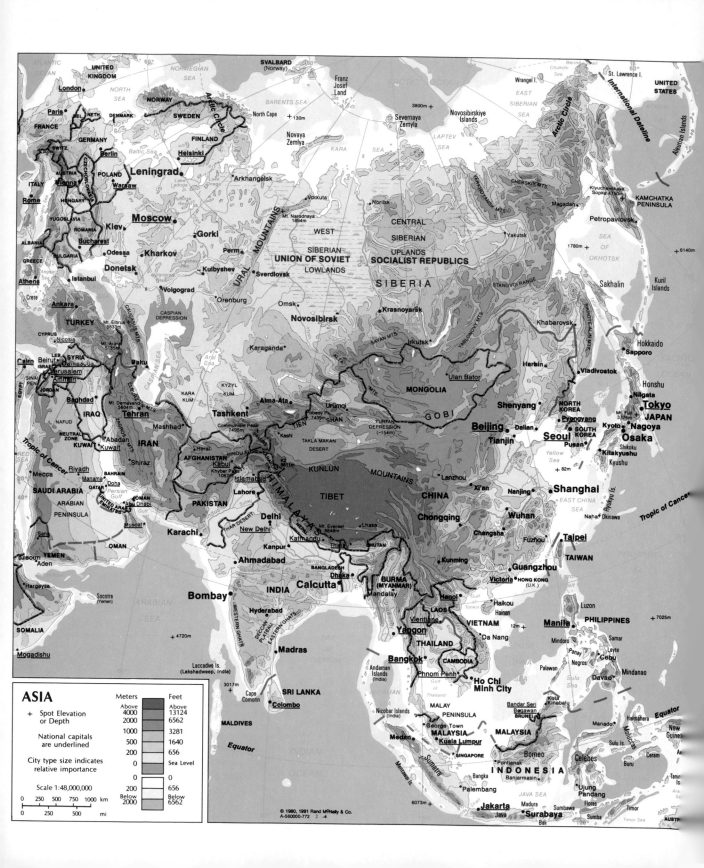

The Himalayas, viewed here from the Siwalik Hills of Nepal, contain all the world's mountains more than 7,620 m (25,000 ft) high. Several of Asia's major river systems—the Ganges, the Brahmaputra, and the Indus—rise in the foothills of the Himalayas.

Numerous islands, arranged in a series of arcs, fringe the Southeast Asian and Pacific coasts of the continent. The islands of the Southeast Asia archipelago pick up the main trend lines of Burma's Arakan Yoma and continue them through the Andaman and Nicobar islands of India and the islands of Sumatra, Java, and Bali in the Indonesian archipelago. Near Bali, the main trend of the mountainous belt splits into two segments. One segment continues eastward through the islands of Timor, the Moluccas, and New Guinea and eventually forms the mountains of New Zealand; the other segment turns northeastward and passes in a series of arcs through Borneo, the Philippine archipelago, Taiwan, the Ryukyu Islands, Japan, and Sakhalin and the Kuril Islands before touching the mainland in the Kamchatka Peninsula (USSR). These island arcs are seismically active, and earthquakes and volcanic eruptions frequently occur.

The most extensive lowlands in Asia are located in the USSR. They are the Western Siberian Plain, a vast, subarctic forested region located east of the Urals, and the Kirghiz Steppe, a semiarid plain located mainly in Kazakhstan. Other important lowlands are mainly in the alluvial valleys and deltas developed by rivers flowing to the south and east. The largest of the alluvial valleys is the Indo-Gangetic Plain, located in the Indian subcontinent

between the Himalayas and the Deccan Plateau. Occupying parts of Pakistan, India, and Bangladesh, it is drained by the Indus, Ganges, and Brahmaputra rivers; river water is diverted extensively across the plain for irrigation, and the region is one of the world's most intensively cultivated and most densely populated places. Other Asian lowlands are the North China Plain, its soils enriched for centuries by loess sediments spread over the valley and deltas of the flood-prone Huang He (Yellow River); the alluvial valleys and deltas of the Chang Jiang (Yangtze, China), Irrawaddy (Burma), and Mekong (Cambodia) rivers; and the Fertile Crescent of the Tigris and Euphrates rivers in Iraq.

Geology. Five Asian "shield" areas (geologically stable areas of ancient crystalline rock) are usually recognized. They are the Arabian and Indian shields in the south and the Tarim Basin (Seridian massif), Northern China (the Chinese massif), and the Siberian (Angara) Shield. Great thicknesses of sediments accumulated between these blocks of stable rocks and were subsequently folded and uplifted in periods of mountain building (orogenies). Asia has had a complex orogenic (mountain-building) history. The Caledonian Orogeny occurred in the Silurian and Devonian periods and is recorded in Asia by the Sayan and other mountains of eastern Siberia. The Hercynian Orogeny occurred in the Late Carboniferous (Pennsylvanian)

Soviet workers completed laying the Baikal-Amur Mainline in 1984. This 3,200-km (2,000-mi) railroad runs parallel, on the northern side, to the famous Trans-Siberian Railroad in southeastern Siberia. It has opened up the area's rich mineral resources and vast forestlands to exploitation.

and Permian periods and created several mountain ranges—the Urals, Tian Shan, Kunlun, and Qin Ling (Tsingling).

According to plate-tectonics theory, by the close of the Permian Period, Asia, together with the ancestral cores of all the other continents, formed the supercontinent known as Pangaea. During the Triassic Period, Pangaea split apart into the northern landmass of Laurasia (from which North America, Europe, and northern Asia later developed) and the southern landmass of Gondwanaland (from which India and the continents of the Southern Hemisphere later developed). A large sea called Tethys separated the two landmasses. By the end of the Jurassic Period, Gondwanaland fragmented, and the Indian plate began a northeastward movement. It eventually collided with and was drawn under the edge of the Eurasian plate, and in the process Tethyan sediments were deformed and uplifted to form the Himalayas, Tibetan Plateau, and other high mountains of southern Asia. The African plate moved northward and collided with Eurasia to thrust up the European Alps and the mountains of Asia west of the Himalayas. Much later, probably during the Miocene Epoch, rifting and seafloor spreading created the Red Sea and the Gulf of Aden, and Arabia split away from Africa to form a separate plate. Earth movements occur today in the Indonesian, Japanese, Philippine, and other Pacific island arcs; in these areas there is widespread seismic and volcanic activity, attesting to the geological instability of the region. (See CONTINENTAL DRIFT.)

Climate. Three broad climatic realms may be distinguished in Asia. They are: monsoon Asia, dry Asia, and cold Asia.

Monsoon Asia. The climate of South, Southeast, and East Asia is strongly influenced by the immensity of the Asian landmass, the barrier presented by its great highland core, and the MONSOON wind system. In summer, warm air above the continental interior of Asia rises and creates low-pressure centers. The air pressures above the Pacific and Indian oceans are relatively high. Consequently, strong, moisture-laden winds are drawn inland

from the oceans into the low-pressure areas of Asia, bringing heavy rainfall wherever they are forced to rise up over low hills, mountains, or other topographic obstacles. The summer monsoon in India interrupts a very hot, dry spell. Elsewhere in Southeast and East Asia the break is not as dramatic, but rainfall in all of monsoon Asia is concentrated in the summer months. In the coastal region of East Asia, tropical cyclones (typhoons) bring additional precipitation and devastating winds.

In winter, the land surface in the interior of Asia cools off more rapidly than the surrounding oceans. As a result, cold descending air currents over the heart of Asia generate high-pressure centers facing the relatively low pressure zones over the Indian and Pacific oceans, where temperatures are higher. From October to about April, cold, dry, continental winds blow offshore from inland Asia. This is the season of the winter monsoon.

Places exposed to the monsoons are warmer in summer and colder in winter than places in corresponding latitudes not under their influence. They are also, for the most part, the wettest parts of Asia.

Within this large monsoon area, important temperature differences exist between north and south. An equatorial climate predominates over much of Indonesia and Malaysia; average annual temperature is about 20° C (70° F) and average annual rainfall more than 2,030 mm (80 in). North of the equatorial region is a tropical monsoon area, in which summers are hot and humid (average temperatures over 27° C/80° F) and winters cool (10° C/ 50° F) and dry. Rainfall is more than 1,270 mm (50 in). Climates in the rest of monsoon Asia range from warm temperate in central China and southern Japan to cool temperate in northern China and Japan. The growing season decreases gradually from almost a full year in Indonesia to about four months in China's northeast.

Dry Asia. Parts of Southeast Asia, Central Asia, and Mongolia have a wide range of dry climates that range latitudinally from the tropical deserts of the Arabian Peninsula in the west to the subtropical steppe climate present in Iran and Afghanistan and the midlatitude steppe and deserts of Mongolia and northern China. Rainfall varies from a low of less than 25 mm (1 in) in parts of the Gobi Desert to 200 mm (8 in) in Soviet Central Asia. Throughout this belt, rainfall is extremely unpredictable. The eastern coastal fringe of the Mediterranean Basin (the Levant) has a typical Mediterranean climate and receives rain in winter; average annual precipitation along this western edge of dry Asia is about 500 mm (20 in).

Cold Asia. Most of Soviet Asia has a cold climate. The southern regions have a subarctic climate, where summers are mild (21° C/70° F) and short, lasting for less than four months. Rainfall decreases from about 510 mm (20 in) in coastal locations to less than 250 mm (10 in) in the interior. The extreme northern section of Asia is dominated by the polar tundra climate, where the low year-round temperatures create a permanently frozen subsoil known as permafrost.

Drainage. The major rivers of Asia, that is, those reaching the sea, include the Ob, Yenisei, and Lena, which flow northward to the Arctic Ocean; the Amur, Huang He, and Chang Jiang (the world's third longest river, after the Nile and the Amazon), which drain eastward to the Sea of Okhotsk, Yellow Sea, and East China Sea, respectively, all coastal seas of the Pacific Ocean; the Ganges, Indus, and Brahmaputra rivers, which flow southward toward the Indian Ocean; the Mekong, Irrawaddy, and Salween, which rise in eastern Tibet and drain southward through the peninsulas of Southeast Asia; and the Tigris and Euphrates system, which flows into the Persian Gulf, an arm of the Indian Ocean. In addition, about 12,950,000 km² (5,000,000 mi²) of land in Central Asia is drained by rivers that do not reach the

sea. The Ili flows into Lake Balkhash; the Syr Darya and the Amu Darya into the Aral Sea; and the Ural River into the Caspian Sea. Others are intermittent streams, which flow only after heavy rains; their waters evaporate in the deserts, and some end in salt lakes or playas, which may be dry part of the year.

The Dead Sea, a saltwater lake whose shore is the lowest point on Earth, is fed by the Jordan River. The Caspian Sea, also saline and the world's largest inland body of water, loses more water by evaporation than it receives from streams and precipitation. The Aral Sea, about 280 km (175 mi) to the east, is also saline and once covered a much larger area. Lake Baikal in southern Siberia is the world's deepest lake (1,741 m/5,712 ft) and has only one outlet, the Angara River. The waters of Lake Baikal are fresh.

Soils. Soil types correspond closely to their respective climatic and natural vegetation regions. In the permafrost region of northern Asia are tundra soils, unusable for agriculture because of the short growing season and impeded drainage. South of the tundra, in the vast coniferous forest region of cold temperate Asia, are podzols with high acidity and low organic content. Farther south, in the zone of mixed coniferous and deciduous forests, the gray brown forest soils have higher humus content and are less acidic than the podzols. Between the temperate forests of northern Asia and the deserts of Central Asia a belt of chernozem and chestnut soils appears. These black to dark brown soils are very rich in humus and mineral nutrients and are very productive when farmed. The desert and mountain soils of dry Asia have little to offer for agricultural production. Even where irrigation is possible, a danger of salt and alkali accumulation in the topsoil ex-

The Laotian provincial capital of Pakse, on the Mekong River, is a market for agricultural produce and forest products. The Mekong River, one of the most important waterways of Southeast Asia, serves as a major commercial avenue in Laos, Thailand, Kampuchea (Cambodia), and Vietnam.

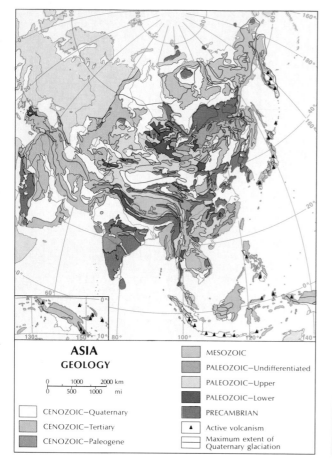

ASIA
GEOLOGY

0   1000   2000 km
0   500   1000   mi

☐ CENOZOIC–Quaternary
▨ CENOZOIC–Tertiary
▨ CENOZOIC–Paleogene

▨ MESOZOIC
▨ PALEOZOIC–Undifferentiated
▨ PALEOZOIC–Upper
▨ PALEOZOIC–Lower
▨ PRECAMBRIAN
▲ Active volcanism
☐ Maximum extent of Quaternary glaciation

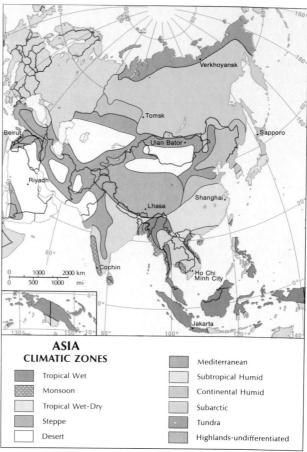

ASIA
CLIMATIC ZONES

▨ Tropical Wet
▨ Monsoon
☐ Tropical Wet-Dry
▨ Steppe
☐ Desert

▨ Mediterranean
☐ Subtropical Humid
▨ Continental Humid
☐ Subarctic
▨ Tundra
▨ Highlands-undifferentiated

ists. Consequently, cultivation in dry Asia is confined to well-drained alluvial soils along major river valleys.

The soils of hot, humid monsoon Asia belong to the major soil category known as pedalfers. These soils are rich in iron and aluminum material. High temperatures promote rapid oxidation and contribute to their reddish or yellowish appearance. Heavy rainfall washes soluble mineral and organic matter from the topsoil to the subsoil, leaving insoluble minerals, such as aluminum, in the topsoil. These tropical red earths are generally infertile, and therefore agriculture in monsoon Asia is confined mostly to alluvial soils along river valleys. Some prominent exceptions exist: soils developed on basic volcanic ash in the northeastern Deccan Plateau (India) and in Java are among the richest soils in monsoon Asia.

Vegetation. Much of the original green cover in monsoon Asia has been replaced by secondary growth or farmlands as a result of centuries of cultivation. Even in the equatorial region of Southeast Asia periodic burning by shifting cultivators has greatly reduced the extent of tropical rain forest, and tropical deciduous forests dominate what little forest area remains. These forests yield

valuable tropical hardwoods, such as teak, sal, ironwood, and bamboo.

In dry Asia limited vegetation, such as short grasses, will occur even on the edges of the most barren desert areas. Most of these desert plants are xerophytic (drought resistant) and halophytic (salt tolerant). More significant vegetation occurs where groundwater is near the surface.

Separating cold Asia from dry Asia is an extensive band of low grasslands called the steppe. Steppe vegetation predominates in Mongolia and southwest Asiatic Russia. North of the steppeland is a narrow transition zone of mixed forest. Farther to the north lies the vast expanse of coniferous forest known as taiga in the Soviet Union. The taiga is a rich storehouse of commercially valuable needleleaf softwoods, such as spruce, larch, fir, and pine. Even farther north, lichens, mosses, and occasional dwarf willows manage to survive in the cold tundra.

Fauna. Arctic animals, although noted for their mobility, are even less diverse than arctic plants. Polar bears, mouselike lemmings, reindeer, and arctic foxes are common animals in the tundra region. The mammals and birds of subarctic Asiatic Russia are of the cold-hardy

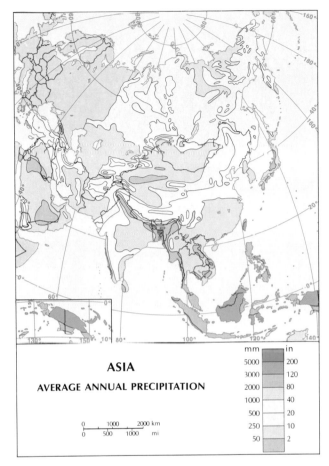

ASIA

AVERAGE ANNUAL PRECIPITATION

mm	in
5000	200
3000	120
2000	80
1000	40
500	20
250	10
50	2

0   1000   2000 km
0   500   1000   mi

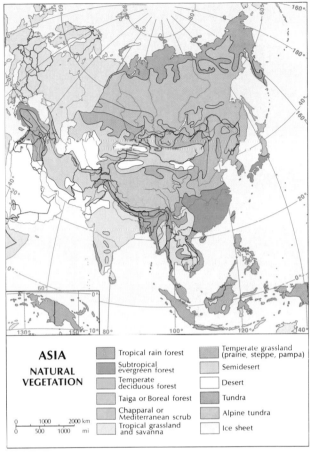

ASIA

NATURAL VEGETATION

0   1000   2000 km
0   500   1000   mi

Tropical rain forest
Subtropical evergreen forest
Temperate deciduous forest
Taiga or Boreal forest
Chapparal or Mediterranean scrub
Tropical grassland and savanna

Temperate grassland (prairie, steppe, pampa)
Semidesert
Desert
Tundra
Alpine tundra
Ice sheet

type. Examples are the Altai elk, brown bear, wolf, ermine, sable, and erne (a Siberian eagle similar to the bald eagle). Birds are prominent vertebrates in Asian deserts. Animals peculiar to dry Asia include the kuland (Mongolian wild ass), Bactrian camel, saiga (an antelope), Tibetan antelope, kiang, yak, argali (wild sheep), and markhor (wild goat). In East Asia are found such indigenous animals as the takin, bharal (wild Himalayan sheep), goral (a rock goat), musk deer, siko, Thorold's deer, Père David's deer, panda, Asiatic black bear, and high-altitude salamanders. Tigers and elephants are still found in some southern parts of the continent.

Mineral Resources. Asia's coal deposits are the largest in the world, with an estimated 60% of the world's total reserves located within the USSR; other coal reserves occur in nearly every province of China, in Korea, and in India. In 1988 the USSR ranked 2d in world coal production, China 3d, India 5th, and North Korea 11th. Asia also has vast oil deposits, especially in the USSR; in the Persian Gulf area, which has an estimated 60% of the total oil reserves of the non-Communist world; and in the South China and Yellow seas and other parts of the conti-

nental shelf off the coasts of East, Southeast, and South Asia. In 1988 the USSR ranked 1st among world crude-oil producers, Saudi Arabia 3d, China 5th, Iran 7th, Malaysia 9th, Iraq 12th, Indonesia 13th, Kuwait 16th, the United Arab Emirates 19th, and India 20th. The USSR has about 39% of the world's natural-gas reserves, and in 1988 it ranked 1st in natural-gas production. Marketing difficulties have limited Soviet production, but this situation began to change in the 1980s with the construction of a new Soviet pipeline that enables the USSR to supply Western Europe as well as increasing domestic supplies.

Iron ore is abundant in the USSR, which ranked 1st in world production in 1988. China ranked 3d, and India 6th. Tin is widely distributed in Southeast Asia, with Malaysia and Indonesia ranking among the top world producers. Asia also has large deposits of bauxite and a variety of other minerals, including major world deposits of chromium, manganese, mercury, selenium, tellurium, tungsten, zinc, graphite, magnesite, mica, pyrite, and talc. Japan, although it is the industrial giant in Asia, has few of the mineral resources needed for modern industry and must import them.

This Mongol clan of the Central Asian steppes still has a traditional nomadic existence. Although programs of economic development have been inaugurated by the government of the Mongolian People's Republic, livestock herding remains the nation's principal economic activity.

Water Resources. Irrigation canals crisscross the Indo-Gangetic Plain, Chang Jiang Valley, and other alluvial lowlands of monsoon Asia. Irrigation during the dry season of the monsoon makes possible a double and triple cropping of land where year-round temperatures are warm enough and has been a major factor in the ability of Asia's river valleys to support such large population clusters. Irrigation and the availability of groundwater for growing crops in oases are also major factors in the settlement and economic development of most of dry Asia in the southwest. Rivers remain the primary means of transportation for most Asian countries outside Japan. Road and rail facilities are generally limited, although India's network is extensive.

Only a small part of the continent's vast hydroelectric power potential has been developed, most of it in such fuel-deficient nations as Japan and Bangladesh or as part of a larger program of river improvements as in the Indus and Mekong river basin projects. Rivers with enormous hydroelectric potential are the Chang Jiang, Ob, Lena, and Yenisei.

Arable Land Resources. Only about 17% of all Asia excluding the USSR is planted in crops and only 14% of all Asia including the USSR. India has the most arable land, with 50% of its total area under cultivation. China ranks second, with 11% of its total area under crops; and Turkey a poor third, with 35% of its total area under crops. Other large arable landholdings are in Iran, which has 12% of its total area under crops; Indonesia, which has 10% of its area cultivated; and Pakistan, which has 24% of its total area planted to crops.

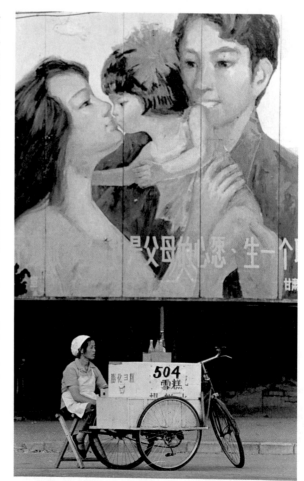

A Chinese street vendor tends her bicycle cart beneath a family-planning billboard. China, with more than one-fifth of the world's population, has vigorously promoted birth control. One-child families receive special privileges. Families with more than three children are subject to penalties.

Forest and Fish Resources. Forests cover about 36% of the USSR and 20% of the rest of Asia. The USSR has the largest reserves of commercial softwoods in the world (mostly east of the Urals in Soviet Asia) and leads the world in timber production. Deciduous forests are extensive in southern Asia, especially in the tropical and subtropical parts of monsoon Asia. Indonesia and India together account for half of all Asian woods cut from deciduous forests. In the wake of industrialization, however, deforestation is occurring in South and Southeast Asia, as it had earlier in China.

Japan and the USSR are the world's two top-ranking fish producers, and both maintain large oceangoing fishing fleets. China is the third-ranking fish producer, and India is fourth. In keeping with the intensive cultivation of land in Asia, fish are also raised in flooded rice fields.

People

Traditional Culture Areas. Asia has a long cultural heritage of great diversity. Sedentary agriculture and the beginnings of urban life and civilization developed before 4000 BC in MESOPOTAMIA (southwestern Asia); about 3000 BC at Harappa and Mohenjo-daro in the Indus Valley, now in Pakistan (see INDUS CIVILIZATION); and about 2000 BC in the unrelated development of Chinese culture in the loess lands of China's middle Huang He, or Yellow River, valley. These three areas of early civilization served as "culture hearths," or centers from which major cultural traditions, modified by later differences in religion, nationalism, and historical circumstance, were transferred outward and adopted over wide areas of Asia (and sometimes beyond).

Six major cultural regions are recognized in Asia. The three dominant ones are Southwest (or Islamic) Asia,

(Above) *Members of this camel caravan in Qatar, like all nomadic traders, have furnished an important means of commerce in southwestern Asia. Before explorers charted water routes to East Asia, caravans constituted the cultural and economic links between Europe and the Orient.* (Right) *The Masjid-i-Shah, or Royal Mosque, is one of the masterpieces of Savafid architecture in Isfahan, Iran. The mosque, richly decorated with glazed tile, was completed in 1637.* (Below) *A group of children pose before the 13th century bronze* Daibutsu, *or Great Buddha, of Kamakura, a city in Japan. Buddhism was introduced into Japan during the 6th century by Chinese travelers.*

The Jordanian (left) *is an Arab, one of the Semitic peoples of southwestern Asia. The young Anatolian boy* (center) *lives in Turkey, the westernmost nation of Asia. Like all Japanese, except for the Ainu, the woman* (right) *is of Sino-Mongoloid descent.*

South (or Indic) Asia, and East (or Sinic) Asia, which developed from the three original culture hearths. The fourth is Southeast Asia. Set between China and India, this region is what political and cultural geographers call a "shatter zone," or a culture area dominated by two or more strong neighboring cultures. The remaining two culture areas are Northern (or Soviet) Asia and Central (or Interior) Asia, both sparsely populated and peripherally located in terms of the major culture hearths.

Racial and Ethnic Groups. Asia has a great diversity of ethnic groups, with two-thirds of all Asian peoples belonging to the Mongoloid group. The largest ethnic group is the Han Chinese, who constitute about 94% of the total population of China and dominate the eastern half of that nation. The remaining 6% of that nation's population includes Mongols, Uygurs, Huis, Zhuangs, Tibetans, and other groups. The second largest Asian group is the Japanese, who except for a few thousand AINU in the northern island of Hokkaido, constitute a single ethnic group in Japan. India, by contrast, is ethnically complex. In general terms, a lighter-skinned people of Aryan origins are characteristic in the north, and a darker-skinned DRAVIDIAN-speaking people are characteristic of the south.

The north central sections are occupied by a great variety of different tribal groups. European Russians constitute about 40% of the population of Soviet Asia, but important minorities in the southern steppes include the Buryat, Kalmyk, Tadzhik, Chukchi, and Tungu. Southeast Asia is fragmented along ethnic lines and includes among its major ethnic groupings Indonesians, Malays, Burmese, Thais, Khmers, Vietnamese, and Filipinos as well as numerous isolated hill peoples. The principal ethnic groups in Southwest Asia are Semites (mostly ARABS but many Jews in Israel), TURKS, Armenians, Persians, KURDS, and BALUCH.

Languages. Chinese, spoken by an estimated 1 billion people in China, Southeast Asia, and other parts of the continent, is the language most widely spoken in Asia; it includes Mandarin Chinese and many distinctive dialects including Cantonese, Wu, Min, and Hakka. Hindi, spoken by about 215 million people, is the second most widely

used language; it is spoken mainly in northern India and Pakistan. Arabic, spoken mainly in Southwest Asia, is the third major language; and Russian, widely spoken and used as a second language in Soviet Asia, is the fourth. These languages cross national boundaries and enjoy international status. The many other languages spoken in Asia enjoy mainly national and regional usage. Languages introduced by colonial powers have also left important marks on Asia. In India, which is fragmented by numerous languages, English remains an official government language and the country's only unifying tongue. Spanish remains important in the Philippines. (See AFROASIATIC LANGUAGES; INDO-IRANIAN LANGUAGES; MALAYO-POLYNESIAN LANGUAGES; SINO-TIBETAN LANGUAGES; SOUTHEAST ASIAN LANGUAGES; URAL-ALTAIC LANGUAGES.)

Religions. The principal Asian religions are Hinduism, Islam, and Buddhism. Hinduism is the main religion of India. Islam is the principal religion in Southwest Asia, Afghanistan, Pakistan, Bangladesh, Malaysia, and Indonesia. Large Muslim minorities exist in India, the Philippines, and Central Asia. Buddhism, which developed in India, is no longer important in that country but constitutes the principal religion in Burma, Thailand, Sri Lanka, Laos, and Cambodia. In the form of a northern sect known as TIBETAN BUDDHISM, it is dominant in Tibet and Bhutan. Buddhism is also well represented in Japan. Taoism, an indigenous Chinese religion, and Confucianism, which is more a philosophy than a religion, were both widespread in China in pre-Communist times. Other important Asian religions are Shinto, or traditional Japanese nature worship; Roman Catholicism, practiced mainly in the Philippines; and Protestantism. Less well represented religions include such sects as the SIKHS, PARSIS, and Jains (see JAINISM) in India.

Education and Health. About 60% of Asia's school-age children attend school. Literacy varies markedly from one Asian country to another. Only 10% of Afghanistan's population is literate, which is defined as persons more than 15 years of age who can read or write. Literacy rates range from about 25% of the population in Iran and Saudi Arabia to about 50% in China, India, Turkey, and Ma-

The Inner Asian nomadic woman (left) *is descended from the Mongol warriors. The Indonesian woman* (center) *is from the island of Flores. A Nepalese porter* (right) *earns a living by carrying goods over the precarious paths of his Himalayan homeland.*

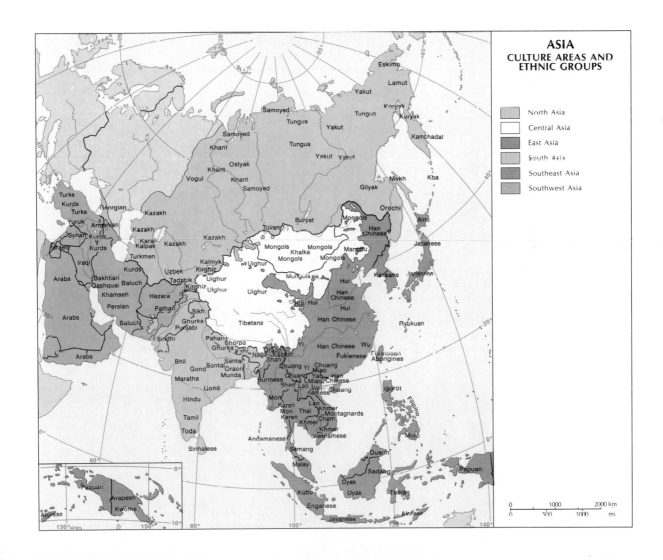

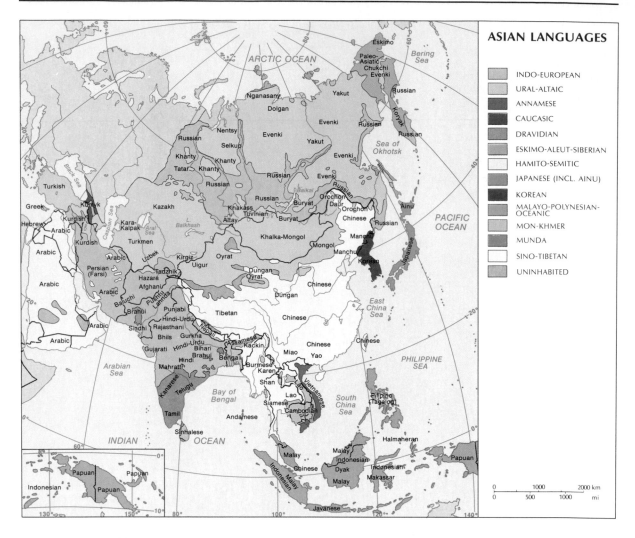

ASIAN LANGUAGES

INDO-EUROPEAN
URAL-ALTAIC
ANNAMESE
CAUCASIC
DRAVIDIAN
ESKIMO-ALEUT-SIBERIAN
HAMITO-SEMITIC
JAPANESE (INCL. AINU)
KOREAN
MALAYO-POLYNESIAN-OCEANIC
MON-KHMER
MUNDA
SINO-TIBETAN
UNINHABITED

laysia and close to 100% in Japan and the Soviet Union.

The average daily per capita protein consumption is inadequate in the majority of Asian countries. Asia's food supply has grown at only a slightly faster rate than the population, and malnutrition is widespread in poorer areas and among the lowest economic groups. The rates of infant mortality are higher in India and the Middle East than in China and are lowest in the industrial developed countries of Japan and the USSR. The average life expectancy of Asians ranges from about 40 to 65 years. Japan and the USSR are significant exceptions; life expectancy is more than 70 years, and infant mortality is very low.

Demography. Population densities in Asia range from the lowest in the world in parts of the Arabian Desert, Tibetan Plateau, and high mountains of South and Inner Asia to some of the world's highest population densities in the Indo-Gangetic Plain and the Chang Jiang Valley. Although average annual population growth in Asia (ex-

cluding Soviet Asia) has declined from the more than 2% of the first half of the 1970s, the annual population growth for the region has averaged 2% a year for the past 30 years. Asia's population is expected to double soon after the end of the century and is expected to account for 65% to 75% of all the world's population at that time. Only Japan, the USSR, Hong Kong, and Singapore have attained low birthrates and death rates. China and India have demonstrated some success in encouraging birth limitation, but birthrates in the rest of Asia continue at a high level characteristic of less developed countries. Death rates have fallen almost everywhere with the advent of better medical care, improved nutrition, and the increasing ability to avert famine by imports from other areas when crops fail. It is generally assumed that economic development and reduction in birthrates are related, but much dispute exists as to which comes first.

Practically all Asian countries, with perhaps the exception of isolated Bhutan and Nepal, have experienced urbanization in recent years. People flock from the countryside to the cities, where they increase unemployment, congestion, and various forms of social disorganization. They also tend to abandon traditional cultures in favor of modern, urban, industrial, and commercial mores. BOMBAY, CALCUTTA, RANGOON (Yangon), BANGKOK, MANILA, HONG KONG, SINGAPORE, and JAKARTA are examples of this process. SHANGHAI, one of the largest cities in the world, was such a city until the Chinese government forcibly relocated part of the population to the surrounding area.

Despite this process of urbanization, however, most Asian countries remain predominantly rural. The exceptions include modernized Israel, where just over 10% of the population live in rural areas, and Japan, where only 23% of the population are classified as rural. In Southwest Asia, with its long tradition of urban living, Iraq and Jordan have only 30% of their populations in rural areas. Elsewhere in Asia, the rural population amounts to 76% of the total in India and Indonesia and nearly 80% in China.

Economic Development

During the Middle Ages, Asia was the most developed part of the world. Syria was famous for its textiles, swords, steel, and silverware; India for the delicacy of its cottons; Iran (Persia) and Central Asia for rugs; Southeast Asia for spices; and China for exquisite porcelains, silks, and other items coveted by Western traders and consumers as late as the 18th century. Today, however, except for the USSR, Japan, Israel, and parts of oil-rich Southwest Asia, most Asian countries are considered part of the developing world. They have not shared in the Industrial Revolution and the higher standards of living that industrialization has provided to the Western world, and in most Asian countries the majority of the people live close to the limits of survival.

Agriculture. Agriculture remains the dominant economic activity throughout Asia except in Israel, where only 4% of the population are engaged in farming; Japan,

Signs proliferate in Tokyo, which is both the capital of Japan and one of the world's leading commercial and financial centers. Its city population is the largest in Asia.

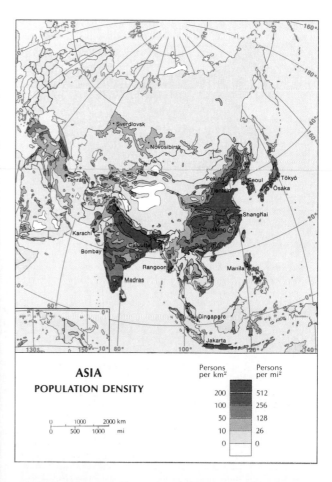

ASIA
POPULATION DENSITY

	Persons per km²	Persons per mi²
	200	512
	100	256
	50	128
	10	26
	0	0

(Above) The Indian elephant, which is smaller and more docile than its African counterpart, has been domesticated and trained to perform heavy labor in southern and eastern Asia.

(Below) On a Honda assembly line in Japan, robots spot-weld car bodies and frames. Japanese industry makes more extensive use of robots than any other in the world. Japan also produces the largest number of motor vehicles.

(Above) These rice paddies in Sri Lanka, formerly Ceylon, are terraced along a hillside to retain water. The paddies will be drained before the crop is harvested. Rice, the staple crop throughout southern and eastern Asia, is intensively cultivated in areas dominated by seasonal monsoon rains.

(Below) Baskets of coal are sold in a Chinese free market. During the 1980s China liberalized its economy, allowing small-scale entrepreneurship and promoting business collaboration with foreign investors.

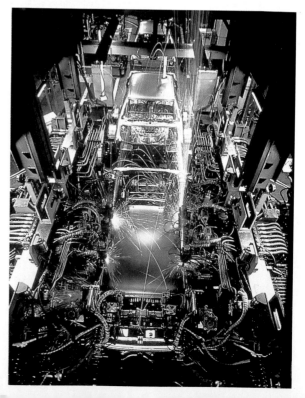

where only 8% are farmers; and Soviet Asia, where only 10% work in agricultural activities. By contrast the proportion of the labor force in farming in the rest of Asia is 60% in China and Indonesia and 52% in India, and ranges as high as 93% in Bhutan and Nepal.

Four distinct agricultural systems coexist in Asia: small-holding agriculture, plantation agriculture, collective agriculture, and shifting agriculture. Small-holding agriculture, in which small private farms produce a combination of subsistence and cash crops for home consumption and local markets, predominates in the capitalist economics. Collective agriculture, in which production is based on central planning, is practiced in China and the Soviet Union. Plantation agriculture, involving the production on large land estates of one or a few agricultural commodities for foreign markets, is most notable in Southeast Asia. Shifting or SLASH-AND-BURN AGRICULTURE is practiced by tribal groups in tropical rain forests.

The principal food crop in Asia is rice, most of it paddy rice grown in flooded fields during the summer, but some upland rice is also grown without irrigation. About 91% of all the world's rice is grown in Asia, some 40% of it in China, 20% in India, 7% in Indonesia, and 6% in Bangladesh. Wheat is the second major food crop; it is grown as a second crop during the dry monsoon season where temperatures are warm enough and is also the chief crop in drier areas such as northern China, the USSR, Turkey, and the shores of the Mediterranean Sea. About 23% of the world's wheat is produced in the USSR, 10% in China, 7% in India, 4% in Turkey, and 5% in the rest of Asia. Other principal food crops are millet, sorghum, maize, barley, soybeans, and kaoliang (kafir corn). Commercial crops include cotton (India, the USSR, and China), silk (China, India, and Japan), jute (Bangladesh and Southeast Asia), rubber and palm oil (Malaysia, Thailand, and Indonesia), sugarcane (Pakistan, Thailand, Indonesia, Taiwan, India, and the Philippines), tea (India, China, Indonesia, and Japan), and copra (Indonesia and the Philippines).

Animals play a major role in Asian agriculture, both as part of the intensive system of agriculture characteristic of the densely populated alluvial plains and as part of a nomadic economy of cold and semiarid regions. China has the largest hog population in the world. Hogs are easy to raise, produce abundant manure, and, as pork, provide a major source of animal protein in the Chinese diet. India has the largest bovine population in the world. Cattle in India, however, are kept for religious and draft purposes; as a sacred animal the cow is not raised for meat. Camels, used mainly for transportation, are ubiquitous animals in dry Asia. Sheep are reared in semiarid environments such as south central USSR, western China, the central Indian plateaus, and the Middle East, and reindeer are herded in the northern parts of Soviet Asia.

Japan, India, and China are largely self-sufficient in food. New strains of wheat and rice, developed in the 1960s and 1970s as part of the GREEN REVOLUTION, have raised crop yields as much as four- to five-fold per hectare in some places. The new strains, however, supply lower yields per hectare than do traditional seeds unless nur-

tured by large amounts of fertilizers and careful irrigation. Fertilizer production has increased greatly, as has the amount of land under irrigation. Except in Japan, Taiwan, and the USSR, however, fertilizers and irrigation are not available to all farmers, and those too poor to afford them have suffered declining yields. This has often accelerated the existing concentration of land ownership, although vigorous land-reform programs have redistributed land in some countries, notably China.

Mechanization holds less promise for raising agricultural productivity because Asia's agricultural methods have been traditionally labor intensive. Indeed, it would pose additional burdens for most Asian nations by increasing the need to provide employment for those displaced by the improvements and unable to find work in the slow-growing industrial sectors.

Forestry and Fishing. In most of Asia, forestry and fishing cater mainly to domestic markets. Both activities, however, are major industries in Japan and the USSR. Teak is a specialty timber export in Thailand and Burma.

Mining. Asia's great wealth of mineral resources furnishes the raw materials for much of the world's industrial establishments. Among the fuels, in 1988, Asia produced 33% of the world's total oil supply, 24% of the bituminous and anthracite coals, and 8% of the marketed natural gas. Among metals, it produced 43% of the world's tin, most of it concentrated in Malaysia, Indonesia, and other parts of Southeast Asia; 18% of the iron ore; 22% of the chromium; 11% of the manganese; 16% of the mercury; 36% of the selenium; 20% of the tellurium; 43% of the tungsten; 19% of the zinc; and 12% of the titanium. Of the world's total production of nonmetals, Asia supplied 35% of the cement, 41% of the graphite, 36% of the magnesite, 40% of the mica, 34% of the nitrogen fertilizers, 19% of the pyrite, 19% of the salt, and 43% of the talc. In total value of mineral output, Asia ranked first among all the continents.

Manufacturing. Industrialization is widely promoted as the solution to Asia's poverty and unemployment problems. Japan has shown the advantages of its "economic miracle," and Taiwan, South Korea, Singapore, and Israel have demonstrated that the Japanese model can work elsewhere. Southwest Asia has benefited from foreign aid to some extent, especially in the case of strategically located Turkey, but oil has contributed much of the capital needed for development.

The USSR and Japan are among the world's leading manufacturing nations. In the USSR, however, the major industrial centers are in the European part; Soviet Asia is essentially a vast storehouse of natural resources still largely unexploited because of their inaccessibility to markets. Japan lacks industrial raw materials and specializes in producing technical machinery, transport equipment, and precision instruments that are high in value but low in bulk. Examples of this type of manufacture are automobiles and electrical and electronic equipment. China experimented briefly with peasant-based industrialization during its GREAT LEAP FORWARD of 1958–60, but this approach was later abandoned as inefficient. After the Cultural Revolution, China began to import ad-

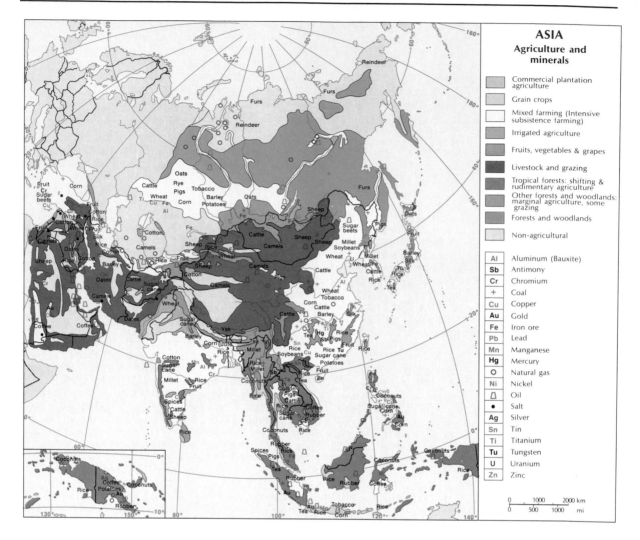

ASIA
Agriculture and minerals

- Commercial plantation agriculture
- Grain crops
- Mixed farming (Intensive subsistence farming)
- Irrigated agriculture
- Fruits, vegetables & grapes
- Livestock and grazing
- Tropical forests: shifting & rudimentary agriculture
- Other forests and woodlands: marginal agriculture, some grazing
- Forests and woodlands
- Non-agricultural

Al	Aluminum (Bauxite)
Sb	Antimony
Cr	Chromium
+	Coal
Cu	Copper
Au	Gold
Fe	Iron ore
Pb	Lead
Mn	Manganese
Hg	Mercury
O	Natural gas
△	Oil
Ni	Nickel
•	Salt
Ag	Silver
Sn	Tin
Ti	Titanium
Tu	Tungsten
U	Uranium
Zn	Zinc

vanced technology from the West to promote its industrialization program. Industries were encouraged to become more autonomous and responsive to market demands, although the pace of reform slowed from the late 1980s. As in India, industry in China is still dominated by light manufacturing. Southeast Asia and the Middle East possess few significant industrial regions. What little manufacturing exists is concentrated in the national capitals and a few commercial cities. In the Middle East, industrial growth was disrupted by the 1990 Iraqi invasion of Kuwait and subsequent (1991) war in the Persian Gulf area.

Power. Energy consumption in Asia is closely related to the degree of industrialization. Per capita energy consumption is highest in Qatar and the USSR and lowest in Cambodia and Nepal. Thermal energy is a major source of power in Asia. India, China, and the Asian portion of the Soviet Union have high hydroelectric power potentials, most of which, however, have not been developed.

Transportation and Communication. With the exception

of Japan, Asian countries generally possess inadequate transportation facilities. Overland transportation in Asia is made difficult by the continent's landforms and the great distances between key population, market, and resource areas. Railroads are extensive only in Japan, India, and eastern China. The TRANS-SIBERIAN RAILROAD, which serves much of Soviet Asia, crosses the Ural Mountains and proceeds across southern Siberia to the Pacific port of VLADIVOSTOK. A parallel rail line, the Baikal-Amur Mainline (BAM), was completed in 1984. Asia's road system is even less developed than its railroads. Consequently, river and local coastal transport are of great importance in much of Asia. More than 45% of all passenger traffic in Japan travels via automobile, but corresponding figures in the rest of Asia are very low.

Trade. Petroleum is the major export in oil-rich countries of the Middle East. It accounts for nearly 90% of total annual exports by value in Saudi Arabia and is the predominant export for Iran, as it was for Kuwait and Iraq prior to the imposition of an international embargo upon both nations after the August 1990 Iraqi invasion of Kuwait. Indonesia is at present the only country in monsoon Asia with sizable petroleum exports. The regional economic impact of the Iraqi invasion and subsequent war in the Persian Gulf included the loss of income from hundreds of thousands of Palestinian, Jordanian, South Asian, and Filipino guest workers in the region; a halt in exports of South Asian commodities to Iraq and Kuwait; the impact of rising oil prices; and the loss of Turkish and Jordanian revenues from Iraqi exports.

Exports from Southeast Asia are mainly tropical crops and minerals (rubber, palm oil, sugarcane, coconut, tin, bauxite), most of which are shipped to the industrialized

nations of the world. The Indian subcontinent exports textiles, machine products, and craft goods. The principal imports are manufactured products and petroleum. China's

This bust was found among the ruins of Mohenjo-daro, one of several cultural centers that flourished along the Indus River during the 3d millennium BC. The Indus River culture was one of Asia's three earliest civilizations, the others developing between the Tigris and Euphrates rivers and along the Huang He in China.

(Above) Two "immortals," archers in the army of Darius I, are portrayed in this relief from the Persian royal palace at Susa. Persia's invasion of Greece was repulsed (490 BC) at Marathon, thus preventing Asian domination of Hellenistic Europe. (Below) The Great Wall of China, the most extensive structure ever built, follows the ancient northern borders of China for about 2,400 km (1,500 mi). The Qin emperor Shi Huang Di (221–210 BC) ordered the Great Wall built to keep out northern barbarian tribes.

Gautama, founder of Buddhism; Laozi, mythical founder of Daoism; and Confucius, founder of a code of social ethics adopted as China's state ideology, appear in this painting. The philosophies of these venerated sages profoundly influenced Chinese thought.

ASIA IN 1294

Maximum extent of the
Great Mongol Empire
Boundaries within the
Great Mongol Empire
Other boundaries
Route of Marco Polo 1271–1295
★ Capital city
• City or town

foreign trade increased dramatically in the 1980s but still lags significantly behind that of Taiwan and Japan.

Regional cooperative ventures include the Columbo Plan, set up in 1960; the Association of Southeast Asian Nations (see ASEAN), set up in 1967 as the successor to the SOUTHEAST ASIA TREATY ORGANIZATION; the often fragmented ARAB LEAGUE, established in 1945; and the South Asian Association for Regional Cooperation, founded in 1985.

History

The origins of Asian history and civilizations developed independently but in similar patterns in three widely separated river-valley systems. The earliest cultural center in western Asia was in the parallel valleys of the Tigris and Euphrates rivers, later called Mesopotamia by the Greeks. The second was the Indus Valley of northwestern India. The third was the flatland section of China's Huang He, or Yellow River.

Ancient Civilizations. The basic contributing factor in the development of all three centers of civilization was the seasonal deposit of sedimentation by silt-saturated floodwaters. In such perennial flood areas, permanently settled agriculturists abandoned their previous hunting, fishing and food-gathering routines and learned to cooperate in village units that were eventually grouped around governmental centers.

Contemporary with the development of such river-val-

(Above) *Minamoto Yoritomo, Japan's first shogun, defeated the Taira clan in 1185 and established a military rule that lasted 700 years.* (Left) *Angkor Wat, in Cambodia, was built by the Khmer kings in the 12th century.*

ley communities during the 4th and 3d centuries BC was a transition from the use of stone tools in the NEOLITHIC PERIOD to the use of metals in the BRONZE AGE. As societies became more complex, regulated trade emerged and writing systems developed.

Southwest Asia in Ancient Times. From about 2800 to 2400 BC, Mesopotamia was controlled by the cities of SUMER, at the eastern end of the FERTILE CRESCENT. Dominance then passed to the more northerly region of AKKAD. Around 2000 BC, after a century of enemy intrusions, the state of BABYLONIA emerged. It produced in time the famous legal Code of HAMMURABI (*c.*1800 BC). KASSITE rule (1600–1200 BC) was followed by the even longer ascendancy of ASSYRIA, an empire based in northern Mesopotamia. Assyria finally fell (612 BC) before a coalition of Medes (see MEDIA) from the north, Persians from the east,

This illustration accompanied Marco Polo's account of his travels in the Orient. The Venetian explorer reached the court of Kubla Khan in 1275. Marco Polo's book about his adventures promoted interest in East Asia and resulted in later explorations by the mercantile nations of Europe.

Genghis Khan, one of the great conquerors in Asian history, appears in a portrait from a 13th-century Chinese album. Commanding an army of Mongol tribes, he subjugated a vast empire stretching from the Pacific Ocean to the Caspian Sea.

A British officer is met by an attendant on his arrival in India. Although the Portuguese, the Dutch, and the French had established earlier trading outposts in India, the British East India Company slowly gained political control with the help of local Indian leaders. Defeating an army of Bengali patriots in 1757, the English established themselves as the leading power in southern Asia.

and a resurgent Babylonia, under the Chaldean dynasty, in the south. The new Babylonian empire was overrun by the Persians in 539 BC.

Persian domination over southwestern Asia was initiated by CYRUS THE GREAT (r. 549–30 BC) as conqueror and DARIUS I (r. 522–486 BC) as adminstrative organizer of the vast empire (see PERSIA, ANCIENT). One noteworthy aspect of Persian rule was the emergence of monotheistic ZOROASTRIANISM, which related directly to the emergence of the other monotheistic faiths of Southwest Asia—Judaism, Christianity, and Islam.

In 330 BC the unity of the Persian Empire was interrupted temporarily by the forces of ALEXANDER THE GREAT, who reached the Indus Valley in 326 BC. After a period of political confusion, a second Persian empire (see PARTHIA) spread across Mesopotamia to the Mediterranean Sea. Roman armies conquered Syria in 63 BC, and for several centuries thereafter the Roman-Persian frontier was the Euphrates River. After the Parthian dynasty collapsed in the early 3d century AD, the Persian SASSANIANS continued the struggle with the Roman Empire and its successor state in the east, the BYZANTINE EMPIRE.

Ancient India. The earliest focal point of historic civilization in India, also dating from the late 4th millennium BC, was the central portion of the Indus Valley, which developed commercial contacts with Mesopotamia and with Southeast Asia. The Aryan conquerors of the Indus Valley were warrior predators from central Asia, whose final conquest occurred between 1500 and 1200 BC. The Aryans introduced their Indo-European language and Sanskrit writing system, and Aryan religious practices coalesced with older forms in the emerging Hinduism. In the 6th century BC, Buddhism and Jainism appeared simultaneously. Buddhism was to spread in East and Southeast Asia, although it eventually disappeared in India.

In the late 4th century BC, CHANDRAGUPTA MAURYA conquered the kingdom of Magadha in the lower Ganges Valley. His famous grandson, ASOKA (r. c274–232 BC), expanded his rule virtually throughout the subcontinent. In about AD 320, after a series of incursions from the north, another Indian conqueror, Chandragupta, restored imperial domination over the entire continent. The GUPTA dynasty ruled India for more than 200 years before succumbing to renewed attacks from the north.

Ancient China. Chinese civilizations began in the fertile valley of the Huang He. The earliest Chinese dynasty, the Xia (Hsia), evolved about 2000 BC. The more powerful SHANG dynasty of northern China, which reached its zenith c.1400 BC, was overthrown in c.1027 BC by a prince of Zhou (Chou). After a major uprising (771–770 BC) reduced dynastic authority, the figure of Confucius emerged against a background of political disorder. China was politically unified during the latter half of the 3d century BC by the state of Qin (Ch'in). In 206 BC, power shifted to the HAN dynasty, whose rulers forced the northern invaders to retire behind the GREAT WALL OF CHINA, reduced Korea to vassal status, annexed Tonkin and Yue, and pushed Chinese political influence into Central Asia.

Early Developments in Southeast Asia, Korea, and Japan. With the exception of the Vietnamese, the peoples of Southeast Asia developed important cultural contacts with India. Korea and Japan were closer to the center of Chinese power and culture and were much influenced by Chinese patterns.

The arrival of American warships in Tokyo Bay in 1854 is portrayed in this Japanese print. The U.S. government dispatched Commodore Matthew C. Perry to establish commercial relations with Japan. Perry's show of U.S. naval strength persuaded the Japanese to open their ports of Shimoda and Hakodate to U.S. trade.

Settled agriculture is thought to have originated in Southeast Asia. Before the Christian era, Austroasiatic Mon tribes migrated south from China into the heart of the Southeast Asian mainland and established commercial and cultural ties with India to the west. On the eastern shores of the Gulf of Siam, the Malay Funanese participated in the north-south seaborne trade, while the Malay Chams established the state of Champa on the lower coast of Annam. The Khmer later pushed down the Mekong Valley from South China, overcame or absorbed the Funanese, and created a major Buddhist cultural center on the eventual site of Angkor. The Khmer Empire lasted from the 6th to the 15th century AD. From the 6th century AD and until about 835, the Tibetan Pyu people moved into northern Burma and established overland contacts with India. After the Pyu capital was destroyed by Thai raiders in 835, leadership among the Tibeto-Burmese peoples passed to the Burmese, who unified Burma in the 10th century with their capital at Pagan. Thai occupation of the upper Mekong Valley occurred considerably later than the Tibetan intrusions into northern Burma. The Thai capital of Ayutthia, destroyed by the Burmese in 1569, was as thoroughly Buddhist-oriented as Pagan or Angkor.

Tungusic tribes migrated into the Korean peninsula by the 4th century BC. China held (108 BC–AD 313) parts of northwestern Korea until driven out by the Koguryo, one of three rival Korean kingdoms. The Buddhist Silla dynasty unified the peninsula in the 660s. The Koryo dynasty that replaced (936) it was overthrown (1392) by

This map illustrates Western influence in Asia at the beginning of the 20th century. European powers—particularly Britain, France, and the Netherlands controlled large areas of the continent until World War II disrupted colonial rule and strengthened nationalist movements.

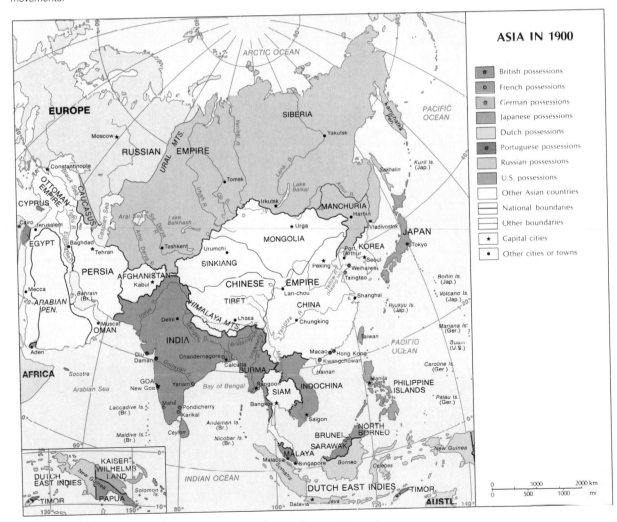

Mohandas K. Gandhi, known as the Mahatma (Great Soul), is regarded as the architect of India's independence movement. Preaching religious tolerance and civil disobedience, Gandhi prevailed upon Great Britain to grant India its independence in 1947.

the neo-Confucianist Yi, who later paid tribute to Manchu-dominated China.

A unified Japanese state, ruled by the tribal leaders of Yamamoto, emerged in about the 4th century AD. Chinese influence reached its height from the 6th to the 9th century. In the 12th century and from the 15th to the late 16th century, Japan was divided into autonomous and warring aristocratic estates. Soon after the establishment (1603) of the TOKUGAWA shogunate, it entered a period of total seclusion.

Period of Nomadic Invasions. From the early centuries AD until the 17th century, a series of nomadic peoples established dominance over large parts of the continent.

The Rise of Islam in Western Asia. From the 7th century, Muslim ARABS embarked on an impressive expansion. Damascus became the capital of the Arab CALIPHATE in 661 and Baghdad in 762. Seaborne expeditions con-

quered the Sind valley of northwestern India in 712 and soon dominated the Indian Ocean. Muslim armies also overran North Africa and most of Spain.

When Arab control weakened in the late 700s, Muslim leadership centered for a time in Persia. In 1055 a Muslim Turkish people, the SELJUKS, seized Baghdad and came to dominate the entire Near East. Their empire was destroyed by the invasions of GENGHIS KHAN and his MONGOL hordes in the early 13th century. Late in the 14th century, Turko-Mongol hordes under TIMUR ravaged Persia and Mesopotamia.

The Ottoman TURKS completed the overthrow of the Byzantine Empire by the capture of Constantinople in 1453. The OTTOMAN EMPIRE, which survived until 1918, came to dominate the Near East (except Persia), North Africa, and southeastern Europe.

Turkic and Mongol Raiding in the South and East. The Afghan ruler MAHMUD OF GHAZNI invaded northern India about 1000. The DELHI SULTANATE (established 1206), the first Muslim state in India, prepared the way for the more lasting Mongol conquests that established the MOGUL Empire in the 16th century.

From the time of Han rule (206 BC–AD 220), China's heartland continued little changed; foreign invader-rulers tended to become sinicized. China attained its peak of power under the T'ANG dynasty (AD 618–906). A southern Song (Sung) dynasty (1127–1279) took over from the successor Northern Song dynasty (960–1127) and created a second cultural golden age. KUBLAI KHAN's thoroughly sinicized Mongol YUAN dynasty was followed (1368–1644) by the indigenous MING. The Ming were overthrown by the invading Manchus.

From the time of Kublai Khan, Mongol bands raided much of Eastern Asia outside of China. Mongol tribesmen continued to control portions of TIBET and the border areas of TURKISTAN long after the Mongol withdrawal from China proper in 1368.

Asia and the West. The Portuguese reached Calicut, India, by 1498 and later extended their influence over the coasts of India and Ceylon and eastward to the MOLUCCAS. Spain acquired territories in the Philippines, while the Dutch directed their attention mainly to the Moluccas and Java. Like the Dutch, Britain and France established

These saluting Chinese Communist troops cooperated with the Nationalist Chinese Army in resisting the Japanese invasion during World War II. Led by Mao Zedong and Lin Biao, Communist forces won control of China in 1949, forcing the Kuomintang army under Generalissimo Chiang Kai-shek to flee to the neighboring island of Taiwan.

U.S. troops were sent to support the government of South Vietnam, an ally by treaty, when the activities of Communist Viet Cong guerrillas were interpreted as an attack on that nation. Two years after U.S. combat troops were withdrawn in 1973, South Vietnam surrendered to the Communists and is presently part of the Socialist Republic of Vietnam.

East India Companies (see EAST INDIA COMPANY, BRITISH; EAST INDIA COMPANY, DUTCH; EAST INDIA COMPANY, FRENCH) to exploit trading opportunities; the British under Robert CLIVE gradually attained a dominant position in southern India. China and Japan escaped major European intervention during this early period, but parts of Northern and Central Asia were colonized by Russians.

By the end of the 18th century the first substantial expansion of European control in Asia had begun. The British occupied Ceylon in 1815 and totally annexed Burma by 1886. Meanwhile, after suppression of the INDIAN MUTINY of 1857, the British government assumed direct rule over India. Farther east, the British founded Singapore in 1819, and the Dutch gradually extended their control over Indonesia. After 1874 the British asserted sovereignty over the entire Malay peninsula; they established protectorates over northern Borneo in 1888.

In Southeast Asia, Siam (now Thailand) alone managed to keep its independence. French attention focused on Vietnam, where national unity had been achieved only in 1802. France also took control of Cambodia (1863) and Laos (1893), which were consolidated with Vietnam to form the colony of Indochina. The United States took possession of the Philippines in 1898 after defeating Spain in the SPANISH-AMERICAN WAR.

Even China fell victim to European intrusion. Although it was never actually colonized, it suffered extreme humiliation. Japan's isolation ended when it was forced to accept a commercial treaty in 1853–54. The ensuing political uproar led to the overthrow of the Tokugawa shogunate and the resumption of imperial authority in the MEIJI RESTORATION of 1868. Japan then pursued an expansionist foreign policy. After defeating China in the first SINO-JAPANESE WAR (1894–95), Japan assumed a virtual protectorate over Korea (formally annexing it in 1910) and forced China to cede Taiwan. Japan also defeated Russia in the RUSSO-JAPANESE WAR (1904–05).

Meanwhile, Russia acquired territories in northern Asia and took over Turkistani SAMARKAND and Bhukara in 1868 and Khiva in 1873. In Western Asia the British seized ADEN in 1839 and later acquired a controlling interest in the Suez Canal. At the oubreak of WORLD WAR I in 1914, most of Asia was under European or U.S. domination, although Asian resistance to such domination had already begun.

Asian Nationalism. Early Asian nationalist movements and efforts at modernization were usually directed against the traditional mores of their own societies as well as against colonialism. China's KUOMINTANG initiated the revolution of 1911 that led to the downfall of the Manchu dynasty, but the subsequent conflict between the Nationalists and Communists aided the Japanese occupation (1931–32) of Manchuria.

World War I had meanwhile produced enormous repercussions in Western Asia. It led to the final breakup of the Ottoman Empire in 1918 and the establishment of the Republic of Turkey in 1923. The Arab provinces of the former empire became virtual colonies of Britain (Palestine, Transjordan, Iraq) and France (Syria and Lebanon). Iraq gained formal independence in 1921 but, like the others, remained under European domination until World War II. In Persia, REZA SHAH PAHLAVI deposed the conservative Qajar dynasty in 1925. Adjacent Central Asian territories became separate republics within the USSR after the Bolshevik Revolution in 1917; Mongolia, which had separated (1911) from China, also came under Soviet influence.

The Impact of World War II. WORLD WAR II permanently ended direct Western domination of Asia. Following Japan's lightning conquest of Southeast Asia in 1942, the British, French, and Dutch found it impossible to recover control, despite Japan's eventual defeat in 1945. The Philippines gained independence in 1946 and India (partitioned into predominantly Hindu India and predominantly Muslim Pakistan) in 1947. In 1948, Britain granted independence to Burma and Ceylon (now Sri Lanka). The Dutch withdrew from Indonesia in 1949, and a Communist-led revolution drove the French from Indochina in 1954. Korea gained formal independence in 1948, with a Communist government in the North and a non-Communist government in the South. In 1949 another Communist regime was established in China; the Chinese Nationalists were forced to retreat to Taiwan. During and soon after World War II, France and Britain relinquished their interwar mandates in the Middle East. The incorporation of most of the mandate of PALESTINE into the new Jewish state of Israel (1948), however, was bitterly opposed by the Arab states.

Recent Developments. In addition to a series of ARAB-ISRAELI WARS, the inclusion of largely Chinese Singapore in the Malaysian federation proved short-lived (1963–65), and one of the INDIA-PAKISTAN WARS led to independence (1971) for Bangladesh. Insurgencies in Burma (now Myanmar), Indonesia, Malaysia, and the Philippines met with less success than those in Indochina, where the United States became involved in the VIETNAM WAR as it had been in the KOREAN WAR. Cyprus was forcibly partitioned (1975) into Greek and Turkish sectors, once-peaceful Lebanon became a battleground of warring factions, and Soviet forces occupied (1979–89) Afghanistan. Nowhere was the continuation of outside involvement in the region more evident than in the international reaction to the Iraqi occupation of Kuwait, which led to war in 1991.

See also: CHINA, HISTORY OF; INDIA, HISTORY OF; JAPAN, HISTORY OF; KOREA, HISTORY OF; MIDDLE EAST; articles on Asian countries.

Asia Minor   see ANATOLIA, ANCIENT; TURKEY

Asian Americans

Asian Americans are Americans whose origins are traced to countries of Asia and the Pacific Islands. Also called Oriental Americans or Pacific Americans according to their geographic origins, they represent diverse peoples with differing historical, linguistic, and social backgrounds. The major population groups originate from three areas: (1) East Asia—Chinese, Japanese, and Koreans; (2) Southeast Asia—Cambodians, Laotians, and Vietnamese; and (3) the Pacific Islands—Fijians, Filipinos, Guamanians, Hawaiians, and Samoans. In 1980 these groups, together with South Asians, numbered an estimated 3.5 million people. The largest groups (in descending order) were Chinese, Filipinos, Japanese, Koreans, Asian Indians, and Vietnamese. Approximately 40 percent of all Asian and Pacific Americans arrived in the United States after 1965, when immigration restrictions were eased. Their largest concentra-

Chinese members of the International Ladies' Garment Workers' Union prepare to participate in the New York City's Labor Day parade. Recent Chinese immigrants have revitalized New York's large Chinatown and other segments of the city's economy.

tions are found in Hawaii and in the West Coast cities of Los Angeles; San Francisco; and Seattle, Wash. Substanial populations also live in other large metropolitan areas, including Chicago, Boston, and New York City.

In common with members of other racial minorities in the United States, Asian Americans have endured a history of racial discrimination and restricted opportunity for full participation in American life. Despite these adversities, the distinctive cultural heritage, industry, and resourcefulness of these people represent a unique contribution to America.

Chinese Americans. The California GOLD RUSH of the 1850s provided the impetus for the initial wave of immigrants from China. These immigrants were also eager to escape problems of overpopulation, poverty, and political unrest in their homeland. They intended to stay only long enough to acquire wealth, but relatively few returned. Many were victimized by employers who paid low wages for long hours of hard labor.

Most Chinese soon gave up mining and turned to the service trades, small businesses, or unskilled labor. An estimated 10,000 Chinese laborers built the transcontinental railroad across the Sierras and the Rockies. Very early the Chinese were targets of racial discrimination. They were prohibited from owning property or securing licenses and were barred from many occupations. In 1882, Congress passed the first of the CHINESE EXCLUSION ACTS to halt further immigration. As a result of their encounter with racial hostility and of their own village tradition of mutual aid, the Chinese congregated in Chinatowns, insular ethnic communities that met their housing, economic, social, and psychological needs. Chinatowns continue to flourish in New York City—where today's largest U.S. Chinatown is located—and other American cities.

With the liberalization of immigration laws in 1965, a new wave of Chinese immigrants arrived, mainly from Hong Kong. In the period between 1960 and 1975, more

Vietnamese fisherman sort their catch of shrimp and crabs in Seabrook, Texas, on Galveston Bay. Refugees from Southeast Asia comprise the newest group of Oriental Americans.

than 200,000 Chinese were admitted, and by 1980 the Chinese American population was more than 800,000. The influx of new immigrants has created problems of economic survival, overcrowding, family tensions, and youth in turmoil; however, the industry and energy of the new immigrants have also revitalized the Chinatowns across the nation.

Today Chinese Americans are a vital force in American urban life. They rank ahead of all other ethnic groups in educational attainment. With more than one-fourth employed in professional and technical fields, they have been called a model minority.

Japanese Americans. The Japanese formed the second wave of immigrants from Asia, beginning in the late 1880s. When Chinese immigration was cut off, Western agriculturists turned to Japan for cheap labor. Most Japanese immigrants were impoverished farmers or young unmarried males wishing to make their fortunes abroad. As with the earlier Chinese, the Japanese also worked in railroad construction, lumbering, and fishing and later moved into service trades and small businesses. With their hard work and efficiency they presented serious competition, and their success angered many Americans. Anti-Japanese legislation followed, such as exclusion from further immigration, denial of land ownership, and segregation of school children.

In response to hostility and discrimination, the Japanese, like the Chinese, found protection and mutual support in "Little Tokyos," ethnic enclaves similar to Chinatowns. They formed their own unions and social organizations, such as the Japanese American Citizens League (founded 1930), to combat anti-Japanese acts. Their efforts, however, were largely ineffectual. Following the attack on Pearl Harbor, the war hysteria of the early 1940s

led to the forced removal and internment of about 110,000 West Coast Japanese (two-thirds of whom were U.S. citizens; see NISEI) in concentration camps in the American interior.

After World War II, American attitudes toward the Japanese changed. A major factor was the brilliant record of the 442d Regimental Combat Team, composed almost entirely of Japanese Americans and the most highly decorated military unit in American history. Today the 700,000 Japanese Americans are among the most acculturated of all Asian Americans in terms of American values and lifestyle. They rank among the highest in education and income of all ethnic groups, and many among them have assumed an increasingly important role in linking the United States with Japan.

Korean Americans. The first Koreans to reach the United States were students and political refugees of the 1880s. Large-scale immigration, mostly of poor farmers, began in 1903 to Hawaiian sugar plantations. In 1905 the Korean government ended further emigration upon learning of harsh working conditions in Hawaii. Thereafter, until 1965, a small number of "picture brides," students, and some political exiles were admitted.

After the quota system was abolished in 1965 immigration from Korea again increased. The 1980 census reported that there were 355,000 Korean Americans living in the United States, in sharp contrast to the 70,000 reported in the 1970 census. Among them are some 5,000 Korean orphans adopted by American families and nearly 30,000 Korean wives of American servicemen.

Korean immigrants are highly educated; more than a third have completed college. Most were previously engaged in professional, technical, and managerial occupations, but in the United States many have been impeded by language difficulties and restricted opportunities. Despite these obstacles Korean Americans are more widely dispersed than any other Asian-American group. More than half are located outside the West Coast and Hawaii, mainly in industrialized urban areas of the Northeast and Middle West.

Filipino Americans. Filipino immigration in many respects has paralleled the Chinese and Japanese immigration that preceded it. Early Filipino immigrants were mostly young men needed to replenish the labor force after the Japanese were excluded in 1924. They worked in seasonal agriculture in California and in salmon canneries in the Northwest and Alaska. They too faced racial discrimination through laws forbidding land ownership, banning of interracial marriages, and imposition of an immigration quota of only 50 per year after 1935. They were frequently refused service in restaurants and barbershops, barred from swimming pools and movies, and forced to live in slum areas.

Filipinos, who were among the lowest-paid farm workers, also found work as busboys, dishwashers, cooks, domestic help, and gardeners. Employment in business and the professions was largely denied by union regluations and state licensing requirements. After World War II some Filipinos found jobs in factories, in trades, and in sales. As late as 1960, most were still employed as unskilled laborers.

Since 1965, when quotas were lifted, the Philippines has led all other nations except Mexico in immigration. Between 1960 and 1970 the Filipino-American population increased from 176,000 to 343,000. At the time of the 1980 census there were 775,000, surpassing the Japanese, and following the Chinese, as the second largest Asian-American group. About 85 percent of Filipino Americans lived in urban areas in 1980, compared to 5 percent in 1940.

The new wave of Filipino immigrants has consisted largely of professionals and single women. By 1970 Filipino women had attained higher median levels of education than the national average for all other women. This and other factors have contributed to a rapid improvement in the socioeconomic status of the Filipino-American community.

Pacific-Islander Americans. The major groups of Pacific-Islander Americans consist of Guamanians, Hawaiians, and Samoans. Approximately 32,000 Guamanians, 167,000 Hawaiians, and 42,000 Samoans were living in the continental United States in the 1980s. Many Pacific Islanders came to the United States during the late 1930s and the 1940s by enlisting in the military services. With their families they settled mainly around military bases in San Diego, San Francisco, and Long Beach, Calif., and Seattle, Wash. A later migration consisted of Islanders who left home in search of a better life or in pursuit of higher education.

Because of vast differences between the relatively simple agricultural economy and village society of the Islands and the complex industrial urban society in America, many Islanders have had great difficulty in adjusting to their new environment. American institutions such as the public schools, health and welfare agencies, and governmental services have been generally unresponsive to the special needs and circumstances of the Islanders. The survival of Islander communities has largely depended on preservation of traditional social institutions. The extended family has continued to provide support for family members and kin. A traditional system of *matai*, or family chief, maintains a sense of authority and order in Samoan communities. The church, an important center of Islander community life, has helped to perpetuate native traditions.

Southeast-Asian Americans. Southeast Asians are the most recent group to arrive in America. They consist mainly of Cambodian, Laotian, and Vietnamese (many of Chinese descent) refugees who fled from South Vietnam in 1975. About 150,000 refugees were admitted initially, and the exodus has continued. By 1980 an estimated 200,000 or more Southeast-Asian refugees were settled throughout the United States, with concentrations in California, Texas, New York, and Pennsylvania. The refugees were mainly young (two-thirds under the age of 24), many arrived in family groups, and 40 percent were Roman Catholics. Two-thirds originated from urban settings. Many were highly educated and had occupied important positions in government, the military, business, and industry in south Vietnam. In the United States, most refu-

gees have had to settle for low-level, low-paying jobs offering little prospect of advancement.

Since their arrival the Southeast-Asian refugees have formed more than 100 ethnic organizations offering job placement, English-language training, recreation, and other forms of mutual aid and support. Like the Chinese and the Japanese, Southeast-Asian Americans have relied heavily on ethnic-group solidarity and self-help for their survival.

Asimov, Isaac   The Russian-born American biochemist and writer Isaac Asimov, b. Jan. 2, 1920, has written prolifically on history and science. *Asimov's New Guide to Science* (rev. ed., 1984) is ranked among the best books of science written for nonscientists. But Asimov is best known for his science fiction, including *I Robot* (1950), *The Foundation Trilogy* (1951–52), and *The Gods Themselves* (1972). Two volumes of his autobiography have apppeared: *In Memory Yet Green* (1979) and *In Joy Still Felt* (1980). Asimov has been professor of biochemistry at Boston University since 1949.

Isaac Asimov, a Russian-American biochemist and educator, is among the most prolific of contemporary authors. His literary fame is largely a result of his imaginative science-fiction writing and his ability to explain difficult concepts of modern science to the lay reader.

Photo Jill Krementz © 1979

Asmara [az-mar'-uh]   Asmara, or Asmera (1984 est. pop., 275,385), is the capital of the autonomous region of Eritrea in northern Ethiopia. The city lies about 65 km (40 mi) southwest of Massawa, inland from the Red Sea, at an altitude of 2,365 m (7,760 ft). It is the center of a fertile region, but drought and civil strife have disrupted the economy. Asmara was occupied by Italy in 1889 and became the capital of Italian Eritrea in 1900. It was the principal base for the Italian attack on Ethiopia in 1935–36. The city was under British military administration from 1941 until 1952, when it was federated into Ethiopia by a United Nations resolution; in 1962 it was forcibly annexed by Ethiopia.

Asoka, Emperor of India [uh-soh'-kuh]   Asoka, d. 232 BC, one of the greatest emperors of India, made

Buddhism the state religion of his realm. The third ruler of the MAURYA dynasty, he was the son of Bindusara and grandson of Chandragupta Maurya. As crown prince, Asoka was viceroy of Taxila and Ujjain. He became emperor on his father's death (c.273 BC) and by the conquest of Kalinga, now Orissa state, c.261 BC, consolidated his kingdom to include most of northern and central India as well as what are now Afghanistan and Baluchistan. His influence extended to southern India and Sri Lanka. After seeing the horrors of war in Kalinga, Asoka converted from Brahmanism to Buddhism and ruled according to Buddhist principles of philanthropy and compassion. He relaxed harsh laws, created an ordered economic expansion, established principles of justice and morality, and pursued a foreign policy that renounced war.

Many of Asoka's edicts were engraved on pillars and rocks erected throughout India. More than 30 of these survive and are the chief source of information on Asoka's reign. He strongly influenced the development of Buddhism, not only by making it the state religion but also by sending Buddhist missionaries to other countries, particularly Sri Lanka, which became the center of classical Buddhism. Asoka's empire was ended only 50 years after his death by a Brahman-led Hindu reaction that virtually extinguished Buddhism in India.

asp The term *asp* is applied to various snakes: the asp viper, *Vipera aspis*, of Europe; the North African asps of the genus *Cerastes*; and the Egyptian cobra, *Naja haje*. The asp is probably most famous as the instrument of death in CLEOPATRA's suicide. The species of snake used is in question, but the most likely candidate is the Egyptian cobra, whose bite is relatively painless and quick in its lethal effect. This snake was worshiped by the ancient Egyptians and appears on the headdresses of their sculptures. Political prisoners were often allowed to commit suicide by using the Egyptian cobra rather than face torture. This species, which has a much narrower hood than its Asian relatives, is widely distributed in Africa.

See also: COBRA; VIPER.

asparagus [uh-spar'-uh-guhs] Asparagus, *Asparagus officinalis*, is a perennial herb of the lily family, Liliaceae, that is cultivated for its tender spring shoots. Indigenous to coastal areas of Europe and Asia, it is widely grown in the United States. Propagation is mostly by seed. The first harvest is made in 2 or 3 years; well-maintained fields produce for 15 years or more.

With suitable environmental conditions, buds on underground rhizomes (rootlike elements) develop into edible spears after dormancy. Spears are harvested when they are 20 to 25 cm (8 to 10 in) long and when leaves tightly clasp the tip. Daily harvests are required when temperatures exceed 25° C (77° F). The harvest season extends for 2 to 3 months.

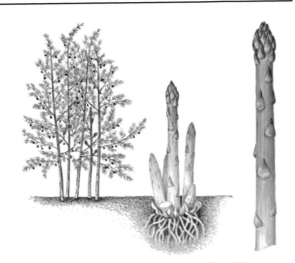

The asparagus is a popular garden vegetable. The edible spears (middle and right) are harvested in spring and early summer, after which the plant (left) grows taller and leafs out.

asparagus fern The asparagus ferns, genus *Asparagus*, are any of 100 to 300 species of perennial herbs, woody vines, or shrubs belonging to the lily family, Liliaceae. Although they are not true ferns, many produce fernlike foliage. Native to the Old World but widely cultivated, they are grown as foliage houseplants. The flowers are white, greenish, or yellowish.

The species most commonly called asparagus fern, or lace fern, *A. setaceus*, has leaf clusters arranged in a flat, triangular spray. Baby smilax, *A. asparagoides myrtifolius*, has broad, glossy leaves. Sprenger asparagus, *A. densiflorus sprengeri*, has drooping stems covered with needlelike leaves. Sickle thorn asparagus, *A. falcatus*, has glossy leaves.

aspartame see SWEETENER, ARTIFICIAL

Aspen [as'-pin] Aspen (1990 pop., 5,049) is a town in west central Colorado, located on the Roaring Fork River at an elevation of 2,400 m (7,875 ft). It is the seat of Pitkin County. Founded as a silver-mining camp in 1878, the town declined when silver prices dropped in 1893. Today Aspen is a fashionable ski resort and the site of the Aspen Institute for Humanistic Studies, the Aspen Music School, and an annual music festival.

aspen Aspens are deciduous hardwood trees belonging to the genus *Populus*, which also includes cottonwoods and balsam poplars, within the willow family (Salicaceae). Aspens can be distinguished from cottonwoods and balsam poplars by their buds, which are essentially nonresinous. Bigtooth aspens, *P. grandidentata*, are medium-sized trees found in the northern quarter of the

The quaking, or American, aspen is so named because the slightest breeze causes its foliage to tremble. The aspen, about 6–18 m (20–60 ft) tall, is used commercially for pulpwood.

United States and adjacent Canada. The bark is greenish, smooth, and thin and becomes dark brown. Leaves are elliptical or nearly round, 6.4 to 10 cm (2.5 to 4 in) long, and coarsely toothed with curved teeth. Quaking aspens, *P. tremuloides*, are small- to medium-sized. The bark is yellowish green or whitish on large trunks that become black with furrows and flat ridges.

Aspergillus *Aspergillus* is a widely distributed fungal genus, subdivision Ascomycotina (see FUNGI). About 80 species are known, many of which form MOLDS on exposed foods. They are also common contaminants of cultures in laboratories.

Several *Aspergillus* species cause respiratory disorders, particularly in birds but also in other animals—infrequently including humans, in whom the disease can produce symptoms resembling those of tuberculosis. These same species can also cause serious human ear infections. *A. flavus*, which contaminates stored foods such as rice, wheat, peanuts, and corn under hot, humid conditions, produces a toxin called aflatoxin. This toxin has caused liver cancers in test animals. Strong circumstantial evidence indicates that it can also trigger liver cancer in humans with chronic hepatitis B.

asphalt see TAR, PITCH, AND ASPHALT

asphyxia [as-fix'-see-uh] Asphyxia is unconsciousness due to suffocation or other interference with oxygenation of the blood. Causes include obstruction of the windpipe by food, foreign bodies, vomit, mucus, or swollen vocal cords; lack of air; crushing injuries to the chest; and anaphylactic shock in severely allergic individuals. Late stages are characterized by bluish purple skin color, dilated pupils, increasingly irregular breathing, and loss of consciousness.

aspirin [as'-prin] Aspirin is the drug most widely used as an ANALGESIC, or pain reliever; antipyretic, or fever reducer; and anti-inflammatory agent. Its activity is based on chemicals called salicylates. It has become the standard by which all other analgesics and antipyretics are measured.

Aspirin is most effective in relieving slight to moderately severe pain, particularly headache, muscle aches, and joint pains. It is less effective against deep-seated pain originating in internal organs. Because it suppresses inflammatory processes while relieving pain, it is still the treatment of choice for arthritis and related disorders. Aspirin reduces fever by increasing blood flow to the surface, thereby promoting sweating and heat loss from the body. There is evidence that all the therapeutic effects of aspirin involve the inhibition of the synthesis of prostaglandins, fatty acids with hormonelike functions. This effect has been linked with the prevention of blood clots in potential stroke and heart-attack victims.

Aspirin is considered a relatively safe drug. Its chief drawback is its ability to irritate the lining of the stomach and cause bleeding. In large doses aspirin is toxic, however, causing kidney damage and, in severe cases, death. Aspirin should never be given to children with viral diseases such as chicken pox or influenza. Such use has been associated with occurrences of the sometimes fatal REYE'S SYNDROME.

Asplund, Erik Gunnar [ahs'-pluhnd] Erik Gunnar Asplund, b. Stockholm, Sept. 22, 1885, d. Oct. 20, 1940, had become the leading figure in the development of the modern style in Scandinavian architecture by the time of his death. The simplified classicism of his early period found ultimate expression in the Stockholm City Library (1924–27). His festive designs for the Stockholm Exhibition buildings (1930; destroyed) led to the spread of the INTERNATIONAL STYLE throughout Scandinavia.

Asquith, Herbert Henry, 1st Earl of Oxford and Asquith [as'-kwith] Herbert Henry Asquith, b. Sept. 12, 1852, d. Feb. 15, 1928, was prime minister of Great Britain's last Liberal cabinet. Born into the middle class, he studied at Oxford University and became a successful London barrister. Following election to Parliament in 1886, Asquith gained recognition as a powerful speaker and debater, as Charles Stewart PARNELL's counsel before a judicial commission (1889), and as a leader of the Liberal party's imperialist faction during the SOUTH AFRICAN WAR. He served as home secretary (1892–95) and as Sir Henry CAMPBELL-BANNERMAN's chancellor of the exchequer (1905–08).

As party leader and prime minister from 1908, Asquith presided over a distinguished cabinet that legislated on old-age pensions; a miners' minimum wage; sickness, accident, and unemployment insurance; and protection for trade unions. The introduction of heavy taxation of the wealthy provoked a crisis when the House of

Herbert H. Asquith was Liberal prime minister of Great Britain from 1908 to 1916. His government brought about substantial social reform and a reduction in the House of Lords' power.

Lords rejected the budget, and the government, in turn, tried to end the veto power of the Lords. After two general elections in 1910, the government achieved its aim by passing the Parliament Act of 1911. Asquith's premiership is also associated with agitation by militant socialists, women suffragists, and Irish Unionists; the latter, by opposing the third HOME RULE BILL (1912), brought Ireland to the brink of civil war in 1914.

After the beginning of World War I, Asquith came under criticism for apathetic leadership. He survived a political crisis in May 1915 and reconstituted his government as a coalition. He resigned in December 1916, and was succeeded by David LLOYD GEORGE. Asquith led the strife-torn Liberal party until his retirement in 1926. In 1925 he went to the House of Lords as earl of Oxford and Asquith.

ass Asses, the smallest members of the horse family, Equidae, comprise the subgenus *Asinus* of the single

The Asian wild ass differs from its larger relative the horse by having long ears, a stiff mane, and a loud bray.

horse genus, *Equus*. The domesticated ass is also called a DONKEY or burro. The animals stand 1 to 1.5 m (3 to 5 ft) at the shoulder and have a brush-tipped tail about 45 cm (17 in) long; their weight ranges up to 260 kg (570 lb). The coat is gray to reddish brown, and the wiry mane is dark. The ears are long and the feet small, with sharp hooves. Wild asses live in desert plains, where they can survive on little food or water for long periods. The ass of northern and eastern Africa, *E. asinus*, has been domesticated for centuries as a sturdy pack animal; introduced into the Americas, it has formed feral herds there. The Asian species *E. hemionus*, called the kulan or onager, is found from Syria to Manchuria; a Tibetan species, *E. kiang*, is known as the kiang.

Assad, Hafez al- [hah-fez ul ah-sahd'] Hafez al-Assad, b. *c.*1928, was elected president of Syria in 1971 and reelected in 1978 and 1985. A member of Syria's Alawite minority, he joined the BAATH PARTY in 1946 and was named air force commander after Baath took power in 1963. He served as defense minister from 1966 to 1970, when he seized the premiership. Assad has faced periodic opposition at home from the fundamentalist Muslim Brotherhood. To advance Syrian interests, he has maintained close ties with the USSR, aided Iran during the long Iran-Iraq war (1980–88), intervened militarily and diplomatically in Lebanon since 1976, and backed Palestinian factions opposed to Yasir ARAFAT. Assad was among the "hard-line" Arab leaders who denounced the 1979 Egyptian-Israeli peace treaty. He has strengthened Syria militarily and has demanded the return of the Israeli-occupied Golan Heights to Syria. At the end of 1990, following the Iraqi invasion of Kuwait, Assad sent Syrian troops to Saudi Arabia, where they joined the U.S.-led anti-Iraqi coalition.

Assam [uh-sam'] Assam, a northeast Indian state situated mainly in the Brahmaputra River valley, has an area of about 78,523 km^2 (30,318 mi^2) and a population of 23,000,000 (1985 est.). The economy is based on agriculture, particularly rice and tea cultivation. Dispur is Assam's capital.

Assam, a word referring to the kingdom of the Ahoms, who ruled the region from 1228 to 1816, was known as Kamarupa in antiquity. After a decade of Burmese invasions Assam came under British rule (1826–1947). After independence traditional Assam was gradually truncated, beginning with the cession of most of the district of Sylhet to Pakistan in 1947. In 1963, NAGALAND became a separate state, and in 1972 the state of Meghalaya and the union territories (now states) of Arunachal Pradesh and Mizoram were also separated. Following attacks by the student-led Assamese movement on Bangladeshi Muslim immigrants, a 1985 accord stated that immigrants who arrived after 1971 were to be deported. Subsequently, there were demands for curbs on migration from elsewhere in India.

Assassins [uh-sas'-inz] Assassins is the Western name for a group of fanatical ISMAILIS, a sect of the Muslim SHIITES, who worked for the creation of a new FATIMID caliphate from 1094 to 1273. On the death (1094) of al-Mustansir, the Fatimid caliphate in Egypt was split between his two sons; the Assassins were partisans of his deposed eldest son, Nizar. From mountain fortresses in northern Persia, they waged a war of terror against orthodox Muslims and the Christian Crusaders. They often murdered prominent individuals; hence, *assassin* in English came to mean a politically motivated murderer.

The extremism of the Assassins began to moderate in the 13th century. They were destroyed in Persia by the Mongols (1256) and in Syria by the MAMELUKES (1273).

assault and battery Assault is a threat against a person, and battery is physical attack. For example, a person who waves a fist in front of another person and threatens to beat that person is guilty of assault; a person who strikes another person with a fist is guilty of battery. The victim can sue the assailant for damages (see TORT), and the state may also prosecute for misdemeanor.

In a civil case alleging assault, the victim must prove that he or she was in imminent danger of injury or had reason to think so. Abusive language alone does not constitute an assault. Threatening with a pistol may be an assault, even if the weapon is unloaded. In a case of battery the amount of contact or force is unimportant, for any touching of another person in an angry, vengeful, rude, or insolent manner constitutes a battery.

Some jurisdictions distinguish the felony of aggravated assault, usually defined as assault with intention to commit some other crime, such as armed robbery.

assembly language Assembly language is the name given to any low-level COMPUTER LANGUAGE that is tailored to the architecture of a specific microprocessor. Although all assembly languages closely resemble one another, each microprocessor has a different configuration of memory addresses—analogous to mail slots—where information can be stored in binary form, a series of ones and zeros, that is difficult to understand. Assembly languages are a more-readable shorthand form of binary code. Assembly programs are, however, still more difficult to write and read than programs in high-level computer languages such as BASIC or Pascal, although assembly programs run much faster. The first assembly languages were developed in the early 1950s.

assembly line The assembly line is a system of manufacturing in which each worker performs a specialized operation on an unfinished product as it is moved by CONVEYOR past his or her station. The system is designed to achieve an uninterrupted production process by organizing and integrating the various operations. The assembly-line technique is primarily an American development.

The concept of a continuous production process, for example, was the essential feature of the system of conveyor belts and chutes installed in 1784 by Oliver EVANS in his Delaware flour mill.

The second major U.S. contribution to the evolution of the assembly line was the utilization of interchangeable parts for use in varied products. Henry Ford (see FORD family) demonstrated how these features could be combined. Early in 1913, Ford began using a moving assembly line in the manufacture of magnetos, with a substantial reduction in assembly time. This success prompted Ford to extend the assembly-line system to the production of the entire automobile. (see AUTOMOTIVE INDUSTRY; MANUFACTURING, HISTORY OF).

This development was soon adopted by the manufacturers of an increasing number of products. The assembly line became the foundation of modern mass production.

Concern over the possible adverse effects of assembly-line work has increased in recent years. In 1973 the U.S. government released a study citing the negative effects of the "dehumanizing" assembly line.

The advent of the robotized assembly line, however, may eventually eliminate human participation altogether (see ROBOT).

Assiniboin [uh-sin'-uh-boyn] The Assiniboin, an Indian tribe of the Great Plains of North America, separated from their neighbors the Dakota and Lakota (Teton) Sioux probably by the mid-1600s. They often formed alliances with the Algonquian-speaking Cree and battled other Siouan-speakers—the Sioux, Crow, Hidatsa, and Mandan. A typical Plains warrior society, the Assiniboin relied upon the buffalo for food, shelter, and clothing, and upon the horse for mobility in war and the hunt. The SUN DANCE was their most sacred ritual, and the long feathered headdress indicated male status and prestige. The women decorated skins and clothing with porcupine quills. The men depicted their war deeds on their TEPEES and on circular war shields.

The Assiniboin call themselves the Nakota, meaning "the allies" or "the people." They number about 3,000 in Canada and 2,200 in the United States. The largest group, now known as Stoney Indians, resides west of Calgary in Alberta. Another large group lives primarily on the Fort Peck and Fort Belknap reservations in Montana.

Assiniboine River [uh-sin'-uh-boyn] The Assiniboine River, 965 km (600 mi) long, rises in southeastern Saskatchewan, Canada, and flows south and east into Manitoba, where it joins the Red River at Winnipeg. It is navigable for about 480 km (300 mi), and its main ports are Brandon and Winnipeg. The river was discovered by the French in 1736 and named for the Assiniboin Indians.

Assisi [ahs-see'-zee] Assisi (1981 pop., 19,000) is a town in Perugia province in central Italy. The home of

Saint FRANCIS OF ASSISI (1182–1226), it is a religious and tourist center in the Apennines. It was an independent commune in the Middle Ages when the Convent of Saint Francis was built.

associationism Associationism is the psychological theory that all mental activity begins with simple ideas that are both compounded into complex ideas and succeeded by other ideas in the stream of consciousness according to certain laws of association. It is most familiar as the psychological doctrine of empiricist philosophers of the 18th and 19th centuries, although similar ideas were postulated much earlier (see EMPIRICISM).

In recent decades in a related approach called *connectionism*, cognitive scientists have explored the neural architecture that enables the brain to make connections between stored memories and new sensory input, as when a person is able to pick a face out of a crowd. Attempts have been made to replicate the brain's neural connections in computers.

associative law SEE ALGEBRA; ARITHMETIC

Assumption of Mary In Roman Catholic doctrine the Assumption means that MARY, the mother of Jesus, was taken (assumed) bodily into heavenly glory when she died. In the Orthodox church the *koimesis*, or dormition ("falling asleep"), of the Virgin began to be commemorated on August 15 in the 6th century. The observance gradually spread to the West, where it became known as the feast of the Assumption. By the 13th century the belief was accepted by most Catholic theologians, and it was a popular subject with Renaissance and baroque painters. The Assumption was declared a dogma of the Roman Catholic faith by Pope Pius XII in 1950.

Assyria [uh-sir'-ee-uh] Assyria was an ancient name for that part of MESOPOTAMIA on the upper Tigris River now included in the northern Iraqi provinces of Ninawa, Sulaymaniya, Tamim, and Irbil. Watered by the Tigris and its tributaries, the Greater and Lesser Zab, ancient Assyria stretched from just west of the Tigris to the Zagros Mountains on the east and from about 34° north latitude up to the hills of Armenia.

Assyria took its name from its original capital, Ashur, situated just north of the junction of the Tigris and the Lesser Zab. Its founders were a Semitic-speaking people who arrived from the southwest shortly after 2000 BC. During the Old Assyrian period (c.1900–1550 BC) the territory was unified by a series of vigorous rulers, and its influence was felt along the middle Euphrates and westward into central ANATOLIA (modern Turkey), where Assyrian traders established commercial colonies. By 1800 BC, however, the coming of the HITTITES drove the Assyrians out of Anatolia, and the rise of Babylon under Hammurabi soon afterward caused a contraction of Assyrian power in Mesopotamia. By 1550 BC, Assyria was part of the

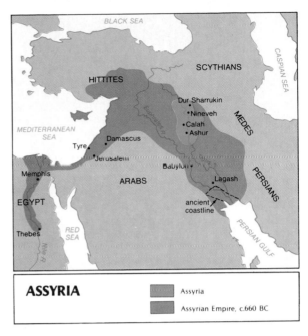

Centered on the upper Tigris River in Mesopotamia, the Assyrian Empire grew to control much of southwest Asia at the height of its influence during the 7th century BC.

Kingdom of Mitanni; it did not regain independence until the collapse of that regime about 1365 BC.

After a slow revival, Assyrian strength quickened after 1000 BC and reached a new peak in the 9th century under Ashurnasirpal II (r. 883–59) and SHALMANESER III (r. 858–24), whose campaigns brought plunder and tribute from little kingdoms westward all the way to the Mediterranean Sea. After 800 BC this mighty dynasty gradually declined and finally collapsed (c.748 BC), but a new era began with the accession of TIGLATH-PILESER III in 745. Babylon was subjected to Assyria, and states to the west were once more made tributary. The formal organization of an empire began with the last Assyrian dynasty, founded by SARGON II. Sargon (r. 721–05), SENNACHERIB (r. 705–681), and ESARHADDON (r. 681–68) made conquests that brought ELAM, MEDIA, Persia, Babylonia, Syria, Palestine, and even part of Egypt under Assyrian rule. A recession commenced under ASHURBANIPAL (r. 668–26), and by 612 the Medes and Babylonians had destroyed the city of NINEVEH and brought an end to the Assyrian Empire.

The four successive capitals of Assyria—Ashur (Qalat Sherqat); Calah (Nimrud), founded by Ashurnasirpal II; Dur Sharrukin (KHORSABAD), the fortress city of Sargon II; and Nineveh, selected by Sennacherib—have all been excavated by archaeologists, revealing the brilliance of Assyrian civilization. Despite the notorious brutality (and efficiency) of the Assyrian army, which the Assyrians themselves assiduously publicized, the great accomplishments of ancient Assyria in art and architecture, and also in literature, are universally recognized.

Actor and dancer Fred Astaire, seen here with his most famous dance partner, Ginger Rogers, in a scene from The Gay Divorcée *(1934), enjoyed acclaim as America's most accomplished dancer. A perfectionist, Astaire insisted that his entire figure appear on screen during all his dance routines.*

Astaire, Fred Fred Astaire was the stage name of Frederick Austerlitz, b. Omaha, Nebr., May 10, 1899, d. June 22, 1987, who brought new distinction to musical comedy with his elegant and witty song and dance routines. First teamed with his sister Adele on the stage—they made their Broadway debut in 1918, dancing in the musical *Over the Top*—Astaire turned to Hollywood on her retirement from show business, making his initial screen appearance in *Dancing Lady* (1933). His greatest success came when he was paired with Ginger ROGERS in a series of romantic comedies featuring their dance numbers, notably *The Gay Divorcée* (1934), *Top Hat* (1935), *Swing Time* (1936), and *Shall We Dance?* (1937). With other partners, Astaire starred in such musicals as *Daddy Longlegs* (1955) and *Funny Face* (1957). He also appeared in dramatic roles. A perfectionist who often choreographed his own dances, he received a special Academy Award in 1949.

Astarte [uh-stahr'-tee] In Near Eastern mythology Astarte was the goddess of fertility and sexual love and of war. Crops, newborn animals, and firstborn children were sacrificed to her to assure fertility. The gazelle, dove, and myrtle were sacred to her. In Phoenician art, Astarte was represented with a cow's horns, symbolizing fertility. Her Babylonian and Greek counterparts were Ishtar and APHRODITE. The Bible refers to Astarte as Ashtoreth, worshiped by the Philistines and, at times, the Israelites.

astatine [as'-tuh-teen] Astatine is a radioactive chemical element, the fifth and final of the HALOGENS, Group VIIA in the periodic table. Its symbol is At, its atomic number is 85, and its atomic weight is 210 (stablest isotope). The name is derived from the Greek *astatos*, meaning "unstable." Astatine is one of the rarest elements in nature, and the Earth's crust is estimated to contain less than 30 g. It was first synthesized in 1940 in a nuclear reaction between alpha particles and bismuth.

Twenty isotopes are known, of which ^{210}At is the longest-lived, with a half-life of 8.3 hours. The melting point of astatine is 302° C, and its boiling point is 337° C. Since it is short-lived, its chemical properties are difficult to investigate, but tracer experiments, in which small amounts of the element are reacted in the presence of iodine, indicate that they are similar to those of iodine. Astatine accumulates in the thyroid gland, and its use has been proposed in the treatment of hyperthyroidism in humans.

aster Asters, genus *Aster*, are any of several large plants, commonly called asters, starworts, Michaelmas daisies, or frost flowers. The genus, in the family Compositae, includes approximately 250 to 500 species. Asters are found chiefly in North America, with some species extending into South America; others are distributed throughout Europe and Asia.

The asters are mostly coarse-growing, leafy-stemmed plants that are occasionally somewhat woody at the base. Although most are perennials, a few are annuals and biennials. All have alternate, simple leaves that are untoothed or toothed but rarely lobed. Asters produce large clusters of flowering heads, although a few species have single heads. Each head contains a central disk of small yellow (sometimes orange, purple, or white), tubular flowers surrounded by numerous showy, ray flowers ranging from blue or violet shades of purple, to red, pink, or white. The ray flowers are never yellow.

The asters are a striking, common component of the flora of late summer and fall. They grow profusely along roadsides and in vacant lots, as well as in prairies and forests. They are also excellent garden ornamentals.

The China aster, *Callistephus cinensis*, is related to the true asters. Native to China, it is a handsome annual herb often grown for its late-summer blooms.

The alpine aster (left) *flourishes in rock gardens. It is native to eastern Europe. The New York aster* (right) *is a North American plant that is popular in cut floral arrangements.*

asteroid   An asteroid is any one of a large number of small solid objects in the SOLAR SYSTEM, sometimes called minor planets. The vast majority are found in a swarm called the asteroid belt, between the orbits of Mars and Jupiter, at average distances of 2.1 to 3.3 astronomical units (AU) from the Sun. CERES, Pallas, and Vesta are the three largest asteroids, having diameters of 1,000, 610, and 540 km (621, 379, and 336 mi). Probably about 500,000 asteroids have diameters greater than 1 km (0.6 mi), and others range down to the size of meteorites. The tiny moons of Mars are thought likely to be asteroids captured by that planet's gravitational field.

Once thought to be debris from a single fragmented planet, asteroids are probably bodies from the first days of the solar system that never grew to planetary size. Most asteroids seen today are probably fragments of once-larger ones, as indicated by their irregular shapes. Some asteroids of the inner solar system may be burned-out comets. The collision of one such object with the Earth 2.3 million years ago has been implicated with the onset of an ice age at that time.

The mineral composition of an asteroid's surface can be inferred from its reflected light. It is estimated that three-quarters of the main-belt asteroids with diameters greater than 50 km (31 mi) have surfaces similar to carbonaceous chondrites and that those of most of the remainder are mixtures of silicates and metallic iron.

asthma   [az'-muh]   Asthma is a respiratory disorder marked by breathing difficulty caused by temporary narrowing of the bronchi, the airways branching from the trachee to the lungs. Attacks usually are brought on by allergic reaction to ANTIGENS such as grass and tree pollens, mold spores, fungi, animal dander, and certain foods but may also be caused by chemical irritants in the atmosphere or by infections of the respiratory tract (see BRONCHITIS). Susceptibility to an asthma attack is based on hyperactivity of the bronchial muscles, which constrict on exposure to one or another of these agents. Research suggests that an enzyme present in the lungs of asthma sufferers may lead to this hypersensitivity by releasing a blood-protein peptide that acts as a potent constrictor of bronchial muscles.

Episodes of asthma vary widely in severity and may last from a few minutes to several days. They may begin at any age but usually occur in childhood. In children, asthma often is associated with eczema, a skin inflammation that may reflect the tendency of the child to develop hypersensitivity reactions. The attacks usually become less frequent and less severe over the years and disappear in about half of all affected children before adulthood. In one form of asthma, called intrinsic asthma, however, the attacks become less frequent and less severe, but recovery between them is less complete. The bronchi in such patients become chronically narrowed, causing a progressive loss of capacity for physical exertion. The prevalence of asthma is only about 1 or 2 percent worldwide but varies greatly from country to country.

In the United States asthma affects about 6.9 percent of children.

Typically, an asthma attack begins within minutes after exposure to a triggering agent. Symptoms include a sensation of tightness in the chest, coughing and wheezing, and difficulty in breathing. Persons having attacks usually find it more difficult to exhale than inhale, which causes overinflation of the chest and impaired lung functions. Attacks that last for hours or days despite treatment are called status asthmaticus. Patients with this condition develop a rapid pulse as the heart attempts to compensate for the lack of oxygen in the blood. They also develop signs of exhaustion and dehydration.

On a long-term basis, asthma usually is managed by determining the agent responsible for the attacks so that the patient can avoid it. When avoidance of allergens is not feasible, patients can sometimes be desensitized by injections of graded doses of the allergen at regular intervals. Relaxation and breathing exercises have also been found helpful. Most asthma attacks can be controlled by the administration of appropriate drugs by injection, orally, or by inhalation of aerosols. Occasionally, oxygen administration or use of a respirator may be required. Asthma attacks can result in death.

Aston, Francis William   The English physicist and chemist Francis William Aston, b. Sept. 1, 1877, d. Nov. 20, 1945, discovered in 1919 that stable elements of low atomic weight are mixtures of ISOTOPES. Using a mass spectrograph (see MASS SPECTROMETRY), which he developed while working with Sir Joseph John THOMSON in Cambridge, and for which he received the 1922 Nobel Prize for chemistry, Aston also found that the masses of most atoms could be expressed as whole numbers when compared with oxygen (mass 16).

Astor   (family)   The Astor family built an immense fortune from the American fur trade, New York City real estate, and other investments. The founder of the fortune, **John Jacob Astor**, born a butcher's son in Waldorf, near Heidelberg, Germany, July 17, 1763, went to London at the age of 16 and emigrated to the United States at the age of 20. He organized the FUR TRADE from the Great Lakes to the Pacific and eventually to the Far East. He also invested profitably in New York City real estate. In 1808 he combined all his holdings into the AMERICAN FUR COMPANY; when he died on Mar. 29, 1848, he was the wealthiest man in the country, with a fortune estimated at more than $20 million. He left $400,000 to establish the Astor Library, now part of the New York Public Library.

John Jacob's son **William Backhouse Astor**, b. Sept. 19, 1792, d. Nov. 24, 1875, directed the building of the Astor Library and, with astute investments in New York City property, came to be known as "the landlord of New York." His son, **John Jacob Astor**, b. June 10, 1822, d. Feb. 22, 1890, was a philanthropist who took a minor part in New York civic and political affairs. William's grandson, **John Jacob Astor** IV, b. July 13, 1864, d. Apr.

15, 1912, built the Astoria section of what later became the Waldorf-Astoria Hotel in New York City. He died in the sinking of the *Titanic*. His mother, originally named Caroline Schermerhorn, was the Mrs. William Astor of legend, queen of New York society's Four Hundred. His cousin, **William Waldorf Astor**, b. Mar. 31, 1848, d. Oct. 18, 1919, built the Waldorf section of the Waldorf-Astoria Hotel and served as U.S. minister to Italy in 1882–85. In 1890 he moved to England and in 1899 became a British subject. He bought the *Pall Mall Gazette* and established the *Pall Mall Magazine*, and was made baron of Hever Castle in 1916 and viscount in 1917.

William Waldorf's elder son, **Waldorf Astor**, the 2d viscount, b. May 19, 1879, d. Sept. 30, 1952, was private secretary to Prime Minister David Lloyd George. From 1919 to 1945 he published *The Observer*, and from 1935 to 1949 he served as chairman of the Royal Institute of International Affairs. His wife was Nancy, Lady Astor. His younger brother, **John Jacob Astor**, b. May 20, 1886, d. July 19, 1971, became chief owner of *The Times* (London) in 1922. In 1956 he was made a baron in his own right.

Astor, Lady   Nancy, Viscountess Astor, b. Danville, Va., May 19, 1879, d. May 2, 1964, became the first woman to sit in Britain's Parliament. Originally named Nancy Witcher Langhorne, in 1906 she married Waldorf Astor, a Conservative member of Parliament. When he succeeded to his father's title in 1919 and entered the House of Lords, she won his seat in Commons and held it until 1945. She worked enthusiastically for temperance and for women's and children's welfare and was known

Lady Nancy Astor is received into Parliament by Arthur Balfour (left) and Prime Minister David Lloyd George (right) in this painting. In 1919 Lady Astor became the first woman to sit in the British House of Commons.

for her outspoken opinions. In the late 1930s, in her country home at Cliveden, she was the focus of a group that favored an appeasement policy toward Nazi Germany. When Britain declared war, however, she strongly supported the war effort.

Astor, Mary   Mary Astor was the stage name of Lucille Vasconcells Langhanke, b. Quincy, Ill., May 3, 1906, d. Sept. 25, 1987, an American screen actress from the 1920s to the 1960s. She played conventional heroines in such silent epics as *Beau Brummel* (1924) and appeared as a *femme fatale* in *Dodsworth* (1936), *Midnight* (1939), *The Great Lie* (1941; Academy Award), and *The Maltese Falcon* (1941).

Astor Place Riot   The Astor Place Riot occurred in New York City on the night of May 10, 1849. It climaxed a longtime rivalry and feud between two famous actors: William Macready, a haughty English tragedian supported by New York's social elite; and Edwin Forrest, the self-made and hot-tempered idol of the masses. As Macready was playing Shakespeare's Macbeth inside the fashionable Astor Place Opera House, rock-hurling b'hoys—Bowery toughs led by the notorious Ned Buntline—stormed the theater. A hundred policemen and militia tried to stop them and finally began firing. The riot resulted in 31 deaths. Those injured in the melee numbered 150.

A 19th-century engraving depicts the Astor Place Riot of 1849, which was precipitated by a feud between the actors Edwin Forrest and William Macready.

Astoria   Astoria is a seaport city and the seat of Clatsop County in northwestern Oregon, situated on the Columbia River near its mouth. Fishing and lumbering are the most important local industries. About half the population of 10,069 (1990) is of Finnish descent. Astoria grew from a trading post established by John Jacob Astor's fur company in 1811. Nearby Fort Clatsop National Memorial marks the site of a Lewis and Clark Expedition encampment (1805–06).

Astrakhan [as'-truh-kuhn]   Astrakhan is the capital of Astrakhan oblast in the Russian republic of the Soviet Union. It is situated in the delta of the Volga River about 100 km (60 mi) from the Caspian Sea and has a population of 503,000 (1986 est.). One of the Soviet Union's largest inland ports, Astrakhan serves as a center for transshipments between the Volga's river vessels and the Caspian's seagoing ships. The city is a major fishing port and the center of the Soviet caviar industry. The pelts of the karakul lamb of Central Asia, which used to be traded through the port, are called "Astrakhan" after the city.

Astrakhan became prominent around 1460 as the capital of one of the Tatar khanates (chiefdoms) that emerged from the breakup of the GOLDEN HORDE. After its conquest by the Russians in 1554–56, it was transformed into a fortress, of which the kremlin, or citadel, survives. Astrakhan flourished as a trading center on the Volga water route to Asia from the 16th to the 19th century. It lost significance with the coming of the railroad era but rebounded when connected by rail with the Caucasus (1942) and with Kazakhstan (1970).

astrochemistry   Astrochemistry is a branch of astronomy that primarily deals with the origin and interaction of the chemical constituents of the universe. Most matter in the universe exists in atomic or subatomic form, and for many years astronomy and chemistry were somewhat divorced, because chemistry is principally concerned with the larger, molecular forms of matter. Since 1963, however, astronomers have discovered more than 60 types of molecules in the space between the stars, including water, ammonia, and formaldehyde.

astrogeology   Astrogeology applies principles of geology, geochemistry, and geophysics in the study of extraterrestrial solid matter (planets, moons, asteroids, comets, and so on). Specific techniques include REMOTE-SENSING observation by satellite or from Earth and the landing of men or instrument packages on other planetary bodies such as the Moon, Venus, or Mars. Astrogeologists also study extraterrestrial objects found on Earth, such as meteorites, and terrestrial objects or geologic structures created by meteorite impact, such as METEORITE CRATERS, TEKTITES, and astroblemes (ancient impact scars). The science is largely an outgrowth of the exploration of the solar system from the 1960s on.

astrolabe [as'-troh-layb]   The planispheric astrolabe was the most important instrument of astronomers and navigators from medieval times through the 16th century. It was used at least as early as the 1st century BC by the Greeks. The word derives from *astro* ("star") and *labio* ("finder"). The function of the astrolabe was to measure the altitudes of celestial bodies, from which time and the observer's latitude, could be determined. The measurement of the altitude of the North Star yields the latitude, and the altitude of the Sun and stars yields the time.

The astrolabe consists of two flat circular disks ranging from about 7.5 to 25 cm (3 to 10 in) in diameter. One disk, known as the rete, is a star map on which the bright stars are indicated by named pointers and the path of the Sun and planets is shown. The other disk, known as the tympan, is engraved to show the zenith, the horizon, and the lines of altitude and azimuth for a specific latitude.

The astrolabe, one of the most ancient scientific instruments, consists of two discs, the rete, or star map, and the tympan. The instrument pictured dates from the 16th century. The astrolabe can be used for telling time; predicting the rising and setting of the Sun, Moon, and stars; surveying; and navigation.

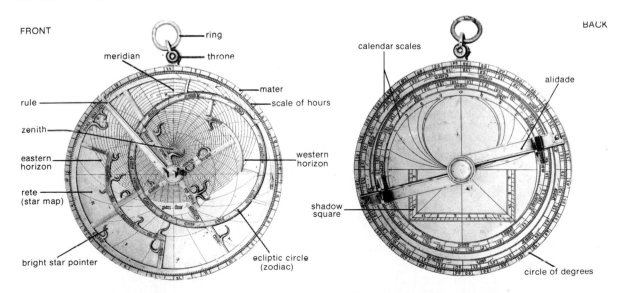

FRONT
ring
meridian — throne
mater
rule
scale of hours
zenith
eastern horizon
western horizon
rete (star map)
bright star pointer
ecliptic circle (zodiac)

BACK
calendar scales
alidade
shadow square
circle of degrees

Both disks are held by a hollow body, with a scale of hours engraved on the rim.

The back of the astrolabe is used to make the observations required. A circle of degrees is engraved around the edge and is used to measure the altitude of the Sun or star with the aid of the alidade, or sighting bar. The astrolabe is held in a vertical position by a ring, and the altitude of a star is measured with the alidade. Then the rete is turned until the proper star point is over the indicated altitude line on the tympan. The altitude and azimuth of the stars above the horizon can then be read. The astrolabe was superseded by the SEXTANT in the 18th century.

astrology   Astrology is the use of astronomical phenomena to predict earthly and human events, in terms of an assumed theoretical system. In its earliest form astrology consisted of simple omens that astrologers read from the sky. In its mature form astrology analyzes the supposed effects of the Sun, Moon, planets, and stars on the Earth for a specific time and place. Although histori-

cally the meanings of the terms *astronomy* and *astrology* sometimes overlapped, astronomy has been concerned only with determining the positions and physical properties of celestial bodies. Natural astrology, on the other hand, assumed that a generalized celestial influence affected weather, crops, and other phenomena related to whole nations of people; judicial astrology made specific predictions about the future of individuals.

Astrology originated in ancient Babylonia and spread to China, India, and the West, where different but related traditions grew up. The earliest known horoscope incorporating the principles of mature astrology dates from 409 BC. In the 2d century AD the astronomer Claudius PTOLEMY prefaced his *Tetrabiblos* with a defense of astrology that proved influential. After the fall of the Roman Empire, astrology declined in the Latin west but flourished in the hands of the conquerors of the Eastern Empire.

In the 12th century astrology began to prosper in Western Europe. By the end of the 17th century, however, astrology was considered a pseudoscience by almost all learned people. Not only was it opposed to the Chris-

An astrology chart as cast by an astrologer indicates the position of the Sun, Moon, and planets in the sky at the moment of a person's birth. Each zodiac sign and each planet is represented by a symbol, or glyph. The chart is divided into twelve houses, which rule spheres of life such as career, health, and marriage. For the birthday charted here, Uranus is in Aries, in the fifth house, which rules sports, romance, and creative expression. The astrologer determines the ascendant (ASC in red lettering) by finding out which zodiac constellation was on the horizon at the moment of birth. The ascendant, in this case Sagittarius, expresses the personality. The midheaven (MC in red lettering) indicates ambition and career. Each planet also has relationships, or aspects, with other planets, as represented in the chart by red, orange, and green lines. When all the planets, signs, houses, and aspects are considered together, the astrologer interprets the chart. The chart here indicates a combination of wit, flair, and talent for the dramatic.

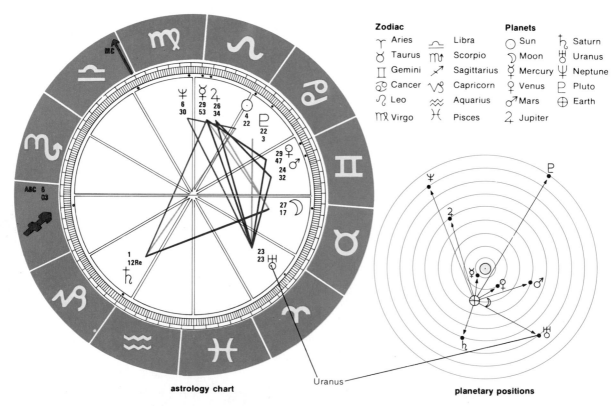

Zodiac				Planets		
♈	Aries	♎	Libra	☉	Sun	♄ Saturn
♉	Taurus	♏	Scorpio	☽	Moon	♅ Uranus
♊	Gemini	♐	Sagittarius	☿	Mercury	♆ Neptune
♋	Cancer	♑	Capricorn	♀	Venus	♇ Pluto
♌	Leo	♒	Aquarius	♂	Mars	⊕ Earth
♍	Virgo	♓	Pisces	♃	Jupiter	

astrology chart

Uranus

planetary positions

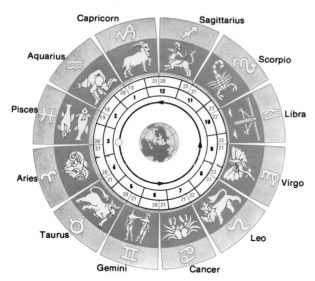

Black numbers on this astrology wheel refer to months, beginning with January; blue numbers indicate the days of the month on which each sign begins and ends. Early scientists thought the Sun revolved around the Earth, as pictured in the center of the wheel. The astrology wheel starts with Aries, which begins on March 21 and ends on April 20; the wheel progresses counterclockwise around the circle through the signs. Each sign has a character that represents its unique traits, and each has a symbol. Accordingly, Aries the Ram rules the personality; Taurus the Bull rules money and resources; Gemini the Twin rules communications; Cancer the Crab rules home and family; Leo the Lion rules romance and creative activities; Virgo the Virgin rules service; Libra the Balance rules marriage, Scorpio the Scorpion rules passion and death; Sagittarius the Archer rules philosophy and higher education; Capricorn the Goat rules career; Aquarius the Water Bearer rules friends and hopes; and Pisces the Fish rules secrets.

tian doctrines of divine intervention and human free will, but also the acceptance of a greatly expanded, Sun-centered universe raised doubt about whether the heavens were created to direct changes on Earth.

In addition to the purported effects of planets on the weather, body types, and personality, astrology also has to take into account the new relationships continually being set up among celestial bodies. To do this it uses the 12 signs of the ZODIAC. *Aspects* are special angles that allow for a discontinuity in astrological influences. For example, there is supposed to be an effect when two planets are 60° apart, but then relatively little effect until a separation of 90° occurs.

The astrological column in a newspaper today is generally based on the sign of the zodiac in which the Sun was located when a person was born. A simplified form of astrology, it implies that all people born under the same sign anywhere in the world at any time share common characteristics and that their daily activities should be so guided. A more individual analysis is possible when casting a horoscope by noting the relationships of the Sun, Moon, planets, and signs of the zodiac to the time and place of one's birth.

For centuries critics have attacked astrology on scien-

tific grounds, questioning the means by which celestial influences could occur, and on moral grounds, since many view humans as creatures of free will. On their side, astrologers, past and present, have often sought to imply that empirical evidence establishes the existence of heavenly influences and have held that erroneous predictions could be attributed to the complexity of the study. They have generally not taken into account the PRECESSION OF THE EQUINOXES, whereby the dates associated with the signs of the zodiac change over time.

astrometry Astrometry, also called positional astronomy, is the branch of astronomy that deals with determining the positions and motions of celestial bodies. This science is also concerned with measuring other quantities, such as the diameter and polar flattening of the Sun and planets, and determining the orbits of double-star components (see BINARY STARS).

Astrometry is one of the oldest branches of astronomy.

Angular distances between stars are determined with a filar micrometer (A) and heliometer (B). Rotatable frame (1), fixed cross hairs (2,3), and position scale (4) permit measurement of the north-south orientation of two stars. Parallel cross hairs (5,6), mounted on movable supports (7,8), are centered on the stars by turning precision screws (9, 10), and their angular separation is read on calibrated heads (11, 12). The heliometer uses a prism system or divided object lens (a) to produce separate images of two stars in each lens half (b). One lens half is moved parallel to the other (c) until the star images coincide (d). The lens's displacement gives the angular distance.

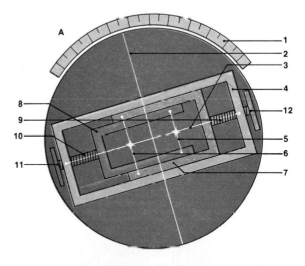

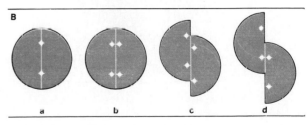

In ancient times the altitude of celestial bodies was determined by the gnomon, the JACOB'S STAFF, the QUADRANT, and the armillary sphere. The accuracy obtained with the best of these instruments was within 2 minutes of ARC. The invention in the 17th century of the TELESCOPE, TRANSIT, micrometer, and pendulum clock improved the accuracy of these measurements immensely. After the discovery in the 18th century that, aside from PARALLAX, the stars had their own motion, known as PROPER MOTION, the determination of their positions and the measurement of stellar parallaxes caused by the Earth's motion around the Sun became the major objects of astrometry.

The position of a celestial object can be given by two coordinates, usually expressed as right ascension and DECLINATION (see CELESTIAL SPHERE; COORDINATE SYSTEMS in astronomy). Two methods for determining the position of stars are used in astrometry. In the absolute method, the coordinates of a star are measured independently of those of any other star, usually by reading the altitude on the transit circle and timing the transit of the star. The second method, known as the differential method, determines a star's position by comparison with the positions of other stars, called fundamental stars. Today the photographic method is predominantly used for differential observations. Stars being measured are photographed with fundamental stars, and the necessary measurements are made on the photographic plate itself.

Despite such achievements as these, the fact that all objects in the sky are in motion necessitates the periodic revision of fundamental catalogs. In addition, parallaxes at present can be established only out to a distance of about 3,000 light-years. Beyond that distance, the motions and distances of celestial objects are estimated only in terms of various astrophysical assumptions (see DISTANCE, ASTRONOMICAL). Radio and, increasingly, optical interferometry (see INTERFEROMETER) are used to establish the positions in the sky of very distant objects. In addition, astrometric satellites such as the European Space Agency's (ESA) *Hipparchos*, launched in 1989, will be increasingly important to the field.

See also: ASTRONOMICAL CATALOGS AND ATLASES; TIME.

---

astronaut   An astronaut, or cosmonaut in Soviet usage, is a person trained for flight beyond the Earth's atmosphere. (The U.S. Department of Defense also calls astronauts the test pilots who fly aircraft higher than 80 km/50 mi above the Earth.) From Apr. 9, 1959, when the

(Above) *The seven original U.S. astronauts for Project Mercury were announced in 1959. They were* (front row, left to right) *Walter M. Schirra, Jr., Donald K. Slayton, John H. Glenn, Jr., Scott Carpenter, and* (back row) *Alan B. Shepard, Jr., Virgil I. "Gus" Grissom, and L. Gordon Cooper. Shepard made the first, suborbital U.S. flight in May 1961 and Glenn the first orbital one in 1962.*

(Left) *The original Soviet cosmonaut corps posed for this group picture in May 1961 at the summer home of Sergei Korolev* (front row center, with wife and daughter), *the chief designer of the Soviet space program. To the right of Korolev is Yuri Gagarin, who the month previously had become the first human being to enter space. To the right of Gagarin is Gherman Titov, who in August of that same year became the second person to orbit the Earth. Many later stars of the Soviet program also appear in the picture.*

Sally Ride, seen here at work aboard the Space Shuttle Challenger in June 1983, became the first woman in the U.S. astronaut program to enter space.

first 7 U.S. astronauts were presented at a press conference in Washington, D.C., through the pre-Space Shuttle era, a total of 73 men were selected by the National Aeronautics and Space Administration (NASA). Of these, 43 flew in the MERCURY, GEMINI, APOLLO, and SKYLAB programs. In 1978, 35 new candidates were selected for the SPACE SHUTTLE program, including 6 women; thereafter, new candidates were recruited annually.

At President Eisenhower's recommendation, the original "Mercury seven" astronauts were selected from the military services. Only qualified test pilots with at least 1,500 hours of flight time were considered. Of the 508 men whose service records were screened, 18 were recommended and 7 were selected. Between 1962 and 1969 six more groups of astronauts, totaling 66, were chosen.

The USSR's corps of cosmonauts was selected on a similar basis and at about the same time as the Mercury astronauts, but women were incorporated earlier in the Soviet program. The total number of cosmonauts roughly equaled that of astronauts in 1970 and has been higher since then. In more recent Soviet missions, cosmonauts from other nations have been included.

See also: SPACE EXPLORATION

astronautics   Astronautics is that area of engineering and technology which is concerned with spaceflight. The discipline encompasses several technical fields, including astrodynamics, propulsion, structures, power supplies, thermal control, and communications. Astrodynamics, the study of spacecraft motion through force fields in space, is the cornerstone of astronautics.

A distinction is made between CELESTIAL MECHANICS and astrodynamics. The former is associated with the natural motion of celestial bodies; the latter refers to the controlled motion of spacecraft. Astronautics may essentially be said to have its origins in the theoretical works of Konstantin TSIOLKOVSKY at the start of the 20th century (see

SPACE EXPLORATION). The knowledge of celestial mechanics preceded the development of astrodynamics by several hundred years.

Basic differences also exist between astronautics and aeronautics, the flight of spacecraft as opposed to that of aircraft. An airplane uses AERODYNAMIC forces (those resulting from the action and reaction associated with air movement) for its flight and the control of flight. The pilot implements this control through devices that change the orientation of deflecting surfaces about the craft. He or she can use visual and instrument cues for knowing when to make altitude and flight-path corrections. An astronaut uses propulsive or internally caused torques to control orientation. Having no horizon or magnetic compass, the astronaut relies on GYROSCOPES and special sensors to make changes in attitude. A spacecraft flies because of a balance between gravitational and centrifugal forces.

The few physical principles underlying the study of spacecraft motion are elementary in their basic form. Sir Isaac NEWTON first formalized the physical laws that determine the motion of a spacecraft. Johannes KEPLER provided the empirical laws (known as KEPLER'S LAWS) that describe planetary motion and allowed a test of Newton's laws.

Spacecraft can follow four different types of flight paths in space. All orbits of Earth satellites are either circular or elliptical. Planetary probes follow parabolic or hyperbolic trajectories when leaving Earth's gravitational influence. Launch is achieved by the use of a single-stage or multistage rocket (see ROCKETS AND MISSILES). The rocket must develop sufficient thrust for a sufficient length of time to lift the payload above the atmosphere and place it in orbit or send it into deep space.

Once the spacecraft is in orbit two categories of orbital maneuvers are of interest. The more common one is raising the altitude of a circular orbit. The other is changing the orbital inclination. To raise the radius of a circular orbit, at least two separate thrusting intervals are required. For most such maneuvers, two such thrusts are optimum if applied properly. This maneuver, called a Hohmann transfer, consists of simply increasing the orbital velocity at one point, waiting exactly one-half the transfer orbit period, and then increasing the orbital velocity again.

Many missions involve the rendezvous and docking of two spacecraft. Such maneuvers were demonstrated in

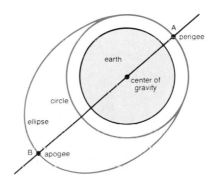

Satellite orbits may be circles or ellipses, depending on the initial speed of the satellite. Higher speeds result in larger ellipses, each with an apogee, or high point from Earth, and a perigee, or low point. Earth's center of gravity is one focus of each ellipse, and the line AB is the major axis.

the APOLLO PROGRAM. Docking involves a sequence of maneuvering phases. Initially, the chase vehicle is launched into an orbit quite close to that of the target. Once in the vicinity, special rendezvous maneuvers are carried out, using carefully applied, small thrusts over a period of several minutes.

As a mission in orbit ends, a spacecraft may simply be shut off, or it may be brought back to Earth. All manned flights, obviously, must end with a return through the atmosphere. This is initiated by slowing the vehicle velocity slightly through the use of retrofiring. A shallow descent is then begun into the upper atmospheric limits. Passage through the upper atmosphere is spread along several thousand kilometers to minimize heat buildup in the spacecraft's thermal protection system. Once the vehicle has slowed, landing can be achieved by parachute deployment or, in the case of vehicles such as the SPACE SHUTTLE, by an unpowered gliding descent.

Many space missions involve planetary probes that leave a low parking orbit on a hyperbolic trajectory away from Earth. The probe will either crash on or fly by the planet, depending on small adjustments in its flight path. Such minute changes are called midcourse corrections.

astronomical catalogs and atlases

An astronomical catalog is a tabular compilation of data about selected celestial objects, whereas an astronomical atlas includes charts or photographs of these objects. HIPPARCHUS of Rhodes compiled the first star catalog in 150 BC; about AD 127, PTOLEMY of Alexandria prepared a catalog of 1,022 stars, listing their brightnesses and positions. In 1603, Johann Bayer codified the existing constellations in the *Uranometria*, an atlas that depicted the naked-eye stars in baroque drawings of the constellations. The Messier catalog of diffuse objects (1771–84), compiled by the French astronomer Charles MESSIER, cataloged numerous objects, now known to be star clusters, galaxies, and nebulae. One of the most useful sets of stellar catalogs and charts ever prepared is the *Bonner Durchmusterung* (Bonn Finding List, 1859–62), containing relatively accurate brightnesses and positions for about 320,000 stars.

Modern catalogs and atlases may contain information on positions, distances, brightnesses, spectra, motions, variability, and other characteristics of celestial objects. They range from the general to the specific. The *Yale Catalog of Bright Stars* contains a wide variety of information on the 9,110 naked-eye stars in the sky, whereas Halton Arp's *Atlas of Peculiar Galaxies* is devoted to the examination of a few hundred galaxies having odd structural characteristics. *The Henry Draper Catalogue* (HD) of stellar spectra (1886–1949) contains 359,082 stars, giving brightnesses, spectral classes, and approximate positions. The *New General Catalogue of Nebulae and Clusters of Stars* (NGC) and two supplemental *Index Catalogues* (IC) contain more than 13,000 objects. Bright galaxies are known by NGC numbers.

The *Franklin-Adams Charts* (1914) was the first photographic atlas that covered the entire sky. An atlas much used at present is the National Geographic Society–Palomar Observatory Sky Survey, covering two-thirds of the sky and consisting of plates taken in the blue and red region of the spectrum down to about magnitude 20. By means of supercomputers and laser readers, a catalog is being developed of the objects that appear on these plates. Also under way is a deeper survey of northern skies, and a comparable southern-sky survey is being developed by astronomers in Chile and Australia.

Astronomers will rely more and more on computerized databases, such as the skymap tapes compiled by NASA's Astronomical Data Center. The goal is to have a complete computer catalog that, on request, will furnish the astronomer with all the existing data on any particular star or group of stars.

astronomical unit see DISTANCE, ASTRONOMICAL

astronomy and astrophysics

Astronomy, the most ancient science, began with the study of the Sun, the Moon, and the visible planets. The modern astronomer is still centrally concerned with recording position, brightness, motion, and other directly observable features of celestial objects and with predicting their motion according to the laws of CELESTIAL MECHANICS. Astrophysics, a 19th- and 20th-century outgrowth of classical astronomy, uses quantum mechanics, relativity theory, and molecular, atomic, nuclear, and elementary-particle physics to explain observed celestial phenomena as the logical result of predictable physical processes. The astrophysicist seeks to characterize the constituents of the universe in terms of temperatures, pressures, densities, and chemical compositions. Although the term *astronomer* is still used, virtually all astronomers have been trained in astrophysics. The broad aim of modern astronomy is to develop encompassing theories of the origin, evolution, and possible destiny of the universe as a whole, a field of endeavor that is known as cosmology.

Astronomy before the Twentieth Century

From the dawn of civilization until the time of Copernicus, astronomy was dominated by the study of the motions of celestial bodies. Such work was essential for ASTROLOGY, for the determination of the CALENDAR, and for the prediction of ECLIPSES. It was also fueled by the desire to reduce irregularity to order and to predict positions of celestial bodies with ever-increasing accuracy. As early as 3000 BC, the collection of massive stones at STONEHENGE in England functioned as an ancient observatory, where priests followed the annual motion of the Sun each morning along the horizon in order to determine the beginning of the seasons. By about 2500 BC, Stonehenge may have been used to predict eclipses of the Moon.

It was almost a millennium later, in the period from about 1800 to 400 BC, that the Babylonians developed a calendar based on the motion of the Sun and the phases of the Moon. The Greeks, taking a geometrical approach to explaining celestial motions, sought to represent the motions of celestial bodies by using spheres and circles.

(Left) *A 1660 engraving from Andreas Cellerius's book,* Harmonia Macrocosmica, *represents the Copernican heliocentric, or Sun-centered, universe, depicting the 5 known planets revolving about the Sun.* (Below) *Johannes Kepler, the German astronomer, discovered the three laws of planetary motion that bear his name.*

This explanatory method of "epicycles," perfected by HIPPARCHUS (*c.*190–120 BC) and PTOLEMY (AD *c.*100–170), was not upset until KEPLER replaced the circle with the ellipse in 1609. These Greek models of celestial motion were put forth within the framework of the geocentric world system, systematized by ARISTOTLE and his disciples since the 4th century BC.

COPERNICUS placed not the Earth but the Sun at the center of the universe; this view was put forth in his *De revolutionibus orbium caelestium* (On the Revolutions of the Heavenly Spheres, 1543). In that work, however, he merely adapted the Greek system of epicycles to the new arrangement. It was left for Kepler to resolve observed anomalies in planetary motions by using the ellipse, enabling him to discover his three laws of planetary motion. KEPLER'S LAWS and the Copernican theory reached their ultimate verification with Sir Isaac NEWTON's enunciation of the laws of universal gravitation in the *Principia* (1687), in which the Sun was assigned as the physical cause of planetary motion. During the 18th century the implications of gravitational astronomy were recognized and analyzed by able mathematicians, mostly in France. The science of celestial mechanics was born, and the goal of accurate prediction was finally realized. The observation of stellar positions, which formed the reference frame for all planetary motions, laid the groundwork for solving the problem of the distribution of the stars and the structure of the universe.

Meanwhile, in the arena of descriptive astronomy, the physical similarity of the Earth and planets became a matter of significant inquiry after Copernicus showed that the Earth and planets are in motion around a central Sun. GALILEO GALILEI first turned his TELESCOPE toward the heavens in 1609. His discovery of the mountainous na-ture of the Moon, the four moons of Jupiter, and the phases of Venus provided more evidence that the planets had Earthlike characteristics. Such discoveries slowly accumulated throughout the 17th and 18th centuries.

Drawings in a diary by the Italian astronomer Galileo disclose his first telescopic views of the Moon in 1609. He found that the Moon, covered with craters, mountains, and valleys, was not a perfect crystalline sphere—as philosophers had claimed—but an imperfect celestial body.

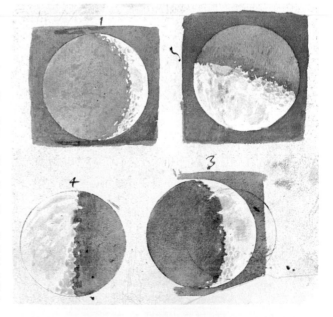

(Above) *The Dutch astronomer Jan Oort points to a picture of Andromeda, a spiral galaxy much like our own. A pioneer in galactic astronomy, Oort discovered that our galaxy rotates.*

(Left) *The American astronomer Edwin Hubble looks through the 1.2-m (48-in) Schmidt camera in California's Palomar Observatory. Hubble was the first astronomer to prove (1923) the existence of galaxies outside our own.*

Christiaan HUYGENS first correctly interpreted the rings of Saturn in 1659, observed dark markings on Mars and belts of clouds on Jupiter, and speculated that Venus was shrouded in clouds. With more refined telescopes, such as those built by Sir William HERSCHEL in England, the details of the solar system became better known. Herschel himself made the spectacular discovery of the planet Uranus in 1781. In 1846, the presence of yet another planet (Neptune), predicted by John Couch ADAMS and U. J. J. Leverrier, was confirmed observationally—a triumph for both theory and observation.

With the invention of spectroscopy in the 1860s, the science of astrophysics was born. Astrophysics yielded its most substantial results in the study of the Sun and stars, where the myriads of observed spectral lines were gradually interpreted as a precise set of chemical fingerprints. With spectroscopy and the almost simultaneous invention of photography, astronomers compiled great catalogs mapping the solar SPECTRUM. Knowledge of the Sun now outstripped planetary astronomy, for the first time other stars were proved to be suns themselves, and a firm foun-

dation was laid for a study of the internal constitution and evolution of stars in the first quarter of the 20th century.

From the time of Aristotle until the Copernican revolution the structure of the universe had been conceived firmly as Earth-centered, in spite of Aristarchus's heliocentric views. The Copernican theory implied a vastly enlarged universe, and the subsequent shift from the closed, tightly structured world to an infinite, homogeneous universe was one of the landmarks in the history of astronomy. The concept of a sphere of fixed stars gradually crumbled during the 17th-century Scientific Revolution, opening the way in the 18th century for investigations of the distribution of stars. In the 1780s William Herschel, through his observational program of star counts, concluded that the stars were distributed in a flattened, disk-shaped system with the sun near the center. Because of the lack of a direct method for determining stellar distances, progress in cosmology lagged for more than a century after Herschel's star counts. Even after the first stellar parallaxes were measured in the 19th century, too few distances were determined to solve the problem of the structure of the stellar system. Real progress in cosmology was finally made only in the early 20th century through an analysis of the extremely small motions of stars, known as proper motions. Jacobus Cornelius KAPTEYN, Jan Hendrik OORT, and others made crucial contributions to the modern view of our galaxy as an enormous disk-shaped rotating assemblage of stars. With the work of Harlow Shapley, Edwin HUBBLE and others, by the 1920s the existence of innumerable independent galaxies was confirmed, along with evidence for an expanding universe.

New Windows on the Universe

In the 20th century, advances in astronomy have been so rapid that the second half of the century can be considered a golden age. Traditional optical astronomy has been revolutionized by the development of new techniques of faint-object detection, including more sensitive photographic emulsions and a plethora of electronic imaging devices. Using standard telescopes, the optical astronomer can now see fainter and more distant objects than ever before. In addition the astronomer is no longer limited to observing the visible light from celestial bodies. New instruments now allow the study of the heavens in entirely new regions of the spectrum.

Radio Astronomy. In 1931, Karl G. Jansky of the Bell Telephone Laboratories discovered extraterrestrial radiation at radio wavelengths and launched the field of RADIO ASTRONOMY. During the 1930s, Grote REBER, an American radio engineer, further investigated celestial radio radiation and single-handedly brought radio astronomy to the attention of professional astronomers.

As a result of theoretical investigations by astronomers in the Netherlands during World War II, an observable radio line, emitted by neutral hydrogen atoms in space, was predicted at a wavelength of 21 cm. Detection of this line caused radio astronomy to advance rapidly after the war. Today, radio telescopes and radio interferometer systems worldwide study radio emission from the stars, the plan-

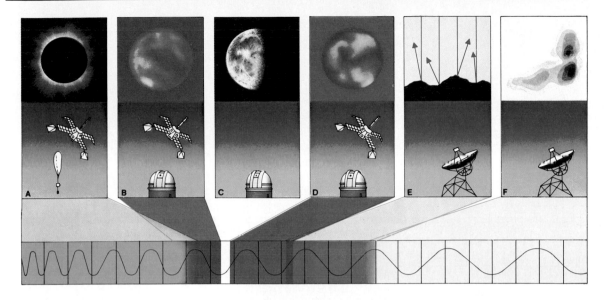

Technological advances have permitted study of celestial objects using all the wavelengths of the electromagnetic spectrum. (A) Balloons and orbiting satellites have recorded intensities of X-ray and gamma-ray radiations from the Sun's corona, providing information about its structure, density, and temperature. (B) Ultraviolet studies of Mars and other planets have revealed atmospheric compositions and pressures. (C) Visual observations of all objects, including the Moon, remain important. (D) Infrared studies of Mars have furnished surface details and temperatures. (E) Radar units have yielded planets' distances and rotation rates. (F) Radio telescopes have revealed radio galaxies, pulsars, and quasars.

ets, the interstellar medium in our galaxy, and extragalactic sources.

Achievements in radio astronomy include the mapping of galactic structure and the discovery of quasars, pulsars, and a large number of complex organic molecules in interstellar space. RADAR ASTRONOMY has also been used within the solar system to determine, for example, the rotational periods of Venus and Mercury.

Infrared Astronomy. Although scientists have known since the time of William Herschel in the late 18th century that infrared radiation from celestial objects can be detected, it was not until the late 1950s and early 1960s that INFRARED ASTRONOMY became the subject of intensive research. Sensitive detectors were developed that allowed astronomers to explore the infrared region of the spectrum. Infrared astronomy has been helpful in studying the very young or evolved stars that are commonly associated with dense clouds of dust observed in interstellar space.

Ultraviolet, X-Ray, and Gamma-Ray Astronomy. In 1957 the USSR launched the first satellite, thus beginning the space age. Few other disciplines have benefited from artificial SATELLITES to the extent that astronomy has. (See SPACE EXPLORATION.) For the astronomer, the atmosphere presents a murky or opaque barrier through which observations of the far infrared, ultraviolet, X-ray, and gamma-ray spectral regions are difficult or impossible. Satellites and, to a limited extent, high-altitude balloons and rockets have become platforms from which to observe these spectral regions. Since 1962 the United States and other nations have launched a wide range of orbiting observatories that are devoted to observing the ultraviolet, infrared,

and X-ray regions (see OAO; OSO; HIGH ENERGY ASTRONOMICAL OBSERVATORY; UHURU). These studies have resulted in a better understanding of very hot stars and have produced evidence of the existence of BLACK HOLES. The

A 1979 photograph of Jupiter taken by the Voyager 1 space probe discloses colored clouds that appear to be swirling around the rapidly circulating Great Red Spot (lower left). To the center right may be seen the satellite Io.

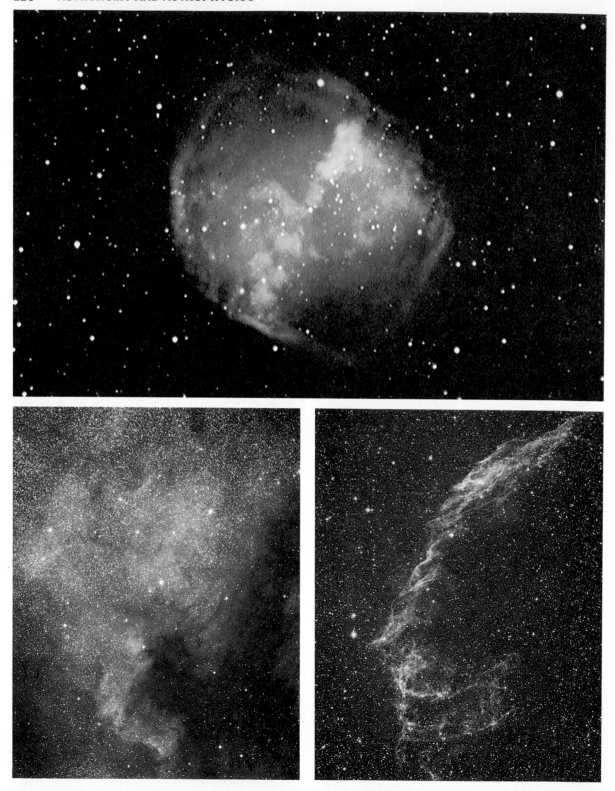

(Opposite page) *Three different types of nebulae are illustrated in these astrophotographs. The Dumbbell Nebula* (top) *is a planetary nebula in the constellation Vulpecula, consisting of a small, hot central star surrounded by a slowly expanding shell of luminous gases. The North American Nebula* (lower left) *in Cygnus is a denser-than-average region of luminous gases, primarily hydrogen. The dark areas are composed of large, relatively dense, opaque clouds of dust. The Veil Nebula* (lower right) *is believed to be the remains of a supernova explosion occurring some 50,000 years ago.*

(Right) *These four radio dish antennas, each 30 m (98 ft) in diameter, are part of the Very Large Array (VLA) radio telescope in San Augustin, N.Mex. With twenty-seven such antennas placed along a 63-km (39-mi) Y-shaped track, the VLA provides the resolving power of a single dish 30 km (20 mi) wide.*

impact of extraterrestrial astronomy in all parts of the wavelength spectrum is being extended by a continuing program of space astronomy supported by the SPACE SHUTTLE (see GAMMA-RAY ASTRONOMY, SPACE TELESCOPE; ULTRAVIOLET ASTRONOMY; X-RAY ASTRONOMY).

The Solar System

The achievements of astronomy and astrophysics are evident in the rapidly growing knowledge of the extraterrestrial environment, from the SOLAR SYSTEM to the most remote galaxies. The solar system, as it is known today, comprises the Sun and nine PLANETS, in order of increasing distance from the Sun: Mercury, Venus, Earth, Mars, Jupiter, Saturn, Uranus, Neptune, and Pluto. The last, Pluto, was discovered in 1930 by Clyde William TOMBAUGH, an astronomer at the Lowell Observatory.

Planets, Asteroids, and Comets. Except for Mercury and Venus, each planet has from 1 to more than 20 natural SATELLITES, including Pluto, whose moon was not discovered until 1978. The planets Saturn, Jupiter, and Uranus are known to have rings, the latter two systems having been discovered in 1979 and 1977, respectively. Sightings in 1985 also confirmed the existence of some manner of ring system around Neptune; the rings may be in the form of broken arcs.

Between the orbits of Mars and Jupiter lies a belt containing thousands of minor planets, or ASTEROIDS. The orbits of most of the asteroids restrict them to the region between Mars and Jupiter, but exceptions exist whose elongated orbits bring them within a few million kilometers of Earth.

COMETS can attain distances 150,000 times greater than that from the Earth to the Sun. In 1950 the Dutch astronomer Jan Hendrik Oort speculated that the solar system is surrounded by a cloud of comets, most of which never enter the inner regions of the solar system. The orbits of only a few are disturbed sufficiently to bring them near the Earth. HALLEY'S COMET, known since 240 BC, swings around the Sun once every 76 years and was observed most recently in 1985–86.

Flyby space probes involving most of the planets, and surface landings on the Moon, Venus, and Mars, have transformed planetary astronomy. No longer must observations be made at great distances; on-site measurement of numerous physical properties is now possible. In studying the planets, the astronomer must also enlist the aid of the chemist, the geologist, and the meteorologist. In spite of the great increase in knowledge, however, the probes and landings have raised more questions than they have answered. The origin of the solar system, for example, remains unknown. The VENERA missions to Venus and the VIKING landers on Mars indicate that life as it is known on Earth does not exist on either planet, nor is life possible on the Moon.

The Sun. The Sun is a star with a surface temperature of 5,800 K and an interior temperature of about 15,000,000 K. Because the Sun is the nearest star and is easily observed, its chemical composition and surface activity have been intensely investigated. Among the surface features of the Sun are SUNSPOTS, prominences, and flares. It is now known that the maximum number of sunspots occurs approximately every 11 years, that their temperature is approximately 4,300 K, and that they are related to solar magnetic activity in a cycle taking about 22 years to complete. Studies of historical records have also shown long-scale variations in sunspot numbers.

Predictions based on theory indicate that energy-generating processes deep within the Sun and other stars should produce a certain number of chargeless, weightless particles called NEUTRINOS. Efforts to detect solar neutrinos have thus far indicated a far lower rate of neutrino production than current theory seems to require, and revisions of theory may in time prove necessary. On the other hand, physicists and cosmologists are equally interested in the concept that at least some forms of neutrino have mass and undergo transformations inside the Sun.

The Stars

The accumulation of precise data on some of the nearer STARS early in the 20th century enabled Ejnar Hertzsprung and Henry Norris Russell, working independently, to plot a graph of brightness and color, two basic stellar properties. When they plotted intrinsic stellar brightness on one axis and stellar color (equivalent to surface temperature) on the other axis, Hertzsprung and Russell found that, instead of being scattered over the graph, the stars fell into distinct regions: a heavily populated, diagonal band, known as the main sequence, that varies from bright, hot, blue stars to faint, cool, red ones; a horizontal band containing bright, cool, red stars (the giants); and a sparsely populated, horizontal band containing very luminous stars of all colors (the supergiants). In honor of these scientists, graphs of the type they plotted are called HERTZSPRUNG-RUSSELL DIAGRAMS, or simply H-R diagrams.

The features found on the H-R diagrams are a key to modern astrophysics because they are basic to an understanding of STELLAR EVOLUTION. The star's initial mass determines exactly the position of the star on the main sequence. The star gradually changes, however, thus changing its position on the H-R diagrams. As the hydrogen that fuels the star's fusion reaction becomes depleted, the outer layers of the star expand, and it enters the giant phase. Eventually they become unstable and begin to lose mass—some smoothly, others catastrophically, depending on their masses. Most stars pulsate smoothly; some may brighten rapidly in older age, blowing material off into space to form a planetary nebula. A few giant, unstable stars explode as SUPERNOVAS. In any case, evolution proceeds to the stellar graveyard. The most common result of evolution is the WHITE DWARF; large stars end up as NEUTRON STARS (PULSARS) and, possibly, black holes.

The Galaxies

The solar system is located in the outer regions of our galaxy. From the Earth, the visible part of THE GALAXY is seen in the night sky as the Milky Way. This part is actually a flattened disk about 100,000 light-years wide and with a central bulge. Around it lies a spherical halo of star clusters (see CLUSTER, STAR) about 200,000 light-years wide, which is surrounded in turn by a much larger corona of dust and gas. The entire system contains matter in quantities equivalent to more than 1,000 billion solar masses. The Sun takes about 200 million years to orbit the galactic center, which lies about 30,000 light-years from the Sun in the direction of the constellation Sagittarius. Prior to the pioneering work of Harlow Shapley in 1917, the Sun was thought to lie near the galactic center. Shapley also demonstrated the galactic halo of star clusters.

The structure of our galaxy has been mapped by now, using the distances of extremely luminous stars as well as radio observations of the 21-cm line of the hydrogen spectrum. It has been shown to take the form of a typical spiral galaxy (see EXTRAGALACTIC SYSTEMS). Three basic galactic types exist: spirals, such as the Milky Way and the ANDROMEDA GALAXY; irregulars, such as the MAGELLANIC CLOUDS; and ellipticals. The last exist at both extremes of galactic size; a dwarf elliptical may contain only a few million stars, whereas a giant elliptical may contain trillions of stars. The fact that extragalactic systems are vast, remote collections of stars was not understood until 1929, when Edwin P. Hubble identified a variable star in the Andromeda galaxy and determined its distance.

The Milky Way, Andromeda galaxy, and Magellanic Clouds are members of a gravitationally bound cluster of galaxies known as the Local Group, which contains about 20 members in all. Other clusters, such as one in the direction of the constellation Virgo, may contain more than 1,000 galaxies, and much larger superclusters also exist; the Local Group may itself be part of a local supercluster.

Cosmology

In 1912, Vesto M. Slipher discovered that more distant galaxies beyond the Local Group are receding from the Earth at high velocities. With a knowledge of the distances of these objects, Hubble was able to demonstrate a relationship between a galaxy's RED SHIFT (a DOPPLER EFFECT observed in the galaxy's spectrum, indicating its recessional velocity) and its distance: the farther away a galaxy is, the greater is its red shift (see Hubble's constant). This is considered good evidence for the BIG BANG THEORY mentioned below.

Since Hubble's computations, a continuous effort has been made to extend the boundaries of the observable universe to more remote, higher red-shift objects. Observation of such distant galaxies contributes to greater understanding of the origin and possible fate of the universe. The search for higher red shifts took an unexpected turn when, in 1960, two radio sources were identified with what appeared to be stars. This was surprising, because stars were not expected to be such strong radio sources, and the spectra of these objects could not be associated with any type of star. It was not until 1963 that Maarten Schmidt correctly interpreted the spectra as having enormous red shifts. These objects, known as QUASARS, are still the subject of great controversy. It is not known whether their red shifts are attributable to their great distance, as is true of normal galaxies, or attributable to other physical phenomena.

Additional evidence has given astronomers a good idea of the origin of the universe—the concern of COSMOLOGY. In 1965, Robert W. WILSON and Arno A. Penzias discovered an isotropic microwave BACKGROUND RADIATION characteristic of that emitted by a blackbody at 3 K. This BLACKBODY RADIATION, whose existence has since been confirmed by numerous observations, is believed to be an artifact of the big bang with which most astronomers believe the universe began. According to the big bang theory, a single, cataclysmic event occurred about 20 billion years ago that disrupted the dense mass composed of all matter and radiation in the universe. The matter then dispersed, cooled, and condensed in the form of stars and galaxies. Most cosmologists now accept the big bang theory rather than the rival STEADY-STATE THEORY and are attempting to account for the exotic physical events that would have been involved in the very first moments of the big bang (see INFLATIONARY THEORY). They have yet to determine, however, whether the universe will expand indefinitely or will ultimately collapse upon itself and perhaps repeat the process indefinitely.

astrophotography Astrophotography is the PHOTOGRAPHY of stars and other celestial bodies for the purpose of obtaining observational data. It has long been an important tool in modern astronomical and astrophysical research. Other techniques have allowed improvements over the photograph in certain areas, but the photographic method has the advantage of providing a two-dimensional image of the sky.

In astrophotography the telescope is furnished with a plateholder so that it can act as a CAMERA. In addition, several types of telescopes are exclusively designed for photography, such as the astrographs used for photographic star catalog observations, and the SCHMIDT TELESCOPE. The advantage of the Schmidt telescope is the excellent images it produces over a large angular field. This is accomplished with a spherical mirror and a nonspherical thin corrector plate of glass located at the center of curvature of the mirror, correcting the spherical aberration introduced by the mirror.

Among the several image-enhancing techniques, the development of the electrographic camera has made it possible to measure stars fainter than those detectable with either the conventional photoelectric or photographic method. In this camera the image is formed on a photographic plate by highly accelerated electrons emitted by a photocathode placed at the optical focal plane of the telescope.

astrophysics see ASTRONOMY AND ASTROPHYSICS

Asturias [ahs-toor'-ee-ahs] Asturias was a small kingdom in northwestern Spain centered on the city of Oviedo. It came into being early in the 8th century under Pelayo (r. 718–37), whose victory over the Muslims at Covadonga in 722 marked the beginning of the Christian reconquest of Spain. Asturias then expanded westward to Galicia and southward to the Douro River. The discovery of the supposed tomb of the Apostle James at Santiago de Compostela in Galicia enhanced the prestige of the kingdom and opened it to pilgrims from northern Europe. Early in the 10th century the kings took up residence at LEÓN, and thereafter Asturias formed part of the kingdom of León. Since 1388 the title "Prince of Asturias" has been given to the heir to the Spanish throne.

Asturias, Miguel Ángel Miguel Ángel Asturias, b. Oct. 19, 1899, d. June 9, 1974, was a Guatemalan-born poet and novelist who won the Nobel Prize for literature in 1967. After receiving a law degree, he left Guatemala in 1923 and settled in Paris. For the next 40 years he alternately served his country as a diplomat and spent long periods in political exile. His most important novel, *The President* (1946; Eng. trans., 1964), a portrait of a modern dictatorship, was translated into 16 languages. In 1963 he wrote *Mulata de tal*, describing a peasant couple preparing for the witchcraft priesthood.

Asunción [ah-soon-seeohn'] Asunción is the capital city of Paraguay. It has a population of 477,000 (1985). Located on a bay of the Paraguay River near its junction with the Pilcomayo River, it is the industrial and cultural center of Paraguay as well as its principal port. Cotton, sugar, grain, tobacco, and cattle are processed there. Local manufactures include textiles, shoes, beverages, and small boats. Asunción was founded as a trading post in 1537 on the day of the Assumption (Aug. 15), the city's namesake. Inhabitants of Buenos Aires sought asylum there after an attack by Pampa Indians in 1541, and soon afterward the city became headquarters for Spain's affairs in eastern South America. The Universidad Nacional de Asunción (1890) and the Universidad Cathólica Nuestra Señora de la Asunción (1960) are located there.

Aswan Aswan (1986 est. pop., 195,700) is the capital of Aswan governorate in southeastern Egypt. About 708 km (440 mi) southeast of Cairo, it is on the east bank of the Nile River about 9.6 km (6 mi) north of the First Cataract. The population swelled as a result of the construction (1960–70) of the Aswan High Dam. About 13 km (8 mi) south of the city, the dam has spurred development of metal, artificial fertilizer, and hydroelectric power industries. The older Aswan Dam is located between the city and the Aswan High Dam.

Aswan has long been a favorite winter resort because of its hot, dry climate. Known to the ancient Egyptians as Suwana and to the Greeks as Syene, Aswan has been an important city since the 1st millennium BC. As the southern frontier of Egypt, it was the gateway to trade with the south. Nearby archaeological sites include the now relocated 4th-century BC temple of Isis, formerly on the island of PHILAE, and the 6th-century Coptic Monastery of St. Simeon.

Aswan High Dam The Aswan High Dam blocks the NILE RIVER near the resort town of Aswan in Upper Egypt. The rock-fill dam, completed in 1970, is one of the world's largest structures. It is 3.26 km (2.3 mi) in length and rises 111 m (364 ft) above the riverbed. Lake NASSER (High Dam Lake), the reservoir it impounds, averages 9.6 km (6 mi) wide and extends upstream 499 km (310 mi). An earlier granite dam, the Aswan Dam, lies 6.4 km (4 mi) downstream. The Aswan Dam was completed in 1902, but its crest has been twice raised.

Ten years in construction, the Aswan High Dam cost $1 billion. The water it stores has opened the way to agricultural expansion. More than 360,000 ha (900,000 acres), most of it formerly desert, were added to the total of arable land; an equal amount was irrigated year round to enable it to produce several crops a year instead of just one. Between 1979 and the mid-1980s overuse and drought led to a 20% drop in the water level of Lake Nasser. The dam has a hydroelectric power capacity of 2.1 million kW and supplies more than 25% of Egypt's power.

Both Aswan dams have been the focus of worldwide archaeological concern. Construction of the Aswan Dam in 1902 partially inundated the Temple of PHILAE. Lake Nasser inundated many ancient sites, including the temples and colossi at ABU SIMBEL. As a result of the creation of Lake Nasser, 100,000 Egyptian and Sudanese Nubians had to be resettled.

A study completed in 1982 found that the incidence of waterborne diseases in the areas along the Nile actually dropped as a result of the dam. Also, evaporation from Lake Nasser is not as high as was predicted. But adverse effects have been recorded: salt buildup on land and in the Nile; the destruction of the sardine fishery in the eastern Mediterranean; erosion in the Nile waterway and in the delta region.

asylum   see RIGHT OF ASYLUM

Atacama Desert   The Atacama Desert is an arid region in northern Chile, extending south from the Peruvian border for about 950 km (600 mi). The area is part of the Pacific Coast desert of South America. The desert is bounded on the west by a coastal mountain range and stretches across a central plain (elevation about 600 m/2,000 ft) to the Andes Mountains. Average temperatures are relatively low, about 19° C (66° F) in summer, and little vegetation grows.

Nitrate production from the region's dry salt basins became so profitable during the latter half of the 19th century that the desert was fought for by Bolivia, Peru, and Chile in the War of the Pacific and annexed (1884) by Chile. Production declined after World War I, due largely to the manufacture of synthetic nitrates. Subsequent mining of copper, now the region's chief source of revenue, has not reversed the trend of declining population.

Atahualpa   [at-uh-wahl'-puh]   Atahualpa, c.1500–1533, was the last independent ruler of the INCA empire of pre-Columbian South America. The son of HUAYNA CAPAC, Atahualpa was victorious in a civil war resulting from a dispute with his brother Huáscar over the rulership of the Inca territory. On Nov. 16, 1532, shortly after he gained control of the empire, Atahualpa was captured by Francisco PIZARRO and a group of Spanish soldiers in Cajamarca, Peru. In a vain attempt to save Atahualpa, his subjects assembled one of the largest ransoms in history, an estimated $30 million worth of gold and silver. He was executed by garroting eight months after his capture.

Atalanta   In Greek mythology Atalanta was a princess famed for her swiftness in running. Warned against marriage by the oracle at Delphi, she nevertheless challenged each of her suitors to a footrace. If Atalanta won, the suitor would forfeit his life, and if he won, she would marry him. None outraced her. Then Melanion (in another version, Hippomenes) sought the help of Aphrodite, who gave him three golden apples. As Melanion and Atalanta raced, he dropped the apples one at a time, and Atalanta paused to retrieve them. She lost the race and married Melanion. Later they were changed into lions by Zeus.

Atatürk, Kemal   [ah'-tah-toork, kuh-mahl']   Kemal Atatürk, b. Mar. 12, 1881, d. Nov. 10, 1938, was the founder and first president of the Turkish Republic (1923–38). Originally named Mustafa Kemal, he joined the YOUNG TURKS as a young military officer and then took an active role in the coup that overthrew the Ottoman sultan ABD AL-HAMID II in 1909. The only Ottoman commander to gain fame during World War I, Kemal foiled the British attempt (1915) to land at Gallipoli and later kept the Turkish army of Syria together as it was pushed back into Anatolia by the British.

Kemal opposed the Turkish government's decision to surrender (1918) to the Allies and sign the Treaty of Sèvres (1920), which gave up large areas of Anatolia to foreign occupation. Assigned to supervise demobilization in Anatolia, he used this authority and his wartime reputation to organize a national army, which ultimately drove out Allied occupying forces, abolished the sultanate, and replaced it with a republic. As reward, Kemal was later given the name Atatürk ("Father of the Turks").

As president of the republic, Atatürk instituted a unicameral parliament (the Grand National Assembly), a responsible government, led mostly by Prime Minister Ismet INÖNÜ;, and a modern bureaucracy. But he allowed only one party—his own Republican People's Party. He emphasized Turkish nationalism to rally popular support for the drastic, revolutionary measures needed to modernize the nation. His reforms included disestablishment of Islam as the state religion, secularization of education and justice, emancipation of women, adoption of modern Western clothing and Latin script, and enforcement of equality for all citizens.

Mustafa Kemal, later called Kemal Atatürk ("Father of the Turks"), won fame as a military commander during World War I and led the revolution that established the Republic of Turkey in 1923. As president, he pursued a vigorous policy of modernization. In 1934, when the Turks were required to adopt surnames, he was dubbed Atatürk by the parliament.

Initial attempts to develop the economy by encouraging private enterprise foundered because of inefficient management as well as the economic crisis of the 1930s; so Atatürk developed statism—state control of the basic means of production through national banks. Friendly relations were maintained with Turkey's former subject peoples, now independent states or mandate territories, through a series of alliances. The rise of Italian Fascism and German Nazism led Atatürk into close relations with Britain and France.

Atchison   Atchison (1990 pop., 10,656) is a city in northeast Kansas. Located on the Missouri River, the city has been an important rail, river, and road terminal since the Atchison & Topeka Railroad was chartered in 1859. It is surrounded by rich farmlands, and grain products and textiles are manufactured there.

Atget, Eugène [aht-gay']   The French photographer Jean Eugène Atget, b. Feb. 12, 1857, d. Aug. 4, 1927, was virtually unknown in his lifetime but is today considered one of the greatest photographers. He had been a sailor, an actor, and a painter before he took up photogra-

This photograph (c.1910) of a lampshade vendor is from Eugène Atget's series documenting French tradespeople. Atget sold his prints for a pittance as records of a vanishing Paris.

phy at the age of 40. Considered a documentary photographer, Atget often photographed the same site from different angles and at different times, thus demonstrating the malleability of photography. Atget sold thousands of his pictures of Paris to antiquarians and libraries. Attention was drawn to his work largely through the efforts of Berenice ABBOTT.

Athabasca, Lake [ath-uh-bas'-kuh]   Lake Athabasca is in west central Canada and straddles the border between Alberta and Saskatchewan. The fourth largest lake in Canada, excluding the Great Lakes, it is 335 km (208 mi) long from east to west and 8–56 km (5–35 mi) from north to south. A part of the Mackenzie River system, Athabasca is fed by the Athabasca and Peace rivers on the southwest and is drained by the Slave River to the northwest. Uranium City is on its northern shore. The lake was discovered in 1771 by Samuel HEARNE. Its name is Cree for "where there are reeds."

Athabasca River   The Athabasca River, in Canada, is the most southerly tributary of the MACKENZIE RIVER. Rising in the Columbia Icefield in southwestern Alberta, it flows 1,231 km (765 mi) across the province to its northeast corner, where it enters Lake Athabasca.

Athanasius, Saint [ath-uh-nay'-zhuhs]   Athanasius, b. c.295, d. 373, was bishop of Alexandria and a defender of the Christian faith during the 4th-century crisis of ARIANISM. As a theological expert at the Council of Nicaea, which gathered in 325 to condemn the Arian rejection of Christ's divinity, Athanasius defended the unity of Christ as both God and man (see NICAEA, COUNCILS OF). Seventeen of his 45 years as bishop of Alexandria (328–73) were spent in exile, imposed on him on five separate occasions between 335 and 366, largely through the maneuverings of the Arianizing party.

Athanasius's writings in defense of Nicene orthodoxy include three *Discourses against the Arians* (c.358). An earlier work, *On the Incarnation of the Word* (c.318), brought to its fullest expression the orthodox doctrine of redemption. His *Life of St. Antony* (c.356) is an important source for early monasticism. After his final restoration to office, Athanasius spent his last years in peace. His feast day is May 2.

Athanasius asserted both the full humanity and full divinity of Jesus Christ. He held that if Christ were not one in being with God the Father, then salvation could not be possible; and if Christ were not fully man, then human nature could not be saved. The CREED named for him is of later origin.

atheism   *Atheism,* from the Greek *a* ("non") and *theos* ("deity"), commonly and loosely refers to the theoretical or practical denial of the existence of a deity. The meaning of *atheism* has varied considerably in history: even the earliest Christians were labeled "atheists" because they denied the existence of the Roman deities. In Western culture, where monotheism has been the dominant mode of religious belief, atheism has generally referred to the denial of the existence of a transcendent, perfect, personal creator of the universe. To be an atheist need not mean that one is nonreligious, for there are religions, such as Buddhism and Taoism, that do not postulate the existence of a supernatural being. Atheism should be distinguished from AGNOSTICISM, which means that one does not know whether or not a deity exists.

Until recently atheism has been widely believed to be both immoral and dangerous to society. Plato not only viewed atheism as irrational but argued that certain atheists deserved the death penalty. When Christianity became the dominant religion in the West, atheism and heresy were thought to be worthy of exile or death because it was a much more serious matter to corrupt the soul than to damage the body. Atheism was also dangerous to the political authority of Western monarchies that claimed to rest upon divine right.

The believability of atheism seems directly proportionate to the growth of the sciences and the emergence of humanism since the Renaissance. In the 19th century the sciences seemed to make theological explanations of the origins of the universe and of the emergence of humankind unnecessary. Particularly important were the writings of David Hume and Immanuel Kant, which established that attempts to prove the existence of God from the world order were invalid. In the mid-19th century explicitly atheistic and humanistic systems of philosophy appeared. Ludwig Feuerbach, Karl Marx, Arthur Schopenhauer, and Friedrich Nietzsche were not only atheists but also militant critics of religion generally and of Christianity particularly.

Theoretically, atheists maintain either that there are no good arguments for believing in the existence of a personal deity, or that the statement *God exists* is incoherent or meaningless. The last type of logical criticism of theism is characteristic of logical positivism. Practically, some atheists have argued that belief in a supernatural and supreme being requires a devaluation of this life or that the belief is an expression of infantile helplessness.

Athelstan, King of Wessex

Athelstan, d. Oct. 27, 939, king of Wessex and Mercia (924–39), carried on the work of his grandfather, ALFRED, and father, EDWARD THE ELDER, in unifying the English kingdoms. He conquered (927) the Norse kingdom of York and defeated (937) a coalition of Scots and Norse Irish at Brunanburh, a battle celebrated in the Anglo–Saxon Chronicle. Athelstan's laws were aimed chiefly at the suppression of lawlessness. The king married his sisters to several powerful princes, including the future German king Otto I, founder of the Holy Roman Empire.

Athena

In Greek mythology Athena was the patron goddess of Athens and an important member of the Olympic pantheon. Born fully armed and from the forehead of the chief god, Zeus, Athena was her father's favorite child. He entrusted her both with the aegis, his breastplate, and with his terrible thunderbolt.

Athena was a major warrior figure, and most images depict her dressed in armor and holding a spear. In the *Iliad* Homer describes her as a fierce battle goddess who continually intervened on the side of the Greeks in the TROJAN WAR. However, she also took an interest in handicrafts and agriculture, and the olive tree, which she is said to have created, was sacred to her. She was also noted for her wisdom and good sense; this explains her close association with the owl, an ancient symbol of wisdom and reason.

The most famous ancient temple to Athena was the Parthenon, named for one of the goddess's epithets, Parthenos ("the Maiden"), which still stands atop the ACROPOLIS in Athens.

Athenagoras

[ath-uh-nag'-uh-ruhs]   Athenagoras I, b. Vasilikon, Greece, Mar. 25, 1886, d. July 7, 1972, was the ecumenical patriarch of Constantinople (Istanbul) and honorary primate among the patriarchs of the Orthodox church from 1949 to 1971. His name was Aristokles Spyrou. He was enthroned as patriarch on Jan. 7, 1949. A brilliant and versatile personality, he responded to the ecumenical initiatives of Pope PAUL VI. After traveling to Jerusalem to meet (1964) the head of Roman Catholicism, he also received the pope in Istanbul (July 1967) and made a historic visit (October 1967) to Rome. He was the first Orthodox patriarch of recent history to engage in such far-reaching steps toward Christian unity.

Athens (Georgia)

Athens (1990 pop., 45,734) is a city in northeastern Georgia on the Oconee River. The seat of Clarke County, it was founded in 1801 as the site of the University of Georgia. The city has many antebellum homes. Textiles, clocks, and electrical transformers are manufactured there.

Athens (Greece)

Athens (Greek: Athínai) is the capital and largest city of Greece. It lies on a small plain that extends southward to the Saronic Gulf, a branch of the Aegean Sea. The city center is 11 km (7 mi) from the coast and is served by the port of PIRAEUS, with which it forms a single metropolitan area. Greater Athens has an area of 427 km^2 (165 mi^2) and a population of 3,027,331 (1981). The population of the city proper is 885,737 (1981).

Athens is surrounded by mountains: Aigaleos to the west, Parnes to the north, Pentelikon to the northeast, and Hymettus to the east. Most are of limestone or marble, from which the ancient buildings of the city were constructed. The plain on which the city lies contains isolated limestone hills, including Lykavittos, now called Hagios Georgios, which rises 339 m (1,112 ft) above the sea, and the flat-topped ACROPOLIS, 156 m (512 ft) high,

The Parthenon (center), perhaps the finest remaining example of classical Greek architecture, commands a panoramic view of Athens. In 1833, Athens was selected as the capital of the independent Greek nation.

around which the city grew. The city is on the Ilissus River, which is dry for much of the year and carries abundant water only after winter storms. Athens has a typical Mediterranean climate, with hot, dry summers and mild winters. Rainfall is slight.

The Contemporary City. Athens, the seat of the Orthodox primate of Greece, is the center of the Greek government and the capital of the department of Attica. The old palace of the kings of Greece is now used to house the parliament. Athens is also the primary financial and commercial center in Greece and is the focus of the road and rail systems. Much of the country's maritime trade takes place at the port of Piraeus. Athens has an international airport. Manufacturing industries have been developed primarily in and near Piraeus. Light engineering, textiles, chemicals, and cement making are important, as are distilling, milling, tanning, tobacco preparation, and the processing of other local agricultural products.

Athens is the principal cultural and educational center of Greece and has a university, founded in 1837, as well as professional schools. The city is noteworthy for its fine archaeological collections, especially those contained in the National Archaeological Museum. The city's most important cultural remains, however, are its numerous architectural monuments, dating from ancient times and later periods. Foremost among these is the Acropolis, the ancient fortified hill on which stand the Erechtheum, Parthenon, and Propylaea, all of the 5th century BC. To the south of the Acropolis are the Theater of Dionysus and the Odeum of Herodes Atticus, and to the west, the AREOPAGUS (council chamber) in which St. Paul spoke. The AGORA is partially excavated. The STOA, or colonnaded walk, of Attalos, which is located there, has been reconstructed and now holds a sizable collection of Greek antiquities. The city also contains a number of fine Orthodox churches of the Byzantine period, including the 12th-century Little Metropolitan Church.

History. The earliest settlement, dating from before 3000 BC, was situated on the summit of the Acropolis, protected on all sides except the west by its steep slopes. Named for the city's patron goddess, ATHENA, the ancient city developed mainly to the north of this hill, around the agora, or marketplace. Parallel walls, called the Long Walls, made a protected thoroughfare between the city and its port of Piraeus. The most glorious period in the city's history was the 5th century BC, when it was the cultural and artistic center of the classical world. Although overshadowed by the rise of Rome, it remained a city of social and intellectual importance during the Roman Empire. St. Paul visited Athens, and the Emperor Hadrian lavished money on its public buildings.

Thereafter the city declined in importance. It was subject to attack by Slavs and was reduced to a petty provincial town in the Byzantine Empire. In 1204, Athens was occupied by the Crusaders and remained under Western rule until its capture by the Turks in 1456. Greece gained independence from the Turks in the war of 1821–32, and in 1833, Athens became the capital of Greece.

In 1833, Athens was a small urban settlement of less than 4,000 people located north of the Acropolis in a district known today as the Plaka. Modern Athens developed to the north and east of the old city. The architect Eduard Schaubert laid out a network of wide, straight boulevards that converge at Synragma (Constitution) Square and the Royal Palace, lying to the east of the early city.

atherosclerosis [ath-uh-roh-skluh-roh'-sis] Atherosclerosis is a disorder of large and medium-sized arteries, most commonly the large CORONARY ARTERIES that supply the heart muscle with oxygen-rich blood. It is considered the most familiar form of ARTERIOSCLEROSIS.

The disorder is characterized by a buildup of fatty deposits, called plaques, on the inner walls of the affected arteries. The plaques consist of materials such as CHOLESTEROL, LIPIDS, and cellular debris. They lead to a loss of elasticity in the artery and to ischemia, or a narrowing of the blood's passageway. The resulting decrease in smooth blood flow may ultimately deprive a vital organ, such as the heart or brain, of its blood supply. Loss of circulation to a limb may also occur.

Atherosclerosis is the most common cause of coronary HEART DISEASE, including HEART ATTACKS, and of other cardiac disorders. It is also a major cause of STROKE.

The incidence of atherosclerosis increases with age. Men show clinical manifestations an average of 10 years earlier than women, and overt manifestations before the age of 40 occur almost entirely in men. Overt manifestations take time to occur because more than a 75 percent narrowing of arteries is required to impede blood flow seriously.

The causes of the disorder are not yet fully understood, but certain characteristics called risk factors tend to be observed in persons prone to atherosclerosis. These include high blood pressure, or HYPERTENSION, and high blood-cholesterol levels. Resistance to these factors appears to diminish with age, especially when accompanied by OBESITY and cigarette smoking. Atherosclerosis may also be manifested fairly rapidly in diseases such as diabetes in which the concentration of blood lipids is raised.

Diets rich in saturated fats and cholesterol are believed to promote atherosclerosis (see NUTRITION, HUMAN). Lipoproteins transport cholesterol in the blood, and low-density lipoproteins (LDL) in particular seem to increase the accumulation of cholesterol in body tissues. A genetic factor also seems to play a role; persons with a low percentage of LDL receptors in their body tend to develop

atherosclerosis more frequently than do persons with a high percentage of the receptors, regardless of other lifestyles. A deficiency in LDL receptors can also be acquired from a high-cholesterol diet. Factors causing high blood pressure are also important; the atherosclerotic process does not normally occur in low-pressure pulmonary arteries and veins. For this reason excessive use of salt in the diet is discouraged by many physicians.

Evidence suggests that a controlled diet, avoidance of smoking, more exercise, and hypertension control can, if implemented early enough, delay atherosclerosis in persons prone to the disease. Anticholesterol drugs have also been developed. When arteries are clogged by plaques, physicians use such techniques as coronary bypass surgery or ANGIOPLASTY in an effort to check the course of atherosclerosis.

athlete's foot   See RINGWORM

Athos, Mount [ath'-ohs]   Mount Athos is in northeastern Greece at the eastern end of Acte (Aktí) Peninsula on the Aegean Sea. The Holy Mountain (Áyion Óros) of the Greek Orthodox church, it is 2,033 m (6,670 ft) high. The mountain and the surrounding area, 48 km (30 mi) long and 10 km (6 mi) wide, make up the theocratic republic of Mount Athos—an autonomous monastic district inhabited by 3,000 monks from 20 monasteries. Monastic communities of the rule of Saint Basil, a code still followed by monks of the Greek Orthodox church, were first established on the mountain in the 10th century. Nineteen monasteries were built during the 10th through the 13th centuries; the 20th and last monastery was founded in 1540. Mount Athos was pillaged by Crusaders in the 13th century and was again damaged during the 19th-century Turkish occupation. The district declared its independence in 1913 and became a theocratic republic under Greece in 1927.

Atkinson, Brooks   Justin Brooks Atkinson, b. Melrose, Mass., Nov. 28, 1894, d. Jan. 13, 1984, was the principal drama critic for *The New York Times* from 1925 to 1960. His reviews and observations, collected in *Broadway Scrapbook* (1947), *Broadway* (1970), and *The Lively Years* (1973), chronicle the development of the American theater. In 1962, Atkinson received a special Tony Award for lifetime achievement in the theater. He won a 1947 Pulitzer Prize for his reporting from the USSR.

Atlanta   Atlanta, the capital of Georgia and seat of Fulton County, is the transportation, commercial, and financial center of the southeastern United States. It has a population of 394,017 (1990). Atlanta is located in north central Georgia in the rolling foothills of the Blue Ridge Mountains. The city's relatively high elevation (320 m/1,050 ft) creates moderate summer weather and four climatically distinct seasons.

Atherosclerosis is a common degenerative disease in which the arteries become constricted. A diseased artery (B) loses elasticity and has less interior space than a normal artery (A), because of accumulating fatty deposits (orange Globules) on its inner lining. When arteries of the head and neck are affected, atherosclerosis can result in a stroke. Fatty deposits in the cardiac arteries can cause a number of types of heart disease. In leg arteries they may lead to gangrene.

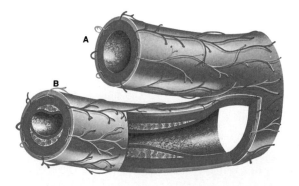

Contemporary City. Atlanta's metropolitan area extends to 15 counties and has a population of 2,833,511 (1990). More than two-thirds of the residents of the city and one-third of the residents of the metropolitan area are black. The city itself, which has grown rapidly in the 20th century, showed the first signs of declining population in the mid-1970s while the suburbs have continued to grow. Tied to the booming economy of the metropolitan area is the development of MARTA, Atlanta's rail rapid transit system.

Atlanta's excellent transportation facilities (it owes its location to a railroad rather than a river) have attracted numerous industries. The most important of them manufacture automobiles, airplanes, and textiles. Nevertheless, distribution (wholesaling, warehousing, trucking) remains the major economic activity. Atlanta has many corporate regional headquarters and has become the center of federal government activity in the Southeast. Hartsfield Atlanta International Airport is one of the country's major airports.

Among the city's major institutions of higher education are Georgia State University (1913), Georgia Institute of Technology (1885), Atlanta University (1865), and Emory University (1836). The Robert W. Woodruff Arts Center houses a theater company, a symphony orchestra, the Atlanta College of Art, and the High Museum of Art. Other places of interest are the Martin Luther King, Jr., National Historic Site, the museum of the Jimmy Carter presidential library, and Grant Park, which has the

Atlanta's skyline is dominated by the 70-story-tall Peachtree Plaza Hotel. With the recent influx of many important corporations, modern Atlanta has become the financial and commercial center of the Southeast.

city zoo and Cyclorama, a Civil War memorial. Stone Mountain state park is nearby.

History. In 1821, Creek Indians ceded land, including the future site of Atlanta, to the state of Georgia. The city sprang up at the southern end of a railroad built (1837) from Chattanooga, Tenn., and was originally called Terminus. Renamed Marthasville in 1843, it was incorporat-

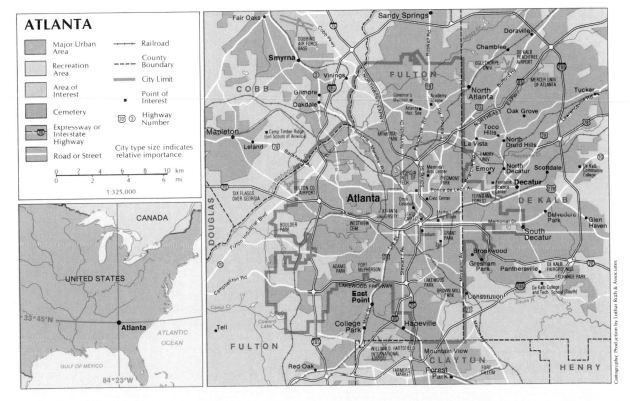

ed as a city in 1847, at which time it received its present name. During the Civil War, Atlanta was, because of its rail connections, a major Confederate supply station. It was occupied by Union forces under Gen. William Tecumseh Sherman on Sept. 1, 1864, and most of its buildings were burned on November 15 (see ATLANTA CAMPAIGN). Sherman's assertion that the burning of the city would enable it to become a great city of the future eventually proved to be true.

After the Civil War, Atlanta regained its position as transportation center of the Southeast. It has served as the state capital since 1868 and was made permanent capital in 1877. In the 20th century the city has actively sought new industries and businesses and has been the leading Southern city in instituting civil rights legislation. In 1990, Atlanta was selected as the site of the 1996 Summer Olympic Games.

Atlanta campaign   The Atlanta campaign in the Civil War began on May 5, 1864, when Gen. William T. SHERMAN, with more than 100,000 Federal troops, advanced from Chattanooga, Tenn., against a Confederate force of some 65,000 under Gen. Joseph E. JOHNSTON.

ATLANTA CAMPAIGN
May 5-Sept. 1, 1864

Union forces
Confederate forces
Battles

SHERMAN

JOHNSTON

2) June 27: Kenesaw Mountain. Sherman repulsed but outflanks Confederate position.
July 17: Johnston replaced by Hood

MARIETTA

1) May 5, 1864: Sherman advances from Chattanooga; Johnston retreats

3) Confederate counterattacks at Peachtree Creek (July 20), Atlanta (July 22), and Ezra Church (July 28) fail (see below). Atlanta captured (Sept. 1)

4) Hood moves north to threaten Tennessee

ATLANTA

5) Nov. 12: Sherman begins "March to the Sea"

CHATTAHOOCHE R.

0 10 15 Km
0 5 10 Mi

THOMAS
PEACHTREE CREEK
II   SHERMAN   July 20
STEWART HARDEE
SCHOFIELD
McPHERSON
EZRA CHURCH
ATLANTA
HOOD
HARDEE   July 22

III   SHERMAN   July 28
EZRA CHURCH
ATLANTA
Aug. 31: Hood abandons Atlanta

Sherman's advance was part of a coordinated Federal drive against the two main Confederate armies in the field in 1864; this drive by George G. Meade against Robert E. Lee and Sherman against Johnston was designed to end the war.

Johnston began one of the great retreats in history, parrying when he could, stalling everywhere, threatening on good ground, evading every trap, backing up with guns and men intact until, at last, he looked down on Sherman's legions from defenses atop Kenesaw Mountain, northwest of Atlanta. There Sherman was checked (June 27), but he flanked the Confederates and besieged Atlanta by the end of July 1864. Johnston was relieved of command on July 17. His replacement was Gen. John B. HOOD, whose more reckless tactics failed to halt Sherman's advance. Hood evacuated Atlanta during the night of August 31, and Sherman moved in the next day.

Atlantic cable   The first transatlantic telegraph cable was completed in 1858, largely through the persistence of Cyrus W. FIELD, its American promoter. The cable stretched across the ocean floor between Trinity Bay, Newfoundland, and Valencia, Ireland. On Aug. 5, 1858, Queen Victoria sent the first official transatlantic message—to President James Buchanan. The cable's current was so weak, however, that the transmission of her 90 words took 67 minutes. Three weeks later the cable's insulation failed. Efforts to lay a new cable succeeded only in 1866, when Field used the largest steamship of its time, the GREAT EASTERN, to pay out the 3,432 km (2,133 mi) of cable.

Transatlantic telephone transmission was not accomplished until 1956. Since that year, numerous telephone CABLES have been laid under most of the world's oceans and seas. The first transatlantic FIBER OPTICS cable, completed in 1988, can carry 40,000 calls simultaneously.

Atlantic Charter   The Atlantic Charter was an Anglo-American statement of common principles issued on Aug. 14, 1941, by President Franklin D. Roosevelt and Prime Minister Winston Churchill. They had conferred for four days (August 9–12) aboard the U.S.S. *Augusta* off Newfoundland. Although the United States had not yet entered World War II, the statement became an unofficial manifesto of American and British aims in war and peace. The charter enunciated eight principles: (1) renunciation of territorial aggression; (2) no territorial changes without consent of the peoples concerned; (3) restoration of sovereign rights and self-government; (4) access to raw materials for all nations; (5) world economic cooperation; (6) freedom from fear and want; (7) freedom of the seas; and (8) disarmament of aggressors. The charter's principles were endorsed by 26 allies in the United Nations Declaration signed in Washington, D.C., on Jan. 1, 1942.

Atlantic City   Atlantic City is a resort and convention center in southeastern New Jersey. The seat of Atlantic

County, it has a population of 37,986 (1990) and a metropolitan population of 319,416. The city lies along the Atlantic Ocean on Absecon Beach, a low, sandy barrier island, and is separated from the mainland by a narrow strait. The economy of the city is based almost entirely on tourism, supplemented by the shipping of seafood.

Permanent settlement of Absecon Beach began in the late 18th century. In 1852, largely through the efforts of Dr. Jonathan Pitney, a local physician, the city became the eastern terminus of the Camden and Atlantic Railroad and began its role as a resort city. The first boardwalk was constructed in 1870, and the first pier, jutting from the boardwalk over the ocean, was built in 1882. The Miss America Pageant was established there in 1921 and has been held annually since (with the exception of 1928–35). With the increase of air travel to other resorts after World War II, Atlantic City experienced a continuous and serious decline in tourist activities. In 1976, however, legalized gambling for the city was approved by state referendum. The first casino opened in 1978, and by 1989, 12 casinos were in operation there. The casinos provided jobs and helped the economy of the surrounding area, but they did little to halt the decline of Atlantic City's poorer neighborhoods.

Atlantic Ocean   The Atlantic Ocean, second largest of the world's oceans, occupies an elongated, S-shaped basin extending in a north-south direction and is divided into the North Atlantic and South Atlantic by equatorial countercurrents at about 8° north latitude. Bounded by North and South America on the west and Europe and Africa on the east, the Atlantic is linked to the Pacific Ocean by the Arctic Ocean on the north and the Drake Passage on the south. An artificial connection between the Atlantic and Pacific is also provided by the Panama Canal. On the east the dividing line between the Atlantic and the Indian oceans is the 20° E meridian. The Atlantic is separated from the Arctic Ocean by a line from Greenland to southernmost Spitsbergen to northern Norway.

Covering approximately 20% of the Earth's surface, the Atlantic Ocean is second only to the Pacific in size. With its adjacent seas it occupies an area of about 106,450,000 km² (41,100,000 mi²); without them it has an area of 82,362,000 km² (31,800,000 mi²). The land area that drains into the Atlantic is four times that of either the Pacific or Indian oceans. The volume of the Atlantic Ocean with its adjacent seas is 354,700,000 km³ (85,093,000 mi³) and without them 323,600,000 km³ (77,632,000 mi³).

The average depth of the Atlantic, with its adjacent seas, is 3,332 m (10,932 ft); without them it is 3,926 m (12,877 ft). The greatest depth, 8,381 m (27,498 ft), is in the Puerto Rico Trench. The width of the Atlantic varies from 2,848 km (1,769 mi) between Brazil and Liberia to about 4,830 km (3,000 mi) between the United States and northern Africa.

The Atlantic Ocean has irregular coasts indented by numerous bays, gulfs, and seas. These include the Caribbean Sea, Gulf of Mexico, Gulf of St. Lawrence, Hudson Bay, Baffin Bay, Mediterranean Sea, Black Sea, North Sea, Baltic Sea, Barents Sea, Norwegian-Greenland Sea, and Weddell Sea. Its relatively small number of islands include Svalbard, Greenland, Iceland, the British Isles, the Azores, the Madeira Islands, the Canaries, the Cape Verde Islands, Bermuda, the West Indies, Ascension, St. Helena, Tristan da Cunha, the Falkland Islands, and the South Georgia Islands.

Ocean Bottom

The principal feature of the bottom topography of the Atlantic Ocean is a great submarine mountain range called the Mid-Atlantic Ridge. It extends from Iceland in the north to approximately 58° south latitude, reaching a maximum width of about 1,600 km (1,000 mi). A great RIFT VALLEY also extends along the ridge over most of its length. The depth of water over the ridge is less than 2,700 m (8,900 ft) in most places, and several mountain peaks rise above the water, forming islands. The South Atlantic Ocean has an additional submarine ridge, the Walvis Ridge.

The Mid-Atlantic Ridge separates the Atlantic Ocean into two large troughs with depths averaging between 3,660 and 5,485 m (12,000 and 18,000 ft). Transverse ridges running between the continents and the Mid-Atlantic Ridge divide the ocean floor into numerous basins. Some of the larger basins are the Guiana, North American, Cape Verde, and Canaries basins in the North Atlantic. The largest South Atlantic basins are the Angola, Cape, Argentina, and Brazil basins.

The deep ocean floor is thought to be fairly flat, although numerous SEAMOUNTS and some guyots exist. Several deeps or trenches are also found on the ocean floor. The shelves along the margins of the continents (see CONTINENTAL SHELF AND SLOPE) constitute about 11% of the bottom topography. In addition a number of deep channels cut across the continental rise.

Ocean sediments are composed of terrigenous, pelagic, and authigenic material. Terrigenous deposits consist of sand, mud, and rock particles formed by erosion, weathering, and volcanic activity on land and then washed to sea. Pelagic deposits, which contain the remains of organisms that sink to the ocean floor, include red clays and Globigerina, pteropod, and siliceous oozes. Covering most of the ocean floor and ranging in thickness from 60 m (200 ft) to 3,300 m (10,900 ft), they are thickest in the convergence belts and in the zones of UPWELLING. Authigenic deposits consist of such materials as manganese nodules. They occur where sedimentation proceeds slowly or where currents sort the deposits.

Water Characteristics

The salinity of the surface waters in the open ocean ranges from 33 to 37 parts per thousand and varies with latitude and season.

Surface water temperatures, which vary with latitude, current systems, and season and reflect the latitudinal distribution of solar energy, range from less than 2° to 29° C (28° to 84° F). Maximum temperatures occur north

Norwegian-Greenland
Sea
▼3970 m.
Iceland
Greenland
3360 m. ▼
REYKJANES RIDGE
North
Sea
Baltic Sea
British
Isles
SCANDINAVIA
CONTINENTAL RISE
LABRADOR
Newfoundland
EUROPE
CARPATHIAN MTS.
ALPS
St. Lawrence R.
Grand Banks
APPALACHIAN MTS.
Bay of
Biscay
Danube R.
PYRENEES
Black
Sea
MID-ATLANTIC RIDGE
**NORTH
AMERICA**
North
American
Basin
Azores
ATLAS MOUNTAINS
Mediterranean Sea
▼5880 m.
Mississippi R.
Mississippi
Fan
5852 m. ▼
Bermuda
*NORTH
ATLANTIC
OCEAN*
Canary
Islands
SAHARA
Gulf of
Mexico
6649 m. ▼
Canaries
Basin
Cuba
PUERTO RICO TRENCH
▼8742 m.
Cape Verde
Islands
Niger R.
*Caribbean
Sea*
Guiana
Basin
AFRICA
PANAMA CANAL
Amazon R.
ROMANCHE TRENCH
MID ATLANTIC RIDGE
Congo R.
WESTERN RIFT VALLEY
EASTERN RIFT VALLEY
SOUTH AMERICA
Angola
Basin
St. Helena
▼6260 m.
ANDES
MATTO
GROSSO
*Brazil
Basin*
▼5207 m.
*SOUTH
ATLANTIC
OCEAN*
KALAHARI
DESERT
*PACIFIC
OCEAN*
ANDES
MID-ATLANTIC RIDGE
WALVIS RIDGE
*Cape
Basin*
Tristan Da Cunha
*Argentina
Basin*
▼6050 m.
Falkland Islands
Strait of Magellan
South Georgia Island
SOUTH SANDWICH TRENCH
TIERRA DEL
FUEGO
▼8428 m.
Atlantic-Indian Basin
Weddell Sea

of the equator, and minimum values are found in the polar regions.

Water in the North Atlantic circulates in a clockwise direction, whereas water circulation in the South Atlantic is counterclockwise—a reflection of the Coriolis force (see OCEAN CURRENTS). The ocean's TIDES are semidiurnal; that is, two high tides occur during each 24 lunar hours. The tides are a general wave that moves from south to north. In latitudes above 40° north some east-west oscillation occurs.

Climate

The climate of the Atlantic Ocean and adjacent land areas is influenced by the temperatures of the surface waters and water currents as well as by the winds blowing across the waters. Because of an ocean's great capacity for retaining heat, maritime climates are moderate and free of extreme seasonal variations. Climatic zones vary with latitude; the warmest climatic zones stretch across the Atlantic north of the equator. The coldest zones are in the high latitudes. Ocean currents contribute to climatic control by moving warm and cold waters to other regions. Adjacent land areas are affected by the winds that are cooled or warmed when blowing over these currents. Hurricanes develop in the southwestern North Atlantic Ocean.

History and Economy

The Atlantic Ocean appears to be the youngest of the world's oceans. Evidence indicates that it did not exist prior to 100 million years ago, when the continents that formed from the breakup of the ancestral supercontinent, Pangaea, were being rafted apart by the process of SEA-floor SPREADING. The Atlantic has been extensively explored since the earliest settlements were established along its shores. The Vikings, Portuguese, and Christopher Columbus were the most famous among its early explorers. After Columbus, European exploration rapidly accelerated, and many new trade routes were established. As a result the Atlantic became and remains the major artery between Europe and the Americas. Numerous scientific explorations have been undertaken, including those by the German *Meteor* expedition, Columbia University's Lamont Geological Observatory, and the U.S. Navy Hydrographic Office.

The ocean has also contributed significantly to the development and economy of the countries around it. Besides its major transportation and communication routes, the Atlantic offers abundant petroleum deposits in the sedimentary rocks of the continental shelves and the world's richest fishing resources, especially in the waters covering the shelves. Threats to the ocean environment include OIL SPILLS, plastic debris, and the incineration of toxic wastes at sea.

See also: CONTINENTAL DRIFT; MID-OCEANIC RIDGE; OCEAN AND SEA; OCEANIC TRENCHES; SUBMARINE CANYON.

Atlantis In Greek legend Atlantis was thought to be a large island in the Atlantic Ocean west of the Pillars of Hercules. The seat of an ancient and advanced civilization, Atlantis and its people were supposedly destroyed by an earthquake. The sources of many Atlantis legends are two dialogues of PLATO. In the *Timaeus*, Plato recounts the story of Egyptian priests who 200 years earlier had reportedly described Atlantis as a powerful island empire seeking to dominate the Mediterranean world more than 9,000 years before Plato's time. The expansionist plans of the Atlantans were ended only when their army was defeated by Athens. Shortly afterward an earthquake caused Atlantis to sink beneath the ocean. In the *Critias*, Plato characterizes Atlantis as possessing an ideal political system.

Later writers were interested in the legend of Atlantis. Many theories suggesting the exact location of the lost island have been advanced, and the nature of its utopian political system has been discussed extensively. Although traditional accounts of Atlantis have been proved false, some archaeologists speculate that the Atlantis legend may have originated with the volcanic eruption that destroyed a highly civilized Minoan town on the island of THERA (Thira) in the Aegean Sea.

Atlas (missile) The Atlas was the first U.S. intercontinental ballistic missile (ICBM), produced in the 1950s to

Three U.S. space-launch vehicles, in order of increasing payload capability, are (left to right) an Atlas D rocket, shown with a Mercury capsule and escape tower, an Atlas D booster with an Agena B upper stage, and an Atlas D with a Centaur second stage.

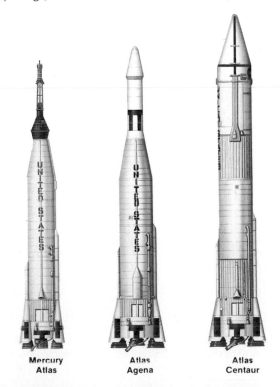

Mercury Atlas   Atlas Agena   Atlas Centaur

counter the threat posed by the Soviet development of large ballistic missiles. Its design profited from the thermonuclear breakthrough of 1954, which led to warheads of lighter weight. Atlas rockets also played a prominent role in the U.S. space program. The Atlas ICBM stood 25.14 m (82.5 ft) high and had a diameter of 3.05 m (10 ft). The lift-off weight was about 120,600 kg (266,000 lb). The range exceeded 14,484 km (9,000 mi). Three Rocketdyne engines provided the thrust.

Atlas was responsible for launching America's MERCURY PROGRAM astronauts into orbit in 1962 and 1963. The missile also launched Lockheed AGENA rocket stages for the U.S. Air Force and NASA. In a subsequent development, a CENTAUR stage was mounted atop a modified Atlas D to provide a versatile, high-energy launch vehicle.

See also: ROCKETS AND MISSILES.

Atlas (mythology)   In Greek mythology Atlas was a TITAN who bore the weight of the sky on his shoulders as a punishment for warring against ZEUS. After the Titans were defeated by the Olympian gods, Atlas was sentenced to support the sky on his shoulders. He was the father of the HESPERIDES, who guarded the golden apples.

atlas   An atlas is a book of maps or charts that may include either a specific region or the entire world. It may also contain thematic information for the subject region on such topics as climate, geology, vegetation, or population. Abraham ORTELIUS's *Theatrum orbis terrarum* (1570) is generally considered to be the first modern atlas. Its name dates from the 16th century, when Gerardus MERCATOR called his collection of maps an atlas and used the figure of Atlas, the Titan, supporting the world on his shoulders, on a cover for books of maps.

Atlas Mountains   The Atlas Mountains are a system of mountain ranges and plateaus in North Africa that extend across Morocco, Algeria, and Tunisia. They have a length of about 2,410 km (1,500 mi), extending from the Atlantic Ocean (where the Canary Islands are their westernmost outcrop) to northeastern Tunisia on the Mediterranean Sea. The highest peak is Toubkal in southwestern Morocco, which reaches a height of 4,165 m (13,665 ft). The Atlas Mountains are separated from the Sierra Nevada of Spain by the Strait of Gibraltar and from the Apennines of Italy by the Mediterranean. The Atlas system is related to the European Alpine system, both having been formed by the movements of the continents of Europe and Africa toward each other during the late Jurassic Period (190–140 million years ago).

The ranges of the Atlas occur in two parallel groups: a coastal group that faces the sea and an interior group that faces the Sahara. The coastal group includes, from west to east, the Great, or High, Atlas in Morocco; the Middle Atlas in Morocco; and the Tell, or Maritime, Atlas, which begins in eastern Morocco and extends across Algeria and Tunisia. The interior group includes the Anti-Atlas range, which is roughly parallel to the Great Atlas; and the Saharan Atlas, which includes the Aurès Mountains in Algeria and Tunisia.

The Atlas Mountains act as a climatic divide between the moderately moist Mediterranean zone and the arid Saharan zone. They are, in addition, a distinctive bioclimatic unit themselves, although temperature, rainfall, and vegetation vary widely along the course of the mountains. Average annual rainfall ranges from 255 to 510 mm (10 to 20 in), and the mean average temperature is 16° C (60° F). The areas with higher rainfall sustain forests (including cedars, oak, and cork), livestock raising (principally sheep and goats), and agriculture. The ranges are rich in minerals, including coal, manganese, copper, iron, lead, cobalt, zinc, and phosphates. The principal inhabitants of the Atlas Mountains are the BERBERS. Spectacular scenery and an equable climate have made tourism an important industry.

atmosphere   The atmosphere is the nearly transparent envelope of gases and suspended particles that surrounds the Earth, profoundly influencing environmental conditions on the planet's surface. Without chemical processes involving several of the atmospheric gases, life could not exist. The physical processes that operate in the atmosphere are also of vital importance because they are responsible for the Earth's varied climates.

Composition and Structure

Many of the physical and chemical processes that occur in the atmosphere are directly related to its composition. The atmosphere is now composed almost entirely of oxygen and nitrogen in their diatomic forms (two atoms bound together by chemical forces). Diatomic nitrogen (N_2) accounts for approximately 78% of the total molecules in the atmosphere, and diatomic oxygen (O_2) represents nearly 21%. The inert noble gas, argon, accounts for about 0.9%, and the remaining 0.1% is composed of many trace gases, the most significant of which are carbon dioxide (CO_2) and water vapor (H_2O). Although concentrations of carbon dioxide amount to only 350 parts per million (ppm), the gas is vital in maintaining the Earth-atmosphere system's heat balance because it absorbs so much infrared radiation. Water vapor, present in highly variable quantities ranging from 0% to 4% by volume, also absorbs considerable infrared radiation and, additionally, is an essential link in the HYDROLOGIC CYCLE. Another important trace gas is the triatomic form of oxygen, ozone (O_3), which is concentrated in a layer centered at about 25 km (16 mi) above the Earth's surface. Although present in maximum concentrations of only about 12 ppm, ozone absorbs so much ultraviolet radiation that the OZONE LAYER shields life on Earth from harmful ultraviolet rays.

Meteorologists usually divide the atmosphere into four layers. In order of increasing elevation these are the TROPOSPHERE, the STRATOSPHERE, the MESOSPHERE, and the THERMOSPHERE. Each has a different temperature range. Temperatures decrease with altitude in the troposphere

An Apollo 9 photograph of a cyclonic storm system above the Pacific Ocean supplies meteorological information than can only be obtained by satellite. Such pictures are important for understanding and predicting large-scale weather patterns.

and mesosphere and increase with altitude in the stratosphere and thermosphere. The troposphere and stratosphere are separated by the TROPOPAUSE, a level of minimum temperature that varies in altitude from about 16 km (10 mi) near the equator to 9 km (5 mi) near the poles. The stratosphere and mesosphere are separated by the stratopause, a level of temperature maximum at an altitude near 50 km (30 mi). The mesosphere and thermosphere are in turn separated by a temperature minimum, the mesopause, which occurs near 80 km (50 mi). These temperature layers are created primarily by the selective absorption of SOLAR RADIATION at various levels in the atmosphere. Radiation in the extreme ultraviolet (wavelength less than 100 nanometers) is absorbed by atoms of oxygen above 100 km (60 mi). This process not only maintains the high temperatures of the thermosphere but also produces electrically charged particles, called ions. For this reason the region of the atmosphere above 80 km (50 mi) is also referred to as the IONOSPHERE. Ultraviolet radiation of somewhat longer wavelengths (200–300 nanometers) penetrates into the stratosphere, where it is absorbed by ozone to produce the temperature maximum near 50 km (30 mi). Visible radiation, on the other hand, penetrates to the surface of the Earth and produces the temperature maximum at the ground level.

Stratification and Static Stability. Temperature distribution alone does not determine the state of the atmosphere. Pressure and density also are important. Atmospheric pressure, usually expressed in units called millibars, is the force that the total mass of air in an imaginary vertical column exerts on a given horizontal area of the Earth's surface. Standard sea-level pressure, 1,013.25 millibars, is equivalent to the pressure exerted by a column of mercury 760 mm (30 in) high. If, like water, the atmosphere were incompressible, pressure would decrease uniformly with height, and the atmosphere, like the ocean, would have a definite upper limit. In reality the atmosphere is compressible; that is, density (mass per unit volume) is proportional to pressure. This relationship, called Boyle's law, for the chemist Robert BOYLE, implies that density decreases with height in the atmosphere: as height increases, less mass remains above a given point; therefore less pressure is exerted. At sea level the density of air is about 1 kg per m^3 (8 oz per ft^3).

Density does not depend only on pressure; for a given pressure, it is inversely proportional to temperature. This relationship, known as Charles's law, for the physicist Jacques CHARLES, implies that the depth of an air column bounded by two constant-pressure surfaces will increase as the temperature in the column increases. Thus the vertical distance over which pressure decreases to half of its surface value ranges from about 5,800 m (19,850 ft) in the tropics to 5,100 m (16,575 ft) near the poles.

When an air mass rises, it expands (because of the reduction in pressure). In expanding, it must work against the pressure force exerted by the surrounding air. According to the principle of conservation of energy (the first law of THERMODYNAMICS), the work done in expansion must be balanced by an equal reduction in the internal energy of the air mass. Since the internal energy is proportional to temperature, an expanding air mass must cool. Conversely, an air mass that is compressed must warm. Compression or expansion of a gas in the absence of heat exchange with the surroundings is called an ADIABATIC PROCESS.

Adiabatic cooling and heating control vertical convection in the atmosphere. A mass of dry air rising adiabatically in the atmosphere cools at a rate of about 10° C per km (17° F per mi). Since, on the average, the decrease of temperature with height in the troposphere is only 6.5° C per km (11° F per mi), an adiabatically ascending air mass becomes cooler and denser than its surroundings and tends to sink back toward its original level. In regions such as DESERTS, where the air near the ground is strongly heated, an air mass displaced vertically upward will become warmer than its surroundings and will be accelerated farther upward. Such statically unstable conditions result in vigorous mixing and upward heat transport.

Moist Processes. Water can exist in all three chemical phases—solid, liquid, and gas—at atmospheric temperatures and pressures. During phase changes, water exchanges heat with its surroundings, a process called latent heating. Condensation and freezing release heat and thus warm the surroundings, whereas evaporation and melting absorb heat and cool the surroundings. CLOUDS and PRECIPITATION are thus essential to the heat balance of the atmosphere.

The amount of water vapor present in a region of the atmosphere is usually expressed in terms of the ratio of the mass of water vapor in a given volume of air to the mass of that volume of dry air, and this in turn is used to determine relative HUMIDITY. When an air mass containing water vapor is forced to rise and cool adiabatically, its humidity will increase to the point of saturation. If the air mass rises beyond this point, condensation will occur and clouds will form.

Condensation causes release of latent heat, which partially offsets adiabatic cooling. The net temperature decrease in an adiabatically expanding mass of saturated air will be less than that in a mass of dry air. Thus, unlike a dry air mass, an ascending saturated air mass tends to become warmer and less dense than its environment, and thus to rise farther, which results in a kind of widespread instability that accounts for the predominance of convective (CUMULUS) clouds. The resulting vertical mixing plays an important role in maintaining the atmosphere's heat and momentum balances.

Radiation and Energy Transfer. In the long-term average, the energy content of the Earth-atmosphere system is nearly constant: energy received from the Sun is almost exactly balanced by energy radiated to space by the atmosphere. Not all of the solar energy that falls on the atmosphere is absorbed. A fraction is reflected back to space by clouds and by the Earth's surface. This fraction, called the ALBEDO, is about 30%. About 19% of the incident energy is absorbed in the atmosphere. The remaining 51% is absorbed at the Earth's surface. The 30% of incident solar energy reflected back into space is balanced by heat transferred to the atmosphere from the Earth's surface primarily through the release of latent heat by evaporation at the surface and subsequent condensation in clouds.

The annual average solar radiation received by the atmosphere varies strongly with latitude—it is four times greater at the equator than at the poles. Radiation emitted to space by the Earth, however, does not vary greatly from one latitude to another. This results in a net radiative energy surplus in the tropics and a net deficit in high latitudes. Thus, in order to maintain the Earth's overall energy balance, energy must be transported poleward. Warm ocean currents, such as the GULF STREAM, account for half of this poleward transport, and the remainder is transported by wind systems.

Circulation

The average distribution of WINDS in the atmosphere is called the general circulation. The general circulation includes not only the more or less steady, global-scale winds but also the many transient disturbances that constitute the weather. To understand the structure of the wind and pressure systems on a global scale, the effects of the Earth's rotation on moving air parcels must be considered.

The Earth's rotation causes the flow of air to be deflected to the right of its direction of motion in the Northern Hemisphere and to the left in the Southern. This is called the CORIOLIS EFFECT, and it is a result of the conservation of momentum. An air flow slows down or speeds up according to whether it moves farther from (equatorward) or nearer to (poleward) the Earth's axis of rotation.

The pattern of air flow then becomes such that flow is parallel to isobars, or lines of constant air pressure at a given height, and the speed of flow is proportional to the pressure gradient. The wind is then said to be in geostrophic balance.

Temperature differences also affect the general pattern of air flow. The cooler the atmosphere is, the more rapidly air pressure decreases with height above the Earth's surface. Therefore, the difference in pressure at two different latitudes also increases with height, and wind velocity must increase with height as well, if it is to maintain geostrophic balance. This increase of velocity with height is called the thermal-wind relationship.

The geostrophic and thermal-wind relationships account for the mean winds being westerly (from the west) in mid-latitudes, where both pressure and temperature decrease poleward, and also account for the winds increasing with height to a maximum of about 30 m/sec in the subtropical JET STREAM core at an average of 30° latitude and 12 km elevation. These upper-level WESTERLIES are among the most important phenomena of the atmospheric general circulation. Transient areas of fair and bad weather originate in, and are carried along by, these upper-level winds. Thus, storm systems tend to move from west to east in mid-latitudes along storm tracks associated with the jet stream. The average jet-stream winds do not, however, blow uniformly in the west-to-east direction; otherwise they could not transport heat poleward. In reality, the disturbing influence of large mountain ranges and land-sea contrasts (see OCEAN-ATMOSPHERE INTERACTION) causes the jet stream to deviate from its mean latitude along a sinuous path circling the globe.

In tropical regions an additional mechanism comes into play. Near the surface, the pressure decreases from the subtropical highs centered at approximately 30° latitude to the equatorial trough, or low-pressure zone. The resulting low-level winds depart from geostrophic balance because of the drag exerted by surface friction, and they form the northeasterly TRADE WINDS in the Northern Hemisphere and southeasterly trade winds in the Southern Hemisphere. The trade winds form the low-level branch of a closed-circulation pattern in the meridional plane known as the Hadley cell, named for the 18th-century Englishman George Hadley, who first described it. Ac-

The Earth's atmosphere generally is divided into four layers (A), based on temperature variations within each divison: the troposphere, stratosphere, mesosphere, and thermosphere. With increasing elevation the troposphere and mesosphere are zones of decreasing temperatures, whereas the stratosphere and thermosphere are regions of increasing temperatures (B) resulting from atmospheric absorption of short-wavelength solar radiation. At any given level, atmospheric pressure depends on the mass of the atmosphere above it, and density depends on the pressure. Both density (C) and pressure (D) decrease rapidly with increasing altitude, particularly above the stratosphere.

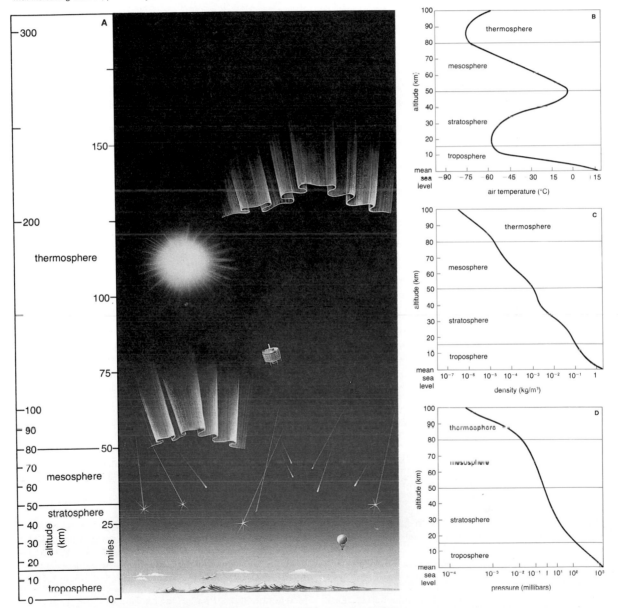

cording to Hadley, surface air heated near the equator rises and moves poleward in the upper troposphere, gradually cooling and sinking back to the surface, where it again moves equatorward to close the loop. This widespread sinking accounts for the predominantly dry conditions in the subtropical zone. The heat and momentum transported out of the equatorial zone by the upper-level poleward flow in the Hadley cell are primarily responsible for maintaining atmospheric heat and momentum balances in the tropical zone.

Weather Disturbances. The transient disturbances that occur in the upper-level jet stream are responsible for much of the weather variations in extratropical latitudes. Small and random perturbations introduced into the jet-stream flow are amplified by drawing energy from the main flow. The resulting disturbances, typically several thousand kilometers in horizontal extent, are the familiar CYCLONES AND ANTICYCLONES seen on the daily weather charts. These systems go through life cycles of growth and decay that last about a week. They tend to concentrate preexisting temperature contrasts into narrow zones of sharp temperature change known as FRONTS. Much of the precipitation associated with extratropical cyclonic systems is concentrated along the warm front (a transition zone from cool, dry air to the warm, moist air pushing it along) that precedes the arrival of the low-pressure minimum at the surface. The low is followed at the surface by passage of a cold front, which pushes out the warm air and marks a return to cool, dry conditions. (See METEOROLOGY.)

Cyclonic storm systems also occur in the tropics, especially in association with the intertropical convergence zone. Tropical disturbances, unlike mid-latitude systems, move from east to west. Wind speeds ordinarily do not exceed several meters per second, although precipitation may exceed 2 cm/day (0.8 in/day). Occasionally, such disturbances intensify into tropical storms, or hurricanes, especially in the western Atlantic and western Pacific (see HURRICANE AND TYPHOON).

Many of the most damaging storms are severe small-scale storms 10–100 km (6–60 mi) in horizontal extent, rather than the cyclonic variety. Isolated THUNDERSTORMS or squalls generated by vertical motions produced by the heating of surface air are common during the summer months in areas where sufficient moisture is present and the atmosphere is conditionally unstable. When several such systems interact, they may generate high winds, hailstorms, and even TORNADOES.

These small-scale disturbances are fairly well understood by now, but little is yet known about the fundamental causes of climatic change (see CLIMATE), which occurs on all time scales. Long-term climatic changes may be related to changing external forces such as variations in the Sun's energy output, but short-term variations seem to be random natural fluctuations in the atmosphere-ocean system.

Human Impacts. Events in recent years have greatly increased awareness of human interactions with the atmosphere. The best-known example of deliberate human impact is the use of cloud-seeding techniques to increase

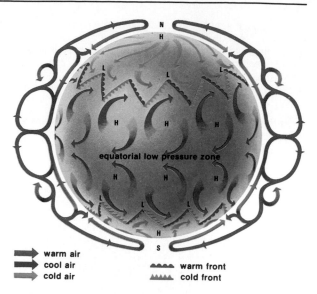

warm air
cool air
cold air

warm front
cold front

The Earth's atmosphere functions as a giant heat engine, in which temperature differences between the poles and the equator provide the global driving force to circulate air masses vertically and horizontally. As warm air rises at the equator and moves toward the poles at high altitudes, cold polar air moves toward the equator at low altitudes to replace it. Winds in any given area are set in motion by movement of air from high pressure cells, H, to low pressure cells, L. Prevailing wind directions at different latitudes, however, depend not only on pressure difference but also on the Coriolis effect, a sideways drift caused by the rotation of the Earth. Thus, the winds, indicated by the curved arrows, tend to spiral out of high-pressure areas in clockwise directions in the northern hemisphere and in counterclockwise directions in the southern hemisphere. Precipitation occurs where cold and warm fronts meet.

precipitation and to prevent hail. Despite many years of extensive efforts, very few successes have been substantiated. (See WEATHER MODIFICATION.)

Inadvertent human modification of the atmosphere, on the other hand, may have both local and global consequences. The local climatic impact of urbanization is well known (see URBAN CLIMATE). Global impacts are harder to assess. In recent years concern has grown over the possible damage to the ozone layer that might occur due to ozone-destroying chemical reactions with FLUOROCARBONS introduced by human activities (see POLLUTION, ENVIRONMENTAL). Scientists established in 1986 that an "ozone hole" (an area of ozone depletion) develops every spring above Antarctica, and evidence gathered since then suggests that a similar phenomenon occurs over the Arctic. At the Earth's surface, ozone levels are increasing as a result of air pollution. Tropospheric ozone damages crops and plays a role in ACID RAIN formation.

The release of carbon dioxide by the burning of fossil fuels has been projected as another serious hazard if it continues unchecked. Concentrations of the gas in the atmosphere have risen from less than 300 parts per million (ppm) before 1900 to about 350 ppm in the late 1980s. The trend could cause a substantial increase in global surface temperatures through the GREENHOUSE EFFECT.

The Origin of the Atmosphere

To understand how the atmosphere formed, scientists must examine 4.5 billion years of geologic time. Then principles from chemistry and biology must be applied to develop a consistent explanation of the changes that must have occurred. The Earth's atmosphere is generally considered to have formed from gases emitted by volcanoes. The composition of volcanic gases today, however, is radically different from the composition of the atmosphere; in particular, volcanoes emit virtually no oxygen. What accounts for the differences?

Volcanic gases would have undergone many changes upon leaving the young planet's interior. Most of the water vapor would have condensed, filling the oceans. Much of the light hydrogen would have escaped into space, and carbon dioxide would have reacted with surface minerals. None of the changes, however, would have produced the atmospheric oxygen observed today.

Considerable evidence exists for the absence of oxygen during the first billion years of the Earth's existence. Two theories have been proposed to explain how oxygen was produced. One attributes it to the breakdown of water vapor by ultraviolet light, a process called photodissociation, which would produce free hydrogen and oxygen.

A second, more likely source of oxygen is life itself, mainly through the process called PHOTOSYNTHESIS, in which carbon dioxide and water combine to produce carbohydrates and oxygen. According to some estimates, approximately 99% of the oxygen added to the atmosphere since the Earth's beginnings was produced by photosynthesis and only 1% by photodissociation. The atmosphere's oxygen content is thought to have increased enough to allow life to emerge from the water onto dry land about 430 million years ago, during the Silurian Period of GEOLOGIC TIME.

See also: METEOROLOGY; WEATHER FORECASTING; WEATHER VARIATION AND EXTREMES.

---

atmospheric sciences The atmospheric sciences focus on the chemical, physical, and dynamic properties of the ATMOSPHERE. Several disciplines are involved: synoptic meteorology, which encompasses much of traditional METEOROLOGY, including simultaneous observations over large portions of the Earth, and analysis of the data as the basis for WEATHER FORECASTING; atmospheric chemistry, the study of atmospheric components such as AEROSOLS, of photochemical reactions, of ozone production and the OZONE LAYER, and of precipitation chemistry; physical meteorology, the study of radiation, optical phenomena, electrical effects in the atmosphere, and the phase changes of water; and atmospheric dynamics, the study of atmospheric motion, both small-scale (turbulence) and large-scale (general circulation).

See also: EARTH SCIENCES.

---

atom An atom is the smallest unit of matter that is recognizable as a chemical ELEMENT. Atoms of different elements may also combine into systems called MOLECULES, which are the smallest units of chemical COMPOUNDS. In all these ordinary processes, atoms may be considered as the ancient Greeks imagined them to be: the ultimate building blocks of matter. When stronger forces are applied to atoms, however, the atoms may break up into smaller parts. Thus, atoms are actually composites and not units, and have a complex inner structure of their own. By studying the processes in which atoms break up, scientists in the 20th century have come to understand many details of the inner structure of atoms.

The size of a typical atom is only about 10^{10} meters. A cubic centimeter of solid matter contains something like 10^{24} atoms. Atoms cannot be seen through optical microscopes, because they are much smaller than the wavelengths of visible light. By using more advanced imaging techniques such as electron microscopes, scanning tunneling microscopes, and atomic force microscopes, however, scientists have been able to produce images in which the sites of individual atoms can be identified (see ELECTRON MICROSCOPE).

Early Atomic Theories

The first recorded speculations that MATTER consisted of atoms are found in the works of the Greek philosophers LEUCIPPUS, DEMOCRITUS, and EPICURUS. Among those who revived the atomic theory in the 17th century were Pierre Gassendi, Robert BOYLE, and especially Isaac NEWTON. The latter part of Newton's *Optiks* is a series of detailed speculations on the atomic nature of matter and light, indicating how some of matter's properties are to be understood in terms of atoms.

In the 19th century, two independent lines of reasoning strengthened the belief of most scientists in the atomic theory and began to reveal some quantitative properties of atoms. One approach, pioneered by John DALTON, involved chemical phenomena and resulted in the concept of ATOMIC WEIGHTS. The other, involving the behavior of gases, was carried out by physicists such as Amedeo AVOGADRO, Rudolf CLAUSIUS and James Clerk MAXWELL.

In 1811, Avogadro suggested that equal volumes of different gases, under the same conditions of pressure and temperature, contain equal numbers of atoms. Avogadro himself never estimated the magnitude of this value, although it is now known as the AVOGADRO NUMBER. Estimates of its value were first given in the mid-19th century by Clausius and Maxwell.

Discovery of the Electron and of Radiation

By the end of the 19th century almost all scientists had become convinced of the truth of the atomic theory. By that time, ironically, evidence was just beginning to accumulate that atoms are not in fact the indivisible particles suggested by their name. One source of such evidence came from studies using gas-discharge tubes, which are similar to neon lights. In such tubes, a gas at low pressure is subjected to intense electrical forces. Under these conditions, various colored glows (now known as glow DISCHARGE) are observed to traverse the tube. A

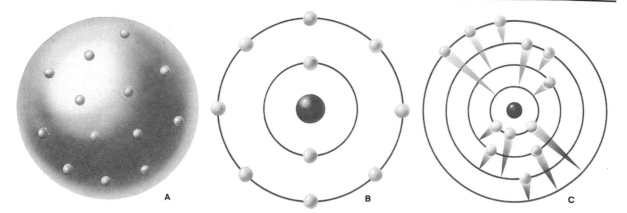

Early in the 20th century the English physicist Joseph John Thomson pictured the atom as consisting of small, negatively charged particles of electricity, or electrons, embedded in a heavier, larger sphere of positive electrical charge, like plums in a pudding (A). Ernest Rutherford, a British physicist from New Zealand, devised (1911) a solar-system model of the atom in which electrons orbit a small, heavy, positively charged central core, or nucleus (B). In 1913 the Danish physicist Niels Bohr revised the planetary model by assuming that electrons can occupy only certain orbits at specific distances from the nucleus (C). Electrons can jump from a low-energy orbit near the nucleus to orbits of higher energy by absorbing energy (green trails). When the electrons return to a lower energy level (purple trails), they release the excess energy in the form of radiation of a characteristic wavelength, such as visible light.

blue glow at one end of the tube, around the electrode known as the CATHODE, was observed for a wide variety of gases. The glow was shown by Sir Joseph John THOMSON in 1897 to involve a stream of negatively charged particles with individual masses much smaller than that of any atom. These particles were called ELECTRONS, and they were soon recognized to be a constituent of all atoms. That is, atoms are not indivisible but contain parts.

In the late 19th and the early 20th century it was also found that some kinds of atoms are not stable. Instead they transform spontaneously into other kinds of atoms. For example, uranium atoms slowly change into lighter thorium atoms, which themselves change into still lighter atoms, eventually ending up as stable atoms of lead. These transformations, first observed by Antoine Henri BECQUEREL, came to be known as RADIOACTIVITY, because the atomic changes were accompanied by the emission of several types of radiation.

Atoms are ordinarily electrically neutral. Therefore, the negative charge of the electrons in an atom must be balanced by a corresponding positive charge. Because the electrons have so little mass, the positive constituents of an atom must also carry most of the atom's mass. The obvious question arose as to how these varied parts are arranged within an atom. The question was answered in 1911 through the work of Sir Ernest RUTHERFORD and his collaborators. In their experiments they passed alpha particles—a type of radiation emitted in some radioactive decays—through thin gold foils. They observed that in some instances the alpha particles emerged in the opposite direction from their initial path. This suggested a collision with a heavy object within the atoms of the gold. Because electrons are not massive enough to produce such large deflections, the positive charges must be involved. Analyzing the data, Rutherford showed that the positive charge in an atom must be concentrated in a very

small volume with a radius less than 10^{-14} meter, or one ten-thousandth the size of the whole atom. This part of the atom was soon called the nucleus. Later measurements showed that the size of a nucleus is approximately given by multiplying the cube root of the atomic weight by 10^{-15} meter.

Rutherford Model

Rutherford proposed an atomic model in which the atom was held together by electrical attraction between the nucleus and the electrons. In this model the electrons traveled in relatively distant orbits around the nucleus. The model eventually proved successful in explaining most of the phenomena of chemistry and everyday physics. Subsequent studies of the atom divided into investigations of the electronic parts of the atom, which came to be known as atomic physics, and investigations of the nucleus itself, which came to be known as nuclear physics. This division was natural, because of the immense difference in size between the nucleus and the electron orbits and the much greater energy needed to produce nuclear as compared with electronic changes.

The Rutherford model of the atom, however, had to face two immediate problems. One was to account for the fact that different atoms of the same element behaved in physically and chemically similar ways. According to the model, electrons could move in any of the infinite number of orbits allowed by Newtonian physics. If that were so, different atoms of the same element could behave quite differently. (This is actually a problem for any atomic model based on Newtonian physics, recognized by Maxwell in 1870.) The other problem was that, according to the principles of electromagnetism, electrons should continuously emit radiation as they orbit. This would cause the electrons to lose energy and to spiral into the nucleus. It was estimated that for the single electron in a hydrogen

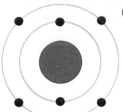

(Left) *A solar-system model of the carbon atom depicts a large nucleus orbited by two electrons in the first orbit and by four electrons in the second orbit. (Below) A three-dimensional view shows electrons circling the nucleus at inclinations to each other. The carbon nucleus contains six protons, which electrically balance the electrons, and six uncharged neutrons.*

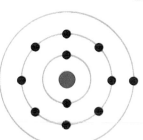

(Left) *A solar-system model of the sodium atom reveals the configuration of the atom's 11 electrons. The two inner orbits are completely filled with two and eight electrons, respectively. Only the eleventh electron, which occupies the unfilled outer orbit, takes part in chemical bonding. (Below) In a modern representation of the sodium atom the electrons are pictured as occupying shells, or layers of space, that are centered on a positively charged nucleus.*

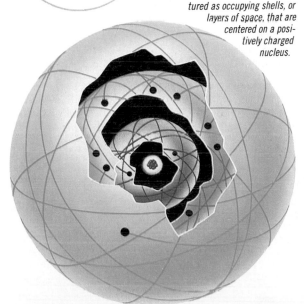

atom, this would take place in 10^{-9} seconds. In reality, hydrogen atoms are indefinitely stable.

An important step toward solving these problems was taken by Niels BOHR in 1913. According to Bohr, the electrons in atoms cannot exist in arbitrary orbits. Instead they are found only in certain "states." The states in which they can exist are those in which the ANGULAR MOMENTUM of their orbits is an integer multiple of $h/2\pi$ where h is a quantity known as PLANCK'S CONSTANT. This constant had been introduced by Max PLANCK in his theory describing BLACKBODY RADIATION.

Bohr Model

According to the Bohr model of the atom, there is a so-called ground state for any atom. This ground state has the lowest energy allowed to the atom, and it is the same for all atoms containing the same number of electrons. An atom normally exists in this ground state, which determined the observed properties of a given element. Furthermore, according to Bohr, no radiation is emitted by an atom in its ground state. This is because energy must be conserved in the radiation process, and no available state of lower energy exists for the atom to balance any energy lost through radiation.

An atom can be removed from its ground state only when enough energy is given to it, by radiation or collisions, to raise an electron to an "excited" state. For most atoms this excitation energy corresponds to several ELECTRON VOLTS. When the atom is excited, it will usually emit electromagnetic radiation rapidly and return to the ground state. The radiation is emitted in the form of individual packets, or quanta, of light, called PHOTONS. Each photon has an energy equal to the difference between the energy of the excited states and the ground state of the atom. According to a formula developed by Planck and Albert EINSTEIN, this energy corresponds to a specific wavelength of the emitted light. Using his assumption about the allowed angular momenta for electrons, Bohr was able to calculate the precise wavelengths in the SPECTRUM of the simplest atom, hydrogen. The agreement of his results with observations did much to convince scientists of the accuracy of his model.

Atomic Physics and Quantum Theory

Bohr was also able to extend his atomic theory to describe, qualitatively, the chemical properties of all the elements. Each electron in an atom is assigned a set of four so-called quantum numbers. (These numbers correspond to the properties of energy, total orbital angular momentum, projection of orbital angular momentum, and projection of spin angular momentum.) It is also assumed—as had first been suggested by Wolfgang PAULI in 1924—that no two electrons in an atom can have the same values for all four quantum numbers. This came to be known as the EXCLUSION PRINCIPLE. This principle influences the way in which the chemical properties of an element depend on its ATOMIC NUMBER (the number of electrons in each atom of the element). A maximum number of electrons can occur for each energy level, and no more than that. For example, the lowest energy level of an atom—

Rutherford found in 1919 that bombardment of a nitrogen nucleus with a helium nucleus produces oxygen and hydrogen nuclei. He concluded that a helium nucleus is absorbed by a nitrogen nucleus and forms an unstable fluorine nucleus, which immediately breaks up into nuclei of hydrogen and oxygen. This was the first artificial transmutation, or transformation, of one chemical element into another element.

alpha particles
(positively-charged helium nuclei)

nucleus (positively-charged)

electrons (negatively-charged)

helium nucleus

nitrogen nucleus

oxygen nucleus

hydrogen nucleus

the one in which the electrons have zero orbital angular momentum—can contain up to two electrons. The one electron in a hydrogen atom exists at this energy level, as do the two electrons in a helium atom. For the next heavier atom, lithium, one of its three electrons must exist in a higher energy state, and as a result this electron can more easily be lost to another atom. Those electrons with approximately the same energy are said to form a "shell." When an atom contains the maximum number allowed for some energy level, that shell is said to be closed. Atoms of INERT GASES, such as helium and argon, have all their shells closed.

Although Bohr's model gives a qualitatively accurate description of atoms, it does not give quantitatively accurate results for atoms more complex than hydrogen. In order to describe such atoms, it is necessary to use QUANTUM MECHANICS. This theory of atomic and subatomic phenomena was created by Erwin SCHRÖDINGER, Werner Karl HEISENBERG, Paul DIRAC, and others in the 1920s. In quantum mechanics, the electron orbits are replaced by PROBABILITY distributions that only indicate in which regions of space each electron is most likely to be found. An equation first written by Schrödinger allows this distribution to be calculated for each atom. From the distribution, properties of the atom such as energy and angular momentum can be determined. Calculations of a wide variety of atomic phenomena have been carried out by means of quantum mechanics. These calculations have proven to give an accurate description of the properties and behavior of atoms. For the simplest atoms, the observations and calculations sometimes agree to better than one part in a billion.

Exploration of the Nucleus

By the late 1920s attention turned from the electronic structure of atoms to the nucleus, a field now known as NUCLEAR PHYSICS. It was already known that nuclei sometimes change into one another through radioactive decay.

Rutherford had also shown, in 1919, that this could be accomplished artificially by bombarding nitrogen nuclei with high-energy alpha particles. In the process the nitrogen nucleus is converted into an oxygen nucleus, and a hydrogen nucleus, or PROTON, is ejected. It had further been discovered by Thomson, Francis William ASTON, and others that for a given element the nucleus sometimes occurs in several different forms that differ in mass. These chemically similar but physically distinct atoms were called ISOTOPES. All of this provided evidence that atomic nuclei also had some kind of internal structure that could be explored through experiments and calculations.

Differences in the integer values of the electric charge and of the mass of many nuclei soon indicated that protons were not the only kind of particle to be found there. That is, the electric charge of a nucleus is always exactly an integer multiple of the charge of a proton, so knowledge of this electric charge always indicates how many protons a nucleus contains. The mass of a nucleus is also approximately—but not exactly—an integer multiple of the mass

In 1932, James Chadwick used a radium source of alpha particles to bombard beryllium foil. He found that a highly penetrating radiation, capable of ejecting high-speed protons from a paraffin block placed in its path, was emitted from the foil. Chadwick also proved that the radiation consists of a beam of uncharged particles, each of which has the mass of a proton. He called these particles neutrons and explained that the direct collision of neutrons with hydrogen atoms in the molecules of the paraffin block had ejected the observed protons.

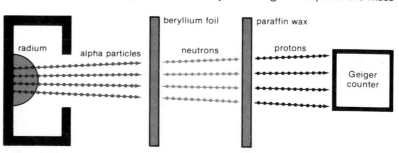

beryllium foil

paraffin wax

radium

alpha particles

neutrons

protons

Geiger counter

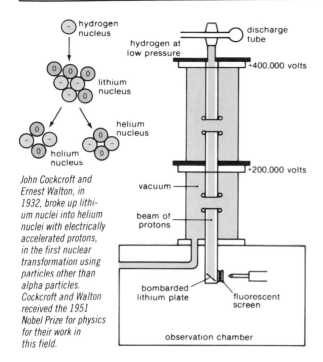

John Cockcroft and Ernest Walton, in 1932, broke up lithium nuclei into helium nuclei with electrically accelerated protons, in the first nuclear transformation using particles other than alpha particles. Cockcroft and Walton received the 1951 Nobel Prize for physics for their work in this field.

of a proton. For many atoms, however, these two integer values are not the same. For example, a helium nucleus has twice the charge but four times the mass of a proton. Clearly, nuclei contain something other than protons.

This problem was solved in 1932 with the discovery by James Chadwick of the NEUTRON. This is a particle that has no electric charge and is slightly more massive than a proton. Thus, most nuclei are composed of both protons and neutrons, which collectively are known as nucleons. A helium nucleus contains two protons and two neutrons, which correctly give the total charge and mass of the nucleus. The isotopes of any given element contain equal numbers of protons but different numbers of neutrons. Thus, an isotope of hydrogen called DEUTERIUM contains one proton and one neutron; a heavier isotope called TRITIUM contains one proton and two neutrons.

The problem then arose as to how atomic particles could be held together in such a small region as the nucleus. The force holding them had to be different from others then known to physicists. It was stronger than the electric forces that can break electrons away from nuclei. On the other hand, the nuclear forces between different nuclei that are far apart are very weak, much weaker than electric forces at such distances. Nuclear forces were studied intensively in the 1930s and '40s, and many details about their properties were learned. Ultimately, such studies became a part of the study of FUNDAMENTAL PARTICLES.

Nuclear physics also revealed that the heaviest known atomic nuclei are the least stable. Very heavy nuclei can break up into two or more smaller nuclei liberating energy in the process. Because of this tendency, all nuclei containing more than about 210 nucleons are unstable

against various kinds of radioactive decay. An important example of this instability of heavy nuclei is nuclear FISSION, discovered in uranium in 1938 by Otto HAHN and Fritz STRASSMANN. This phenomenon was used to produce the ATOMIC BOMB and has been harnessed in reactors to produce NUCLEAR ENERGY. Reactions between two light nuclei, on the other hand, may also release energy in a process known as FUSION. High-energy fusion reactions are the source of energy of most stars.

Recent Work in Atomic and Nuclear Physics

Much recent research in atomic physics has concentrated on atoms in abnormal situations. For example, studies have been made of so-called Rydberg atoms, in which a single electron of a many-electron atom is excited to a very energetic state. Such Rydberg atoms behave similarly to hydrogen atoms, and their properties are accurately described by the energies calculated from the Bohr theory.

There have also been studies of "exotic" atoms in which one of the electrons is replaced by a heavier, negatively charged subatomic particle such as an antiproton (see ANTIMATTER). Because the heavier particle is much closer to the nucleus than an electron would be, such atoms serve as useful probes of nuclear structure.

Nuclear physicists have found methods for studying nuclei heavier than uranium, which do not occur naturally. One way to produce TRANSURANIUM ELEMENTS is by colliding two beams of lighter nuclei. In such a collision, the two nuclei sometimes fuse into a heavier nucleus that can be studied for a short time before it disintegrates. Such heavy-ion collisions have produced nuclei that contain as many as 300 nucleons.

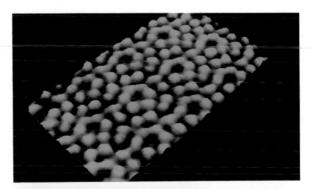

Electron microscopes enable scientists to view the positions of atoms in materials. (Above) A scanning tunneling microscope reveals the pattern of atoms on a silicon surface. (Left) A transmission electron microscope views the atomic lattice of a gold crystal.

atomic bomb

The atomic bomb is an explosive device that depends upon the release of energy in a nuclear reaction known as FISSION, which is the splitting of atomic nuclei. With a release of energy about a million times greater than an equal weight of chemical high explosive, it was the most impressive and disturbing application of science during World War II.

Theory

That mass could be converted into energy was predicted by Albert Einstein early in the century and confirmed experimentally by John D. Cockcroft and Ernest Walton in 1932. But not until 1939, when an entirely new phenomenon was discovered by Otto Hahn and Fritz Strassmann, did a net gain of energy appear possible. Neutrons striking the heavy element URANIUM caused it to fission, the fragments having less mass than the original atom. This mass loss appeared as the energy of motion of the fission fragments and in emitted radiation.

Among the pieces of the split atom were newly produced neutrons, and it was widely recognized that these might encounter other uranium nuclei, cause them to fission, and start a chain reaction. If the chain reaction were limited to a moderate pace, a new source of energy could result. Allowed to progress unchecked, the chain reaction could release energy with explosive force.

Physicists from 1939 on worked to answer such questions as how many neutrons were emitted in each fission, which elements would not capture the neutrons but would moderate or reduce their velocity (thereby increasing the likelihood of uranium fission), and whether only the lighter and scarcer isotope of uranium (U-235) fissioned or the common isotope (U-238) could be used. They learned that each fission releases a few neutrons. A chain reaction, therefore, was theoretically possible if not too many neutrons escaped from the mass or were captured by impurities. Ordinary water moderates the neutrons well but captures too many; heavy water, available only in tiny quantities, and graphite, never before produced at such high levels of purity, were found preferable. The lighter isotope of uranium is, indeed, the fissionable component; but uranium as found in nature consists of only 0.7% U-235, which needed to be separated from the 99.3% U-238.

Development

Frightened by the possibility that Germany might produce an atomic bomb, the Hungarian-born physicists Leo Szilard, Eugene Wigner, and Edward Teller prevailed upon Albert Einstein to address a letter to President Roosevelt. Spurred by the letter, in late 1939 President Roosevelt ordered an American effort to obtain an atomic weapon before the Germans, but significant assistance did not begin until his coordinator of scientific activities for the war, Vannevar BUSH, took charge a few years later. The program was named the MANHATTAN PROJECT when it came under U.S. Army control in mid-1942.

U-235 Gun-Type Atomic Bomb. Because the uncertainties were so great at every step, all processes and techniques were pursued until shown ineffective. Of the several methods investigated for separating the two isotopes, gaseous diffusion and electromagnetic separation were carried into production at Oak Ridge, Tenn. In this manner uranium-235 was enriched from its normal 0.7% to weapons grade of more than 90%. This purified material was then fashioned into the components of a gun-type weapon at the Los Alamos, N.Mex., laboratory headed by J. Robert Oppenheimer. Two pieces of U-235, individually not large enough to sustain a chain reaction, were brought together rapidly in a gun barrel to form a supercritical mass that exploded instantaneously. Confidence in this model was so high that it was not tested. Its first use was in bombing HIROSHIMA, Japan, on Aug. 6, 1945.

Plutonium Atomic Bomb. Well before the U-235 weapon had been developed to the point of seeming assured of success, another type of bomb was proposed. Uranium-238, earlier considered waste material, can capture a neutron without fissioning and become U-239. (All uranium atoms have 92 protons; U-238 has 146 neutrons, and the added neutron raises the total mass to 239.) But the U-239 thus produced is unstable (radioactive) and decays first to neptunium-239 (93 protons and 146 neutrons) and then to plutonium-239 (94 protons and 145 neutrons). Not only was Pu-239 theoretically fissionable, but being a different element it could be separated from uranium by chemical techniques, which would be far simpler than the physical processes that are required to separate isotopes of the same element.

The first successful reactor was assembled on the campus of the University of Chicago under the direction of the Italian physicist Enrico FERMI. On Dec. 2, 1942, it produced a controlled chain reaction. This led to the construction of five large reactors at Hanford, Wash., where

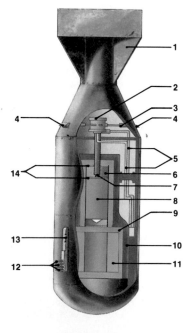

A cross section of the atomic bomb, nicknamed "Little Boy," that was exploded over Hiroshima on Aug. 6, 1945, reveals stabilizing tail fins (1); an air pressure detonator (2), which was used to explode the bomb at a predetermined height; pressure sensors (3); airstream deflectors (4); electronic conduits and fusing circuits (5); a conventional explosive charge (6); a detonating head (7); two U-235 elements; (8, 11) that are driven together to obtain an explosive critical mass; a neutron reflector (9); a cast bomb-casing (10); probes (12); batteries (13); and packing (14).

U-238 was irradiated with neutrons and transmuted into plutonium. After separation, plutonium was also shipped to Los Alamos for fabrication into a weapon.

A new technique called implosion was developed, in which a noncritical shell of plutonium was surrounded by chemical high explosives. When the latter were detonated, intense forces squeezed the plutonium core into an extremely dense, supercritical mass, in which a chain reaction could proceed long enough for a massive explosion. This device was tested at Alamogordo, N.Mex., on July 16, 1945. It was used to bomb NAGASAKI, Japan, on Aug. 9, 1945.

Consequences. After 1945 the United States built thousands of atomic bombs and an array of small-size tactical atomic, or fission, weapons. The far more powerful HYDROGEN BOMB, however, has since come to dominate the U.S. nuclear arsenal. The USSR acquired atomic weapons in 1949, Britain in 1952, France in 1960, the People's Republic of China in 1964, and India in 1974. Despite the 1968 Nuclear Non-Proliferation Treaty (see ARMS CONTROL), a number of additional countries are believed to have acquired some fission-weapons capability. They include Pakistan, Israel, Libya, Egypt, Syria, South Africa, Argentina, and Brazil.

See also: NUCLEAR ENERGY; NUCLEAR STRATEGY; WORLD WAR II.

atomic clock

The atomic clock, the most accurate of timekeeping devices, is based on the measurement of changes in the energy states of atoms. The energy change involved in the most common forms of the atomic clock occurs when the atom absorbs energy, causing an electron to alter its spin characteristics and, subsequently, its magnetic field. The unique frequency (number of complete oscillations per second) of the radiation absorbed by an atom when it undergoes such an energy change is a periodic phenomenon analogous to the swing of a pendulum and may thus be used as a time standard. Because this frequency is largely independent of all normal external conditions, such as air pressure and magnetic fields, the atomic clock is a highly stable device. Atoms especially suitable for atomic clocks include cesium, rubidium, and hydrogen.

The most stable and most commonly used frequency standard is the cesium atom clock. Developed around 1950, it is now being used as a highly stable laboratory standard and as a frequency source in aircraft navigational systems. An international agreement in 1967 defined the atomic second in terms of the resonance frequency of the cesium atom (see METRIC SYSTEM). It can achieve a maximum accuracy of about one second in every 300,000 years.

The rubidium atom clock is a similar atomic frequency standard. Currently, the most accurate atomic clocks are hydrogen MASER devices that operate for restricted periods of time. They lose time at a rate equivalent to only about one second in every 30 million years.

Although atomic frequency standards are too expensive for general use, they can be used as master clocks.

The U.S. Naval Observatory Time Service contains a battery of cesium atomic clocks and also uses other types of atomic clock.

atomic constants

The goal of physics is to understand and formulate the basic laws that govern the various processes of nature, such as gravity and electricity, as well as subatomic processes. These laws must be mathematically precise and must have physical implications testable by accurate laboratory experiments.

To express any law of nature, two kinds of physical quantities are required: one that expresses the variables characterizing a given situation, and another kind that is assumed to be independent of any particular situation in which the laws operate. The latter quantities are called fundamental constants. Some of the more familiar constants are explained below.

Elementary Unit of Charge. It has been observed that all electrically charged bodies in nature carry a charge that is an integral multiple of the charge of a single electron, e. In theory quarks, the constituents of hadrons, have charges that are either $1/3$ or $2/3$ the absolute value of the electron's charge.

Planck's Constant. Energy released in atomic processes comes in extremely tiny bundles, with a fixed amount of energy in each bundle. This discrete nature of energy was first recognized by the German physicist Max PLANCK, who postulated that for a given radiation frequency v, the amount of energy E is given by $E=hv$, where h is a fundamental constant called PLANCK'S CONSTANT. The entire subject of quantum physics is based on this fundamental atomic constant h.

Velocity of Light. The velocities of all moving objects encountered in daily life are known to depend on the frame of reference from which they are measured. Relativity theory, however, states that light or any other form of electromagnetic radiation travels with a speed, c, that is fixed and independent of any frame of reference. The velocity of light, c, is therefore, a fundamental constant.

Gravitational Constant. Newton's laws of GRAVITATION state that any two bodies in the universe attract each other with a force F defined by the law $F = Gm_1m_2/r^2$, where m_1 and m_2 are their masses and r is the distance between them. G is an absolute constant called gravitational constant.

Electron and Proton Mass. Other atomic constants that describe atomic and subatomic systems are the masses of the proton (m_p) and the electron (m_e). These particles, along with the neutron, are constituents of atoms.

Avogadro's Number. In the early days of molecular physics, Amedeo AVOGADRO (1776–1856) postulated that at a given temperature and pressure, equal volumes of different gases contain the same number of molecules. The AVOGADRO NUMBER is the number of molecules in one MOLE of the gas and is a constant for all substances.

Boltzmann's Constant. The description of thermal properties of gases is given by the ideal-gas law relating the pressure P, volume V, and temperature T of the gas as follows: $PV = NkT$, where N is the number of molecules in the gas. The parameter k is an absolute constant called the BOLTZMANN CONSTANT. The determination of Boltzmann's constant was made possible by Avogadro's hypothesis.

In addition to these basic fundamental constants, several other constants can be calculated from those previously defined. These include the Rydberg's constant, used in SPECTRUM analysis, and the BOHR MAGNETON, used to describe the magnetic moment of atomic systems. The values used for the fundamental constants and their derivatives undergo adjustments over the years, as scientific advances make more precise measurements possible.

atomic energy see NUCLEAR ENERGY

Atomic Energy Commission see NUCLEAR REGULATORY COMMISSION

atomic number
The atomic number of an element, which indicates its place in the PERIODIC TABLE of elements, is the number of protons (positively charged elementary particles) in the nucleus of one of its atoms. If an atom is electrically neutral, the same number of electrons is present. Atomic number is often symbolized with the letter Z and is shown as a numerical subscript to the left of its chemical symbol. For example, $^{12}_{6}C$ indicates a carbon atom of atomic mass 12 and atomic number 6, the difference being equal to the number of neutrons in the nucleus.

atomic physics see NUCLEAR PHYSICS

atomic weight
Atomic weight is the average mass of atoms of an element relative to some standard; the present standard is the carbon-12 isotope, which is assigned an atomic weight of exactly 12 atomic mass units (amu). Mass numbers (the sum of an atom's protons and neutrons) are always whole numbers, but the atomic weight of an element is the average of the weights of its ISOTOPES, taking the frequency of their natural occurrence into account, and is not usually a whole number. A gram atomic weight is a quantity of an element in grams that has the same numerical value as the element's atomic weight; the gram atomic weight of carbon is 12 grams. Such a quantity always contains 6.022×10^{23} atoms (one mole). For the atomic weights of the elements, see PERIODIC TABLE.

atomism
[at'-uhm-izm] Atomism (Greek *atomon*, "uncuttable") is the philosophic and scientific theory that reality is composed of indivisible elementary parts called atoms. A theory of physical atoms was first advanced by LEUCIPPUS and DEMOCRITUS; later, it was developed by LUCRETIUS. A much more complex version of the theory is held by scientists today. Atomism also denotes theories that may be psychological (the "simple ideas" of John LOCKE and David HUME) or linguistic (as in the elementary propositions of logical atomism).

atonality
[ay-tohn-al'-it-ee] *Atonality* is a term in music that has been vaguely applied to a wide range of modern Western compositional methods. Their common feature is that they do not use TONALITY in the ways that characterized Western music from the late 17th to the early 20th century. The term is sometimes confined to the music of Arnold SCHOENBERG and that of other innovative composers during the period that led to Schoenberg's development of the twelve-tone system (see SERIAL MUSIC) in the 1920s.

Modern composers, including those who employ twelve-tone or other serial techniques, range widely in their use of tonal centers or emphases. The term *atonality* does not serve a clear function in describing this range. It could more simply be applied to tape or chance assemblages of sound in which questions of tonality do not arise.

atonement
The word *atonement*, constructed from *at* and *one*, means "to set at one" or "to reconcile." In Christian theology atonement denotes the doctrine of the reconciliation of God and man accomplished by the crucifixion and death of JESUS CHRIST. There have been three major theories of atonement: the ransom theory, the Anselmian theory, and the Abelardian theory. The ransom theory, first propounded by ORIGEN (c.185–254), was developed from Mark 10:45 and explained the atonement as a price paid by God in Christ to the devil. Saint ANSELM (c.1033–1109) explained the atonement as an act of satisfaction paid by Christ as man to God, who demanded from man perfect obedience to the law, which he could not fulfill because of his sinfulness. The exemplarist theory of Peter ABELARD (1079–1142) viewed Christ's death as an inspiring appeal of love evoking in the sinner a response of love, thus removing his sin.

In Jewish theology stress is placed on personal acts of atonement; vicarious atonement is given little importance (see also YOM KIPPUR).

Atonement, Day of see YOM KIPPUR

ATP
The main source of immediate energy in all organisms is ATP, or adenosine triphosphate. ATP and closely related compounds furnish the energy for cell growth and cell reproduction, muscle contraction, and other chemical processes. ATP may even be converted into light energy in organisms such as the firefly. The ATP molecule comprises a nitrogen compound, adenine, linked to a molecule of sugar, ribose, to form adenosine. On the adenosine molecule is a chain of three phosphate groups that can be removed one by one to produce ADP (adenosine diphosphate, having two phosphate groups), and AMP (adenosine monophosphate, having only one phosphate). As each phosphate group is removed, the bond that connects it to the rest of the molecule breaks, releasing energy for the cells to use in their various activities. The most important reactions involving ATP are those in which the ATP donates one of its phosphates to

another type of molecule to activate it. For example, glucose (a sugar), which is used by cells as a major energy source, does not react at body temperature unless it receives a phosphate. In the muscle and brain cells of vertebrates, excess ATP molecules are joined to the chemical compound creatine (phosphocreatine), which then serves as a reserve form of energy. In the invertebrates, phosphoarginine serves the same function.

Atreus [ay'-tree-uhs]   In Greek mythology Atreus, the son of PELOPS and the father of AGAMEMNON and MENELAUS, was king of Mycenae. When he discovered that his wife Aerope and his banished brother Thyestes had been lovers, he lured Thyestes home, then killed two sons of Thyestes and served their flesh to him in a feast. On being told what had happened, Thyestes pronounced an irrevocable curse on Atreus and his house. Aegisthus, another son of Thyestes, later slew Atreus and presented the kingdom to Thyestes. Poems and dramas by Homer, Aeschylus, Sophocles, and Euripedes deal with the continuing misfortunes of the House of Atreus.

atrium [ay'-tree-uhm]   The atrium was the central, most important room of the Etruscan and Roman house. Although it may have been used as early as the 5th century BC, by the 3d century BC the atrium house had become overwhelmingly popular in the Italian peninsula. Its use gradually declined under the Roman Empire; it had been replaced by peristyle garden houses by the 3d century AD.

An atrium was rectangular. Its long axis usually pointed toward the street, and its center was open to the sky. In the center of the atrium's floor was a pool (*impluvium*) to catch rainwater, sometimes with a tank underneath. Originally these were made of tufa or terra-cotta, but in the richer houses of the late Roman Republic they were made of marble, sometimes elaborately sculptured.

The other rooms of the house were symmetrically distributed around the atrium, which was the social and religious center of the house. Shrines to the family's gods, busts of their ancestors, and other works of art were displayed there.

In Early Christian and medieval times the term *atrium* applied to a peristyle court (colonnaded quadrangle) built in front of a basilican church (see BASILICA). Everyone had access to the atrium, even non-Christians, but not to the rest of the church.

See also: EARLY CHRISTIAN ART AND ARCHITECTURE; ROMAN ART AND ARCHITECTURE.

atrophy   Atrophy is the shrinking or wasting of cells, tissues, organs, or limbs. Atrophy can result from disuse, as with muscles within a cast; deprivation of motor nerve stimuli, as in poliomyelitis; reduced blood supply (ischemia); starvation, terminal cancer, infection, and other chronic diseases; or deprivation of stimulating hormones. Atrophy of one organ or part can cause hypertrophy, or the enlargement of another tissue or organ to compensate for extra strain or work. In some cases, atrophy is reversible; when it is not, the human body has considerable reserve available in each organ. A person may lose the function of 75 percent of an organ before showing symptoms of disease. For this reason, a kidney donor can function normally with only 50 percent of original tissue. With advancing age, some atrophy is normal.

attachment (law)   Attachment, in law, is a writ issued by a court to take a defendant or his property into custody. It may be used to force the appearance of someone guilty of CONTEMPT or, in the case of property, to ensure that the judgment a plaintiff expects to obtain will actually be paid by the defendant. In issuing a writ of attachment before trial, the court may in some cases attach the defendant's bank account or some of his real estate in the amount that the plaintiff hopes to recover. If the court later decides in favor of the defendant, the plaintiff faces the disagreeable prospect of a countersuit by the defendant for damages he sustained in the attachment of his assets. Garnishment, a common form of attachment, is used to satisfy a creditor. The creditor, or garnishor, obtains a court order requiring the debtor's employer, or garnishee, to deduct the debt from the employee's salary and pay it to the creditor.

attainder, bill of [uh-tayn'-dur]   A bill of attainder was a law directed against a person or a group that pronounced them guilty of treason or felony and denied recourse to normal legal procedure.

The English House of Commons began to pass bills of attainder in the 15th century to punish those who had incurred the king's displeasure. Many distinguished figures were dispatched outside the normal channels of the law and often without any evidence being produced to show their guilt.

The U.S. CONSTITUTION (Article I, sections 9 and 10) forbids bills of attainder. Some American states passed bills of attainder during the Revolution and afterward, prompting the Constitutional Convention to insert the provision against them. Some laws passed by Congress after World War II, including those requiring employees to take loyalty oaths, have been held by the courts to constitute bills of attainder.

Attalus I, King of Pergamum [at'-uh-luhs] Attalus I, 269–197 BC, the greatest ruler of the Anatolian state of PERGAMUM, came to the throne in 241 BC. Although supposedly a vassal-ally of the SELEUCIDS, Attalus was both a strong protector of the Greek cities of Anatolia and an opportunist in trying to expand Pergamum's territory and power. He won a major victory over the Galatians and in 229–228 conquered all Seleucid Anatolia except Cilicia. Most of this territory was lost again (223–222) to Achaeus, the general of ANTIOCHUS III.

Attalus then turned his attention to Greece, becoming involved in wars against PHILIP V of Macedonia. He finally enlisted Roman aid and died toward the end of Rome's Second Macedonian War. By drawing Rome into action in eastern affairs, Attalus brought the ultimate defeat of the Seleucids, but Pergamum itself eventually lost its independence.

Attenborough, Richard and David The English film actor Sir Richard Attenborough, b. Aug. 29, 1923, knighted in 1976, won fame as a cowardly young seaman in *In Which We Serve* (1942). As an actor he also appeared in *Brighton Rock* (1947), *The Guinea Pig* (1949), and *10 Rillington Place* (1971). He later directed such films as *Oh! What a Lovely War* (1969); *Young Winston* (1972); *A Bridge Too Far* (1977); *Gandhi* (1982), for which he received an Academy Award; *A Chorus Line* (1985); and *Cry Freedom* (1987).

His younger brother, Sir David Attenborough, b. May 8, 1926, knighted in 1985, achieved fame as a naturalist, writer, and broadcaster. He joined the BBC in 1952 and was its television director of programs (1969–72). Beginning in 1954 he undertook worldwide zoological and ethnographic filming expeditions for the *Zoo Quest* series. He also wrote and presented the acclaimed series *Tribal Eye* (1975), *Life on Earth* (1978), and *The Living Planet* (1984).

Attica [at'-i-kuh] Attica was a mountainous region of ancient Greece whose important centers included ELEUSIS, Marathon, and its principal city, ATHENS, which dominated the area by the 7th century BC. Attica (Greek, Attiki) is also the name of a modern Greek *nomos* (department) with boundaries somewhat different from those of the ancient region.

Attila the Hun Attila, d. 453, a ruler of the nomadic HUNS, harassed the eastern half of the Roman Empire during the 440s and devastated much of the western half of the empire in 451–52. Because of these exploits he came to be known as the "Scourge of God."

In 434, Attila and his brother Bleda negotiated a treaty with the East Roman (Byzantine) emperor Theodosius II and obtained an immense annual tribute of about 300 kg (700 lb) of gold. After six years of peace, the Huns invaded the empire and defeated several imperial armies. After another treaty and payment of more tribute, peace was made. In 445, Attila murdered his brother and launched a new campaign. He struck again in 447 and forced the emperor to cede large areas south of the Danube to the Huns.

In 450, Attila attacked Gaul. A coalition of imperial forces, Visigoths, and other peoples (especially Alans) was formed by the Roman general AETIUS. Attila's horde was stopped at Orléans and forced to retreat. In 451 at the Battle of the Catalaunian Plains (near Châlons-sur-Marne), Aetius's forces won a decisive victory. Attila retreated, and in 452 he attacked Italy but was turned back by an epidemic.

Clement Attlee was prime minister of Great Britain from 1945 to 1951. His Labour government created sweeping social welfare programs such as the National Health Service.

Attlee, Clement, 1st Earl Attlee Clement Richard Attlee, b. Jan. 3, 1883, d. Oct. 8, 1967, was prime minister of Great Britain's first majority Labour government. Of middle-class origin, he studied at Oxford. In 1907 he joined the Fabian Society and was converted to socialism.

Attlee served as an officer in World War I and then was elected (1919) mayor of Stepney, a London working-class borough. Entering the House of Commons in 1922, he became a minister in the minority Labour cabinet of 1929–31. He refused to follow Ramsay MACDONALD into the National government in 1931 and in 1935 became the Labour party's leader.

A prewar critic of Conservative foreign and defense policies, Attlee held high office in Winston Churchill's wartime coalition of 1940–45. Following Labour's landslide electoral victory in 1945, he headed the cabinet that created Britain's WELFARE STATE. It nationalized major public utilities and several industries, including coal mining; instituted free medical and hospital care; and established or improved numerous relief programs for the underprivileged. The Attlee cabinet was responsible for the granting (1947) of independence to India, Pakistan, Ceylon, and Burma, as well as Britain's charter membership in NATO and alignment with the United States against the Communist powers in the Korean War and the cold war.

Financial and economic problems, especially a trade deficit, forced the Attlee government to resort to austerity measures, including food and fuel rationing and devaluation of the pound. Returned to power by a diminished majority in the 1950 elections, Labour lost a second election to the Conservatives in 1951. Upon retiring from the party leadership in 1955, Attlee was awarded a peerage.

attorney An attorney, or lawyer, is a person trained in the law who is authorized to offer legal advice and represent clients in court. In England a traditional distinction between an attorney who deals with clients and an attorney who pleads for them in court is now less commonly observed: the former is called a solicitor and the latter a barrister (in Scotland, an advocate). In the United States many attorneys specialize in particular branches of the law, such as criminal, corporation, tax, or patent law. Some states, as well as the Supreme Court, distinguish between attorney and counsellor, the former applying to younger members of the bar or those who conduct the formal parts of the suit and the latter to those who advise in their area of expertise. U.S. lawyers are licensed by the individual states.

attorney general   In English-speaking countries an attorney general is the chief legal officer of a government. The attorney general of the United States is the head of the Department of Justice and a member of the cabinet. He acts as the government's attorney in litigation, advises the president and the heads of the executive departments on legal problems, administers the federal prison system, and is the government's legal officer in other matters. In Britain the attorney general represents the crown rather than the government, although some attorneys general have been cabinet ministers.

Attucks, Crispus   Crispus Attucks, b. *c.*1723, was the leader of the mob that defied British troops in Boston on Mar. 5, 1770. He was killed in the ensuing BOSTON MASSACRE. Attucks is believed to have been a black man, perhaps of partly Indian descent.

Atwood, Margaret   The poet and novelist Margaret Eleanor Atwood, b. Ottawa, Ontario, Nov. 18, 1939, is one of Canada's most acclaimed writers. *The Circle Game* (1964; rev. ed. 1966), a volume of poetry, won the 1966 Governor General's Award. Her powerful novel, *Surfacing* (1972), analyzes the heroine's steady isolation from society as she searches in the Canadian wilderness for her missing father. Her other works include 2 volumes of *Selected Poems* (1976, 1988) and the novels *The Handmaid's Tale* (1986; film, 1990) and *Cat's Eye* (1989).

Auber, Daniel François Esprit [oh-bair']   Daniel François Esprit Auber, b. Jan. 19, 1782, d. May 12, 1871, was a French composer who wrote more than 40 comic and serious operas. The best known are *La Muette de Portici* (The Mute Girl of Portici, 1828), the first opera to treat the aspirations of the common people in a heroic manner, and *Fra Diavolo* (Brother Devil, 1830). Auber's ingenious orchestrations, including stirring marches with chorus, influenced Giuseppe Verdi and Richard Wagner.

Aubrey, John   John Aubrey, b. Mar. 12, 1626, d. June 1697, English antiquarian and author, is remem-

bered for sketches of his contemporaries—published in 1813 as *Minutes of Lives* and now known as *Brief Lives*. His *Monumenta Britannica*, a survey of British antiquities long recognized as a pioneering work of British archaeology, was not published until 1980. Aubrey's writings first drew attention to the prehistoric stone circle at AVEBURY and to the burial chambers at STONEHENGE known as the Aubrey Holes.

Aubusson [oh-boo-sohn']   Aubusson, a town in central France not far from Limoges, is a world-famous center of TAPESTRY and rug weaving. The population in 1980 was 5,326. Dating from the 9th-century Saracen occupation or perhaps the Flemish immigration of the 1300s, the weaving industry of Aubusson was well known in the 16th century. The weavers are now famous for their contemporary tapestries as well as for those in earlier styles. A school founded in 1884 provides training for weavers and designers. A blue galloon border (ornamental fabric trim) was devised in the 17th century to identify Aubusson products, which were sometimes marked *Aubusson, MRD*, or *MRDB* (*Manufacture Royal Daubusson* or *Du Buisson*).

Auchincloss, Louis [aw'-chin-klaws]   Louis Auchincloss, b. Lawrence, N.Y., Sept. 27, 1917, is a writer whose novels of manners explore the world of Manhattan high society and the influential Eastern Establishment. Educated at Groton and Yale, he received a law degree in 1941 from the University of Virginia and became a Wall Street lawyer. He drew on his background for his first novel, *The Indifferent Children* (1947), examining the New York social set in World War II. *The Rector of Justin* (1964), a study of the headmaster of a boarding school, won particularly high praise. His 23d book, *The Winthrop Covenant* (1976), was peopled with affluent, upper-class New Englanders and New Yorkers as it analyzed the Puritan character from 1630 to post-Vietnam War days in nine loosely connected stories. Auchincloss's fiction has been likened to that of Henry James and Edith Wharton, and like theirs, his novels—including those of his late career (*Honorable Men*, 1985; *Fellow Passengers*, 1989)—form a geography of a singular fraction of American society.

Auckland [awk'-luhnd]   Auckland is the chief port of New Zealand and is located in north central North Island. The seaport city is situated on a plateaulike isthmus. The city proper has a population of 149,500 (1988 est.), but its metropolitan area is the most populous (911,700) in the country. The central business district is near the commercial docks; factories are in separate areas surrounding the city; and residential areas are in the hills and along the coast. Major industries include heavy engineering and the manufacture of consumer goods. Also important is the trade and export of dairy and lamb products of the region's farming areas. The site of Auckland

Auckland is the major port of New Zealand. Auckland is also important as a distribution center serving the dairy industry, a vital part of the nation's economy.

was once a principal Maori settlement. Established in 1840, the town was until 1865 the colonial capital of New Zealand. The combination of a prosperous rural economy and development of industry resulted in rapid growth, particularly in the 1950s and 1960s. Major institutions include the University of Auckland (1882) and the City Art Gallery (1888).

auction   An auction is a sale of property in which potential buyers compete with each other until one person is acknowledged by the auctioneer as the highest bidder and new owner. An auction stands in sharp contrast to the more familiar practices of face-to-face bargaining and fixed-price sales.

Systems. In the English system of auction, the most familiar one in the United States, participants keep raising their bids. In the so-called Dutch system, the auctioneer begins at a high price and then descends by steps until a bidder indicates an intention to buy at the price level reached. A third arrangement entails setting a time limit for the acceptance of bids. An important, and sometimes controversial, mechanism is the reserve, or undisclosed minimum price, set by the seller jointly with the auctioneer, below which the property will not be sold. The reserve is designed to offset collusive bidding by a consortium of dealers known as a "ring." Otherwise, ring members can refrain from competing with each other and instead place one bid at an unduly low price, later dividing or reauctioning the goods among themselves, thus depriving the original owner of a "fair" price.

The Auctioneer. In conducting the sale, the auctioneer usually acts as an agent for the seller, although he or she may also have a proprietary interest in the goods offered. In recent years, British and American auctioneers have adopted the European practice of charging buyers a premium (usually 10%) as well as being paid a commission by the seller. The auctioneer divides the property to be sold into "lots." Either through a spoken announcement or printed catalog, he describes the lots and outlines the legal and financial conditions governing the auction.

Markets. Stock exchanges, commodity markets, and certain trades and industries—notably fur, fish, and flowers—often buy and sell merchandise by auction. The country auction, where everything may be sold from ordinary household objects to entire farms and their equipment, is an old tradition. Widely publicized in recent years is the glamorous auction of important paintings and art objects, rare books, antiques, jewels, or other items judged to have a value that will increase over time. The fascination with such auctions has grown as art prices have surged to epic proportions.

The oldest and largest art auction firm is Sotheby's, founded in 1744 in England. Joined with New York's Parke Bernet since 1964, it has branches worldwide. Another international firm is Christie, Manson, and Woods International Inc., which has held auctions in London since 1766.

Auden, W. H. [aw'-duhn]   The English-born American writer Wystan Hugh Auden, b. Feb. 21, 1907, d. Sept. 28, 1973, was one of the most important poets of the 20th century. Educated at Oxford, he first attracted attention as a member of a group of young leftist writers who were continuing the artistic revolution of such earlier writers as T. S. Eliot, James Joyce, and Ezra Pound. This group included the poets Louis MacNeice and Stephen Spender and the novelist Christopher Isherwood.

Auden's earliest works are startling. They contain unusual meters, words, and images, juxtapose industrial and natural landscapes, and mix the rhythms of poetry with those of jazz. Some critics feel that Auden's first books, *Poems* (1930) and *The Orators, an English Study* (1932), contain his finest work. With Isherwood, Auden also wrote three plays: *The Dog Beneath the Skin* (1935), *The Ascent of F6* (1936), and *On the Frontier* (1938). Later poems of the 1930s, such as those in *Look, Stranger!* (1936) and *Journey to a War* (1939), express his antiwar sentiments. *Another Time* (1940) contains lighter and more romantic verse.

Auden lived in Germany, where he witnessed the rise of Nazism, and during the Spanish Civil War he served as

W. H. Auden, an English poet who became a U.S. citizen in 1946, achieved critical acclaim during the 1930s as the leader of a left-wing literary movement.

an ambulance driver. In 1936 he married Erika Mann, daughter of Thomas MANN, to provide her with a British passport and enable her to leave Germany. Auden immigrated to the United States in 1939 and at about the same time returned to the religion of his youth, Anglicanism. His wide-ranging intellectual interests and his technical virtuosity in a variety of metrical forms are apparent in such works as *The Double Man* (1941), *For the Time Being* (1944), and the 1948 Pulitzer Prize–winning *The Age of Anxiety* (1947). In 1945 he published *The Collected Poetry of W. H. Auden*, in which poems were so arranged as to defy chronology. In this volume, too, he revised many poems and omitted others, among them two of his most popular political poems.

Nones (1951), *The Shield of Achilles* (1955), *Homage to Clio* (1960), *About the House* (1965), and *City without Walls* (1969) added steadily to the store of his carefully made, irreverent, deceptively simple short poems. Critical essays published in *The Enchafèd Flood* (1950), *The Dyer's Hand* (1962), and *Forewords and Afterwords* (1973) increased his reputation for catholicity of taste. He influenced a generation of new poets by teaching, reading his poems, lecturing in colleges and universities throughout the United States and England, and editing the Yale series of young poets' work.

In his later years Auden spent part of the year at his apartment in New York and part in Italy. Later still, he spent time in Kirchstetten, Austria, where he owned a house memorialized in "Thanksgiving for a Habitat" (1965). With his close friend Chester Kallman he collaborated on opera libretti, including Stravinsky's *The Rake's Progress* (1951). He returned to Oxford as an honorary fellow in 1972.

___

audiencia [ow-dee-en'-see-uh] Audiencias were regional courts of law established in Spain and its American colonies to exercise royal authority in both judicial and administrative matters. In the 16th and 17th centuries they served as powerful arms of the Spanish throne in the New World, mainly to check the independence of the CONQUISTADORS. Four judges usually sat on each case, and their verdict was final in all but the most serious decisions. The judges also functioned as advisors to local administrations and achieved considerable power. By the 19th century, 13 audiencias had been established in the New World.

___

audiovisual teaching aids see COMPUTERS IN EDUCATION; PROGRAMMED LEARNING; TEACHING; TEACHING MACHINES

___

audit see ACCOUNTING

___

Audubon, John James John James Audubon, b. Apr. 26, 1785, d. Jan. 27, 1851, was a French-American ornithologist noted for his bird drawings and paintings. After being educated in France, he came to Mill Grove, the Audubon estate outside Philadelphia where he

The Wood Duck, *from John James Audubon's classic work* The Birds of America, *displays the naturalist's artistic skills as well as his attention to detail. More than 400 handcolored plates were included in the compilation, published between 1827 and 1838. Audubon's work helped the scientists of Europe to classify previously unfamiliar species.*

first experimented with bird-banding and migration. Eventually he devoted his life to painting birds and other animals. Audubon earned a living painting portraits and for a while taught drawing in New Orleans. He took his bird paintings to a publisher in Edinburgh, Scotland, and they were printed in *Birds of America* between 1827 and 1838, with the text, *Ornithological Biography*, appearing in five volumes between 1831 and 1839. William MacGillivray, a Scottish naturalist, collaborated with Audubon on the text and supplied most of the scientific data. Audubon had completed more than 400 paintings by 1838. The Audubon societies of today were named for him.

___

Auer, Leopold [ow'-ur] The great Hungarian violinist Leopold Auer, b. June 7, 1845, d. July 15, 1930, is best known as the teacher of noted performers, including Mischa Elman, Jascha Heifetz, Nathan Milstein, and Efrem Zimbalist. He studied in Budapest and Vienna and with Joseph Joachim in Hanover. From 1868 to 1917 he was professor of violin at the Imperial Conservatory in Saint Petersburg. Auer made his concert debut in New York City in 1918 and settled in the United States, becoming an American citizen in 1926. He taught at the Institute of Musical Art in New York and at the Curtis Institute of Music in Philadelphia.

___

Auerbach, Erich Erich Auerbach, b. Berlin, Nov. 9, 1892, d. Wallingford, Conn., Oct. 13, 1957, was a literary critic and philologist. After teaching Romance philology at German and Turkish universities, he joined the faculty of Yale in 1950. Auerbach's most important book, *Mimesis: The Representation of Reality in Western Literature* (1946; Eng. trans., 1953), spans about 3,000 years and considers works from a variety of cultures and genres. It moves from close examination of texts to broader historical and social considerations. The remainder of Auerbach's work is principally devoted to late Latin antiquity and the French and Italian Middle Ages.

Auerbach, Red   Arnold Jacob "Red" Auerbach, b. New York City, Sept. 20, 1917, a former professional basketball coach, compiled the most successful coaching record in the history of the National Basketball Association (NBA). Auerbach coached the Washington Capitols and Tri-Cities franchises in the late 1940s, then became the leader of the Boston Celtics in 1950. From then until 1966, his teams won 1,037 games and 9 NBA titles. The Celtics won 8 of those titles in a row (1959–66), the longest streak in any major U.S. professional sport. Auerbach retired in 1966 to become full-time general manager of the team.

Augsburg   [owks'-burk]   Augsburg is a city in Bavaria, in southern Germany. With a population of 245,600 (1986 est.), it is the capital of Swabia. Located at the confluence of the Wertach and Lech rivers, Augsburg is a major industrial center for southern Germany—producing textiles, machinery, motor vehicles, and airplanes—and is also an important railroad center. It was founded about 15 BC by the Romans, and in AD 955 Otto I defeated the Magyar invaders there. It was made a free imperial city in 1276 and joined the Swabian League in 1331. The FUGGERS and the Welsers were the most important of the business families who were responsible for the 15th- and 16th-century development of Augsburg into a major banking and commercial center and into a scientific and cultural center as well. The AUGSBURG CONFESSION, which sets forth Lutheran doctrine, was read there in 1530. During the Thirty Years' War the city declined. In 1806 it passed to Bavaria. The noted Fuggerei, a 16th-century housing project for the poor, was damaged in World War II but was restored, as was the town hall (1615). Hans Holbein the Elder, Hans Holbein the Younger, and Bertolt Brecht were natives of Augsburg.

Augsburg, Peace of   see REFORMATION

Augsburg Confession   The Augsburg Confession is a Lutheran confession of faith that was issued (1530) during the Reformation at the Diet of Augsburg. In 1530, Emperor CHARLES V convoked the diet as part of his effort to bring religious peace to Europe. He failed in his efforts, however, because he underestimated the fervor with which the followers of Martin LUTHER had already formulated a distinctive position. Philipp MELANCHTHON, one of the authors of the Confession, designed it to be relatively open to the Roman Catholic church on the right and to other reformed but non-Lutheran parties on the left. It affirmed inherited classic Christian doctrines. Its particular stress on grace, as Luther had interpreted it in the writings of Saint Paul, and its rejection of any righteousness based on human works and merits made it unac-

ceptable to many other Western Christians. The Confession remains the primary statement of faith among Lutherans, who to this day expect their ministers to express fidelity to it at ordination.

Augusta (Georgia)   Augusta (1990 pop., 44,639) is a city in eastern Georgia on the Savannah River. It is the seat of Richmond County and the main trade center for a large area. Its manufactures include textiles, bricks and tiles, and metal, wood, and plastic products. Established in 1735 by order of Gov. James Oglethorpe, Augusta was bitterly contested during the American Revolution. Its subsequent growth paralleled the rapid expansion of the tobacco and cotton industries.

Augusta (Maine)   Augusta is the capital of MAINE and the seat of Kennebec County and has a population of 21,325 (1990). It is located in south central Maine at the head of navigation on the Kennebec River and situated in the heart of rich timberlands. Its main manufactures are paper, textiles, food products, and shoes. Attracted to the location by its navigable tidewater, settlers from Plymouth Colony arrived in 1628. It became the state capital in 1831, and the operation of state government plays a considerable part in its economy.

Augustan age   [uh-guhs'-tuhn]   In Roman literature, the Augustan Age was the reign of the emperor Augustus (27 BC–AD 14), during which VERGIL, OVID, and HORACE wrote. The name has come to designate any eminent period in a nation's literary life. Thus in England the Augustan Age extended from the restoration of the monarchy (1660) to the death of Alexander POPE (1744), and its major writers were Pope and John DRYDEN in poetry, and Jonathan SWIFT and Joseph ADDISON in prose. The literature of this age is distinguished by its clarity and order (in verse the tight heroic couplet is the predominant form), its public tone, and its imitation of Roman models

Augustine, Saint   Saint Augustine of Hippo, a 4th–5th-century North African theologian and bishop, was one of the fathers of the Christian church. Augustine's piety established norms for Christian devotional life, spiritual growth, systematic theology, and patterns of morality. His intellectual probings in Scripture and classical philosophy shaped the academic, ecclesiastical, and political history of medieval and Reformation Europe.

Biography. Augustine was born on Nov. 13, 354, at Tagaste (modern Souk-Ahras, Algeria) and was named Aurelius Augustinus. His father, Patricius, was pagan; his mother, Monica, was a pious Christian. At Carthage, where he studied to be a rhetorician and lawyer, he lived with a woman by whom he had a son, Adeodatus. Adopting MANICHAEISM for a time, and then studying philosophy, Augustine began soul-searching with a group of friends. Eventually, he went to Rome, and then on to Milan, as a

Saint Augustine, shown in a Botticelli fresco, was a major architect of Christian theology. His Confessions *(397–401; Eng. trans., 1620) describes his spiritual journey from paganism to Christian faith.*

teacher of rhetoric. At Milan he met AMBROSE, the city's bishop, whose biblical preaching influenced him profoundly. Ambrose baptized him at Easter in 387.

Returning to Africa the following year, Augustine became a priest and in 395 was made bishop of Hippo (modern Annaba, Algeria). He lived in Hippo for the rest of his life, preaching, writing, ministering, and guiding his church. He died on Aug. 28, 430.

Thought. Augustine's early discovery of Cicero's *Hortensius* inspired his lifelong love of philosophy. He later became familiar with Plato's thought through reading the works of PLOTINUS, and this proved to be a major influence. He adopted a Platonic metaphysics, seeing Absolute Good as the center of reality, transcending thought and the material world. Building on this base, he tried to create a synthesis of the Gospel and Neoplatonic idealism. Having rejected Manichaeism, he came to despise it as a false religion and wrote several works attacking Manichaean beliefs.

As bishop, Augustine became a champion of "Catholic doctrine" as he understood it. Against the DONATISTS, who denied the validity of baptisms and ordinations conferred by those who had repudiated their faith in time of persecution, he defended the Catholic practice of not rebaptizing, arguing that the efficacy of the sacraments does not depend on the personal worthiness of the priest who administers them, but on the saving action of Christ. Against PELAGIANISM, Augustine propounded the doctrine of ORIGINAL SIN, defining the human condition as fallen, incapable of goodness without the grace of God. Salvation, he taught, rests with God alone. (See PREDESTINATION.)

The capture of Rome by the Visigoths under Alaric in 410 prompted Augustine to write his monumental CITY OF GOD, a philosophy of history and critique of Greco-Roman culture, in which he maintained that God's purpose is revealed in the unfolding of historical events. Augustine's sublime devotional *Confessions*, begun in 397, is largely an autobiographical work. In it he unhesitatingly revealed his own painful, struggling spiritual journey.

Augustine was second only to Paul as a shaper of Christian theology. His *On the Trinity*, an answer to Arianism, is a brilliant exposition of the triune Deity and interpretation of the Incarnation, as is *The Enchiridion*. In over 300 sermons he provided insight into the Scriptures. His *On Free Will* and *On Grace and Free Will* explore providence and human freedom. In *On Faith and the Creed, On the Spirit and the Letter*, and *On Nature and Grace*, Augustinian theology is expressed in Latin of matchless beauty. As he was nearing death Augustine reviewed his prodigious literary output, correcting and cataloging in the *Retractations*. Feast day: Aug. 28.

Augustine of Canterbury, Saint   Saint Augustine, d. May 26, 604, called the Apostle of England, was the first archbishop of Canterbury. An Italian missionary, he had been prior of a monastery in Rome until 596, when he and 30 other monks were sent by Pope GREGORY I to convert the Anglo-Saxons. King ÆTHELBERT of Kent, who had married a Christian, allowed them to enter his realm, to preach, and to establish a church at Canterbury. In accord with Gregory's instructions, Augustine freely adapted local customs to Christianity. His policy was to preserve pagan temples and to destroy only the idols, transforming pagan rites and customs into Christian practices whenever possible. Feast day: May 27 (May 26 in England and Wales).

Augustinians   Augustinians are members of various Roman Catholic religious communities of men and women who follow the Rule of Saint Augustine, a code of rules for the monastic life originally drawn up by Saint Augustine of Hippo. The two main groups of Augustinians are the Augustinian (Austin) Canons—or Canons Regular of Saint Augustine—dating from the 11th century, and the Augustinian Hermits or Friars, established by Pope Alexander IV in 1256. Famous Augustinian friars include Martin Luther, in his early career, and the geneticist Gregor Mendel.

Augustus, Roman Emperor   Augustus, b. Sept. 23, 63 BC, d. Aug. 19, AD 14, was the first Roman emperor (27 BC–AD 14). Named Gaius Octavius, he was the son of Gaius Octavius, a Roman senator, and Atia, the niece of Julius CAESAR. Only 18 when Caesar was assassinated (Mar. 15, 44 BC), he became by Caesar's will his adopted son and thereafter used the magic of his new name to win over Caesar's veterans.

Rise to Power. The republican CICERO proposed to use

Octavian (as he is known today) as a tool against Mark ANTONY, and later to remove him from power. Octavian, meanwhile, who had illegally organized a private army, received from the Senate an extraordinary military command and the rank of senator (January 43). Following Antony's defeat at Mutina, Octavian marched on Rome and had himself elected consul. Soon afterward he concluded an agreement with Antony and another Caesarian leader, Marcus LEPIDUS. In November 43, the terrorized popular assembly appointed them triumvirs for five years with responsibility for reorganizing the republic. A bloody purge of their political and personal enemies followed.

In October–November 42, at PHILIPPI in Macedonia, Antony and Octavian defeated the republicans led by BRUTUS and CASSIUS. They then divided the empire, Antony remaining in the East while Octavian received the difficult task of settling the veterans in Italy. The agreements in 40, when Antony married Octavian's sister, and in 37, when Antony and Octavian had their powers extended for another five years, only delayed the new civil war. Antony's affair with CLEOPATRA, queen of Egypt, gave Octavian a pretext to slander him as an oriental despot bent on destroying Rome. In 36, Lepidus, who held Africa, was removed, and Octavian united in his hands all the western provinces. By his marriage (38) to LIVIA DRUSILLA, who became his trusted advisor, he indicated his wish to achieve a compromise with the republican aristocracy. In 32, Italy and the western provinces swore an oath of allegiance to Octavian, but the majority of senators fled to Antony. In September 31, Octavian defeated Antony at ACTIUM, and in 30 he conquered Egypt. The suicides of Antony and Cleopatra left Octavian sole ruler of Rome.

Principate. Octavian proclaimed the restoration of the republic but had no intention of stepping down. In January 27, in a theatrical gesture, he "placed the republic at the disposal of the Senate and the Roman people," but the Senate begged him not to abandon the state. Octavi-

Augustus, who was recognized as the first Roman emperor in 27 BC, extended the boundaries of the empire and reorganized its administration. This statue of the emperor dates from the 1st century AD and is now in the Vatican.

an now received a number of prerogatives that legitimized his position. He was given the military command for ten years (subsequently extended for periods of five and ten years) and the administration of those provinces which required the presence of the army. His official name became Imperator Caesar Augustus, and he was called Augustus (the Exalted). In 23 he received the tribunician power for life and assumed the role of protector of the Roman people. He also received the right to intervene in those provinces administered by the Senate. In 12 BC he became *pontifex maximus*, head of the Roman state religion, and in 2 BC he received the title "Father of His Country." The system he created came to be known as the principate, the rule of the first citizen (*princeps*).

Augustus understood the importance of ideology and propaganda; he sponsored and encouraged the leading writers and artists of his time, such as the historian LIVY and the poets VERGIL and HORACE, who glorified Rome's past and the greatness of his achievement. After years of wars, Augustus brought peace and prosperity. He revived old religious customs and attempted to restore the old stern morality. He extended the Roman frontiers to the Danube and the Rhine in the west and to the Euphrates in the east. After the Roman defeat in the Teutoburg Forest (AD 9), however, he abandoned the idea of conquering Germany.

To prevent civil wars from recurring, Augustus tried to settle the succession during his lifetime, but, for lack of a better alternative, was forced to adopt and appoint as his successor his daughter Julia's third husband, Livia's son TIBERIUS, whom he disliked. Nevertheless, at his death he left the principate strong enough to survive the follies of his successors.

Augustus II, King of Poland   Augustus II (Augustus the Strong), b. May 12, 1670, d. Feb. 1, 1733, king of Poland, was also elector of Saxony (1694–1733) as Frederick Augustus I. When he was elected king of Poland on Sept. 15, 1697, the union of predominantly Roman Catholic Poland with Protestant Saxony appeared useful to the Polish nobles, who hoped that the new king would secure the return to Poland of SILESIA. Instead, together with Emperor PETER I of Russia, Augustus entangled Poland in the Great NORTHERN WAR and briefly (1704–10) lost his throne to STANISŁAW I as a result. A patron of the arts, he was responsible for building the Zwinger Museum in Dresden and for the development of Meissen ware.

Augustus III, King of Poland   Augustus III, b. Oct. 17, 1696, d. Oct. 5, 1763, king of Poland and elector of Saxony, as Frederick Augustus II, was the son of Augustus II. With Russian help, he won the Polish throne in the War of the POLISH SUCCESSION (1733–35). Under the negligent rule of Augustus and his minister Heinrich von Brühl (1700–63), Poland was increasingly prey to the factional rivalries that eventually led to its partition by Russia, Prussia, and Austria. As elector of Saxony, Augustus backed Austria against Frederick I of Prussia in the SEVEN YEARS' WAR, and his army was forced to surrender to Frederick in 1756.

auk [awk]   The auks and their allies, collectively called alcids, are oceanic birds found mostly in Arctic and sub-Arctic regions. Alcids are fish eaters and catch their prey by diving and pursuing it underwater. They also feed on crustaceans, mollusks, worms, algae, and plankton. Their webbed feet are set far back on their short-tailed, compact bodies, and they are clumsy on land. They have large heads and short necks; their bills range from short and stout to moderately long and slender. Most alcids are black or gray above and white below, and some have brightly colored bills and feet.

The name *auk* usually refers to the most famous alcid, the extinct great auk, a flightless bird about 76 cm (30 in) long. The bird nested in great concentrations on North Atlantic islands. Because it showed little fear of humans, it could be easily clubbed to death, and great auks often were herded into corrals or driven on shipboard for slaughter by sailors, fishermen, and sealers who visited the nesting colonies. The feathers were used for bedding, the carcasses for oil, and the eggs for food or fish bait. The colonies dwindled rapidly before 1800, and the last two known specimens were captured on Eldey Island off the coast of Iceland on June 4, 1844.

Other alcids known as auks include the largest living species, the razor-billed auk, *Alca torda*, up to 45 cm (18 in) long; the little auk, or dovekie, *Plautus alle*, 23 cm (9 in) long; the smallest, the least auklet, *Aethia pusilla*, about 16 cm (6.5 in) long; and several other auklets. The dovekie, in particular, is hunted by the Eskimo for food and clothing. Other alcids are the GUILLEMOTS, PUFFINS, and murres.

Alcids gather in dense colonies on islands or rocky coasts, where they nest on the ground, in rock crevices, or on bare ledges. One egg or, rarely, two eggs are laid, and the male shares in their incubation. The murre's egg is pear-shaped and pivots on its axis, which prevents its rolling off the bare ledge when disturbed. Young alcids born on exposed ledges take off for sea in about 2 weeks, but those born in safe burrows may remain there for 6 to 8 weeks. Some alcids are migratory. The 22 species of alcids constitute the family Alcidae, order Charadriiformes.

Aung San [awng sahn']   Aung San, b. Feb. 13, 1915, d. July 19, 1947, was a founder and leader of the Anti-Fascist People's Freedom League (AFPFL), the Burmese political organization that led the struggle for Burma's independence from Great Britain. After Japan invaded Burma during World War II, Aung San was named (1943) defense minister in the puppet regime of Ba Maw. He later joined the underground resistance, however, and in 1944 helped found the AFPFL. In 1945, as commander of the Burma National Army, he brought that force into the Allied camp. In April 1947 the AFPFL won an overwhelming majority in the constituent assembly, which immediately called for total independence. Aung San became head of the provisional government, but he and several other cabinet ministers were assassinated a few months before the signing of the agreement by which Burma became independent. His daughter, Aung San Suu Kyi, emerged as a leader of the democratic opposition during the 1988 uprising in Burma.

Aurangzeb, Mogul Emperor of India [ah'-u-ruhng-zayb]   Aurangzeb, b. Oct. 24, 1618, d. Feb. 20, 1707, was the sixth MOGUL emperor of India and the last

Auks, powerful swimmers and divers, can stay underwater for up to two minutes and reach depths of 10 m (33 ft). They steer with their webbed feet and propel themselves by beating their wings in a flightlike motion. Left to right are the razorbill, common murre, pigeon guillemot, and rhinoceros auklet. They range in size from 23 to 45 cm (9 to 18 in).

to wield effective power. The third son of SHAH JAHAN, he was sent to subdue Golconda (1656) and Bijapur (1657) but returned in 1658 and seized the throne from his sick father, whom he held prisoner at Agra until his death. In the war of succession that followed, Aurangzeb killed his two older brothers and imprisoned his younger brother. He then moved the seat of government from Agra to Delhi and adopted the reign title of Alamgir ("World-holder").

Until about 1680, Aurangzeb's rule was fairly stable. Then, possibly provoked by a revolt (1678–81) of the RAJPUTS, which was supported by his third son, he began a series of fierce campaigns against the Hindu kingdoms. Bijapur and Golconda were finally captured in 1686–87. Thereafter he fought continuously and ineffectively against the Marathas in the south and west. Although Aurangzeb brought the Mogul empire to its greatest extent, his wars depleted his treasury, and his long absences in the south led to a weakening of Mogul control in the north. By his death, the empire was disintegrating.

___

Aurelian, Roman Emperor [aw-reel'-eeuhn]   Aurelian, b. AD 215, became Roman emperor on the death (270) of Claudius II. Coming from a family of modest means, he rose through the ranks to be appointed commander in chief of the Balkan army by Claudius.

During his brief reign Aurelian managed to reclaim large portions of imperial territory that had been lost through war or secession; he thus merited more than most the title "Restorer of the World," which he used on his coinage. He not only recovered (272) Syria from PALMYRA, capturing its queen, ZENOBIA, but also reclaimed (274) several western provinces from the rival emperors of the independent Gallic Empire. Aurelian also began construction of the wall around Rome, reformed the coinage, and installed the Syrian god Sol Invictus ("Unconquered Sun") as the unifying deity of the restored empire. In spite of these achievements, he was murdered as the result of a military conspiracy in 275.

___

Auric, Georges [oh-reek']   Georges Auric, b. Feb. 15, 1899, d. July 23, 1983, was a composer, critic, and opera administrator in Paris. Auric was associated with Darius Milhaud and others in the group of French composers known as Les Six. His compositions include an opera, several ballets, and numerous orchestral, choral, and chamber works. Auric composed music for more than 60 motion pictures, notably the score (1952) for *Moulin Rouge*, which included the popular song "Where Is Your Heart?"

___

Auriga [aw-ry'-guh]   Auriga the Charioteer is a CONSTELLATION prominent during winter in the Northern Hemisphere. Situated between the head of Orion and the north celestial pole, it contains Capella, the sixth brightest star in the sky, three star clusters (M 36, M 37, and M 38) visible through binoculars, and several important double stars. One of these, epsilon Aurigae, has a component 3,000 times the diameter of the Sun and eclipses its

companion, causing a variation of magnitude from 3.7 to 4.5 over a period of 27 years, the longest period of any known eclipsing binary. The other double star, zeta Aurigae, is also an eclipsing binary. It is composed of a hot blue star and a red giant with a period of 972 days.

___

Aurignacian [or-een-yay'-shuhn]   Aurignacian, in archaeology, is a Late Paleolithic tool industry recognized in various forms throughout Europe. The name is taken from the French site of Aurignac. A clearly-defined Aurignacian tool industry occurred from approximately 34,000 to 29,000 years ago. Stone tools include ridged end scrapers, blade scrapers and knives, and burins, many exhibiting a characteristic parallel fluting around the edges. Bone and antler tools are more abundant than in other contemporaneous industries.

The earliest Aurignacian assemblages seem to have occurred with early populations of fully anatomically modern *Homo sapiens*.

See also: MOUSTERIAN.

___

Auriol, Vincent [awr-eeawl']   Vincent Auriol, b. Aug. 27, 1884, d. Jan. 1, 1966, a French Socialist leader, became the first president (1947–54) of the Fourth Republic. Elected to the Chamber of Deputies in 1914, he served as minister of finance (1936–37) and of justice (1937–38) in Popular Front cabinets. In 1940 he was imprisoned by the VICHY GOVERNMENT. Released in 1941, he worked in the French Resistance and then joined the Free French government in exile. In 1947, Auriol was elected president of France. He retired in 1954 but reemerged in 1958 to help swing Socialist support behind Gen. Charles de Gaulle.

___

Aurobindo, Sri [aw-roh-bin'-doh, sree]   Sri Aurobindo, or Aurobindo Ghose, b. Aug. 15, 1872, d. Dec. 5, 1950, was an Indian nationalist and one of India's most original philosophers. During a teaching career in Baroda and Calcutta he became active in efforts to free India from British rule. He was imprisoned in 1908. After his release he retired (1910) to Pondicherry to found an ashram (retreat) that became one of the chief religious centers of India. Assisted by Mira Richard, known as the Mother, he lived there continuously until his death.

According to Aurobindo's philosophy, humanity evolved from matter to the present stage of development called mind and is now in the process of moving to a higher state of supermind, or divinity. On the other hand, human enlightenment and energy come from above. Aurobindo's writings include *The Life Divine* (1940) and *The Synthesis of Yoga* (1948).

___

Aurora   see EOS

___

auroras [uh-rohr'-uhz]   The aurora borealis (northern lights) and aurora australis (southern lights) are beautiful, dynamic, luminous displays seen in the nighttime sky. The most common form of an aurora is a curtainlike luminosity extending east to west. Auroras occur in the upper ATMOSPHERE of both poles and are occasionally visible from middle latitudes as a dark red glow near the poleward horizon. Auroral displays are strongest at times of greatest SUNSPOT activity and resulting MAGNETIC STORMS.

Characteristics. The bottom of the auroral curtain is about 100 km (62 mi) in altitude, and the upper edge rises to 300 km (190 mi) or higher. The curtain often shows a fine pleating or large-scale folds near its lower edge, as it moves toward either the equator or a pole. Seen from above, it appears along oval belts surrounding the geomagnetic poles. Auroras are most common at midnight hours in the north in a circle including southern Hudson Bay, southernmost Greenland, Iceland, the northern tip of the Scandinavian peninsula, the Arctic coast of Siberia, and central Alaska.

Cause. An extensive series of satellite, rocket, and ground-based observations has revealed that auroras result from large-scale electrical discharge processes surrounding the Earth. The discharges are powered by the electromotive force generated by the interaction between the SOLAR WIND and the Earth's magnetic field. The auroral luminosity comes from excited, or ionized, atoms and molecules; energetic electrons, carrying the discharge current, are channeled toward the poles by the Earth's magnetic field and collide with and excite, or ionize, upper atmospheric atoms and molecules. The most common color is the green of energized oxygen atoms, whereas oxygen molecules glow red or yellow; nitrogen atoms emit a purple light, and nitrogen molecules a pinkish one. The folding effect results from the electric field induced on either side of the auroral curtain by the electrons. North of the curtain the field is directed southward, while on the south side it is directed northward. This causes the ionized air on either side to flow rapidly in opposite directions, producing eddylike folds in the curtain.

Auroral activity is controlled by solar activity through the Earth's magnetic field and the speed of the solar wind. A gusty solar wind generated by a solar flare often enhances the auroral discharge, causing the oval belt of the aurora to spread over a larger area. During the declining sunspot period, a fairly intense beam of the solar wind can blow out from a rather quiet region of the Sun and last from a few months to two years. Since the Sun rotates in a period of about 27 days, the beam hits the Earth at 27-day intervals, causing the so-called 27-day recurrence of auroral activity. Auroral activity has a pronounced seasonal variation, reaching a maximum during the months of March and September—the time of the EQUINOXES—but its cause is not well understood. Even during solar flare–induced and recurrent geomagnetic storms, auroral activity is not continuous. Instead, it repeats a quasi-cyclic display that lasts for only a few hours. A typical auroral substorm begins with a sudden brightening of an auroral curtain in the midnight sector. The brightened curtain moves abruptly poleward, and auroral activity subsequently spreads both westward and eastward.

Auschwitz [owsh'-vits] Auschwitz was the German name for Oświęcim, a town in southern Poland, which was the site of a Nazi CONCENTRATION CAMP during World War II. Oświęcim is an industrial town and railroad junction with a population of 45,200 (1982 est.). Large numbers of people, variously estimated at from 1 to 3 million, were killed in the Auschwitz camp. The prisoners were herded naked into gas chambers and exterminated with hydrocyanic gas produced by Zyklon B crystals. Their clothing and valuables were systematically disposed of (even the gold fillings in their teeth were melted down) and the bodies cremated. Most of those exterminated were Jews.

See also: HOLOCAUST.

Austen, Jane Jane Austen, one of the greatest of British fiction writers, had a major impact on the development of the English novel. Her six novels combine 18th- and 19th-century concerns and modes, and have a thematic unity and consistent excellence that make them one of the glories of English literature.

Born Dec. 16, 1775, the daughter of a country clergyman, Austen spent her first 25 years in the village of Steventon in Hampshire. There as a child she wrote sprightly and amusing burlesques of contemporary sentimental fiction, such as Love and Friendship (c.1790; 1922), and composed early versions of her first three novels: Elinor and Marianne (c.1795) became Sense and Sensibility (1811), First Impressions (c.1796–97) became Pride and Prejudice (1813), and Susan, A Novel in Two Volumes became Northanger Abbey (written c.1798–99 and published posthumously in 1818). When her father retired, the family moved to Bath, then briefly to Southampton. Finally they settled in the village of Chawton.

When attempts to interest publishers in her novels failed, Austen published Sense and Sensibility at her own

A view of an aurora in Alaska shows the variously colored displays of light that are common in polar skies at night. The displays are strongest during times of great sunspot activity and are produced by the collisions of atoms and molecules in the upper atmosphere with high-speed particles coming from the Sun.

Jane Austen, a 19th-century English novelist, is portrayed in this pastel sketch by her sister, Cassandra. Despite her lack of formal education, Jane Austen wrote several novels about provincial middleclass society that are regarded as classics of English literature.

expense. In Chawton she issued two of her early novels and wrote her three later ones, *Mansfield Park* (1814), *Emma* (1816), and *Persuasion* (published posthumously in 1818). A final novel, *Sanditon*, was still unfinished when she died on July 18, 1817, in Winchester, where she is buried in the cathedral.

Austen's works are satirical comedies of the domestic and social life of a limited sphere of English society. Her plots constitute variations on the standard theme of female novelists of the late 18th century, definitively established by Fanny BURNEY: a young girl's entry into society climaxed eventually by marriage. Each of Austen's heroines follows this course, by the end of the novel acquiring a husband, often an older man who has been father and guide to her as well as lover. Well aware of the limitations of her fiction, Austen likened herself to a painter of miniatures; yet within the confines of her often predictable plots and narrow focus, she carefully explores an important and universal theme, the adjustments the self must make to family and society.

Austen's early novels look back to the 18th century. *Northanger Abbey* satirizes the Gothic novel and sentimental friendship, and *Sense and Sensibility* mocks the cult of sensibility in which personal feeling and spontaneity were valued to the exclusion of social responsibility and self-restraint. In *Pride and Prejudice*, probably Austen's best-loved work, the vivacious and witty heroine, Elizabeth Bennet, is in the tradition of the articulate women of Restoration and 18th-century comedy. Austen's later works, *Mansfield Park* and *Persuasion*, have themes traditionally labeled Victorian; they describe the loneliness and repression of young women forced into silence and self-effacement by social codes. *Emma*, the sunniest and most satisfying of Austen's novels, has something of the sprightliness of *Pride and Prejudice* but also displays the psychological probing found in the later novels.

In her own time, Austen was a retiring novelist whose name did not appear on her title pages. Yet she had a select band of admirers that included the novelist Sir Walter Scott and the Prince Regent. Her influence on such later writers as Henry James was profound, and her stature as a fiction writer is now unquestioned. There is, however, considerable debate about the tone of her work. Some critics stress the irony of her vision, what D. W. Harding has called her "regulated hatred." They see Austen as responding subversively to a world she knows to be debased, undermining social values while she pays conventional homage to them. Others view her work as an intelligent affirmation of conservative social and religious values, in the same moral tradition as the novelists Samuel Richardson and Henry Fielding and the essayist Samuel Johnson.

Austerlitz, Battle of [ows'-tur-lits]   The Battle of Austerlitz, fought on Dec. 2, 1805, near Austerlitz in Moravia, was a major victory for NAPOLEON I. His opponents, the Austrians and Russians, hoped to cut the French off from Vienna, which Napoleon had just occupied (November 13). Deliberately drawing an attack on his right wing, Napoleon then stormed the weakened allied center, dividing it and inflicting heavy losses. On December 4 the Austrians concluded a separate armistice with the French.

See also: NAPOLEONIC WARS.

Austin   Austin is the capital of Texas and a noted educational center, with five colleges and the enormous main campus of the University of Texas. It is the seat of Travis County in central Texas and has a population of 465,622 (1990) within the city and 781,572 in the metropolitan area. A city with broad, tree-lined streets, Austin is situated on the Colorado River (of Texas), at the foot of the artificial Highland Lakes. Two of the lakes are in the heart of the city, furnishing recreational opportunities. The capitol building is set on one of the hills rising up from the river. Austin's phenomenal growth in industry and research has been spurred by hydroelectric projects on the Colorado and by the facilities available at its educational institutions, although the pace of growth slowed during the 1980s as the economy of Texas declined overall. The city also serves as the trade and financial center of a 10-county grain and livestock-raising area. It is the home of Bergstrom Air Force Base. In 1839 the village of Waterloo was selected as the site for the capital of the new Republic of Texas and was renamed for Stephen F. AUSTIN. Mexican and Indian raids forced the removal of the state offices to Houston in 1842, but they were returned to Austin in 1845. Large-scale growth began with the arrival of the railroad in 1871.

Austin, Stephen F.   Stephen Fuller Austin, b. Austinville, Va., Nov. 3, 1793, d. Dec. 27, 1836, is sometimes called the father of Texas. On the death of his father, Moses Austin, in 1821, he took over a grant to bring U.S. settlers into Spanish Texas. Under the terms of a special act in 1824 and additional contracts in 1825, 1827, and 1828—all of them granted by the newly inde-

Stephen F. Austin organized the first legal settlement of Anglo-Americans in Mexican-owned Texas. Today the capital of the state of Texas bears his name.

pendent Mexican government—the colonizer was responsible for the settlement of more than 1,200 American families in Mexican Texas.

In 1835, following a period of imprisonment in Mexico City, Austin urged Texans to join federalists in Mexico in revolt against the centralist dictatorship of Antonio López de Santa Anna. During the Texas Revolution (1835–36), Austin briefly commanded Texas volunteers and then went to the United States to gain support for the Texan cause. He served as secretary of state of the republic of Texas until his death.

Australia Australia is the world's smallest continent and sixth largest country. With proportionately more desert land than any other continent, Australia has a low population density. Lying completely in the Southern Hemisphere, Australia is bounded by the Indian Ocean on the west and south and by the Pacific Ocean on the east. These oceans merge on the north in the Arafura Sea between Australia and Indonesia and New Guinea, and on the south in the Bass Strait. The coastline length, estimated at 19,200 km (12,000 mi), is remarkably short for so large an area, a result of the relative lack of indentation. Major inlets other than the Gulf of Carpentaria and the Great Australian Bight are few.

Australia is a federation of five mainland states (New South Wales, Queensland, South Australia, Victoria, Western Australia) and one island state (Tasmania), as well as two territories (Northern Territory, Australian Capital Territory). The country's name derives from the Latin *terra australis incognita*, meaning "unknown southern land," which resulted from a confusion between Australia and Antarctica on early world maps.

In many ways Australia is unusual among continents. It lacks major relief features and has a high proportion of dry land. The continent's isolation from other landmasses accounts for its unique varieties of vegetation and animal life, and for the existence of a Paleolithic (Old Stone Age) culture among the Aborigines. Except for Antarctica, Australia was probably the last continent to be inhabited by humans and the last to be explored and settled by Europeans. It is the only continent comprising a single nation-state.

British convicts played an important role in the early history of the territory. The discovery of gold and other ores attracted immigrants, but Australia remained a primarily agricultural country until World War II. Subsequent industrialization has been rapid, and today Australia ranks as one of the world's most economically developed countries, although vast areas of the interior, known as the Outback, remain all but uninhabited.

Land and Resources

Australia is primarily a flat low-lying plateau, with about 95% of the land standing less than 600 m (1,970 ft) above sea level. All its landforms are highly eroded; Australia's mountains reach only 2,228 m (7,310 ft) in Mount Kosciusko.

Physical Regions. Australia can be divided into three major physical regions: the vast Western Plateau, the Eastern Highlands, and the Great Artesian Basin.

Western Plateau. Some 60% of the continent—more than 4,500,000 km^2 (1,740,000 mi^2) of central and western Australia—is the Western Plateau. About half of its area lies between 300 and 600 m (1,000 and 2,000 ft) above sea level. A major fault terminates the plateau on the west, separating a strip of coastal lowland about 50 km (30 mi) wide. The flat, treeless Nullarbor Plain of south central Australia is the southern edge of the plateau. Erosion of the plateau's thick sandstones has produced mesas and buttes in Arnhem Land in the north and in the Kimberley and Pilbara regions of the northwest. In the center of the continent rise the Macdonnell Ranges, carved out of ancient sediments and deformed by open folding. Ayers Rock is to the south of this area. Desert and semidesert lands are extensive. In clockwise order from the south, these deserts include the Great Victoria, Gibson, Great Sandy, Simpson, Tanami, and Arunta. Much of this area is covered with sand ridges reaching heights as great as 30 m (100 ft). Sand-ridge country accounts for nearly a quarter of Australia's total land area. Other large portions of the continent's desert and semidesert country consist of gibber (stony desert), formed by the breakup of surface rocks.

Eastern Highlands. Uplands, to a width of about 500 km (300 mi), serve as an eastern continental rim. These highlands, also known as the Great Dividing Range, are mainly plateau country and are separated from the discontinuous coastal plain by steep, erosional scarps. Elevations exceed 1,500 m (5,000 ft) in parts of the northern rim, but half the ground here is below 300 m (1,000 ft). The New England Range and Blue Mountains to the

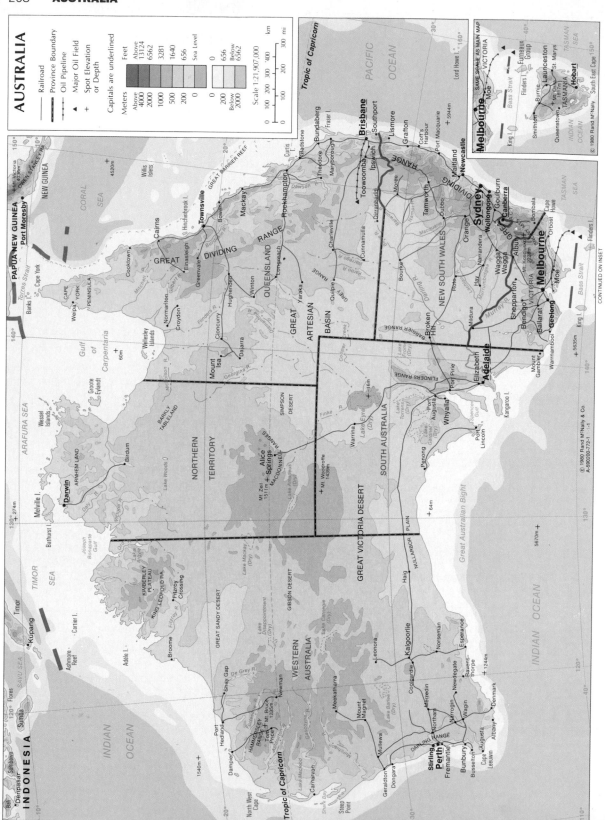

AUSTRALIA

Railroad
Province Boundary
Oil Pipeline
▲ Major Oil Field
+ Spot Elevation or Depth

Capitals are underlined

Meters	Feet
Above 4000	Above 13124
2000	6562
1000	3281
500	1640
200	656
0	Sea Level
0	0
200	656
Below 2000	Below 6562

Scale 1:21,907,000

km
mi

© 1980 Rand McNally & Co.
A-590200-772-1-1-1

CONTINUED ON INSET

SAME SCALE AS MAIN MAP
© 1980 Rand McNally

AT A GLANCE

COMMONWEALTH OF AUSTRALIA

Land: Area: 7,682,300 km² (2,966,151 mi²). Capital: Canberra (1987 est. pop., 289,000). Largest city: Sydney (1987 est. pop., 3,531,000).

People: Population (1990 est.): 17,100,000. Density 2.2 persons per km² (5.8 per mi²). Distribution (1990): 86% urban, 14% rural. Official language: English. Major religions: Protestantism, Roman Catholicism.

Government: Type: federal parliamentary state. Legislature: Parliament. Political subdivisions: 6 states, 2 territories.

Economy: GNP (1988): $204.45 billion; $12,390 per capita. Labor distribution (1987): commerce and services—66%; manufacturing—16%; construction—7%; government and public authorities—5%; agriculture and fishing—6%. Foreign trade (1988): imports—$35.5 billion; exports—$32.4 billion. Currency: 1 Australian dollar = 100 cents.

Education and Health: Literacy (1987): 98.5% of adult population. Universities (1989): 20. Hospital beds (1987): 87,586. Physicians (1986): 36,610. Life expectancy (1987): women—79.5; men—73.0. Infant mortality (1990): 8.7 per 1,000 live births.

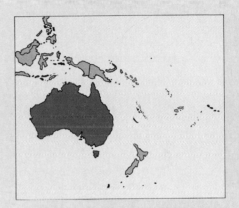

south vary in height from 900 to 1,500 m (3,000 to 5,000 ft). The Australian Alps in the extreme southeast reach more than 1,800 m (6,000 ft) and culminate in Mount Kosciusko in the SNOWY MOUNTAINS. A detached and heavily glaciated portion of the Australian Alps occurs in Tasmania, where it exceeds 1,000 m (3,000 ft) in elevation. The Eastern Highlands form a major drainage divide of Australia. Off the tropical northeastern coast lies the GREAT BARRIER REEF, the world's largest coral reef at 2,000 km (1,250 mi) long.

Great Artesian Basin. Between the Western Plateau and the Eastern Highlands lie three interior basins, called the Great Artesian Basin. Most of this area is less than 300 m (1,000 ft) in elevation and much of it less than 150 m (500 ft). In the north is the Carpentaria Basin, which lies mostly beneath the sea (Gulf of Carpentaria). The vast Eyre Basin contains Lake EYRE, the shore of which is the continent's lowest point, 16 m (52 ft) below sea level. The Eyre Basin is almost separated from the Murray Basin on the south by the projection of high ground (actually worn mountains) in the FLINDERS, Mount Lofty, and Barrier ranges. The overlap of the Simpson Desert from the Western Plateau to the interior basins somewhat blurs the physical distinction between the regions.

Geological History. Geologically, Australia is part of the former southern supercontinent Gondwanaland, which broke up some 160 million years ago, isolating Australia from the other landmasses of the Southern Hemisphere.

The Western Plateau is a stable shield area and has extensive outcrops of Precambrian age rocks (3,000 to 570 million years old). Some Precambrian rocks are also incorporated in the northern half of the Eastern Highlands. Parts of the Western Plateau have from time to time been submerged by shelf seas or have sagged into troughs.

Thick sedimentation in a subsiding trough, now the site of the Eastern Highlands, began some 600 to 500 million years ago, and continued in places until 250 million years ago. Between 400 and 275 million years ago, the trough was twice compressed; mountains were formed, and volcanic chains erupted. Volcanic outbreaks were repeated later throughout the region, especially 25 to 20 million years ago. In the south of the mainland, however, volcanic activity persisted until less than a million years ago.

Sagging basins in coastal areas subsequently collected sediment, much of it deltaic sand, which is now seen as thick sandstone formations. The major sags, however, were to form Australia's interior basins, which contain sediments dating from about 200 million years ago to the present day.

Climate. The climate of Australia varies with latitude. Because the continent lacks relief features and is favored with the moderating influence of the surrounding seas, few dramatic regional variations exist. The northern part of the continent is tropical and influenced by the trade winds. The southern parts lie in the belt of westerly winds and have a more temperate climate. The vast center of

(Above) *Sydney Opera House, perhaps the most famous structure in Australia, rises nearly 61 m (200 ft) above Bennelong Point in the city's harbor. This elaborate center for the performing arts, built between 1960 and 1973, comprises a series of overlapping concrete shells. It was designed by the Danish architect Jørn Utzon.*

(Right) *The Great Barrier Reef, which parallels the coast of Queensland for nearly 2,000 km (1,250 mi), is the largest coral formation in the world. This conglomeration of atolls, cays, and islands consists of the skeletal remains of coral polyps and is the habitat of a wide variety of marine life.*

the continent is arid and extremely hot during the summer (December to March).

The tropical region, and especially the northern coast, experiences a hot, wet (monsoonal) summer. The average January temperature in DARWIN is 28° C (83° F), and the average annual rainfall is 1,240 mm (59 in), nearly 80% of which falls between December and March. In winter, hurricanes tend to develop over the Coral and Arafura seas, some following the path of the East Australian Current as far south as Sydney.

Southern Australia has mild, wet winters, resembling a Mediterranean climate. The southwest experiences hot, dry summers, dominated by subtropical high-pressure systems. Average temperatures at PERTH are 23° C (74° F) in January and 13° C (55° F) in July; the average annual rainfall is 900 mm (35 in). A similar climate affects an area around ADELAIDE. Southern New South Wales, Victoria, and Tasmania receive the most dependable year-round precipitation in Australia. The eastern coast of Queensland and New South Wales receives tropical summer rain. With increasing distance southward, however, temperatures decline and the seasonality of rainfall becomes less marked. On the interior of the southern Eastern

Highlands is a subhumid belt, important for agriculture.

About half of Australia is arid. Dry seasons average eight months in length and a mean annual rainfall of 255 mm (10 in) or less. Summers are hot and winters are warm, and the daily temperature variation is great. The average temperature at ALICE SPRINGS is 26° C (79° F) in January and 12° C (53° F) in July. As with most of Australia, precipitation is undependable, and on rare occasions floods occur.

The arid zone is encircled by a broad belt of semiarid climate. North of the Tropic of Capricorn this belt records a wet summer season, south of the Tropic of Capricorn the average summer is distinctly dry. Because livestock ranches are located in some large eastern parts, prolonged droughts are significant to the economy. Extreme high temperatures in the arid and semiarid regions exceed 38° C (100° F).

Snow is rare except in the higher parts of the southern Eastern Highlands, principally the Snowy Mountains.

Drainage. The Great Dividing Range divides Australia's east-flowing rivers from the west-flowing rivers. About half the continent, however, does not drain into the sea.

Most of the rivers that rise in the Eastern Highlands and flow west either dry up or are seasonal. An exception is the Murray-Darling system. This is Australia's principal river system and includes the DARLING, MURRAY, MURRUMBIDGEE, Barwon, and Lachlan rivers. About 14% of the continent is drained by the Murray-Darling system.

Other than the Murray-Darling system, only 36% of Australia is externally drained. These areas include the island of Tasmania, the area east of the Great Dividing Range, and parts of the coastal north and northwest. Principal rivers range between 350 and 830 km (220 and 520 mi) in length. They have a runoff that averages the equivalent of only 117 mm (4.6 in) of rain a year, although this figure is 690 mm (27 in) in more humid Tasmania.

About 35% of the continent (in the Western Plateau) has uncoordinated drainage, including many ephemeral lakes (those that form after rainfalls and shrink by evaporating) and disrupted streams. Lake Eyre, Australia's largest "lake," is more often a dry depression with a hard salt crust. Until 1950 the lake bed was dry for about a century.

In all regions where drainage is internal or uncoordinated, flow regimes are erratic and usually depend on day-to-day rainfall. The externally flowing rivers generally reflect the seasonal rainfall of the climate, but flow averages conceal strong year-to-year variations. Dams on many Australian rivers (especially those of the Murray-Darling system) aid in the maintaining of relatively steady stream flows.

Soils. Australia's extensive arid regions have sandy or stony desert soils, although large areas on northern tablelands and in the central ranges are devoid of soils. Only the red desert loams possess farming potential.

Light-textured brown soils with high sand content are found in the regions of semiarid climate and support vegetation suitable for livestock grazing. Heavy-textured gray brown soils have formed on silty and clayey alluvium, notably in the Riverina district in southern New South Wales, where irrigation has made for productive agriculture.

The most fertile soils are the black-earth and related red brown soils, which occur in regions receiving from 380 to 650 mm (15 to 25 in) of precipitation annually. The humus-rich and moisture-retentive black-earth soils occur in the subhumid areas of the interior Eastern Highlands, and the red brown soils are found in semiarid areas. Australia's chief wheat and animal products are produced on such soils. In more humid areas with annual precipitation in excess of 650 mm (25 in), leaching can make soils acidic and naturally infertile.

Vegetation. Vegetation is characterized by a dominance of hard-leaf evergreen plants (sclerophylls). The evergreens include some 600 species of eucalyptus trees (called gum trees in Australia) and 800 species of acacia trees (wattles).

Australia's major vegetation belts broadly correspond to climate zones. Tropical rain forest in the north and northwest coastal fringes includes palms, hoop pines, tree ferns, and mangroves in coastal swamps. On the east coast, south of 26° south latitude, tropical rain forest is replaced by subtropical and temperate rain forest of palms, tree ferns, and eucalyptuses, and eventually by

An aerial photograph reveals the parched landscape of the Macdonnell Range in the Northern Territory. The dunelike formations were carved in sandstone by wind erosion.

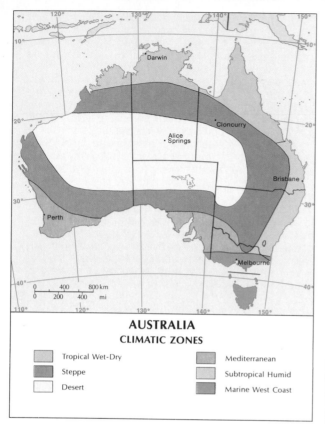

AUSTRALIA
CLIMATIC ZONES

Tropical Wet-Dry | Mediterranean
Steppe | Subtropical Humid
Desert | Marine West Coast

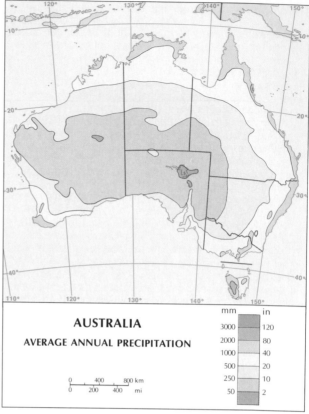

AUSTRALIA

AVERAGE ANNUAL PRECIPITATION

mm	in
3000	120
2000	80
1000	40
500	20
250	10
50	2

beeches and conifers in Tasmania. Rain forests cover about 9% of the continent. On the western slopes of the Great Dividing Range, the vegetation cover thins to subtropical or temperate woodlands of eucalyptus and scrub, accounting for 9% of Australia's land area.

The semiarid belt supports mainly grassland south of the Tropic of Capricorn and savanna woodland to the north. Together these constitute 26% of the continent. In areas of greater dryness, low-growing saltbush and bluebush become common. The extremely dry regions of Australia are distinguished by the highly specialized mulga, a shrubby acacia important as a forage plant. Valuable hardwoods such as jarra and kauri grow in the summer-dry southwest. A belt of mallee, a small, salt-tolerant eucalyptus, grows on sodium-rich soils.

Animal Life. Before the coming of humans, and especially before the landing of Europeans, Australia's pouched mammals (marsupials), such as kangaroos, wallabies, koalas, and wombats, evolved for about 50 million years without predation or competition by placental mammals. Also peculiar to Australia are the egg-laying mammals (monotremes): the platypus and the echidna (or spiny anteater).

Bird life is highly varied and includes the mallee fowl, cockatoo, lyrebird, various parrots, the kookaburra (or laughing jackass), and the large, flightless emu. Numer-

ous species of snakes exist, many of which are poisonous. Among insects, leaf eaters, locusts, termites, and blow-flies (which attack livestock) are destructive.

The introduction from Europe of cattle, sheep, rabbits, foxes, rats, and cats has altered the natural picture and in some cases has been disruptive. Also, some native species have been hunted intensively.

Mineral Resources. Australia possesses enormous mineral resources. Coal reserves are large. New discoveries of iron ore in the Hammersley Range (Pilbara region) of the northwest have helped to increase annual production. Vast bauxite reserves are concentrated in the Grove and Cape York peninsulas. Other abundant metal ores include zinc, lead, nickel, and copper. Gemstones include sapphires from the northern Great Dividing Range and the distinctive Australian fire opals from inland fields in the southeast.

Petroleum, first exploited in Queensland, now comes chiefly from the continental shelf off northwestern Australia and the Bass Strait. Recoverable reserves of natural gas were little tapped before 1969, but by 1987 output was about 15,806 million m³ (558,184 million ft³) a year. At double the present output and consumption rates, coal, oil, and gas would last 100 to 300 years.

Water Resources. The driest of continents, Australia must carefully regulate its existing water resources. Even in some externally drained basins, water supply is at times deficient. Significant groundwater reserves occur beneath one-quarter of Australia, most prominently in the Great Artesian Basin, but they are generally overexploited, and much is unfit for human consumption.

People

In 1990, Australia had an estimated population of 17,100,000 up from 10,100,000 in 1960. Immigration continues to play a major role in population increase, more than 4 million new immigrants having settled in Australia since 1945. Despite a more diversified pattern of immigration in recent years, the population of Australia remains ethnically dominated by a majority that is of British descent or is recently arrived from the United Kingdom. Smaller ethnic groups of European origin include many of Greek, German, Italian, and Yugoslav descent. Aborigines and people of past Aboriginal descent constitute a small minority; there are small but growing Chinese and other Asian minorities.

Australia's pre-European inhabitants, the Aborigines and Torres Strait Islanders, numbered about 185,000 in 1989. Some live on designated tribal lands, and others work on ranches or live in the deteriorated inner-city areas. In general, Aborigines and many part-Aborigines remain far removed from Australia's economic prosperity and social life. (See Aborigines, Australian.)

Language and Religion. The language of Australia is almost universally English, although some immigrant groups form small language blocks in the cities.

About 76% of the total population profess affiliation with some form of Christianity. The predominant religions are Anglicanism (about 26%) and Roman Catholicism (26%), the former reflecting the strong traditional influence of English, the latter of Irish, ancestry. About 11% profess no religion.

Demography. The colonial capital cities (later to be state capitals) were founded from 1788 to 1836. Adelaide, the youngest, was the only one to receive no British convicts. Assisted (subsidized) migration began in the 1830s and continues. Until about 1870, foreign-born population exceeded native-born, and it still amounts to some 20%. Until 1973, immigration was controlled by the effective but unofficial White Australian Policy. Since then there has been a significant increase in arrivals from various Southeast Asian nations.

The population is more than 85% urban. The capital cities have always been demographically dominant, containing 25% to 30% of their individual colonial populations in the mid-1800s and 62% to 72% of their state populations today, except for Brisbane, Queensland (46%), and Hobart, Tasmania (40%). In 1986 the six capital cities and their surrounding metropolitan areas contained more than 60% of all Australians. The largest was Sydney, followed closely by Melbourne. Other large cities include Brisbane, Adelaide, Perth, the industrial center of Newcastle, the ports of Geelong and Wollongong, and the Queensland resort community of Gold Coast. Inland settlements other than Canberra, the federal capital, are generally small.

(Below) *A prospector sifts a load of crushed rock in search of gold. Mineral resources have been vital to the development of Australia. In the 1850s an increase in immigration, resulting from gold strikes, more than doubled the population.*

(Above) *The massive zinc refinery in Risdon, Tasmania's oldest settlement, processes ore from as far away as Broken Hill, in western New South Wales. Tasmania was discovered during the 17th century by the Dutch explorer Abel Tasman. Although this mountainous island is the smallest and least populous state of the Australian Commonwealth, Tasmania's mineral resources and industrial capacity contribute greatly to the nation's economy. Mount Wellington (background) rises to 1,270 m (4,166 ft).*

Education. Education is free and compulsory from the ages of 6 to 15 (16 in Tasmania). From colonial times, education in Australia has been highly centralized. State administrations (the federal government in the territories) controlled the hiring, posting, and promotion of all public school teachers. Until the 1990s, even the overwhelmingly Roman Catholic private schools, were locked together with the public school system by a common external (university entrance) examination taken at the conclusion of secondary education. The federal government has taken an increasing role in education since the 1950s.

All but one of Australia's 20 universities are public institutions; the private Bond University opened in 1989. Entrance is highly selective and competitive.

Australia has developed special programs to meet the needs of children living in isolated areas. The Schools of the Air Program, for example, uses two-way radios for instruction.

Health. Australia has excellent public and private health-care facilities, and the government pays partial medical expenses for citizens. Medical attention in the Outback is supplied by the Flying Doctor Service. The average life span, crude death rate, and infant mortality rate are similar to those of other industrialized nations.

Cultural Activity. A distinctively Australian artistic expression appeared at the end of the 19th century in the works of writers such as Henry Lawson (see AUSTRALIAN LITERATURE). Patrick WHITE, winner of the 1973 Nobel prize for literature, helped focus world attention on Australian literature, and many contemporary authors have garnered international fame. Novelist Peter Carey won England's foremost literary award, the Booker Prize, in 1988.

The growth of cultural institutions and forms of artistic expression reflecting national characteristics was stimu-

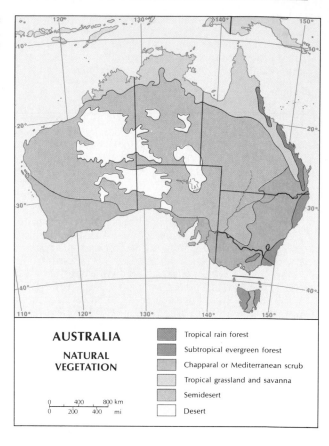

AUSTRALIA

NATURAL VEGETATION

0 400 800 km	
0 200 400 mi	

- Tropical rain forest
- Subtropical evergreen forest
- Chapparal or Mediterranean scrub
- Tropical grassland and savanna
- Semidesert
- Desert

Sheep are driven along a road on a station, or ranch, in New South Wales. Since the introduction of Spanish merinos in 1797, Australia has become a world leader in wool production. The country has more than ten sheep for every person.

lated by government funding, particularly after the establishment of the Australia Council in 1975. Dance companies, museums, musical societies, and arts centers exist in many state capitals. The Australian National Gallery at Canberra (opened 1982) and the Art Gallery of New South Wales in Sydney have large collections of Australian (including Aboriginal) arts, while the Melbourne National Gallery houses a fine collection of European paintings. The Australian Ballet, the Australian National Opera, and the Sydney Dance Company are well known, and Melbourne and Sydney have notable symphony orchestras. The spectacular Sydney Opera House (completed 1973) has attracted an international roster of performers. Melbourne, with its new Victoria Arts Center, became the third venue of the SPOLETO FESTIVAL in 1986. Other Australian contributions to the world of classical music include opera singers Dame Nellie MELBA and Joan SUTHERLAND and composer Percy GRAINGER. Such Australian filmmakers as Gillian Armstrong, Bruce Beresford, George Miller, Fred Schepisi, and Peter Weir have won international acclaim.

In the 1880s, Louis Buvelot and Tom Roberts helped shape a distinctive Australian style of landscape painting that emphasized the quality of local light. More contemporary artists, including William Dobell, Russell Drysdale, Sidney NOLAN, Arthur Boyd, and Fred Williams, often

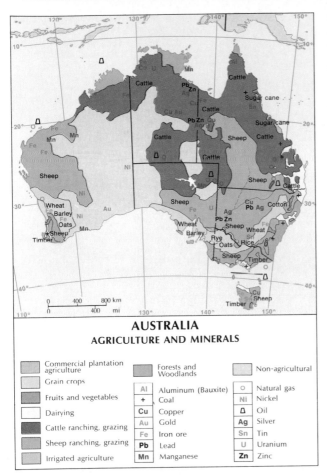

AUSTRALIA
AGRICULTURE AND MINERALS

Commercial plantation agriculture	Forests and Woodlands	Non-agricultural
Grain crops	Al Aluminum (Bauxite)	O Natural gas
Fruits and vegetables	+ Coal	Ni Nickel
Dairying	Cu Copper	Δ Oil
Cattle ranching, grazing	Au Gold	Ag Silver
Sheep ranching, grazing	Fe Iron ore	Sn Tin
Irrigated agriculture	Pb Lead	U Uranium
	Mn Manganese	Zn Zinc

fused modernist ideas with indigenous themes. Attempts are also being made to revive and preserve Aboriginal arts (see OCEANIA, ART OF).

Economy

Australia has a well-diversified economy. Although the country is one of the world's leading exporters of agricultural products, manufacturing accounts for the largest single portion of its income. Most of the continent's mineral production dates from 1960 or later.

Agriculture. Arable land amounts to only 4% of the continent's area, while nearly 60% is in pasture used mainly for low-intensity grazing by cattle and sheep. The arable land, 80% of which is under cultivation, is confined to the nation's humid and subhumid areas located in the southwestern corner of the continent and in a narrow fringe extending inland from the southeastern and eastern coastlands between Cairns and Adelaide. The lands used for pasture are concentrated in the generally drier parts of the continent, some 25% of all Australia being occupied by 16,000 ranches, or stations, averaging 30,000 ha (75,000 acres).

Australia leads the world in wool production and is also an important supplier of wheat, other cereals, dairy products, meat, sugar, and fruit. Australia's sheep yield about 25% of the world's wool as well as substantial quantities of mutton and lamb. Wheat, the chief crop, occupies nearly 70% of all cultivated land and is grown in almost all the states. Sugar is grown in the subtropical areas of coastal Queensland and New South Wales. Major fruits include berries, grapes, apples, bananas, and pineapples.

Forestry and Fishing. Potentially productive forests and woodlands cover less than 6% of all land. About two-thirds are occupied by eucalyptus, a strong, durable wood suitable for building and packaging.

Fisheries are limited, primarily because of the lack of mingling of ocean currents over the extensive continental shelves. The most important fishes, by value, are prawns, rock lobster, tuna, and salmon.

Manufacturing and Industry. Australia is one of the world's most industrialized nations. The most industrialized states are New South Wales and Victoria.

Food processing is the leading industry, in terms of both value and employment. This reflects the continuing importance of processing Australia's traditional meat and wheat exports and the growing importance of wine production, freezing, canning, and other forms of food processing. Second in importance is the manufacture of machinery, and third is metallurgy. Basic steel production is centered at Newcastle, Port Kembla, and Whyalla; Australia also produces specialized steels, aluminum, and refined copper, lead, zinc, and tin. Fourth in value, and associated with the machine and metallurgical industries, is the manufacture of automobiles, aircraft, ships, and other forms of transportation equipment. Other important industries include the manufacture of chemicals, refined petroleum, fertilizers, plastics, pharmaceuticals, textiles, clothing, and footwear. A persistent problem is the limited domestic market and remoteness of overseas markets.

Power. Power is supplied by black coal, brown coal, hydroelectric installations, petroleum, and natural gas. Total production from all sources amounted to 132.2 billion kW h in 1987, about 37% of which was generated and used in New South Wales.

Coal, supplemented by natural gas in South Australia and Victoria and by oil in Western Australia, produces 89% of total electricity; hydroelectric installations, about 11%. The largest hydroelectric installation, producing

An Australian Aborigine, whose ancestors are believed to have migrated from the Malaysian archipelago, wears the dress of a jackeroo, or ranch hand.

(Opposite page) *Alice Springs, an isolated city near the center of Australia, was founded in 1871 as a post on the Overland Telegraph Line.*

(Left) *Sydney, which has one of the world's largest natural harbors, is Australia's busiest seaport and largest city. The first Sydneysiders, as its residents are known, were British convicts exiled to the Australian penal colony in 1788.*

(Below) *Australia's Parliament House, the nation's largest building, opened for the 1988 Australian Bicentennial. The building is located on Capital Hill in Canberra, Australia's capital city since 1927.*

about 5 billion kW h annually, is the Snowy Mountains Hydroelectric Scheme in southeastern New South Wales, a multipurpose power and irrigation project that diverts water into headwaters of the Murray River drainage basin. Unlike other parts of Australia, Tasmania depends wholly on hydroelectricity. In addition to its other energy sources, Australia is also well to the forefront in pioneering the use of solar energy.

Transportation. Most of Australia's railroad lines are concentrated near the coast and radiate inland from the major ports. Reflecting the early development of the states as separate colonies, those in Queensland, Western Australia, and Tasmania operate on narrow-gauge tracks, those in Victoria and South Australia on broad-gauge tracks. Railroad lines cross state lines at only nine points, and at two of them transshipment from one gauge to another is required. Transcontinental routes, converted to standard gauge only since 1969, connect Townsville with Melbourne and Sydney with Perth, and all state capitals are now linked by standard-gauge tracks.

About 50% of Australia's roads are paved. Included in this total are 16,000 km (10,000 mi) of national highways that connect the state capitals and also link them and the Northern Territory with Canberra and the Australian Capital Territory.

Air transportation is important in so large a country. There are six private domestic airlines and one government-owned international airline, Quantas. Most ranches

also have their own aircraft and airstrips.

Trade. Internal trade is dominated by the two most populous states, New South Wales (mainly Sydney) and Victoria (mainly Melbourne). Together these two states account for 55% of all wholesale trade and 75% of all retail sales.

Three-fourths of all foreign trade exports are primary products. Australia leads the world in wool exports and also ranks high among the world's leading exporters of meat, wheat, bauxite, lead, and iron ore. Coal exports are also significant. In the mid-1980s, depressed commodity

prices contributed to a balance-of-trade deficit and a substantial foreign debt. Tourism has become an important source of foreign exchange. About 28% of all imports are materials used in manufacturing; 41% are machinery and transportation equipment.

Notable changes occurred in the direction of trade during the post–World War II era. Exports to the United Kingdom, which had taken 50% of all exports before World War II, fell to 20% in 1965 and only 4.3% in 1988. Conversely, trade with Japan and the United States increased dramatically, the two countries accounting for 37% of exports and 40% of imports in 1988.

Government

The Commonwealth of Australia is a fully independent member of the Commonwealth of Nations. The constitution (1901) resembles that of the United States in that it creates a federal form of government; the powers of the Commonwealth are specified, leaving residual powers to the states.

Supreme executive powers (although more ceremonial than actual) rest in the British monarch, represented in Australia by the governor-general and in each of the six states by a governor. These officials are appointed by the British monarch, but appointments are nearly always recommended by the Australian governments.

Legislative power rests with the Parliament of Australia, which consists of an upper house, the Senate, and the House of Representatives. The leader of the majority party in the House is named prime minister and appoints a cabinet from members of the Senate and House.

The Senate consists of ten senators from each state and two from each territory, each elected for 6-year terms. The number of representatives is proportional to the populations of the states and territories, and House elections are held at least once every 3 years. Members of Parliament are elected by universal adult suffrage, and voting is compulsory.

The principal political parties are the Australian Labor party, the Liberal party, and the National Country party. The latter two, in coalition, have been the dominant parties through most of the period since World War II. Labor, however, was in power in 1972–75 and returned to office in 1983.

The organization of the state governments is similar to that of the Commonwealth. Each state has an appointed governor, an elected premier, and a legislature. Queensland is the only state with a unicameral legislature. State governments are responsible for education, health, public utilities, justice, and transportation. Since 1974 both the Northern Territory and the Australian Capital Territory have had elected legislative assemblies.

History

The original inhabitants of Australia probably arrived from Southeast Asia by way of Indonesia approximately 12,000 years ago. When discovered in 1642 by the Dutch navigator Abel TASMAN, the Aborigines were a Paleolithic people sustaining a meager livelihood in their vast, arid continent. They remained undisturbed until rediscovered in 1770 by Capt. James COOK, who charted a portion of the coastline and took possession of the eastern half of Australia for Britain on his first voyage around the world.

Penal and Free Colonies The British government, looking for an alternative penal settlement to the North American colonies that it lost in the American Revolution, sent Capt. Arthur PHILLIP to establish a penal colony at BOTANY BAY. Landing on Jan. 26, 1788, Phillip actually built the settlement on the better site of Port Jackson (later Sydney). He also opened a second convict post on Norfolk Island. In 1803, to forstall French designs, a further penal extension was made in Van Diemen's Land (Tasmania). The early years were ones of great hardship and near starvation.

Austrailia was spared from being no more than a penal settlement by the introduction of sheep and the opening up of the western plains of New South Wales. British policy broadened to allow emancipists (freed convicts), dis-

Arthur Phillip raised the British Flag at Port Jackson (now Sydney) on Jan. 26, 1788. The anniversary of that event is celebrated annually as Australia Day.

charged prison guards, and free migrants to take up land. By the 1830s they had spilled over from Van Diemen's Land to the mainland to found the free settlement of Victoria, which became a separate colony in 1851. The convict-free British colony of Western Australia, established on the Swan River in 1829, was rescued from mismanagment by the British government a few years later. In 1836 the colony of South Australia was formed on the principles of systematic colonization advocated by Edward Gibbon WAKEFIELD. It, too, fell into chaos and was saved only by official intervention and the stringent economies of Gov. George GREY. Prosperity was later ensured by the introduction of wheat.

In 1825 an expanding New South Wales established a separate penal colony at Moreton Bay (Brisbane); this became the capital of the new colony of Queensland in 1859. Squatters (illegal occupants of land) also opened up the Darling Downs in western New South Wales. By 1844 the free settlers of New South Wales forced the British to stop sending convicts, although transportation to other penal colonies continued.

Apart from the widely separated colonies around its coasts, little was known of Australia until its interior began to be explored, especially after 1840. From then to the end of the century, many intrepid explorers such as Robert O'Hara BURKE, Edward John EYRE, John FORREST, John McDouall STUART, Charles STURT, Thomas Livingstone Mitchell, and Ludwig Leichhardt trekked inland. They found little to induce settlement beyond the eastern seaboard.

With the discovery of gold in the 1850s, however, mining towns sprang up in New South Wales and Victoria. The discovery also produced conflict between the colonial governments and the political demands of the thousands of gold seekers from North America, the British Isles, and New Zealand. As a result, empowered by the Australian Colonies Government Act of 1850, all colonies except

Western Australia adopted representative and responsible forms of government by 1860.

This development accentuated separatism and parochialism as each colony adopted different railway gauges and tariff policies, making intercolonial communication and trade difficult. Common to all, however, was a growing demand by settlers and newcomers for land. This was often frustrated by the intractable nature of the country and the malpractices of squatters. By the 1890s, employer-employee antagonism in the growing industrial sector, prolonged drought, and the failure of many banks led to an economic depression escaped only by Western Australia, through a timely discovery of gold at Kalgoorlie and Coolgardie.

None suffered so grievously in these colonial years as did the Aborigines. Treated almost as animals and hunted down for preying on settlers' livestock, they were virtually annihilated in Van Diemen's Land and nearly so in Queensland.

Federation. Common dangers from without and problems of division within fostered growing recognition of the need for colonial union. After several intercolonial conventions, New South Wales, Queensland, South Australia, Tasmania, Victoria, and Western Australia federated in 1901 into the Commonwealth of Australia. The newly created Northern Territory entered in 1911. The Commonwealth, with its capital first in Melbourne and later transferred (1927) to Canberra, gave the former colonies what they wanted—union, but not unity.

The federal government quickly enacted (1901) the White Australia policy, causing the repatriation of Pacific Islanders (Kanakas) employed in the Queensland sugarcane fields. It also established a common tariff policy, the Commonwealth Court of Conciliation and Arbitration (1904) for industrial arbitration, and the Commonwealth Bank of Australia (1911). The creation (1909) of a separate navy and the institution of compulsory military

The first Federal Parliament of Australia was convened (1901) in Melbourne with an inaugural address by England's duke of Cornwall (later King George V). Under the terms of the new constitution, six colonies were federated to form the Commonwealth of Australia.

training reflected a growing sense of independence from Britain.

At the outbreak of World War I, Prime Minister William M. HUGHES pledged full support to Britain but failed to obtain referendum approval of conscription. Overseas Australian "diggers" served with distinction, especially in the ill-fated Gallipoli campaign. Its sense of nationhood intensified by the war, Australia secured separate representation at the PARIS PEACE CONFERENCE (1919–20) and independent membership in the LEAGUE OF NATIONS. The League granted Australia a mandate over the former German New Guinea and a share in another mandate over the phosphate island of NAURU.

At home, wartime demands had led to the development of heavy industries in the eastern states. Despite labor troubles, the immediate postwar years were prosperous. The federal government attempted to develop the Northern Territory, while the individual states promoted their separate development. In the 1930s, Western Australia even indulged in a short-lived secession movement, and abortive "new state" movements appeared in New South Wales and Queensland. But centralist tendencies prevailed with the deterioration in trading conditions resulting from the worldwide DEPRESSION OF THE 1930s. The states looked to the federal government for aid, all the governments adopted stringent deflationary policies, and Australia sought new markets, which the Imperial Economic Conference at Ottawa (1932) only partly supplied.

When World War II broke out in September 1939, the federal government offered Britain every assistance. To aid the war effort, the states surrendered their taxing rights to the federal government. Soon after Australia entered the war, the Federal Labor party under John CURTIN came to power. After the fall (Feb. 15, 1942) of the British naval base at Singapore to the Japanese and the consequent loss of 22,000 Australian troops as prisoners of war, Curtin insisted upon the return of troops from the Middle East to defend Australia and to assist the U.S. forces stationed in Australia under Gen. Douglas MACARTHUR in their drive back through the Pacific Islands to Japan. But it was undoubtedly U.S. naval supremacy in the Pacific that saved Australia from Japanese occupation.

After World War II. After the war, liberal reconstruction programs were extended to include land settlement as well as full employment and education for all ex-servicemen. In 1948, Labor Prime Minister Joseph Benedict CHIFLEY abandoned all economic controls and introduced large-scale social welfare measures. Of great and lasting significance was the adoption (1946) of a bold federal program to finance immigration. As a result, more than 4 million new Australians, nearly half from continental Europe, diversified and enriched the population, increasing it to more than 14.2 million by 1978. Beginning in 1956 the government also modified its White Australia policy to one of restricted immigration of Asians.

From 1949 to 1972 the government was a Liberal-Country party coalition, led until 1966 by Robert G. MENZIES. This government initiated an extensive water conservation and hydroelectric venture in the Snowy Mountains. Of even greater economic consequences were

rich mineral discoveries. Silver, lead, and copper had long replaced gold as a major source of wealth, but in the 1960s the opening up of almost limitless supplies of iron ore in Western Australia, as well as nickel in Western Australia and bauxite (aluminum) in northern Queensland, changed the pattern of the economy and made Japan Australia's chief export market instead of Britain.

The Labor party returned to power in 1972, but Prime Minister Gough WHITLAM's attempt to speed national economic development through large foreign loans resulted in the dramatic downfall of his ministry. A hostile Senate refused to approve his budget, making it impossible for him to govern. In December 1975, in an unprecedented and much criticized move, Gov. Gen. Sir John KERR dismissed Whitlam and dissolved both houses of Parliament. The Liberal-Country party then easily returned to power under J. Malcolm FRASER. He adopted a policy of economic retrenchment to reduce the alarming unemployment, inflation rate, and overseas indebtedness, but problems triggered by a worldwide recession caused his government to lose popular support. In March 1983 it was replaced by a Labor government under Robert HAWKE, which retained control in the elections of 1984, 1987, and 1990. In keeping with its egalitarian philosophy, the Labor government adopted a universal contributory system of social security and a voluntary health insurance plan (Medibank). More significantly, it extended these programs to include the Aborigines, over whom the nation's conscience has become increasingly sensitive. The federal government has also granted Aborigines the vote and social benefits, hitherto denied them.

In international affairs, Australia has become acutely aware of its position and responsibilities since World War II. Having shed all its traditional ties with Britain, including (in 1986) that of limited appeal to the British privy council, it has become vigorously assertive of its newfound independence. It granted independence to Papua New Guinea in 1975 and plays an active role in Asian and Pacific affairs. Australia has defense links with the United States (see ANZUS TREATY) and New Zealand and sent (1991) a token naval force to join the multinational force fighting Iraq in the Persian Gulf. The country, which celebrated its bicentennial in 1988, also signed (1986) a treaty to establish a nuclear-free zone in the South Pacific.

Australian External Territories

The Australian External Territories consist of islands and Antarctic lands administered by Australia. They differ greatly in climate, population, and physical environment. The islands include CHRISTMAS ISLAND, the Cocos Islands (which voted for union with Australia in 1984; 1986 pop., 616), NORFOLK ISLAND, the tropical Coral Sea Islands Territory, and the uninhabited Heard Island and the McDonald Islands in the subantarctic south Indian Ocean. The Australian Antarctic Territory, formed in 1933, includes all lands (except a portion claimed by France) below 60° south latitude and between 160° and 45° east longitude. The total area is 6,200,000 km^2 (2,400,000 mi^2); there is no permanent population.

Australian literature Written Australian literature in the English language began about 50 years after the Europeans arrived on the continent in 1788. Long before then, the Aboriginal inhabitants had a rich and varied oral tradition, much of which is now lost. In their songs and tales, they celebrated the mythical "dreamtime."

For the first decades after European settlement, transported convicts predominated, and they created out of their new circumstances a wealth of songs and ballads based on English and Irish models. Formal writers also sought to reconcile their experiences in the strange new world with the familiar traditions of the old.

Colonial Period. Most formal poetry and fiction of the late 18th and 19th centuries drew upon models from outside Australia, and much of it was aimed at a European audience. It frequently expressed surprise or alarm at local flora and fauna and emphasized or exaggerated the uniqueness of things Australian, especially bushfires, hostile Aborigines, and escaped convicts. Henry Kingsley spent five years in Australia and inaugurated Australian prose with *The Recollections of Geoffry Hamlyn* in 1859. It avoids the air of a guidebook while transplanting English social customs and aspirations to an Australian setting. The best early Australian novel, *For the Term of His Natural Life* (1874), by Marcus Clarke, is a detailed account of convict life, based on historical records.

Colonial poets such as Charles Harpur and Henry Kendall also sought to unite the traditions of English literature (especially nature poetry) with the local scene, but their efforts were frequently awkward. By the close of the 19th century the colonial phase was ending. Writers were becoming more individual and less self-conscious of their environment. Population growth meant a sustained local readership and indigenous publishing. Magazines such as the Sydney *Bulletin*, founded in 1880, published short stories and poems, especially those dealing with country life.

Nationalist Period. The political nationalism leading to

the establishment of the Commonwealth of Australia in 1901 was reflected in the literature. It sought to depict typically Australian qualities and character traits. Special emphasis was placed upon egalitarianism, loneliness, individualism, and pragmatic materialism. The short stories of Henry Lawson and Barbara Baynton, the verse of Lawson and A. B. "Banjo" Paterson, and the novels of Tom Collins (pseudonym of Joseph Furphy) and Miles Franklin were important in this nationalist phase. The most popular novel of the time, *Robbery Under Arms* (1880), by Rolf Boldrewood (pseudonym of Thomas Alexander Browne), was more a product of the earlier period, however, emphasizing the exploits of bushrangers.

Modern Period. The works of Christopher Brennan, who began publishing poetry about the turn of the century, mark a significant shift in development. Until then, Australian writers had been either expatriate Britons or locals unfamiliar with developments in literature elsewhere. Brennan had lived in Europe for several years and was familiar with current literary innovation, especially French symbolism. His work introduced a note of cosmopolitan sophistication and made Australian writers aware of modernist work overseas.

Other notable writers, such as Henry Handel RICHARDSON, (pseudonym of Ethel Florence Richardson), Vance Palmer, Martin Boyd, and Christina STEAD lived outside Australia during much of their careers. It was not until after World War II, however, that Australian literature ceased to be somewhat old-fashioned and parochial in its concerns and attitudes.

Contemporary Period. The major event in the growth of an identifiable national literature was the international recognition of the novelist Patrick WHITE, the first Australian to win (1973) the Nobel Prize for literature. Although his work explores universal issues, he draws upon traditional local themes, and his interests have had a considerable impact. Thomas Keneally's *The Chant of Jimmie Blacksmith* (1972), in particular, owes a debt to White, although Keneally's later work—*Schindler's List*, for ex-

Miles Franklin (left), *Christopher Brennan* (center), *and Morris West* (right), *have all made significant contributions to the development of Australian literature. The country's literature first attained a national identity with Franklin's My Brilliant Career (1901).*

ample, which takes place in World War II Germany—ranges widely in space and time. Such poets as James McAuley, Judith WRIGHT, and Peter Porter have also established reputations in and beyond Australia. The acclaimed *Summer of the Seventeenth Doll* (1955), a play by Ray Lawler, marked the true beginning of an Australian drama of international stature.

Among women writers, Colleen McCullough has captured legions of admirers with her epic of the Australian outback, *The Thorn Birds* (1977). Long-time novelist Janet Frame continues to publish internationally, as do Dorothy Hewett, Thea Astley, and Elizabeth Jolley. Germaine GREER heads the list of contemporary feminist critics and essayists.

Poets David Malouf and Rodney Hall have both created international audiences for their works in prose, Malouf for several novels including his brilliant evocation of a primitive time in *An Imaginary Life* (1978) and the contemporary *Harland's Half Acre* (1984), and Hall for his huge, encyclopedic novel *Just Relations* (1983).

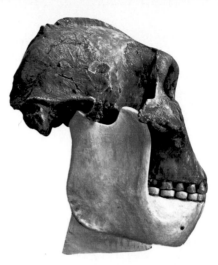

A fossil skull of the hominid known as Australopithecus boisei *was discovered by Mary Leakey in 1959. This prehuman creature, formerly called* Zinjanthropus, *lived in East Africa about 2 million years ago. Although the skull has a small brain capacity and massive jaws, the teeth resemble those of other hominid fossils.*

Australian terrier The Australian terrier is one of the small terriers, standing 25 cm (10 in) at the shoulder and weighing 5.4–6.3 kg (12–14 lb). The rough coat is usually blue black or silver black with rich red markings on the head and legs. Like that of many terriers, the Australian terrier's coat is double, the harsh, straight outer one is about 7 cm (2.5 in) long evenly over the body, and the undercoat is short and soft. Ears and tail are erect.

The breed made its appearance in Australia in the late 19th century, where early settlers interbred the terriers they had brought from England to create an all-purpose hardy little hunter. It is accepted that the cairn, Dandie Dinmont, Irish, Scottish, and Yorkshire terriers are among the breed's progenitors. The breed was slow to gain recognition outside Australia. The Kennel Club in England recognized it in 1933, but the American Kennel Club did not do so until 1960.

The Australian terrier is one of the smallest of working terriers. It was used at one time in Australia to guard mines, herd sheep, and kill vermin.

Australopithecus [aws-truh-loh-pith' uh kuhs]
Australopithecus is a genus of extinct hominid (human-like) fossils generally considered a possible evolutionary ancestor of modern humans. *Australopithecus* came to the attention of the scientific world in 1924 when Raymond DART, a South African anatomy professor, was given the fossil skull of a young child, found at Taung, Cape Province, South Africa. Dart believed he had found the remains of an ancient hominid and named it *Australopithecus africanus*, the "southern ape of Africa."

Scientists remained unconvinced of the hominid status of the australopithecines until the Scottish paleontologist Robert Broom (1866–1951) discovered adult specimens similar to Dart's Taung child at Sterkfontein in the Transvaal. These fossils included pieces of the pelvis and thighbone and demonstrated that *Australopithecus* was an erect biped, one of the most important attributes of a hominid.

The recovery of many additional *Australopithecus* specimens from a number of other South African sites led to the realization that more than one hominid species was represented. Two species, *A. africanus*, the gracile (slight) australopithecine, and a larger, heavier form, *A. robustus*, are now known from the South African deposits. Although it is not possible to date these sites precisely, analyses of the animal bones found with the hominids indicate they lived some time between 3 million and 1.5 million years ago.

In 1959, at OLDUVAI GORGE, Tanzania, Mary LEAKEY discovered a fossil skull that belonged to a creature more massive than the robust australopithecines from South Africa. Originally called "Zinjanthropus boisei," the specimen is now classified as *Australopithecus boisei*. Additional *Australopithecus* specimens have been found at other East African sites. The remains of a more ancient australopithecine, dubbed Lucy, were discovered by Donald Johanson in 1974 at Hadar, Ethiopia, and, together with other fossilized bones found at both Hadar and Laetoli, Tanzania, were called *A. afarensis*. Along with the fossil bones was discovered a remarkable series of footprints that demonstrate the free-striding, fully upright gait of these creatures. Recent research, however, suggests that *A. afarensis* may also have retained anatomical features adapted to arboreal life.

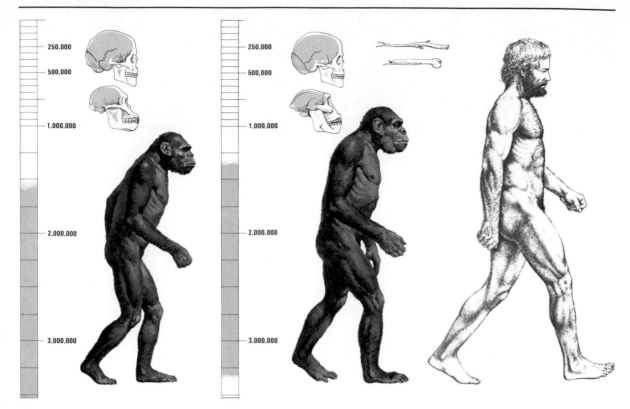

Fossil bones of Australopithecus africanus (left) *and of the larger, heavier* Australopithecus robustus (center), *two extinct hominid species that existed 3.5 to 1.5 million years ago, were discovered in southern Africa. Smaller than modern humans in height and in brain size, the australopithecines walked upright and probably used sticks, bones, and stones as simple tools.*

A controversy ensued in 1985 when a fossil known as the "black skull" was found near Lake Turkana, in northern Kenya. On one side are the paleoanthropologists who place it in the *Australopithecus* line as a precursor to *A. bosei*. Others have proposed that it represents a new species—*Paranthropus*, or "near man." It seems clear that *A. robustus* and *A. boisei* were specialized forms that became extinct about 1.5 million to 1 million years ago. The question remains whether the more gracile *A. africanus* was also an aberrant form that ended in extinction or was the ancestor from which the more advanced members of the genus *Homo* evolved. The relationship of *A. afarensis* to the gracile and robust australopithecines is unclear at present, although it seems reasonable that this species was a precursor to the gracile form. Further research is needed to determine how the "black skull" fits into human evolution.

See also: HOMO HABILIS; PREHISTORIC HUMANS.

Austria   Austria is a landlocked, mostly mountainous country of central Europe whose restricted size and role in world affairs today belie its historic significance. It is bordered to the west by Liechtenstein and Switzerland; to the north by West Germany and Czechoslovakia; to the

east by Hungary; and to the south by Italy and Yugoslavia. Its present boundaries and republican form of government, dating back to 1919, stem from defeat in World War I and the disintegration of the once-vast, multinational Austro-Hungarian empire.

For centuries, Austria's command of vital east-west and north-south trade routes gave it both commercial and strategic importance. Geographically and politically, Austria emerged in the 10th century as the eastern border state (the German name *Österreich* means "eastern state") of the HOLY ROMAN EMPIRE, which it served as a bulwark against invading Slavs and, later, against the Turks. From the late 13th century to the early 20th, Austria's fortunes were synonymous with those of the ruling HABSBURGS, whose dynastic ambitions made it the fulcrum of Europe. The capital city, VIENNA, on the DANUBE RIVER, the Danube Valley, and the Hungarian Plain were the focal points throughout much of Austria's long history.

Land and Resources

The ALPS are the dominant physical feature, covering almost three-fourths of Austria's territory. They can be divided into three ranges: the Northern Alps and the Southern Alps, composed of limestone; and the Central Alps, of crystalline rock. The highest peak, the Grossglockner

AT A GLANCE

REPUBLIC OF AUSTRIA

Land: Area: 83,853 km² (32,376 mi²). Capital and largest city: Vienna (1987 est. pop., 1,479,800).

People: Population (1990 est.): 7,600,000. Density: 90.6 persons per km² (234.7 per mi²). Distribution (1990): 55% urban, 45% rural. Official language: German. Major religion: Roman Catholicism.

Government: Type: federal republic. Legislature: Federal Assembly. Political subdivisions: 9 states.

Economy: GNP (1990): $118.26 billion; $15,560 per capita. Labor distribution (1987): agriculture—8%; manufacturing—28%; construction—8%; government and services—23%; trade—18%; finance and real estate—6%; transportation and communications—7%; other—2%. Foreign trade (1989): imports—$37.9 billion; exports—$31.2 billion. Currency: 1 schilling = 100 groschen.

Education and Health: Literacy (1990): 100% of adult population. Universities (1989): 12. Hospital beds (1988): 82,606. Physicians (1988): 20,502. Life expectancy (1990): 75. Infant mortality (1990): 6 per 1,000 live births.

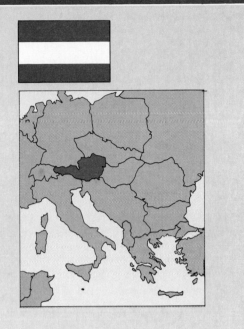

(3,797 m/12,457 ft), stands in the Hohe Tauern range of the Central Alps. Average elevations decrease from west to east. The major ranges are separated by river valleys and depressions, such as the Klagenfurt Basin in south central Austria between the Karawanken and Carnic mountains. Passes such as the BRENNER, leading into Italy, and the Semmering, in eastern Austria, facilitate communications.

To the north of the Alps lies the Danube Valley, which is narrow in the west and broadens at Vienna into the Hungarian Plain. Both these regions contain rich LOESS and alluvial soils, admirably suited to agriculture.

The Bohemian Plateau, north of the Danube Valley, is a hilly upland area composed of granite or covered by forest. Elevations here range from 350 to 900 m (1,150 to 2,950 ft).

Climate. The climate of western and central Austria is generally similar to the moderate Atlantic climates typical of Western Europe. The FOEHN, a warm, dry wind from the south, can set off avalanches when it thaws the snow too suddenly. Eastern Austria has a harsher continental climate, with cold winters, short moderate summers, and only a modest amount of precipitation. Minimum winter temperatures in four major Austrian cities range between -3.3° and 2.2.° C (26° and 28° F); summer maximums, between 17.8° and 20° C (64° and 68° F). These index locations receive between 635 and 990 mm (25 and 39 in) of precipitation annually.

Drainage. The Danube, the country's only navigable river, flows across northern Austria from west to east. All the major rivers of Austria—the INN, Enns, Salza, Mur, Mürz, and Drava—eventually join the Danube. Picturesque finger lakes lie to the north and east of Salzburg and in the Klagenfurt Basin. Neusiedler Lake in Burgenland, on the Hungarian border, with an area of 350 km² (135 mi²), is Austria's largest. Lake Constance in the extreme west is shared with Switzerland.

Vegetation and Animal Life. Deciduous trees, including beech, birch, and oak grow at lower altitudes; higher up, a mixed forest predominates. In Alpine areas, conifers extend from 1,370 to 1,980 m (4,500 to 6,500 ft). Bare rocks and grass slopes continue to the snow line at 2,745–3,048 m (9,000–10,000 ft). Endangered Alpine wildflowers such as the edelweiss grow at the highest altitudes.

The boar, bear, wolf, and lynx have disappeared, but red deer, chamois, marmot, and grouse still flourish in protected Alpine reserves. In the grassy flats of the Neusiedlersee reserve can be found refugee populations of the gray goose, white-tailed and spotted eagles, and breeding colonies of spoonbill and purple and great white herons. In many villages, white storks return annually to their chimney nests.

Resources. Austria's greatest natural resource is its abundant waterpower, which supplies two-thirds of its electrical energy. Timber is supplied by the forests that cover up to 40% of the country and are protected by strict

(Left) *A village in the Salzkammergut district is illustrative of Austria's scenery. The region is noted for its picturesque alpine villages, ancient salt mines, and excavated Iron Age sites.*

(Below) *Salzburg pedestrians stroll along the street where Wolfgang Amadeus Mozart was born in 1756. Salzburg, in addition to being an important manufacturing city, is a noted music center, renowned for its Salzburg Festival, held each summer.*

conservation measures. The most important minerals are magnesite; graphite; iron ore; lignite, a low-grade brown coal; and oil and natural gas. Copper, zinc, lead, and salt are also mined.

People

Austria is basically Germanic in language and ethnic affiliation. The minorities include about 50,000 Croats, principally in Burgenland; about 20,000 Slovenes, concentrated in southern Carinthia; and small groups of Hungarians, Czechs, Slovaks, and Italians. Roman Catholicism is professed by 85% of the population. About 6%, centered in the lowlands and the capital, are Protestants. A Jewish community of fewer than 10,000 is concentrated in Vienna.

The five largest cities in Austria—Vienna, GRAZ, LINZ, SALZBURG, and INNSBRUCK—are home to about a third of the population. A marked population redistribution has occurred since World War II. The eastern provinces have either lost population or made only modest gains, whereas the three western provinces—Vorarlberg, Tyrol, and Salzburg—have shown dramatic increases. Urban areas continue to grow as the farm population leaves the upland valleys and as the tourist industry increasingly develops in the Alpine areas.

Austria's literacy rate of virtually 100% reflects a 200-year history of free and compulsory education. Children are required to attend school from age 6 through 15. After the first four years, students proceed either to a vocational school to train for a trade or to a secondary school

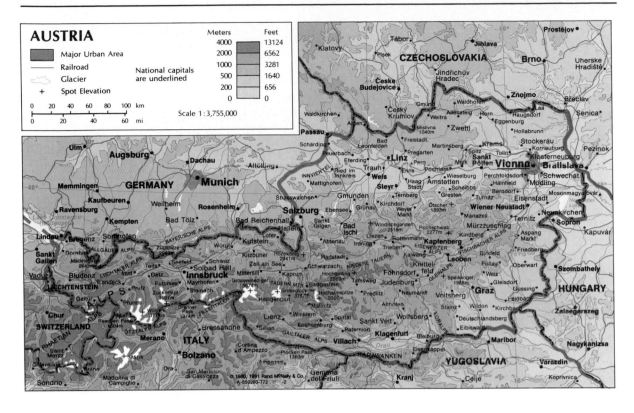

AUSTRIA

- Major Urban Area
- Railroad
- Glacier
- + Spot Elevation

National capitals are underlined

Meters	Feet
4000	13124
2000	6562
1000	3281
500	1640
200	656
0	0

Scale 1:3,755,000

(*mittelschule*) to prepare over an 8-year period to enter a university. The number of students in the university system is modest but increasing. Eighteen universities or colleges are supported by the state.

Austria's standards for health care are indicated by its low infant mortality rate as well as by a ratio of doctors to population of about 1 to 510, one of the highest in Europe. All citizens are covered by national health insurance. In the late 19th and early 20th centuries, Vienna was perhaps Europe's greatest medical center, known particularly for the development of modern psychiatry under Sigmund FREUD.

For the contributions made by Austrians to the arts, see AUSTRIAN ART AND ARCHITECTURE; AUSTRIAN LITERATURE; and GERMAN AND AUSTRIAN MUSIC.

Economic Activity

Manufacturing and Industry. Since the end of World War II, when the country's basic industries were nationalized, the Austrian economy has become increasingly industrialized. Heavy industry tends to concentrate in the Danube Valley, in the Mur-Mürz corridor, and in the capital. Leading manufactured goods include pig iron and steel, automobiles, tractors, locomotives, heavy machinery, electrical parts, chemicals, plastics, paper and pulp, furniture, textiles, and processed foods. Traditional products of Austrian craftsmen include ceramics, glassware, wood carvings, leather products, and optical and musical instruments.

Tourism has become a major industry. It is based on ski and winter sports facilities, on the perennial popularity of medicinal spas, and on the scenic, recreational, and cultural amenities available from the Alps to Vienna. The annual SALZBURG FESTIVAL is an especially popular cultural event.

Agriculture. Two trends have characterized postwar Austrian agriculture: a sharp decline in the portion of the labor force engaged in farming and a decrease in small-scale farming, with farms of fewer than 5 ha (12 acres) either disappearing or being consolidated. Although average farm size remains small and only 20% of the land is arable, scientific methods enable farmers to meet most of Austria's food requirements. Leading crops include barley, wheat, rye, oats, potatoes, sugar beets, and corn. Meat production has risen sharply, and dairy farming is more than adequate to meet national needs.

Forestry. Conifers are the most important commercial wood. Austria produces wood pulp, paper and paperboard, and sawtimber.

Transportation. Austria's transportation system, which is largely state-owned, is modern and efficient. A national airline flies domestic and international routes. About 6,500 km (4,040 mi) of railroads crisscross Austria, traversing all major valleys of the Alps. There are about 11,000 km (6,900 mi) of autobahns (expressways) and federal highways. Both passenger and freight service are available on river vessels on the Danube.

Trade. Austria has had a negative balance of trade since 1945, despite large injections of foreign currency from tourism. Austria must import transport equipment and heavy machinery, fuels, foodstuffs, and raw materials. It exports lumber, paper and pulp, textiles, iron and steel, electric power, and machinery. Its primary trading partner is Germany. Austria is a member of the EUROPEAN FREE TRADE ASSOCIATION.

Government

Austria is a constitutional federal republic composed of nine provinces. A president, popularly elected for a 6-year term, is the head of state, but most governmental power rests with the chancellor and his cabinet, who function for as long as their policies enjoy the confidence of parliament. The chancellor, or prime minister, is usually the head of the political party with the largest number of seats in the lower house of parliament, the National Council (the Nationalrat).

National Council members are elected for 4-year terms. Members of the largely advisory upper house, the Federal Council (Bundesrat), are elected by the provincial legislatures (Landtage), the number from each province being apportioned on the basis of population. Each of the nine provinces (STYRIA, TYROL, Vorarlberg, Salzburg, Upper Austria, Lower Austria, Vienna, Burgenland, and Carinthia) has a governor chosen by its unicameral Landtag.

History

In ancient times, much of the territory later known collectively as "Austria" was called Rhaetia, Noricum, and Pannonia. These became Roman provinces in the 1st century AD. For the next 10 centuries, the area served the more civilized peoples of Europe—initially Roman, later Frankish and German—as a defensive outpost against barbarian invasions.

Roman control collapsed in the 4th century under wave after wave of Germanic and Hunnish invaders. In the 6th century, these tribes were joined by SLAVS and Avars. Nomads from the east, among them MAGYARS, continued to overrun the Danubian area until OTTO I, later Holy Roman emperor, defeated them in the mid-10th century and reorganized the eastern border region as a dependency of the dukes of Bavaria. Under the rule of the Babenberg margraves (976–1246), Austria expanded eastward and southward. Christianity was well entrenched by the early 12th century. The Babenberg lands were occupied (1246–78) by OTTOKAR II of Bohemia. After his defeat by the Habsburg German king RUDOLF I, they passed to the Habsburg family, which provided all but one of the Holy Roman emperors from 1438 to 1806.

The Habsburgs steadily expanded their domains, first by acquiring the Tyrol and Vorarlberg near their hereditary holdings in Switzerland, then by the addition of ISTRIA and TRIESTE to the south. By the marriage (1477) of the future MAXIMILIAN I to MARY OF BURGUNDY, they acquired BURGUNDY and the Low Countries. The accession (1516) of the future emperor CHARLES V to the Spanish throne brought Spain and its empire under Habsburg rule. On

A Habsburg family portrait, painted (c.1515) by Bernard Stigel, shows Emperor Maximilian I (left) with his son, Philip I of Castile; his wife, Mary of Burgundy; his grandsons (foreground) Ferdinand I and Charles V; and Ferdinand's wife, Anne of Bohemia and Hungary.

his abdication (1555–56), Charles left Spain and the Low Countries to his son Philip II and Austria and the empire to his brother FERDINAND I. The Austrian line then oriented its expansion eastward.

Ferdinand's successors proved unable after 1564 to rule coherently or fairly those parts of the empire that had embraced the Protestant REFORMATION. This deficiency was instrumental in causing the THIRTY YEARS' WAR (1618–48). A weakened Austria was forced to recognize the legitimacy of the reformed sects within the empire, but, as the result of the success of the COUNTER-REFORMATION, Catholicism was fully restored in Bohemia and Austria itself.

The efforts of Emperor LEOPOLD I (r. 1657–1705) to undo the Reformation in Hungary led to renewed conflict with the Hungarians and their Turkish allies. In 1683 the Turks besieged Vienna, which was rescued only by the timely intervention of German and Polish forces. A series of imperial victories drove the Turks from Hungary, which Austria formally acquired by the Peace of Karlowitz (1699).

The Austrian empire reached its greatest extent in the first half of the 18th century. Wars over the Spanish and Polish successions brought the addition of the Spanish Netherlands (Belgium) and, in Italy, of Milan, Mantua, Parma, Piacenza, and Tuscany. The War of the AUSTRIAN SUCCESSION (1740–48) grew out of the refusal of the powers to honor the PRAGMATIC SANCTION (issued 1713), the instrument by which Emperor CHARLES VI sought to ensure the indivisibility of his Habsburg possessions and the succession of his daughter MARIA THERESA (r. 1740–80). Maria Theresa's most important contribution lay in measures designed to centralize the administration of an unwieldy empire.

JOSEPH II (r. 1780–90) continued the centralizing efforts of his mother, but he added a humanistic emphasis. He emancipated the serfs, increased the rights of religious minorities, and subordinated the Catholic church to the state. But his reign witnessed losses to the Turks and a revolt in the Spanish Netherlands (1789). Under his brother LEOPOLD II (r. 1790–92), the church and the regional governing bodies won back many of their old powers.

Austria's position in Europe was temporarily shaken by the French Revolution and by the political and geographic changes enacted by NAPOLEON I. In 1806, FRANCIS II laid aside the old imperial title of Holy Roman Emperor, thereafter to reign simply as Emperor Francis I of Austria. Briefly allied with France in the invasion of Russia, Austria subsequently joined with the other powers to defeat Napoleon in 1814.

By the decisions of the Congress of Vienna (1815; see VIENNA, CONGRESS OF), brilliantly orchestrated by the Austrian foreign minister Prince Klemens Fürst von METTERNICH, Austria ceded Belgium to the Netherlands but was compensated by new gains in Italy. Austria also took over leadership of the newly formed GERMAN CONFEDERATION. Under Metternich's aegis, conservatism reigned triumphant over much of the continent for more than 30 years.

The repressive atmosphere, however, could not permanently dampen the liberal or nationalist sentiment that increasingly asserted itself throughout the empire. Dissatisfaction erupted during the REVOLUTIONS OF 1848, forcing Metternich to resign. The revolution was suppressed and under the new emperor, FRANCIS JOSEPH (r. 1848–1916), Austria once more set its course in the direction of centralized, absolutist government, modernized and reformed just enough to make it palatable.

Major setbacks followed. Austria was defeated (1859) in a war with Italy and France, leading to the loss of LOMBARDY to the newly unified kingdom of ITALY. Next came defeat in the SEVEN WEEKS' WAR (1866) against PRUSSIA, which carried with it the loss of Venetia and a number of German territories. Prussia then unified all the German states except Austria into the German Empire in 1871. Austria responded by reshaping its constitutional framework so as to make the Hungarians equal partners in the Austrian Empire. The Compromise (*Ausgleich*) of 1867 created the Dual Monarchy of AUSTRIA-HUNGARY.

Austria remained plagued by the conflicting interests of its multiple nationalities. Its occupation of the Turkish provinces of BOSNIA AND HERCEGOVINA in 1878 and rivalry with Russia for control over the BALKANS in the wake of the Ottoman Empire's decline inevitably intensified the nationalism of the empire's large Slavic minorities. Six years after Austria's outright annexation of Bosnia-Hercegovina, a Serbian nationalist assassinated (June 28, 1914) Archduke FRANZ FERDINAND in Sarajevo. This event led to WORLD WAR I, in which Austria was allied with Germany (see TRIPLE ALLIANCE).

The new Austrian republic was reduced to its essential Germanic core, a quarter of its former size. At the same time, the victorious Allies prohibited Austria from uniting with its potentially still powerful German neighbor, even by means of a customs union. Austria did not adjust well to its straitened postwar circumstances. Politically oriented private armies representing both socialists and conservatives increased the potential for internal strife. The failure of Austria's largest bank in 1931 plunged the nation into economic crisis. Chancellor Engelbert DOLLFUSS assumed dictatorial powers in 1933 and dissolved all rival parties. In July 1934, Dollfuss was murdered by Austrian Nazis determined to force a union (*Anschluss*) with Hitler's Germany. Their aim was accomplished four years later when Dollfuss's successor, Kurt von SCHUSCHNIGG, resigned under pressure from Hitler and German troops occupied (Mar. 12, 1938) the country. From then until the end of World War II, Austria was part of Germany.

Following its liberation by Allied troops in the spring of 1945, Austria was reestablished within its prewar boundaries under a provisional government. This soon gave way to a coalition government that included members of both the Socialist and People's parties. The country was divided into four administrative zones for occupation by U.S., Soviet, British, and French forces. The four powers stayed until 1955. Austria joined the United Nations later the same year.

In the postwar era Austria was governed by a series of political coalitions dominated until 1970 by the conservative People's party, and after that by the Socialists under Chancellors Bruno KREISKY (1970–83), Fred Sinowatz (1983–86), and Franz Vranitzky (1986–). Former UN secretary general Kurt WALDHEIM, who was elected to the presidency in 1986, became a subject of controversy when it was revealed that he had lied about the extent of his activities in the German army during World War II and that Yugoslav sources had accused him of complicity in war crimes. A committee of historians declared the latter charge unproven in 1988, and Waldheim ignored calls for his resignation.

——
Austria-Hungary   Austria-Hungary was the name of the HABSBURG empire from its reorganization into the Dual Monarchy in 1867 to its breakup in 1918. (See AUSTRIA.) Its predecessor, the Austrian Empire, was founded in 1806, when the HOLY ROMAN EMPIRE was dissolved. The major parts of Austria-Hungary were the predominantly German Austrian crown lands, the kingdom of BOHEMIA, GALICIA, the Italian provinces of LOMBARDY and Venetia, and the Kingdom of Hungary.

In 1849, in the midst of the REVOLUTIONS OF 1848, Hungary declared its independence; but with Russian aid, Emperor FRANCIS JOSEPH crushed the rebellion. Subsequent military defeats forced the regime to introduce reforms and deal with the Magyar leaders, Ferenc DEÁK and Count Gyula ANDRÁSSY. In 1867 the latter agreed to the so-called *Ausgleich*, or Compromise, which established the Dual Monarchy.

The Compromise restored historic Hungary with all its non-Magyar peoples and confirmed its constitution of 1848, which allowed the Magyars to dominate. In Austria (the remainder of the empire), the Germans maintained a similar ascendancy over Czechs, Poles, Ruthenians, Slovenes, and the few remaining Italians. The Compromise recognized two separate states joined by a common monarch, who was emperor of Austria and king of Hungary; a single army; common ministries of war, foreign affairs, and finance. Both Austria and Hungary had parliamentary governments, but the electoral laws discriminated against the Slavic majority in the empire.

Austrian politics from 1867 to 1879 were dominated by German liberals, who introduced free compulsory education, enacted guarantees of free speech, press, and assembly, emancipated the Jews, and put through anticlerical legislation. In 1879 conservatives and Roman Catholics formed a ministry under Eduard, Graf von TAAFFE. Taaffe's 1893 bill for universal manhood suffrage failed, and his regime failed as a result. Meanwhile, tensions were increased by the rise of socialism, anti-Semitism, and the Young Czech movement, led by Tomáš MASARYK and Eduard BENEŠ, who demanded ethnic rather than mere provincial autonomy. In 1907 universal manhood suffrage was finally introduced, intensifying class conflict without abating national rivalries.

In Hungary, Magyar control resulted in strenuous efforts to Magyarize the population. A small Independent party, inspired by the exiled hero Lájos KOSSUTH, demanded full independence, and the dominant Liberal party jealously guarded Hungary's rights under the Compromise. The use of German in the army, the economic disparity resulting from industrialization in Austria, and the possibility of democratic suffrage were the main sources of concern.

The cohesive forces in the Dual Monarchy were the army, the bureaucracy, the Catholic church, and a genuine loyalty to Francis Joseph. After the Austrian annexation of BOSNIA AND HERCEGOVINA in 1908, the Yugoslav movement, which aimed at the union of all South Slavs under Serbia, led to the assassination of Archduke FRANZ FERDINAND in 1914. This precipitated the outbreak of WORLD WAR I. In 1916, CHARLES I succeeded Francis Joseph. In 1919–20 the peace treaties of Versailles, St. Germain, and Trianon—negotiated at the PARIS PEACE CONFERENCE—recognized the dissolution of the empire. In the succession states, however—Austria, Hungary, Czechoslovakia, and Yugoslavia—the difficulties of the diverse nationalities continued.

Austrian art and architecture   During the reign (1690–1705) of the Habsburg Holy Roman emperor LEOPOLD I, Austria began to make its contributions to European art history, particularly in the development of BAROQUE and ROCOCO art and architecture. The BIEDERMEIER style emerged and flourished in Vienna in the early 19th

century, and the subsequent revival of Renaissance architectural styles made the city one of the most beautiful in the world by the 1890s. The SECESSION MOVEMENT at the turn of the century brought forth a distinctively Austrian form of EXPRESSIONISM in all the arts; this became a powerful force in much of 20th-century architecture and painting.

Baroque and Rococo Periods. Johann Bernhard FISCHER VON ERLACH and Johann Lukas von HILDEBRANDT, the most outstanding Austrian baroque architects, absorbed the Italian baroque style and developed it independently. Fischer von Erlach's chaste Dreifaltigkeitskirche (Church of the Holy Trinity) in Salzburg (1694–1702) and his spectacular Karlskirche in Vienna (1716–32) echo BORROMINI's and BERNINI's designs in their undulating facades, floor plans in the form of a Greek cross (four equal arms), and use of oval spaces with domed crossings.

Hildebrandt's Upper Belvedere Palace (1721–24) in Vienna expresses secular baroque intentions. The palace, enriched with sculpture on the exterior and with lavish interior stucco decorations and frescoes, is an unmistakable statement of political power. It was intended to equate the Vienna Hofburg (Imperial Palace) and Fischer von Erlach's Schönbrunn (Summer Palace, 1695–1749) with Louis XIV's VERSAILLES. The same exuberance and luxury are found in many of Austria's baroque convents and monasteries, exemplified by the elegant Convent of Saint Florian (1708–11) and the imposing Monastery of Melk (1701–26), both by Jakob Prandtauer.

Balthasar Permoser's statue *Apotheosis of Prince Eugen of Savoy* (1718–21) and Georg Raphael Donner's fountains for the Vienna Flour Market (1737–39) are typical of the late baroque spirit, somewhat calmed by classicist rationality. Johann Michael Rottmayr (1654–1730) broke away from the Italian style by bringing a Rubensesque vitality to his ceiling paintings. Paul Troger (1698–1762) developed a rococo version of this style, although it was weakened by the influence of Correggio and the Roman High Renaissance.

In the reign (1740–80) of MARIA THERESA, painting was the only art form to achieve refinement. The ceiling frescoes of the Heiligenkreuz-Gutenbrunn Church (1757–58) by Franz Anton MAULPERTSCH exhibit a richness reminiscent of Rubens and a compositional strength reflective of Rembrandt. In architecture and sculpture, far less vitality was achieved. Only Franz Xavier Messerschmidt, with his highly theatrical religious sculptures and portrait heads, stands out.

Neoclassical and Romantic Periods. During the reigns of Holy Roman emperors JOSEPH II (1780–90) and LEOPOLD II (1790–92), Austrian cultural life was concentrated in Vienna. The visual arts mirrored the NEOCLASSICISM that dominated all of Europe; the Vienna Academy, under the leadership of the painter Heinrich Füger (1751–1818), became a conservative bastion, against which a successful rebellion was fought by the German painters Johann Friedrich Overbeck and Franz Pforr. They founded (1809) the Lukasbund, a brotherhood of painters who sought to renew their art through a return to the pre-Renaissance system of artists' guilds. In 1810, Overbeck and Pforr

The Upper Belvedere in Vienna, built (1721-24) by Johaan Lucas von Hildebrandt, was designed as the summer residence of Prince Eugene of Savoy. The palace is an example of northern baroque architecture at its opulent peak.

moved to Rome and established the influential group now known as the NAZARENES. Austrian painting took a different turn with the emergence of the Biedermeier, or Old Vienna, painting style, exemplified in the work of Ferdinand Georg Waldmüller. A proto-realist reminiscent of the French BARBIZON SCHOOL, Waldmüller was renowned for his numerous portraits, his naturalistic landscapes, and his affectionate genre paintings, typical of the optimistic world view of the Viennese at this time.

Renaissance Revival in Vienna. Architecture revived in the 19th century with the vast projects of Gottfried Semper, the greatest of the Renaissance-revival architects in the Austro-German sphere. His ensemble of buildings on Vienna's Ringstrasse, including the art and natural history museums (1872–81), part of the Neue Hofburg (1881), and particularly the Burgtheater (1874–88), is

Fulfillment (c. 1909), by the Viennese painter Gustav Klimt, is a preparatory design for his mosaics in the dining room of Palais Stoclet, Brussels, designed by the Austrian architect Josef Hoffmann. Klimt was among the leaders of Jugendstil, the Austrian Art Nouveau movement. (Strasbourg, Musée d'Art Moderne.)

perhaps his finest achievement. In painting, the taste of the upper bourgeoisie and the nobility ran to pompous historical and allegorical subjects exemplified in the huge, brilliantly colored canvases of Hans Makart (1840–84).

20th-Century Movements. In the 1890s a *fin de siècle* decadence settled over all Europe. At the same time protests developed against it. Jugendstil ("youth style"), the Viennese version of ART NOUVEAU, led directly to the founding of the Secession movement in 1897, and to the highly decorative and erotic art of Gustav KLIMT and Egon SCHIELE, and the vivid expressionism of Oskar KOKOSCHKA's paintings and Alfred KUBIN's drawings and prints. Impressionism, by contrast, had little impact on Austrian art. Otto WAGNER and his pupils Josef HOFFMANN, Adolf LOOS, and Joseph Maria Olbrich, the architect of the Vienna Secession building, created a new Austrian architecture of enormous influence in the 20th century, leading directly to the German BAUHAUS school and the dominant INTERNATIONAL STYLE in architecture.

Many artists fled Austria after the Nazi takeover (1938), settling in Switzerland, Paris, and New York and merging in art history with their German fellow expatriate artists. Since World War II, the fantasy paintings of HUNDERTWASSER and the sculptures of Fritz Wotruba (1907–75) have given promise of a resurgence in Austrian art.

See also: GERMAN ART AND ARCHITECTURE; ROMANTICISM (ART).

Austrian literature   Because they share a common language, Austrian literature is usually treated as part of German literature. But the separate cultural and political development of Austria justifies a separate discussion of a specifically Austrian literature, which also includes literature produced in the German-speaking areas of Czechoslovakia, Hungary, Romania, and Yugoslavia.

Medieval Austrian and German literature are inseparable, however. The earliest Austrian literature was the court poems and songs of the minnesingers (see MINSTRELS, MINNESINGERS, AND TROUBADOURS) and the anonymous epic the NIBELUNGENLIED. WALTHER VON DER VOGEL-

WEIDE, in his poems of courtly love, brought the art of the minnesingers to its highest peak. Around 1400, Johannes von Tepl (d. 1414) (also called von Saaz) introduced the Italian Renaissance and humanism into Austrian literature with his *Der Ackermann aus Böhmen*.

Not until the early 19th century, with the fall of Napoleon and the ascendancy of Vienna as a world capital, did great literature blossom again. Among the works of the so-called Biedermeier writers, the historical dramas of Franz GRILLPARZER, the poems of Nikolaus Lenau (1802–50), and the Bohemian tales of Adalbert Stifter stand out. Of equal importance are the folk plays of Ferdinand Raimund and the satirical comedies of the "Viennese Aristophanes," Johann Nestroy. Austrian theater boasts of a long tradition going back to the baroque and the Italian COMMEDIA DELL'ARTE.

In the second half of the 19th century realism began to dominate Austrian literature, especially in the works of Ferdinand von Saar (1833–1906), Ludwig Anzengruber (1839–89), and Ernst von Wildenbruch (1845–1909). Most of these authors wrote village stories and *Heimatroman*, or "regional novels." Anzengruber concentrated particularly on the political and social problems of his time, and Wildenbruch wrote patriotic plays. Saar was the forerunner of Viennese impressionism, of which Arthur SCHNITZLER and Hugo von HOFMANNSTHAL were the most important exponents. Rainer Maria RILKE became the most important German-language poet of the 20th century, and George Trakl was a leading expressionist poet. Other major Austrian influences on German literature were the novelists Hermann BROCH and Stefan ZWEIG and the satirical essayist Karl Kraus.

In the years immediately before and after World War I, three Prague writers attracted serious attention: Franz KAFKA, his friend Max BROD, and the novelist Franz WERFEL. The interwar years were distinguished by the experimental fiction of novelists Robert MUSIL and Heimito von Doderer. After World War II, Ingeborg Bachmann and the Romanian-born poet Paul CELAN added their voices to the war literature. The Wiener Gruppe, formed in the 1960s, were experimental writers interested in concrete poetry and the poetic uses of dialect. They included Friedrich Achleitner, Hans Carl Artmann, and Gerhard Rühm. In more recent years, the novelist and poet Thomas Bernhard and the avant-garde playwright-novelist Peter HANDKE achieved wide acclaim.

Austrian music   see GERMAN AND AUSTRIAN MUSIC

Austrian Succession, War of the   The War of the Austrian Succession (1740–48) was a major European conflict fought to preserve the balance of power in the mid–18th century. The war grew out of competition between Prussia and Austria, conflicts between Austria and France, and a struggle between England and France for superiority in overseas trade and colonial empire. These rivalries were intensified by the problem of the Austrian succession.

On Oct. 20, 1740, Emperor CHARLES VI died and his lands passed to his daughter, MARIA THERESA. Two months later, FREDERICK II of Prussia invaded SILESIA, a province bordering Bohemia. A Prussian victory at Mollwitz in Apr. 1, 1741 hastened the formation of an anti-Habsburg coalition that included Bavaria, Spain, and France as well as Prussia.

Hard pressed by a Franco-Bavarian offensive in the summer of 1741, Maria Theresa made a temporary truce with Prussia and attacked her remaining enemies. Austrian successes brought Prussia back into the war, and victories by Frederick II in 1745 compelled Maria Theresa to accept Prussian control of Silesia. In May, 1745 the French, under Maurice, comte de SAXE, had defeated a combined Austrian, English, and Dutch force at Fontenoy, but French triumphs in the Austrian Netherlands and in India were counterbalanced by losses in Canada and by English domination of the high seas.

A general peace was finally concluded at Aix-la-Chapelle on Oct. 18, 1748. It restored the prewar territorial arrangements in western Europe and the colonial sphere. In central Europe, however, Austria reluctantly recognized Frederick II's annexation of Silesia. Because of the wealth and population of Silesia, Prussia became one of the great European powers. Austria's determination to recover Silesia was a chief cause of the SEVEN YEARS' WAR.

See also: AIX-LA-CHAPELLE, TREATIES OF; FRENCH AND INDIAN WARS.

Austro-Asiatic languages   see SOUTHEAST ASIAN LANGUAGES

Austro-Prussian War   see SEVEN WEEKS' WAR

Austronesian languages   see MALAYO-POLYNESIAN LANGUAGES

authoritarianism   Authoritarianism, in the political sense, is the insistence by government authority of total submission to its will. The authority may be that of a leader, an elite, or a party. Authoritarian movements in democratic countries acquire their greatest following in troubled times when people turn to them for solutions. This happened in Europe between the two world wars. FASCISM and COMMUNISM are strongly authoritarian although in different ways: the former stresses the wisdom of the leader; and the latter, the infallibility of the party. Many contemporary governments are authoritarian without being either Communist or Fascist, for example those of the Persian Gulf states.

See also: TOTALITARIANISM.

autism   Autism is a rare, profound, and poorly understood mental disorder that is present at birth or becomes evident during the first 30 months of life. As children, autistic individuals appear to be physically well developed. The children are, however, severely impaired in their ability to comprehend and communicate.

About 80 percent of those with autism are also classified as mentally retarded. The most distinctive feature of autistic individuals—and this helps to distinguish them from those who are solely mentally retarded—is that autistic individuals seem isolated from the world around them. They appear to be detached, aloof, or in a dreamworld. The word *autism* (derived from the Greek word meaning "self") has been applied because of the individual's superficial resemblance to a person who is self-involved or daydreaming. Such individuals appear to be unaware of the people in their environment, including family members.

About half of all autistic individuals are mute, or speak intelligibly only once or twice during their lifetimes. The rest are able to produce words and sentences, sometimes articulating words clearly before their first birthday, but they do not use speech to communicate. If speech does develop in such children, it generally begins to become intelligible between the ages of five and eight.

The speaking autistic individuals, especially those who fall into the subgroup that exhibits early infantile autism, also known as Kanner's syndrome, display many unusual language mannerisms, such as reversing pronouns (saying *you* for *I*) and repeating a question to indicate *yes*. The Kanner's syndrome subgroup, constituting about 10 percent of all autistic individuals, displays many other unusual and highly characteristic traits, such as an exceptional memory, fascination with mechanical objects, insistence on sameness in the environment (for example, having the furniture in a house always placed in a specific order), and, often, unusual skills in music, art, or computation (see IDIOT SAVANT).

Autism occurs in about 4.5 children per 10,000 live births, and three times as many boys as girls are autistic. Research supports the possibility of a genetic defect, and the discovery of an antibody to brain receptors for the neurotransmitter serotonin in the blood of some autistic individuals suggests that the disorder either might be a form of AUTOIMMUNE DISEASE or else might be an indication of the degeneration of nerve cells in the brain.

In 1988 brain scans using the new technology of MAGNETIC RESONANCE IMAGING revealed that autistic individuals have a large deficiency of brain cells in a part of the cerebellum known as the vermis. The biological mechanism that causes the brain-cell deficiency has not been discovered.

The most pervasive form of treatment for autistic individuals today involves the use of stringent, purposeful BEHAVIOR MODIFICATION programs, in which the subject is taught in small increments and reinforced immediately after an appropriate response is made. Various drugs have been used on autistic children, but drugs currently available have limited effectiveness and some potential for significant side effects. Researchers have found larger-than-normal dosages of vitamin B6 to be helpful to many autistic children and adults. Even so, the programs of treatment have proven effective for a small percentage of cases, and many autistic individuals remain severely impaired, requiring institutionalization or custodial home care for their entire lives.

autobiography   An autobiography, like a BIOGRAPHY, is a record of a life, but it is written (or spoken: see ORAL HISTORY) by the subject. The various kinds of autobiographical writings fall roughly into two groupings. The first focuses primarily on events remembered or participated in by the writer (memoirs and reminiscences). The second emphasizes personal examination or analysis, as in confessional literature. The latter may be loose in form (letters, fragmentary diaries, and incidents in novels) or carefully shaped, retrospective narratives. Examples date as far back as the impulse of Egyptian, Babylonian, and Assyrian kings to record their deeds and wealth. With the exception of the *Confessions of St. Augustine*, however, significant autobiographies are rare in the classical and medieval periods. The closest examples are the *Meditations* of Marcus Aurelius and Julius Caesar's *Commentaries*.

In the Renaissance, as people grew interested in themselves and their relation to the world, autobiographical writing flourished. *The Book of Margery Kempe* (1436), the *Autobiography* (1558–66) of Benvenuto CELLINI, PETRARCH's *Litera ad postero* (c.1367–72), and the autobiography of Lord Herbert of Cherbury (1764) are fine examples.

The late Renaissance and early 18th century were the great ages of autobiography, whether journals (religious and secular), memoirs (political, military, and erotic), or letters. John BUNYAN's *Grace Abounding to the Chief of Sinners* (1666) and Richard Baxter's *Reliquiae Baxterianae* (1696) are examples of religious autobiography; Colley CIBBER's *Apology* (1740) for his own life and Benjamin FRANKLIN's *Autobiography* (1766) are secular ones. The best personal journals and diaries are those of John EVELYN, published in 1818; Samuel PEPYS, published in the 1890s; and James BOSWELL, published in this century.

Possibly because of the romantic movement, the late 18th and early 19th centuries saw the first great modern autobiographies: highly self-conscious, retrospective analyses of an author's life written as a complete work. These include Edward GIBBON's *Autobiography* (1796), *Les* CONFESSIONS (1781, 1788) of Jean Jacques Rousseau, Cardinal John Henry NEWMAN's *Apologia Pro Vita Sua* (1864), Edmund Gosse's *Father and Son* (1907), John Stuart MILL's *Autobiography* (1873), and THE EDUCATION OF HENRY ADAMS (1907).

Several major literary figures have treated their own lives in fictional form, such as Samuel Butler in THE WAY OF ALL FLESH (1903), D. H. Lawrence in *Sons and Lovers* (1913), and James Joyce in PORTRAIT OF THE ARTIST AS A YOUNG MAN.

autogiro [aw'-to-jy'-roh]   The autogiro is an aircraft that obtains its lift from a rotor that freely rotates horizontally. The rotor is not powered directly by the engine but rather by the flow of air past the blades. Forward thrust comes from a propeller. The Spanish engineer Juan de la Cierva designed the first successful autogiro (1923) by hinging the rotor blades so that they could rise and fall freely in response to variations in relative velocity during

An autogiro is a small rotary-winged aircraft. This Wallis autogiro cruises at about 160 km/h (100 mph), weighs about 227 kg (500 lb), and has a range of about 320 km (200 mi).

rotation, thus equalizing the lift. Unlike the HELICOPTER, which eventually took over most of its functions, the autogiro is incapable of hovering flight.

autoimmune diseases

Several serious human diseases result from malfunction of the body's immune system (see IMMUNITY). The so-called autoimmune diseases are best thought of as a lack of proper self-regulation of the normal immune response against foreign substances, such as bacteria, to facilitate their elimination. In autoimmune diseases the system presumably does not properly distinguish between foreign substances and its own "self" substances. Lymphocytes and products of lymphocytes and plasma cells—ANTIBODIES in particular—attack normal cells and tissue constituents, leading to disease. Such diseases include ADDISON'S DISEASE, pernicious ANEMIA, rheumatoid ARTHRITIS, systemic LUPUS ERYTHEMATOSUS, MYASTHENIA GRAVIS, RHEUMATIC FEVER, dermatomyositis, scleroderma, some forms of thyroiditis, and some forms of kidney disease called glomerulonephritis. A similar mechanism has recently been implicated in juvenile DIABETES mellitus.

A limited amount of immune reactivity directed toward "self" antigens exists in the embryo and even in adult life and is thought to be important in regulation of the immune system. When it is not properly controlled, however, an autoimmune disease may ensue. Possibly certain viral and bacterial infections may trigger the disruption of the immunoregulatory apparatus, but the mechanisms are not clear. Generally, treatment of the diseases involves suppression of the immune response. Corticosteroid drugs are frequently efficacious for many of the diseases, and studies of the use of plasmapheresis (removal of plasma containing antibodies) are under way.

automata, theory of [awt-oh-mat'-uh]

The theory of automata deals with the fundamental behavioral principles of automatic machines. It provides the theoretical framework for automated processes in which sensors and detectors replace human sense organs, actuators powered by electric motors or hydraulic forces replace human muscles, and microprocessors replace the human brain. Automata theory was once largely an abstract branch of mathematics that attempted to define the behavior of machines or systems in terms of data inputs and outputs. Specific areas of interest include computing machine theory, language or grammar theory, logic theory, and ARTIFICIAL INTELLIGENCE. Recently, automata theory has been implemented in practical computer-based operations that mimic human processes.

In 1936, Alan TURING, an English mathematician, systematized automata theory by developing, on paper, a model for the digital computer. Turing proved that his "universal computer" could solve virtually any mathematical or logical problem that could be formulated in a logically consistent manner.

In the 1940s, Warren McCulloch and Walter Pitts, of the Massachusetts Institute of Technology (MIT), developed the theory of neural net automation. Essentially an abstract model of the human nervous system, neural net automation theory describes a system of neurons, that, when stimulated above a certain threshold, will fire, and transmit an impulse along connecting fibers. Neural net automation theory has been used in a variety of automata applications.

The 1950s brought a surge of enthusiasm for automata theory. American linguist Noam CHOMSKY showed that automated language analysis could be performed on both human and programming languages. Claude Elwood SHANNON, of MIT, outlined methods whereby a machine could be programmed to play winning chess and learn from its experiences. Additional advances were made by the researcher Herbert A. Simon.

Active areas in modern automata theory include studies in expert systems and man–machine interactions (see CYBERNETICS). Expert systems are computer programs that to some extent encapsulate the expertise of highly trained professionals.

One possibly rich field for basic research is cellular automata. First elucidated by mathematicians John VON NEUMANN and Stanislaw Ulam in the early 1950s, cellular automata are made up of mathematical "cells" that change their value, or state, according to simple rules, or ALGORITHMS. The state of each cell is affected by the states of neighboring cells. Some automata theorists believe it possible to simulate complex physical systems, including the human nervous system, through cellular automata.

Advances in applied areas such as voice recognition and machine-learning have been frustrated by the relatively slow speeds of present-day computers. Higher speeds are needed in order to handle the data involved in such processes.

automation

The term automation refers to a wide variety of systems and processes that operate with little or no human intervention. In the most modern automation systems, control is exercised by the system itself through control devices that sense changes in such conditions as temperature, rate of flow, and volume, and then command the system to make adjustments to compensate for these changes.

History

Automation developed as a result of advances in the design of MACHINES. Most early machines were designed to operate under a specific set of conditions; when these conditions changed, a manual adjustment was necessary to assure proper operation. This was not a major shortcoming, since the machines operated at relatively low speeds. During the 1800s, however, more sophisticated machines were developed and applied to situations requiring a faster response.

Automation was quickly recognized as a valuable way to assure efficiency and accuracy in manufacturing processes. The chemical industries developed the technology of automation to regulate variables such as pressure and temperature that are involved in the production of chemicals. The food industries began to make use of automated systems. The methods of automation were refined with the development of aircraft guidance systems and automatic pilots. The development of digital computers, which can monitor external conditions and make appropriate adjustments to a system, added further impetus to the applications of automation. Industrial robots perform numerous functions on assembly lines, and automated spacecraft on deep-space probes are programmed automatically to make adjustments in operations.

Principles

An automated system adjusts its operations in response to changing external conditions in three steps: measurement, evaluation, and control.

Measurement. In order for an automated system to respond to the external environment, it must be able to measure the physical variables in that environment. If a complex assembly procedure is to occur, a measurement or series of measurements must be made to define the present state of the assembly. These measurements supply the system with information known as FEEDBACK, because the information is fed back to the input of the system and used to exercise some control over it. For example, if the process is self-guidance, the feedback will include the system's location, speed, and acceleration.

Evaluation. The measured information is evaluated in order to determine if corrective action must be initiated. Thus, if a spacecraft evaluates its position and finds itself to be off course, a course correction must be made.

Control. The last step of automation is the action resulting from the measurement and evaluation operations. Thus, the rocket gets an appropriate signal to fire and thereby changes the path of the spacecraft.

Applications

Automation is used in numerous industries throughout the world. Some industries have become more automated than others, and some devices could not work at all with-

out automated features. In many cases, specific applications of the principles of automation have led to new fields.

Process Control. The application of the principles of automation to the control of continuous manufacturing operations is called PROCESS CONTROL. It is used extensively in the chemical and petrochemical industries, where gas and liquid temperatures, flow, pressure, reaction rates, and many other characteristics must be controlled.

Servomechanisms. Many industrial operations require devices, called SERVOMECHANISMS, to control such simple operations as the rotational rate of motor shafts, amount of current, hydraulic or pneumatic pressure within a system, or position of a valve. Servomechanisms function through a feedback process. They are usually actuated by changes in a mechanical situation, although some complex servomechanisms are set in motion by electric or electronic frequencies.

Industrial Robots. The use of automated machines that can be programmed to perform different jobs under various operating conditions has recently become widespread. These machines can properly be called industrial ROBOTS. Robots are employed to drill, machine, and partially assemble automobile engines. The spacecraft sent to the Moon and on deep-space missions are also types of robots. Although radio contact is maintained with these craft, the distances involved are so great that the craft must incorporate devices that can adjust operations—based on the conditions encountered—without human commands.

Future of Automation

As technology continues to be developed and improved, more and more of the routine activities of business and industry will be taken over by automated systems. Microcomputers, based upon the INTEGRATED CIRCUIT, are already causing a vast change in the applications of automation; even a device as small as a washing machine can be put under computer control and thus be programmed to respond to a variety of environmental conditions.

Recent advances in durable miniature systems have made advanced robots of science fiction a near reality. The key characteristic of such a completely automated machine will be self-adaptability, the capacity to evaluate a new overall condition and decide upon a course of action. Realizing this potential will require new developments in computer algorithms, pattern recognition, and control functions. The use of computers to design and manufacture complex systems is becoming increasingly common (see COMPUTER-AIDED DESIGN AND COMPUTER-AIDED MANUFACTURING).

automaton [aw-tahm'-uh-tahn] An automaton is a device that can duplicate certain actions of living things. Greek myth discusses a robotlike guardian devised by Daedalus for King Minos of Crete to awe intruders. In the 1st and 2d centuries BC, HERO OF ALEXANDRIA constructed automatons and described several of them in his book *Epivitalia*. In 1354 the famous Strasbourg clock was built; this mechanism incorporated a metal cock that opened its beak, put out its tongue, crowed, spread its feathers, and flapped its wings. Even more complex clockwork mechanisms followed.

The term *automaton* first appeared in English in 1625 and was related to the idea of ARTIFICIAL INTELLIGENCE. At the time of the Renaissance in Europe, Hero's works were rediscovered, and his accounts inspired automaton makers and inventors.

The golden era of fine automatons, however, was the 18th and 19th centuries. Notable automatons were created by Wolfgang von Kempelen, Jacques de Vaucanson, and Henri Maillardet. The family of Pierre Jacquet-Droz made fabulous toys, including a sheep that bleated in a lifelike manner. Organ-grinders with dancing monkeys were a common automaton theme. By the late 19th century, however, mechanical models had become very crude devices.

See also: ROBOT.

automobile   The automobile is a self-propelled, four-wheeled, steerable vehicle for transporting people on land. This article describes the main parts of the automobile and their components. The history, manufacture, and design of the motorized passenger vehicle are discussed in AUTOMOTIVE INDUSTRY. Technical and operational details are to be found in separate articles on the systems mentioned below.

All passenger cars, trucks, and buses have certain things in common: (1) the power plant, or engine; (2) the chassis, which supports the engine and wheels and includes the frame and the steering and brake systems; (3) the power train, which transmits the power from the engine to the car wheels; and (4) the body.

Engines

A variety of engine types have been used in motor vehicles. They are generally INTERNAL-COMBUSTION ENGINES that burn gasoline or diesel fuel oil. Internal-combustion engines can be classified in several ways. Of the many possibilities, most passenger-car engines run on gasoline, have spark ignition, and are of the liquid-cooled, four-stroke-cycle, overhead-valve, carbureted, reciprocating type. DIESEL ENGINES, which burn fuel oil, are becoming more common in automobiles.

Most gasoline engines have carbureted fuel systems; these mix gasoline with air in the carburetor to form a combustible mixture.

Almost all automobiles use reciprocating engines, which have pistons that move up and down in cylinders. Some automobiles, however, use rotary type Wankel engines.

Chassis

The chassis includes the car frame, power train, wheels, and suspension, steering, and brake systems.

Two types of frames, full and stub, are used. The full frame has side, front, back, and cross members welded

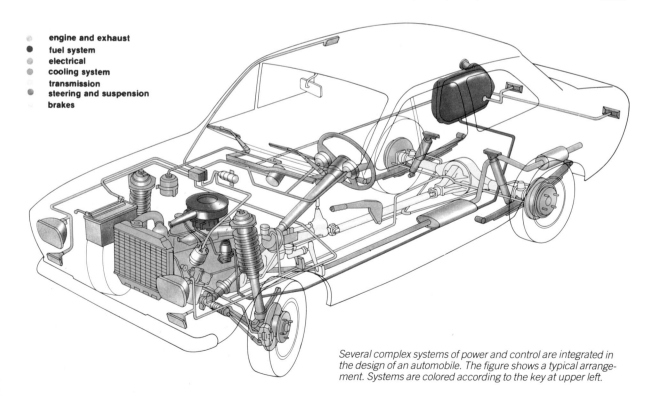

- ◐ **engine and exhaust**
- ● **fuel system**
- ◐ **electrical**
- ◐ **cooling system**
- ◌ **transmission**
- ● **steering and suspension**
- ◌ **brakes**

Several complex systems of power and control are integrated in the design of an automobile. The figure shows a typical arrangement. Systems are colored according to the key at upper left.

into a single assembly that supports all other parts of the vehicle. The stub frame has separate frames for the front and back that are welded to the car body, with the body forming the center and connecting support.

The automobile's wheels are attached to the frame by any of three types of springs: coil, leaf, and torsion bar. All SUSPENSION SYSTEMS use shock absorbers.

The STEERING SYSTEM normally controls the turning of the front wheels. Most cars today have power steering, whereby application of engine power reduces the effort of turning the steering wheel.

In the brake system, a brake fluid in the master cylinder is forced through brake lines to wheel mechanisms when the driver depresses the brake pedal. With power brakes, power from the engine is used to increase the pressure activating the piston in the master cylinder.

Among several impressive new developments are mechanisms that allow all four wheels—rather than simply the two front wheels—to steer the car, permitting easier parking and greater stability at highway speeds; and antilock brakes that prevent skidding, even under wet or icy conditions.

Power Train

The power train includes a manual or automatic TRANSMISSION; a clutch, on cars with manual transmission; a drive shaft; a DIFFERENTIAL; and wheel axles. Although most conventional American cars use a front-mounted engine to drive the rear wheels, an increasing number of newer models use front-wheel drive. In some cars the engine drives all four wheels.

Transmission. The purpose of the transmission is to permit a change in the gear ratio between the engine crankshaft and the driven wheels. The shift is accomplished in manual transmissions by a shift lever operated by the driver. The automatic transmission makes the shifts without driver intervention.

On cars with manual transmissions, a clutch, a device for connecting and disengaging the engine, is used to relieve the driving pressures through the transmission as gears are shifted.

Drive Shaft. The drive shaft, or propeller shaft, connects the transmission with the differential, an arrangement of gears that allows the wheels to rotate at different rates when a car is turning. The drive shaft contains two types of joints: a slip joint and one or more universal joints. This allows the shaft to change its length and direction as the car wheels move up and down.

Body

Of many body designs, the following are the most common. A sedan is a closed body with two or four doors and two cross seats and usually accommodates five or six people. In the two-door model, the backs of the front seats tip forward to give access to the rear seat. A hatchback has an additional door at the rear. A convertible is an open-body design that has a folding top that can be raised or lowered. Open cars are recovering their popularity, after a period when they were not made because of

the dangers of rooflessness in accidents. A hardtop is similar to the two- or four-door sedan except that it has no side members between the front and rear windows. A station wagon has a special body available on a more or less standard chassis. It has cross seats at the front and either cross or side seats at the rear. It may be built to accommodate up to nine people, and it also includes additional luggage or cargo space. A sports car is a low, comparatively small car, usually seating two, that is designed for speed and maneuverability.

See also: BRAKE; CARBURETOR; ENGINE; EXHAUST SYSTEM; IGNITION SYSTEM; TRANSMISSION, AUTOMOTIVE.

---

automobile racing Automobile racing is a competitive sport involving almost every type of automobile. It is open to both professional and amateur drivers and is run on a variety of tracks and courses. The Fédération Internationale de l'Automobile (FIA), the body that governs automobile racing worldwide, has established an elaborate classification system for racing events and the classes and subclasses of cars that may compete in each.

Types of Races

Grand Prix events are the most prestigious, and the title of world champion is awarded to the driver who amasses the highest point total over a series of about 18–20 Grand Prix races during the year. The circuit is open only to Formula One cars—open-wheeled, single-seat, mid-engine vehicles with a strictly limited engine displacement and minimum weight, and with air foils to generate downward thrust. Races are held on specially constructed, closed-circuit tracks (Nürburgring, Germany, for example), as well as on public roads through the heart of a city (Monza [Italy] and Monaco, for example). Because of rigorous qualifying requirements, only about 30 drivers in the world have the required standing to enter a Formula One event. Speeds, held down by winding, rolling courses, range from about 48 km/h (30 mph) to about 290 km/h (180 mph).

The type of car that races at the Indianapolis 500 each year resembles the Formula One car. The 500—consisting of 200 laps on a 4.02-km (2.5-mi) oval track, or 805 km (500 mi)—ranks as the most important event sponsored by the United States Auto Club (USAC). Twenty events count toward the USAC national championship, and most of them are races of 160 to 320 km (99 to 199 mi) held over closed circuits. One notable exception is the Pikes Peak Hill Climb.

Manufacturers World Championship races are open to three classes of vehicles. Most of the races place a premium on endurance (Le Mans 24-hour race, Nürburgring 1,000 km/621 mi) as well as high-speed handling on closed circuits.

The Canadian-American Challenge Cup, or Can-Am series, is an annual 11-race series for two-seater sports cars without limitation on engine displacement. The races do not exceed two hours in duration. Consequently, average speeds may be well in excess of 160 km/h (100 mph).

The cutaway illustration shows the major operational features of the Tyrell Ford Formula One, a Grand Prix racing car. Formula One racers are those built to specifications established by the Fédération Internationale de l'Automobile (FIA), the governing body of Grand Prix racing.

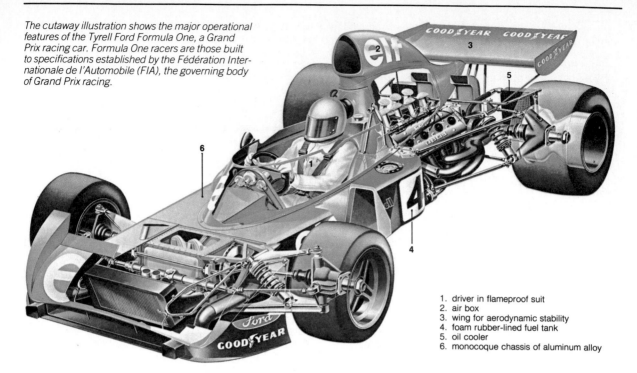

1. driver in flameproof suit
2. air box
3. wing for aerodynamic stability
4. foam rubber-lined fuel tank
5. oil cooler
6. monocoque chassis of aluminum alloy

INDIANAPOLIS 500 WINNERS

Year	Driver	MPH	Year	Driver	MPH	Year	Driver	MPH
1911	Ray Harroun	74.59	1939	Wilbur Shaw	115.04	1969	Mario Andretti	156.87
1912	Joe Dawson	78.72	1940	Wilbur Shaw	114.28	1970	Al Unser	155.75
1913	Jules Goux	75.93	1941	Mauri Rose and	115.12	1971	Al Unser	157.74
1914	Rene Thomas	82.47		Floyd Davis		1972	Mark Donohue	162.96
1915	Ralph De Palma	89.84	1946	George Robson	114.82	1973	Gordon Johncock	159.04
1916	Dorio Resta	84.00	1947	Mauri Rose	116.34	1974	Johnny Rutherford	158.59
1919	Howdy Wilcox	88.05	1948	Mauri Rose	119.81	1975	Bobby Unser	149.21
1920	Gaston Chevrolet	88.62	1949	William Holland	121.33	1976	Johnny Rutherford	148.73
1921	Tommy Milton	89.62	1950	Johnny Parsons	124.00	1977	A. J. Foyt	161.33
1922	Jimmy Murphy	94.48	1951	Lee Wallard	126.24	1978	Al Unser	161.36
1923	Tommy Milton	90.95	1952	Troy Ruttman	128.92	1979	Rick Mears	158.89
1924	L. L. Corum and	98.23	1953	Bill Vukovich	128.74	1980	Johnny Rutherford	142.86
	Joe Boyer		1954	Bill Vukovich	130.84	1981	Bobby Unser	139.084
1925	Peter De Paolo	101.13	1955	Bob Sweikert	128.21	1982	Gordon Johncock	162.029
1926	Frank Lockhart	95.90	1956	Pat Flaherty	128.49	1983	Tom Sneva	162.117
1927	George Souders	97.55	1957	Sam Hanks	135.60	1984	Rick Mears	163.612
1928	Louis Meyer	99.48	1958	Jimmy Bryan	133.79	1985	Danny Sullivan	152.982
1929	Ray Keech	97.59	1959	Roger Ward	135.86	1986	Bobby Rahal	170.722
1930	Billy Arnold	100.45	1960	Jim Rothmann	138.77	1987	Al Unser	162.175
1931	Louis Schneider	96.63	1961	A. J. Foyt	139.13	1988	Rick Mears	149.809
1932	Frederick Frame	104.14	1962	Roger Ward	140.29	1989	Emerson Fittipaldi	167.581
1933	Louis Meyer	104.16	1963	Parnelli Jones	143.14	1990	Arie Luyendyk	185.981
1934	Bill Cummings	104.86	1964	A. J. Foyt	147.35			
1935	Kelly Petrillo	106.24	1965	Jim Clark	150.69			
1936	Louis Meyer	109.07	1966	Graham Hill	144.32			
1937	Wilbur Shaw	113.58	1967	A. J. Foyt	151.21			
1938	Floyd Roberts	117.20	1968	Bobby Unser	152.88			

GRAND PRIX WORLD CHAMPIONS*

Year	Driver	Year	Driver	Year	Driver	Year	Driver
1950	Giuseppe Farina (It.)	1961	Phil Hill (USA)	1972	Emerson Fittipaldi (Braz.)	1983	Nelson Piquet (Braz.)
1951	Juan M. Fangio (Arg.)	1962	Graham Hill (UK)	1973	Jackie Stewart (UK)	1984	Niki Lauda (Aus.)
1952	Alberto Ascari (It.)	1963	Jim Clark (UK)	1974	Emerson Fittipaldi (Braz.)	1985	Alain Prost (Fr.)
1953	Alberto Ascari (It.)	1964	John Surtees (UK)	1975	Niki Lauda (Aus.)	1986	Alain Prost (Fr.)
1954	Juan M. Fangio (Arg.)	1965	Jim Clark (UK)	1976	James Hunt (UK)	1987	Nelson Piquet (Braz.)
1955	Juan M. Fangio (Arg.)	1966	Jack Brabham (Austrl.)	1977	Niki Lauda (Aus.)	1988	Ayrton Senna (Braz.)
1956	Juan M. Fangio (Arg.)	1967	Denis Hulme (N.Z.)	1978	Mario Andretti (USA)	1989	Alain Prost (Fr.)
1957	Juan M. Fangio (Arg.)	1968	Graham Hill (UK)	1979	Jody Scheckter (S.Afr.)	1990	Ayrton Senna (Braz.)
1958	Mike Hawthorn (UK)	1969	Jackie Stewart (UK)	1980	Alan Jones (Austrl.)		
1959	Jack Brabham (Austrl.)	1970	Jochen Rindt (Aus.)	1981	Nelson Piquet (Braz.)		
1960	Jack Brabham (Austrl.)	1971	Jackie Stewart (UK)	1982	Keke Rosberg (Finl.)		

*The first Grand Prix race was held in France in 1906. Unofficial world championship competition started in the 1920s. The first official world title was awarded in 1950.

Stock car races, an American innovation, involve competition among five categories of autos, all of which are modified production passenger vehicles. Thousands of these races are held throughout the country, particularly in the Southern states, under the auspices of the National Association for Stock Car Auto Racing (NASCAR), often on oval dirt tracks. Speeds often exceed 240 km/h (150 mph) for some of the major events (Rebel 500, Firecracker 400).

Drag racing, one of the most popular types of events, is an acceleration event staged on a very short (0.4-km/0.25-mi), straight track. Cars normally race two at a time, and elapsed time, now electronically measured, determines the winner. A drag meet will include several heats. More than 6,000 drag-racing events are held annually in the United States and Canada. For the fastest classification of dragster vehicles, stopping by means of a drag parachute is necessary, because maximum speeds usually exceed 322 km/h (200 mph) and go up to about 400 km/h (249 mph).

(Above) *Stock-car racing, sanctioned by the National Association for Stock Car Racing (NASCAR), is one of the most popular sports in the United States. Stock cars are racing vehicles with passenger-car bodies and modified, factory-built engines.*

Because the object of drag racing is to record the fastest time over a straight, short course, dragsters consist of little more than an aluminum-molybdenum frame (1) propelled by a supercharged engine (2). One front wheel is rimmed with aluminum (3) to ensure that the wheel breaks the beam of the electronic device used to time races. "Header" exhaust pipes (4) are angled back to heat the treadless rear tires (5) and provide traction at the start of the race. Acceleration is so intense that air foils, one in front (6) and another in the rear (7) are used to provide the downward thrust that holds the car on the strip. A braking parachute (8) is often employed to assist the conventional braking system. For safety, the cockpit is surrounded by roll bars (9). Drivers wear a flame-resistant suit (10) and carry an extinguisher (11) in the cockpit.

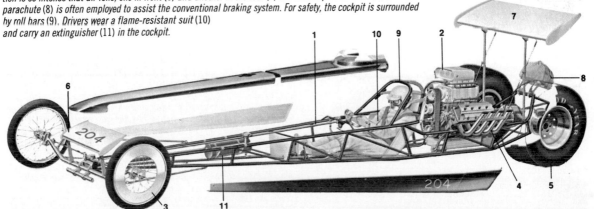

1908 Grand Prix Mercedes

1925 Grand Prix Bugatti Type 35

1930 P2 Grand Prix Alfa Romeo

1937 Mercedes Benz W125

1957 Grand Prix Maserati 250F

1962 Lotus 25

1966 Ford GT Mark II

1977 ELF Tyrell P34

Off-road racing is open to production and modified two- and four-wheel drive vehicles. It is conducted over rugged trails and terrain. Contestants race between checkpoints without being restricted to a specific route. The most famous races of this type in the Western Hemisphere are the Baja 500 and the Mexican 1000, both run in Baja California, Mexico.

Speed trials are races against time; that is, they are attempts to achieve world speed records for an automobile. The vehicles are specially designed, without limitations on weight, engine, or type of fuel. Jet propulsion is the favored propulsion system today. Records are sanctioned only if the trials are run at the BONNEVILLE SALT FLATS in Utah or Lake EYRE, Australia. The current record for one mile is 1,019.469 km/h (633.468 mph), set in 1983.

Rallies are not, strictly speaking, races. They are point-to-point driving competitions in which navigation, disciplined driving, fuel consumption, and other skills count toward victory. Rally courses can be several hundred to thousands of kilometers long, with varying on- and off-road conditions.

History

Automobile racing first appeared as a sport in 1894, when a Paris newspaper organized a competition for mechanically propelled vehicles. The 125-km (78-mi) run between Paris and Rouen was completed by 15 of 21 starting vehicles at an average speed of about 24 km/h (14 mph). A number of races quickly followed, including the first American race, in 1895, between Chicago and Evanston, Ill., won by J. Frank DURYEA, a pioneer U.S. automaker, at an average speed of 12 km/h (7.5 mph). Early races were run on open roads lined with spectators, until an accident on the Madrid–Paris race in 1903 killed ten people and led to a prohibition of this type of racing in Europe. The most famous of the early American races (the Vanderbilt Cup races, held on Long Island, N.Y.) suffered a similar ban in 1911.

The Grand Prix of France, the first competition to take place on a specially constructed circuit, was held at Le Mans in 1906. The Indianapolis Motor Raceway held its

Advances in design efficiency and performance are reflected by these classic racing automobiles. A 1908 Mercedes won the Grand Prix at Dieppe, the race in which service pits were introduced, with an average speed of 110.8 km/h (68.8 mph). The first Grand Prix car offered for sale to private owners, the Bugatti Type 35, won the 540-km (335.5-mi) Targa Florio of Sicily in 1925 with an average speed of 71.58 km/h (44.48 mph). The 1930 P2 Grand Prix Alfa Romeo, a modified version of the 1924 model, featuring increased horsepower and engine capacity, set a new record in the Targa Florio, averaging 77.89 km/h (48.4 mph). Decades of Italian-French domination of international racing prompted Nazi authorities to subsidize the construction of the most powerful Grand Prix car ever built, the 1937 Mercedes Benz W125, to demonstrate German technological superiority. Juan Manuel Fangio, one of the outstanding drivers in the history of international racing, won the last of his five Grand Prix world championships driving a 1957 Maserati 250F. The monocoque frame, an innovative departure from the tubular construction of most racing cars, was introduced in Colin Chapman's 1962 Lotus 25. In 1966, Ford GT Mark IIs finished first, second, and third in the 24 hours of Le Mans. The 1977 Elf Tyrell P34 was the first six-wheeled Grand Prix racing automobile.

first race in 1909 on a dirt track. The track was bricked in 1911, when the first running of the Indianapolis 500 race was held on Memorial Day, which has been its annual race day ever since.

Classifications and events proliferated, with frequent changes in regulations regarding weight and engine displacement. Dominance in certain events was gained, maintained, and then lost over the years by some of the most famous names in automobiles—Alfa-Romeo, Bentley, Bugatti, Ferrari, Ford, Jaguar, Maserati, Mercedes-Benz, and Porsche.

Automobile racing has become one of the world's most popular spectator sports. In the United States it is second only to horse racing. The Indy 500, for example, attracts about 300,000 people, the greatest annual attendance at a sports event in the country.

automotive industry The automobile or automotive industry, more accurately the motor vehicle industry, comprises the manufacture and assembly of AUTOMOBILES, BUSES, MOTORCYCLES, trucks, and components of motor vehicles. The petroleum and rubber industries are not included, nor are manufacturers of batteries and other electrical equipment, unless they are affiliated with a motor vehicle company.

History: From 1890 to World War II

Although the gasoline automobile first appeared in Germany, automotive production on a commercial scale began in France about 1890. Commercial production in the United States began around 1900 and was qualitatively inferior to that in Europe. The industry was an assortment of small firms, each turning out a few cars by handicraft methods. American automobile plants were assembly operations that used parts made by independent suppliers. By contrast, European companies were more likely to build the entire car themselves. The early firms originated in various ways—from bicycle makers, carriage and wagon makers, machinery operations of all kinds, and tinkerers. Attrition was high; in the United States, for example, almost 2,000 separate concerns produced one or more cars. By 1920 the number had shrunk to about 100, and by 1929 to 44. In 1976 the Motor Vehicle Manufacturers Association had 11 members. This trend involved consolidation of some companies as well as elimination of the weakest firms. The same pattern emerged in Europe and Japan.

At the outset it was uncertain whether the automobile would be powered by electricity, steam, or gasoline. At first, the electric car was popular, but its use was limited, because no battery existed that could drive the vehicle either far or fast, although some of the early speed records were set in electric cars.

The steamer lasted into the 1920s. Simply stated, steam automobiles have never been competitive in cost with gasoline cars, either to build or to maintain, and there has always been concern, perhaps unfounded, about the risk of boiler explosions. The problem of cost

might have been resolved by mass production, but pioneers like Ransom E. Olds (1864–1950) and Henry Ford (see FORD family) rejected steam power.

United States. During the first years of the 20th century the United States established a leadership position in automotive production that went unchallenged for half a century. This achievement was largely associated with Henry Ford. After some false starts, he founded the Ford Motor Company in 1903 and five years later brought out the famous Model T, the first car to meet the needs of a mass market. To produce this car in quantity and at low cost, Ford introduced the moving ASSEMBLY LINE technique of mass production in 1913 and thereby secured a dominant position in the industry. The founding of General Motors in 1908 by William C. Durant (1861–1947) appeared to be of secondary importance; yet if Ford devised the technique, General Motors provided the organizational pattern for successful large-scale motor vehicle production over time. Durant's ideas were systematized by Alfred P. Sloan (1875–1966) in the 1920s. An additional important Ford contribution to the growth of the American automobile industry was his successful challenging of the Selden patent, claimed to be a comprehensive patent on the gasoline automobile and controlled by the Association of Licensed Automobile Manufacturers. In 1911 the courts upheld Ford's claim that the Selden patent did not cover the four-cycle engine Ford was using. As a result, the industry adopted a policy (1915) of cross-licensing patents to avoid such litigation.

Both Ford and General Motors were located in the Detroit area, as were other leading producers: Packard, Hudson, Maxwell (reorganized as Chrysler in 1925), and Dodge (acquired by Chrysler in 1928). The effect of this concentration was to make Detroit the center of automotive production. During the 1920s General Motors overtook Ford as the leading manufacturer of motor vehicles. The last Model T was built in 1927. Part of Ford's problem was the emergence of a large used-car market, which meant that a purchaser could buy a secondhand vehicle of higher quality and style for no more than a new Model T. Other companies faced the same situation and met it by devising the annual model, just different enough so that a used car would be clearly identifiable as such. In short, the status symbol became part of the automobile business.

By the time of the great stock market crash of 1929, the annual output of passenger cars in the United States had reached 5 million, and the ratio of registered automobiles to people was 1:5. Cars were produced in quantity by the moving assembly line. The techniques involved were now for the first time integrated as a novel system of production and on a far larger scale than anything previously attempted. This technological revolution had repercussions in other industries. The needs of the automobile industry gave rise to continuous-process manufacture of plate glass and the continuous strip mill for sheet steel, as well as extensive development of alloy steels.

The principal output of the PETROLEUM INDUSTRY changed from illuminants to gasoline. The discovery of vast new oil fields in the early part of the 20th century was a major stimulus to the widespread use of gasoline-powered automobiles, since fuel became plentiful and cheap. The development of the auto industry led to the growth of service enterprises such as gas stations and repair shops. In addition, vehicles created a demand for ROADS AND HIGHWAYS, and an extensive program of highway construction and improvement emerged, much of it financed by taxes on automotive fuels.

Europe. In Europe, the only other major center of automobile production at this time, growth was less rapid. European manufacturers tended to concentrate on luxury and sports cars. Just before World War I, William Morris (1877–1963) in Britain and André Citröen (1878–1935) in France began trying to emulate Henry Ford, but it was not until after the war that they achieved any substantial results. Even then they were handicapped by legislative restrictions, which reflected a continuing attitude that automobiles were luxuries.

Consequently, European manufacturers operated on a considerably smaller scale than the Americans. In Britain, then the leading European producer, no company had enough annual output to justify installing a moving assembly line until 1932, when both Morris and Hillman did so. Indeed, two of the largest firms operating in Europe were the American companies Ford and General Motors.

Surprisingly, these trends, American and European, were little affected by the Depression of the 1930s. Production dropped sharply in the years immediately after the market crash in 1929, but registrations and motor vehicle use remained fairly stable. The principal effect worldwide was to accelerate the elimination of the smaller and weaker companies. In the United States, the Big Three (General Motors, Ford, and Chrysler) controlled 90 percent of the passenger automobile market by 1939. What was left was shared mainly by the Middle Five (Hudson, Nash, Packard, Studebaker, and Willys-Overland). The separate truck manufacturers fared somewhat better, because commercial vehicles come in such manifold and often highly specialized forms that they have never been as completely dominated by mass production methods as passenger cars.

During World War II the automotive industries of the various participants played a major role, in part because military operations were highly mobile and depended on motorized vehicles and, equally important, because the industry possessed productive capacity that could be applied to other military needs. For the United States in particular, the motor vehicle industry was the country's largest single resource in manufacturing capacity, and its contribution to the war effort was impressive. It produced $29 billion worth of military materials, which was one-fifth of the total American output.

The Modern Industry

Since the middle of the 20th century the automotive industry has been global in character. Once some degree of stability was achieved after World War II, motor vehicle production and use surged. Western Europe and Japan began to match the pattern established in the United States and Canada, leading to the steady erosion of the dominant position initially held by the United States. In 1950 the United States produced two-thirds of the world's motor vehicles. In 1980 its share of world production was just over one-fifth. There have been major shifts in position among producing countries. In the 1960s West Germany overtook Great Britain to become the world's second largest motor vehicle manufacturer, a feat largely attributable to the phenomenal success of the VOLKSWAGEN. In the 1970s, Japan overtook West Germany and in the 1980s passed the United States to take first place among motor vehicle producers.

Other countries with substantial automotive industries are Canada, France, Italy, Sweden, and the USSR. Elsewhere, automobile manufacturing has largely been an offshoot of the big firms in the major producing countries.

The heaviest concentrations of motor vehicles in use are in North America, Western Europe, Japan, Australia, and New Zealand, with ratios of 1 car to 2 to 4 persons.

Concentration of Production. Because only large firms can compete successfully in domestic and world markets, the U.S. pattern of concentration of production within a few giant companies has become worldwide. Of the U.S. independents, for example, Nash and Hudson survived by merging as American Motors in 1954. Studebaker and Packard merged in the same year, but the new firm abandoned automobile manufacturing in 1964.

In Great Britain, Morris and Austin joined in 1952 to become the British Motor Corporation (BMC), and two other combines were formed around Leyland Motors and Rootes. Leyland and BMC united in 1968 as British Leyland (BL) Motors, but in the mid-1970s, BL was taken over by the government, which—under the Conservatives' privatization policy—managed to sell off most of the unprofitable automobile groups by the late 1980s. BL was renamed Rover Group in 1986.

The German automobile industry is dominated by Volkswagen, followed by Opel (General Motors), Ford, Daimler-Benz (Mercedes), and BMW (Bayerische Motoren Werke). The French industry has long been focused on Renault (nationalized in 1944), Citroën, Simca, and Peugeot, which merged with Citroën in the 1970s. Fiat, founded in 1899, remains the major Italian automobile manufacturer. Japan's automotive production centers on three giant firms: Toyota, Nissan (Datsun), and Honda.

(Opposite page) *Steam, electricity, and gasoline were all used to power the earliest automobiles. By 1910 the Ford Model T had a hand-cranked four-cyclinder gasoline engine, gas headlamps, and a steering wheel. Electric self-starters and headlights became standard during the next decade, and hydraulic brakes followed in the 1920s, the age of the elegant European touring car. Streamlining was a style feature in the 1930s, along with such improvements as independent front suspension. Tubeless tires and sealed-beam headlights made their appearance in the 1940s, and the end of that decade saw the first Volkswagen "Beetle" imports into the United States. The 1950s was the era of the giant-size car and the tail fin. Safety devices and pollution-control equipment became increasingly important from the 1960s. In the 1970s the rising cost of gasoline created a boom in "compacts" with high fuel economy. By the 1980s, Japanese cars were common on U.S. roads.*

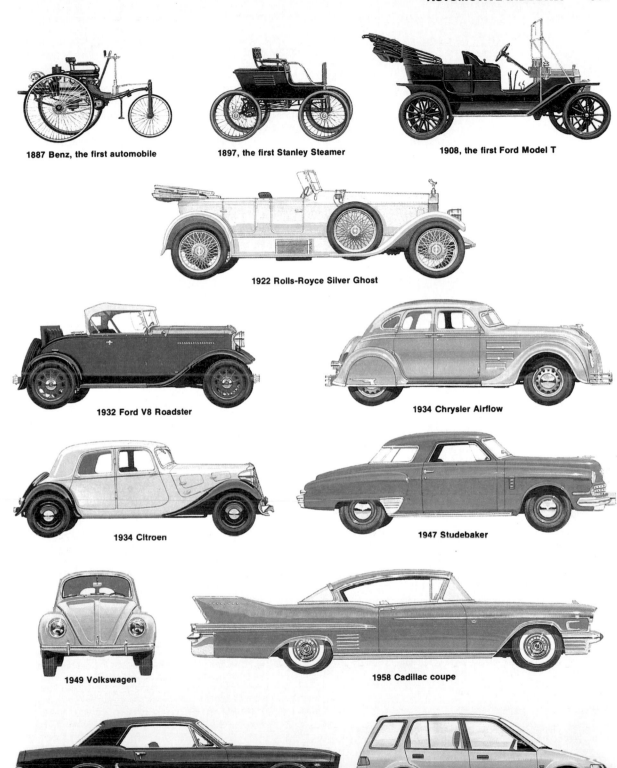

1887 Benz, the first automobile

1897, the first Stanley Steamer

1908, the first Ford Model T

1922 Rolls-Royce Silver Ghost

1932 Ford V8 Roadster

1934 Chrysler Airflow

1934 Citroen

1947 Studebaker

1949 Volkswagen

1958 Cadillac coupe

1965 Ford Mustang

1989 Honda Civic wagon

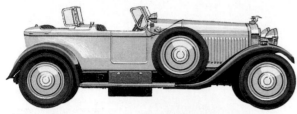

A Hispano-Suiza open touring car (1920–30; France) had a light-alloy, 6-cylinder engine and the first servo-assisted 4-wheel brakes.

A Bentley sport touring car (1931; England) had a 200-hp engine with two carburetors and attained a top speed of 217 km/h (135 mph).

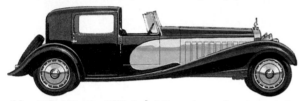

A Bugatti Type 41 sedan (1931; France), the most expensive auto ever built, was limited to a production of only six vehicles.

A Duesenberg SJ roadster (1933; United States) had a supercharged 8-cylinder, 320-hp engine and a top speed of 209 km/h (130 mph).

A Delage D8/120 sedan (1936; France) had a supercharged 8-cylinder engine, a 4-speed transmission, and a top speed of 209 km/h (130 mph).

A Cord Convertible Coupe 812 (1937; United States) had a long hood fitted with louver, retractable headlights, and front-wheel drive.

Crisis Years. For years the U.S. automobile industry emphasized speed, power, and styling in its products. About 1960, however, as first the Volkswagen and then other small foreign cars penetrated the U.S. market, competition pushed U.S. manufacturers into making compacts, cars that—while not as small as the small imports—were considerably smaller than previous American cars.

The market trend to smaller cars developed slowly until a second gasoline crisis in the spring of 1979 brought an abrupt increase in consumer demand for compacts and the new, even smaller, subcompacts. U.S. manufacturers were not prepared for a rapid changeover to smaller models, and when the oil shortage was followed by a prolonged downswing in the economy, the U.S. industry suffered severely. Chrysler, which had already been losing ground, was saved from bankruptcy only by a federally guaranteed $1.5 billion loan. By 1980 the Japanese had captured almost one-quarter of the U.S. market, and high-priced cars from Europe—particularly from Sweden and Germany—were creaming off a significant percentage of the luxury- and sports-car market. So desperate was the U.S. industry's situation that, in the 1982 contract negotiations between the manufacturers and the United Auto Workers, the union made important wage concessions and provided "give-backs" of some benefits in an effort to help the industry back to profitability.

The Chrysler and British Leyland crises seemed to demonstrate that governments will not allow major motor vehicle producers to fail, when that failure might cause economic catastrophe. In 1981 the U.S. government persuaded the Japanese to impose voluntary restrictions on their U.S. exports, restrictions that had the effect of substantially raising the selling prices on all cars, although they also gave U.S. firms time to retool and modernize. From 1978 to 1984 the U.S. industry spent about $69 billion worldwide to redesign its products and modernize its plants.

Although the Japanese industry operated under a quota, cars from newer national industries did not. South Korea began exporting its Hyundai models in quantity in 1984. The South Korean firms Daiwoo, in a joint venture with General Motors, and Kia, working with Ford and Japan's Mazda, have also been successful exporters to the United States.

Mergers and Internationalization. The process of industrial concentration through buyouts and mergers—a process that is almost as old as the U.S. industry itself—

(Left) *Classic cars are generally considered to include the large, luxurious, and expensive high-performance automobiles built between 1925 and 1942. Limited numbers were made, and each was handcrafted to the customer's specifications. In nearly all these cars, only the chassis and engine were made by the car manufacturer; the bodies and interiors were tailored to the individual customer's tastes by American and European custom-coach builders. No two cars were exactly alike, and a greater variety of body types was possible than could be obtained with mass-produced cars. Among others, some classic-car makers, whose names became synonymous with status and quality, were Rolls-Royce and Bently of England, Hispano-Suiza of Spain and France, Bugatti and Delage of France, Mercedes-Benz of Germany, and Duesenberg, Packard, Cord, Pierce-Arrow, Cadillac, and Lincoln of the United States.*

continued in the 1980s. In 1987, Chrysler bought American Motors, hoping to gain from the smaller manufacturer's success with the four-wheel-drive Jeep. Manufacturing agreements have quickened the pace of internationalization, to the point where very few cars can be described as having been made entirely in one country. The three major American automobile companies own factories throughout the world and, in addition, have subassemblies and entire cars manufactured by foreign affiliates.

The rebuilding and modernizing of automobile factories within the country have greatly increased U.S. production capacity. Yet despite the prosperity of the industry, many plants are once again threatened with layoffs and closings. At the end of the 1980s an estimated 20 percent of all auto imports into the United States were "captive imports"—cars sold under U.S. brand names but manufactured in other countries. Auguring particularly ill for the domestic industry, U.S. auto firms increased their production of sophisticated high-tech parts in countries like Mexico and Taiwan, where work was once confined to simple manufacture and assembly. Foreign automakers have established links in the United States with domestic firms, and all major Japanese manufacturers have opened their own factories within the United States, so that in 1990 some 11 percent of North American manufacturing capacity was owned by foreign corporations. The U.S. industry thus faces greatly increased competition and the prospect of overcapacity in the last decade of the 1900s.

Production Methods. The assembly-line technique introduced by Henry Ford continues to be used almost universally in Europe and America. Automation was introduced on the assembly line in the early 1950s, computer-controlled welding robots in the 1970s, and computerized machining of engine parts in the late 1980s.

The Japanese ability to impose high standards of quality control while at the same time improving productivity is challenging the standard assembly-line techniques. The success of the General Motors–Toyota plant—the New United Motor Manufacturing, Inc., or NUMMI—in Fremont, Calif., and of several other Japanese auto manufacturing plants in the United States is considered a triumph for their "team" approach to mass manufacturing. At NUMMI, after U.S. workers are trained in a range of skills, they form small teams that are each responsible for the assembly of a major portion of a car. The team approach requires an educated work force, consid-

(Right) No clear and universally acceptable definition of a sports car exists. For some, a sports car is a small, stylish, "speedy-looking," high-powered automobile, usually seating two persons, that is used more for fun than for transportation. For others, a sports car is one that provides the best possible driving performance, including easy maneuverability, fast acceleration, positive braking, and good steering and handling characteristics and is suitable for both ordinary road driving and high-speed sports competition. The sports-car era began after World War II with the mass production of the inexpensive M.G. T-type Midget that made a sports car affordable to a much greater number of people. Today numerous sports-car events are held throughout the world for enthusiasts who are interested in competitive driving. For many, however, a sports car is to be owned simply for personal enjoyment and is never raced.

An M.G. TC Midget (1947; England) had a 4-cylinder, overhead-valve, twin-carburetor, 1,250-cc engine, running board, and wire-spoke wheels.

A Chevrolet Corvette (1953; United States), America's first production sports car, had a 6-cylinder engine and an automatic transmission.

A Mercedes-Benz 300 SL coupe (1953; Germany) had "gullwing" doors that opened upward and a 6-cylinder, 175-hp engine with fuel injection.

A Jaguar XKE coupe (1961; England) was a high-speed, sleek sports car powered by a 6-cylinder, 265-hp, 3.8-liter engine.

A Porsche 911S (1967; Germany) used a high-performance overhung rear 6-cylinder engine and independent wheel suspension.

A Nissan 300 ZX (1989; Japan) has a 24-valve twin overhead cam engine. Suspension, structure, and aerodynamic shape were computer designed.

erable training inside the factory, and a commitment on the part of management that trained personnel will not be subject to the layoffs and rehirings customary in conventional U.S. auto firms. This new approach to manufacturing had proved so satisfactory that workers in one Japanese-owned plant voted against unionization in 1989.

Safety, Pollution, and Fuel Conservation. Since the 1960s the automobile industry has been subject to legislation limiting the types and quantity of exhaust emissions and dictating safety standards. The use of seat belts and the probable installation of air bags in many car models in the 1990s are among the results of this legislation (see SAFETY, AUTOMOTIVE). Pollution caused by automobile exhausts has proved more difficult to deal with. Although more efficient engines and the use of CATALYTIC CONVERTERS and fuel-injection systems have reduced some noxious emissions, overall auto emissions continue to create problems for such cities as Los Angeles and Tokyo. A plan for stricter emissions-control in Southern California, announced in 1989, anticipates the phasing out of gas-fueled cars by the year 2010. Their place would be taken by electric cars and a new mass-transport system. In the meantime, new engine technologies and the use of alternative fuels such as methanol and propane are intended to reduce pollution significantly.

At the end of the 1980s, fuel conservation was no longer the issue it had been in the 1970s. Larger cars were popular once again, as were gas-guzzling small trucks and four-wheel-drive vehicles. Federal efficiency requirements for new cars and trucks were made less stringent. Yet prototypes for highly efficient vehicles had been made by every major automobile manufacturer. They employed such already-existing technologies as turbochargers that use waste energy to improve engine efficiency; advanced diesel engines; sleeker, aerodynamic designs; and the increased use of plastics and lightweight metals. Some of these prototypes reached fuel efficiencies of more than 160 km (100 mi) per gallon on the highway.

autonomic nervous system   see NERVOUS SYSTEM

autopsy   An autopsy, or postmortem, is a medical examination of a body after death; the basic purpose of an autopsy is to determine the ultimate cause of death, but in the process important medical knowledge can be obtained. Autopsies can reveal mistakes in diagnosis and treatment or confirm their correctness. They can increase understanding of disease processes. By conclusively establishing the cause of death, they can supply more reliable statistics on the incidence of diseases.

Autopsies are also valuable for the training of medical students and other health professionals. They cannot be done without the permission of the nearest relative of the deceased person, except in criminal cases or suspicious deaths, when they can be ordered by a coroner or a medical examiner.

Autopsies include detailed examination of both the exterior and interior of the body. The body is opened by a Y-shaped incision that extends from each armpit to the midline of the chest and continues down the midline to just above the pubic area. The ribs and sternum are cut to expose the chest cavity. The abdominal cavity is exposed by pulling the edges of the incision aside. Organs are removed and dissected for examination of their internal structure, and small pieces of tissue and samples of body fluids may be saved for later chemical and microscopic analysis. The brain is removed through a hole sawed in the skull. After the autopsy is completed, organs not needed for further study are replaced in the body cavities, bones are put back in place, and incisions are sutured.

Auvergne [oh-vairn'-yuh]   A historic region and former province of central France, Auvergne is made up of the departments of Allier, Cantal, Haute-Loire, and Puy-de-Dôme. In 1527 the duchy of Auvergne, created in 1360, was united with the French crown.

In the north is the fertile tertiary basin of the Limagne, where dairying and beef cattle diversify the traditional wheat economy. Clermont-Ferrand (1982 pop., 151,092), on the Allier River, is the center of the French rubber industry. The Puy de Dôme (1,465 m/4,806 ft) is the highest of a chain of recent volcanic peaks that overlook Clermont-Ferrand from the west. In the bleak, depopulated southern part of the Auvergne, the volcanic Plomb du Cantal and Mont Dore reach 1,858 m (6,096 ft) and 1,885 m (6,184 ft).

auxin   see HORMONE, PLANT

avalanche   see LANDSLIDE AND AVALANCHE

avant-garde [ah-vahnt-gahrd']   Avant-garde is a common expression used to describe any experimental or revolutionary form of art, literature, theater, or music. Originally a French military term referring to the vanguard, or spearhead, of an action, it gained wide acceptance as an aesthetic term in the mid-19th century.

At the beginning of the 20th century the term was synonymous with a number of European artistic movements, including Italian and Russian FUTURISM, German EXPRESSIONISM, English VORTICISM, and French CUBISM, Orphism, SURREALISM, and DADA. Each was avant-garde because of its attack on tradition. More recently, the avant-garde has manifested itself not in large-scale movements but in individual artistic and literary genres such as concrete poetry, the new novel (*nouveau roman*), the THEATER OF THE ABSURD, atonal and ELECTRONIC MUSIC, HAPPENINGS, experimental film and television, and PERFORMANCE ART.

Ave Maria [ah'-vay mah-ree'-uh]   The Ave Maria, or Hail Mary, is a prayer to the Virgin MARY. It is widely used by Roman Catholics and is recited as part of the ROSARY. Based on the salutations to Mary by Gabriel (Luke 1:28) and by Elizabeth (Luke 1:42), the prayer was used devotionally as early as the 11th century. It has been set to music, notably by Charles GOUNOD and Franz SCHUBERT.

Avebury [ayv'-bree]   Avebury, a village in Wiltshire, southern England, 129 km (80 mi) west of London, is the site of Avebury Circle, one of the largest prehistoric ritual monuments of Britain. Termed a henge monument (from STONEHENGE, a monument of similar type located about 27 km/17 mi to the south), Avebury Circle consisted of 100 standing stones, up to 4 m (14 ft) high and 335 m (1,100 ft) in diameter, the largest stone circle in Europe. All the stones, termed MEGALITHS, are of local sandstone, called sarsen. An avenue of paired standing stones, now partially restored, linked Avebury with the so-called Sanctuary, a double circle of stones located about 2.4 km (1.5 mi) away, which was destroyed in the 18th century. Avebury was built in late Neolithic times, about 2000 BC, probably by the BEAKER CULTURE. Silbury Hill, the largest prehistoric mound in Europe, is nearby.

Avedon, Richard [av'-uh-dahn]   The American photographer Richard Avedon, b. New York City, May 15, 1923, is noted for his fashion work and his austere, incisive portraits. His long career as a fashion photographer includes work for *Harper's Bazaar* (1945–65) and for *Vogue* magazine since 1966. Avedon's portraits of celebrities, many of which are included in *Portraits* (1976), are characterized by blank, white backgrounds and a frontal, usually unflattering view of his subjects. *In the American West* (1985) presents a bleak picture of an alienated landscape.

average   The average, or mean, of a set of numbers is the sum of all the numbers in the set divided by the total number of elements of the set. Taking as an example the set 50, 60, 65, 70, 75, 80, 80, 85, 92, the mean is 73 (657 ÷ 9). The mean should more precisely be called the arithmetic mean to distinguish it from other, more specialized types of means, such as geometric, harmonic, and weighted means.

A related term is median. The median of a set of numbers is a number such that half of the elements of the set are larger and half smaller than it when the numbers are arranged in order of size. When the number of elements is even, there are two "middle" numbers, and the median is taken to be the average of those two numbers. When the number of elements is odd, a particular number of the set is the middle number, hence, the median. The median of the above set of numbers is 75.

Another term related to average is *mode*, which is the number in a set of numbers that occurs most frequently. The mode of the above set of numbers is 80. If all the numbers are different, there is no mode; if two numbers occur most frequently, there are two modes.

Avernus, Lake [uh-vur'-nuhs]   Lake Avernus (Italian: Averno) is a crater lake in Italy, about 13 km (8 mi) west of Naples. More than 3 km (about 2 mi) in circumference and 36 m (118 ft) deep, the lake was believed by ancient Romans to be the entrance to the underworld because of its sulfuric vapors. A nearby spring was believed to flow from the mythical River Styx. Marcus Agrippa converted the lake into a naval harbor in 37 BC, connected to the sea by a canal and to Cumae by a tunnel, the Grotta della Sibilla.

Averroës [uh-vair'-oh-eez]   Averroës (Arabic: Ibn Rushd), 1126–98, was a Spanish-Arab philosopher, the most noted Aristotelian scholar in Islam. Averroës composed 38 treatises on the various works of Aristotle, as well as original tracts on astronomy, physics, and medicine. His primary work was *The Incoherence of the Incoherence* (c.1180; Eng. trans., 1954), a spirited defense of his Neoplatonic and Aristotelian philosophy.

Averroës studied medicine and law, then served as a judge in Seville and later at Córdoba. In 1182 he became chief physician to the caliph Abu Yaqub Yusuf. His religious views were considered heretical by orthodox Muslims, however, and he was banished from the court by the caliph Mansur in 1195. He was recalled from exile in 1198 but died soon after.

Averroës' commentaries on the Greek philosophers were noted for their clear analysis. Although he enjoyed a high reputation in the Muslim world of learning, he was more influential among Christian and Jewish philosophers. The guiding principle of all his writings was that philosophy and religion must agree. He viewed philosophers as prophets who teach the same principles as religious prophets but in a higher, more abstract form.

Avery, Milton   Milton Avery, b. Sand Bank, N.Y., 1885, d. Jan. 3, 1965, who experimented with color and near-abstraction in his paintings, was a pioneer of modern art in America. He was much influenced by the art of Henri Matisse in the late 1920s. Working in New York City for most of his career, he evolved a vanguard style that, despite its commitment to figuration, influenced the emergence of abstract expressionism after World War II. Eliminating details and dividing the canvas into several zones of essentially flat color, Avery attained a structural simplicity in his mature landscapes that came close to abstraction, as in *Green Sea* (1954; Metropolitan Museum, New York City).

Avery, Oswald T.   Oswald Theodore Avery, b. Halifax, Nova Scotia, Oct. 21, 1877, d. Feb. 20, 1955, a physician and bacteriologist, determined that deoxyribonucleic acid (DNA) is the hereditary material of the cell. In 1944, Avery showed through his work with bacteria that DNA alone, and not protein, was the agent responsible for inducing a heritable change in a living organism. This work influenced James D. Watson and Francis H. C. Crick to start DNA structure studies. Later work showed DNA—the basic unit of heredity—present in all animal cells. These studies were important steps in GENETICS, opening the way to later detailed biochemical studies.

Aves see BIRD

---

aviation

Aviation—the development, operation, and use of AIRCRAFT—refers primarily to the flight of heavier-than-air vehicles, but it also embraces the flight of lighter-than-air vehicles. Human-powered flight began in 1783 with the development of the hot-air BALLOON by the MONTGOLFIER brothers and the hydrogen balloon by Jacques A. C. CHARLES (1746–1823). The birth of practical heavier-than-air aviation came on Dec. 17, 1903, with the flights of Orville and Wilbur WRIGHT near Kitty Hawk, N.C. Aviation basically can be divided into three branches: military, commercial, and general.

Military Aviation

The balloon appeared as an airborne military observation post as early as 1794, in the Battle of Fleurus. Italy employed aircraft for reconnaissance during fighting in Libya as early as 1911. The major contributions made by reconnaissance aircraft during the opening stages of WORLD WAR I gave the airplane major military significance (see AIRCRAFT, MILITARY). During the war specialized fighter-interceptor airplanes were also developed. The next move was to develop a strategic bomber. When its lighter-than-air zeppelin proved unsatisfactory, Germany turned to large multiengine long-range airplanes, employing these in raids against England. In the USSR, Igor SIKORSKY developed similar long-range bombers, based on his pioneering prewar work with large multiengine biplanes.

After 1918 a number of other specialized types were developed for military uses, including troop and cargo transport, medical evacuation, dropping of airborne troops, and operation from naval AIRCRAFT CARRIERS. By 1939 the major air arms (see AIR FORCE) of the world's military forces had a variety of aircraft in service, developed for both strategic and tactical purposes. WORLD WAR II demonstrated the power and importance of fighter, ground-attack, transport, and bomber aircraft and the vulnerability of ships to aircraft strikes.

Postwar military aviation developments have included supersonic fighter, bomber, and strike aircraft, extensive use of aerial refueling and large-scale military airlift operations, and the employment of sophisticated standoff weapons. The air-to-air guided missile has largely supplanted the airborne cannon as the primary armament of modern fighter aircraft. Increasing emphasis has been placed on the military use of HELICOPTERS. Advanced aircraft, such as the Lockheed SR-71A and the Soviet MiG-25 Foxbat (see MiG), are routinely capable of flying at three times the speed of sound (Mach 3). To counter modern fighter, bomber, and attack aircraft, ground forces are using SURFACE-TO-AIR MISSILE (SAM) systems and radar-directed antiaircraft artillery.

Commercial Aviation

Commercial aviation began before World War I with the introduction of passenger-carrying zeppelin AIRSHIPS in 1910. After World War I, aviators around the world quickly initiated primitive air-transport ventures, using modi-fied surplus military aircraft. On Aug. 25, 1919, a de Havilland D.H.4A of Aircraft Transport and Travel Ltd. flew from London to Paris with one passenger and some cargo, initiating the world's first daily international civil airline service. By 1930, several international carriers were already well established. The U.S. Post Office established a federally run AIRMAIL service.

The notable Atlantic flight of Charles A. LINDBERGH in 1927 and the Daniel Guggenheim Fund for the Promotion of Aeronautics, established in 1926, were major forces acting to accelerate U.S. air transportation. The Guggenheim Model Air Line, with an extensive weather-reporting network and radio communications, was the prototype for both future airline management and airways development.

Advances in aircraft technology after World War I led from the open-cockpit biplanes of the 1920s to the high-wing, three-engine Fokker and FORD TRIMOTOR airplanes of the 1920s and early 1930s, and finally to the DC-3 (see DC-3), the first aircraft that could turn a profit simply by carrying passengers. The DC-3 featured such advances as all-metal stressed-skin construction, the radial engine, internally braced wings, retractable landing gear, and the controllable-pitch propeller. By 1938, DC-3s carried 95 percent of U.S. civil air commerce and had won wide foreign acceptance as well.

Following World War I, Germany instituted transoceanic passenger zeppelin flights across the Atlantic, but such operations were slow, disrupted by bad weather, expensive, and dangerous. The 1930s gave rise to the first transoceanic four-engine transports. In May 1919 the U.S. Navy's NC-4 flying boat had been the first airplane to fly (in stages) across the Atlantic. Twenty years later, on May 20, 1939, Pan American Airways launched the first U.S. commercial air operations to Europe, using the Boeing Model 314 Yankee Clipper flying boat. Following the disastrous loss (1937) of the zeppelin HINDENBURG, the flying boat replaced the zeppelin over the Atlantic, rendering the airship obsolete. The flying boat itself, however, soon disappeared (see SEAPLANE).

The world's first major four-engine transport was the Boeing 307 of 1938; it was the first high-altitude transport designed with a pressurized cabin. Soon after came

(Opposite page) *These five early aircraft represent milestones in the history of aviation. The French Henri Farman biplane, a pusher plane (propeller in the rear), was built by the brothers Voisin, who were the first manufacturers of airplanes. This airplane won several early aviation competitions. The Fokker E-III was an extremely effective German World War I fighter plane. It carried the first successful forward-mounted machine gun (synchronized to fire between the propeller blades). The Ford Tri-Motor was a major airline vehicle (1928–32) and one of the first all-metal planes. Charles Lindbergh's Spirit of St. Louis, which made history with the first New York-to-Paris transatlantic flight (1927), was a carefully rebuilt Ryan Brougham. It is 8.4 m (27.7 ft) long and is now on display at the Smithsonian Institution, Washington, D.C. The DC-3 may have made the greatest contribtuion to commercial aviation. It first flew in 1935 and was so successful that even 30 years later more than 500 were still in airline service worldwide. It seated 21–36 pasengers and cruised at about 273 km/h (170 mph). Plane silhouettes (upper left) are drawn to scale.*

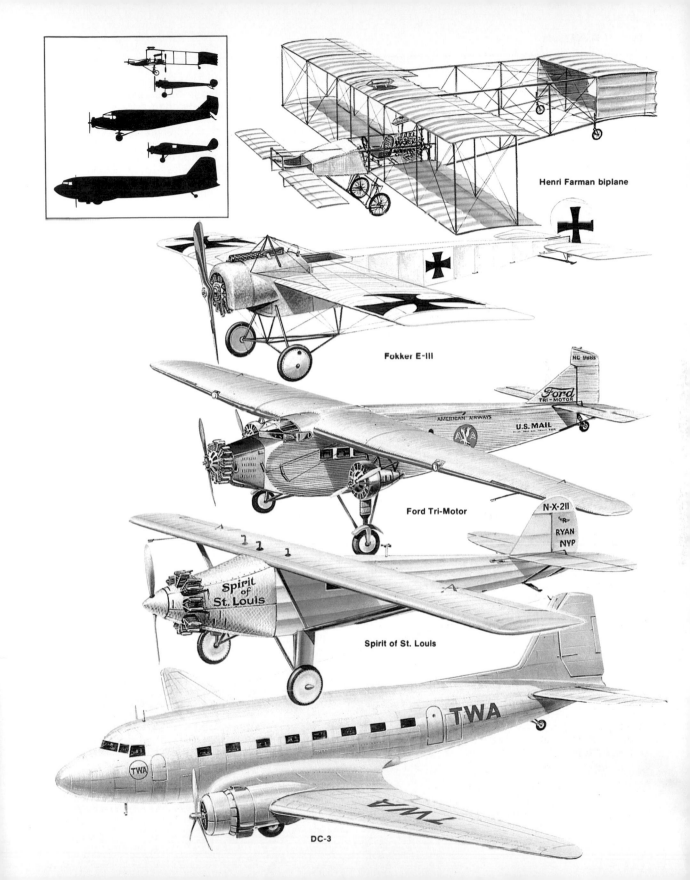

Henri Farman biplane

Fokker E-III

Ford Tri-Motor

Spirit of St. Louis

DC-3

the wartime Douglas DC-4 of 1942. The DC-4 eventually led to the pressurized DC-6 and DC-7 series. U.S. dominance of air transportation continued after World War II. Technology continued to influence transport-aircraft design and operation. Britain developed (1948) the first turbo-propeller airliner, the Vickers-Armstrong Viscount, following this a year later with the first pure-jet gas-turbine-driven airliner, the de Havilland Comet. By 1950, Boeing had embarked on a jet-tanker-transport development program that eventually led to the soon-common sweptwing, podded-engine configuration of the Boeing 707.

The jetliner quickly replaced the ocean liner as the dominant passenger carrier on the North Atlantic; more than 1 million passengers flew the Atlantic in 1958, for the first time surpassing the total carried by ocean liners. As the number of piston-engine transports declined, the number of jetliners in service quickly rose. Feeder airlines to service local regions expanded rapidly. Civil-aviation operations rapidly expanded in the 1960s, encouraging the development of two new ventures in air-transport technology, the jumbo, or wide-body, superjet and the SUPERSONIC TRANSPORT (SST). The first wide-body superjet, the Boeing 747, flew on Feb. 9, 1969. It entered service in 1970 and was quickly followed by other superjet designs. In 1971, as a result of rising environmental and economic concerns, Congress canceled the U.S. SST program. The Anglo-French SST, the CONCORDE, entered scheduled service in 1976, and the Soviet SST, the Tupolev Tu 144, in 1977; serious economic problems, however, were encountered immediately in SST operations.

Air freight operations are a rapidly growing branch of commercial air transport. Shipping cargo by air is particularly advantageous for high-value goods, such as auto parts, chemical and pharmaceutical products, and livestock, and for such trade routes as the North Atlantic, on which alternate modes of transportation are slow. Cargo is shipped in special containers in passenger aircraft with converted interiors.

General Aviation

General aviation is a term that refers to all civil aeronautics with the exception of commercial air-transport operations. It is a diverse field, covering sports flying (see AERIAL SPORTS), business flying, crop-dusting, and numerous other operations. In 1971, fully 97 percent of civil aircraft registered in the United States were classed as general-aviation aircraft.

General aviation is often overlooked because, unlike military and commercial aviation, its aircraft requirements have fluctuated widely and have never been clearly defined Beginning with pre–World War I exhibition flying and post-World War I BARNSTORMING, which popularized aviation, however, general aviation has been a vital part of air traffic. The best-known general-aviation airplane of all time was the ubiquitous PIPER CUB, which first appeared in 1937.

Aircraft Manufacture

The first manufactured aircraft in aviation history was the Lilienthal Type 11 GLIDER, which the pioneer Otto LILIENTHAL built and sold to enthusiasts in Europe and the

United States in the late 19th century. The urgent demands of World War I led to the development of rapid manufacturing techniques for the basically wood-and-wire aircraft of that period. Companies developed forming techniques permitting the construction of wooden monocoque (single-shell) fuselages. During the 1920s, following the work of Hugo Junkers (1859–1935) in wartime Germany, manufacturers developed techniques for metal construction. Claude Dornier (1884–1969), Adolf Rohrbach, and John Northrop made notable contributions to the development of metal aircraft.

During World War II, mass-production techniques and support from outside industries permitted production of U.S. military aircraft to exceed 300,000 airplanes. Postwar challenges to manufacturers included those of transonic and supersonic flight. Once thought to be a barrier to future flight development, the speed of sound (Mach 1) was surpassed by the experimental Bell X-1 rocket-powered research aircraft, piloted by Capt. Charles E. Yeager (1923–   ), on Oct. 14, 1947. The first production supersonic aircraft was the North American F-100 Super Sabre jet fighter.

During the early 1950s the AEROSPACE INDUSTRY took part in the development of long-range guided missiles, and related technologies immediately assumed key importance. These included computer systems, electronic controls, combustion chemistry technology, and advanced structural technology, such as the use of composite structures.

Government Regulation

The development of aviation has required a strong partnership between government and private industry. In Europe before World War I a number of scientifically trained engineers formed research organizations and laboratories, the most notable of these efforts being Britain's Advisory Committee for Aeronautics (1909) and the aerodynamicist Ludwig Prandtl's research center at Göttingen, Germany. In 1915 the United States created the National Advisory Committee for Aeronautics, the predecessor of the NATIONAL AERONAUTICS AND SPACE ADMINISTRATION (NASA), established in 1958. Both agencies developed a number of new concepts.

In addition, governmental regulation has been crucial to the growth of commercial and general aviation, both

(Opposite page) *Jet-age aircraft are among the familiar wonders of the 20th century. An early jet plane, the Messerschmitte Me 262A, which flew at about 860 km/h (530 mph), was used during World War II. The first piloted flight at beyond the speed of sound (Mach 1) was made on Oct. 14, 1947, in a Bell X-1. The rocket-powered North American X-15 research aircraft (active 1964–68) has gone faster 6.72; 7,300 km/h; 4,534 mph) and higher (107,960 m/ 354,200 ft) than any other plane. Nonmilitary use of jet power attained a new plateau of achievement with the advent of the commercial jet airliner. The highly successful Boeing 707 entered service in 1958. The 707, which was 46.6 m (153 ft) long and flew at a speed of nearly Mach 1, could carry 200 passengers over transcontinental distances. The Concorde supersonic jetliner (in service since 1976) has a cruising speed of Mach 2 (2,180 km/h; 1,354 mph) and transports about 125 passengers. It is 62 m (204 ft) long. Silhouettes drawn to scale (upper left) indicate the relative sizes of these aircraft.*

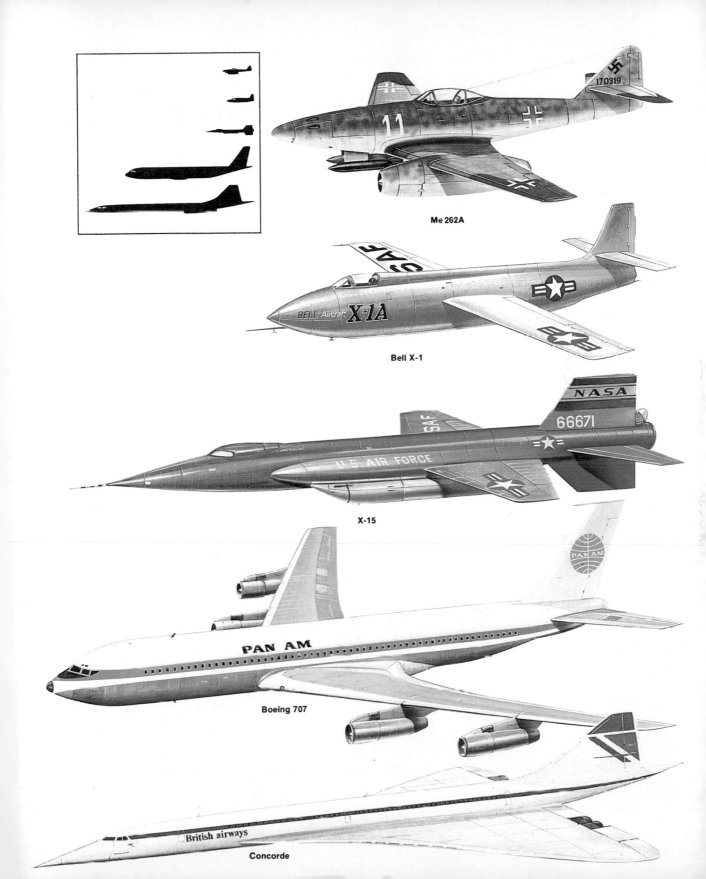

Me 262A

Bell X-1

X-15

Boeing 707

Concorde

abroad and in the United States. In 1925 the U.S. Congress passed the Kelly Act, approving federal subsidy of the airmail service and encouraging the growth of private-sector airmail carriers. The Air Commerce Act of 1926 marked the first federal attempt to impose safety regulations on civil aeronautics and required the registration and licensing of pilots and planes. The FEDERAL AVIATION ADMINISTRATION (FAA), under the Department of Transportation, regulates all aspects of airplane and airport safety and has direct control over the vast air-traffic-control system.

The CIVIL AERONAUTICS BOARD (CAB), an independent agency, had been charged with regulating routes and fares. The passage of the Air Transport Deregulation Act (1978), however, freed U.S. domestic airlines from most governmental restraints on fares and scheduling, and the CAB's authority was slowly scaled back until, in 1984, its functions were taken over by the Department of Transportation.

Airbus Industrie, a five-nation European consortium, competes successfully with U.S. manufacturers with its A300 and A310 widebodies. The mid-range A320 made its first commercial flight in April 1988 and has been selling well. The 320 "flies by wire"—it uses computerized electronic controls rather than the usual hydraulic or cable systems. Airlines in the United States ordered over 100 for delivery in 1989.

An accident in April 1988, involving the tearing away of a large portion of the upper fuselage of a Boeing 737, has brought into focus a major aviation problem. The 737 had made 88,000 flights; cabin air pressure and the corrosive effects of seawater had weakened the fuselage panels. In earlier years aging planes were no problem, because rapidly advancing technology retired aircraft—at least for the regular airlines—before they could suffer the effects of aging. Many older aircraft have now been subjected to metal fatigue tests, and the FAA has proposed a rule that would limit the number of flights a plane can make during its lifetime.

Airports

Regulation of aviation has led to improvements in AIRPORT and airway facilities. The first airports were usually grass strips or open fields. As airways developed, radio navigation aids were increasingly used. The first federal Air Route Traffic Control Center began operating in 1936, and in 1941 the first Instrument Landing Systems were placed in civil aeronautics service.

The postwar Federal Airport Act (1946) accelerated airport expansion and construction. The year 1950 witnessed the first use of VOR (VHF Omnidirectional Range) transmission, which sends a flight-path signal to approaching planes. With the explosive expansion of jet travel, air-traffic control has become increasingly sophisticated. Radar stations now provide coverage of all airspace over the continental United States, and computers are used to automate much of the system.

International air traffic uses Omega, a navigational system in which signals are broadcast from eight global transmission sites. On-plane computers calculate aircraft position by an analysis of the signals. The INTERNATIONAL CIVIL AVIATION ORGANIZATION (ICAO), an agency of the United Nations, facilitates compatibility of navigational equipment and procedures for air traffic on international routes.

The U.S. airlines industry, which had been relatively stable for many years, began to change dramatically after the deregulation of 1978. Price wars erupted on the popular long-haul routes, while fares soared on shorter routes.

By the last half of the 1980s, a completely new structure had evolved. The most powerful lines now included two giants from the days of regulation—American and United—and three others that had begun as regionals but had enlarged by swallowing other, weaker carriers—Northwest, Delta, and Continental. These five shared over 75 percent of all commercial air traffic.

Avicenna [av-i-sen'-uh]   Avicenna (Arabic, Ibn Sina), 980–1037, was a Persian philosopher who spent his life as a physician and scholar-in-residence at many Islamic courts. He died while in service in Isfahan. Many of his writings were translated in the West. Avicenna's works are of a compendious nature, the most notable being a philosophical encyclopedia. As did other Muslim scholars of the Greek school, he attempted to reconcile philosophy and Islam. For Avicenna philosophy was the true path to understanding. His summaries of Aristotle reveal a Neoplatonic outlook, especially in his emphasis on the DUALISM of mind and matter. He saw matter as passive and creation as the act of instilling existence into this passive substance; only in God are being and existence one. Avicenna also wrote numerous works on medicine. His best known is the *Canon of Medicine*, based primarily on Greco-Roman medical tracts. An extraordinarily popular work, it was translated into Latin and served as a foundation of medical learning in European universities for centuries.

Avignon [ah-veen-yohn']   Avignon is the capital of Vaucluse department, southeastern France, on the Rhône River. Located about 80 km (50 mi) northwest of Marseilles, it is a commercial and industrial center that manufactures wine, oil, flour, and textiles. Tourism is also important. The population is 89,132 (1982). Landmarks include the Palace of the Popes (14th century) and a remnant of the Pont d'Avignon (1177–85), a bridge built by St. Bénézet and made popular by the song "Sur le Pont d'Avignon."

Avignon was held successively by the Romans, Germanic tribes, and Burgundian kings until it was purchased (1348) by Pope Clement VI as the site of the papal see. Several popes resided here until 1377, when Pope GREGORY XI returned to Rome. Two antipopes resided in Avignon during the Great SCHISM (1378–1417). The city was annexed to France in 1791.

avocado [ah-vuh-kah'-doh]   The avocado, or alligator pear, *Persea americana*, is a common evergreen tree indigenous to Mexico and to Central and South America. It belongs to the LAUREL family, Lauraceae, which also includes cinnamon, camphor, and sassafras.

The fruit of the avocado takes 9 to 15 months to mature and can grow to 0.3 m (1 ft) long. The buttery flesh that surrounds the seed is about 20 to 30 percent oil.

Propagation is by grafting or budding the desired variety onto seedling stocks. Pollen transfer by bees is necessary. Pear-shaped or oval fruit are borne 2 to 3 years after planting, and well-cared-for trees are productive for many years.

See also: FRUITS AND FRUIT CULTIVATION.

avocet [av'-uh-set]   The avocet is a long-legged, long-necked wading bird of the genus *Recurvirostra*. It has white plumage with contrasting black markings; the sexes cannot be distinguished by their plumage. The long, upturned bill is efficient for catching small crustaceans, mollusks, and insects in shallow or muddy waters. The

The American avocet feeds by running through shallow water and swinging its head to skim off food morsels with its upturned bill. The head and neck are usually white but become buff during the breeding season. The black wing bar is distinctive.

birds nest gregariously. The American avocet, *R. americana*, which is 46 cm (18 in) long, breeds in western North and Central America but strays during migrations to the eastern coast of the United States, where it once nested. Avocets and STILTS constitute the family Recurvirostridae.

Avogadro, Amedeo [ah-voh-gah-'droh]   The Italian physicist and chemist Amedeo Avogadro, b. Aug. 9, 1776, d. July 9, 1856, is known principally for the law in chemistry that now bears his name, AVOGADRO'S LAW. Avogadro received his doctorate in ecclesiastical law in 1796 and occupied (1820–22; 1834–50) the first chair of mathematical physics in Italy at the University of Turin. In his famous law, Avogadro explained Gay-Lussac's law of combining volumes (see GAS LAWS) and established the formula of water as H_2O (rather than the accepted HO). Avogadro also distinguished between atoms and molecules and distinguished atomic weights from molecular weights. He made constant use of a mathematical approach and can be regarded as one of the founders of physical chemistry.

Avogadro number   A mole of any substance is that quantity of the substance which weighs (in grams) the same as its molecular weight. For example, molecular oxygen, O_2, has a molecular weight of 32 (16 for each oxygen atom); one mole of oxygen weighs 32 g. A mole of a substance always contains the same number of molecules—the Avogadro number—as a mole of any other substance. Therefore, Avogadro's law can be stated in terms of moles, namely that equal volumes of gases at the same temperature and pressure contain the same number of moles.

Scientists can measure out an equal number of molecules by simply weighing out an equal number of moles. For gases, this can be done by volume, as one mole of a gas at 0° C and at 1 atmosphere pressure occupies 22.4 liters. The Avogadro number is most reliably determined by X-ray diffraction of crystals. For many years the number was accepted as averaging at about 6.022045×10^{23} molecules; in 1986, however, after more recent studies of silicon crystals, the International Council of Scientific Unions redefined the number as 6.0221367×10^{23}.

Avogadro's law   Avogadro's law states that equal volumes of any two different gases if they are at the same temperature and pressure contain equal numbers of molecules. The law holds except at high pressures, when gases tend to liquefy. Avogadro's law is useful to chemists working with gases because they can simply measure the volumes of reacting gases to determine the equivalent amounts of materials; the difficulties of weighing gases are eliminated.

The law was at first virtually ignored by chemists because when it was tested in 1811, appropriate temperatures were not used by other scientists. It was reintroduced in 1858 by Avogadro's countryman Stanislao Cannizzaro.

avoirdupois   see WEIGHTS AND MEASURES

Avon   Avon, a county in southwestern England, was created in 1974 from parts of Gloucestershire and Somerset. Its area is 1,346 km^2 (520 mi^2), and it has a population of 954,300 (1988 est.). Avon lies outside the industrial complex around BRISTOL and is largely agricultural. Dairy farming is prevalent. Tourists are attracted to BATH and Weston-super-Mare. During the Roman period the area was on an important trade route.

Avon, Anthony Eden, 1st Earl of   see EDEN, SIR ANTHONY

AWACS   see AIRBORNE WARNING AND CONTROL SYSTEM

Awoonor, Kofi [ah-woon'-ohr, koh'-fee]   Kofi Awoonor (original name, George Awoonor-Williams), b. Mar. 13, 1935, is a Ghanaian writer, considered one of the finest English-language poets in Africa. Educated in Ghana, England, and the United States, he has taught at several American universities and at Ghana's University of Cape Coast. Awoonor's poetry draws on the structure and images of traditional African oral verse. His volumes of poetry include *Rediscovery and Other Poems* (1964) and *Ride Me, Memory* (1973). Novelist as well as poet, Awoonor has written *This Earth, My Brother* (1971) and *Fire in the Valley* (1983), and a play, *Ancestral Power* (1970).

---

axiom   In ancient philosophy, an axiom, from the Greek meaning "thought to be worthy of," was a starting point that needed no evidence or demonstration. Axioms are used in the geometry of EUCLID. Axioms were assumed to be self-evident and necessarily true. They were used as foundations for demonstrating other geometrical truths. ARISTOTLE applied the term to certain propositions that he claimed were self-evident.

Axiom is often used interchangeably with *postulate.* However, axiom usually refers to a basic proposition common to many or all subjects, whereas postulate refers to a basic proposition in a specific field.

The philosophers DESCARTES, SPINOZA, and KANT all presented their own views of axioms.

Axioms play a central role in modern mathematical LOGIC. They are the initial premises of a logical system, so that for any set of propositions there can be many different groups of axioms. Beginning with Gottlob FREGE, Giuseppe Peano, Bertrand RUSSELL, and Alfred North WHITEHEAD, various kinds of systems described by axioms have been developed and explored.

---

axion   Axions are hypothetical subatomic particles that preserve symmetry in strong interactions between QUARKS (see SYMMETRY, physics; QUANTUM CHROMODYNAMICS). Physicists theorize that axions are the "dark matter" that may account for much of the universe's mass. Dark matter, if proven to exist, would explain gravitational effects observed in the motion and distribution of galaxies.

Axis   The Axis was the name of the alignment between Nazi Germany and Fascist Italy first formed in October 1936 and strengthened by a formal alliance in May 1939. The term was later used loosely to include Germany's other allies in WORLD WAR II, especially Japan.

---

axolotl [ak'-suh-laht-ul]   Axolotls are salamanders that live in ponds and lakes on the Mexican plateau. They retain most of the characteristics of larvae, such as gills, throughout their lives. The axolotl is known scientifically as *Ambystoma mexicanum* and is classified in the family Ambystomatidae, which inhabits much of North America. Axolotls occur at the lower end of the geographic range of the family, and it is suggested that the relatively harsh conditions of the Mexican plateau resulted in the evolution of these permanently larval forms. In less harsh environments some closely related species are known to occasionally metamorphose into an adult stage. Axolotls are easy to raise in the laboratory and have many genetic variations (including ALBINISM); they are therefore used to test a variety of genetic principles.

Axum   see AKSUM

Ayckbourn, Alan   The English playwright Alan Ayckbourn, b. Apr. 12, 1939, writes witty farces that explore the domestic traumas of middle-class life. More than 35 of his plays have been produced, most notably *Absurd Person Singular* (1972), the trilogy *The Norman Conquests* (1973), *Season's Greetings* (1982), *Woman in Mind* (1985), and *The Revengers' Comedies* (1989). Once an actor, Ayckbourn is now director of productions at the Library Theatre, Scarborough, England.

---

aye-aye [y'-y]   The aye-aye, *Daubentonia madagascariensis,* is a rare primate native to Madagascar that some-

The aye-aye is a primate found in bamboo forests of Madagascar. It is an endangered species because of destruction of its habitat.

what resembles the lemur. About the size of a small fox, it has a long, bushy tail, large eyes, thick fur, and a pair of enlarged front teeth resembling those of rodents. It uses its teeth to break into termite-infested wood, whereupon it probes the termite galleries with its slender, elongated middle finger. The claw on the end of this unusual finger is used to spear insects. The internal anatomy of the aye-aye closely resembles that of the more typical lemurs of Madagascar.

Ayer, A. J.   Sir Alfred Jules Ayer, b. Oct. 29, 1910, d. June 27, 1989, was an English philosopher instrumental in introducing the ideas of LOGICAL POSITIVISM into English philosophy with his book *Language, Truth, and Logic* (1936). Influenced by the thought of Bertrand Russell, Ludwig Wittgenstein, and the earlier empiricism of George Berkeley, Ayer held that philosophy's essential concern is the analysis of language. He denied that metaphysical statements can be meaningful and regarded the value statements of ethics as expressions of emotion.

Ayer's later work reflects more of the traditional emphases of British empiricism.

Ayers Rock   Ayers Rock, in central Australia, is a huge freestanding rock formation, or monolith. Rising above the flat plain of central Australia, the oval-shaped mass is composed of a multicolored, weathered conglomerate. Ayers Rock stands 348 m (1,143 ft) above the desert floor; it is about 2 km (1.5 mi) long and 1.5 km (0.9 mi) wide and is deeply eroded from top to bottom. Its lower portion is pocked with numerous caves that have long been sacred to Aborigines who live in the region. The lower walls and caves contain traditional Aborigine paintings. Sighted in 1872 by the explorer Ernest Giles, Ayers Rock was named for a former South Australian premier, Sir Henry Ayers. The government transferred ownership of Ayers Rock to the Aborigines in 1985.

Ayers Rock looms above the desert of central Australia. The monolith was exposed by wind erosion over the course of eons.

Ayllón, Lucas Vásquez de [yl-yohn'] Lucas Vásquez de Ayllón, b. *c.*1475, d. Oct. 18, 1526, was a Spanish explorer who colonized the Carolina coast. In 1526 he sailed from Hispaniola (Santo Domingo) and founded a settlement at the mouth of what was probably the Cape Fear, Santee, or Pee Dee River. Following his death there during a fever epidemic, the colony was abandoned.

Aylwin, Patricio [ayl'-win] Patricio Aylwin, b. Viña del Mar, Chile, Nov. 26, 1918, became president of Chile in 1990. His 1989 election as the candidate of the Christian Democratic party followed a 16-year period during which Chile was ruled by Gen. Augusto PINOCHET UGARTE, who remains commander in chief of the army. A lawyer by profession, Aylwin was elected to the Chilean Senate in 1965. His opposition to former Socialist president Salvador ALLENDE (1970–73) prompted him to endorse the 1973 military coup, but subsequent repressive policies caused Aylwin to shift his position. As president, Aylwin ordered the release of some political prisoners and an investigation of human-rights abuses.

Aymara [y-mah-rah'] The Aymara are a South American Indian people inhabiting much of the Titicaca Basin in southern Peru and Bolivia. They were part of the INCA empire until the time of the Spanish conquest (*c.*1540), when their large population then came under the administration of the ENCOMIENDA system. The Aymara staged unsuccessful rebellions in the 18th and early 19th centuries. Since the colonial period they have lived as sharecroppers and wage laborers on haciendas, engaging in agriculture. Today they number more than 1 million.

The patrilineal and patrilocal extended family is the basic landowning and economic unit. Endogamous marriages are usually arranged and involve the payment of bride-price in addition to a Catholic service. For centuries Aymara have espoused Catholicism, but many vestiges of the traditional religious beliefs remain.

Ayr [air] Ayr was a county in southwest Scotland until 1975, when it became part of the Strathclyde administrative region. Located south of Glasgow, it is bounded on the west by the Firth of Clyde. The main town is Ayr. The rivers Irvine and Doone divide the region into three traditional sections—the hilly southeast; the central low hills, supporting an extensive dairy industry as well as ironworks and coal mining, which began in Ayr in 1780; and the widely cultivated western lowlands, site of many summer resorts. The poet Robert Burns was born in Ayr, the setting for much of his poetry.

Ayub Khan, Muhammad [ah-yub' kahn] Muhammad Ayub Khan, b. May 14, 1907, d. Apr. 20, 1974, was a field marshal and president of Pakistan. Educated at the Royal Military Academy at Sandhurst, he served in the British Indian army in World War II. After the creation of the Muslim state of Pakistan in 1947, Ayub Khan rose through the army to become the first Pakistani commander in chief (1951–58), also serving as defense minister (1954–55). President Iskander Mirza appointed him administrator of martial law in October 1958. Ayub Khan then proclaimed himself president, thus ousting Mirza. A field marshal from 1959, he was confirmed as president by a referendum in 1960 and was reelected under a new constitution in 1965. Political unrest and riots erupted in 1968, particularly in East Pakistan (later Bangladesh). Ayub Khan resigned amid charges of corruption on Mar. 26, 1969.

Ayutthia [ah-yoo-ty'-uh]   Ayutthia (Ayudhya), a town 72 km (45 mi) north of Bangkok, is the site of the first capital of the kingdom of Siam (present-day Thailand). Founded (c.1350) by the Thai king Ramathibodi I, it remained the southern center of Thai power and culture until 1767, when the Burmese destroyed it.

Ayutthia's Buddhist kings attempted to supplant, by the splendor of their architecture, ANGKOR, the great capital city of the Khmer, which had earlier ruled much of Thailand. Numerous ruined buildings survive at the site, among them tall brick stupas and tower-shrines based on Khmer patterns. These shrines contained Buddhist relics and serenely styled images of the Buddha, of which the colossal bronze sculpture of the seated Buddha in the Phra Monkal Borpitr is the most spectacular. Major temples include the Wat Phra Ram (1369) and the Wat Phra Sri Sanpet (1492). Important pictorial remains include the wall paintings of Buddhist subjects in the royal tomb chambers of Wat Rat Burana (1427) and the late-17th-century examples in the Wat Budhaisawan. Chandrakasem Palace is now a museum.

azalea [uh-zayl'-yuh]   Azaleas are beautiful flowering, semievergreen shrubs or small trees that belong to the

The flame azalea is an evergreen shrub that produces brilliantly hued flowers in spring.

genus *Rhododendron* and the heath family, Ericaceae. Azaleas are native to southeastern Asia, North America, and southern Europe. Horticulturists have developed numerous new varieties for landscape planting; both evergreen and deciduous types are available. Azaleas thrive in acidic soils (pH 4.5–6.5) and where they will receive direct sunlight for part of the day.

Azaña, Manuel [ah-thahn'-yah]   Manuel y Díaz Azaña, b. Jan. 10, 1880, d. Nov. 4, 1940, was a Spanish political leader during the Second Republic. A writer of distinction and a member of the 1931 revolutionary committee, he became war minister in the first republican cabinet and then prime minister (1931–33), inaugurating a number of reforms. When the Popular Front won the February 1936 election, he again became prime minister and then (May 1936) president. During the SPANISH CIVIL WAR he became a mere figurehead. He fled (February 1939) to France just before the republican collapse.

Azande [uh-zahn'-dee]   The Azande (singular, Zande) are an African people who live in Zaire, the Central African Republic, and Sudan. They number more than 100,000 and speak a language of the Eastern subfamily of the Niger-Congo languages. The Azande live by subsistence farming, fishing, and gathering plants and insects.

Descent is traced through the father's line, but communal life is based on the political system rather than on family and kinship ties. Marriage is polygynous, with older men having an advantage over younger men in the acquisition of wives. Traditional Zande religion includes belief in and deep concern with magic (especially sorcery), witchcraft, oracles, divination, and leechcraft, the art of healing.

Azerbaijan [ah-zurby-jahn']   Azerbaijan, one of the 15 constituent republics of the USSR, is located in Transcaucasia, on the Caspian Sea, and borders on Iran. The area is 86,600 km² (33,400 mi²), and the population is 6,808,000 (1987 est.). Azerbaijan's capital is BAKU, with a population of 1,722,000 (1986 est.).

The topography of Azerbaijan is made up of the Greater Caucasus in the north; a central plain of dry steppe; and the uplands of the Lesser Caucasus in the southwest. A distinctive feature is the Apsheron Peninsula jutting out into the Caspian Sea and coinciding with the Baku metropolitan area. The climate is semiarid, with hot summers and cool winters.

The Azerbaijani people, who make up 78% of the population, are Muslim in religion, speak a language related to Turkish, and live mainly in rural areas. Ethnic minorities include Russians (8%) and Armenians (8%).

The leading economic activity is the oil industry around Baku, with refineries in Baku and petrochemical plants in nearby Sumgait. Natural gas is associated with oil production. Alumina is also produced. Cotton is the principal cash crop.

Politically, Azerbaijan includes two subsidiary ethnic autonomous areas: the NAGORNO-KARABAKH Autonomous Oblast, in the Lesser Caucasus, with an area of 4,400 km² (1,699 mi²) and a population of 186,000 (1989 est.); and the Nakhichevan Autonomous SSR—separated from Azerbaijan proper by Soviet Armenia—with an area of 5,500 km² (2,124 mi²) and a population of 278,000 (1987 est.). In the late 1980s the mostly Armenian population of Nagorno-Karabakh repudiated Azerbaijani rule, demanding union with Armenia.

Azerbaijan was governed by a succession of Islamic dynasties between the 7th century AD and its annexation by Russia in 1813. The overthrow of the tsar in 1917 brought a brief period of independence before the Bolsheviks assumed control in 1920.

South of Soviet Azerbaijan, in the extreme northwest of Iran, is another region known as Azerbaijan. Comprising the Iranian provinces of East Azerbaijan and West Azerbaijan, the region is a high plateau of relatively productive farmland. The people, primarily farmers, are ethnically and linguistically related to the Azerbaijanis of the Soviet Union. Soviet troops occupied the area from 1945 to 1946, when it again came under the control of the Iranian government.

azide [a'-zyd] Azides are a group of sensitive, explosive chemical compounds. The molecules of azides all contain three doubly bonded nitrogen atoms attached to an inorganic or organic group. Some have light-sensitive properties like those of silver halides. Most metal azides are explosive under appropriate conditions of heat, shock, or friction and have a limited use in detonation work. Hydrogen azide, a sensitive explosive, is comparable to NITROGLYCERIN. It is also a poison with an action similar to CYANIDE. Lead azide, $Pb(N_3)_2$, the most important member of the group, is used as a primary explosive in industry and by the military. Organic acyl derivatives of azides are acetylating agents that are used in protein synthesis.

azimuth see COORDINATE SYSTEMS (astronomy)

Aznavour, Charles [ahz-nah-voor'] Charles Aznavour is the stage name of Varenagh Aznavourian, b. May 22, 1924, a French-Armenian concert and cabaret singer of international fame. Early in his career he was a protégé of the singer Edith PIAF and wrote songs for her. He has also acted in such films as *La Tête contre les murs* (1958), *Shoot the Piano Player* (1960), *The Games* (1970), *Les Intrus* (1973), *The Tin Drum* (1979), and *Vive la vie* (1984).

azo compound [a'-zoh] An azo compound consists of two organic molecules linked by two nitrogen atoms that share a double bond. This central unit (—N=N—) is called the azo group after azote, an early name for nitrogen. If the nitrogens are linked to atoms other than carbon in the aliphatic or aromatic molecules, the compounds are called diazo compounds.

The simplest aromatic azo compound is azobenzene. Like all compounds containing the light-absorbing azo group, it is colored—in this instance, a bright orange red. Unlike the thousands of other aromatic azo compounds that are industrially important dyes, it has no affinity with fiber, but it is used as an intermediate in the synthesis of such dyes and as an accelerator in the vulcanization of rubber.

Water-insoluble azo dyes that form within the treated material through the reaction of intermediate compounds are called azoic dyes. Most aliphatic azo compounds are not industrially significant, but some of them are used as sources of free radicals.

Azores [ay'-zohrz] The Azores are a group of Portuguese islands in the Atlantic Ocean, located between 37° and 39° north latitude and lying 1,190 km (740 mi) west of southern Portugal. Ten islands, stretching from northwest to southeast over a distance of about 645 km (400 mi), make up the group. Their combined area of 2,247 km² (868 mi²) accommodates a population of 252,200 (1986 est.), which is Portuguese-speaking and mainly of Portuguese descent. The small western islands, Corvo and Flores, are separated by about 240 km (150 mi) of open sea from the central group, which consists of Faial, Pico, São Jorge, Graciosa, and Terceira. Open sea separates these from the southeastern islands of São Miguel, Santa Maria, and Formigas. São Miguel is the largest and most densely populated island. All except Santa Maria are of volcanic origin, rising to heights of more than 900 m (3,000 ft) within a few kilometers of the coast, and most are subject to severe earthquakes.

The climate is temperate, with a very small seasonal range. Rainfall is heavy on the windward sides of the islands. Much of it falls in winter, when severe gales may occur. Bananas, pineapples, and subtropical fruits are grown at lower altitudes. From elevations of about 450 to 900 m (1,500 to 3,000 ft), temperate cereals and fruits prevail, and recently dairying has been introduced. Sardines, tuna, and other fish are caught. The population is declining because of the migration to mainland Portugal and the United States.

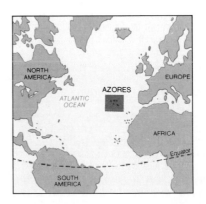

The map indicates the location of the Azores, a group of volcanic islands in the Atlantic Ocean.. The Azores are governed by Portugal, whose navigators discovered them about 1427.

The Azores were discovered by the Portuguese about 1427. They were uninhabited, but the Portuguese began to settle there a few years later. Occupied by Spain from 1580 to 1640, they were used as a staging base for the Spanish fleets. For political and administrative purposes, the islands form three provinces of Portugal.

Azov, Sea of

Azov, Sea of [uh-zawf']   The Sea of Azov is a northern arm of the BLACK SEA in the southern USSR. It covers an area of 38,850 km² (15,000 mi²) and is 370 km (230 mi) long, with a maximum width of 177 km (110 mi). The Azov is the world's shallowest sea, with depths ranging from 0.9 to 14 m (3 to 46 ft). It is fed by the Don, Mius, and Kalmius rivers from the north and by the Yeya and Kuban from the east. It is connected by rivers and the Kerch Strait to the Black Sea. Iron ore and coal are shipped across it, and it is fished commercially. The Azov is frozen for 3 to 6 months during the winter. Major ports are Taganrog and the metal-refining centers of Zhdanov and Kerch.

Aztec

Aztec   According to their own myths and legends, the people known as the Aztecs (who referred to themselves as the Mexica or Tenochca) originated from a place called Aztlán, somewhere in north or northwest Mexico. At that time the Aztecs were a small, nomadic tribe, Nahuatl-speaking, living in the border territory on the margins of civilized MESOAMERICA. Sometime in the 12th century they embarked on a period of wandering; they finally found refuge on a small island in Lake Texcoco where, about 1345, they founded the town of TENOCHTITLÁN.

Aztec Empire.   The Aztecs at first lived under the dominion of Azcapotzalco, the mightiest of the city-states in the valley of central Mexico. They helped this town to conquer territory in the early 15th century, but in 1428 they defeated Azcapotzalco itself with the assistance of allies. By 1431, Tenochtitlán had become an independent state in alliance with the neighboring cities of Texcoco and Tlacopán. This triple alliance soon controlled the entire valley and, with Tenochtitlán as the dominant partner, began a program of military expansion that was still unfinished at the time of the Spanish conquest.

Montezuma I, grandfather of MONTEZUMA II, expanded the empire from the Atlantic to the Pacific. A total of 489 cities paid tribute to the alliance. From these conquered cities came foodstuffs to feed the growing population of Tenochtitlán, together with luxury goods for Aztec nobles and warriors and exotic raw materials—gold, copper, tropical feathers, gemstones, rubber, jade, amber, jaguar skins, and chocolate. Conquest also furnished war captives for sacrifice to the gods.

The alliance powers made no attempt to unify the area they controlled or to change the customs of conquered peoples. The empire was held together by force rather than by loyalty, and the subject states were eager to shake off Aztec control. With the arrival (1519) of the Spanish army of Hernán CORTÉS, several Mexican cities willingly joined forces with the invaders. In 1521,

Tenochtitlán, under the leadership of CUAUHTÉMOC, capitulated to Cortés, and the days of Aztec dominion ended.

Aztec Culture.   For a century, the Aztecs of Tenochtitlán had been the greatest power in Mexico. As they grew in political status, they became sophisticated and civilized. The Aztec empire consisted of numerous loosely connected urban communities. Land ownership was communal; each local group, called a *capulli*, was composed of a few families that jointly owned a piece of land. Part of the yield of cultivated land was given to the state as a kind of tax.

Technology depended more on human skills than on mechanical devices. The wheel was known, but it was used for nothing more important than pull-along toys. No wheeled vehicles existed, nor any machines depending on rotary motion. Iron and steel were unknown, although copper and bronze were used for tools, and Mexican jewelers made magnificent ornaments from gold, silver, and their alloys. Many things that a 16th-century Spaniard took for granted, including glass and glazes, gunpowder, plows, and alphabetic writing, were absent from Mexico, but the lack of these things did not prevent the Aztecs from producing an art and architecture that amazed the

The Aztecs of Mexico built their greatest city, Tenochtitlán, on an island in Lake Texcoco, which was connected to the mainland by several causeways. This center dominated the many other city-states in the Valley of Mexico. Today the lakes Texcoco and Chalco are dry, and Mexico City is built upon the ruins of Tenochtitlán.

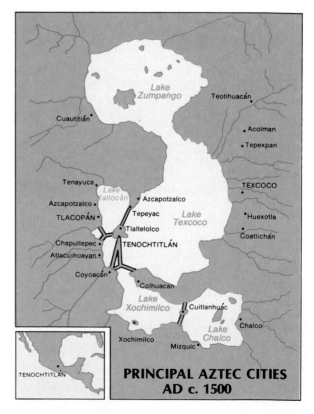

PRINCIPAL AZTEC CITIES
AD c. 1500

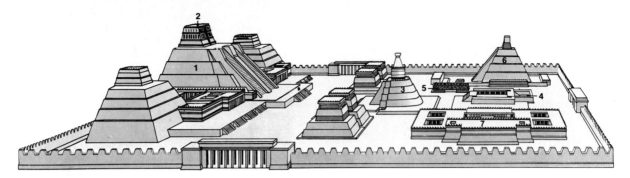

A great pyramid (1) dominates the enclosed sacred compound of Tenochtitlán in this illustration based on archaeological findings. Two temples (2) dedicated to Huitzilopochtli, the Aztec sun and war god, and Tlaloc, the rain god, were built on top of the great pyramid. A round pyramid (3) dedicated to the diety, Quetzalcoatl in his manifestation as wind god, stands between the great pyramid and a ball-court (4). On one side of the ballcourt stands a skull rack (5) and the temple of the Sun (6), and on the other side are living quarters (7) of priests and novices.

Europeans. Although wheat, barley, cattle, horses, sheep, and goats were unknown until introduced from Europe, the Mexicans were efficient farmers who made full use of irrigation, terracing, and fertilization of the fields.

As the Spaniards immediately appreciated, Aztec Mexico was rich and civilized, even if its customs and technology were unlike those of the Old World. The state controlled every aspect of life. Schooling and training in

The Aztecs carried on commerce in a marketplace near the sacred compound of Tenochtitlán. The Aztecs mastered such crafts as weaving, pottery, basketry, and featherwork and created some of the finest works of gold in the world. They traded these products for cocoa beans, rubber, jewels, and other goods from distant regions.

Huitzilopochtli, the sun and war god, was among the most fearsome of deities in the Aztec pantheon. He was worshiped daily with offerings of human blood and the hearts torn from bodies of sacrificial victims.

the martial arts were compulsory for all boys. A centralized bureaucracy looked after the collection and storage of taxes, matters of legislation and punishment, famine relief, and market trading. A special class of merchants devoted themselves to long-distance commerce outside the Aztec empire, and their caravans traveled as far as Yucatán and Guatemala, where they exchanged goods with traders from MAYA territory. These merchants were also used as official envoys and as spies. Religion was in the hands of full-time priests, whose leaders were drawn from the ruling families; thus no conflict of interest existed between church and state.

Aztec Religion. Like all the Mexican peoples, the Aztecs worshiped a multitude of gods, each of whom demanded offerings and sacrifices. Above all, the Aztecs considered themselves the chosen people of HUITZILO-POCHTLI, the sun and war god, in whose name they were destined to conquer all rival nations. Huitzilopochtli shared the main temple at Tenochtitlán with Tlaloc, the rain god, important to the farmers in a land where drought was a constant threat. Another important god was QUETZALCÓATL, the feathered serpent, patron of arts and crafts and the god of self-sacrifice. Religion was ever present. Each place and each trade had its patron deity: each day, and each division of the day, was watched over by its own god. Priests were expected to live in chastity, to mortify their flesh, and to understand astronomy, astrology, the complex rituals and ceremonies, and the art of picture writing. Games also formed part of the religious ritual. A popular ball game was *lachtli*, in which a small rubber ball had to be struck by the hips or thighs and knocked across a special court. In another ritual game, men attired as birds and attached to ropes were slung in a wide circle around a pole. The official state religion of the soldiers and noblemen was concerned primarily with the great and powerful gods: the creators, the solar dei-

ties, the patrons of the warrior orders. By contrast, the common people seem to have preferred the lesser, more accessible gods: the patrons of the craft guilds, the protectors of local shrines, and the deities who looked after the things of everyday life. For everyone, however, rich or poor, each month of the Aztec calendar had its festival, with music, dancing, processions, and sacrifices. All this came to an end with the Spanish conquest and the introduction of the Christian religion, although at the peasant level certain traditions from the Aztec heritage still survive in modern Mexico.

See also: LATIN AMERICA, HISTORY OF; PRE-COLUMBIAN ART AND ARCHITECTURE.

Azuela, Mariano [ah-sway'-lah]   Mariano Azuela, b. Jan. 1, 1873, d. Mar. 1, 1952, a Mexican novelist, inaugurated the cycle of the socially realistic "novels of the Mexican Revolution." A practicing physician from 1899, he served briefly (1915) as a surgeon with Pancho VILLA. Azuela's *The Underdogs* (1915; Eng. trans., 1928), one of the most widely translated of Mexican novels, describes the disillusioning rise and fall of a petty army officer of Indian origins during the revolution. Azuela continued to explore the revolution's impact in such novels as *The Bosses* (1917; Eng. trans., 1956), *The Flies* (1918; Eng. trans., 1956), and *The Trials of a Respectable Family* (1918; Eng. trans., 1963).

azurite   The mineral azurite, which is the basic carbonate of copper, has been used as a decorative stone and a blue pigment. It forms modified monoclinic crystals (see MONOCLINIC SYSTEM) as well as columnar or earthy masses that have a vitreous luster and a distinctive azure blue color. Hardness is 3½–4, streak is blue, and specific gravity is 3.7–3.9. Azurite occurs in the oxidized zone of copper deposits, where it has been precipitated from low-temperature copper and carbonate-rich solutions. It is almost always associated with the more abundant green copper carbonate MALACHITE, to which azurite weathers.

See also: CARBONATE MINERALS; ORE DEPOSITS.

Azurite is a relatively rare mineral found mixed with other copper ores in groups of thin, transparent to translucent, platelike crystals. Its brilliant blue color favors its use in jewelry, although its softness is a disadvantage. In earlier times it was a popular blue pigment used by European and Oriental artists.

GERMAN-GOTHIC	RUSSIAN-CYRILLIC	CLASSICAL LATIN	EARLY LATIN	ETRUSCAN	CLASSICAL GREEK	EARLY GREEK	EARLY ARAMAIC	EARLY HEBREW	PHOENICIAN

B *B/b* is the second letter of the English alphabet; its form and position were inherited from the Latin alphabet by way of the Etruscan and Greek. The Greek letter *beta* was in turn derived from a Semitic (probably Phoenician) writing system, in which the name of the sign is *beth*.

In modern Greek, the letter *beta* is pronounced similarly to *v*. Thus, in the Cyrillic (Eastern Slavic) alphabet, which developed from the late Greek, the symbol *B* represents the sound *v*, and a new symbol for the sound *b*,Б, was devised.

In English, the letter *b* represents a voiced labial stop made by interrupting the flow of air with the lips and vibrating the vocal cords, as in *bat*, *label*, and *slab*. In some instances, *b* is not pronounced when preceded by *m* or followed by *t*, as in *dumb* or *doubt*. Because the sound *b* is very closely related to other labial consonants, such as *p*, *v*, *f* (*ph*), *m*, and *w* (*wh*), these sounds are frequently interchanged in words of different languages that have a common origin: thus Latin *frater*, Greek *phrater*, Sanskrit *bhratr*, German *Bruder*, and English *brother*. At times this interchange is found in words in a single language: English *burse*, *bourse*, *bursar*, *purse*, and *purser* are derived from Latin *bursa*.

See also: WRITING SYSTEMS, EVOLUTION OF.

B-1 bomber The Rockwell International B-1 bomber was developed to replace the obsolescent B-52 STRATO-FORTRESS. The slim, blended-wing fuselage enclosed three internal weapons bays with four missile points under the fuselage, for a total weapons load of 52,160 kg (115,000 lb). Estimated maximum speed of the B-1 at 12,192 m (40,000 ft) was 2,335 km/h (1,450 mph), or Mach 2.2.

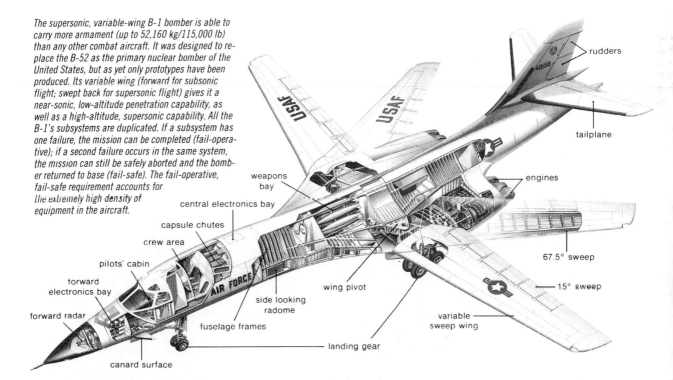

The supersonic, variable-wing B-1 bomber is able to carry more armament (up to 52,160 kg/115,000 lb) than any other combat aircraft. It was designed to replace the B-52 as the primary nuclear bomber of the United States, but as yet only prototypes have been produced. Its variable wing (forward for subsonic flight; swept back for supersonic flight) gives it a near-sonic, low-altitude penetration capability, as well as a high-altitude, supersonic capability. All the B-1's subsystems are duplicated. If a subsystem has one failure, the mission can be completed (fail-operative); if a second failure occurs in the same system, the mission can still be safely aborted and the bomber returned to base (fail-safe). The fail-operative, fail-safe requirement accounts for the extremely high density of equipment in the aircraft.

rudders
tailplane
engines
67.5° sweep
15° sweep
weapons bay
central electronics bay
capsule chutes
crew area
pilots' cabin
forward electronics bay
forward radar
canard surface
fuselage frames
side looking radome
wing pivot
landing gear
variable sweep wing

Maximum designed takeoff weight was 176,810 kg (389,800 lb), and the range was 9,815 km (6,100 mi).

In 1977, President Jimmy Carter canceled the entire B-1 program. In 1981, however, President Ronald Reagan revived the program, with funding going to the development of a new model, the B-1B. Following the crash of a B-1A prototype in 1984, the B-1A was grounded. Reagan's goal of a fleet of 100 B-1Bs was reached in 1988, although the bomber had a turbulent history. The most persistent technical problem involved its electronic radar-jamming defenses. The B-1 remained grounded during the 1990-91 GULF WAR.

B-17 Flying Fortress   see AIRCRAFT, MILITARY

B-2 bomber   see STEALTH BOMBER

B-29 Superfortress   see AIRCRAFT, MILITARY

B-52 Stratofortress   A long-distance U.S. bomber, the Boeing B-52 Stratofortress was first built in the 1950s. The massive 56-m-span (185-ft), 35-degree-sweptwing B-52 entered the Strategic Air Command in 1955 with eight powerful Pratt and Whitney turbojet engines. The B-52G version, developed in 1958, was the most significant bomber in the world's most powerful air force and was able to carry nuclear weapons to any global target at short notice. In January 1962 the B-52H, with TF-33 turbofan engines, demonstrated its ability by flying nonstop without refueling from Okinawa to Madrid (20,147 km/12,519 mi) in 22 hours and 10 minutes. In 1977 the Stratofortress was designated to carry the air-launched CRUISE MISSILE (ALCM). Throughout the 1980s, while the B-1 BOMBER was being developed, the B-52 remained the workhorse of the U.S. bomber fleet.

Ba Xian (Pa Hsien)   In Chineese mythology, the Ba Xian (Eight Immortals) were Taoist holy men, similar in status to saints. Unconnected as historical persons, each was believed to have earned the right to immortality and to be endowed with miraculous powers. The classic group of eight was formed during the Yuan period (1260-1368); they are frequently depicted together in Chinese art.

Baade, Walter [bahd'-e]   Wilhelm Heinrich Walter Baade, b. Mar. 24, 1893, d. June 25, 1960, was a German-born American astronomer who established through extragalactic studies that the universe is twice as large as had been previously thought. Baade's study at Mount Wilson Observatory of the Andromeda galaxy during World War II led to his important distinction between two types of stars, now known as population I and II stars (see POPULATION, STELLAR). Because of its inability to discern a certain type of variable star with the 200-in (508-cm) telescope, Baade also concluded that the Andromeda galaxy must be more than twice as far away as had been previously thought.

Baal [bay'-uhl]   Baal, the name of the fertility god or gods of the ancient Canaanite religions, was one of the chief characters mentioned in the 14th-century BC UGARIT tablets. Called the lord of the universe, he was killed by monsters but restored to life. His death and resurrection were celebrated annually as a part of Canaanite fertility rituals. The cult of Baal—and particularly the human sacrifice and temple prostitution associated with it—was frequently denounced by Old Testament prophets.

Baal Shem Tov [bah'-ahl shaym tohv]   Israel ben Eliezer, b. Ukraine, c.1700, d. 1760, known as Baal Shem Tov ("Master of the Good Name") or by the acronym Besht, was the founder of the Jewish sect of HASIDISM. Little is known of his life, and that little is encrusted with legend.

Baal Shem Tov was reputed to be a wonder-worker and healer by virtue of his knowledge of the secret name of God (hence, "Master of the Good Name"). In reaction to the intellectualism and casuistry of the rabbinical legalists, he stressed the joyous and enthusiastic experience of religious participation. Song and dance, fervent prayer, and ecstatic communion with God were the keys to unlock spiritual powers. Humility completes the list of cardinal virtues. Whatever in his teaching was drawn from the KABBALAH was developed in a way that emphasized the elements of adherence (*devekut*) to God through a recognition of the divine immanence in nature. Attainment of this adherence demanded the total concentrated devotion (*kavvanah*) of the person in fervent communion with God.

Baalbek [bay'-uhl-bek]   Baalbek is a desert oasis village in eastern Lebanon, on the western slopes of the Anti-Lebanon Mountains. It has a population of 14,000 (1982 est.).

Baalbek was probably an ancient center for the worship of the Phoenician god BAAL. The Greeks, who identified Baal with Helios and called the city Heliopolis, occupied the site as part of their conquest of Syria in 332 BC. It became a Roman colony under Augustus in 16 BC. In AD 1759 an earthquake destroyed much of the city. Just west of the village are some well-preserved Roman ruins, including remains of the temples of Jupiter, Bacchus, and Venus and parts of the city wall.

Baath party [bah'-ahth]   The Baath party is a secular Arab political party that advocates a single socialist Arab nation; since 1953 it has been formally known as the Arab Socialist Resurrection Party. The first Baath party congress was held in Damascus in 1947, and the party soon developed organizations in most Arab countries and among Arabs in non-Arab countries. The more conservative and nationalistic military wing of the party eventually seized control of the governments of Iraq (in 1968) and Syria (in 1970), where the Baath party is strongest.

Babbage, Charles The British mathematician Charles Babbage, b. Dec. 26, 1792, d. Oct. 18, 1871, designed an "analytical engine," a mechanical progenitor of the digital computer. Elected (1816) a fellow of the Royal Society, he was Lucasian Professor of Mathematics at Cambridge (1828–39). The computation of logarithms had made him aware of the drudgery and inaccuracy of human calculation, and he became so obsessed with the mechanization of computation that he spent his family fortune in pursuit of it. Although Babbage never built an operational, mechanical computer, his design concepts have been proved correct.

Babbitt *Babbitt* (1922), a novel by Sinclair LEWIS, is a devastating attack on American small-town life. It is set in Zenith, nicknamed Zip City by its inordinately proud and chauvinistic residents. The central character, George F. Babbitt, is a middle-aged real estate broker who devoutly believes in progress and esteems "good fellowship, optimism, and good business." The term *Babbittry* now describes unthinking conformity to prevailing middle-class standards.

Babbitt, Milton Composer Milton Babbitt, b. Philadelphia, May 10, 1916, received traditional training in music and later in mathematics. He studied with Roger Sessions and began writing twelve-tone music (see SERIAL MUSIC), striving for total serial organization of all musical elements in his compositions.

Since 1938, Babbitt has been a member of the faculty of Princeton University, where he works with the Columbia-Princeton Electronic Music Center and with the journal *Perspectives of New Music*.

Babel, Isaak Emmanuilovich [bah'-buhl, ee'sahk em-ahn-weel'-oh-vich] Isaak Emmanuilovich Babel, b. Odessa, July 13, 1894, ranks as one of the finest Russian short-story writers of the Soviet period. He received a traditional Hebrew religious training as well as a secular education. Thus his tales reflect four literary traditions: Russian, Hebrew, Yiddish, and French. Babel's most important works are the short stories contained in the collections *The Red Cavalry* (1926; Eng. trans., 1929) and *Odessa Tales* (1927; *Collected Stories*, 1955). The first is a series of vignettes based on his experience as a soldier in the Polish-Soviet war. The second describes an exotic Jewish Odessa populated with gangsters, beggars, and like characters. In 1939 Babel was arrested on unknown charges; he died or was killed in prison in 1941.

Babel, Tower of [bay'-buhl] According to the Bible the tower of Babel was erected by the descendants of Noah, who were attempting to unite all peoples in building a city and tower that would reach to heaven. God thwarted their efforts by turning their language into bab-blings (Gen. 11). The story may be an early attempt to explain the origin of languages.

Babeuf, François Noël [bah-buf', frahn-swah' nohel'] François Noël ("Gracchus") Babeuf, b. Nov. 23, 1760, d. May 27, 1797, has received considerable attention as a precursor of modern communism. Repeatedly imprisoned after 1789, he gained notoriety in 1795 through his paper *The Tribune of the People*, and on May 10, 1796, he and others were arrested for conspiring to overthrow the Directory. A fiasco, this "Conspiracy for Equality" was also a landmark in the theory and practice of revolution, because Babeuf had evolved both an advanced technique for the seizure of power and a belief that an era of universal equality could be inaugurated by a final revolution in which all private property would be destroyed by a ruthless popular dictatorship. After a prolonged public trial, he was condemned and guillotined.

Babism [bah'-bizm] Babism is a religious movement founded by Mirza Ali Muhammad of Shiraz (Iran), who announced his divine election as the Bab in 1844. This title, meaning "doorway to knowledge," was understood by many to imply that Muhammad of Shiraz claimed to have received a divine manifestation surpassing in significance the revelation granted to the prophet Muhammad, and that his book of revelation, the *Bayan,* overshadowed the Koran. The Bab was executed (1850). His successor fled to Baghdad with his half brother Mirza Husayn Ali, who was later on called the BAHAULLAH ("Splendor of God"). The religious movement led by the Bahaullah became known as BAHA'I.

baboon Baboons are bulky, ground-dwelling monkeys in the order Primate, family Cercopithecidae. They are classified into two genera. Members of the genus *Chaeropithecus* are the blackish gray chacma (*C. ursinus*) of eastern and southern Africa, largest of the baboons; the yellow baboon (*C. cynocephalus*) of central and southern Africa; the brown doguera baboon (*C. doguera*) of east central Africa; and the reddish brown western baboon (*C. papio*) of west central Africa, smallest of the baboons. The sole member of the genus *Comopithecus* is the hamadryas, or sacred Anubis, baboon, which lives in Egypt, Arabia, Sudan, Ethiopia, and Somalia.

Baboons range in length from 50 to 110 cm (20 to 43 in), plus a tail that is 35 to 68 cm (14 to 27 in) long. They weigh from 13.5 to 39.6 kg (30 to 87 lb). The hamadryas grows up to 75 cm (30 in) long, has a 50-cm (20-in) tail, and weighs about 18 kg (40 lb). The body hair is coarse and rough, and the buttocks have naked pads. The adult male hamadryas baboon has an impressive wide mane and side whiskers. In the wild, baboons keep clean by grooming each other's coat. The canine teeth are long, the jaws powerful, and the limbs extreme-

A male hamadryas baboon has a thick, silver mane and coat, as well as long canine teeth, all of which the female lacks. A female carries her young on her back. Common to regions near the Red Sea, these baboons were considered sacred in ancient Egypt.

ly strong, making the baboon a formidable fighter.

Baboons walk or gallop on all fours, sniffing the air with their long, doglike muzzles, and carry their tails in an arch. They are social and travel in large troops of as many as 50. The strongest and most dominant males travel near the center of the troop, along with the infants and their mothers. The older juveniles are nearby in play groups. The young adults on the troop's periphery warn of danger. The dominant males are usually those with the largest canine teeth. They support each other in maintaining order within the troop; thus, fighting among wild baboons is rare. Baboons do, however, fight in captivity. The dominant males also defend the troop against such predators as cheetahs.

Baboons prefer to live on rocky plains or in hilly regions, although sometimes they are found in sparse forests. They usually feed during the day and sleep in trees at night. The usual diet includes scorpions, small animals, and plants.

Baboons breed year round. Gestation lasts 6 months. The infant is born black and changes to adult coloration 4 to 6 months later. Usually, one a year is born.

Babur, Mogul emperor of India [bah'-bur] Babur, b. Feb. 15, 1483, d. Dec. 26, 1530, was the

founder and first emperor of the Mogul dynasty in India. A direct descendant of Genghis Khan and Timur, he became king of the petty principality of Fergana in 1495 and captured Samarkand in 1497. After losing both kingdoms, he occupied Kabul in 1504 and established a kingdom in Afghanistan. In 1525, Babur invaded India. He defeated (1526) the Lodi sultan at Panipat and took Delhi, where he was declared king. During his brief reign Babur conquered northern India as far as Bengal, but he did not have time to establish a secure administration before his death and the succession of his son Humayun.

Babylon The ruins of Babylon (from Bab-ili, meaning "Gate of God"), the 2d–1st millennium BC capital of southern Mesopotamia (Babylonia), stand beside the Euphrates about 90 km (55 mi) south of modern Baghdad, Iraq. Occupied in prehistoric times but first mentioned in the late 3d millennium BC, the city became important when its Amorite king Hammurabi (r. 1792–1750 BC) gained control of all southern Mesopotamia. Raided by the Hittites about 1595 BC, Babylon then came under Kassite rule about 1570 BC, only to be sacked again about 1158 BC by the Elamites, who removed many Babylonian monuments to Susa, including the famous Law Code stela of Hammurabi (now in the Louvre). Dominated by Assyria from the 9th century BC until that country's fall to the Medes in 612 BC, Babylon once more became a major political power under the 6th-century Chaldean kings, in particular Nebuchadnezzar II (r. 605–562 BC). Surrendered to Cyrus the Great in 539 BC and possibly the intended capital of Alexander the Great, who died there in 323 BC, Babylon declined after the founding of Seleucia, the new Greek capital.

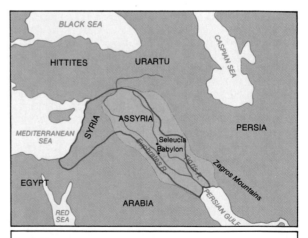

BABYLONIAN EMPIRE

Babylonian Empire *c.*1750 BC

Boundary of Neo-Babylonian (Chaldean) Empire *c.*600 BC

Nebuchadnezzar's triple-walled city measured at least 18 km (11 mi) in circumference. In the old city, on the east bank of the Euphrates, stood Esagila, the temple of Marduk, the city god, and the associated seven-staged ziggurat Etemenanki, popularly associated with the Tower of BABEL. Northward from Esagila, the Processional Way, decorated with animals in glazed and relief brickwork, led through the Ishtar Gate (now in the Pergamon Museum, Berlin) to the New Year (Akitu) temple. Northwest of the Processional Way stood Nebuchadnezzar's palace. Vaulted structures at its northwest corner may be remains of the legendary Hanging Gardens, numbered among the SEVEN WONDERS OF THE WORLD.

The site was first excavated in 1811, but the principal German investigations begun by Robert Koldewey took place from 1899 to 1917. The Iraq Department of Antiquities has carried out recent restoration work.

Babylonia   Babylonia was an ancient name for the lower Tigris-Euphrates valley in MESOPOTAMIA (now in Iraq). It was applied to an area beginning a little north of modern Baghdad and running in a southeasterly direction to the Persian Gulf. Babylonia took its name from its capital city, BABYLON, which first rose to prominence under the Amorite, or Old Babylonian, dynasty shortly after 1900 BC.

The AMORITES were a Semitic-speaking people who came down the Euphrates River from Syria and conquered the northern part of Babylonia (formerly called AKKAD). Under the sixth king of the dynasty, HAMMURABI (r. 1792–1750 BC), famous for his code of laws, all of Babylonia, including SUMER (the south), was united into a single state. The Amorites held sway until the coming (c.1550 BC) of the KASSITES, who established a regime that lasted to the 12th century. Then the Middle Babylonian kings restored native rule, which continued to about 1000 BC. Thereafter the country came under the domination of a succession of foreign masters, of whom the most important were from ASSYRIA. After exacting tribute from the Babylonians for many years, the Assyrian kings finally took (729) the title of king in Babylonia in addition to reigning separately as kings of Assyria. Eventually, a successful revolt against Assyria reestablished (626) Babylonian independence under the so-called CHALDEAN dynasty, the most notable of whose kings was NEBUCHADNEZZAR II (r. 605–562). Chaldean rule ended when the Persians under CYRUS THE GREAT captured Babylon in 539 BC. Henceforth, Babylonia was merely a province in a succession of large empires: Persian, Seleucid, Parthian, and Sassanian (539 BC–AD 650). Its capital was moved from Babylon to nearby SELEUCIA by the Seleucids; later, Ctesiphon was the administrative center of the Parthians and Sassanians.

See also: HAMMURABI, CODE OF; MESOPOTAMIA.

Babylonian Captivity   The Babylonian Captivity is the name given to the period between 586 and 538 BC

when the JEWS of the Kingdom of JUDAH lived in exile in Babylonia. After NEBUCHADNEZZAR II captured Jerusalem and destroyed the first temple in 586, he deported the Judeans to various Babylonian cities (Jer. 52:28–32). When CYRUS THE GREAT conquered Babylonia in 538, he permitted the Jews to return to their homeland.

baby's breath   Baby's breath is the common name for two species of flowering plants, *Gypsophila paniculata* (a perennial) and *G. elegans* (an annual), belonging to the PINK family, Caryophyllaceae. The plants reach heights of 60–90 cm (24–36 in), have lance-shaped leaves, and produce clouds of small, white—sometimes reddish or purplish—flowers. Native to Eurasia but now widespread, they are cultivated as border plants in gardens and for use in bouquets. Some species of bedstraw, *Galium*, are known as false baby's breath.

Bacall, Lauren   [buh-kawl']   Lauren Bacall is the stage name of Betty Joan Perske, b. New York City, Sept. 16, 1924, an actress who achieved overnight stardom with her first film, *To Have and Have Not* (1944). She married the film's star, Humphrey BOGART, in 1945 and appeared with him in *The Big Sleep* (1946) and *Key Largo* (1948). Among her other films are *The Shootist* (1976) and *Mr. North* (1988). She won Tony Awards for *Applause* (1970) and *Woman of the Year* (1981).

baccarat   [bah-kah-rah']   Baccarat is a card game played by a banker, or dealer, and as many as ten other participants. The role of banker is awarded in an auction to the highest bidder, who then finances the bank with the amount of the winning bid. The banker plays against the *table* in an order usually determined by the amount each player has bid.

Baccarat is played with at least three and as many as eight, but usually six, 52-card decks. They are shuffled together and are not reshuffled until the bank changes hands or until seven cards or fewer remain undealt.

The banker deals three hands of two cards each, face down, and one at a time—one to the left, one to the right, and one to himself or herself. The players, called *punters*, may then bet that either the left hand or the right hand, or both, will beat the banker.

Face cards and tens count 0, aces 1 each, and other cards their numerical value. When the total of one hand exceeds 10, the tens unit is dropped. For example, a 7 and a 6, totaling 13, count as 3. The aim of each player, including the dealer, is to be as close to 9 as possible. Each player is entitled to request one more card, dealt face up. The rules require that a player draw another card if his or her count is 4 or less and stand if the count is 6 or more; if the count is 5, the player may stand or draw. The banker is always free to stand or draw.

The banker is committed to pay off only to the amount of money in the bank at the moment of play and may not remove any of the bank's money except to pay losses. The banker may withdraw from play, however, after a deal has been completed and the bets settled. If the banker loses the entire bank or withdraws from the game, the bank is auctioned again and a new game started.

Once a highly popular game most often played for high stakes in the casinos of France, baccarat has never enjoyed favor in the United States and has been replaced worldwide by CHEMIN DE FER.

Bacchus

Bacchus [bak'-uhs] In Roman mythology, Bacchus was the god of wine and revelry. The Bacchanalia was a Roman festival celebrated in his honor—three days characterized by drunken orgies. The son of SEMELE and JUPITER, Bacchus was known to the Greeks as DIONYSUS. His wife was ARIADNE.

Bach, Carl Philipp Emanuel

Bach, Carl Philipp Emanuel [bahk] Known as the "Hamburg" or "Berlin" Bach, Carl Philipp Emanuel Bach, b. Mar. 8, 1714, d. Dec. 14, 1788, was one of the leading composers and keyboard players of the mid-18th century. The second surviving son of Johann Sebastian Bach, he studied law at the universities of Leipzig and Frankfurt on the Oder but received all his training in composition and keyboard from his father. In 1738 he visited the court of FREDERICK II of Prussia, and in 1740 he became his official harpsichordist in Berlin. Bach grew dissatisfied in Berlin and went to Hamburg in 1768 as the musical director for the principal churches of the city. He remained in Hamburg until his death.

Bach wrote much church and chamber music, but his most important compositions are the keyboard sonatas and fantasies written for his favorite instrument, the clavichord. These works were widely known and helped form the transition from the baroque style of his father to the classical style of Wolfgang Amadeus Mozart and Franz Josef Haydn. Like his symphonies, they are notable for their surprise effects and their exceptionally expressive character. His treatise on playing keyboard instruments is the most informative of its kind from the period.

Bach, Johann Christian

Bach, Johann Christian Called the "English" Bach, Johann Christian Bach, b. Sept. 5, 1735, d. Jan. 1, 1782, was a German preclassical composer who had a profound influence on English musical life. The youngest son of Johann Sebastian Bach, he studied in Berlin and Bologna and then moved to England in 1762. Two years later, Bach and Carl Friedrich Abel started the Bach-Abel concerts that lasted two decades and helped end England's musical isolation. Bach's sonatas, concertos, and symphonies were important in the evolution of these forms and influenced Haydn and Mozart.

Bach, Johann Sebastian

Bach, Johann Sebastian Johann Sebastian Bach, one of the greatest composers in Western musical history, created masterpieces of choral and instrumental music,

Johann Sebastian Bach, the great German composer and organ virtuoso, brought baroque music to its peak. Much of Bach's finest music was written for the church, including the St. Matthew Passion (1792) and the Mass in B-minor. His orchestral music includes the six Brandenburg Concertos.

both sacred and secular. Bach was born in Eisenach, Germany, on Mar. 21, 1685, into a family of musicians. His parents died when he was nine years old, and in 1695 he went to live with his brother Johann Christoph, who was an organist at Ohrdruf. He remained there until 1700, learning the fundamentals of the keyboard from his brother and studying composition on his own, using works of older composers as models.

In 1703 he took an orchestral post in Weimar and after six months was appointed organist at the Neukirche in Arnstadt, where he composed his earliest surviving organ works. In 1705 he went to Lübeck (he traveled the 320 km/200 mi, reportedly, on foot) to hear Dietrich Buxtehude, one of the great northern German organist-composers. His Arnstadt tenure lasted two more years and was marked by clashes with the authorities about the scope of his duties. Such difficulties with his employers were constantly to mar his career.

In 1707, Bach married his first cousin Maria Barbara and was appointed organist in Mühlhausen. Almost immediately, the congregation objected to the innovative harmonized music he was introducing, and by the end of the year he moved back to Weimar, where he served as court organist for nine years. When he was not granted the position of music director (*Kapellmeister*) he had hoped for, he sought a post elsewhere. When he found one, at Cöthen, in 1717, he asked for release from his duties at Weimar in a manner so antagonistic that he was imprisoned for a month.

Bach remained at Cöthen until 1723. After the death of his first wife, he married (1721) Anna Magdalena Wilcken. In all he fathered 20 children, of whom several—including Wilhelm Friedemann, Carl Philipp Emanuel, and Johann Christian—became well-known composers. Because his patron at Cöthen, Prince Leopold, enjoyed music, Bach composed both secular and sacred works.

After the prince married, however, music played a less important role in court life, and again Bach sought employment elsewhere.

He found it in Leipzig, where in 1723 he was appointed choir leader and *Kapellmeister* of Saint Thomas Church—a prestigious post that made Bach, in effect, the director of music for the entire city. He remained in Leipzig for the rest of his life and wrote many of his greatest works there. Bach died in Leipzig on July 28, 1750.

Music. Bach's duties required his writing compositions of many kinds organ and choral music for the church, chamber music for court use, and fairly straightforward harpsichord works for teaching the instrument. These compositions make up the bulk of his output. In addition, there are difficult solo works composed either for his own use or for that of friends, and there are also works that are clearly theoretical exercises, such as the Mass in B-minor and the *Art of Fugue*.

One considerable body of Bach's music is his cantata series, of which more than 200 survive. (It is believed that over half of his secular cantatas and more than a third of his sacred ones have been lost.) The secular cantatas, by far the smaller of the two groups, were composed for public and private festivities and use allegorical or mythological texts. Most of the sacred cantatas were composed as parts of cycles, with a specific work intended for each Sunday in the year. Bach is believed to have also composed five Passion settings, although only the *St. John* and *St. Matthew* Passions survive. Also prominent among his sacred works are the Easter and Christmas oratorios, the motets, and the Mass in B-minor.

The sacred works show one side of Bach—that of a composer working in, and responding to, the Lutheran tradition. Another side, that of the keyboard virtuoso, is seen in his organ and harpsichord works. The organ works run the gamut from fairly simple chorale settings to ornate fantasias, toccatas, fugues, and sonatas. Among the harpsichord works, the *Goldberg Variations* and the two books of *The Well-Tempered Clavier* remain at the peak of music for the keyboard.

Bach's command of other instruments and their resources is evident in the six cello suites, the six violin sonatas and partitas, the four lute suites, and the accompanied sonatas for flute, violin, viola, and viola da gamba (now usually played on the cello). For chamber orchestra, he composed four extended suites, as well as the six *Brandenburg Concertos*, and concertos for harpsichord, violin, and oboe.

Significance. At the start of his career, Bach built a distinctive style on the foundations laid by Buxtehude and others of the north German school. Later in his life, as musical fashion moved toward the elegant simplicity of the *stil galant* (the basis of the classical style, of which his son, Johann Christian, was a pioneer), Bach came to be regarded as a musical arch-conservative.

In the last decade of his life he composed works of great complexity using the musical techniques that most interested him. An example is his final work, the *Art of Fugue*. Begun during the 1740s but left incomplete at his death, this compilation is a thorough examination of a sublime musical form by a master who knew that the form was falling out of fashion.

Counterpoint, or the interplay of independent musical strands, is certainly one of the salient features of Bach's work. Yet Bach's appeal lies in the more human qualities his music embodies. Combined with its cerebral aspects are exquisite melodies and complex figuration, and a sense of passion that comes through both in his text settings and in his instrumental works.

Bach, Wilhelm Friedemann   Wilhelm Friedemann Bach, b. Nov. 22, 1710, d. July 1, 1784, was a German virtuoso organist and composer whose compositions, although showing bursts of genius, never fulfilled his early promise. Called the "Halle" Bach, he was the eldest son of Johann Sebastian BACH, who considered Friedemann his most talented son and wrote the instructional *Clavier-Büchlein* for him. After holding organist posts in Dresden (1733–47) and Halle (from 1746 until his dismissal in 1764 for "irregular" behavior), Bach moved in 1770 to Berlin, where he subsisted on recitals, lessons, and charity.

Bacharach, Burt [bak'-rak]   Burt Bacharach, b. Kansas City, Mo., May 12, 1929, is a popular American songwriter. Teamed with lyricist Hal David from 1957, he has written many songs with uncommonly sophisticated harmony and structure, including such hits as "Walk on By" (1964) and "I'll Never Fall in Love Again" (1969) for the pop-soul singer Dionne Warwick. His Academy Award–winning "Raindrops Keep Falling on My Head" (1969) sold 3 million records. Bacharach's stage and film scores include *Promises, Promises* (1969) and *Butch Cassidy and the Sundance Kid* (1969).

---

bachelor's button   Bachelor's button is another common name for the cornflower, *Centaurea cyanus*. The name "yellow bachelor's button" is sometimes applied to a MILKWORT, *Polygala lutea*, also known as candyweed; a biennial of the eastern United States, it grows to about 30 cm (12 in) high. The leaves form a rosette, and the orange yellow flowers develop in racemes.

Bacher, Robert Fox [bak'-ur]   The American physicist Robert Fox Bacher, b. Loudonville, Ohio, Aug. 31, 1905, played a major role in the development of nuclear technology. At Los Alamos, N.Mex., on July 12, 1945, he assembled the first atomic bomb, with his own hands, in an old ranch house. President Harry S Truman awarded him the Medal of Merit and named him a commissioner of the Atomic Energy Commission in 1946. Bacher chaired the physical science division at the California Institute of Technology until 1962 and then served as provost until 1970.

Bacillus   see BACTERIA

bacitracin   SEE ANTIBIOTICS

---

backgammon   Backgammon is a two-person game played on a square or rectangular board that is divided into two equal halves by the *bar*. For purposes of play, one side is called the *inner table*; the other side is the *outer table*.

Projecting toward the center from the edge of each side of the board are 12 elongated triangles called *points*. Each player has a set of 15 pieces, called *men, stones,* or *counters*. The sets are made of contrasting colors, most frequently black and white or red and white. All 30 pieces are placed on the points at the start of the game, in the manner shown here.

The equipment also includes two dice cups, four dice, and a *doubling cube*, whose six faces bear the numbers 2, 4, 8, 16, 32, and 64. This is used to double bets when gambling.

Rules. The object of the game is to be the first to move all 15 men into the inner table and then *bear them off*, that is, remove them from the board. Play commences with each player throwing a single die. Whoever rolls the higher number moves first by playing the numbers on both dice. After that, each player in turn rolls two dice, each of which is counted separately and used to move one or two men, as strategy dictates. Whenever two or more men belong to the same player on a single point, they are safe from attack, and the opposing men may not even stop on such a point, regardless of what numbers a roll of the dice produces.

When a point is occupied by a single man (a *blot*), and an opponent's man can land on that point, the blot is removed from the point, placed on the bar, and made to start over. At this juncture, the player with the man on the bar cannot make another move until that man is able to enter the table, and if the count corresponding to the roll of the dice should block this entrance, the player loses that turn.

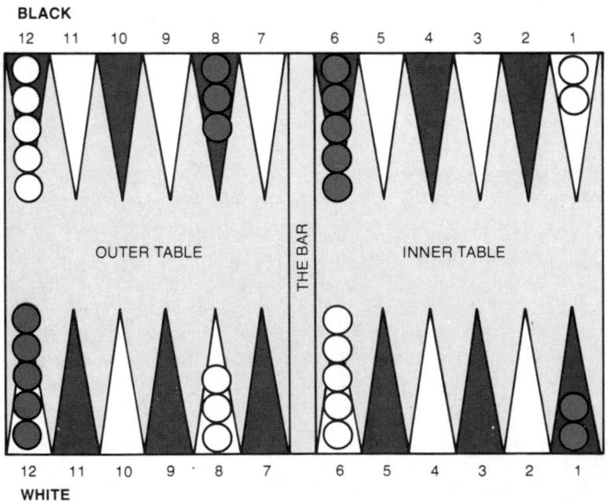

BLACK

OUTER TABLE   THE BAR   INNER TABLE

WHITE

History. Backgammon is thought to be about 5,000 years old, and a reference to the game appears in Plato's writings. Popular in France and England from the 1600s, the game was described by Edmond Hoyle in 1743. With the formulation (1931) of the current set of rules by Wheaton Vaughan and others, the game's U.S. popularity blossomed in the 1930s.

---

background radiation   Background radiation is a low-temperature radiation that pervades the universe at microwave wavelengths. Its source is believed to have been the extremely hot fireball with which the universe began, according to the BIG BANG THEORY. The existence of cosmic background radiation was first predicted in 1948 when Hans BETHE, George GAMOW, and R. A. Alpher proposed a theory of the origin of the elements based on Einstein's theory of general relativity. According to this proposal, the elements were formed under the conditions of extremely high temperature that prevailed in the initial moments of the universe. As the universe expanded and cooled, the radiation field corresponding to the initial high-temperature state decayed in a corresponding manner. Using the data available at that time, Alpher, Bethe, and Gamow calculated that the universal radiation temperature should now be about 25 K, but the radiation could not be detected.

In 1964, during the course of measurements made for another purpose, Arno A. Penzias and Robert W. WILSON of Bell Telephone Laboratories discovered the existence of a uniform background radiation at a temperature about 3.5 K. This was identified as the radiation field predicted earlier. The discovery was soon confirmed by R. H. Dicke and associates at Princeton University. Today the more accurately determined temperature is 2.7 ± 0.2 K. The radiation's spectrum is not entirely uniform.

The discovery of the background radiation supported the singular origin of the universe as expressed in the big bang theory and demonstrated the correctness of the application of Einstein's theory of general relativity to cosmology. The background radiation serves as an effective standard rest frame with which to compare motion in the universe.

See also: COSMOLOGY; INTERSTELLAR MATTER.

Backhaus, Wilhelm [bahk'-hows]   The German pianist Wilhelm Backhaus, b. Mar. 26, 1884, d. July 5, 1969, was renowned for his interpretations of Beethoven and Brahms. After studies in Leipzig and in Frankfurt am Main, the latter under Eugen d'Albert, he began (1900) his career as a concert artist. He taught in London (1905), where he won the Rubinstein piano prize, Sondershausen, Germany (1907), and at the Curtis Institute in Philadelphia (1925–26). His performances were noted for their clarity, force, lack of obtrusive mannerisms, and faithfulness to the scores. He made many recordings, including a notable set of the complete Beethoven piano sonatas.

backswimmer   The backswimmer is any of several aquatic insects that constitute the family Notonectidae, order HEMIPTERA. These insects swim rapidly upside down, using the hind legs as oars.

Backswimmers are predators of other insects, crustaceans, snails, tadpoles, and small fish, sucking out their body juices, and can inflict a painful wound when handled by humans.

bacon   Bacon is the meat product resulting from the curing and smoking of pork. In the United States, about 750 million kg (1.65 billion lb) of bacon annually is produced from pork bellies; Canadian bacon is made from pork loin, and in Europe the ham and shoulder are used.

The ingredients most often used to cure bacon are salt, sugar, sodium nitrite, sodium erythrobate, and the sodium phosphates. These ingredients may be rubbed into the meat or dissolved in water to make a pickling brine. The bellies are then placed in a smokehouse, at temperatures of 54.5° to 60° C (130° to 140° F) and humidities of 25 to 45 percent. The time required for cooking and smoking is from 2 to 10 days, depending on the size of the bellies, the internal temperature desired, and air velocity.

Home-cured bacon is made by rubbing a salt and spice mixture into the meat, or by soaking the meat in brine and then hanging it in woodsmoke. Curing takes up to 4 months.

Bacon, Francis   (painter) Francis Bacon, b. Oct. 28, 1909, is considered by many critics to be the outstanding British painter of the second half of the 20th century. Bacon's subjects—nightmarish distortions of businessmen, ecclesiastics, friends, and animals, all set in ominously confined spaces—seem to be reactions to the calamities of modern civilization, although the artist has avoided clarification of their meaning.

Bacon's painting, in both technique and subject matter, is based largely on works of the old masters. Two famous paintings—*Pope Innocent X* by Diego Velázquez and *Butchered Ox* by Rembrandt—are the sources for Bacon's startling "pope" series, in which an enthroned pontiff, mouth often agape in a shriek, is trapped within the icy perspectives of a glass cage. In *Head Surrounded by Sides of Beef* (1954; The Art Institute of Chicago), the screaming figure is flanked by the split carcass of an ox.

Bacon's subsequent works, many of them triptychs of grotesque male forms writhing across the panels, reveal such disparate influences as Vincent van Gogh and Eadweard Muybridge's photographic motion studies.

Bacon, Francis   (philosopher) Francis Bacon, b. Jan. 22, 1561, d. Apr. 9, 1626, was an English essayist, lawyer, statesman, and philosopher who had a major influence on the philosophy of science. He was first elected to Parliament in 1584. Knighted (1603) after the succes-

sion of JAMES I, Bacon became solicitor-general (1609), attorney-general (1613), lord keeper of the great seal (1617), and lord chancellor (1618); he was also created Baron Verulam (1618), and Viscount St. Albans (1621). Bacon retained James's favor by steadfast defense of royal prerogative, but in 1621 he was found guilty of accepting bribes and was removed from his offices.

Bacon planned a large work, the *Instauratio Magna* (Great Restoration), setting forth his concepts for the restoration of humankind to mastery over nature. It was intended to contain six parts: (1) a classification of sciences; (2) a new inductive logic; (3) a gathering of empirical and experimental facts; (4) examples to show the efficacy of his new approach; (5) generalizations derivable from natural history; and (6) a new philosophy that would be a complete science of nature. Bacon completed only two parts, however: *The Advancement of Learning* (1605), later expanded as *De Dignitate et Augmentis Scientiarum* (On the Dignity and Growth of Sciences, 1623); and the *Novum Organum* (*The New Organon*, 1620), which was to replace Aristotle's *Organon*. Their culmination was an inductive philosophy of nature, in which Bacon proposed to find the "forms," or natural laws, of bodily action. To this end, he devised so-called tables of induction (of

Francis Bacon's Study of Valázquez's Portrait of Innocent X *(1953) transforms the stately image of the 17th-century pope into a symbol of isolation, separation, and entrapment. (Marlborough Gallery, London.)*

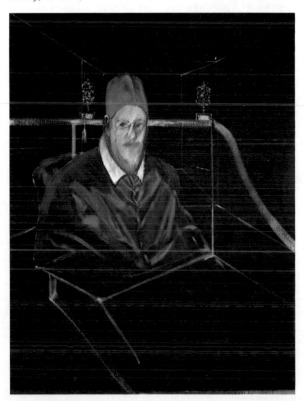

Francis Bacon held high political offices under James I of England but is best known for his philosophical writings. He influenced scientists to rely on knowledge gained through methodical observation rather than on theory.

Honble Francisc.^s Bacon.^s Baro de Very; tam Vice-Comes S.^{ti} Albani mortuus 9 Aprilis. Anno Dni. 1626. Annoq, Aetat 66.

presence, absence, and degrees) designed to discover such forms with the goal of mastery over nature.

Although Bacon was not a great scientist, he gave impetus to the development of modern inductive science. His works were held in esteem by Robert BOYLE, Robert HOOKE, Sir Isaac NEWTON, and Thomas HOBBES. In the 18th century VOLTAIRE and DIDEROT considered him the father of modern science. Other works of Bacon's include his *Essays* (1597–1625) and *The New Atlantis* (1627).

Bacon, Roger   Because of his emphasis on the importance of mathematics and experimentation, the English scholastic philosopher Roger Bacon, *c.*1220–92, is often considered an early advocate of the methods of modern science. He received much of his university training in Paris, where he taught philosophy from about 1240 to 1247; after that he went to Oxford, where he was influenced by the ideas of Robert GROSSETESTE. About 1257, Bacon became a Franciscan friar, and his outspokenness and unorthodox opinions involved him in frequent difficulties with the superiors of his order.

In 1267–68, at the request of Pope Clement IV, Bacon prepared three works, the *Opus maius, Opus minus,* and *Opus tertium,* in which he outlined proposals for a reform of education, arguing that a study of the natural world using observation and exact measurement was the surest foundation for a knowledge of the world's creator. In place of the curriculum followed in medieval universities, he recommended the study of languages, mathematics, alchemy, and experimental sciences—especially optics. In later works, the *Compendium of the Study of Philosophy* (1272) and *Compendium of the Study of Theology* (1292), he harshly criticized the philosophical and theological methods of his day.

Bacon's Rebellion   Bacon's Rebellion was a short-lived revolt in colonial Virginia. It began in May 1676 when Nathaniel Bacon (1647–76), a young, well-placed Virginian, led a small army of his fellow colonists in combat against both the royal governor, Sir William BERKELEY, and the Indians on the frontier. The participants in the rebellion were motivated by a variety of concerns. Some resented Berkeley's growing personal power, others were anxious to strengthen the popular voice in the political process, and nearly all were opposed to the governor's Indian policy, which threatened to restrict their expansion into western lands occupied by Indians.

Bacon and his men enjoyed some initial success. In June 1676 an assembly dominated by Bacon's supporters passed laws extending the rights of freemen and restricting still further the rights of Indians. Bacon died of swamp fever, however, in October 1676, and by January 1677, Berkeley was once again in control of the colony.

bacteria   Bacteria is the common name for a vast group of one-celled microscopic organisms that encompasses the smallest, simplest, and perhaps first form of CELL life that evolved. They constitute one of two divisions in the kingdom MONERA. Bacteria furnish both the raw material and the chemical machinery for their own reproduction, whereas viruses, for example, do not. The oldest sign of life is a fossilized bacterial cell discovered in a rock in Africa and estimated at about 3.5 billion years old. The study of bacteria is called bacteriology, which belongs to the broader science of MICROBIOLOGY, or the study of all types of microorganisms, including one-celled protozoans, yeasts, and algae. Medical microbiology is concerned with the behavior and control of pathogens, which are microorganisms that cause infectious DISEASES in humans and other animals.

Size and Habitat

Thirty trillion bacteria of average size weigh about 28 g (1 oz). Bacteria are measured in microns (0.001 μm, about 0.00004 in) and most types range from 0.1 to 4.0 microns in width and 0.2 to 50 microns in length. Bacteria are found everywhere. Approximately 2,000 species have been identified, many of them living in conditions that would destroy other organisms. They have been found in the almost airless reaches of the upper atmosphere, 10 km (6 mi) below the surface of the ocean, in frozen soil, and on rocks in hot springs. Some bacteria produce a resting stage, the endospore, which is the most resistant living thing known and can be killed only by boiling in steam under pressure for many hours.

Classification

Bacteria are neither plant nor animal. Both bacteria and plants have rigid cell walls, but unlike plants, most kinds of bacteria move about and use organic foods for energy and growth; only a few use photosynthesis.

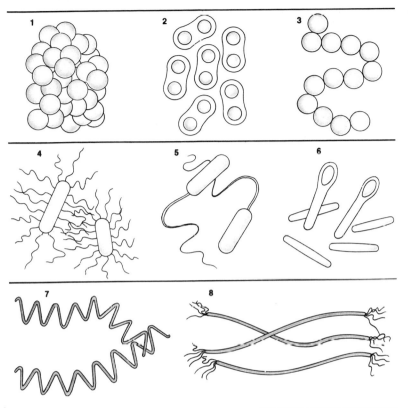

Bacteria are arranged into three basic cell shapes: coccus, or spherical (top); bacillus, or cylindrical (center); and spirillum, or spiral (bottom). Bacteria of the genus Staphylococcus (1) are arranged in clusters. Diplococcus species (2) generally consist of two spheres encased in a membrane, and Streptococcus species (3) form chains. Most cocci are unable to move independently because they lack flagella, which are whiplike appendages.

Most bacilli are freely mobile because they have flagella to propel them through water by a beating motion. Some species have flagella distributed around the body (4) and others have a single flagellum (5). Bacilli form spores (6) that are resistant to heat, lack of water, and toxic chemicals. Each spore germinates and forms new bacilli.

Spirilla may be tightly coiled into an accordion shape, such as Leptospira (7), which is a genus of pathogenic spirochetes. Spirillum species (8) curve in a fairly loose to moderately tight helix. Unlike spirochetes, which are flexible, Spirillum species are rigid and need flagella in order to move. Other spirilla are regularly or irregularly coiled.

On the basis of their shapes, bacteria may be grouped into three main types: the rod-shaped bacilli, which often have small whiplike structures known as FLAGELLA that propel the organism; the spherical cocci (singular coccus), which may grow in chains (STREPTOCOCCI, or "strep germs," as in STREP THROAT) or which may clump together like a bunch of grapes (STAPHYLOCOCCI); and the comma- or spiral-shaped spirilla and SPIROCHETES (one of which is the cause of SYPHILIS). Another kind of bacteria, the mycoplasmas, have no rigid cell walls and consequently are formless. These are the smallest bacteria and are often called pleuropneumonialike organisms, because they cause a contagious pneumonia in cows and human beings (see MYCOPLASMAL PNEUMONIA).

An important, widely used technique for identifying bacteria is gram staining, perfected by the Danish bacteriologist Hans Christian Gram in 1884. In this process the bacteria are treated with a special dye, or stain, and other chemicals. The treated bacteria fall into two groups: gram-positive bacteria, which appear deep violet in color, and gram-negative bacteria, which appear red in color. Physicians often use gram staining in choosing the proper ANTIBIOTIC for treating a bacterial infection. Gram-positive bacteria are more susceptible to penicillin, whereas gram-negative bacteria are usually more susceptible to other antibiotics such as streptomycin. The basis of this difference in staining properties is still a mystery, but evidence indicates that the difference lies in the composition of the bacterial cell wall.

Although bacterial and plant cells are enclosed by rigid walls, the walls differ in composition. Plant cell walls derive their strength largely from cellulose, whereas bacterial cell walls are stiffened primarily by murein (a compound made of amino acids and sugar). This is the basis for the selective activity of certain drugs such as penicillin. Nontoxic to plants and animals, penicillin is toxic to growing bacteria because it inhibits formation of murein and thus interferes with reproduction.

Physiology

The only organisms comparable to bacteria in size and simplicity are the cyanobacteria, still often known as the BLUE-GREEN ALGAE, Cyanophyta. The kingdom Monera is composed of only these two groups. All other forms of cellular life, including human beings, are eukaryotic, that is, their cells contain organelles such as the nucleus, chloroplast, chromoplast, lysosome, mitochondrion, and Golgi apparatus. Cells of monerans are prokaryotic (prenuclear) and lack organelles but not the functions controlled by them.

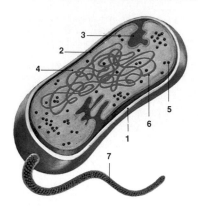

A simplified bacterium has a tough cell wall (1) and a semipermeable membrane (2). A mesosome (3) is an invagination of the membrane into the cytoplasm (4). The cytoplasm contains small bodies such as ribosomes (5), which have the RNA that synthesizes proteins. Bacterial DNA (6) is circular and 1,000 times longer than the cell. Many bacteria have flagella (7).

In terms of metabolism, the diversity of life is much more evident in bacteria (and blue-green algae) than in other organisms. Bacteria display a staggering variety of mechanisms for obtaining energy that have no parallel in higher organisms.

Bacteria may be classified on the basis of their requirements for free atmospheric oxygen. Those requiring oxygen are aerobes; those which cannot live in the presence of oxygen are obligate ANAEROBES; and those which do well with oxygen but can survive without it are facultative anaerobes. Many photosynthetic bacteria are anaerobic. The sulfur bacteria that live in oxygen-poor environments produce sulfur instead of the oxygen gas given off by green plants. Anaerobes obtain sufficient energy for their needs through FERMENTATION (breaking down organic molecules with enzymes). Other bacteria are chemosynthetic; unlike photosynthetic bacteria, which use light as an energy source, they use nitrogen- and sulfur-containing compounds to obtain the necessary energy for food manufacture.

Reproduction

Most bacteria reproduce asexually by binary fission (see REPRODUCTION), in which a single cell divides in two. Many species divide as often as every 20 minutes under favorable conditions. If all the descendants survived, the initial cell would result in about 500,000 new cells after 6 hours. Such rapid increases help to explain the rapid development of disease, food spoilage, decay, and the speed at which certain chemical processes used in industry take place.

Certain bacteria such as *E. coli* reproduce by conjugation, which resembles sexual reproduction in that two bacteria join (mate) and exchange genes. As in true sexual reproduction, the genetic material, or "nuclear" chromosomes, recombine with one another (see GENETICS). In the process of recombination, a fragment of a chromosome transmitted from one bacterium is incorporated in the chromosome of the recipient. Conjugation and recombination increase the total number of different hereditary characteristics in a population of bacteria, increasing the bacteria's chances of survival.

Economic Importance

Most important bacteria are harmless to humans, and many are essential to the existence of plant and animal life. Only a small fraction of bacteria cause disease; most bacteria attack organic matter only after it is dead. Were it not for bacteria that decompose animal waste matter and the bodies of dead animals and plants, these materials would accumulate almost indefinitely. Bacteria also enrich the soil in various ways. The so-called nitrogen-fixing bacteria take nitrogen gas from the atmosphere and convert it to a form (nitrate) that green plants use for growth (see NITROGEN CYCLE). Bacteria also create FERTILIZER by breaking down compost heaps made of soil and dead plant matter.

Bacteria are important industrially in the production of cheese, yogurt, buttermilk, vinegar, and sauerkraut; in the preparation of antibiotics such as streptomycin, which is extracted from soil bacteria; in the tanning of leather and hides and the curing of tobacco; and in sewage disposal plants to render organic wastes harmless. Cattle, sheep, and goats live on grass; yet without bacteria they would not be able to digest the tough fibers of plant cellulose.

Improperly processed foods are subject to spoilage by bacteria. Poisonous toxins are sometimes produced by such food-spoiling bacteria as Staphylococci, Streptococci, and SALMONELLA. They cause severe illness in humans eating affected food. *Clostridium botulinum*, growing in canned or smoked foods that have been improperly processed, produces a toxin that causes BOTULISM, a frequently fatal disease.

Destruction of Bacteria

High temperature usually kills most bacteria. Most disease-producing bacteria in milk, for example, can be killed by maintaining the temperature at 62° C (143° F) for 30 minutes, a process called PASTEURIZATION. "Flash pasteurization," done at 71° C (160° F) for 15 seconds, is now commonly used. Most nonspore-forming bacteria are destroyed by boiling water and can be killed by various disinfectants. ANTISEPTICS may kill bacteria or prevent infection by inhibiting their growth. Among the most potent disinfectants are phenol (carbolic acid), chlorine gas, and alcohol in a 50- to 70-percent solution, as in rubbing alcohol. Certain mercury-containing compounds are often used as disinfectants and antiseptics.

The above chemicals are poisonous in the human body and should not be taken internally. Antibiotics, however, are substances produced by living organisms (usually bacteria and MOLDS) that are used internally for inhibiting the growth of bacteria or destroying them; antimicrobial agents are natural or artificial chemicals having the same use.

Bacteria and Disease

A century ago in the United States, and even today in the less developed countries, at least 25 percent of the children died of bacterial infections before reaching puberty. In the United States and other Western nations, this figure is now below 5 percent as a result of improved sanitation, hygiene, nutrition, and medical care. The control

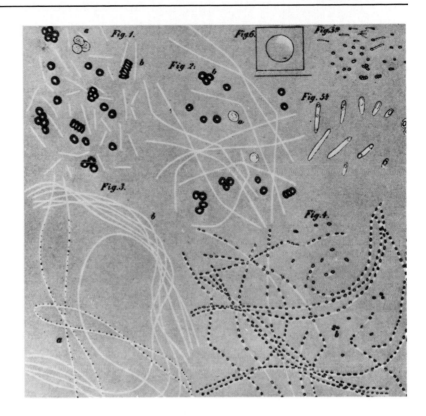

(Above) *Robert Koch, a German bacteriologist, received the 1905 Nobel Prize for his discovery of and research into the bacilli that cause tuberculosis. He also isolated the bacteria responsible for anthrax and cholera.* (Right) *The life cycle of anthrax bacilli as sketched by Koch: New bacilli (1a) are found among red blood cells. These immature bacteria (2a) grow and develop elongated cell bodies (3a). Mature, rod-shaped bacilli (3b) develop spores that form chains (4) when released from the parent bacilli. Eventually the chains break apart so individual spores can develop new bacilli.*

of TYPHOID FEVER alone is perhaps the greatest triumph of organized preventive medicine. As late as 1900 the annual death rate from typhoid fever in the United States was more than 30 per 100,000; by 1944 the rate had decreased to 0.4 per 100,000. For the world as a whole, however, typhoid fever remains a major disease.

History. To account for the spread of certain diseases, thoughtful people since ancient times postulated the existence of transmissible agents of infection invisible to the naked eye. In 1546 the Italian physician Girolamo Fracastoro proposed the germ theory of disease, describing the transmission of disease by "seminaria," or living germs. Visualization of germs could not take place until the microscope had been invented, however. Bacteria and other microscopic organisms were first seen in 1676 by a Dutch linen-draper, Antoni van LEEUWENHOEK, who made single-lens microscopes with sufficient magnification to observe the major types of bacteria as well as protozoans, yeasts, and one-celled algae. Leeuwenhoek is regarded as the father of bacteriology.

The first important classification of bacteria was made in the early 1800s. In 1829, Christian Gottfried established the genus *Bacterium*, using a term formed from the Greek word *bacterion*, signifying a rod. The entire subject of bacteriology has taken its common name from the prominence of rodlike forms of bacteria, now called bacilli. Eventually, bacteria were classified as plants; this remained the dominant view until the 1960s. Bacteria are now classified as Monerans.

An experimental science of bacteriology emerged slowly and required the development of special methodology. The key was the use of sterile (germ-free) materials and antiseptic techniques; a single contaminating cell can ruin an experiment in bacteriology. Only after learning to avoid such contamination could investigators recognize the existing variety of bacteria, their distribution, and their major roles.

Bacteria in Disease. In the 1840s, Ignaz Philip Semmelweiss, a Hungarian obstetrician, tried to convince disbelieving colleagues that the disease that swept through maternity wards and killed hundreds of women each year could be prevented. Childbed fever (puerperal sepsis) was caused by a Streptococcus spread by medical students going from the dissecting room to the patients without first washing. Semmelweiss had the students on his wards wash their hands in disinfectant before each delivery. This precaution greatly reduced the amount of infection and the number of deaths. Nonetheless, he was discredited by his colleagues.

The role of bacteria in a disease was first proved (1876) by the German bacteriologist Robert KOCH for ANTHRAX and was confirmed by Louis PASTEUR. Koch meticulously developed the techniques that are used today in culturing bacteria for study and set down rules still used for proving that a given infection is caused by particular bacteria. These rules are called Koch's postulates and may be summarized as follows: The bacteria must be present in the infected tissue in every case of the infec-

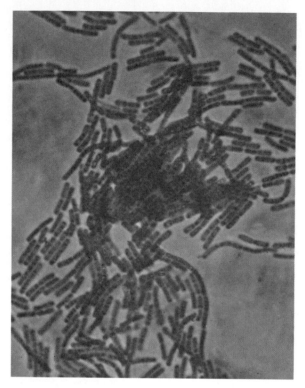

Anthrax bacilli infect the blood and skin of such animals as sheep, pigs, and cattle. Humans who sort wool or handle skins may contract anthrax, but sanitation and vaccination have prevented epidemics in the 20th century.

Plasmids. Many bacteria contain PLASMIDS, which are tiny pieces of DNA that are much smaller than and independent of chromosomal DNA and generally carry nonessential bacterial genes. First observed in *E. coli*, some plasmids carry traits such as resistance to antibiotics. How they acquire their extra DNA controlling resistance and virulence is not known, although many authorities believe that overuse of antibiotics is the main cause.

In GENETIC ENGINEERING, plasmids are isolated, opened up for insertion of pieces of DNA from other sources, and then resealed; this hybrid DNA is called recombinant DNA. The new plasmid is placed into a receptor cell, "infecting" it as if it were a virus. The inserted genes then express themselves along with the normal genetic complement of the cell. A bacterium may be programmed in this way to produce a useful substance; human insulin, for example, is produced when human genes controlling insulin production are placed into a plasmid and then inserted into a bacterium.

Transduction. Bacteria also exchange chromosomal material through transduction, which occurs when bacteria are infected by viruses called bacteriophages. Transduction involves the accidental transfer of bacterial genes between bacterial cells by a bacteriophage and the incorporation of these genes into the recipient bacterium. This transfer requires that the bacteriophage infect a bacterial strain that is destroyed by the virus and that the recipient strain of bacteria be the one that harbors the virus but is not usually destroyed by it. This alternation between destruction of bacterial cells by a bacteriophage and harboring the virus with no sign of infection is called lysogeny.

Bacteria in Modern Biology

Until the 1950s bacteriology was concerned almost solely with pathogenic bacteria. Eventually, however, bacteria were found particularly suitable for studying many basic problems common to all cells, such as metabolism, molecular aspects of genetics, and proteins synthesis. These studies revealed many instances of a resemblance between microbial cells and cells of higher organisms, in their building blocks, enzymes, and metabolic pathways. The advantages of bacteria for such studies include their relatively simple structure; homogenous cell populations (each cell is exactly like the others); extremely rapid growth; and the ease with which billions of individual cells can be cultivated and selected to yield mutants. Mutants obtained in this way have permitted scientists to identify the role of various genes and protein molecules in cell actions as well as reasons for bacterial resistance to antibiotics. These developments have led to an interdisciplinary activity known as molecular biology or biochemical genetics.

bacteriology   see MICROBIOLOGY

Bactria [bak'-tree-uh]   Bactria was an ancient land on both sides of the upper Oxus River, today called the Amu Darya, in present-day northern Afghanistan and the southern Tadzhik republic. The heart of Bactria was the

tion; they must be isolated in pure culture on an artificial medium; inoculation of this culture into experimental animals must cause a similar disease; and the organisms must be recovered from the infected tissue. About ten years before Koch isolated anthrax, Joseph LISTER virtually eliminated wound infections by soaking bandages in carbolic acid. This was the start of modern aseptic surgical techniques.

Following Koch's initial discovery, medical scientists raced to identify other pathogens. Pasteur, however, devoted himself to developing vaccines, which are materials made from specially treated organisms and inoculated into humans and other animals to develop immunity to a specific infectious disease. Studies of the response of the body's defense mechanisms to bacteria later gave rise to the field of immunology.

It is now known that bacteria are transmitted by air, insects, water, food, and direct contact with human beings, animals, and objects. Not all bacteria associated with human beings cause disease. A natural flora exists in the body, and the *E. coli* of the large intestine help to control the body's water balance and to provide certain vitamins. Their presence in drinking water may be taken as a measure of contamination, however, suggesting that pathogens may be present.

plain south of the river and its principal city, Bactra (the present-day Balkh). The northern and southern tributaries of the Oxus made the valleys of Bactria leading to the alluvial plain rich centers of agriculture, but Bactria was more important for its strategic location between China, India, and the West. The prophet Zoroaster is said to have made his first converts in Bactria and to have died there. Bactria became an important province of the ACHAEMENID Empire, and after the conquests of ALEXANDER THE GREAT it became the center of an independent Greek kingdom whose rulers struck fine Greek coins. The kingdom lasted until 128 BC, when northern nomads overran it. Bactria then became part of the Kushan empire and remained so until the 4th century AD, when Sassanian governors became its rulers. The nomadic Hephthalites (White Huns) took control in the following century, ruling until the Arab conquest at the end of the 7th century.

Badajoz [bah-thah-hohs'] Badajoz is the capital of Badajoz province in southwestern Spain, at the Portuguese border on the southern bank of the Guadiana River. Its population is 120,240 (1987 est.). The city is Spain's chief center of trade with Portugal and serves as the market center for the surrounding agricultural region.

Badajoz was settled by the Romans, who built (late 1st century BC) a fortress later occupied (AD 1010–1229) by Moors. The city is still surrounded by walls; also remaining are a Roman bridge, ruins of a Moorish castle, and a cathedral that houses paintings by Luís de Morales, a native of Badajoz. The city was the scene of a massacre after its surrender to General Franco's forces in 1936.

Badalona [bahd-uh-loh'-nuh] Badalona (1987 est. pop., 224,233) is an industrial suburb and port in northeastern Spain, on the Mediterranean coast about 8 km (5 mi) north of Barcelona. Badalona is one of the country's most important and diversified industrial centers, producing metals, textiles, glassware, and petroleum products. As Baetulo, it was important during Roman times.

The American badger is a solitary, fierce animal that hibernates in winter. It is the only New World species of badger.

Baden [bah'-den] Baden is a former state in the extreme southwest of Germany. In 1952 it was combined with two other states to form Baden-Württemberg, one of the ten *länder* (states) of West Germany (see WÜRTTEMBERG). The region's physical relief is dominated by the Rhine River valley in the west and the BLACK FOREST to the south. Baden's historic capital is KARLSRUHE; other important cities include FREIBURG IM BREISGAU, HEIDELBERG, MANNHEIM, and Konstanz.

Baden became a political entity in 1112 when a member of the Zähringen family, Hermann, grandson of Bertold, duke of Carinthia, took the title of margrave of Baden. For the next 600 years, however, the region was divided into numerous petty states, and it suffered particularly from religious rivalries following the Reformation. In 1771, Baden was reunited under the house of Zähringen (combining the margraviates of Baden-Baden and Baden-Durlach). Charles Frederick of Baden allied (1796) himself with Napoléon Bonaparte. In 1806, Baden, with expanded territory, became a duchy in Napoleon I's Confederation of the Rhine. In 1815, Baden became a member of the German Confederation, and in 1836 it joined the ZOLLVEREIN. Revolutionary activity in 1848 was suppressed by Prussian troops. In 1871, Baden became part of the German Empire as a grand duchy. The last grand duke was deposed in 1918, and Baden joined the Weimar Republic. Baden was made an administrative district of Germany in 1933.

Baden-Baden Baden-Baden is a city in the state of Baden-Württemberg in southwestern Germany. Located in the BLACK FOREST, it is a health resort known for hot mineral baths and has a population of 48,700 (1985 est.). The ruins there, dating from the early 3d century, attest to the importance of Baden-Baden as a spa since Roman times. From 1112 to 1705 it was the residence of the margraves of Baden. In the 19th century it became one of Europe's most fashionable resorts.

Baden-Powell, Robert Stephenson Smyth, 1st Baron Baden-Powell of Gilwell [bay-den-poh'-ul] Robert Baden-Powell, b. Feb. 22, 1857, d. Jan. 8, 1941, was a British soldier who founded the Boy Scout and Girl Guide (Girl Scout) movement. During the SOUTH AFRICAN WAR (1899–1902) he won renown for holding MAFEKING against a Boer siege for 217 days. He later organized the South African constabulary. Having formed the Boy Scouts (1908) and, with his sister Agnes Baden-Powell, the Girl Guides (1909), Baden-Powell devoted the rest of his life to the SCOUTING movement. He wrote many books on scouting.

badger Badger is the common name of several nocturnal carnivores belonging to the family Mustelidae, order Carnivora, which also includes weasels and skunks. Six genera and eight species exist. Seven species live in

Eurasia and one in North America, in habitats ranging from prairies to mountain areas.

The badger has a broad, flat body, a small head, and short, heavy-clawed legs. It is a rapid burrower and a fierce fighter. The body may be up to 76 cm (30 in) long, excluding a short tail, and the weight up to 11 kg (25 lb). All badgers have scent glands, which may be used defensively. Most badgers are ground dwellers, but certain badgers of China, Burma, and Java can climb trees. Badgers eat gophers, mice, ground squirrels, other small animals, and some plant material.

badlands

badlands Badlands are elevated areas that have been severely eroded and are deeply incised with gullies. They are usually formed in dry regions and lack a protective vegetation cover. Occasional heavy rainfall will form run-off gullies in the softer strata. Uneven resistance of different rocks can create a tortured landscape of pinnacles and buttes.

The term *badlands* was first used for a region of the northern Great Plains of the United States, specifically in southwest South Dakota and the Little Missouri River region of North Dakota. Two protected badlands areas in the United States remain in natural state. The Badlands National Monument, southeast of Rapid City, S.Dak., covers 985 km^2 (380 mi^2); fossil remains of the saber-toothed cat, the three-toed horse, and other early mammals, reptiles, and birds have been found there. The Theodore Roosevelt National Memorial Park in North Dakota includes 285 km^2 (110 mi^2) of badlands. Little vegetation or animal life exists in these regions, but the multicolored formations of shales and limestones make the parks tourist attractions.

badminton

badminton [bad'-min-tuhn] Badminton is a sport for two or four players in which long-handled rackets are used to hit a shuttlecock (also called a shuttle or bird) over a net stretched across a marked court. Badminton's growth both as a backyard recreation and as a highly developed competitive indoor sport has been greatest since the end of World War II, although the game dates back to the 1800s. The International Badminton Federation (IBF) has members in more than 40 nations, and a world tournament for men and women is held every three years.

History. The game is believed to have been invented in India in a version called *poona.* British army officers learned the game about 1870. In 1873 the duke of Beaufort introduced the sport at his country estate, Badminton, from which the game derives its name. In 1887 the Bath Badminton Club was formed; it was replaced in 1893 by the Badminton Association of England, which codified the rules that still govern competitive play. In the United States, meanwhile, the first badminton club was formed in 1878 in New York City.

The IBF was founded in 1934 with nine nations represented. The introduction of Thomas Cup play for men in 1949 and Uber Cup competition for women in 1957

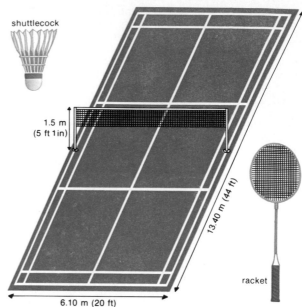

Badminton, introduced by British troops returning from India, grew popular in England, where the first set of rules was codified in 1895.

brought to public attention outstanding stars such as Judy Devlin Hashman, of Baltimore, Md., winner of ten all-England titles.

Equipment. Rackets are lightweight, much smaller than those used in tennis. The 5-g (0.18-oz) shuttlecock is usually made of cork and feathers, which can cause the shuttle suddenly to stop, drop, or turn in midair. The court is about 5.2 by 13.4 m (17 by 44 ft) for singles and 1 m (3 ft) wider for doubles.

Scoring. In order to score a player has to serve, or put the shuttle into play. A server can score when the opponent lets the shuttle fall to the ground or by a fault. A fault occurs when the opponent, in an attempt to return the shuttle safely, allows it to go into or under the net, hits it out of the playing area, touches the net, is touched by the shuttle, or hits the shuttle with the frame of the racket.

In doubles or men's singles, either 15 or 21 points wins a game; in women's singles, 11 points.

Baeck, Leo

Baeck, Leo [bek] Leo Baeck, b. May 23, 1873, d. Nov. 2, 1956, was the chief rabbi of German Reform Judaism and an outstanding leader of progressive Judaism during the Nazi period. His theoretical position developed gradually. In the beginning he espoused an extreme form of rationalism, which is seen in his *Essence of Judaism* (1905; Eng. trans., 1936). Toward the end of his life he promoted a Jewish existentialism, which grew out of his experiences in the concentration camp of Theresienstadt and took expression in *This People Israel* (1955–57; Eng.

trans., 1965). After 1945, Baeck chaired the World Union for Progressive Judaism and taught at the Hebrew Union College in Cincinnati, Ohio.

Baedeker, Karl [bay'-duh-kur] Karl Baedeker, b. Nov. 3, 1801, d. Oct. 4, 1859, was the founder of a publishing firm specializing in travel books extremely popular not only in their original German editions but also in English and French translations. The first of the "Baedekers," a guide to Germany and the Low Countries, appeared in 1839; it was followed by guides to most of Europe, North America, and the Far East.

Baeyer, Adolf von [bah'-yur] The German chemist Adolf von Baeyer, b. Oct. 31, 1835, d. Aug. 20, 1917, carried out important research on DYES. He discovered a new group of dyes, the phthaleins; demonstrated their chemical nature; and, with Heinrich Caro, developed these compounds into dyestuffs. For this research on dyes and his synthesis of indigo, he was awarded the Nobel Prize for chemistry in 1905.

He also carried out notable synthetic and theoretical work on compounds resulting from the reduction of benzene derivatives. Baeyer synthesized (1864) barbituric acid, attained (1892) the first synthesis of a terpene, and investigated the organic peroxides.

Baez, Joan [by-ez'] Joan Baez, b. Staten Island, N.Y., Jan. 9, 1941, is a folksinger and guitarist noted for her strong, pure soprano voice. Several of her recordings in the early 1960s, primarily of Anglo-American folk ballads, sold more than 1 million copies. Baez also recorded her own compostions and songs by Bob DYLAN. Prominent during the 1960s in the civil rights and antiwar movements, Baez more or less retired from singing during the 1970s but returned to the stage in 1985. Her autobiography, *And a Voice to Sing With*, was published in 1987.

Baffin, William [baf'-in] William Baffin, b. c.1584, d. Jan. 23, 1622, was a British navigator who piloted two expeditions searching for the NORTHWEST PASSAGE. On the second voyage (1616), his ship *Discovery* passed north through Davis Strait and went about 485 km (300 mi) beyond previous exploration. Finding it an unlikely route for passage to the Orient, he recommended a search for other routes. Baffin is said to have been the first person to attempt determination of longitude by observing the Moon. Baffin Bay and Baffin Island were named for him.

Baffin Bay Baffin Bay is between Greenland on the east and the Arctic Archipelago of Canada on the west. On the south it connects with the Atlantic Ocean through Davis Strait and on the north with the Arctic Ocean by a chain of sounds. It is 1,127 km (700 mi) long and has a maximum width of 644 km (400 mi). Ice covers the bay much of the year.

Baffin Island Baffin Island is in the Arctic Archipelago of Canada and is part of the Franklin district of the Northwest Territories. The fifth largest island in the world, it is about 1,530 km (950 mi) long and up to 725 km (450 mi) wide. Its area is about 476,100 km^2 (183,800 mi^2). Peaks rise to 2,042 m (6,700 ft).

Bagehot, Walter [baj'-uht] Walter Bagehot, b. Feb. 3, 1826, d. Mar. 24, 1877, was an English social scientist and the editor of the influential journal of international affairs, *The Economist*, from 1860 until his death. He joined the family banking business in 1852 and went to *The Economist* six years later. His knowledge of the money market as it functioned between 1850 and 1870 formed the basis of his influential book *Lombard Street* (1873). Bagehot also wrote *The English Constitution* (1867), which depicted the daily workings of British government; *Physics and Politics* (1869), an application of Darwinism to political theory; and *Economic Studies*, which appeared after his death.

Baghdad Baghdad is the largest city and the capital of Iraq. It is also the capital of Baghdad province. Situated on both banks of the Tigris River in the center of the country, it lies about 40 km (25 mi) north of the parallel river, the Euphrates. The name, which in Persian means the "God-given," has been applied to the city since the 8th century. Baghdad is situated in a rich river valley with an extensive irrigation network and stands at the junction of many of the great trade routes that have shaped the politics and economics of the Middle East. Baghdad has grown greatly in recent decades, and the population of the city is 3,844,608 (1987).

Contemporary City. The ancient city was extensively modernized in the 20th century. Districts destroyed by fire and floods were rebuilt, and the land area increased. Historic landmarks include the 13th-century al-Mustansiriya Madrasah Mosque and the 10th-century minaret of Suq al Ghazi. The University of Baghdad was founded in 1958.

The population, although mostly Arab, also has considerable Persian, Armenian, and Kurdish elements. The major trade of the city is in carpets, hides, wool, gum, and dates. Industries include distilling, oil refining, food processing, tanning, and metalworking. Baghdad continues to fill its traditional roles as an important center of communication and trade. The city is the terminus of the Baghdad Railway (from Istanbul), a project sponsored by the Germans in the early 1900s and a sensitive topic in pre–World War I diplomacy, although traffic on the line was not possible until 1940.

History. The present city was founded in 762 on the west bank by the Abbasid caliph al-Mansur. From that time its commercial supremacy in the region was unchal-

Baghdad, the capital and commercial center of Iraq, crowds banks of the Tigris River. The city suffered extensive damage in bombings by multinational forces during the 1991 Gulf war.

lenged. The period of the city's greatest glory was under Caliph Harun al-Rashid during the 8th–9th centuries, when it was one of the greatest cities of Islam. A period of decline set in, however, and in 1258 the Mongols sacked the city. It was again sacked by Timur (1401) and the Persian shah Esmail I (1508). Thereafter Baghdad was repeatedly conquered by Persians and Turks until 1638, when it became part of the Ottoman Empire. The city was captured by the British in 1917. In 1921 it became the capital of the new Kingdom of Iraq, which was made a republic in 1958. Some of the city was damaged by bombing raids in 1991 as a multinational force attempted to force Iraq to withdraw from Kuwait, which it had occupied since August 1990.

bagpipe   The bagpipe is a musical instrument having reed pipes that are actuated by air pressure from a windbag to which the pipes are attached. The melody is played on one pipe (the chanter) or two (the double chanter) having finger holes. The accompanying pipes—up to six—are called drones; usually rested on the shoulder, they play one sustained tone each. In some bagpipes—the Scottish, for example—air is supplied by the player blowing into a tube connected to the bag. In others, such as the French *musette*, the air is supplied by bellows placed under the arm.

In the earlier, Eastern instruments, both the chanter and the drone pipes have single reeds; in some modern types, all the pipes have double reeds, as in those used in Italy and parts of France, or the drones have single reeds and the chanter has a double reed, as in those of Ireland, Scotland, and Brittany. Bags have been made from the whole skin of a sheep, goat, or other animal, and more recently from leather, rubber, or synthetic material.

The bagpipe is believed to have originated in the Orient, and it was known in ancient Rome. Its penetrating

melody with drone accompaniment made it well suited for medieval music. Since the Renaissance it has been used mostly for folk and military music, notably in the British Isles.

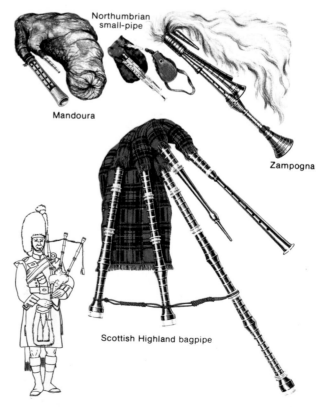

Northumbrian small-pipe

Mandoura

Zampogna

Scottish Highland bagpipe

AT A GLANCE

COMMONWEALTH OF THE BAHAMAS

Land: 13,939 km^2 (5,382 mi^2). Capital and largest city: Nassau (1980 pop., 110,000).

People: Population (1990 est.): 246,491. Density: 18 persons per km^2 (46 per mi^2). Distribution (1985): 57% urban, 43% rural. Official language: English. Major religions: Baptist church, Anglicanism, Roman Catholicism, Greek Orthodoxy, Judaism.

Government: Type: independent state within Commonwealth of Nations. Legislature: Parliament.

Economy: GDP (1988): $2.4 billion; $9,875 per capita. Labor distribution (1986): government—30%; tourism—25%; business services—10%; agriculture—6%. Foreign trade (1987): imports—$1.7 billion; exports—$733 million. Currency: 1 Bahamian dollar = 100 cents.

Education and Health: Literacy (1986): 95% of adult population. Universities (1987): none. Hospital beds (1983): 948. Physicians (1983): 218. Life expectancy (1990): women—75; men—68. Infant mortality (1984): 21 per 1,000 live births.

Baguio [bah-gee'-oh]   Baguio (1980 pop., 119,009), a city on the island of Luzon in the Philippines, is the summer capital of the country and a popular mountain resort. Copper and gold are mined in the rugged surrounding mountains. The city was almost completely leveled by an earthquake in July 1990.

Baha'i [bah-hah'-ee]   Baha'i is a religious movement founded in the 19th century by the Persian BAHAULLAH. It claims members in practically every country of the world. Objecting to polygamy, slavery of any kind, religious prejudices, and politicized religion, Baha'is call for world peace and harmony. The ideals of a world federalist government and a new world language are also a part of their teachings. Recognition of the common ground of all religions is seen as fostering this move toward global unity; Krishna, Buddha, Moses, Zarathustra, Jesus, and Muhammad are all recognized as divine manifestations, a series of prophets culminating in Bahaullah. Nonresistance, respect for persons, and legal recognition of the equal rights of both sexes constitute additional aspects of Baha'i teaching.

(Opposite page) The bagpipe is a musical wind instrument that consists of an air reservoir in the form of a bag, which is inflated by either a mouth pipe or a bellows. The Scottish Highland bagpipe is the most familiar type. A mouth-blown bagpipe, it comprises a tartan-covered bag, a mouthpiece, a conical double-reed chanter with seven finger holes in front and a thumb hole in the rear, two tenor drones, and a bass drone. The Mandoura is a mouth-blown bagpipe from Crete with a kidskin bag and chanter made of a double pipe; each pipe has five finger holes and a single reed. The Zampogna, of Italy and Sicily, is a mouth-blown bagpipe consisting of a sheepskin bag, blowpipe, two conical double-reed chanters, and two double-reed drones. The Northumbrian small-pipe, dating to the late 17th century, is a bellows-blown bagpipe with a cylindrical double-reed chanter and four single-reed drones of which no more than three are used at once.

By the time of Bahaullah's death in 1892, the Baha'i faith had won adherents throughout the Middle East. Under his son Abbas Effendi (or Abdul Baha, 1844–1921), who succeeded him as the movement's leader, it spread to Europe and the United States. Abbas Effendi was succeeded by his grandson, Shoghi Effendi (1897–1957). After Shoghi Effendi's death the Baha'is have been governed by elected leaders. Since the establishment of the Islamic Republic of Iran in 1979, the discrimination to which Baha'is have always been subjected in Iran has escalated into persecution.

Bahamas   The country of the Bahamas, an independent member of the Commonwealth of Nations, is composed of about 700 islands and more than 2,000 cays, islets, and rocks in the Atlantic Ocean. Located about 97 km (60 mi) off the southern Florida coast, they extend about 1,224 km (760 mi) southeastward to within 80 km (50 mi) of Cuba and spread over more than 233,000 km^2 (90,000 mi^2) of the Atlantic. Scenic beaches and mild climate make the Bahamas a major tourist resort.

Land and People. The main islands include Andros (the largest), New Providence, Grand Bahama, Eleuthera, Great Abaco, and Great Inagua. The archipelago generally comprises an undulating limestone platform that is derived from coral. The climate is semitropical, with an average summer temperature of 28° C (83° F) and an average winter temperature of 21° C (70° F). Annual rainfall averages 1,168 mm (46 in) and is concentrated in May–June and September–October. Large Caribbean pine forests thrive on several of the islands.

More than 80% of the population are black. Only 22 of the islands have permanent residents. About half the total population live on the small island of New Provi-

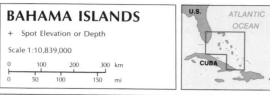

BAHAMA ISLANDS

+ Spot Elevation or Depth

Scale 1:10,839,000

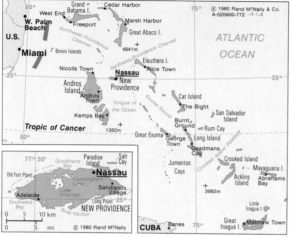

© 1980 Rand McNally & Co.
A-520600-772 -1-1-1

contribute to the continued attraction of tourist revenues. Liberal tax laws have encouraged expatriates to settle in the Bahamas from countries such as the United States, Britain, and Canada. The tax structure has also attracted many foreign banks. Agriculture has played only a minor role in the economy, although the government is promoting agriculture and fishing to lessen the dependence on imported foodstuffs.

The Bahamas has long served as an oil transshipment point to the United States, but the health of oil-related industries (including a government-owned refinery on Grand Bahama) fluctuates with the world demand for oil.

History. Many scholars believe that Christopher Co-LUMBUS made his first landing (Oct. 12, 1492) in the Western Hemisphere on SAN SALVADOR ISLAND of the Bahamas. The first British settlement on the islands was established on Eleuthera in 1648. When the islands became (1670) a British colony, New Providence was made the seat of government. After attempts at farming and fishing proved unsuccessful, the economy eventually settled on tourism after World War II. In 1964 the Bahamas were granted internal self-government, and the first elections under universal suffrage were held in 1967. The islands became fully independent on July 10, 1973. The British monarch appoints the governor-general, but actual governmental control is in the hands of the prime minister and the bicameral parliament. The majority party since 1967 has been the Progressive Liberal party, whose leader, Lynden Pindling, is prime minister. In the 1980s the islands became a major center for trade in illicit drugs, straining U.S.-Bahamas relations.

dence, the site of the capital, NASSAU. Other important settlements are Freeport and West End on Grand Bahama.

Economy. Tourism is the Bahamas' major source of revenue. Climate, gambling casinos, and sport fishing

Tourists are drawn to Nassau's Paradise Beach by the temperate climate and clean, uncrowded recreational areas. Tourism remains the Bahamas' most important source of revenue, despite government efforts to broaden the country's economic base.

Bahaullah [bah-hah-ul-lah']   Bahaullah, or Baha' Allah ("Splendor of God"), is the title assumed by the Iranian religious leader Mirza Husayn Ali, b. Nov. 12, 1817, d. May 29, 1892. He proclaimed (1863) himself to be the person announced by the Bab (see BABISM) as the one who would bring his work to completion. The BAHA'I movement, which arose from Bahaullah's teaching, spread as far as Europe and the United States during the time of Abbas Effendi (1844–1921), Bahaullah's son and successor. Bahaullah died in Acre, Palestine.

Bahia   see SALVADOR

Bahrain [bah-rayn']   Bahrain is an independent emirate comprising a group of low-lying islands located in the Persian Gulf between the Saudi Arabian mainland and the Qatar peninsula. About 40% of the country's population lives in MANAMA, the capital city. Bahrain's importance as an oil-producer is waning, but it continues to be a commercial center because of its strategic location.

Land and People

The two most important islands are Bahrain and al-Muharraq, which are connected by causeway; other islands include Sitra, Umm Nassan, An Nabi Salih, Jidda, and the Hawar group. The islands are generally small and low-

AT A GLANCE

STATE OF BAHRAIN

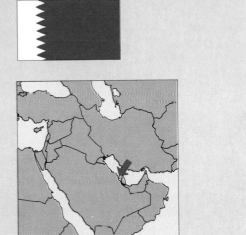

Land: Area: 678 km² (262 mi²). Capital and largest city: Manama (1987 est. pop., 146,994).

People: Population (1990 est.): 520,186. Density: 767 persons per km² (1,985 per mi²). Distribution (1986): 83% urban, 17% rural. Official language: Arabic. Major religion: Islam.

Government: Type: monarchy. Legislature: National Assembly (dissolved 1975). Political subdivisions: 11 municipalities.

Economy: GDP (1987): $3.5 billion; $7,550 per capita. Labor distribution (1984): services—36%; construction—21%; trade—13%; transport and communications—9%; manufacturing—8%. Foreign trade (1988 est.): imports—$2.5 billion; exports—$2.4 billion. Currency: 1 Bahrain dinar = 1,000 fils.

Education and Health: Literacy (1986): 75% of adult population. Universities (1990): 1. Hospital beds (1987): 1,162. Physicians (1985): 518. Life expectancy (1990): women—76; men—71. Infant mortality (1990): 19 per 1,000 live births.

lying, although the central region of the main island is a barren limestone plateau that rises to 135 m (445 ft).

Summer temperatures average 34° C (93° F); winter temperatures average about 17° C (63° F). Relative humidity is 70% to 80% for most of the year, but annual rainfall averages only about 76 mm (3 in).

The population of Bahrain is mostly Arab, more than 65% of Bahrainis being native-born. Many Indians, Persians, Pakistanis, Europeans, and Americans also reside in the country. Arabic is the official language, although Persian and English are understood widely. Islam, practiced by 95% of the population, is the official religion. The SUNNITE sect predominates in the urban centers and accounts for about one-third the population, including the ruling family. The SHIITE sect is important in rural areas. Housing and transportation are state subsidized, and health services and education are free.

Economic Activity

Oil, first discovered in 1931, was Bahrain's principal product for many years, but since reserves are small and will probably be depleted by the end of the 20th century, major efforts have been made to diversify the economy. These include a large oil refinery, a huge gas-powered aluminum smelter, and ancillary industries based on oil refining and aluminum smelting.

Bahrain receives a variety of subsidies from the richer Gulf states. It has become a major regional banking and communications center. Also important are the facilities related to Bahrain's position as a transportation and trade center for the Persian Gulf. The airport at al-Muharraq is

a major international airport, and the port of Mina Sulman offers a free trade zone. A causeway linking Bahrain Island to Saudi Arabia was officially opened in 1986.

History and Government

As early as the 3d millennium BC, Bahrain was the site of the thriving commercial center DILMUN. After nearly eight centuries of independence as an Arab Muslim state, Bahrain came under the rule of Portugal (1521–1602) and Persia (1602–1783). Since 1783 the al-Khalifa family has ruled the country. Bahrain was under British

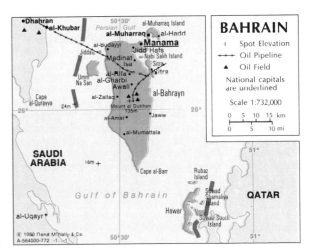

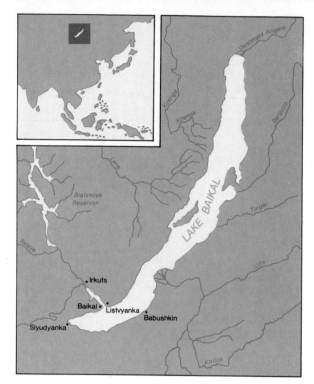

protection from 1861 until independence in 1971, when Bahrain elected not to join the United Arab Emirates. A constitution was adopted in 1973, but the National Assembly, which met for the first time in 1973, was dissolved in 1975, and the emir has since ruled by decree. During the Iraqi occupation of Kuwait, beginning in August 1990, Bahrain accepted thousands of Kuwaiti exiles and was visited by Western soldiers on leave from battlefields in the Persian Gulf region.

Baikal, Lake [by-kahl'] Lake Baikal (or Baykal), located in the USSR in southeastern Siberia west of the Yablonovy Mountains, is the largest freshwater lake in Eurasia. It covers an area of 31,494 km² (12,160 mi²) and measures almost 636 km (395 mi) long and 29–81 km (18–50 mi) wide. With a maximum depth of 1,620 m (5,315 ft), it is the deepest freshwater lake in the world. The Trans-Siberian Railroad passes to the south and the Baikal-Amur Mainline Railway to the north. The lake is a popular summer resort; local forest and mineral resources are processed along its shores. Baikal's exceptionally pure waters support an unusual aquatic population, including many species found nowhere else, and strict pollution curbs have been imposed.

The lake is buffeted by wind-generated storms and the water remains cold year-round; it is frozen from December to May. Baikal is fed by numerous rivers but has only one outlet, the Angara River, at Irkutsk. Olkon Island is in the center of the lake.

Baikonur Cosmodrome [by-kuh-noor'] The Baikonur Cosmodrome, a Soviet space center in Kazakhstan, Soviet Central Asia, is the launch site of all Soviet Sputnik, Luna, Mars, Venera, and manned space shots. It comprises a line of individual launching pads stretching about 95 km (60 mi) from west to east, is just north of the town of Tyuratam, and is known in the West as the Tyuratam space center. The first rocket launchings from Tyuratam were made in mid-1957 in the early intercontinental ballistic missile program headed by Sergei Korolev. It continues to be the center for flight-testing military missiles and space systems, although routine space launchings were shifted beginning in 1966 to another base near the town of Plesetsk, north of Moscow.

bail Bail is the procedure by which a judge releases from custody a person charged with a crime, upon receiving security in the form of cash or a promise that the released prisoner will appear in court at a specified time to answer the charge. The usual form of security is a bail bond provided by a bonding company. Depending on the amount of bail fixed by the judge, the defendant may have to pay a fee of 10 percent and also put up collateral in the form of securities or property.

Bailey, F. Lee Francis Lee Bailey, b. Waltham, Mass., June 10, 1933, has become one of America's best-known criminal lawyers. Among his early successful cases was that of Samuel Sheppard, a Cleveland, Ohio, physician who had been convicted of the 1954 murder of his wife. Bailey became Sheppard's lawyer in 1961, a year after his admission to the bar, and took his case to the U.S. Supreme Court in 1965, where the conviction was overturned. A second trial resulted in a verdict of not guilty. In 1977, Bailey represented Patricia Hearst at her trial for involvement in a bank robbery conducted by the Symbionese Liberation Army.

Bailey, Liberty Hyde Liberty Hyde Bailey, b. South Haven, Mich., Mar. 15, 1858, d. Dec. 25, 1954, an American botanist, systematized the study of horticulture and trained a generation of agriculturists. As a professor of botany and dean of the College of Agriculture at Cornell University (1888–1913), Bailey brought botanists, plant physiologists, and geneticists together to work in the field of horticulture. His published works—about 700 papers and 66 books—include *The Standard Cyclopedia of Horticulture* (1914), still used as a reference source, and *Hortus*, recently revised and republished as *Hortus Third: A Concise Dictionary of Plants Cultivated in the United States and Canada.*

Bainbridge, William The American naval officer William Bainbridge, b. Princeton, N.J., May 7, 1774, d. July 27, 1833, was commissioned (1798) in the newly created U.S. Navy during the undeclared war with France (1798–1800) that followed the XYZ AFFAIR. His first ship, the *Retaliation*, was captured by the French, but he was later so successful in running blockades and convoying American merchantmen in the French West Indies that he was promoted to captain in 1800. Given command of the frigate *Philadelphia* during the TRIPOLITAN WAR (1801–05), Bainbridge was again captured when he ran aground at Tripoli in 1803. During the WAR OF 1812, he successfully advocated a strategy of fleet dispersion and commerce raiding. Commanding the U.S.S. CONSTITUTION, he captured the British frigate *Java* off Brazil on Dec. 29, 1812.

Baird, Bil and Cora   The American puppeteers Bil Baird, b. Grand Island, Nebr., Aug. 15, 1904, d. Mar. 18, 1987, and his wife, Cora, b. New York City, Jan. 26, 1912, d. Dec. 7, 1967, presented puppet shows in theaters and nightclubs and, in the 1950s, on television. They created such well-loved marionettes as Heathcliff the talking horse.

Baja California [bah'-hah]   Baja California (English: Lower California) is a mountainous, arid peninsula of northwestern Mexico. Extending about 1,220 km (760 mi) south from the U.S. border, it ranges in width from 40 to 240 km (25 to 150 mi) and is connected to the Mexican mainland by a narrow strip across the delta of the Colorado River. The peninsula is divided into the Mexican states of Baja California Norte (1989 est. pop., 1,408,774), whose capital city is MEXICALI, and Baja California Sur (1989 est. pop., 327,389), whose capital city is La Paz.

The peninsula retains much unspoiled desert land. Some indigenous plants, including the boogum and elephant trees, exist only there. Most of the peninsula's population is concentrated in the cities clustered near the U.S. border—TIJUANA, Mexicali, and Ensenada. Tourism, the major industry, has grown rapidly.

Bakelite   see PLASTICS

Baker, Sir Benjamin   The English engineer Benjamin Baker, b. Mar. 31, 1840, d. May 19, 1907, helped to design the great railroad bridge across Scotland's Firth of Forth, a 1,630-m-long (5,349-ft) steel structure completed in 1890. He was involved in the building of the first Aswan Dam. He also assisted in the construction of the Eads Bridge across the Mississippi River at St. Louis and designed a pneumatic tunneling shield used to build the Holland Tunnel at New York City.

Baker, Howard   Howard Henry Baker, Jr., b. Huntsville, Tenn., Nov. 15, 1925, Republican senator from Tennessee, gained national prominence in 1973 as a member of the Senate committee investigating Watergate. Elected to the Senate in 1966, Baker became minority leader in 1977. After the Republicans won control

of the Senate in 1980, he became majority leader. He declined to run for reelection in 1984 but in 1987 became President Ronald Reagan's chief of staff during the investigation of the IRAN-CONTRA AFFAIR. Baker resigned that office in mid-1988.

Baker, James A.   James Addison Baker III, b. Houston, Tex., Apr. 28, 1930, became U.S. secretary of state in 1989 under George Bush, whose presidential campaign Baker had managed. A graduate (1952) of Princeton with a law degree (1957) from the University of Texas, Baker practiced law in Houston. He served President Ronald Reagan first as chief of staff (1981–85), earning a reputation as a master of compromise, and then as secretary of the treasury (1985–88).

Baker, Janet   Dame Janet Baker, b. York, England, Aug. 21, 1933, a mezzo-soprano, is world renowned as a recitalist, concert soloist, and opera singer. She studied with Helene Isepp and Lotte Lehmann. Her repertoire ranges from Bach cantatas to the operas of Benjamin Britten. She was awarded a C.B.E. (Commander of the British Empire) in 1976. In 1982, she retired from the operatic stage and published her memoirs, *Full Circle*.

Baker, Josephine   Josephine Baker, b. St. Louis, Mo., June 3, 1906, d. Apr. 12, 1975, an entertainer, personified *le jazz hot* for the French in the 1920s and '30s. In 1924 she was featured on Broadway in *The Chocolate Dandies*. In 1925 she starred in Paris in *La Revue Nègre* and created a sensation as a dancer clad only in a string of bananas. She remained in Paris as a star at the *Folies Bergère*, a blues singer, and a film actress, and became a French citizen in 1937. Baker was honored by France for her work in the French resistance during World War II. She enjoyed Broadway triumphs in 1964 and 1973.

Baker, Newton Diehl   Newton Diehl Baker, b. Martinsburg, W. Va., Dec. 3, 1871, d. Dec. 25, 1937, was secretary of war (1916–21) and administered the U.S. war effort in World War I. He had earlier served (1912–16) as mayor of Cleveland.

As secretary of war, Baker, a pacifist, took little action until the United States entered (April 1917) World War I. Then he proved himself a vigorous administrator. He implemented military conscription, reorganized the War Department, and efficiently administered the huge war budget.

Baker, Russell   Russell Baker, b. Loudoun County, Va., Aug. 14, 1925, is author of the "Observer," a *New York Times* column that is one of the most popular humor commentaries in the country. Formerly a reporter on the *Baltimore Sun* (1947–54) and in the *Times* Washington bureau (1954–62), Baker began the "Observer" in 1962. His columns have been collected in several anthologies, and won him a Pulitzer Prize in 1979. The first installment of his autobiography, *Growing Up* (1982), won another Pulitzer and was followed by *The Good Times* (1989).

Baker, Sir Samuel White

Sir Samuel White Baker, b. June 8, 1821, d. Dec. 30, 1893, was an English explorer in Africa whose expeditions—with those of John Hanning SPEKE—finally settled the question of the source of the Nile. In 1861, Baker and his wife explored the Nile's tributaries in Ethiopia. Two years later they followed the river farther south and discovered (Mar. 14, 1864) Lake Albert Nyanza, determining that the Nile flowed through the lake. Baker was later appointed (1869) governor of the region by the Egyptian khedive and suppressed the slave trade there.

Bakersfield

Bakersfield is a city in the San Joaquin Valley in south central California with a population of 174,820 (1990). Founded in 1859, the city developed rapidly after petroleum was discovered nearby in 1899. It now depends on petroleum-based industries, manufacturing, and agriculture.

Bakhtiari

[bahk-tee-ah'-ree] The Bakhtiari tribe, which numbers more than 800,000, inhabits an area of approximately 67,000 km^2 (25,000 mi^2) that straddles the central Zagros Mountains in Iran. Although only about a third of the tribe is nomadic (the rest are settled agriculturists), the nomads embody the Bakhtiari cultural ideals. They specialize in producing meat and dairy products and migrate seasonally with their sheep, cattle, or goat herds from high plateau pastures where they spend the summer, west of the city of Isfahan, to lowland plains in the province of Khuzistan for winter herd grazing. Their migration across mountain passes at about 3,050 m (10,000 ft) is among the most spectacular known among nomadic pastoralists anywhere.

The Bakhtiari speak a dialect of Persian called Luri and are Shiite Muslims. In the late 19th and early 20th centuries, the Bakhtiari played an important role on the national level in Iran's constitutional movement.

baking industry

The manufacture of bakery products is a significant part of the worldwide food industry. In the United States the industry produces and sells billions of dollars worth of goods annually. Bread and cake products lead in total sales value, followed by cookies, crackers, pretzels, and other products.

The industry consists of large wholesale bakeries, which sell their products to retail outlets or food-service operations; retail bakeries owned, and usually run, by independent bakers; franchised retail outlets; and in-store bakeries, which are specialty sections of supermarkets.

Small neighborhood bakeries owned by the baker, and often staffed by family members, were the main suppliers of bread, rolls, and pastries in the United States until after World War II, when the growth of large wholesale bakeries put small operations at a disadvantage. Large plants mass-produced bread and rolls on automated lines; labor costs per unit of product were lower, as were expenses for ingredients and energy. Better control of processing conditions and ingredient characteristics enabled larger bakeries to maintain more uniform product quality. They had an additional advantage in that they delivered to supermarkets, enabling consumers to buy baked goods without having to visit another store. Factory technologies have since penetrated other countries. Even in such traditionally non–bread-eating countries as Japan, mass-produced bread is becoming a staple.

baking powder

Baking powder is a mixture of baking soda (sodium bicarbonate), an acid salt such as cream of tartar, and small amounts of starch, to simplify measuring and improve the stability of the mixture. It is used as a leavening agent in baking.

Carbon dioxide, the leavening gas produced by baking powder, originates from baking soda. Addition of an acidic compound promotes a rapid release of gas. The rate of gas release controls the size of the bubbles in the dough and influences the grain, volume, and texture of the baked product.

baking soda   see SODA

Bakke case   see UNIVERSITY OF CALIFORNIA V. BAKKE

Bakst, Léon

The Russian artist Léon Bakst, b. Feb. 8, 1866, d. Dec. 24, 1924, is primarily known for his association with Serge DIAGHILEV and his BALLETS RUSSES. His sumptuous decors for such ballets as *Schéhérazade* (1910) and *L'Après-midi d'une Faune* (AFTERNOON OF A FAUN, 1912) contributed to the success of the dance company and, as well, launched a craze for exotic colors and patterns in fashion and interior decoration. Bakst (originally named Lev Samoylovich Rosenberg) met Diaghilev in Saint Petersburg and became cofounder of the luxurious art magazine *Mir iskusstva* (World of Art) in 1899. After his success with the Ballets Russes, he returned to Russia, where he founded a school of painting. His last years were spent in Paris designing sets for plays, ballets, and operas.

Baku

[buh-koo'] Baku is the capital of the Azerbaijan republic in the USSR. It is situated on the south shore of the beak-shaped Apsheron Peninsula on the Caspian Sea. The population of the city proper is 1,150,000, and that of the metropolitan area, which encompasses the entire peninsula, is 1,757,000 (1989).

The city's economy revolves around the historic oil fields on the Apsheron Peninsula and offshore, and several oil refineries, oil-equipment manufacturing plants, and other industries associated with oil are located there. Petroleum, in the form of incoming crude oil and outgoing refined products, constitutes most of the cargo of the port, which is the largest on the Caspian Sea. The population is ethnically mixed, including 46% Azerbaijanis, 28% Russians, and 16% Armenians. First mentioned in the 9th century, Baku passed from Persian to Russian control in 1806. Commercial oil development began in the 1870s. By the start of the 20th century, Baku was the world's largest producer, a position it was unable to maintain with the development of major oil fields elsewhere. In the USSR it now produces only a small percentage of the national total.

Bakunin, Mikhail Aleksandrovich [buh-koon'yin, mee-kuh-yel' ul-yek-sahn'-droh-vich] Mikhail Aleksandrovich Bakunin, b. May 30, 1814, d. July 1, 1876, was a Russian aristocrat who became revolutionist and a leading theorist of ANARCHISM. After taking part in the Revolutions of 1848 in Germany and Austria, he was deported to Russia. Escaping from Siberia in 1861, he went to England and Western Europe and resumed his revolutionary work.

Bakunin taught that man is basically good but corrupted by existing institutions. Accordingly, he advocated the violent overthrow of the state, the churches, and the economic system to permit men to start over again in voluntary associations of free individuals. He was a bitter critic of MARXISM, which he saw as authoritarian. Bakunin was never precise about how his ends would be achieved in practice.

Balaguer, Joaquín [bah-lah-gair', hwah-keen'] Joaquín Balaguer y Ricardo, b. Sept. 1, 1907, was elected president of the Dominican Republic five times. A scholar, poet, and lawyer, he held important posts during the dictatorship of Rafael TRUJILLO Molina. After Trujillo's assassination in 1961, the country fell into disorder and Balaguer went into U.S. exile for three years. He was elected president in 1966 and reelected in 1970 and 1974. A moderate conservative, he attempted to restore financial stability to his country. Balaguer lost the 1978 elections, but in 1986, now 78 years old and blind, he narrowly won a fourth term. He won a fifth term in 1990 in another close election.

Balakirev, Mily Alekseyevich [buh-lahk'-yir-yef, mee'-lee ul-yek-syay'-yih-vich] Mily Alekseyevich Balakirev, b. Jan. 2, 1837, d. May 29, 1910, was a leading Russian nationalist composer. In 1855, Balakirev moved to Saint Petersburg, where he met Mikhail GLINKA, who encouraged him, and for a brief period he was a concert pianist. The leader of a famous group of nationalist musicians known as The FIVE, he wrote a number of works based on Russian folk themes and collected and arranged many Russian folk songs. Balakirev was one of the founders (1862) of the Free Music School in Saint Petersburg and was director (1883–95) of the Court Chapel. Among his best-known works are the piano fantasy *Islamey*, the overture *Russia*, and the symphonic poem *Tamara*. He also wrote symphonies, piano concertos, chamber music, choral works, and many songs.

Balaklava, Battle of [bah-lah-klah'-vah] The Battle of Balaklava, fought on Oct. 25, 1854, in the CRIMEAN WAR, was brought about by an unsuccessful Russian attempt to raise the siege of Sevastopol by British, French, and Turkish forces. It is famous primarily for the senseless but heroic British cavalry charge against Russian field artillery, commemorated in Tennyson's CHARGE OF THE LIGHT BRIGADE.

balalaika [bal-uh-ly'-kuh] The balalaika, a popular Russian instrument of the guitar family, originated in the 17th century. It has a triangular body with a flat back and a slightly arched belly, a long fretted neck, and three rib-fastened gut (or now sometimes metal) strings, played by plucking with the fingers. V. V. Andreyev transformed the balalaika and the dombra, the immediate ancestor of the balalaika, from folk to popular instruments late in the 19th century, creating six sizes of balalaika, from piccolo to contrabass, which he used to form the basis of an all-Russian orchestra.

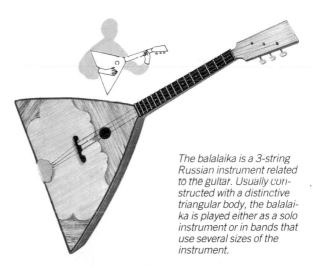

The balalaika is a 3-string Russian instrument related to the guitar. Usually constructed with a distinctive triangular body, the balalaika is played either as a solo instrument or in bands that use several sizes of the instrument.

balance A balance is a mechanical device for weighing. The term is properly applied to an instrument that opposes equal weights in two pans suspended from the ends of a lever that has its fulcrum precisely in the middle. The balance is basically a lever in which equal force is applied to its two arms at points equidistant from the fulcrum. Balances were used by the Egyptians as early as 5000 BC and have been used ever since, especially in commerce, science, and industry.

Analytical Balance. Instruments that weigh very small amounts with extreme accuracy are analytical balances. An accuracy of 1 part in 100,000,000 is theoretically possible using the best equipment. The simplest modern analytical balance is an equal-arm balance with two pans, enclosed in a glass case to protect against dust and air currents. The material to be weighed is placed on one pan, and weights are added to the other until the two are in exact balance. When small weighings are made, the swings of the balance pointer to the right and left are averaged, and the deviation from absolute center is used to calculate the precise weight.

Substitution Balance. In substitution balances, built-in weights counterbalance the load and are removed until the centering pointer comes to rest. The weights may be removed by levers actuated by buttons labeled with the corresponding weight values. The sum of the weights left on the beam may be indicated by a digital readout.

Apothecary Balance. Less-accurate laboratory, or apothecary, balances for weighing heavier samples have a platform or swinging pan on the short end of the beam and sliding weights that may be moved along the long end to offset the load by furnishing greater leverage. Double- and triple-beam balances have riders of different weights on separate calibrated bars. Thus, the heaviest rider may supply 0 to 100 g; the second, 0 to 10 g; and

The balance is an ancient weighing instrument that makes use of various high-sensitivity devices. Screw weights (1) ensure that the long, vertical indicator needle is centered. A rider weight (2) slides along the balance arm for fine adjustment, or a fine gold chain (3) suspended between the balance arm and the vertical scale (4) may be used to increase accuracy; as the vertical scale moves, the weight of the gold chain supported by the balance arm varies. An aluminum plate (5) between poles of a magnet (6) may be used to damp the oscillating balance arm and reduce delay in taking a reading.

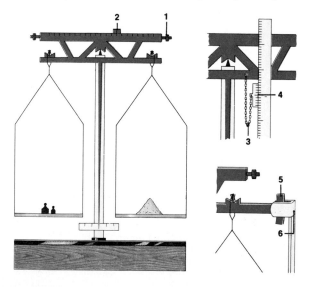

the third, 0 to 1 g. When all riders are in their highest position, they would exactly offset 111 g.

balance of payments

balance of payments   Every country maintains a record of its financial and economic relations with other countries. Just as a household's accounts show various sources of income balanced off against expenditures, so a national government maintains a balance of its international receipts and payments. While each country has its own procedures, the INTERNATIONAL MONETARY FUND (IMF) recommends certain standard practices for all countries to follow. The balance of payments is organized into the current account and the capital account.

The current account covers imports and exports of goods (this part is known as the merchandise account) and of such services as transportation, insurance, and banking. In terms of value the merchandise account is by far the most important component of the current account. Also included in the current account are purchases and sales of military equipment, earnings from investments in other countries, and payments on foreign investments in the home country. Not all of these items will be in balance. The country may have spent more for imported goods than it earned from sales of its own goods abroad; its merchandise account will then be in debit, and it will be said to have a negative balance of trade. Many people feel that their country should export more goods than it imports to have a positive, or favorable, balance of trade, but this is not necessary. A negative balance of trade may be offset by other accounts in the balance of payments—for example, by the export of services or by earnings on investments abroad (see INTERNATIONAL TRADE).

The capital account covers the import and export of capital, both government and private. Capital moves from one country to another in the form of short-term or long-term investments and as debt payments. If a large corporation in one country establishes a plant overseas, that will cause a long-term outflow of capital from the first country—and a long-term inflow to the second—to cover the investment. Short-term capital movements include such transactions as short-term loans or rapid shifts of company funds from one country to another.

When the current and capital account balances are added together, the result shows the total payments and receipts. If a deficit exists, it must be made up in some way. The deficit may be covered by drawing upon the country's previous accumulation of foreign assets, or by borrowing from the central banks of other countries or from the IMF.

When a country runs a sizable balance-of-payments deficit, it means that its currency supply in the international money market will be greater than the demand. Under the system of floating exchange rates in existence since 1973, the value of the currency will tend to fall until demand and supply are equal. In theory at least, the decline in value of the currency will cause foreigners to buy more of the country's goods and services, while its citizens will buy fewer goods from other countries.

balance of power   A balance of power among nations is a state of equilibrium in which no nation or group of nations is able to dominate others. The notion of a balance of power as the goal of foreign policy was adopted by the Italian city-states of the 15th century and by William of Orange (later WILLIAM III of England), whose wars against France between 1672 and 1701 may be seen as an attempt to restore a power balance. In 1713 the Peace of Utrecht prevented either France or Austria from dominating Europe.

The congress system established in 1815 sought to achieve a balance in Europe. Although the formal arrangements made in 1815 broke down quickly, the system whereby the major European powers entered into alliances in order to maintain stable power relations lasted until World War I.

After World War II the COLD WAR rivalry between the United States and the USSR and the development of atomic weapons produced a new bipolar balance—a "balance of terror." Beginning in the late 1980s, however, with the rise to power of Mikhail Gorbachev in the Soviet Union, the U.S. and the USSR renewed their efforts to end this "balance of terror" by concluding new arms-control agreements. By 1991 both nations were declaring that the cold war was over.

Balanchine, George [bal'-uhn-cheen or bal-ahn-sheen']   George Balanchine, b. Georgi Melitonovich Balanchivadze in Saint Petersburg (now Leningrad), Jan. 22 (N.S.), 1904, d. Apr. 30, 1983, is considered the most influential and prolific ballet choreographer of the 20th century. In 1924, while touring Europe with a Soviet company, he joined the BALLETS RUSSES DE SERGE DIAGHILEV and became that company's chief choreographer the following year. Balanchine created ten dances for Ballets Russes, two of which, *Apollo* (1928) and *Prodigal Son* (1929), are still performed. After Ballets Russes was disbanded following Diaghilev's death in 1929, Balanchine worked for various companies before accepting Lincoln KIRSTEIN's invitation to come to the United States to direct a school and, eventually, a company. The School of American Ballet was founded in New York City in 1934. Balanchine choreographed for other dance companies and for Broadway and Hollywood, but from 1948 until his death, he devoted himself almost exclusively to NEW YORK CITY BALLET, for which he created more than 200 ballets.

Balanchine's neoclassical style was based on the classical ballet vocabulary of the French-Russian choreographer Marius Petipa. Balanchine extended, distorted, and recombined this vocabulary in unexpected ways, but always within a classical context. He often used and commissioned scores by composers not yet popularly accepted and closely collaborated with Igor STRAVINSKY for almost 50 years. Balanchine did not alter tempos to suit his dancers; they earned their reputation for being the world's fastest. He was famous for his ability to discern unique

George Balanchine, the artistic director and one of the founders of New York City Ballet, rehearses two of his dancers. One of the most influential choreographers of the 20th century, he emphasized the primacy of pure dance over plot.

qualities in individual dancers, and to reveal these choreographically, but New York City Ballet had no star system.

Most of Balanchine's ballets are nonnarrative, and many are nonrepresentational. Costumes and decor were deemphasized because the dancing was always of primary—and often exclusive—importance.

Balaton, Lake [bal'-uh-tahn]   Lake Balaton (German: Plattensee) is a lake in west central Hungary about 88 km (55 mi) southwest of Budapest. The largest lake in central Europe, it is 77 km (48 mi) long and an average of 13 km (8 mi) wide. It is shallow and fed mainly by the Zala River. Its outlet is the Sío River. Many resorts are on its shores, and prehistoric artifacts have been found.

Balboa, Vasco Núñez de   Vasco Núñez de Balboa, b. 1475, d. January 1519, a Spanish conquistador and explorer, was the first European to sight the eastern shore of the Pacific Ocean; he opened the way for Spanish exploration and settlement of South America's western coast. The son of a poor nobleman, he set sail for the New World in 1500 as part of an expedition to Colombia. He settled on the island of Hispaniola and tried his hand unsuccessfully at farming. In 1510, to escape his creditors, he stowed away on a ship heading for the mainland, where he founded the colony of Darién on the Isthmus of Panama.

In 1513, Balboa led an expedition to the west, and on September 25 or 27 he sighted the Pacific Ocean, which he named the South Sea. King Ferdinand II of Aragon appointed Pedrarias Dávila as governor of Darién and named Balboa to serve under Pedrarias as governor of an area on the Pacific coast, where Balboa founded the settlement of Acla. Pedrarias had Balboa beheaded in Acla on false charges of treason.

bald cypress   The bald cypress, *Taxodium distichum,* is an attractive coniferous tree of the southeastern United States. It grows mainly in swampy areas, sometimes reaching a height of 45 m (150 ft). Not a true cypress, the tree is deciduous, shedding its needlelike leaves and short branches in winter—hence its name. It is noted for its long life; trees as old as 1,200 years have been reported. When it stands in water, unique structures called "knees" (conical outgrowths of lateral roots) develop and usually project above the water. Bald cypress wood is decay-resistant and is valued for construction. The taller Montezuma, or Mexican, cypress, *T. mucronatum,* of Mexico is not deciduous, although it may be so in cooler regions. The two species are members of the redwood family, Taxodiaceae.

Bald cypress grows in swamps and rivers of the southeastern United States and Mississippi Valley. Its needlelike leaves alternate along stems, and its flowers harden into cones by October. Its root growths, or "knees," project above the water.

Balder   In Norse mythology Balder was the god of light and beauty. The most beloved of the gods, he was the son of Odin and Frigg and the husband of Nanna, goddess of the Moon. A famous Norse myth tells how LOKI, the evil

giant, had Balder killed with a dart made of mistletoe, the only thing in the world that had not promised his mother it would never harm him. By his refusal to weep for Balder, Loki also thwarted the gods' effort to secure Balder's release from death and return to Asgard, home of the gods.

baldness   SEE HAIR

Baldung-Grien, Hans   [bahl'-doong-green]   Hans Baldung, or Baldung-Grien, b. *c.*1484, d. 1545, was a German painter who spent most of his artistic life in the Rhineland. His works included altarpieces, isolated panels, designs for stained glass, woodcut prints, BOOK ILLUSTRATIONS, drawings, and portraits of nobility. He signed and dated paintings and other works throughout his career.

Most important and extensive of the Baldung altarpiece commissions is the giant *Mary* altarpiece (1513–16) for the high altar of the cathedral at Freiburg im Breisgau. In this work, Baldung revealed his assimilation

The Three Ages of Women and Death *(1539) by Hans Baldung-Grien is an allegory that displays this German Renaissance artist's typical combination of the macabre and the erotic. The young woman, the old woman, and Death have linked their arms, while the infant clasps Death's flail. (Prado, Madrid.)*

of the massive, full-scale figures of DÜRER, which were combined with the energetic motion, vibrant colors, and spiritual passion found in the work of another great German painter, Mattias GRÜNEWALD.

Baldung's fascination with both the supernatural and the erotic gave rise to his most bizarre subjects. An early woodcut (1510) with color-toned blacks (CHIAROSCURO) depicts a witches' sabbath in the depths of a nocturnal forest. Witches, shown as old and young nude women, are featured in a large number of Baldung's drawings. He also used images of nude women to convey allegorically the ages of humankind and the vanity of sensual pleasures in the face of death. Several panels on the theme of "Death and the Maiden" contrast a lustrous fleshy female nude with the spectral skeleton of Death. A typical masterwork in this genre is the image *Eve, the Serpent, and Death* (c.1510–12; National Gallery of Canada, Ottawa), where original sin is presented as the cause of human mortality.

Baldwin, James   James Arthur Baldwin, b. Harlem, New York City, Aug. 2, 1924, d. Nov. 30, 1987, was a vital literary voice during the era of civil rights activism in the 1950s and '60s. The son of a minister, at the age of 14 Baldwin himself became a preacher in a small evangelical Harlem church. His first novel, *Go Tell It on the Mountain* (1953), is a partially autobiographical account of his youth. The essay collections—*Notes of a Native Son* (1955), *Nobody Knows My Name* (1961), and *The Fire Next Time* (1963)—influenced a large white audience. Later novels include *Giovanni's Room* (1956), about a white American expatriate who must come to terms with his homosexuality, and *Another Country* (1962), about racial and sexual tensions among New York intellectuals. His play, *Blues for Mister Charlie*, was produced in 1964. The short-story collection *Going to Meet the Man* (1965) and the novel *Tell Me How Long the Train's Been Gone* (1968) added to his bitterly incisive descriptions of American racism. *The Evidence of Things Not Seen* (1985) is Baldwin's analysis of the Atlanta child murders of 1979 and 1980.

James Baldwin, the acclaimed black American author, conveys in his writing attitudes of blacks living in a white-dominated society. Baldwin's plays and short stories established him as a leading literary figure in the American civil rights movement.

Robert Baldwin, a 19th-century political reformer, was a leader in establishing parliamentary rule in Canada. Baldwin promoted responsible government by a system that made Canada's executive and cabinet accountable to an elected parliament.

Baldwin, Robert   Robert Baldwin, b. May 12, 1804, d. Dec. 9, 1858, was a respected political leader of pre-Confederation Canada who has become identified with the theory and practice of responsible government. Baldwin was a lawyer who first entered the Upper Canada (Ontario) legislature in 1829 as a moderate reformer. While serving as a minister in 1836 and 1841, Baldwin pressed his view that the British-appointed governor should act on the advice of ministers who possessed the confidence of the majority in the popular legislature.

In 1842, Baldwin joined with his French-speaking colleague Louis Hippolyte LAFONTAINE to form an administration devoted to the achievement of responsible government. When the governor, Sir Charles (later Baron) METCALFE, failed to take their advice on appointments, Baldwin and Lafontaine and most of the cabinet resigned. In 1847 the reformers won victory in the elections, and early in 1848 Baldwin and Lafontaine formed a second ministry as joint premiers for their sections of the Province of Canada (created by the union of Upper and Lower Canada in 1840). Responsible government became firmly established when the new governor, the 8th earl of ELGIN, accepted the ministry's recommendation of a bill granting compensation for losses in the rebellions of 1837–38. The Baldwin-Lafontaine government, sometimes called the Great Ministry, provided amnesty to those taking part in the Rebellions of 1837–38 and established municipal institutions for Canada West (Ontario). Baldwin resigned his office in 1851.

Baldwin, Stanley, 1st Earl Baldwin of Bewdley   Stanley Baldwin was prime minister of Great Britain three times between 1923 and 1937. Born on Aug. 3, 1867, he was the son of a prominent industrialist in Worcestershire and a cousin of Rudyard Kipling. He was elected to Parliament as a Conservative in 1908, became parliamentary private secretary to Andrew Bonar LAW (1916) and joint financial secretary of the treasury (1917), and in 1921 entered the cabinet as president of the Board of Trade.

In 1922, Baldwin played a leading part in persuading the Conservatives to withdraw their support of David LLOYD GEORGE's coalition government. After a general election, he became chancellor of the exchequer in the new Conservative government and then found himself unexpectedly prime minister when Bonar Law had to resign in 1923. Although the Conservatives lost the general election at the end of that year, Baldwin returned to office in November 1924 and remained in power until 1929. During a period of rising unemployment and unrest culminating in the General Strike of 1926, Baldwin gained a reputation for reasonableness and political skill.

After losing the election of 1929, Baldwin spent an unhappy two years as leader of the opposition. When the Labour government collapsed during the economic crisis of 1931, he joined the coalition government of Ramsay MACDONALD as lord president of the council. Baldwin preferred this post to the premiership; he was much less gifted as an executive than as a parliamentarian and conciliator. By the time he succeeded MacDonald as prime minister in the summer of 1935, Baldwin was tired and aging. He won an election that year on a platform that included substantial rearmament but was severely shaken by the government's failure to settle the crisis provoked by the Italian invasion of Ethiopia in 1935–36. Nonetheless, he managed the abdication (1936) of King EDWARD VIII with dignity and sensitivity. Baldwin retired in May 1937, was created a peer, and died on Dec. 14, 1947.

Stanley Baldwin was prime minister of Great Britain three times between World Wars I and II. He was a skilled political leader who retained confidence through a series of crises, including the General Strike of 1926 and the abdication of Edward VIII ten years later.

Balearic Islands

Balearic Islands [bal-ee-ar'-ik] The Balearic Islands, an archipelago in the western Mediterranean, form the Spanish province of Baleares. The population of 673,351 (1988 est.) is concentrated on the densely inhabited four main islands—IBIZA, MAJORCA, MINORCA, and Formentera. The numerous smaller islands are mostly uninhabited. Total area is 5,014 km² (1,936 mi²), and the highest elevation, Torrellas (Puig Mayor), is 1,363 m (4,471 ft). The Balearics are actually partially submerged peaks that are a continuation of the mountains of southeastern Spain. The climate and good soil promote the

The locator map shows the position of the Balearic Islands, an archipelago in the Mediterranean that is part of Spain.

growing of grapes, olives, citrus fruits, and pines (for lumber). Other economic activities include fishing and livestock raising, and some minerals (lead, lignite, and marble) are found, but the economy is heavily dependent on tourism. PALMA, the capital, on Majorca, has a permanent population of 304,422 (1981).

Successively occupied by the Phoenicians, Carthaginians, Romans, and Byzantines, the Balearics came under Moorish control in the 8th century and were used as pirate bases. James I of Aragon captured them in 1235. After maintaining independence from 1276 to 1343, they returned to Spanish control. During the Spanish Civil War (1936–39), Majorca and Ibiza were held by insurgents; Minorca remained Loyalist.

Balenciaga, Cristóbal

Balenciaga, Cristóbal [bah-len-see-ah'-gah, krees-toh'-bahl] Cristóbal Balenciaga, b. Spain, Jan. 21, 1895, d. Mar. 24, 1972, was a master couturier from the 1930s through the 1960s; he was the only designer, beside Madeleine Vionnet, who could cut, fit, and sew his own designs.

In 1947, Christian DIOR introduced the "new look," with lengthened skirts and softened shoulders, but by the 1950s Balenciaga's ideas were dominant. He feminized the suit and popularized the chemise dress in 1955. His puffed evening dresses were marvels of engineering and yet devoid of excess; in his clothes the mature woman could be fashionable. Balenciaga's disciples were André Courrèges and Hubert de Givenchy.

Balfour, Arthur, 1st Earl of Balfour

Balfour, Arthur, 1st Earl of Balfour [bal'-fur] Arthur James Balfour, b. July 25, 1848, d. Mar. 19, 1930, succeeded his uncle, the 3d marquess of SALISBURY, as British prime minister (1902–05) and was leader of the Conservative party until 1911.

Balfour was born into a family with political connections. Entering Parliament in 1874, he received his first cabinet appointment in 1886. As chief secretary for Ireland (1887–91) he earned the nickname "Bloody Balfour" by firm suppression of unrest.

Acting as government leader in the House of Commons in 1891–92 and again from 1895 to 1902, Balfour established a reputation as an excellent debater. When he became prime minister, his government introduced (1902) educational reforms, concluded (1904) the Anglo-French Entente (see TRIPLE ENTENTE), and established (1904) the Committee of Imperial Defence. The government split, however, over Joseph CHAMBERLAIN's tariff proposals, and in 1905 Balfour resigned. After the defeat of the Conservatives in 1906, he led the party in opposition until 1911.

Later, Balfour served as first lord of the Admiralty (1915–16) and as foreign secretary (1916–19). In 1917 he issued the celebrated Balfour Declaration in favor of a Jewish national home. At the PARIS PEACE CONFERENCE he mitigated some of the harsher terms of the Treaty of Versailles (1919). Balfour was created a peer in 1922.

Balfour enjoyed a considerable reputation as a philosopher. His writings include *A Defence of Philosophic Doubt* (1879), *The Foundations of Belief* (1895), and *Chapters of Autobiography* (1930).

Balfour Declaration

The Balfour Declaration was a statement of British policy concerning ZIONISM contained in a letter from Foreign Secretary Arthur Balfour to Lord Rothschild, head of the British Zionist Federation, dated Nov. 2, 1917. Ultimately written into the mandate for Palestine (1922) of the League of Nations, the declaration endorsed the establishment of "a national home" for the Jewish people in Palestine, stipulated that such a national home not prejudice the rights of non-Jewish communities in Palestine, and added that the rights and political status enjoyed by Jews in other countries should not be compromised by the creation of this national home.

Bali

Bali, a province of Indonesia, is part of the Lesser Sunda Islands, 3.2 km (2 mi) east of Java. Its area is about 5,623 km^2 (2,171 mi^2), and its highest peak, Mount Agung, reaches 3,142 m (10,308 ft). The population is 2,766,000 (1988 est.); cities include Denpasar, the capital, and Singaradja. Volcanic in origin, Bali has a dry, mountainous north coastal section and a southern plain with a rainy monsoon season. The annual mean temperature is 28° C (82° F).

The Balinese, the major ethnic group occupying the island, are of Malayan origin. Balinese culture was indirectly influenced in the past by Indian civilization as traders passed through the Indonesian islands. During the 16th century the ruling class of predominantly Hindu Java adopted Islam. As a result many Javanese took refuge in Bali, carrying with them Hindu beliefs and traditions. Today nearly all Balinese live in villages in narrow river valleys or along the coastal lowlands, where they raise rice, maize, cassava, pigs, and cattle for local use and copra, coffee, and tobacco for export. They practice a blend of Hinduism, Buddhism, and animism that stresses dramatic rituals rather than philosophy and mysticism and have adopted a modified form of the Hindu caste system. The Balinese are noted for their graceful dances, lively music, and superb handicrafts—silver and gold jewelry, painting, and woodcarving.

The Dutch EAST INDIA COMPANY traded with Bali from 1597, but the Dutch gained full control only in 1908. After Japanese occupation during World War II, Dutch rule was reestablished until Indonesia received independence in 1949.

Balinese cat

The Balinese cat originated as a sport, or mutation, from the Siamese cat in the early 1950s, when some purebred Siamese produced long-haired kittens. The long-hairs bred true, and eventually the new breed was established. The Balinese has the same body conformation and color points as the Siamese but has a medium-long silky coat. The ears are large and the eyes blue.

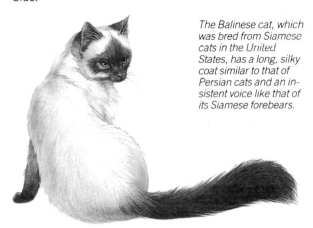

The Balinese cat, which was bred from Siamese cats in the United States, has a long, silky coat similar to that of Persian cats and an insistent voice like that of its Siamese forebears.

Baliol, John de

[bay'-lee-ul] John de Baliol (or Balliol), c.1250–1314, king of Scotland (1292–96), was the youngest son of John de Baliol (d. 1269), the founder of Balliol College, Oxford. In 1290, after the death of King Alexander III's heir, Margaret, "Maid of Norway," EDWARD I of England was made adjudicator between the claimants for the Scottish crown and decided in favor of Baliol.

By 1296, John had fallen out with Edward, who had invaded Scotland and reduced the Scottish king to a *toom tabard* ("empty cloak"). John was later imprisoned in the Tower of London. In 1299 the pope intervened for his release, and John fled to Normandy. John's son **Edward de Baliol**, d. 1364, was crowned king in 1332 and soon acknowledged EDWARD III as overlord of Scotland. He later resigned (1356) his kingdom and title to the English king.

Balkan Wars

The Balkan Wars of 1912–13 were two short wars fought over the disposition of the Ottoman Empire's former Balkan territories. Tsarist Russia supported the efforts of Bulgaria and Serbia in 1911 to establish an alliance that would check Austria-Hungary's advances southeastward into the Balkans. In the aftermath of the 1908 revolt of the YOUNG TURKS, these two smaller states were additionally interested in dividing the remaining Turkish-controlled territory in Europe, specifically MACEDONIA. On Mar. 13, 1912, Serbia and Bulgaria signed a treaty of mutual assistance. Greece joined in a pact with Bulgaria on May 29, 1912, and Montenegro arranged agreements with Bulgaria and Serbia in late September.

With Turkey already involved in a war with Italy over Libya, and despite protests from the great powers, the Balkan League began its war against the Ottoman Empire on Oct. 8, 1912. To the surprise of most observers, the Balkan allies won quick, decisive victories. The Treaty of London (May 30, 1913) forced the Ottoman Empire to cede virtually all of its remaining European territory—except for the region immediately adjacent to Constantinople—to the Balkan states.

Subsequently, the allies disputed the division of the territorial gains. Bulgaria challenged, in particular, Greek and Serbian claims to Macedonia. Overestimating its strength, Bulgaria launched an attack on its former allies on June 30, 1913. This second Balkan War soon found Romania and Turkey joining the fighting with Greece and Serbia. Thus attacked from all sides, Bulgaria had to sign an armistice on July 31. The Treaty of Bucharest (Aug. 10, 1913) stripped Bulgaria of some recently conquered territory. Greece, which in the earlier conflict had taken Crete and some Aegean islands from Turkey, now formally acquired the important port of Salonika (Thessaloníki) and most of coastal Macedonia, while Serbia received north and central Macedonia. Romania obtained a large section of the DOBRUJA from Bulgaria, which also had to yield the greater part of Thrace to Turkey.

Although all the Balkan states significantly increased the size of their territories at the expense of Turkey, Bulgaria remained embittered by its defeat in the second Balkan War, and its neighboring states sought still other lands for expansion. The Balkan disputes were to be continued in the larger context of WORLD WAR I.

Balkans The Balkans are the states that occupy the forested, mountainous Balkan Peninsula of southeastern Europe, a region that for centuries was part of the Ottoman Empire. Although the peninsula's boundaries are imprecise, it is often defined as the region south of the Danube and Sava rivers, thus including the modern states of Albania, Bulgaria, Greece, and most of Yugoslavia, as well as that part of Turkey lying within Europe. Romania, although north of the Danube, is also usually considered a Balkan country. The Balkans are bounded on the west by the Adriatic and Ionian seas, on the south by the Mediterranean, and on the east by the Black and Aegean seas.

Ball, Lucille Lucille Ball, b. Jamestown, N.Y., Aug. 6, 1911, d. Apr. 26, 1989, was a comedienne and TV producer best known for her television series "I Love Lucy," which ran almost continuously from 1951 to 1957 and also featured her husband, bandleader Desi Arnaz. Ball began her career as a model, then appeared—first as bit player, then as featured star—in more than 50

Lucille Ball, an American actress, comedienne, and producer, rose to stardom as the scatterbrained housewife in "I Love Lucy" (1951–57), one of television's most successful situation comedies. Two later series, "The Lucy Show" (1962–68) and "Here's Lucy" (1968–74), established Ball as one of America's most durably popular performers.

Hollywood films. After the success of the "Lucy" series, and her divorce from Arnaz, she became head of two major TV production companies and the star of three subsequent "Lucy" series. She also starred in the Broadway show *Wildcat* (1960), the film *Mame* (1974), and occasionally in TV specials.

Balla, Giacomo Giacomo Balla, b. July 18, 1871, d. Mar. 1, 1958, the oldest of the Italian painters who signed (1910) the *Technical Manifesto of Futurist Painting* in Milan, was the link to the second generation of futurists (see FUTURISM).

After early work in the divisionist (pointillist) technique, Balla, in 1912, adopted cubist fragmentation, evident in such works as *Speeding Automobile* (1912; Museum of Modern Art, New York). His studies, during that same year, of the interpenetration of light were among the earliest abstract paintings.

ballad A ballad is a poem that tells a dramatic story in a simple, direct style suitable for setting to music. The form is characterized by informal diction, a narrative dependent on action and dialogue, thematic intensity, and repetition. The four types are folk, literary, broadside, and sentimental. English folk ballads were first collected by Bishop Thomas Percy in his *Reliques of Ancient English Poetry* (1765). These were supplemented by the more definitive *English and Scottish Popular Ballads* published (1883–98) by Francis Child, an American. (See FOLK MUSIC.) A literary ballad is the result of a deliberate attempt to capture the naive charm of the folk ballad. Wordsworth's "Preface" to his *Lyrical Ballads* (1798) is a manifesto of this urge. Broadside ballads were printed on large, double-columned sheets that included a suggested tune in keeping with the rhythm. In the 18th century they were sold for a penny, and hence became known as penny ballads. Sentimental ballads, songs with banal tunes and melodramatic lyrics, were popular at the turn of the 20th century.

ballade [bal-ahd']   The ballade is both a musical and an Old French poetic form. Originally, it was a dance form as well. The ballade consists of three stanzas and an envoy, written in iambic or anapestic meter, with an octave stanza in the rhyme scheme *a b a b b c b C* and an envoy in the scheme *b c b C* (see VERSIFICATION). Thus the rhymes are carried throughout the poem; stanzas and envoy both end with a refrain (*C*).

Sung ballades were popular in 14th- and 15th-century France. Guillaume de Machaut, poet and musician to French nobility, excelled at the courtly ballade and influenced the work of the English poet Geoffrey Chaucer. François VILLON, however, was the greatest master of the ballade.

Thomas Morley, in his *Plaine and Easie Introduction to Practical Musicke* (1597), speaks of the ballade as a dance form lighter than the villanelle. By the time that Charles Burney had published his encompassing *General History of Music* (1776–89), the ballade had long been dissociated from dancing. Composers in the 19th century turned to the ballade as a romantic musical form. Brahms, Chopin, Grieg, and Liszt all wrote ballades for the piano; and Schubert used the ballade as a song form.

Ballard, J. G.   James Graham Ballard, b. Nov 15, 1930, is an English novelist who has extended the boundaries of science fiction. Ballard was born to English parents residing in Shanghai, but his comfortable childhood was abruptly ended when the Japanese attacked Pearl Harbor. His recollections of the war years provide the substance of his autobiographical novel, *Empire of the Sun* (1984; film, 1987). Among Ballard's most successful science fiction novels are *The Crystal World* (1966), *The Atrocity Exhibition* (1970), *Concrete Island* (1974), and *The Day of Creation* (1988).

ballet [bal-lay']   Ballet is a formalized type of dancing in which the performers, through planned movement to accompanying music, present a story or develop an abstract concept. It is an elaborated form of lyric theater, and its history is a 400-year record of invention and performance. Like opera, with whose history it frequently intermingles, ballet is a tradition European in origin and Renaissance in its ideal of harmonious collaboration between artists—dancers, mimes, choreographers, musicians, and designers of costumes and decor. Since World War II, ballet has achieved a renaissance of its own throughout the world with the establishment of national companies, or private companies with national identities, supported variously by government subsidy, philanthropic funding, and burgeoning public enthusiasm.

Ballet History

The roots of ballet are in the public parades, masques, pageants, and equestrian demonstrations of Italy and France in the 15th, 16th, and 17th centuries. In Italy the impulse toward dramatic representation resulted in the *balletto*—from *ballo* ("dance") and *ballare* ("to dance")—an enormous spectacle lasting hours (or even days) and utilizing dance, recited poetry, song, and elaborate scenic effects, all organized around an allegorical plot and with the masked and richly costumed men and boys of the local court taking the principal roles. The spectacles were presented in large halls or on tennis courts. (Modern theaters as such were not built until the late 16th century.) The audience was the courtiers, who themselves employed dancing masters for instruction in social skills and for mounting amateur theatricals. In 1460, Domenico da Piacenza wrote one of the first dance manuals.

French Court Ballets.   When Henry II of France married Catherine de Médicis, in 1533, she imported the Italian *balletto* to her new home in France, where it became the *ballet*. In 1573, she staged *Ballet des Polonais* to music of Roland de LASSUS, the poetry of Pierre de RONSARD, and the dances of Balthazar de Beaujoyeux. Beaujoyeux's most famous work was *Ballet Comique de la Reine*, presented in 1581.

Louis XIV, patron of the arts and himself a dancer in court ballets (*ballets de cour*), founded L'Académie Royale de Danse in 1661, which brought this form to a culmination. His dancing master, Pierre Beauchamps, codified the positions of the feet in classical ballet technique (the *danse d'école*) and invented many ballets, divertissements, and *comédies-ballets* (a spoken comedy with dance scenes interspersed) in collaboration with MOLIÈRE and the composer Jean Baptiste LULLY. *Le Triomphe de*

Karen Kain and Frank Augustyn dance in the National Ballet of Canada's version of Swan Lake, *a four-act ballet with music by Peter Ilich Tchaikovsky. Although considered a failure when first performed in 1877,* Swan Lake *has since become one of the world's most popular full-length ballets.*

The French dancer Marie Camargo, as portrayed by Nicolas Lancret, was the most popular and accomplished ballerina of the 18th century. She is also credited with raising the skirts of the ballet costume just above the ankle.

l'Amour (1681) was the masterpiece of Beauchamps and Lully; in it appeared LaFontaine, the first woman to dance professionally in a ballet. The French love of *la danse* found a home at the Paris Opéra, and the terminology for ballet technique was henceforth in the French language (see the accompanying *Glossary of Ballet Terms*).

Emergence of Professional Ballet. In the early 18th century, ballet became a profession, with schools, theaters, paid performers, and rival aesthetic movements. The dominant progressive style of dance theater in the century was the *ballet d'action*, an attempt to unify the spectacle around clear narrative indicated in heroic mime and dance. No present-day equivalent to such a style exists, except perhaps in some of the dance-mimes of Mikhail FOKINE. The choreographers John Weaver of England, Franz Hilverding of Vienna, Gaspardo Angiolini of Italy, and Jean Georges NOVERRE of France spread the form throughout Europe and into Russia. The new realism of stage action finally banished masks, and costumes began to suggest period style. Testifying to the international dynasties of dancers now possible, the Italian dancer and dancing master Gaetano Vestris (see VESTRIS family) fathered Auguste Vestris in Paris in 1760, and the son danced at the Paris Opéra for almost four decades as the "god of the dance," a title inherited from his father.

Romantic Ballet. At the end of the 18th and the beginning of the 19th century ballet began to produce works that are still revived. The French ballet *La Fille Mal Gardée* (1789) is the oldest regularly performed work in current world repertoire. The technical reforms that resulted in the romantic movement were achieved by the Italian ballet masters Salvatore VIGANÒ; and Carlo Blasis, and by the Frenchman Charles Didelot, who encouraged the use of *pointe* technique in "toe shoes" (shoes with blocked toes) for women.

The romantic ballet announced itself in Filippo Taglioni's *La Sylphide* (1832), a ballet for his daughter, Marie

Taglioni (see TAGLIONI family). The supernatural subject was expressed through the long, calf-length *tutu* of the sylphs' costume as well as by dancers "flown" by means of wires and pulleys. More importantly, *La Sylphide* marked an advance in dance technique for the simulation of an "unearthly" floating continuity in the dance movement. The work allowed some pointwork for Taglioni, and its choreography featured reactive effects for the *corps de ballet* and waltzlike partnering and adagio passages for the leads. In this ballet and in Adolphe Adam's *Giselle* (1841) the modern idea of the ballerina was born, not only in her sheer authority but in her mastery of dance discourse. Carlotta GRISI was the first Giselle; her dances were choreographed by Jules Perrot, who is known as well for the *Pas de Quatre* (1845), a dance divertissement choreographed for Taglioni, Fanny Cerrito, Grisi, and Lucile GRAHN, the four reigning ballerinas of their age. French ballet music reached a peak of expression in the ballets composed by Léo DELIBES: *Coppélia* (1870), choreographed by Arthur Saint-Léon, and *Sylvia* (1876), choreographed by Louis Mérante.

In addition to the French, the other major—although little known at the time—European school of ballet was the Danish under the direction of August BOURNONVILLE, a pupil of Auguste Vestris. Bournonville's version of *La Sylphide*, which premiered in 1836, is still performed today. Bournonville's many works include *The Conservatory, Napoli,* and *The Guards at Amager.*

Russian Ballet. In Russia, the tsars' rapt imitation of European court manners included the importation of dancing masters, choreographers, and dancers throughout the 18th century. The French ballet master Didelot and the Swedish teacher Christian Johansson brought their art to St. Petersburg (now Leningrad). The great achievement of establishing a Russian classical school of dance, however, was the work of a Frenchman, Marius PETIPA, the chief ballet master of the Imperial School and the Maryinsky (now Kirov) Ballet from 1869 to 1903. His

Anna Pavlova and Mikhail Fokine dance in Marius Petipa's Les Millions d'Arlequin, *or* Harlequinade, *based on commedia dell'arte and first performed (1900) at St. Petersburg's Maryinski Theater.*

The dancer-choreographer Vaslav Nijinsky and the composer Igor Stravinsky collaborated on the ballet Petrouchka. The ballet was first performed in Paris in 1911 by the Ballets Russes de Serge Diaghilev.

many ballets (at least 60 full-length) form the Western idea of Russian theatrical art, especially those ballets set to the music of Peter Ilich TCHAIKOVSKY, *The Sleeping Beauty* (1890) and *Swan Lake* (first perf. 1877; Petipa version 1895). Petipa was assisted by Lev IVANOV, and together their *corps de ballet* experiments, sophistication of *pointe* technique, and clear differentiation between classical and character dance styles remain as definitive of ballet. Ivanov choreographed *The Nutcracker* to Tchaikovsky's score and to Petipa's scenario in 1892. *The Nutcracker* is believed to be the most frequently staged ballet in history.

Fokine and Diaghilev. The beginnings of American theatrical dance proved influential on Russian ballet through the work of Isadora DUNCAN as dancer and choreographer in the first years of the 20th century. Performing barefoot to serious concert scores not intended for dance and wearing light "Greek" costumes, Duncan revolted against the declining French ballet and its European and American progeny, declaring the birth of a "free dance." Her immediate influence was less on American choreographers—Ruth ST. DENIS, Martha GRAHAM, or Doris HUMPHREY—than on the Russian choreographer Mikhail FOKINE. As chief choreographer for the impresario Serge DIAGHILEV, Fokine conquered Paris and all Europe when the BALLETS RUSSES DE SERGE DIAGHILEV opened in the French capital in 1909. For the next 20 years Diaghilev's company ruled world ballet. The greatest of his choreographers was Fokine, whose *Petrouchka* (1911) combined the music of Igor STRAVINSKY, the decor of Aleksandr Benois, and the dancing of Vaslav NIJINSKY (the new "god of the dance"), Tamara KARSAVINA, and Enrico Cecchetti. Fokine's mastery of plastic values and his effects of dance-mime created a new theatrical style. His ballets include *Les Sylphides* (1909; orig. *Chopiniana*, 1907), *Le Pavillon d'Armide* (1907), *Le Carnaval* (1910), and *L'Oiseau de Feu* (*Firebird*, 1910). Among the dancers associated with the Diaghilev company were Alexandra

DANILOVA and Alicia MARKOVA. The Russian ballerina Anna PAVLOVA danced only briefly with Diaghilev's company; with her own troupe she traveled throughout the world educating audiences in classical dance.

From the Diaghilev period a tradition of great collaboration was born. Such world-famous choreographers as Vaslav Nijinsky, his sister Bronislava NIJINSKA, Leonid MASSINE, and George BALANCHINE were all sponsored by Diaghilev. Splendid scenic contributions were made by Benois, Léon BAKST, Michel LARIONOV, and Natalia Goncharova. The greatest ballet composer of this century, Stravinsky, began his career with the Ballets Russes.

Contemporary Ballet

Following Diaghilev's death in 1929, various national ballet companies were established, many of them by his former associates. The earliest to emerge (1932) was the BALLETS RUSSES DE MONTE CARLO, in the first of its several forms. The British school combined the teaching of Marie RAMBERT and the directorial skills of Ninette de VALOIS. The resultant national company, the Sadler's Wells (later the ROYAL BALLET), developed a great classical choreographer in Frederick ASHTON, whose many ballets achieved world acclaim. The choreographer Kenneth MACMILLAN produced such widely admired full-length ballets as *Romeo and Juliet* (1965), *Anastasia* (1971), and *Manon* (1974).

The French ballet has achieved no renaissance in the 20th century, despite the efforts of such longtime Opéra Ballet choreographers as Léo Staats and Serge LIFAR and other influential French choreographers, including Roland PETIT and Maurice BÉJART, or the direction, since 1983, of Rudolf NUREYEV. The ROYAL DANISH BALLET periodically retrenches itself around its Bournonville riches, and its academy continues to produce great male dancers. The Stuttgart Ballet, with a history dating from the 1600s, gained new prominence under John Cranko, who was its director (1961–73). The Russian schools associated with the BOLSHOI BALLET of Moscow and the Leningrad KIROV BALLET have produced such great performers as Galina ULANOVA, Maya PLISETSKAYA, Irina Kolpakova, and Vladimir Vasiliev, as well as the sensational Kirov defectors to the West, Rudolf Nureyev, Natalia MAKAROVA, and Mikhail BARYSHNIKOV.

Ballet in North America. Canada has three major ballet companies: Royal Winnipeg Ballet (1939) received its Royal Charter from Queen Elizabeth II in 1953; NATIONAL BALLET OF CANADA (1951) is based in Toronto; Les Grands Ballets Canadiens (1956) makes its home in Montreal.

In the United States, three companies dominate. The JOFFREY BALLET (1960) offers a museum repertoire of modern classics and occasional works by contemporary choreographers. AMERICAN BALLET THEATRE (1939) presents a repertoire of 19th-century classics along with modern works by Jerome ROBBINS, Britain's Antony TUDOR, Twyla THARP, and Eliot Feld, interpreted by a continually changing performance roster of international stars.

The largest ballet academy in the Western Hemisphere is the School of American Ballet, established in 1934 by

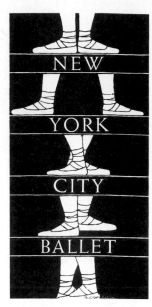

(Left) *Robert Kovich and Chris Komar dance in* Summerspace, *by the revolutionary choreographer Merce Cunningham. The sets and costumes of the dance, first performed in 1958, were designed by Robert Rauschenberg.* (Right) *A poster from the New York City Ballet, with the drawings by Edward Gorey, illustrates the five basic positions of the feet in classical ballet.*

Lincoln KIRSTEIN and choreographer George Balanchine and today the official school of NEW YORK CITY BALLET. In a series of great modern works—*Apollo* (1928), *Serenade* (1934), *The Four Temperaments* (1946; revised 1951), *Orpheus* (1948), *Agon* (1957)—Balanchine re-created the idea of dance classicism and ballet technique. His collaborations with Stravinsky are models of sensitivity to musical values. The core of Balanchine's repertoire, including *Concerto Barocco* (1940), *Symphony in C* (1947, as *Palais de Cristal*), *Divertimento No. 15* (1956), *Liebeslieder Walzer* (1960), *Jewels* (1967), and *Violin Concerto* (1972), has made him the most influential ballet choreographer in the second half of this century.

A number of great dancers have associated with New York City Ballet, among them Mikhail Baryshnikov, Jacques D'AMBOISE, André EGLEVSKY, Suzanne FARRELL, Melissa HAYDEN, Patricia McBride, Peter MARTINS, Maria Tallchief, and Edward VILLELLA. Arthur MITCHELL, a principal dancer with the company, withdrew to found the first black classical ballet school and company, DANCE THEATRE OF HARLEM, following Martin Luther King's assassination in 1968; the company made its auspicious debut two years later.

The oldest American company, the Atlanta Ballet, was founded in 1929. Among the prestigious companies now presenting regular seasons are the Dayton Ballet (1937) in Ohio, the San Francisco Ballet (1938), the Tulsa Ballet (1956), the Boston Ballet (1963), the Minnesota Dance Theater (1962) in Minneapolis, the Houston Ballet (1968), and the Pennsylvania and Milwaukee Ballet (merged 1987) in Philadelphia and Milwaukee. Ballet West, founded (1952) in Salt Lake City by the University

of Utah, is the most notable of university-affiliated companies. These groups, and the many professional ballet and dance schools in the United States, have become the source of fresh talent for ballet companies throughout the Western world.

See also: CHOREOGRAPHY; DANCE; FOLK DANCE; MUSICAL COMEDY; OPERA; THEATER ARCHITECTURE AND STAGING.

GLOSSARY OF BALLET TERMS

Adagio 1. A sequence of exercises in slow tempo, performed in ballet class to develop strength in sustaining extensions and balances. 2. A passage in a *pas de deux* in which the man supports the woman in turns and balances. 3. The technique of partnering.

Air, en l' "In the air." Used to describe steps performed with the working leg off the floor, such as *rond de jambe en l'air*; or jumping steps, such as, *tour en l'air*.

Allegro Sequences of steps in fast tempo, performed in ballet class to develop speed and clarity of execution.

Arabesque A position in which the dancer stands on one leg, straight or bent, with the other extended to the back, usually at right angles to the body, but higher in *arabesque penchée* (leaning), when the dancer leans forward and raises the leg higher to follow the line of the torso.

Assemblé A jumping step in which the dancer thrusts one leg up and out to the front, side, or back, at the same time springing off the other, and brings the legs together in the air before landing.

Attitude A position originally derived from Giovanni da BOLOGNA's statue of Mercury, in which the dancer stands on one leg with the other extended to the front or back and bent at the knee, which is held at a higher level than the foot.

Ballabile   A group dance, usually for the *corps de ballet*.

Ballerina   Literally, "female dancer," but usually used of one who dances leading roles, *prima ballerina*, first dancer.

Ballet master/mistress   Before the word *choreographer* was used in its contemporary sense, the ballet master was responsible for arranging ballets. Today, the term more usually denotes the person who rehearses ballets created by someone else and also performs administrative duties such as drawing up rehearsal schedules; casting of minor roles is often the province of the ballet master.

Ballon   Literally, "bounce." The quality of smooth, springing ascent and descent in jumping steps, achieved primarily by the pliant use of the feet.

Barre   The horizontal wooden bar that runs around the wall of the ballet studio at waist height, and that the dancer holds on to during the first part of class; by extension, this part of ballet class is also usually referred to as the *barre*.

Basque, saut de   A jumping step in which the working leg is raised to the side and the foot of the other is drawn up to the knee of the working leg as the body turns in the air, landing in that position.

Battement   A generic term to describe the various movements in which the leg makes a beating motion. They are performed at the *barre* in a systematic progression to exercise all the leg muscles: *Battement tendu*, in which the leg is extended to front, side, and back with the toe resting on the floor; *battement tendu jeté*, in which the leg is extended to front, side, and back with the toe leaving the floor very slightly (also called *glissé*; or *dégagé*); *battement frappé*, in which the foot is sharply extended to front, side, and back from the ankle of the supporting leg; *petit battement*, in which the working foot beats from front to back, or back to front, against the ankle of the supporting leg; *battement fondu*, in which the working leg is extended to front, side, or back, either to point *tendu* or in the air, from a position in which the working foot is pointed in front or in back of the supporting ankle; both knees are bent at the beginning and straighten simultaneously; *grand battement jeté*, in which the leg is lifted, straight, to front, side, and back, attaining waist level or higher; *grand battement développé*, in which the foot is drawn up to the knee of the standing leg and then extended to front, side, or back, until the leg is straight.

Batterie   A generic term referring to steps in which the feet beat together or cross in the air, either as an embellishment to add brilliance to jumping steps, or as the essential characteristic of the step, as in *entrechats* or *brisés*.

Bourrée, pas de   A linking step in which the weight is transferred from one foot to the other in three small steps. *Pas de bourrée chaîné* or *couru* is a series of small, even steps on *pointe* which give the impression that the dancer is gliding across the surface of the stage.

Brisé, pas   Literally, "broken step." A small traveling *assemblé*; embellished with a beat. *Brisé volé*: a series of *brisés* to front and back alternately, landing on one foot, giving the impression that the dancer is skimming over the surface of the stage.

Cabriole   A jumping step in which the dancer beats straight legs together in the air.

Changement de pieds   The dancer jumps straight up in the air with legs together and reverses the position of his feet before landing.

Chassé, pas   A linking step in which the dancer slides one foot out to front, side, or back, bringing the other up to it in fifth position before continuing into the next movement.

Chat, pas de   Literally, "cat's step." A light, jumping step in which the knees bend, bringing the feet together beneath the body before landing again in fifth position.

Coda   The fast final section of a *pas de deux*, in which the dancers may have brief solo passages as well as dancing together in a brilliant conclusion.

Corps de ballet   The ensemble of dancers in a ballet company, who appear in support of the soloists.

Coryphée   A dancer (of either sex) who has moved out of the *corps de ballet* to dance minor solo roles.

Croisé   Literally, "crossed." A position of the body in which the dancer turns obliquely to the audience, so that when the working leg is raised, it crosses the supporting leg.

Divertissement   1. A section of a ballet comprising dances

These are the five basic positions:

first   second   third   fourth   fifth

that have no connection with the plot, for example, the fairy-tale dances in *The Sleeping Beauty*, Act III. 2. A short dance or excerpt from a longer ballet given as a separate item in a program.

Effacé A position of the body in which the dancer turns slightly away from the audience; the working leg is the one farther from the audience.

Elevation The ability to jump high in the air and give the impression of remaining suspended there for an instant.

Enchaînement A combination of steps into a dance phrase.

Entrechat A vertical jump in fifth position, with the feet changing in the air, twice (*entrechat quatre*), three times (*entrechat six*), four times (*entrechat huit*), and, exceptionally, five times (*entrechat dix*). The term *entrechat deux* is not used: when the feet beat once and change this is called *changement battu* or *royale*. In all of these the dancer returns to fifth position. In *entrechat trois, cinq*, and *sept* the dancer lands on one foot with the other touching the supporting leg after one, two, or three beats.

Épaulement Literally, "shouldering." The slight turning of the shoulders, *croisé*; or *effacé*;, in relation to the head and legs, distinguishes the classic style, particularly of the Italian, Russian, and British Schools. In the old French and the Danish Schools it is rarely used.

Fouetté Literally, "whipped." A turning step, usually done in a series, in which the working leg whips out to the side in a *rond de jambe* and then in to the knee as the dancer turns on the supporting leg, rising on to the *pointe* at each revolution. The 32 *fouettés* performed by Odile in *Swan Lake*, Act III, are a supposed touchstone of female virtuosity.

Glissade Literally, "sliding." A linking step in which the dancer moves to the side, front, or back from fifth position to fourth or fifth position, with a moment of transition in which the feet should be fully stretched.

Jeté Literally, "thrown." A jump from one foot on to the other. It may be a small jump, or large (*grand jeté*;), landing in a position such as *arabesque* or *attitude*. The jump

may be beaten (*battu*) or done with a turn (*en tournant*).

Leotard A one-piece garment covering the whole torso, with or without sleeves, worn with tights for practice or, in modern ballets, as a stage costume. Originally designed by the French acrobat Jules Léotard (1830–70).

Maître or maîtresse de ballet See *ballet master/mistress*.

Pas Literally, "step." The technical terms for ballet steps often include the word *pas*, or sometimes *temps* (literally, "time"), as in *pas de chat* or *temps de poisson*. *Pas* is also used in the sense of "dance," as in *pas de deux/trois/quatre* (dance for two, three, four people) or more, or as in *pas des patineurs* (dance of the skaters). *Pas d'action* signifies a sequence in a ballet in which the narrative is carried forward by means of dancing, as in the so-called Rose Adagio in Act I of *The Sleeping Beauty*.

Pirouette A complete turn of the body performed on one leg; the working leg may be placed against the ankle or drawn up to the knee of the supporting leg, or extended to the side or to the back, in *arabesque* or *attitude*.

Plié Literally, a "bending." The first exercises done in every class to loosen the muscles, the foundation of the dancer's technique. The dancer stands erect at the *barre* and slowly bends the knees, keeping them in line with the turned-out feet. *Pliés* are practiced in all five positions. Nearly every step begins and ends in *demi-plié* (half-), giving impetus to a jump and cushioning a landing.

Pointe The tip of the toe. Women, and infrequently men, dance *sur les pointes* in blocked shoes. The introduction of this technique in the early 19th century made possible the development of female virtuosity, with such feats as multiple *fouettés* and sustained balances on one leg. *Demi-pointe* is when the dancer stands with the toes spread flat on the floor and the rest of the foot raised (*relevé*) from the metatarsal.

Port de bras Literally, "carriage of the arms." Used in this general sense, and also to denote exercises designed to develop the graceful and harmonious use of the arms. For instance, when a dancer, at the *barre*, bends the whole

attitude devant   attitude derrière   arabesque   battement

torso forward and back, this exercise is called *port de bras* even though its correct execution involves the entire body. Positions of the arms correspond to positions of the feet.

Positions   There are five basic positions of the feet in which all steps in classic ballet begin and end, with the legs turned out from the pelvis: First position: heels touching, feet in a straight line; Second position: feet wide apart, in a straight line; Third position: one foot in front of the other, and heel against the instep; Fourth position: feet apart, one in front of the other, opposite fifth; Fifth position: one foot in front of the other, the heel against the joint of the big toe.

Relevé   Literally, "lifted." The raising of the body on to half or full *pointe*.

Rond de jambe   Literally, "circle of the leg." The working leg describes a circle either on the floor (*à terre*) or in the air (*en l'air*).

Sissonne   A jump from both feet on to one foot with the working leg opening to the side, front, or back in a scissor-like motion. May be performed with a beat.

Tour   A complete turn of the body. See *pirouette. Tour en l'air*, a turn in the air, executed as the dancer jumps up vertically. Male dancers are expected to perform double *tours en l'air*, and some are capable of triples. Rarely performed by women.

Tournant, en   Literally, "turning." Many steps may be performed, either singly or in series, while the dancer makes a revolution of the body or describes a circle on the floor.

Turn-out   (French: *en dehors*.) The turning out of the legs from the pelvis, essential for speed, flexibility, elegance, and the ability to move in any direction.

Tutu   Ballet skirt, either calf-length (as in *Les Sylphides*) or projecting straight out at hip level (as in *Swan Lake*), with many layers of ruffles underneath. The term *tutu* is actually a slang word referring to the latter part of the costume, or rather to the part of the anatomy it conceals.

Variation   Solo dance.

Ballets Russes de Monte Carlo [bah-lay roos duh mahn'-tay kahr'-loh]

Ballets Russes de Monte Carlo, an outgrowth of the great BALLETS RUSSES DE SERGE DIAGHILEV, was created in 1931, two years after the death of DIAGHILEV. The new company included the best dancers and choreographers from the parent company, such as Leonid MASSINE, George BALANCHINE (until 1933), André EGLEVSKY, and Alexandra DANILOVA, under the joint directorship of René Blum and Colonel W. de Basil. It opened to great acclaim at Monte Carlo in 1932. In 1936 the company split into two factions, one headed by Blum and the other by de Basil. After litigation Blum's company emerged as the Ballets Russes de Monte Carlo. Its rival, called by de Basil the Original Ballets Russes, died after a decade of unsuccessful world tours.

Ballets Russes de Monte Carlo, on the other hand, triumphed immediately under the leadership of Blum and Massine. The outbreak of World War II in 1939 forced the company to remain in the United States where, headquartered in New York, it continued to tour. Blum was seized by the Gestapo in Paris and died at Auschwitz in 1942. Ballets Russes gave its final New York season in 1957, and toured occasionally until it was dissolved in 1962.

Ballets Russes de Serge Diaghilev [sir-gay' dee-ah'-gil-yif]

A ballet company that became legendary in its own time for its brilliant synthesis of dance, decor, and music, the Ballets Russes de Serge Diaghilev, founded in 1909 by the impresario DIAGHILEV, revolutionized and revitalized BALLET by departing from the romantic style of such full-length ballets as Adolphe Adam's *Giselle* to create shorter, more novel ballets in a modern, expressive style. Despite the company's name, it never performed as a group in Russia.

cabriole   croisé derrière   croisé devant   entrechat   jeté

The poster of Vaslav Nijinsky in L'Après-midi d'un faune *is by Léon Bakst, who also designed the scenery and costumes for the ballet. First performed by the Ballets Russes in 1912, the ballet was choreographed and danced by Nijinsky to music by Debussy.*

Schéhérazade and *Firebird* (both 1910) are typical of Diaghilev's preference for exotic themes and colorful fairy-tale settings and costumes. Léon Bakst's designs and Mikhail FOKINE's choreography were an escape into a febrile world of sensuality and fantasy. At the 1913 premiere of *Le Sacre du printemps* (*The Rite of Spring*), which represented a primitive fertility rite ending with a human sacrifice set to Igor STRAVINSKY's wild and searing music, with Nikolai Roerich's strange designs and Vaslav NIJINSKY's highly controversial choreography, the audience, violently divided in opinion, rioted and almost halted the performance. The Ballets Russes production of *Parade* (1917), half-danced and half-pantomimed, had a scenario by Jean COCTEAU and was choreographed by Leonid MASSINE; it became a major influence on postwar French productions, largely because of Pablo PICASSO's cubist settings and costumes and Erik SATIE's score, a collage of sounds incorporating typewriters and street noises with instrumental music.

During the 1920s Nijinsky's sister, Bronislava NIJINSKA, became an important choreographer for the troupe, and in 1925 George BALANCHINE was appointed chief choreographer. For Serge LIFAR, the last of the great male dancers, after Nijinsky and Massine, to be discovered by Diaghilev, Balanchine created both *Apollo* (1928) and *The Prodigal Son* (1929), two of his most important works.

During the two decades of its existence the Ballets Russes presented about 68 ballets. Many of its dancers and choreographers later joined the BALLETS RUSSES DE MONTE CARLO; others such as Balanchine and Ninette de VALOIS went on to found their own companies.

Ballinger, Richard A.   Richard Achilles Ballinger, b. Boonesboro, Iowa, July 9, 1858, d. June 6, 1922, U.S. secretary of the interior (1909–11) under President William H. TAFT, became the focus of attacks upon Taft's conservation policies. An expert in mining law, he served (1907–08) as commissioner of the General Land Office. As interior secretary, Ballinger in 1909 fired a subordinate who had accused him of impeding investigation of allegedly fraudulent Alaskan coal-land claims. He was denounced by Forestry Bureau chief Gifford PINCHOT and others who felt Taft was betraying former president Theodore ROOSEVELT's conservationist policies. A joint congressional committee cleared Ballinger of wrongdoing, but he resigned in March 1911. The controversy helped create the split in the Republican party that led to the formation of the BULL MOOSE PARTY in 1912.

ballistic missile   SEE ROCKETS AND MISSILES

Ballistic Missile Early Warning System   see BMEWS

ballistics   Ballistics is the scientific study of the propulsion and motion of projectiles such as bullets, ARTILLERY shells, rockets, and guided missiles (SEE ROCKETS AND MISSILES). The field of ballistics also includes the study of the destructive action of such projectiles. The theory and techniques of ballistics have broad applications in technology. These applications include the formation of metal parts by explosive means, the development of cartridge-actuated devices for industry, and the development of heat shields and aluminum bumpers for spacecraft. Scientific research in fields such as geophysics, geodesy, meteoritics, and planetary exploration may also make use of the science of ballistics.

The first systematic treatment of the ballistics of gunnery was given by the Italian Niccolò Fontana, better known to historians of science as Tartaglia, in his *Nuova scienzia*, published in 1537. The theory of exterior ballistics was rapidly developed early in the 18th century, after the principles of dynamics and the methods of the calculus had been established by Galileo, Newton, and Leibniz. This important work in theory was largely an exercise in pure mathematics that had no immediate effect on practical gunnery, because no acceptably accurate way existed to measure the muzzle velocity of any firearm. Such a method was first suggested by the astronomer Cassini in 1707; the instrument itself, the ballistic pendulum, was invented by the Englishman Benjamin Robins in 1740.

Interior Ballistics. Interior ballistics is the study of the propulsion of projectiles by forces derived from the expansion of gases burning within a gun or rocket motor. Although the burning proceeds by similar stages in a gun and in a solid-propellant rocket, the pressures developed within a closed gun breech are much higher than those in a nozzled rocket motor; therefore, the metal parts of a gun system—the chamber, barrel, and recoil mechanism—are more complicated and must be much stronger than those of a nearly recoilless rocket launcher. In addition, motion is imparted in quite different ways to projectiles fired from guns and to missiles carrying both warheads and gas-reaction motors.

Exterior Ballistics.

Exterior Ballistics. Exterior ballistics, in the classical sense, deals with the flight of projectiles moving under the influence of gravitational and aerodynamic forces. The study of certain types of projectile, however, may require that forces not treated in the classical theory of the subject be considered. Guided missiles, for example, may be acted upon by corrective forces, such as motor thrust or aerodynamic lift due to fin movement, when their trajectories depart from prescribed paths in space.

Galileo and Newton were both greatly interested in the force called air resistance, now usually called aerodynamic drag, which reduces the speed of a projectile. The drag of a projectile moving head on is now usually divided into three parts: bow resistance, due to air pressure at the head of the projectile; skin friction, caused by the friction of air moving along the middle portion of the body; and base drag, due to the under-pressure and disturbance of the air behind the base. At speeds slightly greater than that of sound, head drag can be diminished by a sharp, extended point; skin friction by a smooth, somewhat streamlined body; and base drag by a boattail. At Mach numbers of about 3, projectiles with slender, sharply pointed heads and boattails have about half the drag of more obtusely coned, square-based projectiles of the same diameter.

The equations of motion of a particle acted upon by aerodynamic drag and terrestrial gravity can be written by using Newton's second law of motion. In the early 18th century, Johann Bernoulli of Switzerland examined the problem of a particle moving under the influence of gravity and drag proportional to the nth power of the velocity. He changed the equations of motion by substituting, for time, the angle of inclination of the tangent to the trajectory as the independent variable. The Bernoulli solution, obtained in 1719, was widely employed to compute trajectories during the 19th century and continues to have some application for the motion of projectiles fired at low velocities.

Leonhard EULER of Switzerland was the first major writer on ballistics whose work was presented in analytical rather than geometrical form. In the mid-18th century he wrote equations of motion for a particle projectile and devised approximate methods of solving them that have been used repeatedly by later writers. A somewhat more convenient method was devised by James Gregory about the same time and served as the basis for the important method for computing trajectories developed by American astronomer F. R. Moulton during World War I.

At sufficiently great altitudes and ranges, exterior ballistics merges with the field of CELESTIAL MECHANICS. Problems encountered under such conditions fall within the province of a new science, sometimes called geoballistics.

Terminal Ballistics. Terminal ballistics deals with the destructive actions and effects that occur at the end of the projectile's flight as an integral and undeformed body. The flight may end in one of two ways: the projectile may strike a solid obstruction, or its metal case may be broken by the explosion of a bursting charge. The phenomena of impact of a solid missile on a solid target develop as a continuous physical process; they have been extensively studied by flash radiography and are more readily predictable than those of the bursting of a high-explosive charge, whatever the nature of the surrounding medium.

balloon

balloon   A balloon is a type of AIRCRAFT that becomes airborne because of the buoyancy, or lift, supplied by a gas that is less dense than the air surrounding the balloon.

The first public balloon flight was made by the MONTGOLFIER BROTHERS, Joseph and Etienne, at Annonay, France, on June 5, 1783. Made of linen and paper, this unmanned balloon had a volume of 660 m³ (23,308 ft³) and was buoyed up by heated air. The balloon rose to an altitude of 1,800 m (5,906 ft) and flew 1.6 km (1 mi) from its starting point. On Nov. 21, 1783, Pilâtre de Rozier and the marquis d'Arlandes used a Montgolfier balloon to make the first manned flight, from the center of Paris to the city's suburbs. On Aug. 27, 1783, French chemist Jacques A. C. CHARLES inflated a balloon with hydrogen and launched it on an unmanned flight from the Champ de Mars in Paris. In December of that year he and an assistant made the first manned flight in a hydrogen balloon, from Paris to the village of Nesle, 104 km (65 mi) to the north.

Hydrogen was found to be superior to hot air for filling a balloon because hydrogen has inherent buoyancy,

Double Eagle II floats above France toward the end of its historic Atlantic crossing in 1978, the first such flight made by a balloon. The craft was piloted by an American team.

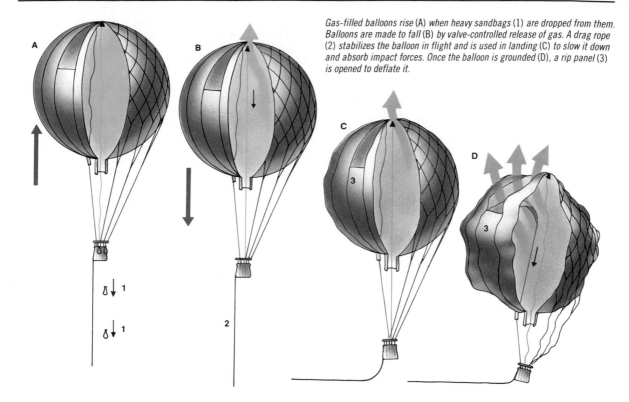

Gas-filled balloons rise (A) when heavy sandbags (1) are dropped from them. Balloons are made to fall (B) by valve-controlled release of gas. A drag rope (2) stabilizes the balloon in flight and is used in landing (C) to slow it down and absorb impact forces. Once the balloon is grounded (D), a rip panel (3) is opened to deflate it.

whereas the ability of hot air to supply lift decreases as the air cools. Helium, discovered in 1895, did not become commercially available until after 1918; it was also expensive and could not supply as much lift as hydrogen. The great advantage of helium, however, is its safety. Hydrogen is highly flammable and potentially explosive, but helium is not.

Once launched, a balloon will rise until its average density exactly equals that of the surrounding atmosphere. In order to go higher, the pilot must discard some ballast (bags of sand are often used). To descend, the pilot releases some of the buoyant gas through a valve.

From the end of the 18th century until the 1930s a balloon craze swept Europe and the United States. On Jan. 9, 1783, at Philadelphia, Jean Pierre BLANCHARD made the first U.S. balloon flight.

Military Use

The balloon was put into early use by the military. In the Battle of Fleurus between France and Austria (June 26, 1794), the French used a tethered balloon to observe the battlefield and direct artillery fire.

When the Austrians besieged Venice in 1849, they used 200 small hot-air balloons to carry bombs that were released by preset controls. Balloons were also used in the American Civil War (1861–65). In both cases, however, results were negligible.

The spherical balloon was excellent for free flight, but tethered spherical balloons were subject to bucking and rotation about their anchor cables. This made them unsuitable for military operations, for which a steady platform was required. By 1900, sausage-shaped balloons had been developed that combined the aerodynamics of the KITE with the aerostatics of the balloon. They foreshadowed the motorized AIRSHIP. Thousands of these kite balloons were used during World War I as observation posts and as aerial barrages (aprons of cables were suspended between the balloons to create hazards for enemy airplanes). Barrage balloons were also used during World War II.

Transcontinental Crossing

The great dream of 19th-century balloonists was intercontinental air travel. Because the prevailing wind in the Northern Hemisphere blows from west to east (see JET STREAM), the Atlantic crossing is easier from North America to Europe; thus most attempts have been eastward.

In 1978, 1980, and 1981, respectively, the first transatlantic, transcontinental (North America), and transpacific flights were made, in helium balloons. In 1984 the first solo transatlantic flight was made.

Sport Ballooning

In the 1960s hot-air ballooning was revived as a sport. The Montgolfiers had had to place their heat source on the ground, so their flights were short. The recent development of a small, lightweight, propane burner, however, now allows the heat source to be carried aloft. New, tough, synthetic balloon fabrics have also been produced.

The first hot-air-balloon crossing of the Atlantic was achieved in 1987.

Scientific Use

Since the 1890s the main scientific use of balloons has been in meteorological research. Small pilot balloons are regularly launched and tracked to determine wind direction and velocity; other balloons containing packages of METEOROLOGICAL INSTRUMENTATION record data from the upper atmosphere. Until the development in the 1930s of the RADIOSONDE, a small and inexpensive radio transmitter, it was necessary to retrieve these packages in order to obtain their data.

Extremely high-altitude balloons are used to detect cosmic rays and gamma rays arriving from outer space. These balloons are sometimes several hundred meters high, and their reusable instrument packages are returned to Earth by parachute. Development of very thin, tough balloon materials such as Astrofilm E accelerated such balloon use in the 1980s.

balloonflower The balloonflower, *P. grandiflorum*, is the only species of the genus *Platycodon* in the BELL-FLOWER family, Campanulaceae. Balloonflowers are perennial herbs native to eastern Asia and Japan. The large flowers are dark to pale blue, lilac, or white and are borne at the ends of the branches. The leaves are oval, and the buds are balloonlike before opening, hence the name. The balloonflower and its varieties are commonly planted as garden borders.

ballot A ballot is a means for indicating a choice between alternatives in an ELECTION. The devices used have ranged from balls and shells in ancient times to tickets, printed forms, and voting machines in the present day.

The so-called Australian ballot, introduced to eliminate corruption in elections, requires that all candidates' names appear on a single, official ballot, which is printed at public expense and distributed at a polling place. It also allows secrecy while voting.

The length of the ballot and the arrangement of candidates' names on it are often controversial because they are thought to influence the decisions of voters.

balm A balm is an aromatic substance. Several species of plants in the MINT family, Labiatae, are known as balm. The common balm, *Melissa officinalis*, is native to Eurasia but is widely cultivated in temperate areas as a garden herb. It is sometimes called bee balm or lemon balm. It is a leafy perennial bearing white, yellowish, or pinkish flowers that attract bees. The lemon-scented flowers can be used for seasonings.

The Mecca balsam, *Commiphora opobalsamum*, of the torchwood family, Burseraceae, yields balm of Gilead, a resin used for incense.

Balmain, Pierre see FASHION DESIGN

Balmer, Johann Jakob [bahl'-mur] Johann Jakob Balmer, b. May 1, 1825, d. Mar. 12, 1898, was a Swiss mathematician and physicist who developed the first mathematical organization of spectroscopic data. Balmer taught mathematics at a girls' secondary school in Basel from 1859 until his death and did not become involved in spectroscopy until late in life. Other workers had tried to establish a mechanical acoustical relationship among spectral lines of an element; Balmer found, by empirical means, a simple formula for accurately generating the known lines of the HYDROGEN SPECTRUM. Using this formula, he also predicted other spectral series that were subsequently discovered.

balsa The balsa, *Ochroma pyramidale*, is a tropical American tree of the Bombax family, Bombacaceae, found in the West Indies and Central and South America. It is best known for its low-density and lightweight wood. The peoples who navigate the coastal and inland waters of Central and South America have used it extensively for canoes and rafts.

Balsa trees may grow to a height of 18 m (about 60 ft), with the trunk growing up to 76 cm (30 in) in diameter in about 6 years. They are now produced most successfully in plantations. The wood's commercial use exploits its insulating qualities against heat or cold, its lightness for flotation equipment, and its capacity for deadening sound or mechanical vibrations. It is widely used for toys and for model building.

balsam fir The balsam fir, *Abies balsamea*, is a small- to medium-sized evergreen conifer tree of the northern forest regions of North America. It belongs to the pine family, Pinaceae. Sensitive to warm temperatures, this

The balsam fir flourishes in moist soil, reaching a height of 12–19 m (40–60 ft). The cones have fanlike scales and a covering of short, fine hairs. The needles are flat.

tree cannot stand hot, dry summers and seldom survives being brought to elevations much below its natural mountain habitat. Balsam fir is short-lived, often decaying after 70 to 80 years.

Balsam fir is a popular Christmas tree. Canada balsam, a liquid resin collected from the bark blisters of balsam fir, is used to mount specimens on microscope slides.

Baltic languages

The Baltic languages are classified among the Northern INDO-EUROPEAN LANGUAGE group, which includes the Slavic and Germanic languages. Two Baltic languages, Lithuanian and Lettish, or Latvian, survive. In addition are some scant traces of Old Prussian as well as evidence of a fourth language, Curonian. These four languages retain elements of ancient Indo-European and of their common ancestor Proto-Baltic. The Baltic, Slavic, and Germanic are the only Indo-European languages to have the sound *m* in the dative plural ending, which indicates their close relationship.

Baltic has been more closely associated with the Slavic languages than with the Germanic. Indeed, the term *Balto-Slavic* has been used to imply an especially close relationship between the two. Many scholars, however, contend that the term is not appropriate and that the two subgroups, Baltic and Slavic, should be kept separate. Efforts to form a Balto-Germanic subgroup have received little support. Scholars, particularly in the USSR, have recently attempted to demonstrate that the Baltic languages correspond to Dacian and Thracian, the ancient languages of the Balkans.

The extant languages, Lithuanian and Latvian, are divided into dialects; Prussian is known only from manuscripts; and Curonian has been absorbed into the living languages.

Lithuanian. This East Baltic language has existed in written form since the late 16th century and is spoken by more than 3 million people. Lithuanian has retained more features of the original Indo-European than any other surviving language. For example, its declension of nouns has retained the dual—a grammatical number indicating two, used in addition to the singular and plural. Its accentuation patterns have retained early Indo-European characteristics, as have its vowels and most of its consonants. It has two principal dialects, Samogitian, or Low Lithuanian, and High Lithuanian. These have been further refined, and the western dialect of High Lithuanian has become the basis for the modern literary language.

Lettish, or Latvian. The East Baltic language Lettish is spoken by 2 million people and has three principal dialects: Tamian, or Livonian; High Latvian; and a central dialect, which is the basis for the modern literary language. As for Lithuanian, texts exist only from the late 16th century. Lettish is less conservative than Lithuanian. For example, it no longer has a movable accent (all words are accented on the initial syllable), no neuter gender exists, and the dual appears only rarely.

Prussian. This West Baltic language, sometimes called Old Prussian, became extinct near the end of the 17th century and is known only slightly from documents, the

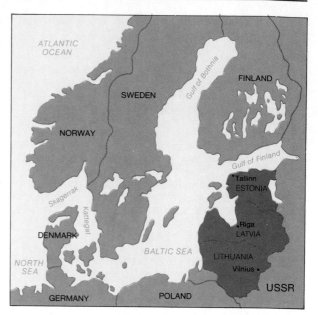

oldest being the *Elbing Vocabulary*, a short German-Prussian glossary between 1300 and 1400. Prussian texts did not appear until the mid-16th century. These writings indicate that Prussian is the most conservative of all Baltic languages, containing more archaisms than Lithuanian and differing significantly from that language and from Lettish.

Curonian. This East Baltic dialect was absorbed into Lithuanian and Lettish by the mid-16th century. No texts exist, and knowledge of Curonian comes primarily from proper names that survived after the language became extinct.

Baltic Sea

The Baltic Sea is an arm of the Atlantic Ocean and is connected to the North Sea by two relatively narrow passages, the KATTEGAT and SKAGERRAK. Touching on Finland, the USSR, Poland, Germany, Denmark, and Sweden, the sea has long been important in trade and commerce. With an area of about 420,000 km^2 (160,000 mi^2), the Baltic is a shrinking remnant of a large water body created by Ice Age glacial melt and is generally shallow. Many rivers feed it, notably the ODER and VISTULA, and it has a shallow outlet to the Atlantic Ocean; the water is brackish (5 to 15 parts salt per 1,000), and the tide is negligible. Ice hampers shipping in winter.

In the Middle Ages the Baltic Sea was the center of trade between ports of the HANSEATIC LEAGUE dealing in fish—particularly herring—timber, grains, furs, and amber. In the 17th century Sweden dominated the area, and from the late 17th century, Russia. Its importance declined when modern ships became too large to pass through the Kattegat, its shallow entrance between Denmark and Sweden. The Kiel Canal crosses the base of the

Danish peninsula, shortening distances to southern Europe. Connecting the Baltic and North seas, it can accommodate medium-sized ships and is one of the most heavily used canals in the world.

Baltic States

The Baltic States are ESTONIA, LATVIA, and LITHUANIA, three small countries located between Poland and the Gulf of Finland on the forested eastern shore of the Baltic Sea. Before 1918 they were part of the Russian empire. After World War I they became independent, but in 1940 they were forcibly annexed by the USSR. Nationalist movements developed in the Baltic States under the stimulus of the PERESTROIKA campaign of Soviet president Mikhail GORBACHEV. In 1990, Lithuania declared its independence, and Estonia and Latvia made preliminary moves in the same direction, causing a crisis in their relations with the USSR. (See also LIVONIA.)

Baltimore

Baltimore, the largest city in Maryland and among the largest in the United States, has one of the nation's biggest seaports and is a wholesaling and manufacturing center. Situated about 65 km (40 mi) northeast of Washington, D.C., the city occupies about 204 km^2 (79 mi^2) along the Patapsco River estuary on Chesapeake Bay.

The population of the city is 736,014 (1990); that of the metropolitan area is 2,382,172. Baltimore's population is about 50% black and also includes many people of Italian, German, and central European ancestry.

The climate is moderate, with temperatures averaging 2° C (35° F) in January and 25° C (77° F) in July. Rainfall averages about 1,065 mm (42 in) annually.

The Contemporary City. Industry and port activities are the main employers. The manufacturing and service industries are especially important. The port has extensive shipbuilding and repair facilities and modern freight-handling equipment. Baltimore has excellent rail, road, and air connections with other major U.S. cities.

Among the colleges and universities in the Baltimore area are the JOHNS HOPKINS UNIVERSITY (1876), the College of Notre Dame of Maryland (1873), the Peabody Conservatory of Music (1868), and Goucher College (1885) in suburban Towson, Md. The Baltimore Museum of Art, the Peale Museum, and the Walters Art Gallery have notable collections of art, and the B & O Railroad Museum houses an impressive collection of railroad memorabilia. Meyerhoff Symphony Hall, FORT MCHENRY (the defense of which, in 1812, inspired Francis Scott Key to write "The Star-Spangled Banner"), the first Roman Catholic cathedral built in the United States, and the National Aquarium are other major attractions. Pimlico Race Track, site of the Preakness Stakes, is nearby. Druid Hill Park contains the city zoo and a natural history museum. The U.S.S. CONSTELLATION, launched in Baltimore in 1797 and the oldest U.S. warship afloat, is docked in the harbor.

Plagued for years by urban deterioration, Baltimore underwent a dramatic rejuvenation in the 1980s, sparked by a commercial and residential building boom particularly alongside the Inner Harbor. Charles and Baltimore streets divide the city; at their intersection the Charles Center, a renewal area of office and apartment buildings, and the Civic Center dominate the skyline.

History. Baltimore, founded in 1729, was named for the baronial title of the CALVERT family, the proprietors of Maryland. The city's strategic location spurred its growth, and by the time of the American Revolution it was a thriving seaport. The city served (1776–77) as the seat of the Continental Congress while Philadelphia was under British siege. The threat to Baltimore's commercial position posed by the opening of the Erie Canal in 1825 prompted construction of the first U.S. railroad here, the Baltimore and Ohio, begun in 1827.

The site of numerous riots between Southern and Northern sympathizers during the Civil War, Baltimore remained within the Union but under martial law throughout the war. During the latter half of the 19th century the city was transformed from a mercantile to an industrial center. In 1904 a fire destroyed most of the downtown business district, but recovery was rapid. Baltimore's continued growth in the 20th century has been due in large part to its port facilities.

Baltimore, David

The American biochemist David Baltimore, b. New York City, Mar. 7, 1938, shared the 1975 Nobel Prize for medicine with Renato Dulbecco and Howard Temin for the discovery of reverse transcriptase, an enzyme that carries out one of the basic molecular processes in a cell. A graduate of Swarthmore College (1960) and Rockefeller University (1964), Baltimore worked at the Salk Institute of Biological Studies before becoming a professor of microbiology at the Massachusetts Institute of Technology in 1968 and then director of its institute for biomedical research. In 1990 he became president of Rockefeller University. At the Salk Institute, Baltimore worked with Dulbecco on the mechanism of replication of the poliovirus in a cell. This led to his discovery of reverse transcriptase in 1970, independently of Temin. Because it had previously been thought that genetic information can be passed only from DNA to RNA and proteins, the discovery that viral RNA can pass information to DNA and replicate was a conceptual breakthrough in molecular biology. It has also been an important tool in the study of viruses and cancer.

Baluch

[buh-looch'] The Baluch (Baloch) are a group of tribes that inhabit the province of Baluchistan in western Pakistan; smaller groups are scattered throughout the Middle East. Of an estimated total Baluch population of more than 2,000,000, about 60 percent reside in Pakistan. Numerous Baluch migrations from the early 19th century, primarily for raiding and for employment as mercenaries, have resulted in their present wide distribution. The groups that stayed in what is now Afghanistan and Turkmenia developed the famous styles of Baluchi rugs.

Although the name *Baluch* is known from earlier records in Iran, the present tribes cannot be traced back beyond the 17th century, when they rose to power under their chief Kambar. The Baluch share a common identity based on Baluchi—an Iranian language—and adherence to Sunni Islam. They have never formed a political unit. Traditional Baluch society consists of pastoral nomadic groups, small agricultural settlements, and remnants of a Negroid slave population that earlier functioned as agricultural serfs and personal retainers for the chiefs.

Baluchistan [buh-loo-chi-stahn']

Baluchistan, meaning "land of Baluchs," is a province in western Pakistan, bordered by Afghanistan on the northwest, the Arabian Sea on the south, and Iran on the west. The area, approximately 347,188 km² (134,050 mi²), is mainly mountainous with barren and rugged terrain.

Primitive agriculture, nomadism, and karez (tunnel-type) irrigation are the main bases of economic life. Some coking coal is mined near Quetta, the capital. The most important food crops are wheat, rice, and millet. Most of the 4,611,000 (1983 est.) inhabitants are Muslim. Baluchistan was a part of the Indian Maurya Empire (3d century BC) and fell under the control of various Turk and Arab empires until it was annexed by the Mogul Empire in 1595. It came under British rule in 1879. Since 1947 it has been a part of independent Pakistan. In 1972, 55,000 Baluch tribesmen launched a revolt for autonomy, which was harshly suppressed.

Baluchitherium [buh-loo-chi-thir'-ee-uhm]

Baluchitherium is an extinct rhinoceros that lived during the

The Baluchitherium was a hornless rhinoceros of late Oligocene and early Miocene times. Considered the largest land mammal ever to have lived, it stood nearly 5.5 m (18 ft) at the shoulder.

middle of the Tertiary Period (about 20–30 million years ago) of GEOLOGIC TIME. It is believed to be the largest land mammal that ever lived. The first baluchitheres were found in central Mongolia. Unlike its modern descendants, *Baluchitherium* was hornless. Its skull was about 1.2 m (4 ft) long, and it stood about 5.5 m (18 ft) high at the shoulder. A long neck and huge, pillarlike legs enabled the animal to browse among the higher branches of trees.

Balzac, Honoré de [bahl-zahk', oh-nohr-ay' duh]

A traditionalist in morality and a reactionary in politics, the great French novelist Balzac was a product of the bourgeois society he so vehemently criticized. Produced between 1829 and 1847, his monumental creation, *La Comédie humaine,* consists of nearly 100 completed novels and some 50 others left in drafts. Presenting the human character as fixed but often possessed by its hereditary, geographical, historical, and social environment, Balzac's microcosm of French society consists of 2,000 recurring characters and spans five decades of postrevolutionary France.

Early Life. Born in Tours on May 20, 1799, Balzac (who later added the *de* to his name) was particularly devoted to his unobliging mother, who dominated him all his life and outlived him. At the age of 8, he was sent to a boarding school, where he read to such excess that by the age of 14 he suffered from nervous exhaustion and returned home to attend the local *lycée* (secondary school). In 1814, he moved to Paris with his family and reluctantly began to study law. He was apprenticed to a law firm but finally persuaded his family to subsidize his literary career for two years. In a miserable Paris garret, with a meager stipend, Balzac embarked on his lifelong regimen: a 16-hour workday and the innumerable cups of coffee.

Balzac's first and abiding ambition was to write for the theater. His first play, *Cromwell* (1819), was so bad, however, that he was advised to try anything but writing. He then turned his hand to Gothic thrillers, using a variety of pen names and working with several collaborators.

Debts and Success. In 1825 a venture that was to publish new editions of French classics turned into a financial disaster. Within three years Balzac ran up 100,000 francs in debts for his triple failures: publishing, a printing establishment, and a type foundry. He was rescued by his family, but for the rest of his life he was plagued by debts and driven by a hunger for renown. His capacity for work was titanic: three or four novels a year, scores of articles and reviews, historical dramas, and a voluminous correspondence.

The first novel published under his own name, *The Chouans* (1829; Eng. trans., 1921), attracted considerable notice; *The Physiology of Marriage* (1829; Eng. trans., 1943) was a major success; and *The Wild Ass's Skin* (1831; Eng. trans., 1954) definitively launched his career. His expenses, however, always exceeded his income, and by 1838 he was 230,000 francs further in debt.

On Mar. 2, 1850, after an 18-year courtship, Balzac married the Polish countess Mme. Hanska, who had

Honoré de Balzac, a French novelist of the 19th century, is renowned for his fictional work concerning French middle-class society. The major portion of his work, a vast collection of novels and shorter fiction, was published as La Comédie humaine *(1829–47).*

signed herself *L'Étrangère* ("the foreign lady") in an anonymous fan letter. Her wealth would have protected him from bill collectors, but on August 18, five months after the wedding, he was dead, worn out by having been what he called "a galley slave of the pen."

Bamako [bah-mah-koh']   Bamako, the capital of Mali in western Africa, is situated in the southwestern section of the country, on the upper Niger River. Bamako has a population of 801,500 (1985 est.). A bustling river port and trade hub, the city is also an administrative and military center. Bamako has several colleges, a notable national museum, a large zoo, and botanical gardens. Although it was a Muslim center in the ancient Mali empire, it had declined to a village of fewer than 1,000 when the French arrived in 1880. Its growth was spurred by the opening of the railroad in 1904 and by the city's designation as colonial capital in 1908.

bamboo   Bamboos are plants of great economic importance in several regions of the world. The name is applied in general to members of the tribe Bambuseae in the GRASS family. Some 76 genera and more than 1,000 species have been described. Most are tropical or subtropical, but a few reach the temperate zones or grow at high altitudes.

Bamboos are perennial plants. Their woody stems are hollow and segmented, with partitions between the segments. The leaves, usually long and narrow, rise from the nodes of the stems. Some species are only shrublike, but others grow to heights of 30 m (100 ft) or more, with stem diameters of 20–30 cm (8–12 in). Bamboo stems are light, strong, durable, flexible, and easily split lengthwise. Depending on size, they are used in making houses, furniture, piping, a wide range of domestic goods, baskets, and musical instruments. They are also pulverized for paper pulp. Bamboo hay is a protein-rich food for livestock, and the fresh sprouts of some species are widely used in cookery. In the United States, bamboo is grown mainly as an ornamental.

One striking characteristic of bamboo is that most species produce seeds only once in their lifetime, which may range to more than 100 years. (They can also reproduce asexually by producing seedless clones, or rhizomes.) Researchers in 1990 announced development of a promising technique for making bamboos flower more rapidly, which would be of major importance to bamboo cultivators.

Bamboo, a fast-growing grass of tropical Asia, Africa, and America, has hollow, segmented stems. It provides material for furniture, wickerwork, poles, and other products.

Bamian [bahm-yahn']   Bamian (Bamiyan), a town in the Bamian River valley (elevation 2,590 m/8,480 ft) northwest of Kabul, in Afghanistan, was for centuries an important commercial and religious center on the caravan route between central Asia and India. During the 2d to 9th century, numerous Buddhist monuments were constructed along the valley cliffs. They include caves fashioned into temples and monasteries, many containing well-preserved frescolike wall paintings, and a famous colossal statue of the Buddha, standing 53 m (175 ft) high, the tallest stone sculpture of its kind in the world. This standing Buddha and another measuring about 37 m (120 ft) are set within niches carved into the cliff. Mongol invaders under Genghis Khan destroyed the town in 1221.

Ban Chiang   The village of Ban Chiang, in northeastern Thailand, is the site of a large and rich Late Neolithic settlement occupied through the Bronze and Iron ages. Some scientists believe that metallurgy developed there independently. It is now thought that the area was settled about 4000 BC, with pottery dating back to 3500 BC, bronzework between 2500 and 1500 BC, and iron implements about 1000 to 500 BC. Since excavation of the site began in 1967, the red-on-buff painted Ban Chiang pottery has become renowned in the international art market.

banana The banana family consists of large plants that flourish in moist areas throughout the tropics. The edible fruit is rich in carbohydrates and is a source of vitamins A and C and the minerals potassium and phosphorus. The most familiar banana is the yellow-skinned, sweet, pulpy fruit of international trade. Of the many varieties, only a few are widely grown and only two are exported. Wild banana plants tend to spring up where tropical forest has been felled or burned.

Bananas are a significant food crop in the tropics. From 80 to 85 percent of the world's banana crop is grown locally for domestic consumption. Consumers in the tropics not only eat the raw, ripe fruit but also cook bananas as a starchy vegetable food. Some fruits are fermented to make beer, and others are dried.

Origin and Types. Bananas originated primarily in Malaysia and the neighboring archipelago probably about 4,000 years ago. Diversity developed over a much wider area, from India to the Philippines and New Guinea. About 2,000 years ago, travelers carried bananas eastward through the Pacific and westward across the Indian Ocean to tropical Africa. Shortly after the discovery of America, Europeans took banana plants from Africa or the Canary Islands to Hispaniola (modern Haiti and the Dominican Republic).

The banana family, *Musaceae*, contains only two genera, *Ensete* and *Musa*. The plants range in height from 1 m (3 ft) to more than 9 m (30 ft) and are actually gigantic herbs. What looks like the trunk of a banana plant is

The banana plant is among the largest herbaceous plants. Its trunk is formed by the bases of overlapping leaves. A banana plant flowers and fruits only once in its life span and then dies. The flower is seen at right.

neither woody nor a true stem. The true stem is underground, and the above-ground portion is called a pseudostem. Even when as large as 60 cm (2 ft) across, the pseudostem is made solely of overlapping, concentric leaf sheaths wrapped tightly.

A slender flowering stalk several centimeters across grows up through the center of the pseudostem and bears a terminal cluster of flowers. The flowers emerge from a purple bract and are tubular, with yellow petals. In the wild, bees and bats pollinate the female flowers, each of which produces a banana. Wild banana fruit is seedy and inedible; the edible, cultivated types are seedless because they are set without pollination and have evolved sterility.

A Southeast Asian species, *M. textilis*, supplies the Philippine Islands with a principal export—Manila HEMP, or abaca. In parts of Ethiopia the 6-m (20-ft) leaves of *E. ventricosum* provide building material, fiber, and a starchy food. Several smaller *Musa* species are grown as ornamentals.

World Production and Trade. The world crop of bananas (including plantains) is estimated to vary from about 35 million to more than 40 million metric tons (39.5–44 million U.S. tons). Many countries, including those in Africa, consume most of what they grow. Banana exporters, who supply the North American and European markets, are led by Brazil, which is by far the world's largest producer. India follows, growing somewhat less than half as much as Brazil. The Philippines, Ecuador, Colombia, and Honduras are also important producers. In the United States only Hawaii grows significant amounts.

From small beginnings in the early years of the 19th century, the trade became important toward the end of that century, aided by the development of fast refrigerated sea transport, improved local transport in the producing countries, and vertical integration of production from plantation to point of retail. In the early days, fruit bunches were mostly shipped unwrapped. Today most fruit is cut and boxed for transport. Fruit is always cut and carried green, and ripened just before delivery to retail stores by the use of ethylene gas in special chambers.

Export production has been bedeviled by epidemic diseases promoted by large-scale monoculture. Efforts are being made to breed new, disease-resistant varieties.

Bancroft, Anne Anne Bancroft is the stage name of Anna Maria Italiano, b. New York City, Sept. 17, 1931, a stage and film actress. She achieved Broadway and Hollywood fame in the role of Annie Sullivan, Helen Keller's teacher, in *The Miracle Worker* (1960; film, 1962), for which she won an Academy Award. Other notable films include *The Graduate* (1967); *The Turning Point* (1977); and *Fatso* (1979), which she also wrote and directed. Bancroft won an Emmy award in 1970 for her television work, and starred in the Broadway production *Golda* (1977), about the life of Israeli leader Golda Meier.

Bancroft, George George Bancroft, b. Worcester, Mass., Oct. 3, 1800, d. Jan. 17, 1891, was a historian, diplomat, and statesman whose comprehensive 10-volume work, *A History of the United States, from the Discovery of America to the Inauguration of Washington* (1834–74; rev. in 1876 and 1883–85, is considered a classic. Bancroft served as secretary of the navy (1845–46) under James K. Polk, actively supporting American expansion even at the cost of war with Mexico. He then served (1846–49) as U.S. minister in London. Opposed to slavery, he abandoned the Democratic party during the sectional crisis to support Abraham Lincoln. From 1867 to 1874, Bancroft was the U.S. minister in Berlin.

band Bands originated in the outdoor ensembles of the Renaissance. In modern usage, the term *band* denotes an instrumental ensemble consisting mainly or entirely of wind instruments and percussion instruments. In its broadest sense, the term may designate almost any instrumental group, such as a jazz band, dance band, or balalaika band. The various types of bands include brass, marching, military, and concert or symphonic. The largest of these, the concert band, usually includes a full complement of woodwinds (piccolos, flutes, oboes, clarinets, bassoons, and saxophones), a large brass section (cornets, trumpets, horns, trombones, and tubas), and a large percussion section. Cellos and double basses are sometimes used to reinforce the bass.

Notable concert bands were the Grand Boston Band founded by Patrick S. Gilmore in 1859 and the famous John Philip SOUSA band founded in 1892. Gilmore, who took his 22d Regiment Band of New York on a worldwide tour, is generally regarded as the father of the concert band in the United States.

Marching bands use neither oboes nor bassoons, the number of clarinets and saxophones is much reduced, and flutes are usually replaced by fifes. Brass bands are smaller yet, eliminating all woodwind instruments except, sometimes, the alto saxophone.

Banda, H. Kamuzu [ban'-duh, kah-moo'-zoo] Hastings Kamuzu Banda, b. 1906?, is president of Malawi, formerly Nyasaland, which he led to independence in 1964. Banda received a medical degree in the United States in 1937 and later practiced medicine in England and the Gold Coast (Ghana) Long active in the African independence movement, Banda returned to Nyasaland in 1958 and was imprisoned (1959–60) for his nationalist activities. In 1961 his Malawi Congress party won a majority in the legislature. Banda became prime minister in 1963, when Britain granted Nyasaland internal self-government, and retained the post after independence. When Malawi became a republic in 1966, Banda became president; he became president-for-life in 1971.

Bandaranaike, Sirimavo [bahn-drah-ny'-kee, see-ree-mah'-voh] Sirimavo Bandaranaike, b. Apr. 17, 1916, twice the prime minister of Sri Lanka, was the world's first woman prime minister. She married political leader Solomon W. R. D. Bandaranaike in 1940. After her husband, then prime minister, was assassinated in 1959, she led her husband's Sri Lanka Freedom party to victory in the election of 1960 and served as prime minister until 1965. She returned to office in 1970 at the head of a left-wing coalition. In the election of 1977 her party suffered a heavy defeat, and J. R. JAYAWARDENE became prime minister.

Bandaranaike, Solomon W. R. D.
Solomon West Ridgeway Dias Bandaranaike, b. Jan. 8, 1899, d. Sept. 26, 1959, was a political leader and prime minister of Ceylon (now Sri Lanka). A lawyer educated at Oxford University, he was elected (1931) to the legislative assembly. When Ceylon became independent (1947), he was a leader in the new House of Representatives. He resigned (1951) from the ruling United National party and the government to found the Sri Lanka Freedom party, and in 1956 he formed the People's United Front, an alliance of four leftist parties, which won the elections of 1956. As prime minister Bandaranaike adopted a neutralist position in international affairs and fostered Sinhalese nationalism at home. He was assassinated by a Buddhist monk in 1959; in 1960 his widow, Sirimavo Bandaranaike, became prime minister.

bandicoot A bandicoot is any of 8 genera and about 19 species of marsupial mammals that constitute the family Peramelidae. Bandicoots are found in Australia, New Guinea, and several South Pacific islands. Several species are endangered or perhaps extinct; in Australia bandicoots are now protected.

The bandicoot's coarsely haired body is from 28 to 76 cm (11 to 30 in) long, including the usually ratlike tail. The muzzle is long and pointed, and the hind legs are longer than the forelegs. The forefeet look three-toed because the outer toes are vestigial. The second and third toes of the hind feet are fused, and the first toes are sometimes absent. The female usually bears a litter of two to six young, and her marsupial pouch opens backward and downward.

Bandicoots are solitary, lively, mainly nocturnal animals that feed on insects, worms, and plants and build

The long-nosed bandicoot is common to eastern Australia. It often lives close enough to towns to be a garden pest.

grassy nests in burrows. Their digging can damage crops, and some species have been considered pests.

Bandung Bandung (1985 est. pop., 1,633,000) is the capital city of West Java province on the island of Java, Indonesia. About 120 km (75 mi) southeast of Jakarta, the city is a Sundanese cultural and educational center. Bandung is hemmed in by a series of volcanic peaks covered with tangled upland vegetation and is the center of Indonesia's quinine industry. It is also noted for its ceramics and textiles.

Settled around 1810, the city has grown rapidly in the 20th century. It is the home of the Institute for Technical Research, the Padjadjaran State University, and a nuclear research center. Just outside the city is the Tangkubanprahu (Upside-Down Boat), a volcanic crater that can be entered.

In 1955, Bandung was the site of a conference of 29 African and Asian nations—the first of its kind—which helped prepare the way for the establishment of the NONALIGNED MOVEMENT.

Banff (Alberta) Banff is an uncorporated Canadian town on the Bow River in southwestern Alberta, near the British Columbian border. It is situated in the Rocky Mountains at an altitude of 1,382 m (4,534 ft) and is mainly a tourist center with a seasonally fluctuating population. The town is the headquarters of Banff National Park (established 1885), renowned for its magnificent mountain and glacier scenery, including Lake Louise, and for its abundant wildlife. The Banff School of Fine Arts, part of the University of Alberta, is located there.

Banff (Scotland) Banff (also called Banffshire) was a county in northeastern Scotland until 1975, when it became part of the Grampian administrative region. On the south shore of Moray Firth, it is between the North Sea coast, to the north, and the Cairngorm Mountains, a range of the Grampian Mountains, to the south. Banff, a seaport at the mouth of the Deveron River, was the county town. The rivers Avon, Deveron, and Spey drain the mainly livestock-raising and dairy-farming region.

Because of the commercial advantages afforded by membership in the HANSEATIC LEAGUE, Banff was an important port during the Middle Ages. The entire county was a center of the JACOBITES after 1689.

Bangalore [bang'-guh-lohr] Bangalore, the capital of Karnataka (formerly Mysore) state of India, is situated on a ridge in the southern Mysore Plateau at an elevation of 949 m (3,113 ft). The city comprises an area of 175 km² (67 mi²) and has a population of 2,482,507 (1981). Bangalore is a center of diversified industries, producing cotton textiles, electronics, machinery, and aircraft. The city has several institutes of learning, including the Indian Institute of Science.

Kempe Gowda, founder of the city in 1537, erected a mud fort, which was rebuilt in stone in 1761. Some remains of TIPPU SULTAN's palace are in the center of the oval fort. Lord CORNWALLIS captured the fort in 1791 for the British. It became the administrative capital in 1831 and was the center of British rule until 1881. The notable botanic gardens of Lal Bagh were laid out in the 18th century.

Bangkok [bang'-kahk] Bangkok is the capital and chief port of Thailand and one of the most important cities in Southeast Asia. It is located on the east bank of the Chao Phraya River 40 km (24 mi) upstream from the Gulf of Thailand. Bangkok's Thai name is Krung Thep ("City of Angels"). The population of Bangkok Metropolis, which includes that of the industrial city of Thon Buri on the west bank of the river, is 5,972,000 (1987 est.).

Bangkok was known during the 19th century as the Venice of the East because of its many canals, which served as streets and commercial thoroughfares. The city has undergone extensive development in recent years, however, and many of the canals have been paved over. Although the city has many modern skyscrapers and buildings that reflect a European influence, perhaps its most distinctive features are the approximately 400 Buddhist temples, called *wats*. Bangkok is a regional center for many United Nations agencies and the site of Chulalongkorn, Kasetsart, Thammasat, Mahidol, and other universities.

Bangkok is Thailand's economic center. The city's industries are based primarily on the products of the surrounding region. Processed rice and lumber are most important. Others include sugar, paper, textiles, cigarettes,

The spires of a Buddhist wat, or monastery, rise above the Chao Phraya River, Bangkok's major avenue of commerce. Bangkok has been the capital of Thailand since the city's founding in 1782.

AT A GLANCE

PEOPLE'S REPUBLIC OF BANGLADESH

Land: Area: 142,776 km² (55,126 mi²). Capital and largest city: Dhaka (1987 est. pop., including Narayan-ganj, 4,770,000).

People: Population (1990 est.): 118,433,062. Density: 830 persons per km² (2,148 per mi²). Distribution (1990): 87% rural, 13% urban. Official language: Bengali. Major religions: Islam, Hinduism, Buddhism, Christianity.

Government: Type: republic. Legislature: Parliament. Political subdivisions: 4 divisions, 64 districts.

Economy: GNP (1989 est.): $20.6 billion; $180 per capita. Labor distribution (1989): agriculture and fishing—55%; commerce and services—18%; government and public authorities—12%; manufacturing—11%; construction—4%. Foreign trade (1989 est.): imports—$3.1 billion; exports—$1.3 billion. Currency: 1 taka = 100 paisa.

Education and Health: Literacy (1985): 33% of adult population. Universities (1985): 6. Hospital beds (1987): 33,038. Physicians (1987): 16,929. Life expectancy (1990): men—54; women—53. Infant mortality (1990): 136 per 1,000 live births.

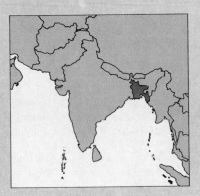

soap, matches, metal, and processed foods. Tourism is also important.

Bangkok is the center of Thailand's transportation system. The modern port of Klongtoi, 7 km (4 mi) downstream from central Bangkok, handles about 90% of Thailand's foreign trade. The busy Don Muang international airport is nearby.

At first a small agricultural community, Bangkok became the capital of Siam in 1782 when Chao Phraya Chakkri (Rama I), founder of the Chakkri dynasty, moved his government from Thon Buri. Rama I built the walled Grand Palace, which contains the Wat Po and the Wat Emerald Buddha. The first major secular construction projects were undertaken during the reign (1851-68) of Mongkut (Rama IV). During the 20th century, and especially since World War II, the city has grown rapidly.

Bangladesh [bahng-glah-desh']   Bangladesh (formerly East Pakistan) is an independent country in southern Asia located on the Bay of Bengal, bounded on most of its borders by India and to the southeast by Burma. It occupies a total area of 142,776 km² (55,126 mi²) and is one of the world's most densely populated and fastest-growing countries. The capital city is Dhaka. Bangladesh is an overwhelmingly agricultural country, with rich farmland and major crops of rice and jute. Before 1947 most of the territory now in Bangladesh was part of the province of British-ruled India known as East BENGAL, which in 1947 joined with the Sylhet district of Assam and became East

Pakistan in the new state of Pakistan. Growing economic and political differences with West Pakistan led East Pakistan to declare independence in 1971 as the new nation of Bangladesh. The name *Bangladesh* means "the Bengal nation." Not all who speak the Bengali language and otherwise identify with the cultural history of Bengal, however, are included within Bangladesh boundaries; many Bengalis live to the west of Bangladesh in the Indian province of West Bengal.

The Land and Resources

The Chittagong Hills in eastern and southeastern Bangladesh include the highest and most rugged parts of the nation, with elevations rising to more than 1,200 m (4,000 ft) above sea level. The remainder of Bangladesh is generally low-lying, with elevations approaching only 300 m (900 ft) in the hills of the northwest and northeast and considerably lower on the vast deltaic plains on the BRAHMAPUTRA, GANGES, and Meghna rivers in southern Bangladesh.

About 6% of the total land area of Bangladesh is permanently under water, and two-thirds is flooded for part of the year. The floods often result in great loss of life, crops, and property damage but are, nonetheless, of special value to agricultural Bangladesh for the nutrient-rich sediments (alluvium) that the muddy floodwaters deposit on the land. The fertility of the soil has attracted thousands of landless laborers to shifting silt islands (*chars*) off the coast, despite their vulnerability to natural disasters.

Climate. Bangladesh has a tropical monsoon-type climate, with a hot and rainy summer and a pronounced dry season in the cooler months. January is the coolest month of the year, with temperatures averaging near 26° C (78° F), and April the warmest month, with temperatures ranging between 33° C and 36° C (91° F and 96° F). The climate is one of the wettest in the world; most places receive more than 1,525 mm (60 in) of rain a year, and areas near the hills receive 5,080 mm (200 in). Most rain falls in the monsoon (June-September) season.

Vegetation and Animal Life. About 15% of Bangladesh is still forested; the three principal forest regions are the Madhupur jungle, the tidal forest in the coastal Sundarbans (a swamp region in the Ganges delta), and the tropical rain forest of the Chittagong Hills. Bamboo and rattan are abundant. Tigers and other game are found in the Madhupur jungle and Sundarbans, crocodiles in the Sundarbans, and elephants, rhinoceroses, and leopards in the hill areas.

Natural Resources. The principal resources of Bangladesh are the fertile soils of the delta region, the long growing season, and the heavy rainfall suitably distributed over the year for growing rice and jute. The nation's abundant water supplies are used to produce hydroelectric power and for irrigation. The country has large reserves of natural gas and some petroleum deposits. Natural gas is piped into Dhaka and CHITTAGONG for industrial use. Large deposits of low-grade coal are mined at Jamalpur.

People

About 98% of the people are Bengalis; most of the remainder are tribal peoples, who live mainly in the hills. About 83% of the population are Muslim and, except for the tribal peoples who are mainly animistic in religious outlook, most of the remaining people are Hindu. Bengali, the national language, is spoken by all but the tribal hill people, who speak a variety of languages.

Bangladesh has one of the highest birthrates and population densities in the world. Nearly half of the total population are under 15 years old. Cholera, tuberculosis, leprosy, and malaria occur widely, and medical personnel, facilities, and supplies are in chronically short supply. Most people live in the countryside. The largest cities are Dhaka and Chittagong (the major seaport).

About one-fourth of the population is literate; and for each literate woman, three men can read and write. About 60% of all children attend primary schools; far fewer attend a technical school or one of the six universities. The largest university is the University of Dhaka.

Bengali literature—rooted in folk legend, ballads, and religious stories—has long flourished. Rabindranath TAGORE, the renowned Bengali poet, remains popular today. Art and architectural traditions conform distinctly to 16th- and 17th-century Islamic styles.

Economic Activity

Before the Industrial Revolution, Bangladesh was known for its fine cotton textiles, but this industry was eclipsed in the 18th and 19th centuries by the production of cheaper mill cloth overseas in Europe. Thereafter, the economy of Bangladesh was primarily agricultural, with major exports in the 18th and 19th centuries of opium and indigo and, in the 20th century, of jute and jute products. Industrial development was not encouraged by the British, and many factories established following partition from India in 1947 were destroyed in the struggle for independence from Pakistan.

Agriculture. Nearly two-thirds of the land area is under cultivation. Double and triple crops are obtained where water is available for irrigation during the dry season. Farms are generally small, and many are so small that normal agricultural crises, such as floods, other natural disasters, and price fluctuations, have forced some owners to sell their land and seek other employment. Rice, planted on 90% of the cultivated land, is the leading crop, but even in good years the output is insufficient to feed the rapidly growing population. The government is encouraging increased planting of wheat as a food crop. The principal cash crops are jute and tea.

Manufacturing. Jute processing is the principal factory industry. Bangladesh supplies more than half of the world's jute, but the paper and plastic-packaging revolution has reduced world demand for jute products, and the

BANGLADESH

Major Urban Area

Railroad

Scale 1:6,000,000

	km
0 50 100 150	

	mi
0 50 100	

Meters	Feet
4000	13124
2000	6562
1000	3281
500	1640
200	656
0	0
200	656

Sailing and motor vessels move along the Burhi Ganga River as it flows past Dhaka (Dacca), the capital and largest city of Bangladesh.

Bangladesh economy has suffered accordingly. Other manufactures include textiles, cigarettes, steel, cement, fertilizers, and chemicals. Many of the industries nationalized by the government in 1972 have since been returned to private ownership.

The chief sources of power are natural gas and thermal electricity produced from oil, natural gas, and coal. Hydroelectric supplies less than 15% of total electricity output put.

Transportation and Trade. The transportation and communication system was severely damaged during the war of independence and again in 1988, when the worst flooding in 70 years left three-quarters of the country under water. Inland waterways are used by river steamers and nonmotorized boats. Bangladesh Biman provides commercial air services.

Bangladesh has an unfavorable balance of trade and depends heavily on international aid and large economic development loans from overseas to feed its large population and finance economic development. Remittances from overseas workers, an important source of foreign exchange, were reduced by the Persian Gulf crisis of the early 1990s.

Government

Bangladesh's constitution of 1972 provided for a parliamentary government with a prime minister selected by the majority party in the legislature. This was revised in 1975, and a presidential government, with a strong, elected president as chief executive, was introduced. In 1975, however, the first president, Sheikh MUJIBUR RAHMAN, was assassinated and the constitution amended. Since then, periods of military rule have alternated with elected governments.

History

Bangladesh, independent only since 1971 and thus one of the world's youngest nations, has a long history of domination by larger political entities. In the late 16th century the area that is now Bangladesh was conquered by the Mogul emperor AKBAR. Under Mogul rule, most of the population was converted to Islam. After 1707, Mogul control weakened, and Bangladesh was caught up in the struggle by European trading and financial interests, including the British EAST INDIA COMPANY, for control of the Indian subcontinent. In 1757, Robert CLIVE led British forces in the famous victory over the French at Plassey, and in 1764 the Mogul emperor acknowledged the dominance of the British, who remained in control until 1947.

When the British withdrew, the nations of Pakistan, which was predominantly Muslim and included modern Bangladesh, and India, which was largely Hindu, were created. In this partition, East Bengal, where most of the jute was produced, became part of East Pakistan, and West Bengal, where the jute-processing factories were located, became part of India.

The two provinces of the new Pakistan nation had almost nothing in common other than the shared Islamic faith; moreover, East Pakistan was separated by more than 1,600 km (1,000 mi) from West Pakistan, and, with more than half the population of the new nation, it felt underrepresented in a government dominated by West Pakistan. In the 1970 national elections, East Pakistan's Awami League, under Sheikh Mujibur Rahman, won a majority of seats in the Pakistan National Assembly but was denied power by delays in the opening of the assembly. On Mar. 26, 1971, East Pakistan proclaimed its independence as the new state of Bangladesh. The national government of Pakistan responded by invading the eastern province, but, with assistance from India, the Pakistani army was driven back before the end of 1971 (see INDIA-PAKISTAN WARS). Sheikh Mujibur Rahman became the first prime minister and, under the amended constitution of 1975, the first president. Mujibur was overthrown and assassinated on Aug. 15, 1975. Gen. Ziaur Rahman, who assumed power after a counter-coup in November, was president from 1977 until his assassination in an unsuccessful military coup in May 1981. Former vice-president Abdus Sattar, elected president in November 1981, was deposed in March 1982 in a military coup led by Lt. Gen. H. M. ERSHAD. Ershad proclaimed himself president in 1983, and in a 1985 referendum voters approved his policies. In 1986 martial law was lifted and the constitution revived after Ershad's Jatiya party won a majority in parliament and Ershad won the presidency in an election boycotted by the opposition. New parliamentary elections held in 1988 after a wave of antigovernment protests were also boycotted by the opposition; further violence took place when Islam was declared the state religion later that year. In December 1990, Ershad suddenly resigned under pressure; he was later arrested. A caretaker government headed by Supreme Court Chief Justice Shahabuddin Ahmed took power until new presidential and legislative elections could be held.

See also: INDIA, HISTORY OF.

The banjo is a stringed musical instrument brought to America during the slave trade from West Africa, where it was called a bania. The standard five-string banjo is used as both a rhythm and a solo instrument in Dixieland jazz and country music.

Bangor   Bangor (1990 pop., 33,181) is a city in east central Maine and the seat of Penobscot County. A port of entry, it is located at the head of navigation on the Penobscot River, 29 km (18 mi) from the Atlantic Ocean. Bangor is a commercial and industrial center that manufactures paper, electronics equipment, and machinery. It is surrounded by Maine's vast timber stands and is a leading lumber port. Settled in 1769, it grew considerably after 1830 with the advent of shipbuilding and expansion of the lumber industry.

Bang's disease   SEE BRUCELLOSIS

Bangui   [bahn-gee'] Bangui (1988 est. pop., 596,776) is the capital city of the Central African Republic in central Africa and lies at the head of navigation of the Ubangi River. Bangui has many small industries and handles the country's exports, mainly timber, cotton, sisal, and coffee. A network of road and rail lines connects it with Cameroon, Chad, and Sudan. The University of Bangui was founded in 1969.

Bani-Sadr, Abolhassan   [bah'-nee-sah'-duhr, ah-bohl-hah'-sahn]   The economist Abolhassan Bani-Sadr, b. 1933, was president of Iran from 1980 to 1981. Bani-Sadr returned to Iran in 1979 after 16 years' exile in Paris and was elected president in January 1980. Although he gained 75 percent of the popular vote, he lacked support in parliament, where the fundamentalist clerics had a majority. In his power struggle with the fundamentalists, he eventually lost the support of the Ayatollah KHOMEINI. In June 1981 he was dismissed. He fled to Paris and formed the National Council of Resistance to oppose the Khomeini government.

banjo   The banjo is a plucked string instrument that has a long fretted neck piercing a circular frame over which a membrane is tightened with thumb screws, often containing a resonator over the open back. A descendant of the West African long-necked lute, it came to the Americas with the slave trade. In the 19th century a more

highly developed banjo, popular especially in blackface minstrel shows, was exported to England. In the early 20th century it became an important rhythmic instrument of the jazz band, and it is now cultivated as a folk instrument. The standard form is the finger-style banjo, originally gut-strung, its five strings plucked with bare fingers. A plectrum banjo with four metal strings is another type.

Banjul   [bahn'-jool]   Banjul, the capital city of Gambia, has a population of 44,536 (1983 est.). The city is located on Saint Mary's Island at the mouth of the Gambia River and is connected to the mainland by ferry. It is the economic center and major port of the country. Its major industry is groundnut processing, beaches and abundant birdlife attract increasing numbers of tourists. Founded as a British trading post in 1816, the city was a British crown colony until independence (1965).

Bank of Canada   The Bank of Canada is that country's CENTRAL BANK. Founded in 1934 and nationalized in 1938, it was assigned the task of regulating credit and currency in the national interest. Although Canada's highly centralized banking system consists (1984) of only 13 Canadian-owned commercial banks, these have a total of almost 7,000 branches. The Bank of Canada is both the note-issuing authority and the holder of reserve deposits for the commercial banks. It can therefore influence the national economy by adjusting interest rates on the loans it makes to commercial banks, by changing the banks' reserve requirements, and by buying and selling securities.

Bank of England   The Bank of England was the first CENTRAL BANK. It serves as the banker to the government of the United Kingdom, with sole authority to issue notes in England and Wales, and also as the banker to the country's commercial banks. Until 1946 the bank was privately owned, but it had long governed its operations in the national interest. Chartered as a joint-stock company in 1694, the bank helped fund the national debt arising from William III's wars in Ireland and against France. Today the bank is able to adjust the country's supply of money through the purchase and sale of securities. It also controls interest rates and sets limits on the amount of bank credit.

Bank of the United States

The first Bank of the United States was established in 1791. A private corporation operating under a federal charter, the bank was designed by Secretary of the Treasury Alexander HAMILTON as a way to secure the safety of public funds, stabilize the currency, and provide a source of credit for the federal government and private business.

The federal government subscribed for 20 percent of the bank's stock of $10 million. In return the bank served as the government's fiscal agent. Although it had no direct legal power to regulate state banks, the Bank of the United States was able to prevent abuses by state-chartered banks by collecting their notes and demanding redemption in specie. Doubts about the constitutional power of the federal government to charter a private corporation, however, had been raised by Thomas Jefferson in 1791, and despite the bank's excellent record in the handling of public funds and in stabilizing the currency, these doubts persisted. In 1811, when the bank's charter expired, it was not renewed.

The instability of state banks, however, led to the chartering of the Second Bank of the United States in 1816. Under its first president, William Jones, the bank engaged in inflationary lending policies that undermined the bank's stability, but the second president, Langlon Cheves (1819–23), restored the bank's role as a conservative influence in the nation's economy. He was succeeded in 1823 by Nicholas BIDDLE.

President Andrew JACKSON, disturbed by misgivings about the bank's constitutionality and angered by political opposition from some of the bank's officers, opposed renewal of the bank's charter. Jackson vetoed a recharter bill and by executive order withdrew all federal deposits from the bank in 1833. Crippled by loss of government patronage, the bank had ceased to be an effective force for national economic stability by the time its charter expired in 1836.

Bankhead, Tallulah

Tallulah Brockman Bankhead, b. Huntsville, Ala., Jan. 31, 1903, d. Dec. 12, 1968, an American actress, won the New York Drama Critics best actress awards for *The Little Foxes* (1939) and *The Skin of Our Teeth* (1942). Her most memorable film role was in Alfred Hitchcock's *Lifeboat* (1943). Her autobiography *Tallulah* (1952) was a best-seller.

banking systems

Commercial banks in the United States are institutions that provide checkable accounts to the public and have a substantial proportion of their assets invested in loans to business firms. The partial deregulation of the depository system effected by the Depository Institutions Act of 1982 has diminished or eliminated many of the functional differences between commercial banks and "thrift" institutions, such as savings and loans. Thrift institutions now compete with commercial banks on a more or less equal basis.

Banks provide the public with checkable deposits, such as DEMAND DEPOSITS and NOW (Negotiable Order of Withdrawal) accounts, as well as time deposits, and use their depositors' funds mainly to make loans and buy securities. U.S. banks make a substantial volume of MORTGAGE loans and consumer loans as well as business loans. Banks operate as financial intermediaries, standing between the ultimate lender (depositor) and the ultimate borrower. By pooling many loans banks reduce the risk of failure, because someone who makes a thousand loans can calculate more accurately what proportion of the loans will be repaid than can someone who makes only a single loan. Because a depository institution has many depositors who usually want to withdraw deposits at different times, a bank with a small portion of its assets available in reserves can allow depositors to withdraw their deposits at any time. By contrast, someone who makes a loan directly to an ultimate borrower cannot turn this loan into cash immediately. Also, depository institutions are experts at finding potential borrowers and lenders and in appraising the quality of loans. Banks face a potential conflict of interest, however. They have an incentive to make risky loans that pay a high rate of return, but part of the risk of failure is borne by depositors or an insuring agency. Hence banks are heavily regulated by the government.

Fractional Reserve System. The banking system can create deposits. To understand this concept, one must realize that deposits are not physical objects but abstract property rights reflected by entries on computer tape. There is nothing magical about multiple-deposit creations. No physical objects are being created; it is all a matter of book entries. As an example of multiple-deposit

The First Bank of the United States, with headquarters in Philadelphia, was chartered by the U.S. government in 1791 to serve as a repository for federal funds and as a loan source for private citizens and businesses. Its charter lapsed in 1811.

creation, imagine someone depositing $1,000 of currency. The bank credits the $1,000 to the depositor's account and then uses this $1,000 to make a loan. The bank cannot lend the total amount because the law, as well as prudence, requires the bank to keep a reserve against the deposit, 10%, for example, or $100. It therefore lends out only $900. The borrower then buys something with this $900, and the seller deposits this $900 check in a bank. That bank then keeps $90 as a reserve against this deposit and lends out $810, which then becomes a deposit in a third bank that keeps $81 as a reserve and lends out $729. Ultimately, all of the original $1,000 is held as reserves by banks. Because reserves are 10% of deposits, total deposits must then be 10 times the original deposit. Thus, in this hypothetical example, on the basis of an original $1,000 deposit of currency, the banking system has $10,000 of deposits outstanding. The numbers used in this example were chosen arbitrarily to simplify the arithmetic. The actual "deposit multiplier" is closer to 2 than to 10. An individual bank cannot lend out more than its deposits because the borrower is likely to spend the amount of the loan and hence withdraw it from the bank. But the banking system as a whole can create multiple deposits because the deposit lost by one bank reappears as a deposit in another bank.

History. Banking existed in ancient Babylon, and Rome had an extensive banking system. In medieval Europe banking declined, largely because the Roman Catholic church condemned the practice of USURY. Banking revived in Renaissance Italy by the early 14th century, and government supervision of banking was established in 1502. During the 14th century the Florentine Bardi and Peruzzi banks had agencies in many countries. The most famous of the Florentine bankers were the Medici. English banking developed from the custom of goldsmiths safekeeping their customers' precious metals. The goldsmiths discovered that they could lend these metals out. They gave their customers receipts, which the customers used to pay their own bills. The BANK OF ENGLAND was established in 1694; in return for a loan to the government it was allowed, among other things, to issue its own notes, thus fulfilling two functions of a CENTRAL BANK.

In the United States the first bank, in the modern sense, was established in 1782. In 1791, Congress established a national bank, the First BANK OF THE UNITED STATES, but its charter lapsed in 1811. In 1816 the Second Bank of the United States was chartered, but its charter was not renewed in 1836. Subsequently, the states allowed the establishment of banks, with little restraint, and many of these banks failed. In 1863 the federal government started a system of nationally chartered banks that were required to back their notes by government securities. In 1913 this system was superseded by the FEDERAL RESERVE SYSTEM.

Banking in the United States. To open a NATIONAL BANK one needs a charter from the federal government, and to open a state bank one needs a charter from a state. All national banks must, and state banks may, become Federal Reserve member banks and be regulated by the Federal Reserve. All member banks must, and most others

do, join the FEDERAL DEPOSIT INSURANCE CORPORATION (FDIC) and are both insured and regulated by this agency. National banks account for about 55% of all deposits, and member banks for more than 70%, and nearly all deposits are insured. The FDIC insures deposits only up to $100,000. Frequently, however, when a bank fails, the FDIC, instead of paying off depositors, merges the failing bank with another bank.

Traditionally, branch banking has been tightly regulated. Most states limited, or altogether prohibited, branching, and banks could not open branches in other states. There are now few constraints on banks having branches within their own states, and banks can even cross state lines in many cases. Many states now allow entry to banks owned by companies owning banks in other states, thus, in effect, allowing banks to operate in several states.

Commercial banks compete with other institutions that offer some of the same services. Savings and loan associations, savings banks (also called mutual savings banks; see SAVINGS INDUSTRY), and CREDIT UNIONS compete with banks for deposits of households and nonprofit institutions. Their accounts are also insured up to $100,000 by government agencies. Savings and loan associations and savings banks invest most of their funds in mortgages and compete with commercial banks in this market. Along with credit unions and FINANCE COMPANIES, they also compete with banks for consumer loans and are now allowed to invest up to 10% of their total assets in commercial loans. Money market funds also compete with banks. They invest in very short-term, extremely safe securities and generally allow their customers to write large checks against their accounts. Competition among banks is strong in cities with many banks, and for the business of large firms that borrow outside their localities. In smaller towns, however, the one or two banks have considerable market power.

Banking in Other Countries. The banking systems of many countries differ sharply from the U.S. system. Other countries are generally much less hostile to banking concentration than is the United States. Relative to the size of the economy, U.S. banks are quite small, and no other country has nearly the number of banks the United States has. For example, in Great Britain four banks hold the great bulk of domestic deposits, and in Canada there are nine chartered banks. Control over banks also differs. The United States, with about 15,000 banks, relies on formal regulation. By contrast, Great Britain relies much more on moral suasion. Another way in which banks differ in various countries is by the type of assets they hold. U.S. commercial banks make business loans in more or less arms-length transactions, whereas in many other countries ordinary banking activities and INVESTMENT BANKING activities are carried out by the same institutions. Thus, German banks, for example, finance firms by making loans and by buying stock in them and place their managers on the boards of these companies.

In many of the less-developed countries much of the banking activity is carried out by branches of large multinational banks, although some countries prohibit foreign banks. In the USSR government banks provide the working-capital needs of factories and ensure that the latter carry out government plans. They also hold consumers' deposits.

International Banking. In recent years banking has become more internationalized. U.S. banks have about a thousand branches and subsidiaries in foreign countries, whereas foreign banks (mainly European and Japanese) account for one-fifth of all industrial and commercial bank loans in the United States. Some large U.S. banks derive more than half their income from international activities. Some small islands, such as the Cayman Islands, have become "monetary havens" akin to tax havens.

An important asset used in international banking is the Eurodollar. Eurodollars are not "dollars," either in the sense of consisting of U.S. currency or of being claims on the domestic branches of U.S. banks. They are just deposits—often time deposits—denominated in dollars in foreign banks or foreign branches of U.S. banks. They are not claims on the United States.

Retrenchment. The banking system, especially in the United States, has experienced several severe shocks since the 1970s. Dramatic oil-price increases imposed by the Organization of Petroleum Exporting Countries (OPEC) coupled with worldwide economic slowdown hit the economies of the less-developed countries (LDCs) very hard. Many were unable to repay or service large loans from major U.S. banks, which were forced to write off some loans and increase reserves against others. Negotiations averted major damage to the stability of the banking system, and a number of proposals have been put forward to limit losses to the banks while still giving relief to the hard-pressed developing economies.

The booming domestic economy of the mid-1980s seemed to offer bright prospects for U.S. banks. Reduced regulatory oversight and the security of insurance by the FDIC prompted many banks to overextend themselves and to enter risky areas of investment. With the end of the rapid growth of the 1980s came a historic number of bank failures, especially among savings and loan institutions (S&Ls) that had invested heavily in home mortgages. In 1990 one of the nation's largest banks, the Bank of New England, was taken over by government regulators after it suffered massive losses as the result of the depressed economy in the Northeast. Mergers of weak institutions with stronger ones are occurring at an unprecedented rate, even as the FDIC insurance fund has been reduced to levels many consider to be dangerously low. Calls are increasing for reregulation of banks, while also freeing them to compete more fairly with other financial institutions.

◼

bankruptcy   Bankruptcy, in law, is a system of procedures by which an insolvent debtor may be released from, or can modify, DEBT obligations. Under the U.S. Constitution, bankruptcy is a matter of federal law and is currently governed by the Bankruptcy Reform Acts of 1978 and 1984. Generally, individuals, corporations, and associations whose assets are less than their liabilities can file.

Major Types. The Bankruptcy Code provides for three major types of bankruptcy proceedings. In Chapter 7, or liquidation, cases, the debtor's property is sold off by a trustee to pay the debts owed to creditors. An individual debtor can keep a modest amount of household property or realty under federal or state exemptions. Individuals with a regular income who cannot pay their debts can, instead of liquidation, elect adjustment (Chapter 13) proceedings. In these cases, claims of creditors are frozen until the individual, with the assistance of a trustee, presents a plan to pay off the creditors from income. With court and creditor approval, the debtor may retain all property. In Chapter 11, or business reorganizations, the business is continued by its management or a trustee while creditors' claims are frozen pending their approval of a plan. With court approval, the plan can modify or forgive debts, recapitalize a corporation, provide for mergers or takeovers, or dispose of assets.

Procedure. The 1984 law gave U.S. district courts original jurisdiction over all Title II bankruptcy proceedings. Trustees are either elected by the creditors in a particular proceeding or appointed by the government. Almost all U.S. bankruptcy cases are voluntarily instituted by debtors, although creditors can force a debtor into involuntary liquidation.

In liquidations the trustee inventories the debtor's assets and lists creditors and their claims. The trustee also administers the property and distributes the proceeds. In nonliquidation cases the trustee and the debtor split these duties.

England and Canada. English law follows a similar approach. Creditors may petition a court to appoint an official receiver as a trustee of the insolvent debtor's estate. If efforts at settlement fail, a formal adjudication of bankruptcy will follow. Canadian law also allows both voluntary and involuntary bankruptcy.

◼

Banks, Sir Joseph   Sir Joseph Banks, b. Feb. 13, 1743, d. June 19, 1820, was an English botanist, a patron of the sciences, and president of the Royal Society of London for 42 years. His interest in botany and the natural sciences prompted him to make voyages of scientific exploration. From his first, to Labrador and Newfoundland in 1766, he brought back botanical specimens that were the beginning of the Banks Herbarium, a collection now in the British Museum. In 1768 he financed and accompanied a botanical expedition to the South Seas with Capt. James COOK, collecting more than 800 previously unknown specimens. Banks was also instrumental in efforts to grow tropical crops throughout the British Empire.

◼

banksia [bank'-see-uh]   The banksia is any of a number of Australian evergreen trees or shrubs of the genus *Banksia* in the family Proteaceae. The leaves are lance-shaped or linear and are variously toothed or incised. They are leathery, dark green above and whitish or brown beneath. The yellowish and occasionally reddish flowers are borne in densely crowded spikes that are terminal or rise from the axils of the leaves; they mature as conelike

The giant banksia flourishes in western Australia and has the largest flower spikes, 30 cm (1 ft), of the Banksia genus. The tree grows to 12 m (40 ft), and its leaves are 30 cm (1 ft) long.

structures. The genus is characteristic of the scrub vegetation found in the mountains of southeastern and southern Australia, and also in southwest Australia.

Banneker, Benjamin   Benjamin Banneker, b. near Ellicott's Lower Mills, Md., Nov. 9, 1731, d. Oct. 9, 1806, achieved fame as a compiler of almanacs. A free black tobacco farmer, he acquired his astronomical knowledge through self-teaching, aided by the loan of books by George Ellicott, a Quaker millowner. He served (1791) as scientific assistant to Maj. Andrew Ellicott in surveying the boundaries for the new District of Columbia. Banneker's series of six almanacs (1791–1802) were widely distributed to counter the prevailing opinion that blacks were inherently intellectually inferior to whites.

Bannister, Roger   Roger Gilbert Bannister, b. Mar. 23, 1929, an English runner, made track history on May 6, 1954, when he became the first person to run a mile in less than 4 minutes. Then an Oxford medical student, he broke the so-called 4–minute barrier with a time of 3:59.4. John Landy set a new record (3:58.0) just 46 days later, but Bannister beat Landy on August 7 in a historic Commonwealth Games mile, retired shortly thereafter, and then wrote *First Four Minutes* (1955). Bannister, who became a neurologist, was knighted in 1975.

Bannock   The Bannock are a North American Indian people whose traditional homeland was the Snake River drainage basin in present-day Idaho and neighboring states. They spoke a Shoshonian language related to that of the Northern PAIUTE. A hunting and gathering people,

the Bannock lived in small, seminomadic bands. Their total population probably never exceeded 2,000. They exploited bison herds and acquired many other cultural traits typical of Plains peoples.

The Bannock remained only loosely united until threatened by whites with the encroachment of their hunting lands. Several outbreaks of hostility toward the whites occurred between 1859 and 1863. In 1866, Fort Hall Reservation was established for the Bannock and the Shoshoni. NEZ PERCÉ resistance in 1877 incited the Bannock to further conflict with the U.S. government. In 1878, Buffalo Horn, a former cavalry scout, led the uprising known as the Bannock War, which ended that year in the massacre of about 140 Bannock warriors, women, and children. Today the combined Bannock and Shoshoni population at Fort Hall reservation numbers about 3,000.

banteng   The banteng, *Bos banteng*, is a wild OX belonging to the family Bovidea, order Artiodactyla; this family includes other wild and domestic cattle (see CATTLE AND CATTLE RAISING). The banteng is about 2 m (6.5 ft) long and 1.2 to 1.5 m (4 to 5 ft) tall at the shoulder. It has slender, curved horns and a black to reddish brown coat. These shy cattle roam in herds through Southeast Asian lowlands and forested hills, eating grass, bamboo shoots, and other plants. Some have been domesticated.

The male banteng has a darker coat than a female, whose hide is reddish brown. Domesticated bantengs are called Bali cattle.

Banting, Sir Frederick G.   The Canadian physician Sir Frederick Grant Banting, b. Alliston, Ontario, Nov. 14, 1891, d. Feb. 21, 1941, extracted, with his assistant Charles H. BEST, the hormone insulin from the pancreas. This breakthrough made possible the treatment of DIABETES mellitus, a disease in which an abnormal buildup of glucose takes place in the body. Earlier work had indicated that a substance produced in the pancreas regulates glucose metabolism. In 1922, Banting and

Best announced that they had successfully isolated a substance from the islets of Langerhans in the pancreas that, when given to diabetic dogs, restored their health. This substance, insulin, also proved effective in treating diabetes mellitus in humans. For his work Banting was a corecipient of the 1923 Nobel Prize for physiology or medicine.

Bantu [ban'-too]

Bantu, meaning "the people," is the name of a major linguistic group in Africa. In the southern projection of the continent from Cameroon's port of Douala on the Atlantic coast to Kenya's Tana River on the Indian Ocean, nearly 90 million people speak Bantu languages, which number nearly 700 and include numerous dialects.

Linguists have tried to explain the enormous geographical spread along with the considerable degree of linguistic convergence in Bantu grammar and vocabulary. Whether the ultimate source of the Bantu people was in the central Benue Valley in eastern Nigeria or in the north, perhaps central Cameroon or the Central African Republic, areas of higher rainfall were gradually colonized as the Bantu speakers, who subsisted mainly by fishing and agriculture, spread south and east of the equatorial forest.

The archaeological evidence for the latter part of the last millennium BC points to expansion by Iron Age invaders, cultivating sorghum and millet, at the expense of indigenous Late Stone Age communities, who subsisted primarily by hunting and gathering. At least by the 5th century AD the invaders, presumably Bantu speakers, had brought the Iron Age as far south as Swaziland and, by the 9th century, into the north of Namibia. Archaeologists are in general agreement that the ancestors of such Bantu speakers as the Kalanga, Karanga, and Venda achieved a peak of material cultural development in the 10th–15th centuries and built the elegant structures, terraces, pits, and fortresses (including the celebrated ZIMBABWE RUINS site) that appear across Zimbabwe into Botswana and at the site of MAPUNGUBWE in the Transvaal.

See also: AFRICAN LANGUAGES; AFRICAN PREHISTORY; individual countries.

banyan

The banyan, *Ficus benghalensis*, is a large fig tree belonging to the mulberry family, Moraceae. It grows in India and Bangladesh and is held sacred in both places. The tree begins life as an epiphyte on a host tree, gathering its nourishment and water from the air. As it grows, its lateral branches send down aerial supporting roots that become absorbing roots when they reach the ground. Eventually, the host tree is smothered as the banyan sends out more branches and roots. The mature banyan's canopy may cover an area more than 300 m (1,000 ft) in diameter. The stems below the canopy form a kind of columned room, sometimes used as a market shelter by merchants in India. The leathery, evergreen leaves are up to 20 cm (8 in) long. The reddish figs are eaten by birds and bats.

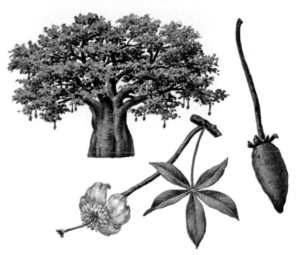

Baobab, one of the largest trees in the world, is one of the few trees found on the African savanna. It has compound leaves, fragrant flowers, and a woody, elongated fruit.

baobab [bow'-bab]

The baobab tree, *Adansonia digitata*, is one of the most unusual deciduous trees of Africa. The interior of its trunk, which may reach 9 m (30 ft) in diameter, and the lower branches are soft and spongy and can store large quantities of water. Baobabs are specially adapted for long dry seasons. They are leafless during this time of year, thus reducing transpiration, or water loss. The baobab is an extremely slow-growing tree, reaching up to 18 m (60 ft) in height, and giant specimens may be several thousand years old. Pollination of the flowers is performed by bats.

The banyan, sacred to Hindus, may shade a huge area beneath its canopy. Secondary, supporting trunks are formed by aerial roots growing from the branches. The paired, edible figs (bottom right) are about 1.25 cm (0.5 in) in diameter.

The baptism of Christ, as portrayed in this early fresco, shows Christ being immersed in the River Jordan by John the Baptist.

baptism   Baptism is a SACRAMENT of the Christian church in which candidates are immersed in water or water is poured over them in the name of the Father, Son, and Holy Spirit. It is derived from the practice of John the Baptist, who baptized Jesus, and probably from the Jewish *tebilah* (a ritual bath). Matthew 28:19 calls upon Christians to make disciples and to baptize them.

In the early church baptism was administered after a period of preparation (catechumenate), preferably at Easter. It was performed in conjunction with the rites later called confirmation and Eucharist. The effects of baptism were believed to be union with Jesus in his death and resurrection, forgiveness of sin, the gift of the Holy Spirit, membership in the church, and rebirth to new life in Christ. Some scholars believe infants were included among the candidates from the beginning; others believe that infant baptism began in the 3d century. Today Baptists and Disciples of Christ do not practice infant baptism and do insist on immersion. Most other churches baptize infants and permit the pouring of water. A few Protestant groups, such as the Quakers, reject outward baptism altogether. The Christian rite is in some ways similar to rites of purification used in other religions.

baptistery   A baptistery is a building adjacent or attached to a church, or sometimes a chamber within a church, in which the ritual of baptism takes place. Baptisteries probably derived their form from ancient Greek and Roman *tholoi*, or round temples, such as the Temple of the Vestal Virgins in the Roman Forum. The domed octagonal baptistery adjoining the basilica of Saint John in the Lateran in Rome, built during the reign (430–40) of Pope Sixtus III, was the prototype for many centuries. Since total immersion was widely practiced at that time, the central feature was usually a large basin or pool directly beneath the dome.

The octagonal form for baptisteries was preferred through the Romanesque and Gothic periods, particularly in Italy. The Florence Baptistery (consecrated in 1059) is

The Florence Baptistery, an octagonal Romanesque structure dedicated to St. John the Baptist, is famous for its gilded bronze doors, the great "Gates of Paradise" (1424–52) by Lorenzo Ghiberti, which depict ten scenes from the Old Testament.

perhaps the best known: sheathed in white marble with green marble trim, the large slant-roofed octagon is directly opposite the central door of the Duomo (Cathedral), a symbolic reminder that baptism is the first rite of Christian life. Inside the baptistery a huge octagonal dome is revealed, completely covered with mosaics, part of an exceedingly rich decorative scheme.

As baptismal practices became simplified, separate baptisteries became a rarity. They survive most frequently today as a font placed near the church door. In churches of religious groups that practice baptismal immersion, the basin or pool is usually placed prominently behind the chancel.

Baptists   The Baptists form one of the largest Protestant denominations. The following distinguish the Baptists from other Protestant communions: (1) their insistence on baptism of adult believers only; (2) their concern for freedom of speech and conscience and for freedom from interference by any civil or ecclesiastical authority; (3) the primacy they seek to give to Scripture in matters of faith, doctrine, and morals; and (4) the authority they give to the congregation in church affairs.

The forerunners of present-day Baptists were the ANABAPTISTS of the REFORMATION period. Some Anabaptist congregations were settled in Holland in the early 17th century when groups of Puritan Independents, or Congregationalists, fled from England to Holland. Influenced by the Anabaptists, some of these Independents were persuaded that Christian baptism was appropriate only for adults with a personal faith and commitment. Returning to England, this group formed the first Baptist congregation in 1611. Shortly thereafter Roger WILLIAMS formed (1639) the first Baptist congregation in Providence, R.I. The Baptists grew rapidly in the United States. The democratic, informal, Scripture-centered, relatively untheological mode of Baptist service was ideal for any unsettled, rural, or frontier situation. Thus the South, the Midwest, and the Far West were heavily populated—more than were the Northeast or the Middle Atlantic—by Baptists, a pattern that remains true to this day.

Baptists view the Christian life as one of personal faith and of serious dedication to live according to the highest Christian precepts. Each person is thus to be born again, converted into a new life, and gathered into the church community. For Baptists the church is essentially the result of conversion and of GRACE, a gathered community of committed believers; it is not the source (rather than the effect) of grace. The church has in itself no authority over its members, over their freedom of conscience, or over their churchly affairs.

Because of their emphasis on the Bible, on a strict puritan ethic, and on the absolute necessity of personal faith and personal holiness, most Baptists around the world have remained conservative, even fundamentalist, in matters of both faith and morals (see FUNDAMENTALISM). Many Baptist conventions refuse to join the ecumenical movement in any official way. They have also largely ignored the social gospel (a concern for establishing social justice in political, social, and economic life) while retaining a deep loyalty to the efficacy of individualistic revivalism. On the other hand, because of their emphasis on freedom of conscience and of personal believing, on the importance of Christian life and works rather than on ritual, on their distaste for creeds, dogmas, and ecclesiastical authority, some Baptists have been leaders in theological and social liberalism.

Bar Harbor   The town of Bar Harbor (1990 pop., 4,443), on Mount Desert Island in southeast Maine, was settled in 1763 and became a famous 19th-century resort. In 1947 most of the town was destroyed by fire. Acadia National Park is located nearby.

Bar Kochba [bar kohk'-buh]   Bar Kochba, also known as Simeon ben Koseva, d. AD 135, was the leader of the Jewish rebellion against Rome, in AD 132–35. The rebels avoided open battles, fighting instead from underground fortifications. Jersualem was conquered. Emperor HADRI-

AN recalled Severus from Britain to oppose Bar Kochba. After a lengthy and heroic defense, the rebellion failed. Bar Kochba died in battle.

bar mitzvah   A bar mitzvah ("son of the commandment") is a male Jew who has reached his 13th birthday and is recognized as fully responsible for his own religious and moral actions. A bat mitzvah is the corresponding female Jew. A rite in the synagogue, which is also commonly referred to as bar mitzvah, marks the attainment of the status of bar mitzvah. In Conservative and Reform Judaism, a similar rite is used for the bat mitzvah as well. When reaching puberty, a young man or woman is called upon to read a prophetic passage from Scripture to the synagogue congregation. Thereupon he or she is recognized as a full member of the congregation, able to count as a member of the required quorum of ten. On that occasion the parents say a blessing: "Blessed is God who has now freed me from bearing full responsibility for this person." In the 19th century, Reform Judaism created the rite of confirmation, either instead of, or in addition to, the bar mitzvah celebration. It is held on the festival of Shavuoth, or Pentecost, which marks the revelation of the TORAH. This rite is now common in Reform and Conservative synagogues.

Bara, Theda   Theda Bara was the stage name of Theodosia Goodman, b. Cincinnati, Ohio, July 20, 1890, d. Apr. 7, 1955, who was molded by Hollywood into the screen's first sex symbol. She was hired by the producer William Fox to play a femme fatale in the silent film *A Fool There Was* (1914) and was immediately dubbed "the vamp." A vast publicity campaign continued to promote this image. Even after leaving Hollywood in 1920, she could not escape typecasting. Bara retired from show business in the late 1920s.

Theda Bara, an American star of the silent screen, achieved widespread popularity for her many roles portraying a cold-hearted seductress. During her 5-year screen contract, she appeared in about 40 films, including Carmen *(1915),* Romeo and Juliet *(1916),* Cleopatra *(1917), and* Salome, the Vixen *(1918).*

Barabbas [buh-rab'-uhs]   In the Bible, Barabbas was the prisoner who, by popular choice of the Jews, was released instead of Christ (Matt. 27, Mark 15, Luke 23, John 18). The Roman governor customarily granted one such pardon each year at Passover time.

Baraga, Frederick [bahr'-uh-guh]

Frederick Baraga, b. June 29, 1797, d. Jan. 19, 1868, was an Austrian-born Catholic missionary to the American Indians in the Great Lakes region. Educated in Vienna, he sought ordination to the priesthood and volunteered for missionary work in the United States.

After learning the Ojibwa (Chippewa) dialect, Baraga published an important grammar of that language (1850) and a comprehensive dictionary (1853). In 1853 Baraga was made bishop and vicar-apostolic of Upper Michigan. In the following years he traveled widely, recruiting clergy, raising funds, and preaching several times a day in a number of languages. He became the first bishop of Marquette (1865). Preliminary steps have been taken toward his canonization.

Baraka, Imamu Amiri [bah-rah'-kah, ee-mah'moo ah-mee'-ree]

A poet, playwright, and community leader, Imamu Amiri Baraka, originally named Everett LeRoi Jones, b. Newark, N.J., Oct. 7, 1934, is best known for his play *Dutchman* (1964), which depicts blacks and whites in a shocking symbolic confrontation. The play won a 1964 Obie Award. As LeRoi Jones, Baraka produced his first major work, the volume of poetry *Preface to a Twenty-Volume Suicide Note* (1961). His increasingly militant stance was reflected in two plays, *The Slave* and *The Toilet*, both produced Off Broadway in 1965. In 1968 he discarded his "slave name" for a Muslim one and assumed leadership of his black Muslim organization, Kawaida, dedicated to coalescing black power in Newark. His *The Autobiography of LeRoi Jones* was published in 1984.

Imamu Amiri Baraka, formerly LeRoi Jones, is an American playwright and poet whose works express hostility toward and mistrust of white society. Baraka also founded the Black Community Development and Defense Organization, a Muslim group, and was a leader of the National Black Political Caucus.

Baranov, Aleksandr Andreyevich [buh-rah'nawf, ul-yik-sahn'-dur un-dray'-uh-vich]

Aleksandr Andreyevich Baranov, b. 1747, d. Apr. 28, 1819, was head of the RUSSIAN-AMERICAN COMPANY and the first governor (1799–1818) of Russian Alaska. Baranov Island is named for him. A successful fur trader, he reached Alaska in 1790, extended the Russian settlements, and sold furs to the United States, to the Spanish in California and Manila, and to Canton, China. In 1808, Baranov's new settlement at Sitka replaced Kodiak as the trading capital.

Barbados

Barbados is an independent country, formerly a British colony, and the most easterly island of the West Indies. Its capital and only port of entry is Bridgetown.

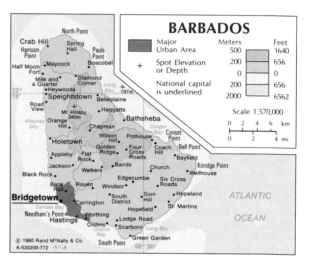

The island is underlain with folded sedimentary deposits, and a surface layer of coral attains 90 m (300 ft) in thickness. In the northeastern parts, erosion has exposed rugged ridges and ravines. The climate is warm and pleasant. The average annual temperature is about 27° C (80° F), and little daily or annual variation occurs. A dry season (from December to May) alternates with a wet season. The average annual rainfall is about 1,500 mm (60 in).

Barbados is one of the world's most densely populated countries. Nearly 90% of the population is black.

The production of sugarcane and its by-products, molasses and rum, long a mainstay of the Barbadian economy, has been replaced by tourism as the chief industry. The development of light industry and the diversification of agriculture have been encouraged by the government.

Barbados was settled by English colonists in 1627. To work the sugarcane plantations, slaves were brought from Africa, a practice that continued until slavery was abolished in the British Empire in 1834. A political-rights movement in the early 20th century resulted in the founding of the Barbados Labour party in 1938. Barba-

AT A GLANCE

BARBADOS

Land: Area: 436 km^2 (166 mi^2). Capital and largest city: Bridgetown (1980 pop. 7,517).

People: Population (1990 est.): 262,688. Density: 602 persons per km^2 (1,582 per mi^2). Distribution (1985): 42% urban, 58% rural. Official language: English. Major religions: Anglicanism, Methodism.

Government: Type: independent state within Commonwealth of Nations. Legislature: Parliament. Political subdivisions: 11 parishes, Bridgetown.

Economy: GDP (1988): $1.3 billion; $5,250 per capita. Labor distribution (1985 est.): commerce and services—68%; manufacturing and construction—22%; agriculture—8%. Foreign trade (1988): imports—$582 million; exports—$173 million. Currency: 1 Barbados dollar = 100 cents.

Education and Health: Literacy (1990): 99%. Universities (1987): 1. Hospital beds (1980): 2,126. Physicians (1983): 213. Life expectancy (1990): women—77; men—73. Infant mortality (1990): 16 per 1,000 live births.

dos became independent on Nov. 30, 1966; it has a parliamentary form of government. Errol Barrow, the first prime minister, was succeeded by Tom Adams, who held office from 1976 until his death in 1985. Since 1987, the prime minister has been Erskine Sandiford.

Barbary ape   The barbary ape, so called since ancient times, is a monkey, not an ape. More precisely, it is a MACAQUE, *Macaca sylvana*. The Barbary ape is 38–76 cm (15–30 in) long and weighs up to 13 kg (28 lb). The thick fur is yellowish brown to black, and the hairless face is whitish pink. Barbary apes are the only wild monkeys now living in Europe; they occupy caves on the Rock of Gibraltar. They also live in rocky areas of Morocco and Algeria. The young are usually born singly. The life span in captivity is more than 30 years.

Barbary States   The Barbary States is a former name for the coastal region of North Africa extending from the Atlantic Ocean to Egypt and comprising the present states of Morocco, Algeria, Tunisia, and Libya. The name is derived from the BERBERS, the oldest known inhabitants of the region.

In the 16th century the Arab principalities of North Africa came under the nominal rule of the Ottoman Empire. They were in fact conquered for Turkey by a corsair, or pirate, known as Barbarossa (d. 1546) to prevent their falling to Christian Spain. Thereafter, the Barbary States became a base for piracy against European shipping in the Mediterranean. The booty—and tribute paid to gain immunity from attacks—were the chief source of revenue for the local rulers.

In 1801 the newly independent United States, whose ships had also been attacked, launched the TRIPOLITAN WAR (1800–05) against Tripoli (now Libya). In 1815 the United States also fought against Algiers, which was then bombarded by an Anglo-Dutch fleet (1816). Nevertheless, it was not until the French conquest (1830) of Algeria that the piracy was effectively ended. Subsequently, the entire region came under colonial rule (by France and Italy) until the mid-20th century.

barbel   see CARP

Barber, Samuel   Samuel Barber, b. West Chester, Pa., Mar. 9, 1910, d. Jan. 23, 1981, was a prominent American composer. After studying at the Curtis Institute of Music in Philadelphia, he attracted notice in 1933 with his overture to *The School for Scandal*. In 1935 his Symphony no. 1 (in one movement) became the first work by an American to be played at the Salzburg Festival. Arturo Toscanini conducted Barber's Adagio for Strings (based on the slow movement of his String Quartet) and First Essay for Orchestra in 1938. Barber won a Pulitzer Prize in 1958 for his opera *Vanessa* and again in 1963 for his Piano Concerto. His major works include *Capricorn Concerto* (1944), *Knoxville: Summer of 1915* (1948) for soprano and orchestra, and *Prayers of Kierkegaard* (1954) for soprano, chorus, and orchestra. Barber's music is characterized by full-blooded lyricism and rich orchestration.

Barber of Seville, The   Although the premiere of Gioacchino Rossini's opera buffa *The Barber of Seville*, at the Argentina Theater in Rome on Feb. 20, 1816, was far from successful, the work won popularity within a short time. Young Rosina is jealously kept under lock and key by her guardian, Doctor Bartolo, who plans to marry her himself. The dashing Count Almaviva has seen the girl in Madrid and pursued her to Seville. The opera's two acts chronicle how the Count and the barber Figaro match wits with Doctor Bartolo (and his scheming music master Don Basilio) to win Rosina's hand in marriage to the Count.

The Barber of Seville is beloved for such brilliant individual numbers as Figaro's "Largo al factotum" and Rosina's "Una voce poco fa" and for its sparkling ensembles. The libretto, by Cesare Sterbini, is based on the first play of a trilogy by the French playwright Caron de BEAUMARCHAIS.

barbershop quartet   The American barbershop quartet probably assumed its present form in the late 19th century, when the informal group singing associated with barbershop bonhomie became formalized and professional quartets became popular. Present-day quartets specialize in songs from the turn of the century, such as "Sweet Adeline" and "Down by the Old Mill Stream." The Society for the Preservation and Encouragement of Barber Shop Quartet Singing in America was founded in 1938.

barbet [bahr'-bit]   The barbet is any of a number of birds of the family Capitonidae. They are small or medium sized, stocky and big headed, heavy billed, and often gaudily colored; many are bright green with contrasting markings of other brilliant hues. Of 72 species, 12 are found in tropical America; the rest inhabit tropical Africa or southern Asia. Forest birds, barbets tend to be seden-

The toucan barbet is one of the New World's tiniest barbets, 21 cm (8.3 in) long. It makes its home in tropical forests of the Andes in Ecuador and Colombia.

tary, but they are extremely noisy. They eat both vegetable and animal food and nest in holes; both sexes incubate and care for the young.

barbiturate   Barbiturates are habit-forming drugs used as sedatives and hypnotics. They are white, crystalline, odorless derivatives of barbituric acid ($C_4H_4N_2O_3$). Medically, they are used to induce sleep, relieve anxiety and neuroses by inducing drowsiness, and control epileptic seizures. Barbiturates are widely abused, being taken to cause a state of euphoria. Sometimes they are used in suicide attempts.

Barbiturates act to depress the central nervous system. The duration of action depends on how quickly one of the drugs passes through the blood-brain barrier and affects the brain. Long-acting barbiturates, such as amobarbital, penetrate this barrier slowly; short-acting drugs, such as secobarbital, penetrate faster and are used to alleviate an inability to sleep. Ultrashort barbiturates, such as thiopental, pass through the blood-brain barrier so rapidly that sleep occurs in seconds; these are used as adjuncts to anesthesia.

Side effects of barbiturates include drowsiness and an effect similar to that of an alcoholic hangover. Judgment and motor control are usually impaired, and mood changes (such as depression) may occur. An overdose depresses the respiratory rate and may result in coma and death. Other depressant drugs (such as alcohol, antihistamines, and tranquilizers), if taken simultaneously, increase the effect of barbiturates. The human body develops a tolerance for barbiturates, and withdrawal symptoms occur once a person who is physically dependent on these drugs stops taking them.

Barbizon school   The term Barbizon school refers to a group of French landscape painters active between 1830 and 1880. They include Théodore ROUSSEAU, Charles François DAUBIGNY, Narcisse Virgile DIAZ DE LA PEÑA, and Constant Troyon. Less well known are Jules Dupré, Achille Etna Michallon, and Georges Michel. Two other painters, Camille COROT and Jean François MILLET, are sometimes included in this group because they also painted at Barbizon, a village bordering the Fontainbleau forest, about 50 km (30 mi) south of Paris.

The members of the Barbizon school were primarily landscape painters interested in both the look and the mood of their native countryside. Because they usually painted in restrained hues and often at twilight, their work differs from the classical, mythological scenes based on Nicolas POUSSIN and the bright, deliberately picturesque landscapes of such romantic painters as Eugène DELACROIX. The school had its roots in the LANDSCAPE PAINTING of such 17th-century Dutch artists as Meindert HOBBEMA and Jacob van RUISDAEL.

The Barbizon artists painted outdoors, *en plein air*. Unlike the later impressionists, however, whom they influenced, they usually finished their works in the atelier. Although they had the support of the influential critic

Théophile Thoré, they were often criticized for the "sketchy" unfinished qualities of their canvases. At the Paris World Exhibition of 1855, however, the Barbizon painters finally achieved both success and popularity.

Barbour, John   John Barbour, b. *c.*1316, d. Mar. 13, 1395, is often considered Scotland's first identifiable poet. While archdeacon of Aberdeen (1357–95) he wrote the national epic romance *The Bruce* (1375). This work, based largely on fact, celebrates Scotland's victory under King Robert the Bruce over the English at the Battle of Bannockburn (1314).

Barcelona   Barcelona is the second largest city and leading seaport of Spain, with a population of 1,703,744 (1987 est.). The capital of Barcelona province and chief city of CATALONIA, it is located on a narrow Mediterranean coastal plain of northeastern Spain.

The Contemporary City. Barcelona's metropolitan area includes many small industrial towns. The city is the leading manufacturing center of Spain and an important banking and financial area. It is linked by road and rail with most of the country.

The old city lies close to the harbor. Its chief feature is Las Ramblas—a broad, tree-lined avenue leading to the Plaza de Cataluña. The old city contains remains of a Roman settlement, a medieval cathedral, and many ancient palaces and houses. Residential and industrial suburbs enclose the area on the north and west and extend over the outlying foothills toward the mountains.

Approximately one-fifth of all industrial production in Spain is from Barcelona. Traditionally, the textile industry, especially woolens and cottons, dominated. Recently, engineering industries, including automobile producers and chemical manufacturers, have been added. Quays and a number of specialized docks for oil, grain, and other commodities facilitate transport for domestic consumption and export.

Barcelona is the site of the University of Barcelona. Founded (1430) by Alfonso V, king of Aragon, it is one of the largest and most important universities in Spain. In 1968 a second university was established with a greater emphasis on graduate studies. A number of museums and galleries, including an important collection of Picasso's works, are also there. The city is a cultural center, especially for the Catalans, and a focus of sports activity, preeminently soccer. New facilities were constructed when the city was chosen to host the 1992 Olympics. Perhaps its most famous building is Antonio GAUDÍ's unfinished Sagrada Familia church, begun in the late 19th century and characterized by its cluster of openwork spires.

History. Barcelona was a Carthaginian city, and the name is believed to have been derived from the Punic family of Barca. The Romans developed the city, and it was later ruled briefly by the Moors. It achieved independence in the 11th century under the counts of Barcelona. After the city had been absorbed (1137) into the king-

The Plaza de Cataluña, the largest of Barcelona's public squares, stands in the heart of the city's commercial district. Barcelona is Spain's leading port on the Mediterranean Sea.

dom of Aragon, it grew to be one of the leading Mediterranean centers of commerce, rivaling Venice and Genoa in wealth. Barcelona declined in the 16th century. Toward the end of the 19th century, the port was modernized, and Barcelona again became a center of commerce. Catalan nationalism has remained strong, and several revolts against Spanish authority have occurred. In the 1930s the city was briefly the capital of an autonomous Catalan state. It was a stronghold of republicanism in the Spanish Civil War.

Bardeen, John   The American physicist John Bardeen, b. Madison, Wis., May 23, 1908, d. Jan. 30, 1991, shared the 1965 Nobel Prize for physics with William B. SHOCKLEY and Walter H. Brattain for the invention of the TRANSISTOR, and the 1972 Nobel Prize for physics with Leon N. Cooper and John Schrieffer for the development of the theory of SUPERCONDUCTIVITY. A graduate of the University of Wisconsin (1928) and Princeton University (1936), Bardeen served as an assistant professor of physics at the University of Minnesota (1938–41) and as a physicist at the U.S. Naval Ordnance Laboratory in Washington, D.C. (1941–45), and at Bell Telephone Laboratories (1945–51). From 1951 to 1975 he was a professor of physics at the University of Illinois, Urbana.

Bardot, Brigitte [bahr-doh']   The French film actress Brigitte Bardot, b. Sept. 28, 1934, achieved international celebrity for the sexy image she projected on and off screen. She was most successful in the films *And God Created Woman* (1956), *The Devil Is a Woman* (1958), *The Truth* (1961), *Contempt* (1964), and *Viva Maria* (1965).

Barenboim, Daniel [bar'-en-boym]   Daniel Barenboim, b. Buenos Aires, Nov. 15, 1942, pianist and conductor, became musical director of the Orchestre de Paris in 1975, a post he held until 1987, when he was appointed artistic director of the new Paris Opéra de la Bastille. In 1989, however, he was dismissed amid controversy, allegedly because of his large salary (over $1 million) and costly plans. He has been named to become head of the Chicago Symphony in 1991. Barenboim's marriage to the supremely talented English cellist Jacqueline du Pré (b. 1945) ended with her tragic death from multiple sclerosis in 1987.

Barents, Willem   The Dutch navigator Willem Barents, b. c.1550, d. June 20, 1597, is the most famous of the early explorers of the Arctic. Seeking the NORTHEAST PASSAGE, he reached the archipelago of Novaya Zemlya on his first two voyages (1594, 1595). He embarked again in 1596, discovering Spitsbergen and rounding the northern point of Novaya Zemlya. Caught in the ice, Barents and his crew survived the winter in a shelter built on Novaya Zemlya. In June 1597 they set out for the mainland in two open boats, but Barents soon died. The Barents Sea is named for him.

Barents Sea   The Barents Sea (formerly called the Murmean Sea) is an extension of the Arctic Ocean lying north of Norway and the USSR, named in 1853 for Willem Barents, the 16th-century Dutch explorer. Its area is about 1,400,000 km^2 (540,000 mi^2). In northern sections of the sea, the average winter air temperature is -25° C (-13° F), but the Soviet port of MURMANSK remains ice-free in winter, partly due to the North Cape Current.

barge   A barge is a flat-bottomed boat of heavy construction used to transport materials in bulk on rivers and canals and in short-distance coastal traffic. Animal haulage of unpowered (dumb) canal barges was used from the Middle Ages to the early 19th century. Mechanical cable haulage, and later steam and diesel power, largely replaced the unpowered barge, although today, on large rivers and canals, several dumb barges are sometimes lashed together in an assembly known as a push tow, which is propelled by a tugboat. On the Mississippi River, barge assemblies of as many as 40 barges may extend 457 m (1,500 ft) ahead of the tug. New barge technology has created the LASH (Lighter Aboard Ship), a vessel that carries cargo in small steel barges that can be stowed on deck or lowered into the water by crane.

Bargello [bahr-jel'-oh]   The Bargello, or *Palazzo del Podestà*, in Florence, Italy, was built between 1254 and 1346 as the armory, city jail, and residence of the chief of police. Remodeled in the 19th century as the Museo Nazionale, it now houses a rich collection of Tuscan

sculpture, ceramics, and medieval armor. Its principal monuments include Lorenzo Ghiberti's and Filippo Brunelleschi's competitive bronze reliefs for the Florence Baptistery doors (1401); Donatello's *St. George* (c.1415–1420) and *David* (c.1430); glazed terra-cottas from the della Robbia workshop (active c.1440–1530); four marbles by Michelangelo; bronzes and marbles by Benvenuto Cellini, and Giovanni da Bologna's *Mercury* (1580).

Bari [bah'-ree]   Bari is the capital city of Bari province and of the Apulia region in southeast Italy. Situated on the Adriatic Sea, it is a major seaport. Bari has a population of 358,906 (1988 est.). Its industries include food processing, flour milling, oil refining, and textiles, chemicals, and tobacco.

Possibly inhabited since 1500 BC, Bari was first under Greek, then Roman, control. During the early Middle Ages it was controlled by Goths, Lombards, Saracens, and Byzantines, until the Normans took it in 1071. An important Crusader embarkation point from 1096, it was revitalized under the German emperor Frederick II (1194–1250) and was later ruled by the Sforzas of Milan before being passed to the kingdom of Naples in 1557. Bari was badly damaged during World War II; its remaining monuments include the 11th-century Romanesque Basilica of San Nicola, a 12th-century Romanesque cathedral, and the Hohenstaufen castle (1223).

barite   The chief ore and most common mineral of barium is barite, barium sulfate, $BaSO_4$. It forms vitreous, white or tinted, tabular or prismatic crystals (see ORTHORHOMBIC SYSTEM) and crystal aggregates ("desert roses"), as well as coarsely laminated or granular masses, STALACTITES, and nodules. Hardness is 3–3½; specific gravity is 4.3–4.6, high for a nonmetallic mineral. Barite mud is used in drilling oil wells to help control oil and gas pressure and prevent drill-hole cave-ins. Barite is the chief component of the white pigment lithopone. Also called heavy spar, it occurs in ORE DEPOSITS and EVAPORITE beds.
   See also: SULFATE MINERALS.

Barite minerals are found in various forms of transparent to opaque crystals with a glassy luster. Normally white to light gray, they are often tinged blue, green, yellow, brown, or red. Illustrated here is a concentric group of crystals called "desert rose."

baritone   *Baritone* is the term applied to the singing voice midway between bass and tenor. The baritone quality may be either lyric or robust; the range is generally from G on the lowest line of the bass staff to G two octaves above. The term *baritone* is also used to designate an instrument next in range to the bass of a family, such as baritone horn and baritone saxophone.

barium   Barium is a chemical element—a silvery, soft metal—and it is the fifth of the ALKALINE EARTH METALS forming Group IIA in the periodic table. Its symbol is Ba, its atomic number is 56, and its atomic weight is 137.34. The density of barium is 3.75 g/cm³ at 20° C; its melting point is approximately 725° C, and its boiling point is approximately 1,640° C. The name *barium* is derived from the Greek *barus*, meaning "heavy."

Barium is widely distributed in nature. The principal ore is barite (barium sulfate), also called heavy spar. The presence of barium oxide in barite was discovered (1779) by C. W. SCHEELE, and the metal was first isolated (1808) by Sir Humphry DAVY. Pure barium oxidizes readily, a property that makes it useful as a "getter" for removing oxygen from vacuum tubes. Useful alloys of barium and aluminum or magnesium are made by reacting these metals with barium oxide. Barium is highly electropositive and very reactive. It readily forms the Ba^{2+} ion, which behaves as a typical divalent ion and can be used to precipitate larger anions. Barium hydroxide, $Ba(OH)_2$, is soluble in water and is a strong base. Barium oxide, BaO, is used as a laboratory source of small amounts of peroxide. The oxidation of BaO in air produces BaO_2, barium peroxide, which, reacting with diluted sulfuric acid, H_2SO_4, yields hydrogen peroxide, H_2O_2.

Barium carbonate, $BaCO_3$, is used as a raw material for other barium compounds, as an ingredient in optical glass and fine glassware, and in the preparation of ceramic permanent magnets for loudspeakers. It is also used as a rat poison.

Barium sulfate, $BaSO_4$, is used medically as a contrast agent when taking X-ray images of the gastrointestinal tract to look for tumors, polyps, or other abnormal conditions (see RADIOLOGY). The procedure is known as a barium enema.

bark   Bark is the external, relatively impervious covering on the stems of TREES and SHRUBS. Two different tissues in the mature stems of PLANTS continuously produce cells as the stem grows: an inner vascular cambium and an outer cork cambium. (Cambium is an embryonic tissue in vascular plants.) The vascular cambium produces inner layers of xylem (water-conducting) cells, which become wood, and an outer layer of phloem (nutrient-conducting) cells, which eventually become part of the bark. The cork cambium produces cork cells, which constitute most of the bark.

As the plant stem increases in girth, the layers from the vascular cambium outward rupture and die and produce the characteristic bark patterns of the different types of plants. The layer of dead cork cells is the outer bark of the older stem or root. The inner bark is the phlo-

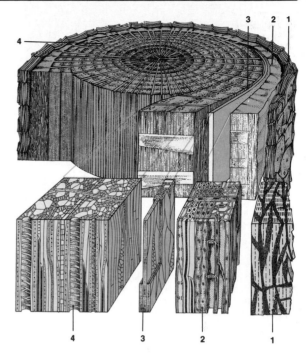

Bark protects trees just as skin protects people. It comprises two basic layers, the cork cambium, or periderm (1), and the secondary phloem (2). Cork cambium is old tissue, which consists of cork cells and dead phloem tissue. Cork cells contain fatty material that makes the entire tissue impermeable by air and water. Old bark cracks, splits, or peels off as the tree trunk grows; a tree can be identified by the outer bark's distinct color and pattern of splitting. Phloem is vascular tissue of a tree and transports or stores food from photosynthetic sites such as leaves. If the phloem is damaged by gouging or chopping, the food supply is cut off and the tree dies. Bark insulates and provides nutrition for inner cambium (3) and xylem (4).

em tissue. In some species the outer bark is slowly and continuously sloughed off; in others it is held tightly to the stem. The thickness of the bark in mature plants varies from less than 3 cm (1.2 in) to the more than 30 cm (1 ft) found in giant redwoods.

bark beetle   The bark beetle is an insect of the family Scolytidae of the order Coleoptera and is also known as the engraver beetle. It is elongate and cylindrical and usually lives beneath the bark of trees, where it tunnels between the bark and wood. Adult and larval tunneling can greatly weaken or kill a tree.

The ELM bark beetle, *Scolytus multistriatus*, is the chief vector, or transmitter, of Dutch elm disease, which has killed millions of elms in North America and Eurasia.

bark cloth   Bark cloth, made by beating the inner bark of certain trees, was traditionally and widely used in the non-Western world for clothing, bed coverings, decorative objects, and ceremonial gifts. It was particularly important in areas where the loom was not known. Bark cloth is often referred to as *tapa*, a word adopted from the Polynesian area.

In making bark cloth, the outer and inner bark is removed from the tree and the outer bark scraped away. The thick inner bark is softened by soaking, then beaten on anvils with special wood or stone implements. The beating thins and greatly widens the bark. Pieces are then pasted, felted, or sewn to form larger pieces. In areas such as Tonga, huge ceremonial pieces might measure about 5.5 m (18 ft) wide and hundreds of feet long. The quality of the product depends on the plant species, the care of the growing plant, and the skill of the craftsperson.

The finished product is often elaborately decorated with geometric or other patterns. The bark cloth might be dipped into a dye, or colored substances such as charcoal or ocher might be beaten into it. Freehand or stamped designs are sometimes also used to decorate the surface. Among the finest bark cloth was that made in Hawaii in the early 19th century.

Barkley, Alben W.

Alben William Barkley, b. Graves County, Ky., Nov. 24, 1877, d. Apr. 30, 1956, was vice-president of the United States (1949–53) under President Harry S. TRUMAN. Son of a Kentucky tobacco farmer, Barkley graduated (1897) from Marvin College in Clinton, Ky., and attended the University of Virginia Law School. Returning to Kentucky, he began legal practice in the town of Paducah and was a county judge from 1909 to 1913.

Barkley, a Democrat, represented Kentucky in the U.S. House of Representatives (1913–27) and Senate (1927–49). In the Senate he was majority leader (1937–47) and a key spokesman for President Franklin D. Roosevelt's New Deal legislation. After serving as vice-president, Barkley sought the 1952 Democratic presidential nomination, but criticism of his age caused him to bow out of the race. In 1954, Barkley was again elected to the Senate and served until his death. His autobiography, *That Reminds Me*, was published in 1954.

Barlach, Ernst

[bahr'-lahk]   Ernst Barlach, b. Jan 2, 1870, d. Oct. 24, 1938, was a German sculptor, graphic artist, and dramatist whose work is a sculptural form of EXPRESSIONISM and of social protest, opposed to the laws of classical beauty. Barlach used distortion and grotesque interpretations of the human form to express spiritual states rather than to achieve individual representations.

Barlach's expressionist sensibilities were stirred by the Russian peasants, who became prototypes for his heavy, blocky forms, which are closely related to both Russian peasant woodcarving and German medieval art. In 1908, he carved his first works in wood, *Seated Woman* (Herbert Kurz collection, Wolframs-Eschenbach, Germany) and *Shepherd in a Storm* (Künsthalle, Bremen); he had cast his first bronzes, *Beggarwoman with Child* (William Landmann collection, Toronto) and *The Melon Eater* (Beloit College Art Collections, Beloit, Wisc.), in 1908.

By the outbreak of World War I in 1914, Barlach was producing works such as *In Time of War* (lithograph),

The Reunion, *carved in 1926 in walnut by Ernst Barlach, is one of his many wood sculptures in the medieval German tradition. A sculptor, graphic artist, and playwright, Barlach was a major German expressionist. (Ernst Barlach House, Hamburg.)*

Hunger (wood relief, location unknown), and *The Avenger* (plaster, Barlach Estate, Güstrow, Germany; bronze, Wallraf-Richartz Museum, Cologne). His major works in bronze are massive groupings of figures or single forms usually swathed in heavy, deeply folded drapery.

During the 1930s, Barlach's works were under constant attack by the Nazis. As he was being made an honorary member of the Vereinigung bildender Künstler (Artists' Alliance) of the Vienna SECESSION MOVEMENT in 1936, his work was removed from the jubilee exhibition of the Berlin Akademie der Künste (Art Academy) before its opening. In 1937 his *Warrior of the Spirit* (1928) in Kiel was damaged by the Nazis (restored 1954), and his Güstrow Memorial, *The Hovering Angel* (1927), was removed. In America, the 1931 exhibition of Barlach's works at New York's Museum of Modern Art exerted considerable influence on younger artists, especially those committed to social realism.

barley

Barley is probably the world's oldest domesticated grain crop, having been cultivated in Egypt as early as 6000 BC. It is a grass of the family Gramineae, generally classified in three types: six-row, two-row, and hull-less. The two- and six-row types—referring to the arrangement of the grains in the head—commercially are the most important.

Barley can be grown under a greater variety of climatic conditions than can any other grain. The normal height of the plant is 76 cm (30 in), with grain heads forming at the tops of the stems. The plant can be harvested by a combine, or cut and windrowed in swaths to dry. The kernels require careful threshing to avoid the skinning or breaking that will harm germination, if they are to be used for seed.

Barley is the fourth most important cereal crop, after wheat, rice, and corn. Total annual world production in the mid-1980s was 185 million metric tons (204 million U.S. tons), with the USSR producing almost four times as much as Canada and the United States, the next most important producers.

Approximately 60 percent of all barley produced is ground or rolled and mixed with other ingredients to produce animal feeds. The major food use of barley is in the production of malt for the brewing of BEER. The grain is eaten in soups and porridge, and is used in making flour for flat breads.

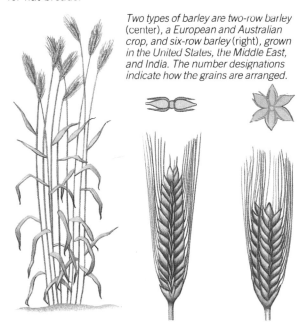

Two types of barley are two-row barley (center), a European and Australian crop, and six-row barley (right), grown in the United States, the Middle East, and India. The number designations indicate how the grains are arranged.

Barlow, Joel

Barlow, Joel   The development of the early American poet and statesman Joel Barlow, b. Redding, Conn., Mar. 24, 1754, d. Dec. 24, 1812, closely paralleled that of the young nation. His poems, "The Prospect of Peace" (1778) and *The Vision of Columbus* (1787), reflect the conservative religious, political, and literary ideas that made him one of the Connecticut Wits. His *Vision* received its final epic form in the more self-consciously poetical *The Columbiad* (1807). Barlow's most popular poetic work is "The Hasty Pudding" (1796), a mock-heroic praise of the uniquely American cornmeal mush.

Barnabas, Saint   St. Barnabas was one of the earliest Christian converts at Jerusalem and one of the first missionaries. He introduced St. PAUL to the apostles after Paul's conversion (Acts 9). Barnabas led the missionary effort in Antioch and went to Cyprus with St. Paul, although he and Paul later disagreed over an assistant named John Mark (Acts 15) and separated. Feast day: June 11.

barnacle   Barnacles comprise the invertebrate subclass Cirripedia in the class Crustacea of the arthropod phylum. This group of about 1,000 exclusively marine species includes the only crustaceans that are sessile (permanently attached to a surface). Most live attached to rocks, shells, ship bottoms, and other submerged objects; some live on whales, turtles, and fish; and two groups are parasitic on other marine invertebrates.

Larval barnacles have six pairs of thoracic limbs, reduced abdomens, and mouthparts. A carapace forms a bivalvelike pair of shells around the body. Upon metamorphosis to the adult stage, the larva settles and attaches to a substrate head-down, using cement secreted by glands at the base of the first pair of antennae. Calcareous plates replace the carapace and surround the animal. Within the protective plates, the barnacle body consists of a cephalic region and thoracic region containing six pairs of long, feathery appendages (called cirri) that rhythmically emerge to catch food.

Internally, the barnacle possesses a U-shaped gut with a simple stomach and a blood pump to aid circulation. Gills are absent, and gas exchange occurs across the mantle and cirri surfaces. The barnacle is mostly hermaphroditic.

Barnacles form encrustations on ship bottoms that can cut ship speed by 30 percent, significantly increasing fuel costs.

Barnard, Christiaan   Christiaan Barnard, b. Nov. 8, 1922, is the South African surgeon who, on Dec. 3, 1967, performed the first successful human heart transplant. In 1974 he was the first to implant a second heart in a human being and to link the hearts to work together to provide blood circulation. Barnard served as professor of surgical science at the University of Cape Town from 1968 until 1983, when he retired from active surgical practice.

Barnard, Edward Emerson   The foremost American observational astronomer of his time, Edward Emerson Barnard, b. Nashville, Tenn., Dec. 16, 1857, d. Feb. 6, 1923, worked at Lick and Yerkes Observatories. Barnard was well known for his frequent discovery of comets and nebulae, for the novel application of photography to astronomy on a regular basis, and for his discoveries of BARNARD'S STAR and the fifth moon of Jupiter. Especially remarkable were his photographs of the Milky Way, an achievement that required long exposures and extreme patience.

Barnard, Henry   Henry Barnard, b. Hartford, Conn., Jan. 24, 1811, d. July 5, 1900, was the first U.S. commissioner of education. Educated at Yale, Barnard served three terms (1837–39) in the Connecticut legislature, where he introduced the bill creating a state board of "commissioners of common schools." After moving to Rhode Island, Barnard wrote the bill creating the office of commissioner of public schools in that state and then served as its first commissioner (1843–49). In 1849 he returned to Connecticut to become superintendent of common schools. In helping to establish successful school systems in Connecticut and Rhode Island, Barnard was following in the steps of Horace MANN.

Barnard was chancellor of the University of Wisconsin (1858–60) and president of St. John's College, Annapolis, Md. (1866–67). In 1867, when Congress established the Bureau of Education, he became commissioner, serving until 1870.

Barnard College

Barnard College   Established in 1889, Barnard College (enrollment: 2,250; library: 155,000 volumes) is a private 4-year liberal arts college for women in New York City. Although it declined to merge with its coordinate college, Columbia, the two institutions continue to cross-register courses and share facilities.

Barnard's Star

Barnard's Star   Barnard's Star is the star of largest known PROPER MOTION, 10.3 seconds of arc per year. Its velocity is 140 km (87 mi) per second. The fourth nearest star to the Sun (after the three stars of the Alpha Centauri system), it is located 5.9 light-years away in the constellation Ophiuchus. It is a faint, cool dwarf star of spectral type M5 and magnitude 9.54. Evidence that planets orbit Barnard's Star is inconclusive.

Barnburners   see HUNKERS AND BARNBURNERS

Barnes, Djuna

Barnes, Djuna   Djuna Barnes, b. Cornwall-on-Hudson, N.Y., June 12, 1892, d. June 18, 1982, was an American writer and illustrator whose fame came with the novel *Nightwood* (1936). Barnes had previously published the novel *Ryder* (1928). Her later verse drama, *The Antiphon* (1958), was produced in Stockholm. Other books include *Selected Works* (1962) and *Smoke and Other Early Stories* (1982).

barnstorming

barnstorming   Barnstorming is a form of aerial showmanship that reached its peak in the 1920s. In the years preceding World War I, flying-exhibition teams thrilled spectators at carnivals, county fairs, and flying meets across the United States. After the war, when thousands of surplus military planes were sold at bargain prices, ex-military pilots earned money by taking adventurous passengers up for a ride. Many also entertained at fairs and air shows, demonstrating wartime aerobatics, parachute jumps, wing-walking, and other stunts. Barnstorming accidents in the 1920s and '30s gave aviation a poor reputation, although many fliers established reputable fixed-base operations, offering flight training, charter flights, aerial photography, and other services that helped develop commercial aviation. With stringent safety precautions, the tradition of barnstorming continues in present-day air shows and other events.

Barnum, P. T.

Barnum, P. T.   Phineas Taylor Barnum, b. Bethel, Conn., July 5, 1810, d. Apr. 7, 1891, was the most famous U.S. showman and a self-proclaimed "Prince of Humbugs." After starting out as a merchant and lottery-ticket salesman, he fell into the occupation of showman in 1835 with the purchase of a decrepit hymn-singing black woman, Joice Heth, said to be 161 years old, whom he brazenly exhibited as the nurse of George Washington. Graduating to the equally sensational "Feejee Mermaid" (in reality the upper half of a monkey sewn to the body of a fish), he later made fortunes out of the midget TOM THUMB and the Swedish singer Jenny LIND. In these, as in all his enterprises, Barnum was one of the first impresarios to realize the value of massive, carefully planned publicity campaigns.

Between 1841 and 1868, Barnum was the proprietor of the American Museum in New York City, where he produced melodramas and thousands of curiosities, freaks, and wild animals were displayed. Over 41 million tickets were sold during Barnum's management. In 1871 he launched a mammoth traveling CIRCUS, museum, and menagerie. A merger with James A. Bailey's London Circus ten years later led to the concern that eventually became known as the Barnum & Bailey Show, which in turn was acquired by the Ringling Brothers in 1907.

Besides an active life as a showman, Barnum was a journalist, real-estate speculator, and a popular lecturer. He served four terms in the Connecticut state legislature and one term as mayor of Bridgeport, where the Barnum Museum exists today.

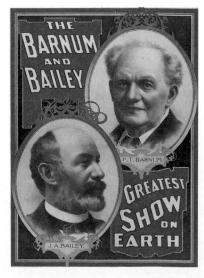

A 19th-century handbill advertises the "Greatest Show on Earth," the famous circus formed in 1881 by P. T. Barnum and his competitor James Bailey. A consummate showman, Barnum made a fortune exhibiting such sensational attractions as Siamese twins, midgets, and exotic animals.

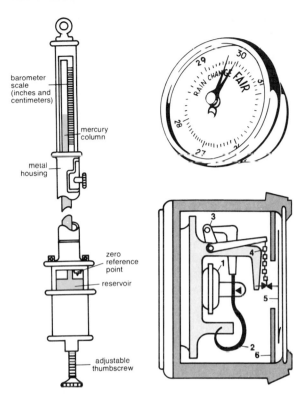

A mercury barometer (left) *consists of an upright mercury-filled glass tube with its lower end submerged in an adjustable mercury reservoir and a vernier-equipped scale for reading the mercury column height. A cross-section of an aneroid barometer* (right) *reveals a small metal box* (1), *from which air has been withdrawn, with a movable end that expands and contracts with changes in air pressure. Any motion of the movable end is transmitted by means of a spring* (2), *a system of levers* (3), *and a chain* (4) *to a rotating needle* (5), *which indicates the air pressure on a graduated scale* (6).

barometer   The barometer, the single most important meteorological instrument, measures atmospheric pressure.

Mercury Barometer. The invention of the mercury barometer (1643) by Evangelista TORRICELLI depended on his realization that air has weight. He noted that if the open end of a glass tube filled with mercury is inverted in a bowl of mercury, the atmospheric pressure on the bowl of mercury will affect the height of the column of mercury in the glass tube. The greater the air pressure, the longer is the mercury column. The atmospheric pressure may be calculated by multiplying the height of the mercury column by the mercury density and the acceleration due to gravity. At sea level, atmospheric pressure is equal to about 15 lb per in^2, or 29.9 in of mercury.

Aneroid Barometer. Most barometers are of the aneroid type and function without liquid. The aneroid barometer, dating from 1843, consists of a small metal box, almost totally evacuated of air. One side is immovable, and the opposite side is connected to a strong spring to keep the box from collapsing. The movable side will expand if the air pressure decreases and will compress if the air pressure increases. The position of the movable side is indicated by a pointer. The aneroid barometer can be easily converted into a barograph, or recording barometer, by adding a pen to the pointer. The ink in the pen describes a trace (barogram) on the paper wrapped around a cylinder. The cylinder usually rotates once a day or once a week. An aneroid barometer is checked regularly against a mercury barometer for calibration.

The mercury barometer is used in research laboratories and in the most important weather stations. Aneroid barometers, used in the home, on board ships, and in all weather stations, are also a prominent part of RADIOSONDE instruments.

baron   see TITLES OF NOBILITY AND HONOR

baroque art and architecture [buh-rohk']   Baroque art and architecture, broadly speaking, is the art and architecture of Europe and its Latin American colonies in the 17th and the first half of the 18th centuries. In a more specific sense, the term refers to the most characteristic of the styles created in that period—that is, to the art that arose in Italy and Flanders soon after 1600, dominated ITALIAN ART AND ARCHITECTURE until the classical revival of the mid-18th century, and produced echoes of varying intensity in all other countries. This style is associated, above all, with Peter Paul RUBENS and Giovanni Lorenzo BERNINI.

Origins

The label *baroque* was first applied to the art of this period in the late 18th century, when the style itself had gone out of fashion. The word may be derived either from the Portuguese *barocco*, meaning an irregularly shaped pearl, or, as is perhaps more likely, from *baroco*, a scholastic term coined as a mnemonic aid for a tortuous argument in logic. As used by late 18th-century art critics, it signified "absurd," "willful," "grotesque"—in other words, a wanton defiance of the classical rules.

Baroque art at its greatest and most intense is found in Roman Catholic countries, and a close association, if not an ideological link, existed between the style and the Roman Catholic church in the later stages of the COUNTER-REFORMATION, when the church was reemphasizing its traditional spiritual doctrines. Because of its associations with authoritarian regimes in both church and state, the baroque succeeded best in traditional societies, such as those of Italy, Spain, and central Europe, whereas it met with some resistance in the more progressive societies of northern Europe (including France).

Characteristics

Formally, the baroque style owed much to RENAISSANCE ART AND ARCHITECTURE and the intervening phase, MANNERISM; it was also influenced by the antique Greek and Roman art and architecture—particularly the classical orders of architecture and the idealized human figure. A

Peter Paul Rubens's opulent style is shown in Rape of the Daughters of Leucippus *(c.1616). Its warm colors, voluptuous female nudes, and dramatic vitality are characteristic of the baroque Flemish painter. (Alte Pinakothek, Munich.)*

strong connection exists also between baroque and Renaissance (bypassing Mannerist) methods of representing reality. Some of the features correctly regarded as most typically baroque, such as inward-curving facades and oval groundplans, were anticipated by prototypes occurring as sidelines, often in underdeveloped form, in the art of the past. (By the same token, baroque ILLUSIONISM was not without precedents, either.) Baroque artists and architects did create some, although not many, entirely new forms, of which perhaps the most important was the double curve—inward at the sides, outward in the middle—used for facades, doorways, and furniture. In architecture, other primary features are twisted columns and fantastical pediments. In sculpture, the style is characterized by fluttering draperies, realistic surfaces, and the use of bronze, white and colored marbles, and sometimes other materials in the same work. In painting, the main features are illusionistic ceilings, bold foreshortening, and a new, powerful kind of realism, obtained chiefly through the use of light and shade. The expression of emotion was increasingly emphasized in both painting and sculpture. In larger works, such as tombs and church interiors, two or more arts were often harnessed into one overwhelming effect. The result was a style of great richness and flexibility.

Historical Development

The development of the baroque style began in Italy around 1600, when a group of painters, of whom the most important were Michelangelo da CARAVAGGIO and

Annibale CARRACCI, brought about a revival of art in Rome following the breakdown of Mannerism.

The first to turn this revival decisively toward a baroque aesthetic was the Flemish painter Rubens, who, after studying in Italy from 1600 to 1608, created a baroque style of marvelous color, vitality, and realism. An example is his series of allegorical paintings (1629–35) glorifying the Stuart monarchy, on the ceiling of Inigo JONES's Banqueting House, WHITEHALL PALACE, London.

The main center of the baroque was Rome. The dominant personalities were the sculptor and architect Bernini, the architect Franceso BORROMINI, and the architect and painter Pietro da CORTONA, the latter a master of illusionistic ceiling painting (*Triumph of Divine Providence*, 1633–39; Palazzo Barberini, Rome). Bernini's most outstanding contribution is to be seen in his additions to ST.

The enormous baldachino (1624–33) in St. Peter's, Rome, designed by Giovanni Lorenzo Bernini, stands over the high altar. The gilded bronze canopy combines architecture and sculpture in its twisting columns and ornamental decoration.

PETER'S BASILICA (1624–78), the most astounding group of baroque works in any one place. Although Borromini's architecture was confined to a narrower compass, his small churches, such as San Carlo alle Quattro Fontane (1638–41; 1662–67), with its undulating walls and facade and its highly original ornament, are in some ways even more ingenious than its larger baroque counterparts.

Influence in Northern Europe, Iberia, and Colonial America

Outside Italy and Flanders, the baroque was mainly a late 17th- and 18th-century phenomenon. Probably its most radiant flowering was in Germany, in such churches as Vierzehnheiligen (Fourteen Saints; 1743–72), near Bamberg, by Johann Balthasar NEUMANN. In Spain and Portugal and their American colonies, the interpretation was more pious and popular, as can be seen in Bartolomé MURILLO's painting of the *Immaculate Conception* (c.1660; Prado, Madrid) or in the facade of Santiago de Compostela Cathedral (finished 1750). In France, full acceptance of the baroque was prevented by the cult of reason, which favored classical restraint, but the resulting "classical-baroque" style produced the greatest of all royal palaces, VERSAILLES (1669–1703). In the Protestant Netherlands the full baroque was confined to sculpture, but the art of REMBRANDT was affected by the style (*The Night Watch*, 1642; Rijksmuseum, Amsterdam). In Protestant England a temperate form of baroque was applied in the design of large country houses and, most notably, SAINT PAUL'S CATHEDRAL, London (1675–1708), by Sir Christopher WREN.

In the early 18th century the baroque gave way in France and Germany to the ROCOCO STYLE, and in the second half of the century both styles were superseded by NEOCLASSICISM.

▬

baroque music   The term *baroque* refers to music written during the period extending roughly from 1600 to 1750, beginning with the first attempts at opera, in Italy, and ending with the death of Johann Sebastian BACH, whose works represent the zenith of the era's contrapuntal style.

In the late 18th century—a period during which the dominant style stressed elegance and simplicity—writers began to use the word *baroque* to describe earlier music (as well as painting, sculpture, and architecture) that seemed to them to be distorted by a profusion of unnatural ornamentation. (*Baroque*, a French word, means an irregularly shaped pearl, of the type often used in the extremely fanciful jewelry of the post-Renaissance period.)

By the end of the 16th century, Italian composers had perfected the MADRIGAL, a popular form of polyphonic text setting in which the music reflected the intensity of the emotions suggested in the poetry. Claudio MONTEVERDI was chief among the early experimenters in vocal music; his operas and books of madrigals stand as the high points of this early period of the baroque.

The early Italian CANTATA was a form in which a story—usually secular—was related by a solo singer through recitatives and arias, to a sparse basso continuo (a lute or harpsichord, usually with a bass viol emphasizing the bass line). Over the course of 150 years, this form traveled through Europe and was greatly transformed, particularly in Germany, where it evolved into works that could include several singers and a chorus. The ORATORIO, an extended dramatic work on a religious theme, had its roots in Rome and spread throughout Europe through the work of the German-English composer George Frideric HANDEL.

In Italy the term SONATA meant a group of slow and fast dance movements, or an abstract work in contrasting slow and fast sections, the latter known as a "church sonata." The early sonatas could be either for solo instruments or for small ensembles. Toward the end of the 17th century, as the middle baroque period gave way to the late, or high, baroque, the ensemble sonata gave way to the concerto grosso, where an opposition is set up between the full ensemble (the ripieno, or "filling") and a smaller group, typically composed of two violins and continuo (the concertino). From the concerto grosso emerged the solo CONCERTO, in which a solo instrument is set against the forces of the full ensemble.

Central in the development of the sonata and the concerto, and the various vocal forms as well, is another of the baroque era's novel elements: tonality. By the middle of the 16th century the old system of church modes was being replaced by a new concept of key relationships (see MUSIC). Bach's *Well-Tempered Clavier* illustrates these relationships. It also demonstrates two other important baroque forms, the freely invented PRELUDE and the complex, tightly structured FUGUE.

Distinct national schools emerged during the late baroque. One French trait was the use of dotted rhythms, which gave dance movements, as well as preludes and overtures, an especially lively character that came to be associated with France, even when used by composers elsewhere. In Germany, elements of both Italian basic style and French fashion were prevalent, but these were tempered by a more staid Lutheran musical tradition and by a fascination with contrapuntal complexity.

In all countries, musicians were expected to add ornamentation and embellishment to the music they found on the printed page. Some of the era's music—Bach's, for instance—is notated so densely that it probably includes a great deal of what might originally have been ornamentation. Most scores of the time leave ample room for the interpreter's input.

▬

Barr, Alfred H., Jr.   The American art historian and museum administrator Alfred Hamilton Barr, Jr., b. Detroit, Jan. 28, 1902, d. Aug. 15, 1981, founded the MUSEUM OF MODERN ART, New York City, and became, at the age of 27, its first director. During his tenure as director (1929–43), and later as director of museum collections (1947–67), Barr was responsible for building an unprecedented collection comprising outstanding examples of all the contemporary visual arts, including architectural designs, cinema, photography, and the decorative and industrial arts. Through exhibitions and writings, he was instrumental in developing popular interest in modern art in the United States.

---

barracuda [bair-uh-koo'-duh]   Barracuda are predaceous fish of the family Sphyraenidae, order Perciformes, that inhabit temperate and tropical waters throughout the world. They have a long-bodied form with a sharp set of fangs and jutting lower jaw. The most common species along the western Atlantic coast is the great barracuda, *Sphyraena barracuda*, which is most abundant in the West Indies. The great barracuda may grow to more than 3 m (10 ft) in length; the larger ones tend to live in the deeper waters of the coral reefs, where they feed on fish. Barracuda can be dangerous to humans when provoked, being attracted to erratic movement and bright colors. Overall, however, the low number of alleged attacks does not completely support the fish's dangerous reputation.

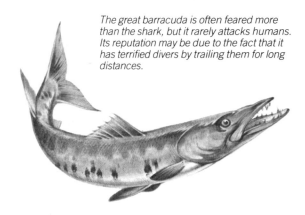

The great barracuda is often feared more than the shark, but it rarely attacks humans. Its reputation may be due to the fact that it has terrified divers by trailing them for long distances.

---

barracudina [bair-uh-koo-dee'-nuh]   Barracudinas are among the most common midwater (to a depth of 3.2 km/ 2 mi) marine fishes found in all oceans. Barracudinas are slender-bodied and resemble their namesakes, the barracudas, in having an impressive array of teeth. Unlike most midwater fishes, the majority of barracudinas lack luminescent organs, the genus *Lestidium* being an exception. The largest measured species, *Paralepis barysoma*, grows to about 61 cm (24 in). Barracudinas are the favorite food of many larger fishes, including the tunas. The barracudinas are members of the family Paralepididae.

Barragán, Luis [bah-rah-gahn']   The Mexican architect Luis Barragán, b. 1902, d. Nov. 22, 1988, is known for his abstract minimalist building designs and visually dramatic landscape settings, which often include the evocative use of still or running water. In numerous residential buildings in Mexico City, notably the luxurious Jardines de Pedregal (1945–50), and at the spare and ascetic chapel for the Capuchinas Sacramentarius in

Tlalpan (1952–53), he used vast unbroken walls that give the impression of abstract, planar sculpture.

Barragán's frequent use of such vibrant colors as coral, pink, lemon, and magenta on the exteriors of his buildings evokes the richness of traditional Mexican village and ranch architecture. He also found inspiration in SURREALISM, in the French architect LE CORBUSIER, and in Moorish gardens.

Barranquilla [bah-rahn-kee'-ah]   Barranquilla (1985 pop., 889,781), a port city on the Río Magdalena in northern Colombia, 16 km (10 mi) from the Caribbean Sea, is the capital of Atlántico department. Diversified industries produce ships, aluminum products, textiles, glass, shoes, beverages, cement, and chemicals. Barranquilla draws tourists to its colorful carnivals. Atlántico University (1941) and the University of the North (1967) are located there. Settled in 1629, the city grew in importance when steamboats began to navigate the river.

Barras, Paul François Jean Nicolas, Vicomte de [bah-rahs']   The vicomte de Barras, b. June 30, 1775, d. Jan. 29, 1829, a French revolutionary, was a leading member of the five–man DIRECTORY government (1795–99). He joined the Jacobins and was elected to the National Convention in 1792.

Becoming opposed to the Reign of Terror, he helped depose (July 1794) Maximilien ROBESPIERRE and subsequently commanded the Army of the Interior and the police. In 1795 he chose Napoléon Bonaparte (later NAPOLEON I) to put down a revolt in Paris against the Directory. As a director he lived in luxury, sustained by bribes. Bonaparte's coup of Nov. 10, 1799, forced him to retire from government.

Barrault, Jean Louis [bah-roh']   A French actor, director, and mime, Jean Louis Barrault, b. 1910, was a student of Charles Dullin's at Théâtre de l'Atelier and of the mime Étienne Decroux. His performances in Ben Jonson's *Volpone* and William Faulkner's *As I Lay Dying* brought him to the attention of Antonin ARTAUD, who taught him not to intellectualize his roles but to feel them. Barrault joined the Comédie-Française in 1940 and staged plays by Aeschylus, Shakespeare, and Paul Claudel. With his wife, Madeleine Renaud, he founded the Compagnie Renaud-Barrault (1947), where he directed and acted in André Gide's translation of *Hamlet*, Franz Kafka's *The Trial*, Albert Claudel's *Break of Noon*, and plays by Albert Camus, Jean Anouilh, Eugène Ionesco, Samuel Beckett, and Jean Genet. His most noteworthy film role was in *Children of Paradise* (1944) by Marcel Carné.

Barre [bair'-ee]   Barre (1990 pop., 9,482) is a city in Washington County in central Vermont. The area was settled in 1788; the city, originally named Wildersburgh, was renamed for Barre, Mass. Since the War of 1812 its chief industries have been granite quarrying and finishing, which have attracted skilled European stonecutters to the area. The Rock of Ages granite quarry, the world's largest, is open to visitors. Goddard College (1863) is also nearby.

Barre, Raymond [bahr]   Raymond Barre, b. Apr. 12, 1924, was prime minister of France under President Valéry Giscard d'Estaing from 1976 until 1981. He also served as minister of finance and economic affairs from 1976 to 1978. Backed by the conservative Union pour la démocratie française, he was an unsuccessful candidate for the presidency in 1988. Barre has been a professor of economics since 1951 (at Tunis, Caen, and Paris) and was vice-president (1967–72) of the European Commission.

barrel organ   The barrel organ, a mechanical instrument operated by a handle or clockwork, was popular in English country churches beginning in the 18th century. This instrument is often confused with the HURDY-GURDY, a medieval instrument, and with the barrel piano, a mechanical instrument used by street musicians. The action of the barrel organ operates the bellows and rotates a barrel from which pins project. These open valves on the pipes, allowing air to enter and the pipes to sound. Barrel organs had as few as eight pitches and as many as the full chromatic range.

Barrie, Sir James   James Matthew Barrie, b. May 9, 1860, d. June 19, 1937, was a Scottish novelist and playwright whose works include the enduring children's play PETER PAN. Barrie received a strict upbringing in the village of Kirriemuir, which, as the imaginary Thrums, furnished the setting and material for much of his fiction, including *Auld Licht Idylls* (1888) and *A Window in Thrums* (1889). He went to Edinburgh University and then became a journalist in Nottingham. He later moved to London as a free-lance writer, but soon relied solely on literature for his livelihood. With the publication in 1891 of the novel *The Little Minister* and the play *Richard Savage*, he became prominent. His other early work includes *The Professor's Love Story* (1892), a play characterized by humor and sentimentality, and *Margaret Ogilvy* (1896), a biography of his mother. His dramatic reputation was established with the romantic *Quality Street* and *The Admirable Crichton* (both 1902) with its social satire. Despite the influence of IBSEN at that time, Barrie wrote only one problem play, *The Wedding Guest* (1900), in which the former mistress of the bridegroom, with their child, invades his wedding. His later plays include *What Every Woman Knows* (1908) and, perhaps his best, *Dear Brutus* (1917), a mixture of fairy tale and realism. *Peter Pan or the Boy Who Would Not Grow Up* was first performed on Dec. 27, 1904, and was published as the story *Peter and Wendy* in 1911 and as a play in 1928.

Barrow   Barrow is a village in northern Alaska, located 14 km (9 mi) southwest of Point Barrow, the northern-most part of the United States. Its population of 3,469 (1990) is predominantly Eskimo. Whaling and handicrafts are important industries, and the area has vast oil and gas reserves. The U.S. Navy maintains the Barrow Arctic Science Research Station, and a U.S. Air Force installation is nearby.

barrow   The term *barrow* is applied to a variety of burial monuments in European prehistory, ranging from the stone-built chambered tombs of the NEOLITHIC PERIOD in the Atlantic west to the Iron Age burial mounds of the HALLSTATT and LA TÈNE cultures of Britain and Europe. Specifically, however, it refers to the unchambered earthen tumuli, often originally built over internal structures of timber, that characterize BRONZE AGE cemeteries. The cemeteries of the WESSEX CULTURE of southern England are of this type; some are outstanding for the wealth of their grave goods, including bronze weapons, gold ornaments, and necklaces of amber and faïence.

Barrow, Clyde   Clyde Barrow, b. Tellice, Tex., Mar. 24, 1909, was a murderer and bank robber whose story was dramatized in the film *Bonnie and Clyde* (1967). For four years he and Bonnie Parker (b. Rowena, Tex., Oct. 1, 1910) wandered the southwestern United States, holding up gas stations, luncheonettes, and small-town banks. The pair killed 12 people before they themselves were killed in a police ambush in Louisiana on May 23, 1934.

Barry, Sir Charles   Sir Charles Barry, b. May 23, 1795, d. May 12, 1860, one of the leading architects of his time in England, is best known for designing the Houses of Parliament (1836). His most characteristic works include the Reform Club (1837–41) in London, in the Italian *palazzo* mode; the Royal Institution in Manchester (1824–35; now City Art Gallery) in the Greek Revival manner; and Gothic Revival churches such as Saint Peter, Brighton (1824–28).

Barry, John   John Barry, b. 1745, d. Sept. 13, 1803, was a U.S. naval commander in the AMERICAN REVOLUTION. Born in Ireland, he immigrated to America in the early 1770s. In 1776 he was commissioned a captain in the Continental Navy. Commanding the brigantine *Lexington*, Barry captured (Apr. 17, 1776) the British tender *Edward*—the first British ship to be taken at sea by the Americans. His subsequent commands were the *Effingham*, the *Raleigh*, and the *Alliance*; in the last, he captured two British ships in 1781 and fought (Mar. 10, 1783) the final naval engagement of the war, against the British *Sybil*.

During the undeclared war with France (1798–1800), Barry was in command of U.S. forces in the Caribbean. Because of his role in training Stephen DECATUR and other prominent second-generation naval officers, Barry is sometimes called the father of the U.S. Navy.

Barrymore (family) The Barrymores were an Anglo-American family of actors who became prominent first on the New York stage and then in Hollywood films. Their close-knit, imperious, and tempestuous lives were the thinly disguised subject of *The Royal Family* (1927), a play by George S. KAUFMAN and Edna FERBER.

The patriarch of the family, **Maurice Barrymore** (1847–1905), made his debut in London in 1872 and immigrated to America in 1875. He acted opposite most of the famous actresses of his day, and in 1876 married one, **Georgianna Drew** (1856–93). Together, the Barrymores appeared in such plays as *Diplomacy* (1886) and as leading players in Helena Modjeska's company.

Their eldest son, **Lionel Barrymore**, b. Apr. 28, 1878, d. Nov. 15, 1954, achieved fame in such plays as *The Copperhead*. He won the Academy Award as best actor in *Free Soul* (1931), and appeared in *Grand Hotel* (1932) and *Dinner at Eight* (1933). He also played the gruff but kindly Dr. Gillespie in 15 Dr. Kildare movies, beginning with *Young Dr. Kildare* (1938).

Lionel's sister, **Ethel Barrymore**, b. Aug. 15, 1879, d. June 18, 1959, achieved immediate success in 1901 as Madame Trentoni in *Captain Jinks of the Horse Marines*. She played Shakespeare's heroines Juliet and Portia, Dumas *fils*' Camille, and Ibsen's Nora in *A Doll's House*. Her most notable performance was Miss Moffat in *The Corn Is Green* (1940). She also received an Academy Award for her supporting role in the film *None But the Lonely Heart* (1944).

Lionel's brother, **John Barrymore**, b. Feb. 15, 1882, d. May 29, 1942, known for his superb profile and erratic temper, was the most famous member of the family. In 1922–23 he appeared in a record 101 performances as Hamlet, considered his finest stage role. Barrymore also acted in the screen comedies *A Bill of Divorcement* (1932) and *Twentieth Century* (1934).

The Barrymores never appeared together on stage, but they all acted in the film *Rasputin and the Empress* (1932).

The Barrymores (left to right), John, Ethel, and Lionel, belonged to the second generation of a prominent family of American actors. In 1932 the three starred in the film Rasputin and the Empress, *the only production in which the family appeared together.*

Barth, John John Simmons Barth, b. Cambridge, Md., May 27, 1930, is one of the first American writers to win both popular and academic acclaim for his experimental fiction. His early novels *The Floating Opera* (1956) and *The End of the Road* (1958; film, 1970) drew heavily on the philosophy of EXISTENTIALISM and the fiction of Albert CAMUS and Jean Paul SARTRE. With *The Sot-Weed Factor* (1960), Barth abandoned conventional storytelling and moralizing in favor of a literature that criticizes itself through burlesque and parody. Barth's theory of fiction, explained in "The Literature of Exhaustion" (*Atlantic Monthly*, August 1967), is perhaps best illustrated in his novel *Giles Goat-Boy* (1966) and his collection of short fiction entitled *Lost in the Funhouse* (1968). He argued in the essay that the apparent exhaustion of all literary forms makes it imperative that the contemporary writer "confront an intellectual dead end and employ it against himself to accomplish new human work." His collection of three novellas, *Chimera* (1972), received a 1973 National Book Award for fiction; *Letters* (1979), *Sabbatical* (1982), and *The Tidewater Tales* (1987) are more recent novels.

Barth, Karl (bahrt) Karl Barth, b. Basel, Switzerland, May 10, 1886, d. Dec. 9, 1968, inspired and led the renaissance of Protestant theology that took place from about 1920 to 1950. He studied at the universities of Bern, Berlin, Tübingen, and Marburg and held pastorates in Switzerland between 1909 and 1921. During this time he became known as a radical critic both of the prevailing liberal theology and of the social order. Liberal theology, Barth believed, had accommodated Christianity to modern culture. The crisis of World War I was in part a symptom of this unholy alliance. In his famous commentary on Romans (1919) Barth stressed the discontinuity between the Christian message and the world. God is the wholly other; he is known only in his revelation; he is not the patron saint of culture, but its judge.

Between 1921 and 1935, Barth held professorships at Göttingen, Münster, and Bonn. He engaged in controversy with Adolf von HARNACK, holding that the latter's scientific theology is only a preliminary to the true task of theology, which is identical with that of preaching. With the rise of Adolf Hitler, Barth emerged as a leader of the church opposition to Nazi control, expressed in the Barmen Declaration of 1934.

He returned to Switzerland and was professor at Basel (1935–1962), exercising a worldwide influence. During this period he worked on his *Church Dogmatics* (1932–67), a multivolume work of great richness that was unfinished at his death. Although he modified some of his early positions, he continued to maintain that theology is concerned only with unfolding the revealed word attested in the Bible and has no place for natural theology or the insights of non-Christian religions. He held that religion is humankind's attempt to grasp at God and is therefore diametrically opposed to revelation, in which God has come to humans through Christ.

Barthelme, Donald [bahr'-tuhl-mee]   Short-story writer and novelist Donald Barthelme, b. Philadelphia, Apr. 7, 1931, d. July 23, 1989, was a major figure among Americans who write outside the realist tradition. A newspaper reporter, art-museum director, and university publicist, Barthelme became a full-time writer after the publication of his first short-fiction collection, *Come Back Dr. Caligari* (1964). Barthelme's novels, *Snow White* (1967), *The Dead Father* (1975), and *Paradise* (1986), deftly satirize American life and reveal a sharp eye for the absurdities concealed beneath familiar customs. *60 Stories* (1981), *Overnight to Many Distant Cities* (1983), and *40 Stories* (1987) are short-story collections.

Donald's brother Frederick, b. Houston, Tex., Oct. 10, 1943, is both artist and writer. His spare style mimics the emotional sparseness of the suburban lives he describes in short-story collections (*Moon Deluxe*, 1983) and such novels as *Two against One* (1988).

Barthes, Roland [bahrt]   The distinguished French literary critic and intellectual Roland Barthes, b. Nov. 12, 1915, d. Mar. 25, 1980, was a leading exponent of the application of STRUCTURALISM and SEMIOTICS to the study of literature. He carried this out in *Writing Degree Zero* (1953; Eng. trans., 1977) and *Critical Essays* (1964; Eng. trans., 1972). *The Empire of Signs* (1970; Eng. trans., 1982) applies semiotics to Japanese culture. Other influential works include *S/Z* (1970; Eng. trans., 1974) and *The Pleasure of the Text* (1973; Eng. trans., 1975).

Bartholdi, Frédéric Auguste [bahr-tohl-dee']   The French sculptor Frédéric Auguste Bartholdi, b. Aug. 2, 1834, d. Oct. 4, 1904, is best known for public monuments, notably the huge red sandstone *Lion of Belfort* (1875–80) in Belfort, France, and the colossal bronze STATUE OF LIBERTY (1886) in New York Harbor. Other works reflecting Franco-American friendship include his statues of the Marquis de Lafayette (1873–76) for Union Square, New York City, and of George Washington and Lafayette (1896) for the Place des États-Unis, Paris.

Bartholomew, Saint   Saint Bartholomew was one of the APOSTLES, mentioned only in the lists of the Twelve (Matt. 10:3; Mark 3:18; Luke 6:14; Acts 1:13). His name means "son of Tolmai," and he is frequently identified with Nathanael (John 1). According to tradition he was martyred in Armenia. Feast day: Aug. 24 (Western); June 11 (Eastern).

Bartók, Béla [bahr'-tohk, bel'-uh]   Béla Bartók, b. Mar. 25, 1881, d. Sept. 26, 1945, was one of the greatest composers of the 20th century. A Hungarian, he studied piano and composition at the Budapest Academy of Music, where he was appointed professor of piano in 1907.

Béla Bartók, the 20th-century Hungarian composer, was a student and collector of folk music. He combined its rhythmic, melodic, and textural elements with traditional classical forms to produce a highly individual style.

Until 1936, Bartok traversed Hungary, the Balkans, Turkey, and parts of North Africa searching for indigenous material, and with the composer Zoltán KODÁLY he produced a series of important studies, anthologies, and arrangements of folk songs.

During the 1920s, Budapest performances of his one-act opera *Duke Bluebeard's Castle* (1911) and ballets *The Wooden Prince* (1914–16) and *The Miraculous Mandarin* (1919) were well received. Bartók traveled widely in Europe as a pianist, and in 1927–28 he toured the United States.

The Piano Sonata of 1926 initiated Bartók's most fruitful period, which includes *Mikrokosmos* (1926–37), a large set of piano pieces designed for students; Piano Concertos nos. 1 (1927) and 2 (1931); String Quartets nos. 3–6 (1927–39), widely considered the most important contributions to the genre by a 20th-century composer; Music for Strings, Percussion, and Celesta (1936); Sonata for Two Pianos and Percussion (1937); and Violin Concerto no. 2 (1937–38). In 1940, in reaction to the growing Nazification of Hungary, Bartók went to the United States. There he suffered disappointment, financial hardship, and illness, yet he also completed the Concerto for Orchestra (1943) and all but the final bars of Piano Concerto no. 3. Bartók died of leukemia in New York City.

The stark strength of Bartók's music (particularly the rhythmic drive of the fast movements), as well as its percussive quality and novel tone color, all derive from his affinity for folk music. His harmony is often dissonant, full of irregular chords and tone clusters; many of his melodies are based on the folk patterns of the pentatonic (5-tone) scale.

Bartolommeo, Fra [bahr-toh-loh-may'-oh]   Fra Bartolommeo, also called Baccio della Porta, b. Mar. 28, 1472, d. Oct. 31, 1517, was the foremost painter in the High Renaissance in Florence after Leonardo da Vinci. His monumentalized style combines the geometrical compositions developed in the 15th century with the classical figural style that he helped to develop from Leonardo's work. A typical large altarpiece is *The Mystic Marriage of Saint Catherine* (1511; Louvre, Paris), which displays faultless technique, complex spatial organization, and subtle use of color.

Barton, Clara   Clarissa Harlowe Barton, b. North Oxford, Mass., Dec. 25, 1821, d. Apr. 12, 1912, founded the American RED CROSS. Known as the "Angel of the Battlefield," she cared for the wounded during the Civil War and helped gather identification records for the missing and the dead. After becoming familiar with the work of the International Red Cross in Europe, she organized a similar group in the United States in 1881.

Barton, Derek   The English chemist Derek Harold Richard Barton, b. Sept. 8, 1918, received, with Odd Hassel, the 1969 Nobel Prize for chemistry for his work on the three-dimensional structure of complex organic molecules. He also discovered (1960) a method for synthesizing the hormone aldosterone.

Barton, Sir Edmund   Edmund Barton, b. Jan. 18, 1849, d. Jan. 7, 1920, was the first prime minister of the Commonwealth of Australia (1901–03). From 1891 he led the federal movement, helping to draft the Commonwealth constitution. He served in the government of New South Wales in several positions, including that of acting prime minister. Knighted in 1902, he served as a senior judge of the Australian High Court from 1903 until his death.

Baruch, Bernard M.   [buh-rook']   Bernard Mannes Baruch, b. Camden, S.C., Aug. 19, 1870, d. June 20, 1965, an American financier and confidant of presidents, began his career in a Wall Street brokerage house and made a fortune in stocks while still a young man. During World War I he was chairman of the War Industries Board, and following the war he was a U.S. delegate and an economic advisor to the Paris Peace Conference. In later years he often served as an economic advisor to government, and every president from Woodrow Wilson to John F. Kennedy consulted Baruch. He wrote about his life in *Baruch: My Own Story* (1957) and *Baruch: The Public Years* (1960).

Baruch, Book of   [bair'-uhk]   Baruch, considered a canonical book of the Bible by Roman Catholics, follows the Book of Lamentations. It is not found in the Hebrew Bible and is included in the APOCRYPHA by Protestants. The book, a brief compilation of verses from the books of Job, Daniel, Isaiah, and Jeremiah, is named after Baruch (fl. 600 BC), secretary of the prophet Jeremiah. Its dependence upon later works such as Daniel, however, suggests a composition date in the 2d century BC. Written in

three sections, it contains liturgical prayers and a homily on wisdom.

Barye, Antoine Louis   [bah-ree']   Antoine Louis Barye, b. Sept. 24, 1796, d. June 25, 1875, was a French sculptor renowned for his bronzes of wild animals. He made direct observations of animals in Paris zoos and attended lectures on animal physiology. The resultant watercolors are among the world's finest animal paintings.

Barye's bronze *Tiger Devouring a Crocodile* (Louvre, Paris) won a medal in the Paris Salon of 1831, but five large hunting groups (Walters Art Gallery, Baltimore) were rejected for the Salon of 1837, a rebuff he answered by not submitting any works for years. Barye's studies in Greek art gave a neoclassic monumentality to his later works, as in the dynamic bronze *Theseus and the Minotaur* (1846; Hirschhorn Museum, Washington, D.C.) and in his powerful stone allegories *War, Peace, Force, and Order* (1854; Louvre).

baryon   [bair'-ee-ahn]   A baryon is any member of a class of relatively heavy FUNDAMENTAL PARTICLES (from the Greek *barys*, meaning "heavy") that comprises the proton (the lightest member), the neutron, and several particles called hyperons, denoted by the Greek letters *lambda, sigma, xi,* and *omega.* The hyperons have lifetimes of about 10^{-10} seconds and decay into nucleons and some number of MESONS or lighter particles. Each baryon is assumed to have a corresponding antibaryon.

    See also: HADRON.

Baryshnikov, Mikhail   [buh-rish'-ni-kawf, meek-hyl']   Mikhail Nikolaievich Baryshnikov, b. Riga, Latvia, Jan. 27, 1948, is considered by many the greatest male classical dancer of his generation. He joined the Kirov Ballet in 1967, creating the title role in Konstantin Sergeyev's *Hamlet* (1970). While on tour with Soviet dancers in Canada in 1974, he defected, wanting to

Mikhail Baryshnikov, the Latvian-born virtuoso dancer, performs (1978) in Jerome Robbins's version of Afternoon of a Faun. *Famous for his brilliant but highly disciplined technique, Baryshnikov left the Kirov Ballet in 1974 for the chance to extend his repertoire in modern ballets.*

dance a more extensive repertoire, particularly of contemporary works, than was available to him in the USSR. Soon afterward, he joined American Ballet Theatre (ABT). Although he continued to dance such classic ballets as *Giselle, La Bayadère*, and *La Sylphide*, he also added to his repertoire ballets by Frederick Ashton (*Les Patineurs*), George Balanchine (*Theme and Variations*), and Antony Tudor (*Shadowplay*). Twyla Tharp created *Push Comes to Shove* for him in 1976. Baryshnikov also appeared with other companies. Although he is capable of prodigious feats of virtuosity, his dancing is notable for the concealment of effort and of obvious preparation.

In 1976, Baryshnikov made his debut as a choreographer with *The Nutcracker* for ABT. A *Don Quixote* followed in 1978. That year he left ABT and joined New York City Ballet to work with George Balanchine. He returned to ABT as director in 1980 and continued to choreograph (*Cinderella*, 1984) and to dance (premiering *The Mollino Room*, 1986). He resigned as director in 1989 and soon after premiered in a revival of Martha Graham's *American Document*. Baryshnikov also has pursued an acting career, appearing in the films *The Turning Point* (1977), *White Nights* (1985), and *Dancers* (1987), and on Broadway in *Metamorphosis* (1989).

Barzun, Jacques [bahr'-zuhn] Jacques Barzun, b. Créteil, France, Nov. 30, 1907, is an American historian, author, and teacher. He graduated from Columbia University in 1927 and received a doctorate in French history from Columbia in 1932. He taught there from 1929, later serving as dean of the graduate faculties (1955–58) and as dean of faculties (1958–67).

Barzun is best known for his studies in intellectual history and education. These include *Darwin, Marx, Wagner* (1941), *Berlioz and the Romantic Century* (1950), the controversial *The House of Intellect* (1959), and *Science: The Glorious Entertainment* (1964).

bas-relief [bah-ree-leef'] Bas-relief, or low relief, is a sculptural term used to describe an object with a design slightly projecting from the surface. It is the opposite of high relief, in which the design appears almost wholly detached by undercutting from its background, being attached only where functionally necessary. Bas-reliefs incorporate both surface plane and carving in their design; the degrees of projection from the surface plane depend on style, function, placement, or material.

The ancient Egyptians used a simple outline cut into the stone, with virtually no modeling and no projection. The reliefs decorating the palaces of the Assyrian kings, in very low relief with a particular interest in the naturalistic modeling of animal details, exemplify the narrative use of bas-reliefs: battle scenes and lion hunts are depicted in long friezes. Narrative friezes were also commonly used to decorate Greek temples, where an interest in representing depth was emphasized by an increasing number of superimposed planes. In parts of the Parthenon frieze, five or six planes are sometimes used, yet the actual thickness of

This Assyrian bas-relief is from the palace of Ashurbanipal at Nineveh in present-day Iraq. Dating from about 700–650 BC, the relief represents scenes from a royal lion hunt. The relief is in the British Museum, London.

the relief is only a little more than 5 cm (2 in).

Ornamental reliefs are found in Indian temple-sculpture and in such Khmer temples as Angkor Wat. In Europe, bas-reliefs were widely used for sculptured CAPITALS, varying from simple geometric ornamentation, as in English Norman cathedrals, to depictions of figures and vegetation, as in Romanesque and Gothic sculpture, or the elegant stylization of Early Christian and Byzantine sculpture. The leafy basket capitals in HAGIA SOPHIA (AD 532–37), Istanbul, and the delicate marble pluteus (panel; 6th century) in Sant' Apollinare Nuovo, Ravenna, are prime examples of Byzantine sculpture.

Pictorial illusionism, fully exploited in the *rilievo schiacciato* ("flat relief") refined by DONATELLO during the Renaissance, suggests a much greater depth through a trick of optical perspective, as for example in Donatello's alterpieces *Ascension and Delivery of the Keys to St. Peter* (1428–30; Victoria and Albert Museum, London). The durability of bas-reliefs, as opposed to the relative fragility of paintings, was a consideration in decoration of tombs, fonts, pulpits, and portals. Lorenzo GHIBERTI's east doors, called the *Gates of Paradise* (1425–52), of the Florence Baptistery are a supreme example of bas-relief in gilded bronze.

This marble relief, a classical Greek work from the west frieze of the Parthenon, represents two horsemen. Dating from about 440 BC, it stands 103 cm (43 in) high. The relief, displayed at the British Museum, London, is part of the Elgin Marbles.

Low relief is particularly suitable for the decoration of smaller objects. Private devotional images in the form of diptychs (two panels) carved of ivory or cast in metal were common in Byzantine art and in the art of the Middle Ages, when manuscript covers were frequently decorated with ivory bas-reliefs. They have also been used for jewelry. Coincidental with the development of ornamental reliefs in Greek art, the CAMEO flowered as an art form in the classical and the Hellenistic periods. The *Gemma Augustea* (1st century AD; Kunsthistorisches Museum, Vienna) is one of the largest (20 by 23 cm/8 by 9 in) and most sumptuous extant examples. Low relief was also used to decorate Chinese BRONZES, jade amuletic jewelry, and lacquer work. Pre-Columbian jade ornaments are an example of the profusion of bas-reliefs in PRIMITIVE ART. Two of the earliest types of relief are on coins and seals; examples of seal stones date from about 5000 BC in West Asia and were also widely used in the ancient Near East.

See also: IVORY CARVING; SCULPTURE; SCULPTURE TECHNIQUES.

basalt [buh-sawlt'] Basalt is the most abundant of the Earth's volcanic rocks (see IGNEOUS ROCK). It is dark, dense, and hard and is usually so fine-grained that individual crystals can be seen only under a microscope. Basalts typically consist of the following chemical compounds, in order of decreasing abundance: silicon dioxide, aluminum oxide, iron, magnesium oxide, calcium oxide, sodium oxide, titanium oxide, potassium oxide, and minor amounts of manganese oxide and other substances. These compounds combine to form the SILICATE MINERALS—chiefly plagioclase FELDSPAR, PYROXENE, and AMPHIBOLE—of which basalt is composed. Small amounts of other minerals, including magnetite, ilmenite, apatite, and sphene, are always present. Natural glass is common in the matrix. Basalts of suboceanic origin may also contain abundant OLIVINE. Near rapidly cooled edges of LAVA flows or DIKES, escaping gas produces a basalt full of holes, or vesicles, which may be filled with gemstones such as opal and chalcedony or with ZEOLITES.

Basaltic MAGMA is believed to form by partial melting of mantle rocks near the base of the crust and deeper in the mantle. It then rises through oceanic or continental rifts to cover vast areas of the ocean floors or continents.

See also: RIFT VALLEYS; SEAFLOOR SPREADING; VOLCANO.

base (chemistry)   see ACIDS AND BASES

base (mathematics) In any NUMERAL system, the base of the system is the number that determines the place values for numerals written in that system. For example, in the numeral 3467, the separate numerals 3, 4, 6, and 7 each occupy a distinct place in the numeral as a whole, and each separate numeral indicates a multiple of the value of the place it holds.

In the DECIMAL system, which is the one most widely used worldwide, the number 10 is the base. This means that each place in a numeral written in the base-10 system has the value of increasing powers of 10, reading from right to left. Thus, using the example 3467, the 7 indicates $7 \times 1 \ (10^0) = 7$; the 6 indicates $6 \times 10^1 = 60$; the 4 indicates $4 \times 10^2 = 400$; and the 3 indicates $3 \times 10^3 = 3000$.

It is not necessary to use base 10; any positive integer greater than 1 may also be used. For example, BINARY NUMBERS use base 2 and are useful in digital computers; octal numbers, base 8, are useful in reading the cumbersome binary numbers; and duodecimal numbers (see DUODECIMAL SYSTEM), base 12, are used because they simplify certain calculations.

baseball Baseball is an immensely popular American game, known as the "national pastime," played between two teams of nine players each. The basic implements used in the game are a leather-covered ball, wooden bats for hitting the ball, and gloves for catching it. Baseball is played on a large scale in Latin America, Japan, and other places besides the United States, but it is in the United States that it thrives most both as a participant and spectator sport. It is played at its highest level in the United States and two Canadian cities, where 26 teams make up the American and National Leagues (each with two divisions, East and West). Combined, these leagues are called major-league (professional) baseball.

Most players who reach the major leagues have worked their way up through Little League, scholastic, college, and minor-league (professional) ball. The vast majority of major-league players are American-reared, although since the 1960s the sport has seen an influx of Latin American players.

Following a regular season of 162 games, the division winners vie for each league's pennant; the American and National League champions then compete in the World Series. Both rounds of competition employ best-of-seven series of games.

Baseball's popularity is in part a result of the fact that almost every American boy plays the game at one time or another, and the lore of the game is intertwined with

American life. Baseball has supplied the American culture with a wide range of legendary heroes, as well as books, magazines, movies, and songs. The game has contributed hundreds of words and phrases to the American language.

The History of Baseball. The popular myth that Abner DOUBLEDAY invented baseball in Cooperstown, N.Y., in 1839, is without foundation. Actually, baseball evolved from cricket and rounders, with town ball and the New York game, popular in the eastern United States by the 1820s, as intermediaries.

On June 19, 1846, a New York team defeated the Knickerbocker Baseball Club of New York, which had drafted (1845) rules establishing the nine-player team and the four-base diamond. The score at Elysian Fields in Hoboken, N.J., that day was 23-1 in four innings.

In 1857 a convention of baseball clubs established the length of a game as nine innings instead of 21 runs. One year later the first organized league, the National Association of Base Ball Players, was formed.

The first professional team, the Cincinnati Red Stockings, won 91 and tied 1 of their first 92 games in 1869-70. Their success helped spread professionalism, and the National Association of Professional Base-Ball Players operated a loose league for five years (1871-75) until the owners formed the National League of Professional Base Ball Clubs in 1876 and made baseball a business.

The independent American Association (1882-91) prospered by allowing Sunday games and the sale of beer in the stadium. Both leagues survived the rival Union Association's challenge in 1884, but in 1890 the athletes formed the Players League, which financially pressed the National League and mortally wounded the American Association. In 1892 the eight-team National League absorbed four American Association teams, but it reverted to eight teams after 1899.

In 1901 the American League declared itself a major league, invaded National League cities, and raided the older league for players. The result of the eventual truce was the World Series, which has been played every year since 1903—except 1904, when the New York Giants refused to meet the American League champions (Boston).

The major leagues successfully met the challenge of the Federal League (1914-15). But further problems arose with the revelation that eight members of the Chicago White Sox had conspired to throw the 1919 World Series to Cincinnati. Only the appointment of Judge Kenesaw Mountain LANDIS as commissioner and the introduction of a livelier ball saved the game. Landis enforced strict regulations regarding integrity of players, and the livelier ball significantly increased the number of crowd-pleasing home runs.

Star players, reared in a minor-league system that comprised 59 leagues in 1949, increased baseball's popularity and caused it to be called America's pastime. The annual All-Star Game between teams composed of the best players in each league was begun in 1933.

The introduction of night baseball (1935) and the entry to the majors of black players (1947), previously consigned to all-black leagues, changed the style of play and expanded the potential talent pool. Then, in the 1950s, dramatic organizational changes occurred. In 1950 a $6-million World Series television contract made baseball the financial giant among sports, but it thereby became inordinately dependent on television. In 1953 the Na-

Opening-game ceremonies for the 1983 World Series—between the Baltimore Orioles (American League) and the Philadelphia Phillies (National League)—were held at Memorial Stadium in Baltimore, Md.

Spectator enthusiasm for baseball, even during the sport's formative years, is evident in this Currier and Ives print from 1866. The game depicted, between the Brooklyn Atlantics and the Philadelphia Athletics, was played only three years before the first professional team—the Cincinnati Red Stockings—was organized.

tional League Boston Braves moved to Milwaukee, and one year later the American League St. Louis Browns became the Baltimore Orioles, breaking up a city roster that had been constant for 50 years.

In 1958 the Brooklyn Dodgers moved to Los Angeles and the New York Giants moved to San Francisco, making big-league baseball a truly national game. The American League added two cities in 1961, and the National League did the same in 1962. In 1969 another expan-

sion by both leagues necessitated divisional play, the winners in each division within each league meeting in a best 3-out-of-5 championship play-off to determine the World Series contestants. Finally, the American League added two teams for the 1977 season.

The following teams are currently active: National League East—Chicago Cubs, Montreal Expos, New York Mets, Philadelphia Phillies, Pittsburgh Pirates, and St. Louis Cardinals.

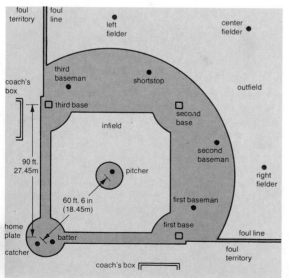

(Left) *The diagram illustrates the layout and standard dimensions of a baseball field, known as a diamond. Dots indicate a batter and the typical fielding positions of the nine defensive players.*

(Right) *The pitching circle (top) is a gently sloping mound topped by a rectangular plate. The batting area (bottom), consisting of the batter's boxes, the catcher's box, and home plate, is the focal point of offensive activity.*

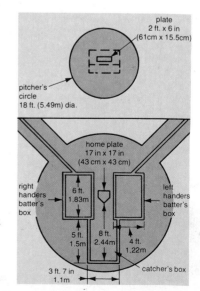

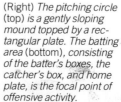

Baseball, at its most fundamental level, requires only a bat (1), or tapering cylinder of wood, and a ball (2), usually a multilayered sphere covered with hide. Formal competition requires more specialized equipment, either for protection or to enhance an athlete's performance. Outfielders, pitchers, and infielders wear a standard fielding glove (3), except for the first baseman, whose glove (4) is adapted for his position. At the plate, a batting helmet (5) is worn, its flap covering the ear and temple. Shoes (6) are cleated for added traction. The catcher's mitt (7), wider and less flexible than other fielding gloves, has additional padding to protect its wearer's hand. A catcher's mask (8) affords protection for the face, while the body is guarded by a chest protector (9) and shin guards (10). During a game, the plate umpire (11) is positioned behind the catcher (12), where both the batter (13) and the pitcher (14) can be observed. Like the catcher, the umpire wears protective gear. Once the ball is pitched, the batter attempts to drive it along a path that will elude the defense presented by outfielders (15) and infielders (16) or over the outfield fence in fair territory before touching the ground.

National League West—Atlanta Braves, Cincinnati Reds, Houston Astros, Los Angeles Dodgers, San Diego Padres, and San Francisco Giants.

American League East—Baltimore Orioles, Boston Red Sox, Cleveland Indians, Detroit Tigers, Milwaukee Brewers, New York Yankees, and Toronto Blue Jays.

American League West—California Angels, Chicago White Sox, Kansas City Royals, Minnesota Twins, Oakland Athletics, Texas Rangers, and Seattle Mariners.

Baseball's popularity diminished somewhat in the 1960s and early '70s, particularly with the rise of professional football. But despite its heavy television coverage and schedule of night games, baseball's popularity as a family spectator sport rose again in the late 1970s, the early 1980s, and the early 1990s.

Playing the Game. Baseball is played on an area divided into an infield of standard proportions and an outfield of varied dimensions. The infield is square, with 90 ft (27.4 m) on each side. The corner farthest from the outfield fence is home plate, and the other bases—first, second, and third—run counterclockwise. The pitcher's mound, an 18-ft (5.5-m) circle inclining upward toward a small rectangular rubber slab in the center, lies inside the square 60 ft 6 in (18 m) from home plate. The outfield ends at an outer fence, the distance of which from home plate varies with the shape of the field. It is usually about 76 to 137 m (250 to over 450 ft).

The teams play nine innings, alternating in the field and at bat, with the home team batting last. The infielders—first baseman, second baseman, shortstop, and third baseman—usually position themselves along the two sides of the square between first and second and second

MAJOR LEAGUE WORLD SERIES
(Series Winner in Italics)

Year	National League Team (Wins)	American League Team (Wins)	Year	National League Team (Wins)	American League Team (Wins)	Year	National League Team (Wins)	American League Team (Wins)
1903	Pittsburgh (3)	*Boston* (5)	1934	*St. Louis* (4)	Detroit (3)	1964	*St. Louis* (4)	New York (3)
1905	*New York* (4)	Philadelphia (1)	1935	Chicago (2)	*Detroit* (4)	1965	*Los Angeles* (4)	Minnesota (3)
1906	Chicago (2)	*Chicago* (4)	1936	New York (2)	*New York* (4)	1966	Los Angeles (0)	*Baltimore* (4)
1907	*Chicago* (4)	Detroit (0)	1937	New York (1)	*New York* (4)	1967	*St. Louis* (4)	Boston (3)
1908	*Chicago* (4)	Detroit (1)	1938	Chicago (0)	*New York* (4)	1968	St. Louis (3)	*Detroit* (4)
1909	*Pittsburgh* (4)	Detroit (3)	1939	Cincinnati (0)	*New York* (4)	1969	*New York* (4)	Baltimore (1)
1910	Chicago (1)	*Philadelphia* (4)	1940	*Cincinnati* (4)	Detroit (3)	1970	Cincinnati (1)	*Baltimore* (4)
1911	New York (2)	*Philadelphia* (4)	1941	Brooklyn (1)	*New York* (4)	1971	*Pittsburgh* (4)	Baltimore (3)
1912	New York (3)	Boston (4)	1942	*St. Louis* (4)	New York (1)	1972	Cincinnati (3)	*Oakland* (4)
1913	New York (1)	*Philadelphia* (4)	1943	St. Louis (1)	*New York* (4)	1973	New York (3)	*Oakland* (4)
1914	*Boston* (4)	Philadelphia (0)	1944	*St. Louis* (4)	St. Louis (2)	1974	Los Angeles (1)	*Oakland* (4)
1915	Philadelphia (1)	*Boston* (4)	1945	Chicago (3)	*Detroit* (4)	1975	*Cincinnati* (4)	Boston (3)
1916	Brooklyn (1)	*Boston* (4)	1946	*St. Louis* (4)	Boston (3)	1976	*Cincinnati* (4)	New York (0)
1917	New York (2)	*Chicago* (4)	1947	Brooklyn (3)	*New York* (4)	1977	Los Angeles (2)	*New York* (4)
1918	Chicago (2)	*Boston* (4)	1948	Boston (2)	*Cleveland* (4)	1978	Los Angeles (2)	*New York* (4)
1919	*Cincinnati* (5)	Chicago (3)	1949	Brooklyn (1)	*New York* (4)	1979	*Pittsburgh* (4)	Baltimore (3)
1920	Brooklyn (2)	*Cleveland* (5)	1950	Philadelphia (0)	*New York* (4)	1980	*Philadelphia* (4)	Kansas City (2)
1921	*New York* (5)	New York (3)	1951	New York (2)	*New York* (4)	1981	*Los Angeles* (4)	New York (2)
1922	*New York* (4)	New York (0)	1952	Brooklyn (3)	*New York* (4)	1982	*St. Louis* (4)	Milwaukee (3)·
1923	New York (2)	*New York* (4)	1953	Brooklyn (2)	*New York* (4)	1983	Philadelphia (1)	*Baltimore* (4)
1924	New York (3)	*Washington* (4)	1954	*New York* (4)	Cleveland (0)	1984	San Diego (1)	*Detroit* (4)
1925	*Pittsburgh* (4)	Washington (3)	1955	*Brooklyn* (4)	New York (3)	1985	St. Louis (3)	*Kansas City* (4)
1926	*St. Louis* (4)	New York (3)	1956	Brooklyn (3)	*New York* (4)	1986	*New York* (4)	Boston (3)
1927	Pittsburgh (0)	*New York* (4)	1957	*Milwaukee* (4)	New York (3)	1987	St. Louis (3)	*Minnesota* (4)
1928	St. Louis (0)	*New York* (4)	1958	Milwaukee (3)	*New York* (4)	1988	*Los Angeles* (4)	Oakland (1)
1929	Chicago (1)	*Philadelphia* (4)	1959	*Los Angeles* (4)	Chicago (2)	1989	San Francisco (0)	*Oakland* (4)
1930	St. Louis (2)	*Philadelphia* (4)	1960	*Pittsburgh* (4)	New York (3)	1990	*Cincinnati* (4)	Oakland (0)
1931	*St. Louis* (4)	Philadelphia (3)	1961	Cincinnati (1)	*New York* (4)			
1932	Chicago (0)	*New York* (4)	1962	San Francisco (3)	*New York* (4)			
1933	*New York* (4)	Washington (1)	1963	*Los Angeles* (4)	New York (0)			

and third bases. The outfielders—left, center, and right fielders—cover those portions of the outfield. The pitcher stands on the rubber, and the catcher crouches behind the batter. The American League decided in 1973 to allow a 10th player, a designated hitter, to bat for the pitcher. U.S. colleges also adopted the rule.

The team at bat sends its nine players to the plate in a specified sequence. Each batter attempts to hit the pitcher's deliveries, which the latter tries to vary in speed and in placement within the strike zone (the area over home plate and between the batter's knees and armpits). Substitutions are allowed throughout the game but preclude a player's return.

The defending players wear a leather glove on one hand. The catcher's glove, the largest, is round and heavily padded. The first baseman's mitt is more flexible and has one compartment for the thumb and another for the other fingers. The remaining players use gloves with separate compartments for each finger and a webbing between the thumb and index finger. The bat, up to 2.75 in (7 cm) thick and 42 in (106.7 cm) long, is round and wooden (in amateur games aluminum is allowed). The ball consists of three layers: a cork-and-rubber sphere forms the central core; woolen yarn is then tightly wound around the core; and a leather casing is stitched together around the whole. A regulation baseball is 9–9.25 in (22.9–23.5 cm) in circumference and weighs 5–5.25 oz (141.7–148.8 g).

Each team's half-inning consists of three outs. An out

Ty Cobb played 24 seasons (1905–28) in the major leagues, winning the American League batting championship a dozen times en route to his .367 lifetime batting average.

(Right) *Babe Ruth, the great New York Yankee of the 1920s and '30s and the most famous baseball player in history, crashes one of his 714 career home runs, a record that stood until 1974.*

(Below) *Joe DiMaggio, regarded as one of the most graceful outfielders ever to play baseball, set one of the sport's most durable records in 1941, hitting safely in 56 consecutive games.*

CY YOUNG AWARD WINNERS*

Year	Player, Team, League
1956	Don Newcombe, Brooklyn, NL
1957	Warren Spahn, Milwaukee, NL
1958	Bob Turley, New York, AL
1959	Early Wynn, Chicago, AL
1960	Vernon Law, Pittsburgh, NL
1961	Whitey Ford, New York, AL
1962	Don Drysdale, Los Angeles, NL
1963	Sandy Koufax, Los Angeles, NL
1964	Dean Chance, Los Angeles, AL
1965	Sandy Koufax, Los Angeles, NL
1966	Sandy Koufax, Los Angeles, NL
1967	Jim Lonborg, Boston, AL; Mike McCormick, San Francisco, NL
1968	Dennis McLain, Detroit, AL; Bob Gibson, St. Louis, NL
1969	Mike Cuellar, Baltimore, and Dennis McLain, Detroit, tied in AL; Tom Seaver, New York, NL
1970	Jim Perry, Minnesota, AL; Bob Gibson, St. Louis, NL
1971	Vida Blue, Oakland, AL; Ferguson Jenkins, Chicago, NL
1972	Gaylord Perry, Cleveland, AL; Steve Carlton, Philadelphia, NL
1973	Jim Palmer, Baltimore, AL; Tom Seaver, New York, NL
1974	Catfish Hunter, Oakland, AL; Mike Marshall, Los Angeles, NL
1975	Jim Palmer, Baltimore, AL; Tom Seaver, New York, NL
1976	Jim Palmer, Baltimore, AL; Randy Jones, San Diego, NL
1977	Sparky Lyle, New York, AL; Steve Carlton, Philadelphia, NL
1978	Ron Guidry, New York, AL; Gaylord Perry, San Diego, NL
1979	Mike Flanagan, Baltimore, AL; Bruce Sutter, Chicago, NL
1980	Steve Stone, Baltimore, AL; Steve Carlton, Philadelphia, NL
1981	Rollie Fingers, Milwaukee, AL; Fernando Valenzuela, L.A., NL
1982	Pete Vuckovich, Milwaukee, AL; Steve Carlton, Phila., NL
1983	LaMarr Hoyt, Chicago, AL; John Denny, Philadelphia, NL
1984	Willie Hernández, Detroit, AL; Rich Sutcliffe, Chicago, NL
1985	Bret Saberhagen, K.C., AL; Dwight Gooden, New York, NL
1986	Roger Clemens, Boston, AL; Mike Scott, Houston, NL
1987	Roger Clemens, Boston, AL; Steve Bedrosian, Phila., NL
1988	Frank Viola, Minnesota, AL; Orel Hershiser, L.A., NL
1989	Bret Saberhagen, K.C., AL; Mark Davis, San Diego, NL
1990	Bob Welch, Oakland, AL; Doug Drabek, Pittsburgh, NL

*Best pitcher as selected by Baseball Writers Association.

occurs most commonly when a ball is caught before bouncing (a fly ball), when a ground ball is caught and thrown or carried to first base before the batter arrives, when a base runner is not touching a base and is tagged by a fielder holding the ball, when a fielder who has the ball touches a base other than first when there is a runner approaching that base and each previous base, when a player has left a base and is unable to get back before a caught fly ball is thrown to the base, and when the pitcher gets three strikes on a batter.

A strike is any pitch the batter swings at and misses, any pitch that travels through the strike zone, and any batted ball that lands outside the straight lines running from home plate through first base and from home plate through third base to the outfield fence (called a foul). If the batter has two strikes, a foul is not considered a strike unless it is a foul bunt or a tipped foul caught by the catcher before it bounces.

The team at bat tries to get players on base and advance them until they round all four bases to score runs. The team with more runs after nine innings wins. If the score is tied at the end of nine innings, the teams play extra innings until one team scores more than the other and both teams have had an equal number of turns at bat.

A batter reaches base if hit by a pitch, if he or she receives a walk by taking four pitches (called balls) outside the strike zone, if a defensive player misplays the ball for an error, if the catcher interferes with a swing, and if the catcher fails to catch the pitcher's throw on a third strike and does not throw the ball to first base before the batter reaches the base. But the most common way of reaching base is with a hit.

MOST VALUABLE PLAYER*

Year	Player, Team (AL)	Player, Team (NL)
1931	Lefty Grove, Philadelphia	Frank Frisch, St. Louis
1932	Jimmy Foxx, Philadelphia	Chuck Klein, Philadelphia
1933	Jimmy Foxx, Philadelphia	Carl Hubbell, New York
1934	Mickey Cochrane. Detroit	Dizzy Dean, St. Louis
1935	Hank Greenberg, Detroit	Gabby Hartnett, Chicago
1936	Lou Gehrig, New York	Carl Hubbell, New York
1937	Charley Gehringer, Detroit	Joe Medwick, St. Louis
1938	Jimmy Foxx, Boston	Ernie Lombardi, Cincinnati
1939	Joe DiMaggio, New York	Bucky Walters, Cincinnati
1940	Hank Greenberg, Detroit	Frank McCormick, Cincinnati
1941	Joe DiMaggio, New York	Dolph Camilli, Brooklyn
1942	Joe Gordon, New York	Mort Cooper, St. Louis
1943	Spurgeon Chandler, New York	Stan Musial, St. Louis
1944	Hal Newhouser, Detroit	Marty Marion, St. Louis
1945	Hal Newhouser, Detroit	Phil Cavarretta, Chicago
1946	Ted Williams, Boston	Stan Musial, St. Louis
1947	Joe DiMaggio, New York	Bob Elliot, Boston
1948	Lou Boudreau, Cleveland	Stan Musial, St. Louis
1949	Ted Williams, Boston	Jackie Robinson, Brooklyn
1950	Phil Rizzuto, New York	Jim Konstanty, Philadelphia
1951	Yogi Berra, New York	Roy Campanella, Brooklyn
1952	Bobby Shantz, Philadelphia	Hank Sauer, Chicago
1953	Al Rosen, Cleveland	Roy Campanella, Brooklyn
1954	Yogi Berra, New York	Willie Mays, New York
1955	Yogi Berra, New York	Roy Campanella, Brooklyn
1956	Mickey Mantle, New York	Don Newcombe, Brooklyn
1957	Mickey Mantle, New York	Henry Aaron, Milwaukee
1958	Jackie Jensen, Boston	Ernie Banks, Chicago
1959	Nellie Fox, Chicago	Ernie Banks, Chicago
1960	Roger Maris, New York	Dick Groat, Pittsburgh
1961	Roger Maris, New York	Frank Robinson, Cincinnati
1962	Mickey Mantle, New York	Maury Wills, Los Angeles
1963	Elston Howard, New York	Sandy Koufax, Los Angeles
1964	Brooks Robinson, Baltimore	Ken Boyer, St. Louis
1965	Zoilo Versalles, Minnesota	Willie Mays, San Francisco
1966	Frank Robinson, Baltimore	Roberto Clemente, Pittsburgh
1967	Carl Yastrzemski, Boston	Orlando Cepeda, St. Louis
1968	Dennis McLain, Detroit	Bob Gibson, St. Louis
1969	Harmon Killebrew, Minnesota	Willie McCovey, San Francisco
1970	John Boog Powell, Baltimore	Johnny Bench, Cincinnati
1971	Vida Blue, Oakland	Joe Torre, St. Louis
1972	Dick Allen, Chicago	Johnny Bench, Cincinnati
1973	Reggie Jackson, Oakland	Pete Rose, Cincinnati
1974	Jeff Burroughs, Texas	Steve Garvey, Los Angeles
1975	Fred Lynn, Boston	Joe Morgan, Cincinnati
1976	Thurman Munson, New York	Joe Morgan, Cincinnati
1977	Rod Carew, Minnesota	George Foster, Cincinnati
1978	Jim Rice, Boston	Dave Parker, Pittsburgh
1979	Don Baylor, California	Willie Stargell, Pittsburgh
		Keith Hernandez, St. Louis
1980	George Brett, Kansas City	Mike Schmidt, Philadelphia
1981	Rollie Fingers, Milwaukee	Mike Schmidt, Philadelphia
1982	Robin Yount, Milwaukee	Dale Murphy, Atlanta
1983	Cal Ripkin, Jr., Baltimore	Dale Murphy, Atlanta
1984	Willie Hernández, Detroit	Ryne Sandberg, Chicago
1985	Don Mattingly, New York	Willie McGee, St. Louis
1986	Roger Clemens, Boston	Mike Schmidt, Philadelphia
1987	George Bell, Toronto	Andre Dawson, Chicago
1988	Jose Canseco, Oakland	Kirk Gibson, Los Angeles
1989	Robin Yount, Milwaukee	Kevin Mitchell, San Francisco
1990	Rickey Henderson, Oakland	Barry Bonds, Pittsburgh

*Selected by Baseball Writers Association.

Jackie Robinson, a daring base runner, slides safely into home plate. Robinson made his debut with the Brooklyn Dodgers in 1947, becoming the first black to play in modern major league baseball.

Hits come in many forms: gentle bunts to unreachable parts of the infield, hard-hit ground balls that travel between infielders, bloopers popped in an arc beyond the infield but out of the outfielders' reach, line drives in front of or between the outfielders, and clouts smashed over the fence. Both the batter and runners may advance as far as possible on any hit. A one-base hit is a single, a two-base hit a double, a three-base hit a triple, and a four-base hit a home run. The most common kind of home run is a fair ball over the fence on a fly, but a batter may also run around all the bases before the fielders can retrieve a

Willie Mays hit 660 home runs in the major leagues, a number surpassed only by Henry Aaron and Babe Ruth. Mays's unorthodox "basket" catches and a powerful throwing arm made him one of baseball's finest outfielders.

(Left) *Sandy Koufax, star lefthander of the Los Angeles Dodgers, pitched four no-hit games. Plagued by arm injuries, he retired in 1966 at the height of his career.*

ball hit inside the ballpark and throw it to the plate.

Runners may also advance by stealing a base, on a balk (improper procedure by a pitcher), on a sacrifice (a bunt intended to move the runner even though the batter probably will be out), or on a sacrifice fly (a fly ball caught by an outfielder but not returned to the proper base before the runner reaches it—provided the runner does not leave his or her original base before the ball is caught).

Four umpires, one near each base, regulate the game, enforce the rules, and call balls and strikes, foul and fair balls, and safe or out. The umpires may also eject players from the game for improper behavior and call a forfeit for serious infractions. Some amateur games have only one or two umpires; the play-off series in both the American and National leagues and the World Series have six.

Baseball has two basic styles of play. Inside baseball, prevalent until the 1920s, emphasizes speed, defense, and good pitching. The second style emphasizes power hitting. The New York Yankees dominated baseball with the latter, winning 29 pennants and 20 World Series between 1921 and 1964. The use of relief pitchers and artificial turf has returned inside baseball to favor, but power hitting remains an appealing factor in the game.

Basel [bah'-zuhl] Basel (also Basle; French: Bâle) is the capital of the half canton of Basel Stadt, in northern Switzerland. The population of the city proper is 171,574 (1988 est.), and that of the conurbation, 363,029. Located on the Rhine River where it joins with the Birs and Weise rivers, Basel is a major industrial center and commercial port.

Manufactures include chemicals, pharmaceuticals, machinery, and textiles. Basel is also a center for banking and finance; the Bank for International Settlements has its headquarters there. Basel University, founded by Pope Pius II in 1460, is the oldest in Switzerland. Landmarks

include the cathedral (consecrated 1019), a Romanesque and Gothic building containing the tomb of Erasmus; the town hall (1504–14); the Church of Saint Martin; and several museums, including a gallery exhibiting the works of Hans Holbein.

Known as Basilia to the Romans, Basel became the seat of a bishopric in the 5th century. It was an imperial free city of the Holy Roman Empire from 1096 to 1501 and was the site of the ecumenical Council of Basel in 1431–49. Basel joined the Swiss Confederation in 1501 and quickly became an intellectual center of the Swiss Reformation, with Holbein residing in the city and Erasmus teaching at the university. In 1831 the original canton was divided in half when the rural population revolted and proclaimed independence from the city.

Basel, Council of The Council of Basel convened in 1431 as the 17th ecumenical council of the Roman Catholic church. Almost from the beginning the council fell into conflict with Pope Eugene IV, who was suspicious of it. When in 1437 he ordered the council transferred to Ferrara (see FERRARA-FLORENCE, COUNCIL OF), some of its members refused to comply. They declared the pope deposed and, to replace him, elected a layman, Amadeus VII, duke of Savoy, who took the name Felix V. Thereafter the Basel assembly became increasingly involved in the political quarrels of Germany. Although the council accomplished a partial reconciliation with the HUSSITES, its efforts at reform were largely ineffective. Moreover the failure of its challenge to papal authority marked the triumph of the papacy over CONCILIARISM.

basenji [buh-sen'-jee] The basenji is a smooth-coated dog that stands about 41–43 cm (16–17 in) at the shoulder and weighs about 10–11 kg (22–24 lb). Its glistening coat ranges in color from red to tan or pure black, and it has white markings on the chest, muzzle, legs, and tip of the tail. The ears are erect, and the tail is carried erect and tightly curled to one side of the back.

The basenji was raised in ancient times in Central Africa. The first basenjis brought to England in 1895 died

The basenji is a short-coated African dog that does not bark but sometimes produces a yelping sound. It is one of the oldest breeds of dogs and was first raised to kill small predators. The name is Bantu word meaning "natives."

before the breed became established, and the dog did not reappear in England—or arrive in the United States—until the mid-1930s. It was recognized by the American Kennel Club in 1943.

Basho [bah-shoh]   Basho was the pseudonym of Matsuo Munefusa, b. 1644, d. Oct. 12, 1694, the finest writer of Japanese HAIKU during its formative years. His attention to the natural world transformed this verse form from a frivolous social pastime into a major genre of Japanese poetry. From 1684, he traveled widely, keeping diaries, such as *The Narrow Road to the Far North* (1689; Eng. trans., 1974), and collaborating with local poets on the linked-verse forms known as *renga*.

BASIC   see COMPUTER LANGUAGES

Basie, Count   The pianist and bandleader William "Count" Basie, b. Red Bank, N.J., Aug. 21, 1904, d. Apr. 26, 1984, was one of the great exponents of SWING. He studied with Fats Waller, a major influence on his work, and played with New York and Kansas City jazz groups in the 1920s and early '30s before forming his own band in 1935. Basie's band was celebrated for its polished, rhythmic versions of blues melodies. Famous musicians who performed with Basie include the singer Billie Holiday and saxophonist Lester Young.

---

basil   Basil are herbs of the genus *Ocimum*, belonging to the mint family, Labiatae. Native to tropical Asia and Africa, common, or sweet, basil, *O. basilicum*, grows about 30 cm (1 ft) high. Crushed basil leaves are used to flavor tomato products, meats, fish and egg dishes, and salads. Basil's essential oil is used in perfumes, and it is one of the herbs used in the production of chartreuse liqueur.

Common, or sweet, basil is an annual herb that produces shiny, green leaves that have a spicy fragrance. Its small, white flowers bloom in August and can be pinched off to promote more leaf growth.

Basil I, Byzantine Emperor (Basil the Macedonian)   Basil I, b. *c.*812, d. Aug. 29, 886, ruled the Byzantine Empire from 867 to 886 and founded the Macedonian dynasty, which governed until 1056. Born of Armenian parents in Macedonia, he rose as a favorite of Emperor Michael III, whom he then murdered (Sept. 24, 867). By conquering the PAULICIANS, Basil continued Byzantium's expansion eastward toward the Euphrates. In church affairs he reconciled the moderate and extremist factions led by patriarchs PHOTIUS and St. Ignatius of Constantinople.

Basil ordered a recodification of Byzantine law similar to that of JUSTINIAN I. His construction of the Nea Ecclesia (New Church) set a pattern for later Byzantine architecture. Basil was succeeded by his son LEO VI.

Basil III, Grand Duke of Moscow   see VASILY III, GRAND DUKE OF MOSCOW

Basil the Great, Saint   Saint Basil the Great, b. *c.*329, d. Jan. 1, 379, was one of the Cappadocian Fathers, the other two being his brother, Gregory of Nyssa, and his friend, Gregory of Nazianzus. The Cappadocians brought to fulfillment the theological work of Athanasius against ARIANISM.

Basil was born at Caesarea in Cappadocia. He received higher education in Constantinople and Athens but settled as a hermit near Neo-Caesarea by the Iris River. In 364 the bishop of Caesarea, Eusebius, persuaded Basil to accept ordination. Basil agreed and became an able defender of orthodoxy among the churches of Anatolia. In 370 he succeeded Eusebius as bishop. Basil established hospitals, fostered monasticism, and reformed the liturgy. His Rule, a code for monastic life, became the basis of eastern monasticism, and the liturgy of Saint Basil, probably compiled by him though later revised, is still used on certain Sundays in Orthodox churches.

Basil is known mainly for the treatise *On the Holy Spirit* (375) and three books entitled *Against Eunomius* (363–65), who was an Arian protagonist. Feast day: Jan. 1 (Eastern); Jan. 2 (Western; formerly June 14).

---

basilica [buh-sil'-i-kuh]   In the Roman Catholic church *basilica* is an honorary name given to certain churches. The original and still the most important basilicas are the four principal churches of Rome: SAINT PETER'S BASILICA, San Giovanni in Laterano, Santa Maria Maggiore, and San Paolo Fuori le Mura.

The term *basilica* also refers to a particular architectural form. In Roman architecture a basilica was a large, oblong building used particularly as a court of law and a place of public assembly. In Early Christian and Merovingian times the function of the basilica became exclusively religious, and the plan was often varied.

Although the name is derived from the Greek *Basilikē* (meaning "royal"), the Basilica Porcia, the earliest known, was built (184 BC) by Cato the Elder in republican Rome. It was so useful that others were built throughout the Roman world, usually adjoining the FORUM or AGORA of a town. The earliest preserved basilica (2d century BC) has been found in POMPEII. VITRUVIUS (active 46–30 BC) gave detailed directions for building such basilicas in his treatise on Roman architecture.

The form of the basilica lent itself to public assembly for religious rites. A rare pagan religious basilica dating from the reign (AD 14–37) of Tiberius was discovered in Rome near Porta Maggiore. The form was widely used for synagogues in Palestine and at Sardis, Turkey, from at least the 2d century AD. When early Christian congregations grew too large to meet in *titulae* (houses), they adopted the basilican form. Constantine's 4th-century donations of monumental basilicas at all the major holy sites throughout the Roman world strengthened the popularity of the form.

In many basilicas the ceiling of the nave was raised by placing a wall pierced with windows (the clerestory) above the side colonnades. The hall might be beam-roofed, vaulted, or domed. An altar took the place of the Roman tribunal. Rooms on either side could be used as the *prothesis* and *diakonikon* (rooms in which the sacraments, books, and vestments were stored) in the Byzantine church. In Western churches they became side altars, chapels, and sacristies as Romanesque and Gothic architecture developed.

The basilica thus served as the basic plan for the majority of churches in the past, and it continues to be the most popular form for houses of worship today.

See also: CATHEDRALS AND CHURCHES; MONASTIC ART AND ARCHITECTURE.

basilisk [baz'-uh-lisk]   In Greek and Roman mythology, the basilisk, or cockatrice, was a serpent with the head and wings of a cock and the tail of a dragon. Its glance killed whatever it encountered.

basin and range province   The most familiar basin and range province is found in the western United States. In such an area, fault-block mountains trending north to south rise abruptly above intermontane (between-mountain) DESERT basins. Most of Nevada and parts of Oregon, Idaho, California, Arizona, New Mexico, and northern Mexico are included in the area. Much of the province has interior drainage; rivers terminate either in salt lakes that have no outlets (such as Great Salt Lake, Utah) or in the low parts of desert basins (bolsons), where they feed PLAYA lakes that evaporate during dry seasons. The mountains have been so deeply eroded that in places only remnants (inselbergs) remain. Material washed down from the mountains by flash floods fills the intermontane basins and piles up as ALLUVIAL FANS that slope away from the canyon mouths..

See also: EROSION AND SEDIMENTATION; MOUNTAIN.

Baskerville, John   John Baskerville, b. Jan. 28, 1706, d. Jan. 8, 1775, was an English type designer and printer. His beautiful round Roman typeface had an important influence on type design (see TYPE AND TYPESETTING). Baskerville made outstanding contributions to modern typography through other innovations, such as the use of woven paper and the invention of rich black inks. In 1757 he printed his first book, a quarto edition of Vergil. He was printer to Cambridge University from 1758 to 1768. His printed folio Bible of 1763 ranks as one of the finest examples of printing in the 18th century.

Basket Makers   see ANASAZI

basketball   Basketball, extremely popular around the world, is a court game played by two teams of five players each. The object is to put a ball through a hoop, or basket, and thus score more points than the opposing team.

Although basketball can by played outdoors, it was invented to serve as an exciting indoor exercise for the winter months in a northern climate. It quickly became a spectator sport, however, and now attracts large audiences to gymnasiums and arenas, especially in the United States, South America, and Europe.

The sport is played on the amateur level by high schools, colleges, other groups, and, since 1936, by national teams in the Olympic Games. It also is played by professional athletes, notably in the United States and Europe. The foremost championships contended for are those of the National Basketball Association (U.S. professionals), the National Collegiate Athletic Association (U.S. colleges), and the Olympic Games.

History

James Naismith, an instructor in physical education at the International Young Men's Christian Association (YMCA) Training School in Springfield, Mass., devised basketball in December 1891. Naismith, who later became a doctor of medicine, hung two peach baskets, one at either end of the gymnasium, as goals. His YMCA athletes played the first game with a soccer ball, passing it back and forth until one team was able to throw it into its assigned basket. That first game was governed by 13 axioms formulated by Naismith. The rules of basketball, based on those axioms, were established later by the YMCA and the Amateur Athletic Union. All 13 axioms are still incorporated in today's rules.

Word of the new game spread swiftly, and basketball soon was being played in YMCA gymnasiums throughout the eastern United States. Its growth was so rapid that the first men's intercollegiate game was played in 1897, the first professional league was founded in 1898, and the first collegiate association—the Eastern Intercollegiate League—was formed in 1902. Women also took up the game before 1900.

The growing popularity of basketball resulted in improvements in equipment and skills. The metal hoop was

(Above) *Towering Kareem Abdul-Jabbar relied on agility and swift reflexes to become the NBA's all-time leading scorer.*

(Left) *The fourth Madison Square Garden, built (1968) above the Pennsylvania Railroad Station, is home for the New York Knicks.*

Three diagrams illustrate layouts and standardized dimensions used in basketball. Basketball courts (A) vary in size depending on the level of competition. Backboards (B) may be either rectangular (professional and collegiate) or fanshaped (some high schools), but the basket's height (C) is a globally recognized 10 ft (3.05 m).

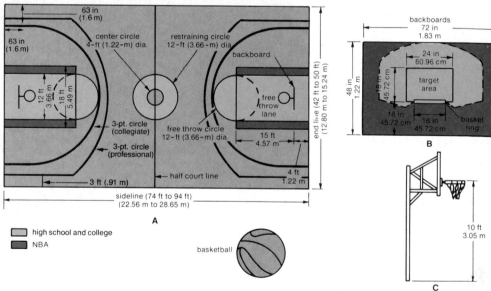

introduced in 1893, and backboards in 1895. The soccer ball was replaced by the first basketball. As playing skills also became more sophisticated, the game attracted more and more spectators.

Until the late 1930s, scores were low, sometimes in single digits. After each score, opposing centers (one of the five positions, the others being two guards and two forwards) lined up in the middle of the court and jumped for the ball. Then the team that got the ball would pass or

dribble until a player was about 3 m (10 ft) from the basket before trying a shot. The slow pace did not inhibit the growth of the game, however. By the 1920s, basketball was being played all over the United States, and tournaments were being conducted in high school and college gymnasiums. Most states held high school championships for boys.

Several events in the 1930s spurred the growth of the game as a spectator sport and at the same time made basketball more exciting for the players. The first of these came in the 1932–33 season (basketball seasons tend to be between football in fall and baseball in spring), when rules designed to speed up play were adopted. It became mandatory, under penalty of losing possession, to move the ball past midcourt in less than ten seconds. In addition, no offensive player was permitted to remain within the foul lanes for more than three seconds. Then in 1934 a New York sportswriter, Ned Irish, persuaded the promoters at New York's Madison Square Garden, a large arena, to schedule doubleheaders between college teams. These events proved successful, and similar promotions followed in other cities. Before long, colleges began building their own arenas for basketball.

Another significant advance occurred in 1936, when a Stanford University team traveled from California to a Madison Square Garden promotion to challenge the eastern powers in the "cradle of basketball." Opponents and fans were stunned by the Stanford style of shooting—one-handed while jumping, which contrasted to the prevalent method of taking two-handed shots while standing still. One Stanford player, Hank LUISETTI, was so adept at the "jump shot" that he could outscore an entire opposing team. The new style gained universal acceptance, and basketball scores rose remarkably.

In the 1937–38 season the center jump following each field goal was eliminated. At the end of the next season, Madison Square Garden brought in college teams from around the nation for the National Invitation Tournament (NIT), a postseason play-off that was adopted (1939) on a wider scale by the National Collegiate Athletic Association (NCAA). Although the NIT is still held annually, the NCAA tournament serves as the official intercollegiate championship.

The first basketball team poses with the game's inventor, James Naismith (suited, center row). Naismith, a physical education instructor, developed basketball in 1891 to provide young men with an indoor athletic diversion during winter.

Wilt Chamberlain, 7 ft 2 in (2 m 18 cm) tall, the National Basketball Association's all-time leading rebounder, works the ball in toward the net.

The University of Kentucky (coached, 1930–72, by Adolph Rupp), St. John's (in New York), the University of North Carolina, Duke University, Kansas University, and Indiana University have been among the leading college basketball teams for years. From 1964 to 1975 the University of California at Los Angeles (UCLA), coached by John WOODEN and led by the centers Lew Alcindor (see ABDUL-JABBAR, KAREEM) and Bill WALTON, dominated the intercollegiate play-offs, winning the title an unprecedented 10 times in 12 years. The 1,250 college teams in the United States now draw about 30 million spectators per season.

Although women have played the game since the 1890s, and even though a few states (Iowa, for instance) have shown great participatory and spectator interest in secondary-school women's basketball for some decades, significant growth and serious recognition of women's basketball in the United States and elsewhere did not occur until the 1970s. Almost all U.S. states now hold girls' high school tournaments, and basketball is the fastest-growing women's intercollegiate sport.

Professional Basketball

From 1898 on, many attempts were made to establish professional basketball as a spectator sport but success did not come until 1946. The best of the early efforts was

NBA* PLAYOFF WINNERS
(NBA champion in italics)

Year	Eastern Conference	Western Conference
1947	*Philadelphia Warriors*	Chicago Stags
1948	Philadelphia Warriors	*Baltimore Bullets*
1949	Washington Capitols	*Minneapolis Lakers*
1950	Syracuse Nationals	*Minneapolis Lakers*
1951	New York Knickerbockers	*Rochester Royals*
1952–53	New York Knickerbockers	*Minneapolis Lakers*
1954	Syracuse Nationals	*Minneapolis Lakers*
1955	*Syracuse Nationals*	Ft. Wayne Pistons
1956	*Philadelphia Warriors*	Ft. Wayne Pistons
1957	*Boston Celtics*	St. Louis Hawks
1958	Boston Celtics	*St. Louis Hawks*
1959	*Boston Celtics*	Minneapolis Lakers
1960–61	*Boston Celtics*	St. Louis Hawks
1962	*Boston Celtics*	Los Angeles Lakers
1963	*Boston Celtics*	Los Angeles Lakers
1964	*Boston Celtics*	San Francisco Warriors
1965	*Boston Celtics*	Los Angeles Lakers
1966	*Boston Celtics*	Los Angeles Lakers
1967	*Philadelphia 76ers*	San Francisco Warriors
1968	*Boston Celtics*	Los Angeles Lakers
1969	*Boston Celtics*	Los Angeles Lakers
1970	*New York Knickerbockers*	Los Angeles Lakers
1971	Baltimore Bullets	*Milwaukee Bucks*
1972	New York Knickerbockers	*Los Angeles Lakers*
1973	*New York Knickerbockers*	Los Angeles Lakers
1974	*Boston Celtics*	Milwaukee Bucks
1975	Washington Bullets	*Golden State Warriors*
1976	*Boston Celtics*	Phoenix Suns
1977	Philadelphia 76ers	*Portland Trail Blazers*
1978	*Washington Bullets*	Seattle SuperSonics
1979	Washington Bullets	*Seattle SuperSonics*
1980	Philadelphia 76ers	*Los Angeles Lakers*
1981	*Boston Celtics*	Houston Rockets
1982	Philadelphia 76ers	*Los Angeles Lakers*
1983	*Philadelphia 76ers*	Los Angeles Lakers
1984	*Boston Celtics*	Los Angeles Lakers
1985	Boston Celtics	*Los Angeles Lakers*
1986	*Boston Celtics*	Houston Rockets
1987	Boston Celtics	*Los Angeles Lakers*
1988	Detroit Pistons	*Los Angeles Lakers*
1989	*Detroit Pistons*	Los Angeles Lakers
1990	*Detroit Pistons*	Portland Trail Blazers

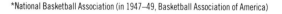

*National Basketball Association (in 1947–49, Basketball Association of America)

Jerry West, the outstanding guard of the Los Angeles Lakers, drives past defensive players en route to a field goal. West's single-season record for free throws testified to the aggressiveness of his playing style.

arenas in major cities. Another professional league, the National Basketball League, was already in existence, with franchises in medium-sized midwestern cities. The two leagues merged in 1949 as the National Basketball Association (NBA) and pared away the weaker franchises.

With the signing of the country's best collegians through what was called a player draft, the NBA could display both talent and balance. The NBA's greatest spurt of growth occurred in the 1960s and '70s. Although the Boston Celtics, led by Bill RUSSELL, Bob COUSY, and John HAVLICEK and coached by Red AUERBACH, won 11 of 13 NBA titles beginning in 1957, fans also closely followed such stars as Philadelphia's Wilt CHAMBERLAIN, Cincinnati's Oscar ROBERTSON, and Los Angeles's Jerry WEST and Elgin BAYLOR. The NBA of the 1970s and 1980s exhibited a welcome balance of power: from 1970 until 1988 no team won consecutive NBA titles, though the New York Knicks (with Willis Reed, Walt Frazier, and Bill BRADLEY) won twice; the Boston Celtics, 5 times (3 with Larry BIRD); and the Los Angeles Lakers, 6 times (5 with Kareem Abdul-Jabbar and Magic JOHNSON).

In the 1970s the NBA expanded from 9 teams to 22. Some of the new franchises were acquired when the American Basketball Association (1968–76) merged with

Oscar Robertson, who became the NBA's all-time leader in assists while with the Cincinnati Royals and Milwaukee Bucks, attempts a jump shot. A superb scorer and rebounder as well as passer, Robertson is considered by many experts to have been the game's greatest all-around player.

made by the HARLEM GLOBETROTTERS, an all-black team that first toured only the United States and then internationally to play local professional or semiprofessional teams. The Globetrotters, founded in 1926, were not affiliated with a league. Their style was and is often showy because, at least into the early 1950s, they could dominate all opponents.

In 1946 serious professional basketball had acquired a following among American sports fans, who wanted to see the former collegians in action. That year the Basketball Association of America, with teams from the United States and one from Toronto, began competing in large

NBA SCORING LEADERS

Year	Player, Team	Average
1947	Joe Fulks, Philadelphia	23.2
1948	Max Zaslofsky, Chicago	21.0
1949	George Mikan, Minneapolis	28.3
1950	George Mikan, Minneapolis	27.4
1951	George Mikan, Minneapolis	28.4
1952	Paul Arizin, Philadelphia	25.4
1953	Neil Johnston, Philadelphia	22.3
1954	Neil Johnston, Philadelphia	24.4
1955	Neil Johnston, Philadelphia	22.7
1956	Bob Pettit, St. Louis	25.7
1957	Paul Arizin, Philadelphia	25.6
1958	George Yardley, Detroit	27.8
1959	Bob Petit, St. Louis	29.2
1960	Wilt Chamberlain, Philadelphia	37.9
1961	Wilt Chamberlain, Philadelphia	38.4
1962	Wilt Chamberlain, Philadelphia	50.4
1963	Wilt Chamberlain, San Francisco	44.8
1964	Wilt Chamberlain, San Francisco	36.5
1965	Wilt Chamberlain, San Fran., Phila.	34.7
1966	Wilt Chamberlain, Philadelphia	33.5
1967	Rick Barry, San Francisco	35.6
1968	Dave Bing, Detroit	27.1
1969	Elvin Hayes, San Diego	28.4
1970	Jerry West, Los Angeles	31.2
1971	Lew Alcindor, Milwaukee	31.7
1972	Kareem Abdul-Jabbar (Alcindor), Milwaukee	34.8
1973	Nate Archibald, Kansas City-Omaha	34.0
1974	Bob McAdoo, Buffalo	30.6
1975	Bob McAdoo, Buffalo	34.5
1976	Bob McAdoo, Buffalo	31.1
1977	Pete Maravich, New Orleans	31.1
1978	George Gervin, San Antonio	27.2
1979	George Gervin, San Antonio	29.6
1980	George Gervin, San Antonio	33.1
1981	Adrian Dantley, Utah	30.7
1982	George Gervin, San Antonio	32.3
1983	Alex English, Denver	28.4
1984	Adrian Dantley, Utah	30.6
1985	Bernard King, New York	32.9
1986	Dominique Wilkins, Atlanta	30.3
1987	Michael Jordan, Chicago	37.1
1988	Michael Jordan, Chicago	35.0
1989	Michael Jordan, Chicago	32.5
1990	Michael Jordan, Chicago	33.6

Julius Erving ("Doctor J"), one of the game's most acrobatic players, leaps high toward the basket for a lay-up.

NBA MOST VALUABLE PLAYER*

Year	Player, Team	Year	Player, Team
1956	Bob Pettit, St. Louis	1975	Bob McAdoo, Buffalo
1957	Bob Cousy, Boston	1976–77	K. Abdul-Jabbar, L.A.
1958	Bill Russell, Boston	1978	Bill Walton, Portland
1959	Bob Pettit, St. Louis	1979	Moses Malone, Houston
1960	Wilt Chamberlain, Philadelphia	1980	K. Abdul-Jabbar, L.A.
1961–63	Bill Russell, Boston	1981	Julius Erving, Philadelphia
1964	Oscar Robertson, Cincinnati	1982–83	Moses Malone, Houston, Phila.
1965	Bill Russell, Boston	1984–86	Larry Bird, Boston
1966–68	Wilt Chamberlain, Philadelphia	1987	Earvin Johnson, L.A.
1969	Wes Unseld, Baltimore	1988	Michael Jordan, Chicago
1970	Willis Reed, New York	1989–90	Earvin Johnson, L.A.
1971–72	Lew Alcindor (Kareem Abdul-Jabbar), Milwaukee		
1973	Dave Cowens, Boston		
1974	K. Abdul-Jabbar, Milwaukee		

*Selected by NBA players.

the NBA. Also, a Dallas, Tex., franchise was added in 1980; Charlotte, N.C., and Miami, Fla., in 1988; and Minnesota and Orlando, Fla., in 1989.

During the late 1970s and early 1980s several women's professional leagues were begun; all of them failed financially.

Rules and Equipment

Professional, college, and high school games are similar except in length and in range of basic skills. Professional games are 48 minutes long, divided into quarters; college games, 40 minutes, played in halves; and high school games, 32 minutes, broken into quarters. If a game is tied at the end of regulation time, an overtime (3 to 5 minutes, depending on the level of competition) is played. Several overtimes may be played before the outcome is decided.

Although no set of dimensions for a basketball court is universally accepted, the recommended size is 94 ft (28.65 m) long and 50 ft (15.24 m) wide.

Two points are given for a field goal, which is a shot that goes through the hoop—10 ft (3.05 m) high—while the ball is in play. The NBA instituted, beginning with the 1979–1980 season, the 3-point field goal, awarded to a player who scores from beyond a semicircle (see diagram) at least 22 ft (6.71 m) from the basket. The NCAA followed suit, beginning in 1986–87, with a 3-point semicircle that averages 19.75 ft (6 m) from the basket. One point is awarded for a free throw, or foul shot, which is attempted by a player who has been fouled, or impeded physically, by an opponent. Free throws are attempted, undefended, from a line drawn 15 ft (4.57 m) from the basket.

NCAA* BASKETBALL CHAMPIONS

Year	Team	Year	Team
1939	Oregon	1966	Texas Western
1940	Indiana	1967–73	UCLA
1941	Wisconsin	1974	North Carolina State
1942	Stanford	1975	UCLA
1943	Wyoming	1976	Indiana
1944	Utah	1977	Marquette
1945–46	Oklahoma A & M	1978	Kentucky
1947	Holy Cross	1979	Michigan State
1948–49	Kentucky	1980	Louisville
1950	CCNY	1981	Indiana
1951	Kentucky	1982	North Carolina
1952	Kansas	1983	North Carolina State
1953	Indiana	1984	Georgetown
1954	La Salle	1985	Villanova
1955–56	San Francisco	1986	Louisville
1957	North Carolina	1987	Indiana
1958	Kentucky	1988	Kansas
1959	California	1989	Michigan
1960	Ohio State	1990	Univ. of Nevada, Las Vegas
1961–62	Cincinnati		
1963	Loyola (Ill.)	1991	Duke
1964–65	UCLA		

*National Collegiate Athletic Association.

On the offensive, a player may advance the ball by passing or even rolling it to a teammate or by dribbling, which is bouncing it along the floor with one-hand taps. The defensive team can get the ball back by intercepting passes, blocking shots, or even by literally stealing it out of an opponent's hand, provided that no illegal body contact occurs. After a basket is made, the ball is awarded to the other team, which puts it back in play. If a field-goal attempt is missed and the ball remains in bounds, it is kept in play by the team that recovers (rebounds) it.

basketry   Basketry, the art of twisting together strands of material to form objects, is one of the oldest and most widespread handicrafts. Basketry is most often employed to make containers, but it has also been used in the construction of such other items as houses (of osier, or willow), boats, sails, carts, coffins, clothing, armor, masks, fish weirs, and furniture.

Most of the baskets that survive from ancient times have been found in dry caves or burials located in arid or semiarid places, including coastal Peru, the Nile Valley, and the Southwest region of the United States. Among the oldest known examples are basket fragments dating from about 10,000 years ago, found at Danger Cave, Utah. Basketry has also been found preserved in peat bogs, in permafrost, and under water, or in a carbonized state. In regions with wet climates, ancient basketry is best known from impressions left in mud or pottery or from its representation in paintings and carvings.

Construction Methods. Basketry is generally either woven or sewn. Basket-weaving requires that one element, called the weft, be passed over and under a foundation element called the warp. Techniques include plaiting or checkerwork, when warp and weft elements are of equal width, thickness, and flexibility; twilling, when two or more weft strands are passed over and under two or more warps; wickerwork, when relatively inflexible warp and relatively slender and flexible weft elements are used; and twining, when two or more weft elements are passed around each warp.

In sewn or coiled baskets a foundation is coiled around itself and then stitched in place. Technical variations of sewn baskets are defined by stitch, stitching patterns, the shape of the foundation, and the materials of which it is composed.

Materials. Among the materials used are metal wire, baleen (whale bone), leather, porcupine quills, and other animal or mineral products. Most baskets, however, are made of vegetal materials. Willow has been the favored basketmaking material of northern Europe for millennia. Bamboo is frequently used in the Far East, rattan in tropical Asia and Indonesia, and cane in parts of tropical Africa and America. All of these materials are usually woven or plaited. In areas where softer and more flexible materials such as palm leaf, tree roots, bark, yucca, or grasses are available, plaiting, twining, and coiling are generally the dominant techniques.

Decorative Methods. Self-patterns are those which are woven or sewn into a basket as it is made. Additive designs are those which are applied to completed baskets. The most basic self-patterns are textural and are created by the construction method used: chevrons or diamonds woven with twill or twine techniques or small-scale chevrons sewn by split-stitch methods. Additive decorations include false embroidery, imbrication (overlapping), and the sewing of beads or feathers to the foundation of a coil basket as it is made. Because of their flexibility, the twine and coil methods are most conducive to decoration.

The greatest variety of decorated baskets come from East Africa and the Southwest and Northwest Coast regions of aboriginal North America. The elaborately decorated baskets of the Pomo Indians of California are among the finest in the world.

Baskin, Leonard Leonard Baskin, b. New Brunswick, N.J., Aug. 15, 1922, is an artist who is known as a sculptor in wood and bronze, as a watercolorist, engraver, maker of woodcuts and lithographs, and as an illustrator and occasional author of books. In his work with the human figure, Baskin often uses biblical or mythological themes—as in *A Passover Haggadah* (1974), for which he provided watercolors of events in the biblical Exodus and hand-lettered much of the Hebrew text as well. He may be better known for his animal prints—his illustrations for poet Ted Hughes's *Crow* (1970), for example, or his own *The Raptors and Other Birds* (1985), which makes birds seem messengers of a malign nature.

Basque language Basque, or Euskara, is a language spoken by about a million people in northern Spain and southwestern France. Although attempts have been made to link it to ancient Iberian, the Hamito-Semitic group, and Caucasian, its origins remain uncertain. The sound pattern resembles that of Spanish, with its five pure vowels and such peculiarities as a trilled *r* and palatal *n* and *l*. In spite of this and numerous Latinate loan words, Basque has maintained its distinctiveness throughout two millennia of external contacts. For example, it still places a unique emphasis on suffixes to denote case and number and to form new words. Attempts are now being made to standardize Basque orthography.

Basques The Basques are a people whose homeland is the westernmost part of the Pyrenees Mountains: four provinces in Spain (Guipúzcoa, Vizcaya, Álava, and Navarra) and the department of Pyrénées-Atlantiques in France. Known to the Spanish as *vascos* and to the French as *basques*, the Basques call themselves *Euskaldunak* and their homeland *Euskadi*. Basque speakers number about 890,000 in Spain and 80,000 in France (1987 est.), but a larger number identify themselves as Basques in each country.

The origins of the Basques are still a mystery; their language is unrelated to any Indo-European language. Traditionally a fiercely independent peasant and fishing people, they were known as early as the Middle Ages as skilled boat makers and courageous whale hunters and cod fishermen who often ranged far into the Atlantic. Isolated in their mountainous homeland, the Basques repulsed incursions by Romans, Germanic tribes, Moors, and others until the 1700s. They lost their autonomy in France after the French Revolution (1789) and in Spain by the early 1800s.

A large number of Basques have migrated to North and South America. Historically, this migration has been the result partly of adverse political circumstances (most Basques opposed the Franco regime in Spain) and partly of the inheritance rule known as primogeniture, by which the oldest son inherits the family farm. Younger sons generally have either sought employment in coastal settlements as industrial workers or fishermen, or they have migrated to the New World, frequently finding work as sheepherders.

A movement for Basque separatism arose in the 19th and 20th centuries, which since 1959 has been led by the militant separatist organization ETA (a Basque acronym for "Basqueland and Freedom"). Spain's Basques were granted home rule in 1980, but ETA violence continued. In 1988 the ETA and the Spanish government agreed to hold talks.

Basra [bas'-rah] Basra (Busra, Bussora, or Bassorah) is an oil-shipping port of southeastern Iraq and the capital of Basra province. It is situated on the Shatt-al-Arab, about 115 km (71 mi) from the Persian Gulf. The population is 616,700 (1985 est.). Industries include oil refining and the manufacture of petrochemicals and fertilizer. Petroleum products, wheat, wool, barley, and dates are exported.

The city was founded in 636 by Caliph Umar I. An important center of letters, science, poetry, finance, and commerce under the early ABBASIDS, it declined in later centuries but was revived with the completion of the railroad to Baghdad in the early 20th century. Occupied by the British in World Wars I and II, it was an important staging post on the Allied supply route to the USSR after 1941. Basra's rapid commercial development after World War II was due to its advantageous location as a port and to the major oil fields nearby. The port was virtually closed, however, first by war with Iran (see IRAN-IRAQ WAR, 1980–88) and then by the GULF WAR that began in January 1991.

bass (fish) [bas] The bass is any of several percoid, or perchlike, fish, including some important food fish and some of the most popular game species. Most bass are members of three related families: Serranidae, or sea bass, including GROUPERS; Percichthyidae, or temperate bass; and Centrarchidae, or SUNFISH, including the CRAPPIE and some bream. The first two families are primarily marine shore fish distributed worldwide in tropical and temperate seas, but a few species are found in brackish or fresh water; together they number more than 400 species. The Centrarchidae, about 30 species, are freshwater fish of temperate North America.

Bass are spiny-finned fish with generalized, laterally compressed bodies and usually only slightly forked tail fins. They range in size from the giant sea bass, *Stereolepis gigas*, a temperate bass of the Pacific coast of North America that reaches lengths of 2.1 m (7 ft) and weights of more than 250 kg (550 lb), to sea bass species that reach lengths of no more than 10 cm (4 in). The majority of bass are carnivorous.

Among common sea bass of North America are the Pacific coast's kelp bass, *Paralabrax clathratus*; the barred sand bass, *P. nebulifer*; and the spotted sand bass, *P. maculatofasciatus*. On the Atlantic coast, the black sea bass, *Centropristis striata*, is a popular game fish.

Several temperate bass, including the giant sea bass,

Bass are popular North American food and game fish. Shown are the striped bass (top); *the yellow bass* (middle), *and the largemouth bass* (bottom).

are important game fish as well. The most desirable species, the striped bass, *Morone saxatilis*, can weigh more than 45 kg (100 lb). It is native to the Atlantic coast and was introduced to the California coast in the late 19th century.

Probably the best-known bass to North American freshwater anglers are the various sunfish species of the genus *Micropterus*. The largemouth bass, *M. salmoides*, occurs naturally in eastern North America but has been introduced throughout the rest of the continent. It is one of the most popular of all freshwater game fish; the angling record is 10 kg (22.25 lb). The smallmouth bass, *M. dolomieui*, is a more northern species that grows to about half the size of the largemouth. Another common species is the spotted bass, *M. punctulatus*, found from Ohio to Florida and westward into Kansas and Texas; it grows to about 1.8 kg (4 lb).

The white sea bass, *Cynoscion nobilis*, of California is actually a drum, family Sciaenidae.

bass (music) [bays]   The bass is the lowest part of a musical composition, the foundation on which the HAR-MONY, in the traditional sense, is built. The lowest adult male singing voice is also called the bass. When referring to a musical instrument, the term *bass* indicates either the lowest member of a family, or, when a contrabass instrument is used, the next lowest, as in bass CLARINET. The DOUBLE BASS, the lowest instrument of the violin fam-

ily, is sometimes called simply the bass. The bass clef is the F clef on the fourth line of the musical staff.

Bass, Sam [bas]   Sam Bass, b. near Mitchell, Ind., July 21, 1851, d. July 21, 1878, was an outlaw in the American West. In 1869 he left Indiana for Texas, where he became a cowboy and a deputy sheriff. About 1875 he began robbing stage coaches to recoup gambling losses. Bass participated in a $65,000 Nebraska train hold-up in 1877. Returning to Texas, he organized a gang that robbed four trains. He was shot by Texas Rangers during a bank robbery at Round Rock, Tex., and died two days later.

Bass Strait [bas]   The Bass Strait lies between Australia and its island state, Tasmania. It was named in 1798 for George Bass, a British surgeon and navigator. The strait is 298 km (185 mi) long and varies from 129 to 242 km (80 to 150 mi) wide. Its average depth is 70 m (230 ft).

Bassani, Giorgio [bah-sah'-nee]   The Italian poet and novelist Giorgio Emilio Bassani, b. Apr. 4, 1916, is regarded as one of his country's most interesting contemporary writers. A rigorous, elegant stylist, he is at his best in depicting his native Ferrara, particularly its Jewish community, during the fascist era and the persecutions of the late 1930s and '40s. His work includes the novel *The Garden of the Finzi-Continis* (1962; Eng. trans., 1965; film, 1971), *Five Stories of Ferrara* (1965; Eng. trans., 1971), *The Heron* (1968; Eng. trans., 1986), and a collection of poems published in English (1982) as *Rolls Royce and Other Poems*.

Bassano (family) [bah-sah'-noh]   The Bassano family of Venetian painters was active for about 100 years from the early 16th century to the early 17th century. Their name was derived from the town of Bassano, where the family lived at various times. The painters were Francesco da Ponte, the Elder, *c*.1480–1540; Jacopo, *c*.1517–1592; Giovanni Battista, 1553–1613; Leandro, 1557–1622; and Gerolamo, 1556–1621.

Francesco the Elder painted for churches in and near Bassano. His style was somewhat provincial; a painting such as *Madonna Enthroned between Saints Peter and Paul* (1519; Museo Civico, Bassano) reflects the work of Bartolommeo Montagna, Giovanni Battista Cima, and Giovanni Caroto.

Francesco's son **Jacopo** was far more important. *The Holy Trinity* (Church of the Trinity, Angarano), with elongated figures and decorative effects achieved through bold swirls of drapery, owes much to the Florentine MAN-NERISTS. Jacopo often portrayed groups of rustic figures in compositions such as *Adoration of the Shepherds* (*c*.1568; Galleria Nazionale, Rome), sensitive renderings of realistic genre figures combined with an often dramatic CHIAROSCURO.

Jacopo's increasingly realistic style was continued both in the family's workshop in Bassano and in the Venice studio of his sons. Of the sons, **Leandro** was probably the most gifted. He was well known for his numerous portraits in the style of TINTORETTO.

See also: RENAISSANCE ART AND ARCHITECTURE.

basset hound   The basset hound is a long-bodied, heavy-boned breed of hound that stands 28–35 cm (11–14 in) at the shoulder and weighs 18–27 kg (40–60 lb). Its long, soft, drooping ears, wrinkled brow, and short legs give it a distinctively wistful appearance. The smooth coat is accepted in any color and markings at breed competitions; for such shows, the dew claws may be removed.

The breed is an old one and has been known for centuries in continental Europe. Having better scenting ability than any breed except the bloodhound, it was used by royalty as a slow-working, steady trailer of game. Because it is low-slung, the basset hound is particularly good in rough, dense terrain. The breed has been known throughout the United States since the late 19th century.

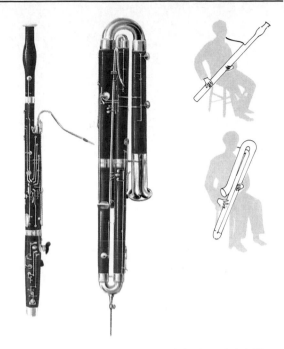

The bassoon (left) *is a double-reed, low-pitched woodwind. The contrabassoon, or double bassoon* (center), *has a range one octave lower than the bassoon. The instruments are shown* (right) *in their playing positions.*

The basset hound, known for its melancholy expression, was bred to slowly trail rabbits and hares.

bassoon for effective tenor-range solos and for humorous effects.

The modern French bassoon more closely approximates the sound of the 18th-century instrument. The German bassoon, which produces a warm, rich tone, is used in America and England and increasingly in other European countries.

basswood   see LINDEN

basso continuo   see FIGURED BASS

bassoon [buh-soon']   The bassoon is a double-reed woodwind, the bass of the OBOE family. Its normal range is from B flat below the bass staff to the D in the second octave above middle C. The tube, 2.79 m (9 ft 2 in) long, is bent to make a height of 1.22 m (4 ft) and consists of a metal crook on which the reed is placed and four sections of maple or pearwood: the tenor, the butt, the bass, and the bell.

In the mid-17th century the woodwind makers in the court of Louis XIV created the sectional bassoon from the Renaissance double-bored curtal, and its use immediately spread rapidly from Jean Baptiste LULLY's orchestra throughout Western orchestras as the proper woodwind bass for ensembles. Classical composers exploited the

Bastille [bah-steel']   A fortress and prison in Paris, the Bastille was a symbol of royal absolutism before the French Revolution. Begun in 1370, it was originally intended to augment the city's defenses. By the 17th century it was being used as a prison; Voltaire and the Marquis de Sade were among its most famous prisoners.

On July 14, 1789, at the beginning of the French Revolution, a mob gathered outside the Bastille, demanding the munitions that were stored within. The commander refused to surrender and the building was stormed. Ironically, only seven prisoners were inside. The Bastille was demolished soon after.

July 14, Bastille Day, has been as the French national holiday since 1880. As with the American Independence Day, the holiday in France is celebrated with the setting off of fireworks and with parades and other festivities.

Basutoland   see LESOTHO

ILLUSTRATION CREDITS

The following list credits or acknowledges, by page, the source of illustrations used in this volume. When two or more illustrations appear on one page, they are credited individually left to right, top to bottom; their credits are separated by semicolons. When both the photographer or artist and an agency or other source are given for an illustration, they are usually separated by a slash. Those illustrations not cited below are credited on the page on which they appear, either in the caption or alongside the illustration itself.

3 Bodleian Library
8 Rand McNally & Company
9 Charles Swithinbank; Photo Researchers/Russ Kinne
12 Popperfoto, London; The Bettmann Archive
15 Ardea/Hans and Judy Besti
16 Superstock/Shostal/Kapoor
17 The Bettmann Archive
19 Magnum Photos/John Nance
21 Courtesy Collins Publishers
22 Courtesy American Museum of Natural History; UPI/Bettmann Newsphotos
23 Frederick Sutter/International Defense Images; Sipa Press/John Gunston
25 Scala, Florence
34 Paul C. Pet
36 National Portrait Gallery, London
37 Photo Researchers/John Mass
39 The Bettmann Archive
40 Photo Researchers/G. Tomsich
47 Photographie Giraudon
47 NASA; NASA; NASA; NASA
48 NASA
50 Freelance Photographers Guild; Rand McNally & Company
56 Scala, Florence
57 Sygma/Andy Hernandez
62 Bibliothèque Nationale, Paris
63 Sipa Press/Kol Al Arab; Photo Researchers/George Holton
64 Sipa Press/Aral; Sipa Press/Aral; Black Star/Sclarandis
65 Magnum Photos/Abbas; Magnum Photos/Marc Riboud
68 UPI/Bettmann Newsphotos
73 Picturepoint, London
74 Big Horn National Forest, USDA Forest Service; Audrey Topping
75 Magnum Photos/Ian Berry; Photo Researchers/Bill Belknap
76 © Aerofilms, Ltd.
77 Photo Researchers/John Veltri
78 Photo Researchers/Georg Gerster
79 Aldus Archives; The British Museum
80 Ashmolean Museum, Oxford
81 Ashmolean Museum, Oxford; Robert Harding Picture Library Ltd.
82 Prothmann Associates; © National Geographic Society/George F. Mobley; Peruvian Embassy
87 Aldus Archives; H. H. Baudert
88 Art Resource/Scala
89 Photographie Giraudon
90 Art Resource; Art Resource
92 Wolfe Worldwide Films; Art Resource
93 Art Resource; Art Resource
94 A. F. Kersting; Picturepoint, London; Photri; Hendrich Blessing
95 Photo Researchers/Jan Moline; Photo Researchers/Van Bucher
96 Fred Bruemmer
97 Rand McNally & Company

100 The Mansell Collection
101 Brown Brothers; The Granger Collection
102 Charles Swithinbank; Arecibo Observatory
105 Rand McNally & Company
106 Photo Researchers/Carl Frank
107 Photo Researchers/Lisl Steiner
108 Photo Researchers/George Holton; Photo Researchers/George Holton
113 New York Public Library Astor, Lenox, and Tilden Foundations
114 Scala, Florence
118 Rand McNally & Company
119 The Image Bank/Harald Sund
120 Photo Researchers/Paolo Koch
121 The Image Bank/Robert Philips; Photo Researchers/Björn Bölstad
124 Rand McNally & Company
125 The Image Bank/Stephen Green-Armytage
126 Photo Researchers/Betsy Blass; Courtesy Arkansas Department of Parks and Tourism
127 Photo Researchers/Betsy Blass; Photo Researchers/Betsy Blass
132 Staatliche Museum, Berlin
133 Metropolitan Museum of Art, New York, Peabody Museum, Salem; Metropolitan Museum of Art, Rogers Fund, 1904, New York
135 FMC Corporation
136 Wide World Photos
137 ANP-Foto; NASA
139 Leeds Museum; Aldus Archives
142 The Bettmann Archive
143 National Portrait Gallery, London
146 Musée des Antiquites Nationales, St. Germaine-en-Laye, France
147 Art Resource/Scala
148 Aerofilms, Ltd.
149 The Bettmann Archive
151 Art Resource/Scala; Art Resource/Scala
154 Scala, Florence
156 Culver Pictures
158 Gianfranco Gorgoni
159 Photo Researchers/Porterfield-Chickering
160 National Gallery, London; National Gallery, London; Louvre, Paris
164 Het Spectrum
165 Culver Pictures
172 National Portrait Gallery, Washington, D.C.
173 Bibliothèque Nationale, Paris
175 United Kingdom Atomic Energy Authority, London
178 Het Spectrum
183 UPI/Bettmann Newsphotos
186 Rand McNally & Company
187 Anthony-Verlag/Scharf
188 Sovfoto
189 The Image Bank/Morton Beebe

192 Photo Researchers/Paolo Koch; Wide World Photos
193 Hoa-Qui/Richer; Kees Scherer; AGE
194 The Image Bank/Harvey Lloyd; Sem Presser; The Image Bank/Joseph Hettis
195 Kees Scherer; Mirèille Vautier; Het Spectrum
197 Gamma-Liaison/Kaku Kurita
198 Photo Researchers/Bernard Pierre Wolff; Roel Burgler; Photo Researchers/Joan Lebold Cohen; Photo Researchers/Saito
201 National Museum of Pakistan, Karachi; Louvre, Paris; Courtesy Museum of Fine Arts, Boston; Magnum Photos
203 Photo Researchers/Susan McCartney; Jingo-ji, Kyoto; Sem Presser; National Palace Museum, Taipei, Taiwan, Courtesy Aldus Books
204 Scala, Florence; Sem Presser
206 Courtesy The High Commission of India/Aldus Books; Foto-archief Spaarnestad
207 Rob Brijker Press Agency
208 Magnum Photos/Eve Arnold
209 Black Star/Herman Kokojan
213 The Bettmann Archive
216 Het Spectrum
218 City Museum and Art Gallery, Plymouth Courtesy Aldus Books; Culver Pictures
219 Adler Planetarium/Roderick Webster
222 NASA; © Peter Pesavento Collection
223 NASA
225 Sem Presser; Courtesy The Foundation Saint Thomas, Strasbourg/Aldus Books; Scala, Florence
226 Sem Presser; UPI/Bettmann Newsphotos
227 NASA
228 Lick Oberservatory; California Institute of Technology; California Institute of Technology
229 The Image Bank/Harald Sund
232 The Bettmann Archive
233 International Museum of Photography at George E. Eastman House
235 Photo Researchers/John Veltri
237 Photo Researchers/Allen Green; Lothar Roth and Associates
240 Librarie Hachette, Paris
243 NASA
251 IBM/Thomas J. Watson Research Center; Photo Reseachers/G.J. Hills, John Innes Institute Science Photo Library
256 Culver Pictures
258 Photo Researchers/Mario Fantin; Photo Trends
261 Scala, Florence
262 Scala, Florence
265 © Malcolm Lockwood Photography
266 National Portrait Gallery, London
267 The Bettmann Archive
268 Rand McNally & Company
270 AGE/Forester; Sem Presser
271 Photo Researchers/Georg Gerster
273 Photo Researchers/A. B. Joyce; AGE/Forester
274 Scala, Florence
275 The Image Bank/Luis Villota
276 The Image Bank/J. L. Stage; Australian Overseas Information Service

277 Photo Researchers/Carl Purcell; Sem Presser
278 Courtesy Australian Information Center
280 All pictures—Courtesy Australian Information Center
281 Bruce Coleman Ltd.
284 Photo Researchers/Andy Bernhaut; Superstock/Shostal/Jacobs
285 Rand McNally & Company
286 Kunsthistorisches Museum, Vienna
289 Photo Reseachers/Paolo Koch
297 Dave Houser
313 The Image Bank/Morton Beebe
318 Sem Presser; Photo Researchers/G. Tomsich
324 The Bettmann Archive
328 The Mansell Collection
331 The Bettmann Archive; Arete Archives
332 Photo Researchers/Russ Kinne
336 Photo Researchers/Georg Gerster
338 Rand McNally & Company; Photo Researchers/Slim Aarons
339 Rand McNally & Company
345 The Image Bank/Farrell Grehan
347 Camera Press Ltd./Gerson; Public Archives of Canada
348 Photo Researchers/Van Bucher Collection
350 UPI/Bettmann Newsphotos
351 Martha Swope Associates
352 Photographie Giraudon; Aldus Archives
353 The Bettmann Archive
354 Cunningham Dance Foundation; New York City Ballet/Edward Gorey
355 Martha Swope Associates
356 Martha Swope Associates
357 Martha Swope Associates
358 Snark International
359 Gamma-Liaison
365 Slidemakers
368 Photo Researchers/George Holton
370 Rand McNally & Company
371 Photo Researchers/Bernard Pierre Wolff
373 Culver Pictures
378 Scala, Florence
379 UPI/Bettmann Newsphotos
380 Magnum Photos/Bob Adelman
383 AGE/Viñals
384 Geocom BV
388 The Bettmann Archive
390 Scala, Florence
394 Brown Brothers
395 The Bettmann Archive
396 Martha Swope Associates
397 Robert Harding Picture Library Ltd.
398 Robert Harding Picture Library Ltd.
399 Focus on Sports
400 The Bettmann Archive
402 Wide World Photos
403 UPI/Bettmann Newsphotos; UPI/Bettmann Newsphotos
404 UPI/Bettmann Newsphotos; UPI/Bettmann Newsphotos
405 UPI/Bettmann Newsphotos
408 Photo Researchers/Carl Schofield; The Image Bank/Walter Iooss, Jr.
409 Basketball Hall of Fame; Focus on Sports
410 Wide World Photos; UPI/Bettmann Newsphotos
411 Focus on Sports